Social Cognition
The Basis of Human Interaction

FRONTIERS OF SOCIAL PSYCHOLOGY

SERIES EDITORS:

Arie W. Kruglanski, *University of Maryland at College Park*
Joseph P. Forgas, *University of New South Wales*

Frontiers of Social Psychology is a new series of domain-specific handbooks. The purpose of each volume is to provide readers with a cutting-edge overview of the most recent theoretical, methodological, and practical developments in a substantive area of social psychology, in greater depth than is possible in general social psychology handbooks. The editors and contributors are all internationally renowned scholars whose work is at the cutting edge of research.

Scholarly, yet accessible, the volumes in the *Frontiers* series are an essential resource for senior undergraduates, postgraduates, researchers, and practitioners and are suitable as texts in advanced courses in specific subareas of social psychology.

PUBLISHED TITLES

Negotiation Theory and Research, Thompson
Close Relationships, Noller & Feeney
Evolution and Social Psychology, Schaller, Simpson, & Kenrick
Social Psychology and the Unconscious, Bargh
Affect in Social Thinking and Behavior, Forgas
The Science of Social Influence, Pratkanis
Social Communication, Fiedler
The Self, Sedikides & Spencer
Personality and Social Behavior, Rhodewalt
Attitudes and Attitude Change, Crano & Prislin
Social Cognition, Strack & Förster

FORTHCOMING TITLES

Exploration in Political Psychology, Krosnick & Chiang
Social Psychology of Consumer Behavior, Wänke
Social Motivation, Dunning
Intergroup Conflicts and Their Resolution, Bar-Tal

For continually updated information about published and forthcoming titles in the *Frontiers of Social Psychology* series, please visit: **www.psypress.com/frontiers**

Social Cognition
The Basis of Human Interaction

Edited by
Fritz Strack and Jens Förster

Psychology Press
Taylor & Francis Group

New York   London

Psychology Press
Taylor & Francis Group
711 Third Avenue,
New York, NY 10017

Psychology Press
Taylor & Francis Group
27 Church Road
Hove, East Sussex BN3 2FA

First issued in paperback 2015

Psychology Press is an imprint of the Taylor and Francis Group, an informa business

© 2009 by Taylor & Francis Group, LLC

International Standard Book Number-13: 978-1-138-87674-3 (pbk)
International Standard Book Number-13: 978-1-84169-451-1 (Hardcover)

Except as permitted under U.S. Copyright Law, no part of this book may be reprinted, reproduced, transmitted, or utilized in any form by any electronic, mechanical, or other means, now known or hereafter invented, including photocopying, microfilming, and recording, or in any information storage or retrieval system, without written permission from the publishers.

Trademark Notice: Product or corporate names may be trademarks or registered trademarks, and are used only for identification and explanation without intent to infringe.

Library of Congress Cataloging-in-Publication Data

Social cognition : the basis of human interaction / edited by Fritz Strack, Jens Forster.
    p. cm. -- (Frontiers of social psychology)
Includes bibliographical references and index.
ISBN-13: 978-1-84169-451-1 (alk. paper)
ISBN-10: 1-84169-451-7 (alk. paper)
  1. Social perception. 2. Social psychology. I. Strack, Fritz, 1950- II. Forster, Jens, 1965-

HM1041.S624 2008
302'.12--dc22
                                        2008024861

Visit the Taylor & Francis Web site at
http://www.taylorandfrancis.com

and the Psychology Press Web site at
http://www.psypress.com

Contents

Social Cognition: An Introduction — vii
About the Editors — xi
Contributors — xiii

1 **Attention, Perception, and Social Cognition** — 1
   Galen V. Bodenhausen and Kurt Hugenberg

2 **Representing Social Concepts Modally and Amodally** — 23
   Paula M. Niedenthal, Laurie Mondillon, Daniel A. Effron, and Lawrence W. Barsalou

3 **Unconscious, Conscious, and Metaconscious in Social Cognition** — 49
   Piotr Winkielman and Jonathan W. Schooler

4 **Conversational Inference: Social Cognition as Interactional Intelligence** — 71
   Denis Hilton

5 **Induction: From Simple Categorization to Higher-Order Inference Problems** — 93
   Klaus Fiedler and Henning Plessner

6 **Mental Construal in Social Judgment** — 121
   Norbert Schwarz

7 **Comparison** — 139
   Thomas Mussweiler

8 **Metacognition** — 157
   Herbert Bless, Johannes Keller, and Eric R. Igou

9	**Intuition**	179
	Fritz Strack and Roland Deutsch	
10	**Spontaneous Evaluations**	199
	Karl Christoph Klauer	
11	**Emotion**	219
	Roland Neumann	
12	**A Social-Cognitive Perspective on Automatic Self-Regulation: The Relevance of Goals in the Information-Processing Sequence**	245
	Jens Förster and Markus Denzler	
13	**Language and Social Cognition**	269
	Gün R. Semin	
14	**Culture and Social Cognition in Human Interaction**	291
	Bettina Hannover and Ulrich Kühnen	

Author Index   311

Subject Index   327

Social Cognition: An Introduction

The power of scientific explanations depends on the right level of analysis. For psychology, there is no doubt that the cognitive level has led to a deeper understanding of human behavior.

After a pioneering period with a strong focus on behaviorism, it became clear that much more is needed to understand human behavior. Instead, knowledge about how people think and feel has contributed much more to understanding how they behave. In modern social psychology, theorizing has always been at the cognitive level of analysis. This was the case long before the "cognitive revolution" took place. In fact, social psychology was even considered "the repository of underground cognitive wisdom during the behaviorist interlude" (Mandler, 1985, p.18). Lewin's (1936) concept of "life space," Festinger's (1957) idea of "cognitive dissonance," or Heider's (1946) construct of "cognitive triads" and Bem's (1967) self-perception processes were elements of powerful cognitive explanations of social behavior. Specifically, characteristics of mental structures (e.g., the imbalance) were found to cause behavioral consequences.

However, the dynamics of these structures were mainly driven by inherent motivational properties and were often at conflict with a view of the human as a seeker of knowledge and truth (Nisbett & Ross, 1980). Therefore, subsequent cognitive accounts were normatively oriented. Specifically, they described mental operations in their capacity of generating judgments that corresponded to reality (e.g., Bem, 1967, Kelley, 1967). Surprisingly, systematic deviations from these prescriptions were found to be the rule rather than the exception and required explanation. As a consequence, various judgmental heuristics were invoked to account for these biases (Tversky & Kahneman, 1974).

With the advent of the "cognitive revolution" in experimental psychology, a unifying model emerged on the scene. Specifically, the paradigm of information processing has offered a temporal structure for cognitive phenomena. It starts with the encoding of information, continues with its internal representation, and ends with its retrieval from memory. This standard sequence of information processing was readily embraced not only by researchers in experimental psychology but also by social psychologists, who had already adopted the cognitive level of analysis. The idea of "processing" has added a sequential component that has greatly stimulated new research. New questions about existing findings have been raised, and innovative research has been stimulated.

Thus, this shift of the research paradigm has immediately exerted its impact on social psychology. Specifically, it has helped create the field of "social cognition" (e.g., Fiske & Taylor, 1991) to which the present volume is dedicated. Social cognition has since become one of the most vibrant domains in social psychology. It has facilitated the conceptual integration of related areas, such as emotion and motivation, and it has brought about one of the most innovative lines of research, namely, that of "implicit" processes.

In this volume, a number of accomplished researchers address a list of issues that have emerged as central topics of social cognition. In discussing their importance, the authors combine a report of the state of the art with their own cutting-edge research. In summary, the present chapters yield a comprehensive picture of this important domain of social psychology.

Specifically, some chapters explain how the information enters into the system (Chapter 1 by Bodenhausen and Hugenberg) and how it is represented (Niedenthal, Mondillon, Effron, and Barsalou's Chapter 2; Winkielman and Schooler's Chapter 3). Others describe specific cognitive operations that are particularly important in the processing of social information (Hilton's Chapter 4; Chapter 5 by Fiedler and Plessner; Schwarz's Chapter 6; Mussweiler's Chapter 7; Chapter 8 by Bless, Keller, and Igou; Chapter 9 by Strack and Deutsch) and address evaluation and affect as important determinants of judgment and behavior (Klauer's Chapter 10; Neumann's Chapter 11). The final chapters demonstrate how the principles of social cognition can be fruitfully applied to phenomena of self-regulation (Chapter 12 by Förster and Denzler) and be harnessed for a deeper understanding of global topics like language (Chapter 13 by Semin) and culture (Hannover and Kühnen's Chapter 14).

In summary, the present volume attempts to provide both an introduction into the processing of social information and an overview of the flourishing field of social cognition. We would like to express our gratitude to Rita Frizlen and her team for their editorial assistance and particularly for providing the author and subject indices.

Fritz Strack
University of Würzburg

Jens Förster
University of Amsterdam

REFERENCES

Bem, D. J. (1967). Self-perception: An alternative interpretation of cognitive dissonance phenomena. *Psychological Review, 74*, 183–200.

Festinger, L. (1957). *A theory of cognitive dissonance*. Oxford, England: Row, Peterson.

Fiske, S. T., & Taylor, S. E. (1991). *Social cognition* (2nd ed.) New York: McGraw-Hill.

Heider, F. (1946). Attitudes and cognitive organization. *Journal of Psychology, 21*, 107–112.

Kelley, H. H. (1967). Attribution theory in social psychology. In D. Levine (Ed.), *Nebraska Symposium on Motivation* (pp. 192–238). Lincoln: University of Nebraska Press.

Lewin, K. (1936). *Principles of topological psychology*. New York: McGraw-Hill.

Mandler, G. (1985). *Cognitive psychology*. Hillsdale, NJ: Erlbaum.

Nisbett, R. E., & Ross, L. (1980). *Human inference: Strategies and shortcomings of social judgment*. Englewood Cliffs, NJ: Prentice Hall.

Tversky, A., & Kahneman, D. (1974). Judgment under uncertainty: Heuristics and biases. *Science, 185*, 1124–1131.

About the Editors

Fritz Strack received his PhD in 1983 from the University of Mannheim. Subsequently, he has held positions at the Max Planck Institute for Psychology, the University of Trier and the University of Würzburg where he currently holds a chair in social psychology. During his academic career, he studied at Stanford University, was a postdoctoral fellow at the University of Illinois, and was a visiting professor at the New School for Social Research in New York. He has served on the editorial boards of the leading journals in social psychology and has been editor of the *European Journal of Social Psychology*. Dr. Strack has received the Wilhelm Wundt Medal, the Thomas M. Ostrom Award and the Theoretical Innovation Prize of the Society of Personality and Social Psychology (SPSP). He is a fellow of several learned societies and has been president of the European Association of Social Psychology.

Jens Förster attended high school at Lübbecke/Westfalia, majoring in German and French literature, biology, and religious sciences. He earned a Diploma in Psychology and a Dr. rer. nat. from Trier University in 1992 and 1994, respectively. His advisor was Fritz Strack. He also studied German literature, linguistic data processing, and philosophy in Trier and opera and performing arts in Saarbrücken, receiving his "Vordiploma" (BA) in 1991 and 1994. From 1996–1998, he was a post doctoral candidate at Columbia University, New York, where his advisor was Tory E. Higgins. He also taught at the New School for Social Research in New York. In 2000, Dr. Förster received his habilitation at Würzburg University. Before moving to Amsterdam, he held positions at the Universities of Trier, Würzburg, and Duisburg and at Jacobs University, formerly known as International University Bremen. He is author or coauthor of more than eighty book chapters or articles on topics including embodiment, metacognition, stereotypes, social judgments, mood, and self-regulation. He serves or has served on a variety of boards of leading journals in social psychology, such as the *European Journal of Social Psychology*, *Journal of Personality and Social Psychology*, *Social Cognition*, *Social Psychology*, and *Self and Identity*. He was elected speaker of the German Social Psychology Association for the 2003–2005 term, and in 2008 he became director of the Kurt Lewin Institute.

Contributors

Lawrence W. Barsalou
Emory University
Atlanta, Georgia, USA

Herbert Bless
University of Mannheim
Mannheim, Germany

Galen V. Bodenhausen
Northwestern University
Evanston, Illinois, USA

Markus Denzler
University of Amsterdam
Amsterdam, The Netherlands

Roland Deutsch
University of Würzburg
Würzburg, Germany

Daniel A. Effron
Stanford University
Stanford, California, USA

Klaus Fiedler
University of Heidelberg
Heidelberg, Germany

Jens Förster
University of Amsterdam
Amsterdam, The Netherlands

Bettina Hannover
Freie Universität Berlin
Berlin, Germany

Denis Hilton
University of Toulouse
Toulouse, France

Kurt Hugenberg
Miami University
Oxford, Ohio, USA

Eric R. Igou
University of Tilburg
Tilburg, The Netherlands

Johannes Keller
University of Mannheim
Mannheim, Germany

Karl Christoph Klauer
Albert-Ludwigs-Universität Freiburg
Freiburg, Germany

Ulrich Kühnen
Jacobs University Bremen
Bremen, Germany

Laurie Mondillon
University of Clermont-Ferrand
Clermont-Ferrand, France

Thomas Mussweiler
University of Cologne
Cologne, Germany

Roland Neumann
University of Dortmund
Dortmund, Germany

Paula M. Niedenthal
Centre National de la Recherche
Scientifique (CNRS) and
University of Clermont-Ferrand
Clermont-Ferrand, France

Henning Plessner
University of Heidelberg
Heidelberg, Germany

Jonathan W. Schooler
University of California, Santa
Barbara
Santa Barbara, California, USA

Norbert Schwarz
University of Michigan
Ann Arbor, Michigan, USA

Gün R. Semin
Utrecht University
Utrecht, The Netherlands

Fritz Strack
University of Würzburg
Würzburg, Germany

Piotr Winkielman
University of California, San Diego
San Diego, California, USA

1

Attention, Perception, and Social Cognition

GALEN V. BODENHAUSEN and KURT HUGENBERG

INTRODUCTION

At the most basic level, minds are structured in ways that permit the successful navigation of challenges related to survival and reproduction. In general terms, the mental operations that are most central to achieving success in the face of such challenges involve the recognition of opportunities and threats and the generation of appropriate strategies for exploiting (or avoiding) them. Although the minds of our hominid ancestors might have been primarily concerned with tasks such as recognizing edible substances and dangerous predators, the modern human mind often has a vast array of preoccupations (e.g., science, philosophy, entertainment, etc.) that bear little direct relation to survival or reproductive concerns. What can explain our comparatively rich cognitive capacities as a species? One compelling answer to this question lies in the extremely social nature of human beings. From early ancestral times, the *homo* genus has been typified by a high degree of sociality, with individuals living in highly interdependent groups (e.g., Leakey, 1978). To survive and thrive in such a context, the ability to understand other humans is key. Few skills would afford greater advantages than the ability to understand the minds of other group members—to understand their intentions (e.g., to cooperate or compete), to learn what they know (e.g., where threats and opportunities lie), and to manipulate what they believe. Possession of such cognitive skills would greatly increase the probability of successful reproduction, and progeny who inherited these skills would enjoy similar advantages. Indeed, this particular repertoire of skills appears to be fundamental in setting humans (and perhaps their closest primate relatives) apart from other animals (e.g., Tomasello, Carpenter, Call, Behne, & Moll, 2005). From this perspective, the human cognitive architecture owes its sophistication to the affordances and constraints of sociality (e.g., Brewer, 2004; Byrne, 2000; Cummins, 1998; Seyfarth & Cheney, 1994).

To know the minds of others, we must attend to and perceive the available cues, whether in their verbal or nonverbal behavior, that contain information about their inner qualities. The field of social cognition emerged from the study of this process of person perception, which focused on the perceiver's ability to discern others' states (e.g., emotions) and traits (Bruner & Tagiuri, 1954; for a review, see Jones, 1990). Researchers in this tradition have generally assumed that cognitive representations of actors (and of the contexts in which they behave) mediate behavioral responses to the social world (e.g., Fiske & Taylor, 1991; Wyer & Carlston, 1979). These representations confer meaning onto the sensory input that is received, and in so doing, they potentiate corresponding responses. In short, thinking is for doing. The underlying model is schematically depicted in Figure 1.1.

When conceptualized in this way, perception is essentially the interface between the outer and inner worlds. Social targets and the contextual stimuli of the outer environment create signals (visual, auditory, etc.) that can be sensed, and the perceiver receives these signals and converts them into psychologically meaningful representations that define our inner experience of the world. The process of perception is governed both by "bottom-up" sensory input and by "top-down" imposition of meaning based on template matching and other pattern recognition processes that allow for the structuring and interpretation of the input (e.g., Marr, 1982; Triesman & Gelade, 1980). Once a meaningful percept is achieved, it serves as input to higher-order cognition, including inferences about the target's goals and intentions. This interpretation of target input then guides the perceiver's response.

As a simple example, consider walking into your kitchen and observing a person brandishing an object that appears, on the basis of various visually detectable features, to be metallic and pointed. The ability to infer the states and traits of this person will clearly be of some use here. Is the person smiling? If so, is the smile serene or maniacal? If it is maniacal, is it sincerely or playfully so? Prior knowledge about the specific actor (e.g., one's spouse) or general type of actor (e.g., females), as well as other contextual cues, will be used to determine whether the actor is menacing and, correspondingly, whether approach or avoidance is appropriate. This

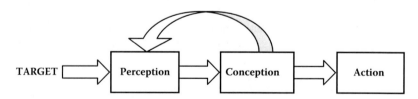

Figure 1.1 Simple schematic model of social information processing.

kind of simple perception-appraisal-response sequence is implemented innumerable times in the course of any given day and, to a great extent, is completed without effort (Choi, Gray, & Ambady, 2005). Indeed, this sequence can run to conclusion with such efficiency that we often fail to recognize its constructive aspects. With perception positioned at the front end of this process, it is a suitable place to start the analysis of social cognition, and indeed there are now several decades of research examining the initial processing of social information; unfortunately, there is much less work following the sequence through to the realm of naturalistic behavioral responses (Zebrowitz, 1990). We provide an overview of the "front end" of the social information-processing apparatus. We begin with a discussion of attentional processes and the social psychological factors that modulate them. Next, we consider the mechanisms by which attended stimuli are initially processed into meaningful representations. Finally, we discuss the direct and indirect connections between perception and action.

SELECTIVE ATTENTION IN PERCEPTION

While perception is the first step in social cognition, attention is commonly considered the first step in perception. One of the most common, yet most powerful, metaphors for understanding attention is that it functions as something akin to a "spotlight" (e.g., Derryberry & Tucker, 1994). This spotlight of attention can illuminate only a limited amount of information at any one time, facilitating the perception of those focal stimuli. Thus, not all stimuli in the perceptual field receive equal attention; instead, some stimuli are selected for relatively intense scrutiny, making them more likely to reach the threshold of awareness (Posner, 1994), while others are processed only superficially, receiving little of our precious attention. This model of attention recognizes the processing bottleneck inherent in our cognitive system (Broadbent, 1958). We can only keep so many things in focal attention at any given time.

Indeed, this problem of selecting which stimuli will receive attention and which will be ignored is one of the central problems of the cognitive system. From shoppers searching the supermarket shelves for their favorite brand of dishwashing detergent, to entomologists searching the forest floor for a particular species of insect, our attentional systems must select important or goal-relevant stimuli from the environment while simultaneously ignoring or even suppressing the processing of distracting detergents, bugs, or other stimuli in general. These two separate needs, attention and inattention, are subserved by different cognitive mechanisms, leading to an outcome called *selective attention*.

Despite the phenomenological experience of attention being a unitary construct, recent theory and research in both psychology and neurology suggest that the orienting function of attention is actually composed of at least three separate processes (e.g., Posner, Walker, Friedrich, & Rafal, 1984): disengaging attention from an initial target, moving attention to a new target, and then reengaging attention.

This disengage-move-engage model of attention has been very influential in recent research on visual attention.

PREATTENTIVE SCANS AND ATTENTION CAPTURE

For some stimuli to be selected and others ignored, and thus for attention to be engaged in the first place, information must initially be processed to a certain extent without attention, or processed *preattentively*. Information selectively attended to would then undergo more extensive cognitive processing. In the visual modality, this preattentive processing is generally understood as a parallel scan of all available loci within the visual field.[1] The attentional system then selects some stimuli for more processing than others. Preattentive scans of the environment are necessarily fast and automatic, and they operate on low-level stimulus features. One of the primary functions of such preattentive scans is to parse the visual field into meaningful objects. Which stimuli are selected for attention or which stimuli capture attention depends both on the nature of the stimuli and qualities of the perceiver.

Capturing Attention: From the Bottom Up

In 1890, William James made the prescient distinction between passive and active attention capture. This distinction between passive and active maps quite well onto more modern views of attention capture as driven simultaneously by bottom-up and top-down processing, respectively. Some stimuli seem to automatically capture attention in an entirely bottom-up fashion. For example, stimuli that appear without warning (e.g., Jonides & Yantis, 1988; Yantis & Johnson, 1990), certain luminance and contrast changes that signal motion (e.g., Theeuwes, 1995), as well as stimuli that appear to be "looming" (i.e., appearing to approach the observer; Franconeri & Simons, 2003) all appear to automatically capture attention. Franconeri and Simons noted that although the perceptual qualities of attention-grabbing stimuli do not seem to share many perceptual features, the stimuli that capture attention in a bottom-up fashion seem to all require immediate behavioral responses (e.g., a rock flying in your direction). It seems quite functional that the attentional system is tuned to attend quickly to moving and looming stimuli as those stimuli will commonly have more immediate survival implications than their more stable brethren.

Using that same logic, Öhman and colleagues (e.g., Öhman, Flykt, & Esteves, 2001; Öhman, Lundqvist, & Esteves, 2001) argued that biologically important fear-relevant stimuli, such as snakes, spiders, and angry facial expressions, also automatically draw attention. Indeed, they argued that, because of the survival benefits of quickly recognizing and dealing with such evolutionarily relevant threats, such stimuli get prioritized by the attentional system in a manner similar to other behaviorally urgent events such as looming stimuli and sudden visual onsets. For example, Öhman, Flykt, and Esteves (2001) found that fear-relevant pictures such as those of snakes and spiders were found more quickly in visual search tasks than fear-irrelevant pictures such as flowers or mushrooms. In a related task, Öhman, Lundqvist, and Esteves (2001) replicated Hansen and Hansen's (1988) earlier findings that angry facial expressions are found more quickly than any other expression in a visual search. Indeed, some theorists argued that threat-relevant stimuli in general, regardless of the evolutionary significance of the specific stimulus, will attract visual attention. For example, Pratto and John (1991) presented positive and negative trait words in different color fonts in a color-naming task and found slower response latencies to negatively as compared to positively valenced words, which they interpreted as an indicator that attention was drawn toward the negative as compared to the positive words.

Capturing Attention: From the Top Down

Although it appears that certain stimulus properties (e.g., sudden onset) or stimulus types (e.g., threatening stimuli) do seem to attract attention in a relatively bottom-up fashion, the power of such stimuli to capture attention is clearly moderated by the state of the perceiver in a relatively top-down manner. Classic research by Erdelyi (1974) documented the ways in which affectively potent stimuli can capture attention. For example, in a task that required ignoring distracter stimuli, Jewish participants performed well unless the to-be-ignored stimulus was a swastika. More recent research corroborated the tendency to orient to threatening cues and further indicated that this tendency is particularly potent for individuals high in state or trait anxiety. For example, MacLeod and Mathews (1988) found that individuals in a high-anxiety state (i.e., 1 week before an important exam) tended to shift attention toward threatening, examination-relevant words, whereas those low in anxiety (i.e., 12 weeks before an exam) shifted attention away from threatening words, a pattern of data that also appears to be conceptually similar for high trait anxiety individuals (e.g., Broadbent & Broadbent, 1988; Li, Zinbarg, & Paller, 2007; MacLeod, Mathews, & Tata, 1986). Similarly, attention to threatening facial expressions (i.e., of anger) also appears to be moderated by the influence of anxiety. A growing body of literature using dot-probe tasks has found that threatening facial expressions tend to most powerfully draw the attention of individuals high in trait anxiety (e.g., Bradley, Mogg, Falla, & Hamilton, 1998; Fox et al., 2000). More generally, Niedenthal, Halberstadt, and Innes-Ker (1999) documented that emotional states tend to direct perceivers' attention to the emotional aspects of encountered stimuli, further confirming the importance of affect in guiding attention.

Beyond affective states, the expectancies and goals of perceivers are also a powerful determinant for how attention is focused. Indeed, for our entomologist to be able to find a favored insect among the swarm, selective attention must be modulated in a top-down fashion. Such top-down, conceptually driven processing is one cardinal interest of social psychological research, and as such it is perhaps not a surprise that many cases of top-down processing in the attention literature seem to have clear manifestations within the social cognitive literature.

Perhaps the best known of the top-down effects in attention is that contextually unexpected stimuli attract attention. For example, in their now-classic experiment, Loftus and Mackworth (1978) found that visual attention was drawn earlier and more frequently by "oddball" objects that had a low probability of appearing in a scene (e.g., an octopus on a farm) than by contextually expected objects (e.g., a tractor on a farm). In this case, there is no inherent property of the stimulus that attracts attention, but instead it is the conceptual dysfluency of a particular object (i.e., the octopus) with the observed context (i.e., the farm) that leads to attention being captured. Within the social psychological literature, this closely mirrors Sherman's (2001) encoding flexibility model, which posits that attention and thus subsequent processing are drawn to violations of a stereotype. Thus, when an individual encounters stereotype-inconsistent information, attention is drawn, and the perceptual details of an event are encoded. Conversely, when stereotype-confirming information is encountered, detailed attention need not be allocated to the information because the conceptual gist of the stereotype-consistent information can be quickly and easily extracted and encoded (see also von Hippel, Jonides, Hilton, & Narayan, 1993).

Not only conceptually, but also perceptually dysfluent stimuli draw visual attention. Unique or novel stimuli that are unlike adjacent stimuli also draw visual attention during a visual search (e.g., Johnston, Hawley, Plew, Elliott, & DeWitt, 1990). This is particularly relevant when applied to the social psychological theory on token status and social categorization. For example, a European American among a group of African Americans will tend to draw a great deal of attention simply due to perceptual uniqueness, a condition that may be exacerbated by conceptual dysfluency (e.g., a lone African American at an otherwise all-White Ku Klux Klan rally would likely be a quite salient figure indeed).

More recent neuropsychological research by Ito and Urland (2003, 2005) provided further evidence for the relevance of social categorization on early attentional processes. Using event-related potentials, Ito and Urland (2003) found that White participants' early waveform components (N100, P200) tended to show stronger attention to Black than to White targets, showing stronger attention to targets from less-frequently encountered social categories. Importantly, later in the attentional stream, Whites' attention appeared to shift toward members of their racial in-group and away from Black targets. Ito and Urland (2005) interpreted the early attentional findings as a vigilance process for potentially threatening stimuli. In line with this explanation, Black men, about whom negative, violent stereotypes are quite common, elicit a stronger early vigilance effect than other social categories. However, insofar as the stimuli in these tasks do not require continued vigilance, attention reverts to in-group targets (targets that are presumably more evaluatively positive). Chiao, Heck, Nakayama, and Ambady (2006) provided particularly compelling evidence of the role of social categorization in attention and visual search. They showed that the performance of biracial (Black/White) individuals in a visual search task was moderated by whether or not their Black or White identity had been primed. When primed with the White side of their identity, these biracial individuals evinced faster detection of Black faces compared to when they had been primed with their Black identity.

Importantly, these top-down effects on selective attention also appear to be powerfully influenced by the attitudes and the motivational states of the perceiver (Bruner, 1957). For example, Roskos-Ewoldsen and Fazio (1992; see also Fazio, Roskos-Ewoldsen, & Powell, 1994) argued from a functional perspective of attitudes that one of the purposes that attitudes can serve is an orienting function. In particular, Fazio and colleagues argued that attitude objects toward which perceivers have highly accessible attitudes, regardless of their valence, will tend to attract attention during the preattentive scan. However, only attitude objects with relatively strong hedonic consequences (i.e., highly accessible attitudes) are proposed to grab attention. Across four studies, Fazio and colleagues found that perceivers have better memory for attitude-evoking targets that are both integral (Experiments 1 and 2) and incidental (Experiment 3) to perceivers' task goals as well as attitude-evoking targets interfering with perceivers, visual searches (Experiment 4).

As discussed, affective states such as anxiety can lead to a focus of attention on anxiety-provoking stimuli. Affective states influence not only the direction of attention, but also the breadth of attentional focus (see Derryberry & Tucker, 1994, for a review). Although the spotlight metaphor is one of the most common in the discussion of attention, a competing metaphor is one of the zoom lens (Eriksen & Yeh, 1985). For attention to be at its most functional, we should be able to broaden or constrict the scope of attention, depending on our goals and motivations. During a particularly intensive search or a very challenging task, it may be quite useful to focus our attention on a very small number of relevant stimuli, whereas during other tasks, focusing on global at the expense of local information may be of greater use.

One motivational variable that influences the scope of attention is an orientation toward approach versus avoidance. Specifically, people who are exposed to approach-related cues or who are enacting approach-related behaviors appear to adopt a wider attentional focus and show greater flexibility in attention allocation compared to people in an avoidance orientation (Förster, Friedman, Özelsel, & Denzler, 2006; Friedman & Förster, 2005). Other research suggests that emotional states may similarly modulate attentional breadth, with anxiety narrowing attention (Easterbrook, 1959; Tyler & Tucker, 1982), whereas happiness is associated with a broader focus (e.g., Isen & Daubman, 1984). Clearly, affective and motivational factors can exert marked effects on both the scope and direction of attention.

HOLDING ATTENTION

As noted, the phenomenological experience of attention is that it is a unified process; however, attention is constituted by not just what grabs our attention, but also what holds our attention. In fact, despite the relatively large literature described regarding attention capture, relatively recent theory regarding attention suggests that much of what was previously thought to capture attention instead influences the *hold* component of attention. Indeed, distinguishing what attracts versus what holds attention is an increasingly important focus within attention research.

For example, Fox and colleagues (e.g., Fox, Russo, Bowles, & Dutton, 2001; Fox, Russo, & Dutton, 2002) called into question the attention-capturing power of negative stimuli, such as angry faces and negative words. In particular, much of this previous literature relies heavily on Stroop or Stroop-like tasks (e.g., Pratto & John, 1991) and dot-probe paradigms (e.g., MacLeod et al., 1986) in which critical to-be-ignored stimuli appear within foveal vision, whose sudden appearance will already automatically draw visual attention. In both tasks, perceivers must simultaneously attend to one stimulus characteristic (Stroop) or one stimulus (dot-probe), while ignoring another stimulus characteristic or stimulus. In both cases, an inability to ignore the to-be-ignored stimuli has been commonly interpreted as stronger attention-capturing power of that class of stimuli. For both Stroop and dot-probe tasks, however, it is unclear whether longer response latencies are due to visual attention being directly drawn to the stimuli during the preattentive scan, or whether, once attention has been engaged due to the sudden presentation, attention is difficult to *disengage*.

In fact, it does seem that threatening stimuli, both words and faces, do hold visual attention more strongly than nonthreatening stimuli. Fox and colleagues (2002) used a modified exogenous cueing paradigm in which a participant's attention was drawn away from a fixation point by a briefly presented stimulus word or face (either threatening or nonthreatening). This stimulus was then immediately replaced with a probe. Importantly, the probe either appeared at the exact location of the threatening or nonthreatening stimulus (the stimulus served as a valid cue for the probe) or appeared across the screen on the other side of the fixation point (an invalid cue). If threatening stimuli draw attention, participants should be faster to respond to the probe when it appears at the same location as a threatening (as compared to a nonthreatening) stimulus. Conversely, if attention is more powerfully held by a threatening stimulus, there should be longer response latencies to respond to invalid trials for threatening than for nonthreatening stimuli. Fox et al. (2002) found only the latter to be true. The cue validity effect was stronger for threatening than for nonthreatening stimuli. It seemed that participants had a more difficult time tearing their attention away from the location of a threatening stimulus than from a nonthreatening stimulus.

INHIBITING COMPETING SENSORY INPUTS

For some stimuli to be selected for the relatively intense scrutiny of attention, the stimuli that are nonfocal and unattended must be ignored. Thus, for our entomologist searching the forest floor, the attention spotlight must focus on the favored insect while simultaneously inhibiting the representations of the dozens of other bugs competing for attention.

There is an extensive literature that addresses this problem of how the cognitive system deals with competing inputs in selective attention. For example, in one of the first displays of what has become known as negative priming, Tipper (1985) simultaneously showed participants two superimposed stimuli, one of which was to be attended to and the other unattended. On critical trials in which a subsequent probe was identical to the previously unattended stimulus, naming latencies were slowed. Subsequent research has used a number of related paradigms, which have repeatedly indicated that the representations of unattended stimuli are inhibited by the cognitive system, an effect that a number of theorists have argued is a functional mechanism in efficient attentional selection (e.g., Dagenbach & Carr, 1994; Milliken & Tipper, 1998). In support of the claim that inhibition is a critical component of efficient attentional selection, Tipper and Baylis (1987) found that this negative priming effect is quite weak for individuals who commonly have everyday attentional failures. In any case, the available evidence makes it clear that the interplay of facilitatory and inhibitory processes, as modulated by the goals, emotions, and motives of the perceiver, guide attention to just a subset of the available stimulus field. Once captured, these attended stimuli can receive additional processing. Although the importance of facilitatory processes in biasing attention has long been appreciated, only relatively recently have several social psychological studies confirmed that inhibitory processes constrain the focus of attention in both person perception (e.g., Macrae, Bodenhausen, & Milne, 1995) and self-perception (e.g., Hugenberg & Bodenhausen, 2004); for a review, see Bodenhausen, Todd, and Becker (2007).

EXTRACTING MEANING FROM ATTENDED STIMULI

Once stimuli are transfixed in the spotlight of visual attention, the stage is set for further perceptual processing, although the task of discerning the meaning of attended stimuli seems a daunting one. Visual sensory input consists of features such as lines, texture gradients, and colors that are, in themselves, devoid of meaning. Feature detectors in the visual system are able to use these low-level features to permit the construction of more meaningful representations of the sensory world. One of the fundamental challenges of visual perception is to partition the stimulus array into discrete, meaningful objects ("wholes"), not just disjointed features. The Gestalt psychologists were among the first to characterize the principles governing this process of perceiving meaningful wholes. Similarly, social psychologists are interested in how various perceived features of social targets cohere into meaningful, holistic impressions (e.g., Asch, 1946). Given that many of the most influential pioneers of social psychology, including Asch himself, came from the Gestalt psychology tradition, the common focus on emergent meaning is not surprising.

In a fundamental sense, the challenge posed by the goal of "making sense" of the stimulus input is one of recognizing patterns. This challenge can only be surmounted by the joint application of top-down and bottom-up processes. Although the stimuli carry their own structure, as the ecological perspective emphasizes (McArthur & Baron, 1983), the perceiver must in most instances draw on prior experience to recognize that structure and appreciate its implications. When the target is a person, the richness and complexity of the stimulus person may be experienced in very different ways by perceivers. For example, some research suggests that to perceive the intentions of others, we typically simulate the same action mentally and map it onto our own intentions (when we have performed similar actions in the past; Blakemore & Decety, 2001). In this sense, social perception is necessarily highly egocentric. As social psychologists have long emphasized, different perceptions of the social world will emerge from perceivers who bring different expectancies, attitudes, motives, emotional states, or prior experiences to the top-down aspects of person perception (Bruner, 1992; Kelley, 1950).

EXPECTANCIES AND ATTITUDES

An extensive amount of research has investigated the impact of expectancies on perception, with a majority of this work emphasizing one of two opposing effects of expectancies. *Assimilation effects* emerge when the meaning of stimulus input is shifted toward a preexisting (expected) concept or prototype. *Contrast effects* emerge when the meaning of stimulus input is shifted away from the expected prototype. Assimilation is commonly found when the input bears sufficient general similarity to the prototype or is ambiguous with respect to prototype fit (e.g., Heider & Simmel, 1944); contrast is commonly found when the input contradicts the expected pattern to a sufficient degree (e.g., Biernat, 2005; see Schwarz & Bless, 2007, for a conceptual review elaborating the conditions under which assimilation versus contrast effects are likely to emerge). Massad, Hubbard, and Newtson (1979) provided particularly interesting evidence that fundamental aspects of perceptual organization are shaped by expectancies. They showed participants an ambiguous dynamic display of abstract geometric stimuli after having induced different "interpretive sets" by applying particular concepts to the stimuli (e.g., "bully" vs. "guardian"). The perceived structure of the event sequence was assessed by having respondents segment the sequence into meaningful units. The same sequence was perceptually segmented (and interpreted) in very different ways, depending on the expectancies evoked by the labels.

Although studied in many domains, these top-down processes have been particularly thoroughly explored in research examining the influence of an actor's social category membership on perceptions of his or her behavior. In many instances, a target's social identities (e.g., race, sex, age) can be rapidly perceived and can immediately establish expectancies that will influence the perception of the target's subsequent behavior. For example, compared to European American targets, African American targets displaying the very same behavior are judged to be more threatening or aggressive (Duncan, 1976; Sagar & Schofield, 1988). These effects can arise either from assimilating the perceptual input to specific stereotypic expectancies about the target's social group or from a more general evaluative assimilation based on attitudes toward the group. Evaluation is fundamental to the construction of meaning (Osgood, Suci, & Tannenbaum, 1957), and attitudes often provide the top-down context for disambiguating incoming information. Indeed, a primary function of social attitudes is to provide a global appraisal of the reward or punishment potential embodied in a stimulus. After a target is assigned to a particular category, such as a racial group, general attitudes toward that group create expectancies of positive or negative characteristics that can bias perception of the target's behavior. In support of this notion, Hugenberg and Bodenhausen (2003) showed that European American participants had a greater readiness to attribute hostility to African American (vs. European American) faces, but only when the participants had relatively high levels of implicit (automatic) racial prejudice. Participants who showed little evidence of implicit prejudice did not perceive the target faces differentially as a function of race. Thus, depending on the perceiver's racial attitudes, different constraints are imposed on the top-down aspects of extracting meaning from otherwise identical stimulus input. In this case, consciously reported, deliberated attitudes did not predict patterns of perceptual bias. The fact that it is automatic attitudes that guide these kinds of perceptual distortions speaks to their great rapidity. A growing number of studies show automatic perceptual biases of this sort (e.g., Correll, Park, Judd, & Wittenbrink, 2002; Payne, Lambert, & Jacoby, 2002). An important consequence of the automaticity of these biases is the fact that perceivers typically remain unaware that any subjective interpretations have occurred; instead, they experience their perceptions of the social world as veridical and objective, a phenomenon known as *naïve realism* (Ross & Ward, 1996).

The research just reviewed emphasized the role of social categorization in social perception, but an intriguing recent line of research has documented the role of category-correlated features in shaping social perception and judgment independently of category membership per se. Blair, Judd, Sadler, and Jenkins (2002) showed that the presence of Afrocentric features in a target person's face influenced the degree to which social perceptions aligned with stereotypes of African Americans, and this was true regardless of whether the target was explicitly categorized as an African American or European American. Similarly, within each racial group, Blair, Judd, and Chapleau (2004) found that persons who possess more Afrocentric facial features received harsher judgments in criminal sentencing. In this instance, facial features create a bottom-up pathway for activating racial stereotypes that appears not to be moderated by social categorization per se. Once activated, these stereotypes can insinuate themselves into social perception by the previously documented processes of assimilation (e.g., Bodenhausen, 1988). In general, social attitudes and expectancies can exert many noteworthy effects on what people perceive and how they perceive it (for a review, see Fazio, 1986).

PRIOR EPISODIC EXPERIENCE

Whereas the preceding section emphasized the role of generic knowledge (e.g., attitudes, stereotypes) in shaping perception, it is also the case that episodic experiences can play an important role in influencing how social perception unfolds. One of the more interesting examples of this phenomenon comes from studies conducted by Lewicki (1985). Participants in one study were required to make choices that depended on perceptions of the friendliness of experimental confederates. The participants had previously been exposed to another (un)friendly confederate whose hairstyle was similar to that of one of the newly encountered confederates. Although the confederates behaved the same way in all conditions, and they in fact did not give much information that would permit the determination of their level of friendliness, their superficial similarity to the previously encountered person exerted a reliable assimilative influence on their perceived friendliness.

A vast literature has accumulated confirming that recent experiences routinely influence subsequent perception, judgment, and behavior. Most of this research has been conducted under the rubric of "priming effects," which come in two main varieties: semantic priming and affective priming. The major lesson of this research is that recently encountered exemplars and recently activated concepts can exert surprisingly potent influence on the processing of subsequently encountered information, even if the new information is ostensibly completely unrelated to the prior information. In the case of semantic priming research, recently activated cognitive representations produce highly accessible concepts that are used to interpret the meaning of incoming stimuli. In one classic demonstration, Srull and Wyer (1979) showed that frequent prior activation of hostile concepts in one task produced a tendency to interpret the ambiguous behavior of a subsequently encountered person as more aggressive compared to a control condition that did not experience frequent activation of the hostile concepts. Although priming can sometimes produce contrast effects, the most common pattern is for ostensibly unrelated (or subliminal) primes to produce assimilation effects. For such effects to occur, the to-be-perceived target stimuli must be sufficiently ambiguous that they permit multiple interpretations, and the activated concepts must be sufficiently applicable to the target (Higgins, 1996). In addition to influencing the manner in which ambiguous stimuli are perceived, semantic priming also influences the speed with which unambiguously semantically related stimuli can be perceived and interpreted, with semantically congruent stimuli receiving more efficient processing (see McNamara, 2005, for a review).

In the case of affective priming, the general evaluative tone of a recent experience influences subsequent information processing. Murphy and Zajonc (1993) showed that subliminal presentations of simple affective cues (happy or scowling faces) resulted in significant shifts in participants' perceptions of novel stimuli (Chinese idiographs). They postulated a misattribution mechanism by which the diffuse affective reaction generated by the prime stimulus is applied to the subsequently encountered target. As with semantic priming, affective priming is also evident in the more efficient, rapid processing of stimuli that are affectively consistent with recently experienced stimuli (see Klauer & Musch, 2003, for a review).

AFFECTIVE AND MOTIVATIONAL STATES

The "new look" in perception that emerged in the mid-20th century was organized around the idea that attention and perception are tuned by the emotional and motivational states of the perceiver. One of the more famous early demonstrations documented a perceptual bias in a simple perception estimation task: estimating the size of coins. Specifically, perceivers consistently overestimated the size of relatively more valuable coins, but this general tendency was moderated by socioeconomic status: Poor perceivers were prone to exhibit a larger "value bias" than wealthy ones (Bruner & Goodman, 1947). Personal values were found to generally influence perceptual thresholds (Postman, Bruner, & McGinnies, 1948), and Postman and Bruner (1948) showed that emotional distress influences perception, and that perceptual defenses are sometimes raised to avoid processing unpleasant or threatening stimuli. Findings such as these accord with the general proposition that affective and motivational states convey important information about a person's current priorities, and it makes a great deal of sense that processes of perception are tuned and oriented toward these priorities.

Over the subsequent decades, researchers have explored a variety of mechanisms by which ego defense and other self-related motives color all aspects of social cognition (e.g., Dunning, 2003). A classic study by Hastorf and Cantril (1954) documented how the partisan motives of football fans colored their perceptions of game events, leading to systematically different, in-group-favoring perceptions of the same events, depending on one's team allegiance. More recently, Balcetis and Dunning (2006, 2007) showed that perceptions of ambiguous stimuli are resolved in ways that serve the current goals of the perceiver (such as self-enhancement or the reduction of cognitive dissonance). Fein and colleagues (e.g., Fein, Hoshino-Brown, Davies, & Spencer, 2003) showed that a perceiver is more likely to organize his or her perceptions of an out-group target in stereotypic ways after experiencing a self-image threat. These examples are drawn from an extensive literature showing how our perceptions are tuned toward self-serving meanings.

Other examinations of motivational bias have expanded beyond the realm of self-enhancing social perceptions. For example, recent research (Sacco & Hugenberg, 2008) suggested that motivational states not only bias the direction of perception (e.g., causing a coin to loom larger) but also enhance the perceptual acuity of the visual system. In this research, participants were put in a cooperative mindset, a competitive mindset, or a control mindset unrelated to either motivational state. In line with classic evidence from the new look, interpretations of morphed angry-happy expressions were directionally biased by motives: Competitively motivated participants interpreted ambiguous expressions as angrier than did cooperatively motivated participants. In a separate perceptual discrimination task, however, the same participants were presented with two morphed stimuli from the same morph continuum and were required to decide whether the stimuli were identical or were similar but subtly different. Participants in both cooperative and competitive mindsets became better able to make this fine-grained perceptual discrimination. In other tasks, cooperatively and competitively motivated participants became better able to distinguish real (Duchennne) from fake smiles and even became better able to accurately perceive motivationally relevant happy and angry expressions in increasing levels of visual noise. Thus, motives can certainly affect the interpretation of stimuli, but they also appear to tune perceivers into fine-grained perceptual details of motivationally relevant stimuli.

Broader attentional shifts also seem subject to perceivers' level of regulatory focus (e.g., Higgins, 2006), which is concerned with whether perceivers are more oriented toward advancement and opportunity (i.e., a promotion focus) or security and the avoidance of loss (i.e., a prevention focus). Förster and Higgins (2005) argued that perceivers who are (chronically or momentarily) focused on prevention concerns are likely to adopt a vigilant perceptual style that is oriented toward details, whereas perceivers who are focused on promotion concerns are likely to adopt an eager perceptual style that is oriented toward the "big picture." This notion maps onto a classic distinction between local versus global perception. They adopted a classic test devised by Navon (1977) to study whether perceivers are more oriented toward seeing the forest or seeing the trees. In line with their hypotheses, Förster and Higgins found that the degree of promotion focus was related to the speed with which perceivers could discern the global pattern, whereas the degree of prevention focus was related to the speed with which perceivers could discern the local details within the global pattern. Thus, perceptions are organized not only in terms of self-serving motivations but also in terms of the general orientations toward self-regulation that are captured in regulatory focus theory.

INDIVIDUAL DIFFERENCES IN THE EXTRACTION OF MEANING IN PERCEPTION

The foregoing discussion underscores several ways in which perceptions of the social world can be idiosyncratic. The very same social stimulus can be experienced in distinctly different ways by individuals who have different motives, attitudes, expectancies, and recent experiences. All of this work underscores the crucial role of top-down processes in constraining social perception. Research by Lewicki (2005) suggests another potentially important individual difference dimension: internal versus external encoding style. An *external encoding style* refers to a conservative, data-driven approach to perception in which reactions to stimuli are more strongly governed by bottom-up aspects of perception. *Internal encoding styles*, in contrast, reflect a greater readiness to make theory-driven assumptions and rely on top-down processing. Individuals appear to show reliable variation in their adoption of these encoding styles. Compared to the external style, the internal encoding style confers both advantages and disadvantages. Perceivers with an internal style are better at identifying rapidly presented pictures and words and are better at seeing the pattern in an incomplete display; however, they are also more prone to priming effects and more likely to overlook information that is inconsistent with their expectations (see Lewicki, Czyewska, & Hill, 1997). Thus, this research suggests that individual differences in perception arise not only from differences in the cognitive content governing top-down processing, but also in the overall potency of the top-down side of perception relative to the reality constraints provided by incoming, bottom-up data.

FROM PERCEPTION TO ACTION

Perception is linked to action in some fairly obvious ways. To navigate the environment, manipulate objects, and interact with others, we must be able to perceive external stimuli and use this perceptual input for motor guidance. The connections between perception and action are sufficiently intimate that some theorists have postulated that both systems rely on the same underlying representations (i.e., common-coding theories; see Prinz, 1997). Indeed, much attention has been devoted recently to the workings of mirror neurons, which are cortical neurons that fire both when a given action is actually performed and when the same type of action is merely perceived (i.e., when conspecifics are seen to perform analogous actions; for a review, see Rizzolatti & Craighero, 2004). The traditional social psychological view, reflected in Figure 1.1, has relied on the assumption that perception guides action by virtue of the meaning that is conferred on perceived stimuli.

One specific model that captures this perspective very well is Fazio's attitude-to-behavior process model (Fazio, 1986), which has been incorporated into his more recent MODE model (e.g., Fazio & Roskos-Ewoldsen, 2005). The model assumes that selective perception is a key mediator of attitude-behavior consistency. When an attitude is activated in memory, it can influence online processes of perception that imbue the attitude object and the surrounding circumstances with meaning and thereby inform overt behavioral responses. For example, if proenvironmental attitudes are accessible and become activated, an empty beverage container on the ground may be perceived as a recyclable object. Once so defined, the perceiver may pick it up and carry it to a suitable recycling bin. If the proenvironmental attitude had been inaccessible, the same object might have merely been perceived as garbage and left lying on the ground (or put into a garbage can). The meaning conferred in the process of perceiving the environment is therefore critical in determining how the perceiver will act. Thus, the social psychological view has been that differences in the way different people react to the same stimulus or situation are attributable to the different attitudes, beliefs, emotional states, motives, and past experiences that have shaped their construals of the environment (Ross & Nisbett, 1991).

This traditional view has been challenged in provocative ways by recent research that questions the necessity of conceptual mediation of the linkages between perception and action. According to this view, perception can sometimes directly produce action without any intervening process of appraising the meaning of the perceived stimuli. The growing body of supportive literature suggests the necessity of amending our schematic model (see Figure 1.2).

Some neuroanatomical evidence supports the possibility that perceptual input is indeed processed in two separate pathways, one for appraising its meaning and one for directly organizing behavioral responses (Norman, 2002). Thus, there appear to be good biological reasons for expecting both direct and indirect (construal-mediated) influences of perception on action.

The evidence for direct perception–behavior linkages comes from studies of automatic behavior (for a review, see Dijksterhuis, Chartrand, & Aarts, 2007). In these studies, researchers use priming techniques to expose participants to particular stimuli and then show that exposure to the stimuli exerts measurable effects

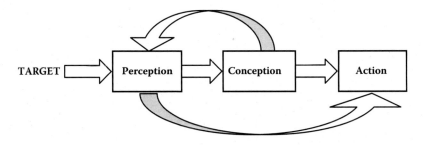

Figure 1.2   Modified schematic model of social information processing.

on behavior, even though perceivers would have no logical reason to see any connection between the prime stimuli and their own responses (i.e., there is no plausible conceptually mediated pathway connecting perception of the prime to the measured behavior). For example, Bargh, Chen, and Burrows (1996) showed that activation of words associated with the elderly caused participants to walk more slowly (an elderly behavioral trait). Although conscious appraisals do not appear to be relevant for effects of this sort, it is clear that the conceptual system is playing a role in that perception of the elderly related primes is governed by top-down expectancies that have presumably been learned. Indeed, automatic behavior effects resulting from stereotype activation have been shown to vary with the idiosyncratic strength of the relevant stereotype (Dijksterhuis, Aarts, Bargh, & Van Knippenberg, 2000). In this case, the conceptual system (specifically, the meaning associated with the category "elderly") biases the perceptual system, which then exerts a direct influence on the action system. As Dijksterhuis et al. (2007) pointed out, perceived environmental stimuli can influence behavior by directly activating motor programs, as may be the case in some forms of the phenomenon of motor mimicry (Chartrand & Bargh, 1999), or by activating traits or goals that in turn potentiate relevant behavioral responses.

Given the available evidence for both a relatively conscious, indirect, construal-based pathway connecting perception to action as well as a more unconscious, direct pathway, it is likely that the most satisfying theoretical accounts of the connections between perception and action will incorporate (at least) two distinct mediating causal processes. One such model is the reflective-impulsive model (RIM) proposed by Strack and Deutsch (2004). According to the RIM, perception of a stimulus can result in the direct activation of behavior representations via spreading activation processes, potentially producing corresponding impulsive behaviors (e.g., seeing a bowl of peanuts may trigger eating of the peanuts even if one is not at all hungry, with little in the way of thoughtful construal taking place). In contrast, perception can also activate relevant knowledge and conscious reasoning processes (i.e., reflection) that produce a more thoughtful construal of the stimulus and may result in quite different behavioral consequences (e.g., thinking about the facts that one is not really hungry and that one is trying to lose some weight, the visually detected peanuts are construed as a high-calorie impediment to a more swimsuit-ready physique and are passed up). Although a clear distinction is drawn between these two pathways connecting perception and action, the RIM also recognizes that the pathways can and do interact in significant ways.

CONCLUSION

There is a long and venerable tradition of studying social perception and seeking to understand how meaning is extracted from incoming information about the social world. This interest extends back even into the heyday of behaviorism, reflecting the adamant belief of social psychologists that, no matter how influential the external environment is in shaping behavior, that impact is mediated by cognitive mechanisms occurring within the active mind of a perceiving organism. Nevertheless, a major trend in recent decades has been the increasing appreciation that many vital aspects of social perception happen very rapidly and automatically, in ways that are often completely opaque to the perceiver's conscious mind. Perception often seems inextricably linked to conscious experience, in that we are aware of that which we attend to and perceive. But, the top-down shaping of attention and perception typically occurs behind the curtain of consciousness, in the patented black box of the behaviorists. However, as we develop ever-more-powerful techniques for studying these unconscious mental processes, much has been learned—and much remains to be learned—about the perceptual processes that transform the buzzing confusion of the outer world into a meaningful and coherent inner world and that permit organized and adaptive action.

NOTE

1. We focus our attention primarily on the visual modality of perception because the bulk of the available research on social perception has focused on visual information. However, analogous processes undoubtedly operate in auditory perception, and recent research has even documented subtle influences of olfactory perception in directing social preferences (e.g., Li, Moallem, Paller, & Gottfried, 2007).

REFERENCES

Asch, S. (1946). Forming impressions of personality. *Journal of Abnormal and Social Psychology, 41*, 258–290.

Balcetis, E., & Dunning, D. (2006). See what you want to see: Motivational influences on visual perception. *Journal of Personality and Social Psychology, 91*, 612–625.

Balcetis, E., & Dunning, D. (2007). Cognitive dissonance and the perception of natural environments. *Psychological Science, 18*, 917–921.

Bargh, J. A., Chen, M., & Burrows, L. (1996). Automaticity of social behavior: Direct effects of trait construct and stereotype priming on action. *Journal of Personality and Social Psychology, 71*, 230–244.

Biernat, M. (2005). *Standards and expectancies: Contrast and assimilation in judgments of self and others*. New York: Psychology Press.

Blair, I. V., Judd, C. M., & Chapleau, K. M. (2004). The influence of Afrocentric features in criminal sentencing. *Psychological Science, 15*, 674–679.

Blair, I. V., Judd, C. M., Sadler, M. S., & Jenkins, C. (2002). The role of Afrocentric features in person perception: Judging by features and categories. *Journal of Personality and Social Psychology, 83*, 5–25.

Blakemore, S.-J., & Decety, J. (2001). From the perception of action to the understanding of intention. *Nature Neuroscience, 2*, 561–567.

Bodenhausen, G. V. (1988). Stereotypic biases in social decision making and memory: Testing process models of stereotype use. *Journal of Personality and Social Psychology, 55*, 726–737.

Bodenhausen, G. V., Todd, A. R., & Becker, A. P. (2007). Categorizing the social world: Affect, motivation, and self-regulation. In B. H. Ross & A. B. Markman (Eds.), *Psychology of learning and motivation* (Vol. 47, pp. 123–155). New York: Elsevier.

Bradley, B. P., Mogg, K., Falla, S. J., & Hamilton, L. R. (1998). Attentional bias for threatening facial expressions in anxiety: Manipulation of stimulus duration. *Cognition and Emotion, 12*, 737–753.

Brewer, M. B. (2004). Taking the social origins of human nature seriously: Toward a more imperialist social psychology. *Personality and Social Psychology Review, 8*, 107–113.

Broadbent, D. E. (1958). *Perception and communication*. London: Pergamon Press.

Broadbent, D. E., & Broadbent, M. H. (1988). Anxiety and attentional bias: State and trait. *Cognition and Emotion, 2*, 165–183.

Bruner, J. S. (1957). On perceptual readiness. *Psychological Review, 64*, 123–152.

Bruner, J. S. (1992). Another look at New Look 1. *American Psychologist, 47*, 780–783.

Bruner, J. S., & Goodman, C. C. (1947). Value and need as organizing factors in perception. *Journal of Abnormal and Social Psychology, 42*, 33–44.

Bruner, J. S., & Tagiuri, R. (1954). The perception of people. In G. Lindzey (Ed.), *Handbook of social psychology* (Vol. 2, pp. 634–654). Reading, MA: Addison-Wesley.

Byrne, R. W. (2000). Evolution of primate cognition. *Cognitive Science, 24*, 543–570.

Chartrand, T. L., & Bargh, J. A. (1999). The chameleon effect: The perception-behavior link and social interaction. *Journal of Personality and Social Psychology, 76*, 893–910.

Chiao, J. Y., Heck, H. E., Nakayama, K., & Ambady, N. (2006). Priming race in biracial observers affects visual search for black and white faces. *Psychological Science, 17*, 387–392.

Choi, Y. S., Gray, H. M., & Ambady, N. (2005). The glimpsed world: Unintended communication and unintended perception. In R. R. Hassin, J. S. Uleman, & J. A. Bargh (Eds.), *The new unconscious* (pp. 309–333). New York: Oxford University Press.

Correll, J., Park, B., Judd, C. M., & Wittenbrink, B. (2002). The police officer's dilemma: Using ethnicity to disambiguate potentially threatening individuals. *Journal of Personality and Social Psychology, 83*, 1314–1329.

Cummins, D. D. (1998). Social norms and other minds: The evolutionary roots of higher cognition. In D. D. Cummins & C. Allen (Eds.), *The evolution of mind* (pp. 30–50). New York: Oxford University Press.

Dagenbach, D., & Carr, T. H. (Eds.). (1994). *Inhibitory processes in attention, memory, and language*. San Diego, CA: Academic Press.

Derryberry, D., & Tucker, D. M. (1994). Motivating the focus of attention. In P. M. Niedenthal & S. Kitayama (Eds.), *The heart's eye: Emotional influences in perception and attention* (pp. 167–196). San Diego, CA: Academic Press.

Dijksterhuis, A., Aarts, H., Bargh, J., & Van Knippenberg, A. (2000). On the relation between associative strength and automatic behavior. *Journal of Experimental Social Psychology, 36*, 531–544.

Dijksterhuis, A., Chartrand, T. L., & Aarts, H. (2007). Effects of priming and perception on social behavior and goal pursuit. In J. A. Bargh (Ed.), *Social psychology and the unconscious: The automaticity of higher mental processes* (pp. 51–131). New York: Psychology Press.

Duncan, B. L. (1976). Differential social perception and attribution of intergroup violence: Testing the lower limits of stereotyping of blacks. *Journal of Personality and Social Psychology, 34*, 590–598.

Dunning, D. (2003). The zealous self-affirmer: How and why the self lurks so pervasively behind social judgment. In S. J. Spencer, S. Fein, M. P. Zanna, & J. M. Olson (Eds.), *Motivated social perception: The Ontario symposium* (Vol. 9, pp. 45–72). Mahwah, NJ: Erlbaum.

Easterbrook, J. A. (1959). The effect of emotion on cue utilization and the organization of behavior. *Psychological Review, 66*, 183–201.

Erdelyi, M. H. (1974). A new look at the New Look: Perceptual defense and vigilance. *Psychological Review, 81*, 1–25.

Eriksen, C. W., & Yeh, Y. (1985). Allocation of attention in the visual field. *Journal of Experimental Psychology: Human Perception and Performance, 11*, 583–597.
Fazio, R. H. (1986). How do attitudes guide behavior? In R. M. Sorrentino & E. T. Higgins (Eds.), *Handbook of motivation and cognition* (pp. 204–243). New York: Guilford.
Fazio, R. H., & Roskos-Ewoldsen, D. R. (2005). Acting as we feel: When and how attitudes guide behavior. In T. C. Brock & M. C. Green (Eds.), *Persuasion: Psychological insights and perspectives* (pp. 41–62). Thousand Oaks, CA: Sage.
Fazio, R. H., Roskos-Ewoldsen, D. R., & Powell, M. C. (1994). Attitudes, perception, and attention. In P. M. Niedenthal & S. Kitayama (Eds.), *The heart's eye: Emotional influences in perception and attention* (pp. 197–216). New York: Academic Press.
Fein, S., Hoshino-Brown, E., Davies, P. G., & Spencer, S. J. (2003). Self-image maintenance goals and sociocultural norms in motivated social perception. In S. J. Spencer, S. Fein, M. P. Zanna, & J. M. Olson (Eds.), *Motivated social perception: The Ontario symposium* (Vol. 9, pp. 21–44). Mahwah, NJ: Erlbaum.
Fiske, S. T., & Taylor, S. E. (1991). *Social cognition* (2nd ed.). New York: McGraw-Hill.
Förster, J., Friedman, R. S., Özelsel, A., & Denzler, M. (2006). Enactment of approach and avoidance behavior influences the scope of perceptual and conceptual attention. *Journal of Experimental Social Psychology, 42*, 133–146.
Förster, J., & Higgins, E. T. (2005). How global versus local perception fits regulatory focus. *Psychological Science, 16*, 631–636.
Fox, E., Lester, V., Russo, R., Bowles, R. J., Pichler, A., & Dutton, K. (2000). Facial expressions of emotion: Are angry faces detected more efficiently? *Cognition and Emotion, 14*, 61–92.
Fox, E., Russo, R., Bowles, R., & Dutton, K. (2001). Do threatening stimuli draw or hold visual attention in subclinical anxiety? *Journal of Experimental Psychology: General, 130*, 681–700.
Fox, E., Russo, R., & Dutton, K. (2002). Attentional bias for threat: Evidence for delayed disengagement from emotional faces. *Cognition and Emotion, 16*, 355–379.
Franconeri, S. L., & Simons, D. J. (2003). Moving and looming stimuli capture attention. *Perception & Psychophysics, 65*, 999–1010.
Friedman, R., & Förster, J. (2005). The influence of approach and avoidance cues on attentional flexibility. *Motivation and Emotion, 29*, 69–81.
Hansen, C. H., & Hansen, R. D. (1988). Finding the face in the crowd: An anger superiority effect. *Journal of Personality and Social Psychology, 54*, 917–924.
Hastorf, A. H., & Cantril, H. (1954). They saw a game: A case study. *Journal of Abnormal and Social Psychology, 49*, 129–134.
Heider, F., & Simmel, M. (1944). An experimental study of apparent behavior. *American Journal of Psychology, 57*, 243–259.
Higgins, E. T. (1996). Knowledge activation: Accessibility, applicability, and salience. In E. T. Higgins & A. W. Kruglanski (Eds.), *Social psychology: Handbook of basic principles* (pp. 133–168). New York: Guilford.
Higgins, E. T. (2006). Value from hedonic experience and engagement. *Psychological Review, 113*, 439–460.
Hugenberg, K., & Bodenhausen, G. V. (2003). Facing prejudice: Implicit prejudice and the perception of facial threat. *Psychological Science, 14*, 640–643.
Hugenberg, K., & Bodenhausen, G. V. (2004). Category membership moderates the inhibition of social identities. *Journal of Experimental Social Psychology, 40*, 233–238.
Isen, A. M., & Daubman, K. A. (1984). The influence of affect on categorization. *Journal of Personality and Social Psychology, 47*, 1206–1217.
Ito, T. A., & Urland, G. R. (2003). Race and gender on the brain: Electrocortical measures of attention to race and gender of multiply categorizable individuals. *Journal of Personality and Social Psychology, 85*, 616–626.

Ito, T. A., & Urland, G. R. (2005). The influence of processing objectives on the perception of faces: An ERP study of race and gender perception. *Cognitive, Affective, & Behavioral Neuroscience, 5,* 21–36.
James, W. (1890). *Principles of psychology.* New York: Holt.
Johnston, W. A., Hawley, K. J., Plew, S. H., Elliott, J. M., & DeWitt, M. J. (1990). Attention capture by novel stimuli. *Journal of Experimental Psychology: General, 119,* 397–411.
Jones, E. E. (1990). *Interpersonal perception.* New York: Freeman.
Jonides, J., & Yantis, S. (1988). Uniqueness of abrupt visual onset in capturing attention. *Perception & Psychophysics, 43,* 346–354.
Kelley, H. H. (1950). The warm-cold variable in first impressions of persons. *Journal of Personality, 18,* 431–439.
Klauer, K.-C., & Musch, J. (2003). Affective priming: Findings and theories. In J. Musch & K.-C. Klauer (Eds.), *The psychology of evaluation* (pp. 7–49). Mahwah, NJ: Erlbaum.
Leakey, R. E. (1978). *The people of the lake: Mankind and its beginnings.* New York: Avon.
Lewicki, P. (1985). Nonconscious biasing effects of single instances on subsequent judgments. *Journal of Personality and Social Psychology, 48,* 563–574.
Lewicki, P. (2005). Internal and external encoding style and social motivation. In J. P. Forgas, K. D. Williams, & S. M. Laham (Eds.), *Social motivation: Conscious and unconscious processes* (pp. 194–209). New York: Cambridge University Press.
Lewicki, P., Czyewska, M., & Hill, T. (1997). Nonconscious information processing and personality. In D. Berry (Ed.), *How implicit is implicit learning?* (pp. 48–72). Oxford, England: Oxford University Press.
Li, W., Moallem, I., Paller, K. A., & Gottfried, J. A. (2007). Subliminal smells can guide social preferences. *Psychological Science, 18,* 1044–1049.
Li, W., Zinbarg, R. E., & Paller, K. A. (2007). Trait anxiety modulates supraliminal and subliminal threat: Brain potential evidence for early and late processing influences. *Cognitive, Affective & Behavioral Neuroscience, 7,* 25–36.
Loftus, G. R., & Mackworth, N. H. (1978). Cognitive determinants of fixation location during picture viewing. *Journal of Experimental Psychology: Human Perception and Performance, 4,* 565–572.
MacLeod, C., & Mathews, A. (1988). Anxiety and the allocation of attention to threat. *Quarterly Journal of Experimental Psychology: Human Experimental Psychology, 40,* 653–670.
MacLeod, C., Mathews, A., & Tata, P. (1986). Attentional bias in emotional disorders. *Journal of Abnormal Psychology, 95,* 15–20.
Macrae, C. N., Bodenhausen, G. V., & Milne, A. B. (1995). The dissection of selection in social perception: Inhibitory processes in social stereotyping. *Journal of Personality and Social Psychology, 69,* 397–407.
Marr, D. (1982). *Vision.* San Francisco: Freeman.
Massad, C. M., Hubbard, M., & Newtson, D. (1979). Selective perception of events. *Journal of Experimental Social Psychology, 15,* 513–532.
McArthur, L. Z., & Baron, R. M. (1983). Toward an ecological theory of social perception. *Psychological Review, 90,* 215–247.
McNamara, T. P. (2005). *Semantic priming: Perspectives from memory and word recognition.* New York: Psychology Press.
Milliken, B., & Tipper, S. P. (1998). Attention and inhibition. In H. Pashler (Ed.), *Attention* (pp. 191–221). East Sussex, England: Psychology Press.
Murphy, S. T., & Zajonc, R. B. (1993). Affect, cognition, and awareness: Affective priming with optimal and suboptimal stimulus exposures. *Journal of Personality and Social Psychology, 64,* 723–739.

Navon, D. (1977). Forest before trees: The precedence of global features in visual perception. *Cognitive Psychology, 9*, 353–383.
Niedenthal, P. M., Halberstadt, J. B., & Innes-Ker, Å. H. (1999). Emotional response categorization. *Psychological Review, 106*, 337–361.
Norman, J. (2002). Two visual systems and two theories of perception: An attempt to reconcile the constructivist and ecological approaches. *Behavioral and Brain Sciences, 24*, 73–96.
Öhman, A., Flykt, A., & Esteves, F. (2001). Emotion drives attention: Detecting the snake in the grass. *Journal of Experimental Psychology: General, 130*, 466–478.
Öhman, A., Lundqvist, D., & Esteves, F. (2001). Face in the crowd revisited: A threat advantage with schematic stimuli. *Journal of Personality and Social Psychology, 80*, 381–396.
Osgood, C., Suci, G. J., & Tannenbaum, P. H. (1957). *The measurement of meaning*. Urbana: University of Illinois Press.
Payne, B. K., Lambert, A. J., & Jacoby, L. L. (2002). Best laid plans: Effects of goals on accessibility bias and cognitive control in race-based misperceptions of weapons. *Journal of Experimental Social Psychology, 38*, 384–396.
Posner, M. I. (1994). Attention: The mechanism of consciousness. *Proceedings of the National Academy of Sciences, 91*, 7398–7402.
Posner, M. I., Walker, J. A., Friedrich, F. J., & Rafal, R. D. (1984). Effects of parietal injury on covert orienting of attention. *Journal of Neuroscience, 4*, 1863–1874.
Postman, L., & Bruner, J. S. (1948). Perception under stress. *Psychological Review, 55*, 314–323.
Postman, L., Bruner, J. S., & McGinnies, E. (1948). Personal values as selective factors in perception. *Journal of Abnormal and Social Psychology, 43*, 142–154.
Pratto, F., & John, O. P. (1991). Automatic vigilance: The attention-grabbing power of negative social information. *Journal of Personality and Social Psychology, 61*, 380–391.
Prinz, W. (1997). Perception and action planning. *European Journal of Cognitive Psychology, 9*, 129–154.
Rizzolatti, G., & Craighero, L. (2004). The mirror-neuron system. *Annual Review of Neuroscience, 27*, 169–192.
Roskos-Ewoldsen, D. M., & Fazio, R. H. (1992). On the orienting value of attitudes: Attitude accessibility as a determinant of an object's attraction of visual attention. *Journal of Personality and Social Psychology, 63*, 198–211.
Ross, L., & Nisbett, R. E. (1991). *The person and the situation: Perspectives of social psychology*. New York: McGraw-Hill.
Ross, L., & Ward, A. (1996). Naive realism: Implications for social conflict and misunderstanding. In T. Brown, E. Reed, and E. Turiel (Eds.), *Values and knowledge* (pp. 103–135). Hillsdale, NJ: Erlbaum.
Sacco, D. F., & Hugenberg, K. (2008). *Social motives tune the perceptual system*. Manuscript submitted for publication.
Sagar, H. A., & Schofield, J. W. (1988). Racial and behavioral cues in black and white children's perceptions of ambiguously aggressive acts. *Journal of Personality and Social Psychology, 39*, 590–598.
Schwarz, N., & Bless, H. (2007). Mental construal processes: The inclusion/exclusion model. In D. A. Stapel & J. Suls (Eds.), *Assimilation and contrast in social psychology* (pp. 119–141). Philadelphia: Psychology Press.
Seyfarth, R. M., & Cheney, D. L. (1994). The evolution of social cognition in primates. In L. Real (Ed.), *Behavioral mechanisms in evolutionary ecology* (pp. 371–389). Chicago: University of Chicago Press.

Sherman, J. W. (2001). The dynamic relationship between stereotype efficiency and mental representation. In G. B. Moskowitz (Ed.), *Cognitive social psychology: The Princeton symposium on the legacy and future of social cognition* (pp. 177–190). Mawah, NJ: Erlbaum.
Srull, T. K., & Wyer, R. S., Jr. (1979). The role of category accessibility in the interpretation of information about persons: Some determinants and implications. *Journal of Personality and Social Psychology, 37*, 1660–1672.
Strack, F., & Deutsch, R. (2004). Reflective and impulsive determinants of behavior. *Personality and Social Psychology Review, 8*, 220–247.
Theeuwes, J. (1995). Abrupt luminance change pops-out: Abrupt color change does not. *Perception & Psychophysics, 57*, 637–644.
Tipper, S. P. (1985). The negative priming effect: Inhibitory priming by ignored objects. *Quarterly Journal of Experimental Psychology: Human Experimental Psychology, 37*, 571–590.
Tipper, S. P., & Baylis, G. C. (1987). Individual differences in selective attention: The relation of priming and interference to cognitive failure. *Personality and Individual Differences, 8*, 667–675.
Tomasello, M., Carpenter, M., Call, J., Behne, T., & Moll, H. (2005). Understanding and sharing intentions: The origins of cultural cognition. *Behavioral and Brain Sciences, 28*, 675–735.
Triesman, A., & Gelade, G. (1980). A feature integration theory of attention. *Cognitive Psychology, 12*, 97–136.
Tyler, S. K., & Tucker, D. M. (1982). Anxiety and perceptual structure: individual differences in neuropsychological function. *Journal of Abnormal Psychology, 91*, 210–220.
von Hippel, W., Jonides, J., Hilton, J. L., & Narayan, S. (1993). Inhibitory effect of schematic processing on perceptual encoding. *Journal of Personality and Social Psychology, 64*, 921–935.
Wyer, R. S., Jr., & Carlston, D. E. (1979). *Social cognition, inference, and attribution*. Hillsdale, NJ: Erlbaum.
Yantis, S., & Johnson, D. N. (1990). Mechanisms of attentional priority. *Journal of Experimental Psychology: Human Perception and Performance, 16*, 812–825.
Zebrowitz, L. A. (1990). *Social perception*. Pacific Grove, CA: Brooks/Cole.

2

Representing Social Concepts Modally and Amodally

PAULA M. NIEDENTHAL, LAURIE MONDILLON,
DANIEL A. EFFRON, and LAWRENCE W. BARSALOU

INTRODUCTION

Social cognition can be defined as the study of the mental processes that mediate the perception of social entities and behavior. These mental processes are sometimes called the "thoughts people have about people" (Wegner & Vallacher, 1977, p. viii) or the "organized thoughts that people have about social interaction" (Roloff & Berger, 1982, p. 21). Discrimination, for example, is a behavior we wish to predict, and its prediction is enhanced by an understanding of ways in which the discriminating person thinks about the group they are discriminating against, by an understanding, that is, of their concept or stereotype of the target group (e.g., Devine, 1989; Dovidio & Gaertner, 1998; Fazio, Jackson, Dunton, & Williams, 1995; Lepore & Brown, 1997). A *concept* is a mental representation of a category, natural or artifactual, that exists in the world or in the introspective experience of the individual. So, social psychologists who study social cognition study concepts. Of course, just how concepts are represented and used can be viewed in a number of ways. Implicitly or explicitly, students of social cognition adopted a variety of different models of concepts from cognitive psychology. There have been some challenges to the currently fashionable models of the conceptual system. Why these challenges should be taken seriously is at issue here.

In the first part of the chapter, we review three different models of the conceptual system that have been of interest to social psychologists. We also discuss the ways in which they account for or implement some basic preoccupations of researchers in social cognition, including concept learning, information retrieval, and induction or inference. The models we review are associative network models, exemplar models, and distributed processing (connectionist) models. Then, we present recent and not so recent findings that seem not to fit, at least in a rigorous a priori way, these models. Most such findings implicate the use of sensorimotor and affective systems in information processing, not implicate by association but implicate as a causal mechanism. To make sense of such findings, we describe a different approach to concepts that has been variously called sensorimotor-based models, embodied simulation models, or more broadly, theories of embodied cognition. After making comparisons between these models and the standard models described in the first part of the chapter, we present new findings from our laboratory that seem to underscore the utility and productivity of such embodiment models from the point of view of researchers in the area of social cognition.

A secondary goal of the chapter is to stimulate concern among social psychologists about the details of the representational models that they adopt. This is important because when sharp details and assumptions of the representation model are not made explicit and not evaluated empirically, then the model becomes a heuristic or a story. Because it is easy to tell stories about patterns of data, this leads to theoretical imprecision and an inability of the model to be falsified. Leaving these details to cognitive psychologists is fine in some cases as long as those details are then maintained as fundamental to the model, and are directly transferable to the domain of social cognition, that is, to the domain of how people think about other people. Unfortunately, this is not always the case. In fact, some of the authors of the present chapter consider current symbolic models of the conceptual system inadequate for the modeling of emotional information processing and consider alternative models, such as the more recently (re)proposed models of embodied cognition as more biologically and psychologically plausible representational models (e.g., Barsalou, Niedenthal, Barbey, & Ruppert, 2003; Niedenthal, Barsalou, Winkielman, Krauth-Gruber, & Ric, 2005).

WHAT ARE CONCEPTS, AND WHY DO WE CARE ABOUT THEM?

To begin, we need to start by being clear about what we mean when we talk about concepts. We have mentioned that concepts represent categories of entities, situations, and experience. They are important because they are used in almost every act of higher-level cognition, such as thinking, reasoning, and language use, and also participate in lower-level processes such as perception, identification, and recognition. When in a crowded marketplace we suddenly *see* our friend Isabelle as such, we are relying on our concept of Isabelle to categorize the input as this particular friend. Other experiences with the social world also involve concept use. Choosing the right person in a crowded store to ask where to buy gloves involves applying our concept of a *salesperson*. We distinguish children from teachers in the schoolyard, conductors from passengers on a train, and protesters from government officials from police at a demonstration. Each of these discriminations involves the use of a concept.

Complementing the substantial literature in cognitive psychology (see Goldstone & Kersten, 2003, for review), the literature in social psychology shows that concepts facilitate the encoding of information (e.g., Klatzky et al., 1982), the retrieval of information from memory (e.g., Cohen, 1981), and the ability to make inferences about never-before-seen entities (e.g., Cantor & Mischel, 1979). This last consequence of using concepts, powerful induction, is probably the most interesting implication of concepts for social psychologists and is a reason to spend substantial theoretical and empirical effort discovering the principles of social cognition. If finding out that concepts support induction is exciting, then formulating a theory about how the conceptual system supports such inference is essential. All such theories need to deal both with representation, or what constitutes knowledge about a category, and with process, or how that concept gets used.

TRADITIONAL MODELS OF CONCEPTS IN SOCIAL COGNITION: AMODAL ARCHITECTURES

Two of the most recently relied-on models of the conceptual system within cognitive psychology and social cognition are associative network models and exemplar models. For our purposes, they are initially grouped together because they both assume that high-level cognitive processes such as categorization and induction operate on symbols that have been abstracted out of the perceptual system in which they were initially encoded and do not necessarily preserve anything about the initial state of the organism during perception and learning (Newell & Simon, 1972; Pylyshyn, 1984).

From these two approaches, then, here is how an entity is processed: First, the experience of an encountered entity is represented in modality-specific systems in the brain. (The term *modality-specific systems* in its present usage includes the sensory systems [vision, audition, touch, taste, smell] that underlie perception of the entity, the motor systems that support resulting action, and the introspective systems that support conscious experiences of emotion, motivation, and cognitive operations.) This first step is not debated; it is an accepted account of perception. However, models of the conceptual system that rely on the computer metaphor then go on to claim that these modality-specific states are subsequently redescribed and stored in an abstract, amodal form, a form something like language (Fodor, 1975). These are the *amodal* symbols to which we refer throughout the chapter. This redescription can only occur if there is a mental transduction process that takes the sensory input and recruits an abstract symbol that stands for that input (Barsalou, 1999b). It is the amodal symbol that is used directly in later processing about the entity. For example, when perceiving a social entity, such as a crowd of people, for the first time, the information is initially processed in at least the visual, auditory, and probably affective systems (because crowds can be energizing or frightening). Then, this information is transduced to an abstract symbol that might be implemented as *crowd* (or alternatively as a series of Xs and Os). In some way, this symbol will be stored with others such as *loud*, *cheering*, and *happy*. These might form a feature list, which by some accounts (although not all) constitutes the concept in memory. Later, when one is questioned about one's concept of crowds, what is extracted from memory and used to make inferences are (at least) these three pieces of information in their abstract form, that is, a label for the concept and a list (structured or not) of its features.

The full set of abstracted symbols thus constitutes the person's knowledge, or conceptual system, and supports inference, categorization, memory, and other forms of higher cognition. A theorist can use the language of feature lists, semantic networks, propositions, schemata, statistical vectors, and so on to account for people's redescriptions of their perceptual, motor, and introspective states. In most such cases, he or she is assuming that representation is amodal, and that the mind is modular (e.g., Kunda, 1999; Smith, 1998; Wyer & Srull, 1984). In the next section, we briefly review two models of concepts that possess these characteristics and that have been relied on in social cognition, and we mention how they account for some basic concerns in the field.

Associative Network Models

Associationism began as a theory about how ideas combine in the mind. According to the theory, the mind is the result of the combination, according to the law of association, of simple and irreducible elements derived from sense experiences. For Aristotle, British empiricists (e.g., Berkeley, 1685–1753; Hartley, 1705–1757; Hume, 1711–1776; Mill, 1806–1876), structuralists (e.g., Titchener, 1867–1927; Wundt, 1874–1983), and French sensationalists (e.g., de Condillac, 1715–1781; La Mettrie, 1709–1751), these elements were sensations, perceptions, and ideas. Also, essentially all associationists believed that the elements that are associated (representations) are not innate but are acquired through learning and experience (Locke, 1979). According to the theory, the mind is as a mirror of representations of nature than can be investigated with experimentation.

Associative network models within cognitive psychology were proposed to apply the ideas of associationism to model semantic memory (e.g., Anderson, 1983; Collins & Loftus, 1975). In these accounts, discrete nodes, which are interconnected by links, represent elements, and the patterns of associations constitute knowledge. This binding occurs when the elements are thought about together, and its result is a unified representation that can be entirely or partially retrieved when activated by a component. For example, the concept of *elderly people* is represented as a link between the node (an abstracted symbol) that stands for *the elderly* and the node corresponding to a feature such as *walking slowly*. Although associative network models of semantic memory within cognitive psychology usually specify distinct types of links such as *feature* links (indicating that an object possesses the feature) or linguistic-structural links, both of which imbue important structural power to the knowledge network, such labeling of links is often not preserved in associative network models within the field of social cognition (see Smith, 1998, for discussion).

When a node is activated, all nodes linked to it are activated according to the strength of association and via a mechanism of spreading activation; the more a node is interconnected, the greater the probability that it will be activated by its neighbors. Importantly, activation to a node can vary quickly over time but not the strength of the link. The strength of the associative link is relatively stable and changes only very slowly over time.

A large number of substantive results in social psychology have been explained by associative network mechanisms. Such research has examined how information about social knowledge is acquired, stored in memory, formed into impressions, retrieved, and used in making judgments of individuals.

Concept Learning In the view of associative network models, an individual's concept of an entity such as a person, a social situation, or the self is represented by a node to which additional information about that entity becomes linked during initial and subsequent exposures to it. Specifically, during encoding, if the individual thinks about or integrates a behavioral element with another one, an associative link connecting the two nodes will be established (Hastie, 1980; Srull, 1981; Srull & Wyer, 1989). These nodes do not constitute perceptual information but rather redescriptions of the perceptual experience.

Retrieval of Information Later retrieval of information within associative network models relies, as mentioned, on a mechanism of spreading activation. Activation is assumed to spread in parallel over connected nodes until some threshold of activation has been reached. Of interest to social psychologists, and as evidenced in many relevant studies, when individuals recall information, they are often influenced by their expectancies and stereotypes as well as biases introduced during encoding.

A well-known effect that can be accounted for within associative models is the memory advantage for the retrieval of expectancy-incongruent information (Stangor & Duan, 1991). According to the associative network account, when individuals try to reconcile incongruent information to previous expectations about a target (person or a group), they think about these behaviors in relation to other relevant behaviors. As a result, associative links are formed not only between the incongruent elements and other incongruent and congruent elements but also between the incongruent elements and the social target. As a result, congruent content is not thought about in relation to the other behaviors and therefore has fewer established associations (Srull & Wyer, 1989; Stangor, & McMillan, 1992). Because these structures of associations are activated in the recall of information, incongruent elements may be better recalled than congruent ones.

Social Judgments When a node representing a group or a group member is activated, associated stereotypic traits or evaluations also become active, thereby affecting judgment, attitudes, and behaviors toward the social target. Differences in strength of association allow for relatively easy implementation of individual differences in the relationships between concepts and judgments. For example, some White experimental participants may respond more quickly to positive trait words following the prime *white* than following *black* because their concept of *white* is more strongly associated with positive trait terms than is their concept of *black* (Devine, 1989; Gaertner & McLaughlin, 1983).

The associationist position has been relied on heavily to inspire and guide research in social cognition. Nevertheless, it is true that the very notion that associations can constitute concepts, that is, that association alone can ground the conceptual system, is itself debatable (e.g., Strack & Deutsch, 2004). Thus, a number of alternative models have been proposed.

Exemplar models

Exemplar models were developed in part as a challenge to the idea, contained in most associative network models of semantic memory, that concepts are abstract and decontextualized, preserving nothing in particular about the situation or context in which category instances were actually encountered. The notion of abstraction, realized specifically in prototype models (e.g., Posner & Keele, 1968), had a difficult time accounting for a number of observations, including changes in the gradient of prototypicality observed across situations. For instance, if a robin is prototypical of the category *BIRD* and a chicken far less prototypical, then how and why do the prototypicality ratings of these birds change in the context of a farmyard or an imagined voyage to another country or culture (Barsalou, 1987)?

Represented, for example, by the context model of Medin and Schaffer (1978) and including Nosofsky's generalized context model (1986), exemplar models developed in cognitive psychology propose that each experience of a category member is preserved as a trace in memory, although not in photo-like form since top-down conceptual and attentional influences at encoding can bias encoding to some degree. The entire body of exemplars constitutes the concept. Although some exemplar models see traces as similar to images, or episodic memories, most assume that the exemplars preserve nothing about the perceptual experience during exemplar acquisition. Exemplars may be points in multidimensional space (Nosofsky, 1992) or attribute values such as *X*s and *O*s (Medin & Schaffer, 1978), but for most theorists, they are redescriptions of the original input.

Concept Learning Acquiring a new concept, from this perspective, has a boot-strapping quality. Or as Kruschke has noted, "One way to learn a category is merely to memorize its instances" (Kruschke, 2005, p. 186). All of the instances of a category are indeed represented, but how do we know that those things are all the *same kind of thing*? In most category learning models that rely on an exemplar account, computations of perceived similarity and feedback about success in making classifications does this work. Thus, acquiring a concept involves repeated exposure to similar things, and having a concept involves the ability to judge the similarity between new and old instances. For person concepts, the exemplars might be individual persons, a possibility suggested by Smith and Zarate (1992), but such models can also handle the notion that incomplete representations support the use of subtypes (e.g., Judd & Park, 1993).

Retrieval of Information An exemplar is retrieved, or used to categorize a new instance of a category, to the extent that it is judged as most similar to an input. The similarity between the perceived entity and represented exemplars, computed in parallel, determines categorization. Importantly, the use of specific dimensions of similarity, from the world of possible dimensions of similarity, can in some models be guided by selective attention to dimensions relevant in the situation, prior sensitizing to dimensions, and so forth. Specific exemplar models have then been developed to account for different aspects of retrieval. For example, Logan's (2002) instance model of automaticity is concerned with memory retrieval and how skilled performance becomes automatic, that is, through retrieving stored exemplars of the skill that is involved. Nosofsky's exemplar-based random walk model generalizes the Logan model and is also concerned with different types of retrieval.

Social Judgments The exemplars that are activated and judged most similar to the input are used to make judgments about the specific entity. What is particularly powerful about exemplar models is that they can predict the effects of situational information on which an exemplar is judged most similar and therefore used in judgment. Because in theory the exemplars retain at least some information about the situation in which the instance was encountered, we can predict that a particular judgment will show sensitivity to context. Thus, the concept that one uses to make judgments or predictions about a typical child playing in the context of a nursery school will not be exactly same as the judgments and predictions about a typical child playing in the context of a beach vacation. Likewise, a priest will not be expected to say and do the same things in a religious service as at a high school soccer game (Barsalou, 1987; Cantor & Mischel, 1977).

Parallel Distributed Processing (Connectionist) Models

The view of the cognitive system represented by the two accounts just discussed was one that was inspired and dominated by the metaphor of computer as serial processor. When challenged about this analogy, David Rumelhart (1989) responded by saying that:

> The inspiration for our theories and our understanding of abstract phenomena always is based on our experience with the technology at the time. I pointed out that Aristotle had a wax tablet theory of memory, that Leibniz saw the universe as clockworks, that Freud used a hydraulic model of libido flowing though the system, and that the telephone switchboard model of intelligence had played an important role as well. (p. 133)

Parallel distributing processing (PDP) or connectionist models of the cognitive system are *neurally inspired* and attempt to replace serial computer-style computation with brain-style computation. Because in reality the brain is comprised of billions of neurons that operate in parallel, neurally inspired computation has to involve many parallel connections rather then extremely fast (and biologically implausible) serial connections, as implemented in (serial) computer-inspired processing models.

Connectionist models conceptualize memory as a set of units and connections between units. The patterns of these connections and their connection weights represent concepts. Each time the connections are realized in the use of a concept, the concept is slightly different from when last used because the connections and their weights are influenced by recent experiences with similar patterns and the state of the system at the point that the concept is used. There are three important implications of this. One is that there is no static representation. Rather, memory is entirely dynamic and involves reconstruction at the time when particular knowledge is needed. Another implication is that no single unit represents a concept or idea; concepts are not local. Rather, concepts are distributed across units in memory. Finally, there is no distinction between representation and process because the job of having and using a conceptual system is performed by a set of units and their connections. The units and their connections constitute both representation (such as associations in associative network models) and processing (such as the process of spreading activation). The general architecture is conceptualized as discussed next (Rumelhart, 1989; Shanks, 1997; Smith, 1996, 1998).

First, there is a set of processing units that are considered to perform the simple task of computing a weighted algebraic sum of their inputs. The units and their connections constitute the system. In many, although not all, connectionist accounts, there are three types of units. First, there are *input* units, which receive information from the environment through the sense systems. Second, there are *hidden* units, which produce input and output within the system but do not have links to the other units. Finally, there are *output* units, which produce the response (motoric or otherwise) that is the consequence or implication of the work of hidden units (e.g., a categorization of a perceived object). The units are in some state of activation at all times; there is no time when some state or some pattern of activation is not present.

What is important is the pattern of connectivity between units because this pattern represents the knowledge contained in the system and how the system will respond to new input. Changing knowledge, as in category learning, in such models amounts to modifying the patterns of interconnectivity in the system. Such updates can involve the development of new connections, the loss of existing connections, and the modification of the strength of existing connections (Rumelhart, 1989).

Concept Learning   In connectionist models, learning a new concept amounts to acquiring a set of new connection weights. An interaction with each new entity causes changes in the state of activation of the system, and the system comes to know the set of input features that produce the output of (correct) category membership. As noted by Smith (1996), the most important features of learning in connectionist accounts are that learning is incremental, that learning is implemented as changes in connection weights, and that such changes take the form of reducing the difference between the network's response to an input and the known correct output. Most examples of learning of interest to social psychologists can be modeled in this way.

Retrieval of Information   In connectionist models of explicit recall, memory involves the reactivation of patterns of connections that stand for some entity. Memory is thus reconstructed, and as mentioned, because of the nature of any momentary state of activation of the system, each reconstruction of memory will be slightly different, reflecting prior states of activation. Associative memory can be modeled as the reconstruction of a pattern of connection weights that represent more than one idea, through a pattern completion process, quite easily (e.g., McClelland, McNaughton, & O'Reilly, 1995; see Carlston, 1994, for applications in social cognition).

Social Judgments   The notion of going beyond the information given, *social inference*, is also implemented by a pattern completion mechanism. Behavioral findings of specific interest in the area of social perception have been implemented in connectionist models. For instance, Kashima and Kerekes (1994) published a model of the evaluation of target individuals based on the input of personality traits. They reproduced the previously observed effect by which the evaluation of an individual can be correctly predicted from the weighted average of the evaluations of the input information, the traits (e.g., Anderson, 1981). Smith and DeCoster (1998) relied on the *autoassociative connectionist* model of McClelland and Rumelhart (1985) to reproduce a number of interesting effects, including exemplar-based social inference; group-based stereotyping; the use of several stereotypes to generate new, emergent characteristics; and the effects of recency and frequency of exposure to an entity on its accessibility in memory.

Similarities Between Associative Network, Exemplar, and Connectionist Models

There are many ways to compare models of the conceptual system. Barsalou (2003) compared the three types of models examined here (specifically considering feedforward versions of connectionist models) along five dimensions: architecture, representation, abstraction, stability, and organization. He noted that all three models implement modular architectures, meaning that the conceptual system is encapsulated from the sensory (input) and motor (output) systems. In addition, all three models represent concepts amodally as redescriptions of the input from the sensory system into an abstract language. On the three remaining features of abstraction, stability, and organization, the models did not always agree. We focus on abstraction and stability here.

First, regarding abstraction, although an associative network model of semantic memory represents concepts in a symbolic or language-like format that is entirely devoid of contextual information, exemplar models and connectionist models preserve the situated nature of knowledge. In different ways, those models show sensitivity to context and produce different output depending on the context in which the knowledge is used. Thus, unlike associative network models, exemplar and connectionist models can account for the fact that objects can be categorized in one category within one context and another way within another context (Goldstone, Medin, & Halberstadt, 1997).

From associative network and exemplar accounts, knowledge is very stable. That is, the same concept is used repeatedly, and it changes only very slowly. Similarly, although in theory all exemplars are used to provide the correct categorization in a given task, the addition of one new or even many new exemplars does not fundamentally change what the system knows. In contrast, connectionist models are dynamic. As mentioned, the state of the distributed system that is a concept is influenced by recent exposures to the concept and by other patterns of activation that precede the use of a specific concept. Figure 2.1 summarizes similarities and differences between the different representational models just briefly reviewed.

EMBODIMENT FINDINGS IN SOCIAL COGNITION

There are many findings in the social cognition literature that are hard to account for using associative network, exemplar, or connectionist models without making changes to their basic assumptions or adding new ones in an unprincipled way (see Barsalou et al., 2003; Niedenthal, Barsalou, Ric, & Krauth-Gruber, 2005; Niedenthal, Barsalou, Winkielman, et al., 2005, for discussion). For example, Schubert (2004) instructed male and female experimental participants to make a fist under the pretext of producing the *rock* gesture from the children's game *rock-paper-scissors*. Schubert found that while making a fist, males appraised depictions of situations in which power is ambiguously at issue as related to having power or being powerful. Females appraised the same situations as related to loss of power or being powerless. In a second study, men and women made judgments about a hypothetical target. Schubert observed that men and women also diverged in that while making a fist men judged an assertive person as more positive and women judged the person as more negative.

How or why should making a fist influence social judgment and processes of impression formation? According to Schubert (2004), assertive physical behavior,

	Model of representation			
Dimension	Associative network	Exemplar	Connectionist	Multimodal simulation
Architecture	Modular	Modular	Modular	Nonmodular
Representation	Amodal	Amodal	Amodal	Modal
Abstraction	Abstracted	Situated	Situated	Situated
Stability	Stable	Stable	Dynamic	Dynamic

Figure 2.1 Comparisons of different representational models (based on Barsalou, 2003).

such as making a fist in preparation for fight, has a different relationship to the concept of power for men and women. He cited work suggesting that for men such behavior is associated with feelings of powerfulness in the sense that males strike out when feeling powerful. For women, on the other hand, assertive physical behaviors are associated with feelings of powerlessness in that sense that women strike out when feeling helpless, not when feeling powerful. But, precisely how does the motor behavior of making a fist influence social judgment?

Or, consider the following findings: In a study of text comprehension of interest to social psychologists, Glenberg and Kaschak (2002) had participants read sentences in which the described actions involved movement away from the author of the action (e.g., "You handed Courtney the notebook") or in which the described actions involved movement toward the author of the action (e.g., "Courtney handed you the notebook"). Other sentences were nonsensical. The participants' task was to judge whether the sentences made sense. For participants in one condition, the response that a sentence made sense was made by pressing a button that involved reaching away from the body. In a second condition, the response that a sentence made sense was made by reaching toward the body. Results revealed that participants judged sentences as sensible faster when the actions described in the text and the action used for making the correct response were compatible (i.e., both moving away or moving toward the body). These findings are consistent with those of Buccino et al. (2003), who showed that when individuals listened to sentences that described hand or leg movements, motor cortex and the distal muscles in the arm and leg were differentially and systematically activated.

A final example of a result that seems difficult to account for was reported by Mussweiler (2006). In a series of studies, he showed that having experimental participants engage in motor movements that typified a particular social category primed the use of that category in social judgment and even in automatic perceptual processing. For instance, in one study individuals were led to behave in a *portly* way (for which portly meant slowly and heavily). Specifically, participants were led to walk around with weights on their ankles and their wrists while wearing life preservers on their upper bodies. After having this motor/bodily experience, the participants read about a hypothetical person and had to communicate their impression of the person by rating traits, some of which constituted the stereotype of *overweight people*. Results showed that participants who had been led to move in a portly way rated the hypothetical person as more characterized by traits typical of overweight people than did participants who had not been led to move in a portly way.

Taken together, these representative findings, and many others summarized elsewhere, seem to implicate the environment, body, and modality-specific systems in the representation and processing of meaning (e.g., Barsalou et al., 2003; Niedenthal, Barsalou, Ric, et al., 2005; Niedenthal, Barsalou, Winkielman, et al., 2005). For these reasons, they are often called *embodiment effects*. According to the types of amodal accounts of representation summarized here, embodied states are peripheral associations linked to amodal concepts. So, for instance, knowledge of elderly people might be linked to embodied states of walking slowly and favoring a particular bodily posture. From the amodal accounts, however, these states do not constitute the grounding of the concept. Rather, the embodied states are represented by amodal symbols that stand for them. The embodied state of walking slowly, for example, is linked to an amodal symbol for slow walking. When knowledge about the elderly is used, the amodal symbol for walking slowly is activated, and it supports the inference that older people tend to walk slowly. Embodying slow walking is not, however, required to represent the conceptual relation between slow walking and the elderly. Actually, walking slowly is a peripheral state that can trigger the concept for elderly people, or that can result from its activation, but always is mediated by the amodal symbol for this motor state. Thus, the modality-specific states that occur in action, perception, and introspection about social entities are peripheral appendages linked to amodal symbols that stand for them.

There are at least three reasons to question this account. One is that sensorimotor behavior as represented in amodal representational models has been largely added as an afterthought to account for somewhat dazzling findings. The original models did not contain this idea. Second, there is no clear theory of the transduction process. With the exception of some ideas on this matter by Kosslyn (e.g., 1975; Kosslyn & Pomerantz, 1977) regarding visual imagery, the process by which perceptual information is redescribed has been assumed without being demonstrated. Finally, this account is not parsimonious in that if the perceptual states could be reused rather than redescribed, the models could be in fact more parsimonious.

Embodiment Theories: Amodal Architectures

There exist a number of recent theories, sometimes called *theories of embodied cognition*, that implicate modality-specific systems in knowledge acquisition and use. Examples include Damasio's (1994) theory of emotion, Glenberg's (1997) theory of memory, Barsalou's (1999) theory of the conceptual system, Gallese's (2003a) theory of intersubjectivity, and Decety's theory of empathy (e.g., Decety & Jackson, 2004). The theory of embodiment that we describe in detail here was proposed by Barsalou (1999a, 1999b), and it is of interest because, as just noted, it seeks specifically to propose an alternative model of the conceptual system to the amodal and modular accounts discussed in the chapter. Furthermore, it makes quite naturally the predictions tested in the three examples of embodiment effects summarized.

Multimodal Simulation Theory In Barsalou's theory, which we call the multimodal simulation account, the neural states that occur in interaction with an entity or a situation represent that entity or situation in memory. Furthermore, these states do not represent the entity in a static way. Rather, in this view, information processing is a dynamic skill. It comprises, as the name implies, simulations that involve parts of the sensorimotor system as if an actual entity or situation were experienced. Thus, in this approach, the modality-specific states that represent perception, action, and introspection when one is actually in interaction with a particular entity, or in a specific situation, are also used to represent these ideas when the original entity or situation is not actually present. For example, retrieving the memory of a person involves the reactivation of parts of the visual states that were active while perceiving the person. In the same manner, thinking about an action involves partial activation of the motor states that originally produced it (see Figure 2.1 for a comparison to the other models discussed).

What having a concept is, then, is having the ability to reactivate parts of the neural states that occurred when one was actually with—physically or introspectively—instances of a category. Put differently, having a concept means having the ability to simulate experiences with its members. Concepts in this approach are therefore also called *simulators*. According to Barsalou's account, a simulator develops for any object, event, or aspect of experience that has been repeatedly attended to. Due to its exquisite flexibility, attention can be allocated to different parts of overall experience. For example, individuals can attend to whole objects (e.g., motorcycles), features of objects (e.g., sour), types of people (e.g., skinheads), emotional states (e.g., joy), motivational states (e.g., interest), actions (e.g., pushing), events (e.g., weddings), contexts (e.g., amusement parks), physical relations (e.g., next to), and so on. Across development, a large number of simulators are established in long-term memory to represent this rich and varied experience. Once a simulator is established, it can be used to reenact aspects of experience, thus supporting the capacity to perform conceptual tasks. But, note that the notion of multimodal simulations is not the same as the idea of holistic images. In this view, photo-like images of external scenes do not constitute the conceptual system. Rather, componential bodies of accumulated information about the modality-specific components of experience comprise the conceptual system.

The use of a given simulator, a concept, in performing a conceptual task is called *simulation*. The number of ways that a simulator can simulate a category is, in theory, unlimited. This is because in different situations, different subsets of the modality-specific knowledge in the simulator can be activated to represent the category. For instance, when asked what typical *terrorists* are like, an individual might simulate, in a number of modalities (e.g., visual, auditory, and introspective), the impressions of terrorists that he or she has learned through exposure to the media (or, less fortunately, in real life). But, the sampling within these modalities changes depending on which instance of terrorism drives the simulation (i.e., where it happened, when it happened, and who was there). Because terrorists are associated with strong emotional reactions, simulations within the affective system should be highly marked and negative. Note that if part of knowing what a terrorist is involves simulations within systems for negative affect, then we do not necessarily need to assume that a *tag* for the concept *terrorist* is associated with another *tag* that stands for, and somehow generates, negative affect (e.g., Fiske, 1982). Because thinking about a terrorist involves a multimodal simulation, the negative affect is construed as a partial grounding of the concept, not as a reaction that is activated by access to the concept's tag in associative memory.

Judgments and inferences are based on a simulation for a category. Because the simulation of a category is influenced by the constraints of the context in which the knowledge is needed, these simulations should thus be tailored for making useful and informed judgments in the current situation. The simulation account similarly specifies that only the parts of the representation that are required for effective functioning are actually simulated. As an example of this, behavioral studies have demonstrated that simulations occur only in the modality required to perform a given task. Recent functional magnetic resonance imaging (fMRI) studies have also revealed selective activation of relevant parts of sensory cortex when property verification tasks were performed in different modalities (Kan, Barsalou, Solomon, Minor, & Thompson-Schill, 2003; Kellenbach, Brett, & Patterson, 2001).

EXPERIMENTAL EVIDENCE IN FAVOR OF EMBODIMENT THEORIES

Object Concepts

Although many experimental findings could be called evidence supportive of the general sense of embodiment theories, until recently very few studies have been designed to pit predictions of modal and amodal representational models directly against each other. Barsalou and collaborators designed and conducted a number of such studies of natural object categories. Using property verification tasks and property generation tasks, these researchers compared the nature of processing that would be predicted straightforwardly by modal versus amodal models and found rather better support for modal models (see Barsalou, Solomon, & Wu, 1999; Barsalou, 2003; and Barsalou, Simmons, Barbey, & Wilson, 2003, for a review and discussion of such findings).

The basic prediction is that behavioral and neuroimagining evidence will reveal the use of modality-specific systems in conceptual tasks that rely on those modalities, and that conceptual processing will show evidence of perceptual grounding of knowledge. For instance, the study by Kan and colleagues (2003) demonstrated that when a property that is typically processed in one modality (such as *sour* or *loud*) is verified as true for a particular concept (such as *LEMON* or *BOMB* for the examples, respectively), the relevant brain areas that support processing of those sensations are selectively activated. This suggests that the property is in effect simulated to perform the task (see Pecher, Zeelenberg, & Barsalou, 2003, 2004, for related behavioral findings). An amodal model of representation would not make such a prediction because the amodal symbol for the property of interest would be accessed, and this would require no activation in sensorimotor areas.

Social Concepts

The specifics of an embodiment account of social information processing cast new light on results in the social cognition literature and thereby also provide support for such an approach. For example, we think that the Schubert (2004) and the Mussweiler (2006) findings reviewed here are predicted, a priori, from an embodiment theory such as that of Barsalou. This is because both are examples that show that the processing of social information is causally related to the reexperience of the defining motor behavior.

In a related vein, other recent research has demonstrated that the activation of the stereotype of the elderly automatically primes stereotype-consistent behavior (e.g., reduced motor speed; Dijksterhuis & Bargh, 2001; Ferguson & Bargh, 2004;

Wheeler & Petty, 2001). A classic study by Bargh, Chen, and Burrows (1996) showed that when students were primed by the category *elderly people*, they walked more slowly when leaving the laboratory than nonprimed students. In other research, Dijksterhuis, Spears, and Lépinasse (2001) had student experimental participants form an impression of a group composed of either young or old people. They then had participants perform a lexical decision task. Participants who had just formed an impression of the elderly made lexical decisions more slowly than those who had just formed an impression of young people. Likewise, Kawakami, Young, and Dovidio (2002) found longer latencies on a lexical decision task for participants who had previously been exposed to photographs of elderly people relative to participants who were not.

The interpretation of the effects of category activation on motor behavior developed by Bargh and his colleagues (1996) relied on a marriage of associative network models of memory with the principles of ideomotor action described by James (1890). The effects were thus interpreted as showing that exposure to some traits contained in the category *elderly* primed, by association, amodal representations of the stereotypical traits of the category (e.g., slowness), which in turn activated behavioral representations associated with each trait (e.g., walking slowly), thereby increasing the tendency to perform these behaviors (Bargh et al., 1996; Dijksterhuis & Bargh, 2001).

We would interpret the findings slightly differently. From the present embodied simulation view, processing the concept of the elderly involves simulating an example of the concept. Thus, slow walking would be a result of simulating in multiple sensorimotor systems interactions with older people. In other words, the slowed walking is viewed as part of the simulation of the category not the result of the priming of an amodal symbol for the category and, through the diffusion of activation, for slow walking. Chambon, Droit-Volet, and Niedenthal (under review), conducted a study in which some aspects of the two accounts of the effects of priming the elderly come into opposition. They specifically examined the perception of time for which time was represented by photographs of faces of the elderly versus faces of young people. An amodal stereotype activation account predicts that when duration is represented by images of the elderly, then (young) individuals will tend to estimate time as longer than it actually is. This is because a proposition contained in the stereotype is that the elderly move slowly (take more time). If the stereotype is activated by the presentation of an elderly face and used as the basis for judgment, then the duration of a presentation of that face on a computer screen would be seen as longer than that of a younger person.

However, if the elderly are embodied in the sense of simulating their behavior in motor systems, then standard time perception models make an entirely different prediction. According to internal clock models of time judgment (Gibbon, 1977; Gibbon, Church, & Meck, 1984), the raw material for subjective time comes from the number of pulses emitted by a (biologically based) pacemaker; the pulses are accumulated in a timer during the event to be judged. Subjective time thus depends on the number of pulses accumulated during the stimulus to be judged: The more pulses accumulated, the longer the duration is judged to be (for a review, see Meck, 2003). In studies of temporal perception, there is much evidence that subjective time varies as a function of the speeding up or the slowing down of the pacemaker in certain circumstances (e.g., Drew, Fairhurst, Malapani, Horvitz, & Balsam, 2003). Specifically, when arousal decreases, the number of pulses is lower, and time is estimated as shorter. Combined with an embodiment approach, then, this model predicts that the perception of time represented by the elderly will be seen as shorter, not longer. In particular, if perceivers reproduce the sensorimotor states of *being there* with elderly people, arousal should decrease, as it does when movements are slower (Jennings & van der Molen, 2002). This should slow the speed of the pacemaker, fewer pulses should accumulate, and time should appear shorter rather than longer (i.e., underestimated).

An embodiment account would also make another specific prediction. That is, studies of the embodied simulation of other individuals' gestures and expressions have demonstrated that the behavior of all perceived individuals is not inevitably and automatically reproduced. For example, individuals are more likely to imitate behaviors of in-group members, suggesting that people tend to imitate the gestures of people with whom they are identified or wish to empathize (e.g., LaFrance & Ickes, 1981; Zajonc, Adelmann, Murphy, & Niedenthal, 1987). The implication of these past demonstrations is that processes of identification and motivation to empathize impose limits on the extent to which the behaviors of other people are embodied (Decety & Jackson, 2004; Jackson & Decety, 2004). Furthermore, as noted by Blakemore and Decety (2001), the perception and simulation of human movement are influenced by a perceiver's knowledge of and experience with his or her own movement constraints (Viviani, 2002). This reasoning suggests a refinement of the present prediction regarding the perception of duration represented by the elderly. Specifically, a sex-specific effect could be expected to occur because the (relatively young) participants may not be sufficiently identified with the elderly of the opposite sex to internally simulate their motor behavior.

In their study, Chambon and colleagues employed the temporal bisection task, a frequently used task developed to test the predictions of the clock-based model (e.g., Droit-Volet, 2003; Wearden, 1991). In the bisection task, participants learn to categorize two standard durations, one short and one long, in an initial training phase. In a test phase, they are presented with comparison stimulus durations (i.e., intermediate duration values and the standard values). The task is to classify the durations as representing either the short or the long standard duration. In Chambon et al., the comparison stimulus durations in the test phase were represented by pictures of faces of elderly and young males and females (expressing neutral emotion). Results showed that female participants underestimated the time that an elderly woman's face was presented on a computer screen. This underestimation was not observed when duration was represented by faces of young women or men of any age. In addition, male participants underestimated the duration that the face of an elderly man was presented on a computer screen. This underestimation was not observed when duration was represented by faces of young women or men. These findings thus show that specific predictions that are made from an embodied cognitive model of representation are not necessarily the same as those derived from a model in which stereotypes prime amodal symbols that represent the typical motor behavior of the category members. Thus, the utility of the approach is illustrated in this example.

Gallese (2003b) came to the same conclusion regarding social cognition when he noted that, according to amodal models of representation:

> When faced with the problem of understanding the meaning of others' behaviors, adult humans must *necessarily* translate the sensory information about the observed behavior into a series of *mental representations* that share, with language, the propositional format. This enables one to ascribe others' intentions, desires and beliefs, and therefore to understand the *mental antecedents* of their overt behavior ... (but this is a) *disembodied view*. ... I think that there is now enough empirical evidence to reject a disembodied theory of the mind as biologically implausible. (p. 520)

Emotion Concepts

What does it mean to possess general knowledge about emotions? How is an emotion concept grounded? Could it be that conceptual processing of emotion also involves the (re)experience of an emotion? This is exactly what a modal representation model would propose, and we find this a compelling answer. That is, maybe what it means to have emotion knowledge is the ability to simulate emotional experience. So, when someone tells us the "movie was scary," we know just how to understand this because we can simulate fear, specifically the type that is experienced in the cinema.

Evidence in favor of simulation in the use of emotion concepts was demonstrated in a series of two studies by Mondillon, Niedenthal, Vermeulen, and Winkielman (in preparation). In the first of those studies, individuals had to make judgments about whether words referring to concrete objects (e.g., VOMIT) were associated with an emotion (they did not have to say which emotion; they provided simply a yes or no response). The list of concepts to which the experimental participants were exposed included concepts that were associated with joy, disgust, and anger as well as no particular emotion. While the participants were exposed to the concepts and making their judgments, the activation of four facial muscles were recorded (with a technique called electromyographic [EMG] recording). Two of the muscles, the orbicularus occuli (around the eyes) and the zygomaticus (around the mouth) muscles, are typically enervated when an individual is smiling with happiness. The corrugator (over the eyebrows) is typically enervated when an individual is frowning with anger. The levator muscle is activated when an individual makes the grimace of disgust.

According to amodal representational models, the judgment that, for example, a SLUG is associated with disgust does not require the simulation of being there with a slug. That it engenders disgust is another feature of slugs that is represented in a feature list by an amodal representation. It can be accessed without recourse to the emotion itself. On the other hand, modal models would predict that the judgment is based on a simulation of being there with a slug. Consequently, the first models would predict that judgments about whether an object is associated with an emotion are not accompanied by the specific emotional experience (a simulation, which can be detected by activation of facial muscles), whereas the latter models do.

The results of the study just described, as well as a second study in which the words to be judged were abstract emotion words (i.e., RAGE, ANGER, and CONTEMPT for the broad category of anger) and the judgment was whether the concept was an instance of an emotion, the results supported predictions of a modal account of representation. Specifically, in both studies, judgments about words that refer to objects that elicit joy or that are synonyms for joy were accompanied by specific activation of the obicularus occuli and the zygomaticus muscles; judgments about words that refer to objects that elicit anger or are synonyms for anger were accompanied by specific activation of the corrugator muscle; and judgments about words that refer to objects that elicit disgust or are synonyms for disgust were accompanied by activation of the levator muscle. Thus, the findings support a proposed process by which conceptual processing involves simulation of the concept in sensorimotor systems.

Recently, Niedenthal, Barsalou, Ric, et al. (2005) reviewed many additional findings from the emotion literature to further reinforce this view of how emotion concepts are grounded. They summarized evidence that individuals embody other people's emotional behavior, that embodied emotions produce corresponding subjective emotional states in the individual, that imagining other people and events also produces embodied emotions and corresponding feelings, and that embodied emotions mediate cognitive responses. Taken together, then, the logical and experimental evidence in favor of modal accounts of emotion concepts are very strong and motivate many important questions for the field.

OBJECTIONS TO EMBODIMENT THEORIES

If things were so easy and modal representational systems were so powerful, then cognitive scientists, including social psychologists, would certainly be converted to embodiment models. This is not the case because things are not so easy and because there are many issues remaining to be debated and resolved. Here, we discuss several of them (see Barsalou, 2005, for a fuller discussion).

Amodal Symbols

A first issue concerns the existence of amodal representations per se. The question is whether amodal symbols are necessary to account for the classic symbolic functions that sensorimotor simulations might arguably not implement. There are a number of possible responses to this question. One is that the classic amodal representations that constitute the conceptual system in most models such as those reviewed in this chapter do not exist, but that there are other types of (relatively) amodal representation.

To understand one possible way to think about other types of amodal representation, it is necessary to describe the representational architecture endorsed by some theories of embodied cognition. Damasio's (1989) theory of convergence zones (CZs) has been used to understand how the sensorimotor states that occur in interaction with the world and during introspection can be stored and used in simulations (e.g., Simmons & Barsalou, 2003, for discussion). To begin, when a stimulus is perceived, the activation of groups of neurons that code its featural information in the relevant perceptual modality are organized into hierarchically arranged *feature maps* (e.g., Palmer, 1999). The idea of CZ theory is that conjunctive neurons in the brain's association areas capture and store the patterns of activations on the feature maps for later use in high-level cognitive processes; these are the CZs. Importantly, higher-level CZs integrate patterns of activation across modalities, and in this way the full complexity of a stimulus, across modalities, is preserved.

Simmons and Barsalou (2003) suggested that the sets of conjunctive neurons in association areas that activate simulations in feature systems could be viewed as *amodal vectors*. In response to this challenge, however, Damasio (1989) pointed out that conjunctive neurons function only to control simulations and thus do not function fully as free-standing representations. Simmons and Barsalou (2003) also suggested that conjunctive neurons have modality-specific tunings and as such are therefore not really amodal.

A related issue is whether certain tasks necessarily rely on simulation. The use of associative strength in the lexical system rather than simulation to perform some cognitive task has been demonstrated and discussed by Solomon and Barsalou (2004). However, the fact that associations between lexical items are represented and used to perform some tasks says nothing about the grounding of the conceptual system. It merely shows that recourse to conceptual content is not always required in information processing.

Abstract Concepts

One of us noticed that at the age of 4 her son started to represent time spatially with the distance between his hands. Although time is considered an abstract concept, this type of concrete spatial conception and associated motor behavior may easily constitute the conceptual content. These observations are familiar to students of Piaget, of course (e.g., Piaget, 1929). For some people, it is easy to see also how other apparently abstract notions such as *liberty* and *motivation* could be grounded in the affective and motor systems. Still, most people more readily appreciate how the modal simulation account implements concrete concepts than abstract concepts. Consistent with the thought problem concerning time just presented, Barsalou (1999b) suggested that abstract concepts are grounded in specific events and introspections, and that this content can be later simulated in relevant modality-specific systems.

Some evidence in favor of this view of abstract concepts was reported by Barsalou and Wiemer-Hastings (2005). These researchers had participants generate properties for abstract and concrete concepts. In so doing, the participants also had to generate contextual descriptions for both types of concepts, including agents, objects, settings, actions, and introspections. An analysis of the content of abstract and concrete concepts showed that they were highly similar. The differences between the types of concepts were that in general participants generated more information about physical objects, background settings, and simple behaviors for the concrete concepts. For the concepts, participants generated somewhat more information about people, social interactions, complex relations, and introspections. However, in both cases the properties seemed to be based on situation simulations.

Perhaps the study of emotion concepts will lead researchers to more fully appreciate the ways in which sensorimotor and introspective simulations can provide the content of abstract concepts. Furthermore, this will perhaps only prove satisfactory if studied from a developmental perspective.

REPRESENTATIONAL LIMITATIONS OF THE BODY

Related to the problem of defining the content of abstract concepts, the endorsement of embodiment theories relies in part on their ability to reasonably summarize and find sufficiently powerful the body's representational capacity. Focusing specifically on affective and introspective experience, some critics have argued that bodily feedback is too undifferentiated and too slow to serve as a basis of such experience. Moreover, it has been argued that the same bodily state may be associated with a number of different cognitive and emotional representations (Zajonc & McIntosh, 1992). This kind of objection to embodiment theories, broadly defined, is long-standing and has been very persuasively used by Cannon (1927, 1929) and many others to argue against the James-Lange theory of emotion (James, 1896/1994).

We have noted elsewhere (Niedenthal et al., 2005) that there are a number of possible responses to this objection. Zajonc and Markus (1984), for instance, pointed out that the motor system can support extremely subtle distinctions, a point that has been made by Gallese (2003a), among others. Furthermore, even a limited number of motor states can support a very large number of experiential distinctions. The facial muscles alone can combine to produce many different representational distinctions.

More important, and a point to be made repeatedly, recent embodiment approaches, sidestep such criticisms by their emphasis on the brain's modality-specific systems and not on the body's muscles and viscera. The circuits in modality-specific brain areas are as fast and refined as any other form of cortical representation (e.g., Pulvermüller, Shtyrov, & Ilmoniemi, 2005) and are thus able to dynamically process a large number of bodily states at the same time (Damasio, 2003).

CONCLUSION

We briefly reviewed some of the dominant representational models in social cognition and the way in which basic processes of interest to social psychologists are implemented by such models. Many findings in both the cognitive and social cognition literatures indicate that there is a closer relationship between sensory and motor experience of and with entities in the world and the knowledge we possess about them. Therefore, we tried to summarize the principles and the utility of more recent theories that hold that meaning is grounded in the sensorimotor states that occur in interaction with them. These models will not suffice for accounting for all cognitive phenomena that we observe, and no one is making that argument (see Simmons & Barsalou, 2003). We believe, however, that these theories should be viewed not as threatening recent currently fashionable models of representation relied on in social cognition, but as evolving from them toward *a priori* accounts of embodied phenomena that, traditionally, have been difficult to explain. We believe, therefore, theories of embodied cognition can provide social psychologists with powerful new ways of theorizing about social representations and the mechanisms that process them. Such theories offer new ways of conceptualizing attitudes, attitude change, impression formation, stereotyping, emotion, and empathy.

REFERENCES

Anderson, J. R. (1983). *The architecture of cognition*. Cambridge, MA: Harvard University Press.

Anderson, N. H. (1981). *Foundations of information integration theory*. New York: Academic Press.

Bargh, J. A., Chen, M., & Burrows, L. (1996). Automaticity of social behavior: Direct effects of trait construct and stereotype activation on action. *Journal of Personality and Social Psychology, 71*, 230–244.

Barsalou, L. W. (1987). The instability of graded structure: Implications for the nature of concepts. In U. Neisser (Ed.), *Concepts and conceptual development: Ecological and intellectual factors in categorization* (pp. 101–140). Cambridge, England: Cambridge University Press.

Barsalou, L. W. (1999a). Language comprehension: Archival memory or preparation for situated action? *Discourse Processes, 28*, 61–80.

Barsalou, L. W. (1999b). Perceptual symbol systems. *Behavioral and Brain Sciences, 22*, 577–609.

Barsalou, L. W. (2003). Situated simulation in the human conceptual system. *Language and Cognitive Processes, 18*, 513–562. (Reprinted in H. Moss & J. Hampton, *Conceptual representation,* Psychology Press, East Sussex, England, 2004, pp. 513–566.)

Barsalou, L. W. (2005). Situated conceptualization. In H. Cohen & C. Lefebvre (Eds.), *Handbook of categorization in cognitive science* (pp. 619–650). St. Louis, MO: Elsevier.

Barsalou, L. W., Niedenthal, P. M., Barbey, A., & Ruppert, J. (2003). Social embodiment. In B. Ross (Ed.), *The psychology of learning and motivation* (Vol. 43, pp. 43–92). San Diego, CA: Academic Press.

Barsalou, L. W., Simmons, K., Barbey, A., & Wilson, C. D. (2003) Grounding conceptual knowledge in modality-specific systems. *Trends in Cognitive Sciences, 7*, 84-91.

Barsalou, L. W., & Wiemer-Hastings, K. (2005). Situating abstract concepts. In D. Pecher and R. Zwaan (Eds.), *Grounding cognition: The role of perception and action in memory, language, and thought* (pp. 129–163). New York: Cambridge University Press.

Barsalou, L. W., Solomon, K. O., & Wu, L. L. (1999) Perceptual simulation in conceptual tasks. In M. K. Hiraga, C. Sinha, & S. Wilcox (Eds.), *Cultural, typological, and psychological perspectives in cognitive linguistics: The proceedings of the 4th conference of the International Cognitive Linguistics Association* (vol. 3, pp. 209–228). Amsterdam: John Benjamins.

Blakemore, S.-J., & Decety, J. (2001). From the perception of action to the understanding of intention. *Nature Reviews/Neuroscience, 2*, 561–567.

Buccino, G., Riggio, L., Melli, G., Binkofski, F., Gallese, V., & Rizzolatti, G. (2003). Listening to action related sentences modulates the activity of primary motor system: A combined TMS and behavioral study. *Cognitive Brain Research, 24*, 355–363.

Cannon, W. B. (1927). The James–Lange theory of emotions: A critical examination and an alternative. *American Journal of Psychology, 29*, 444–454.

Cantor, N., & Mischel, W. (1977). Traits as prototypes: Effects on recognition memory. *Journal of Personality and Social Psychology, 35*, 38–48.

Carlston, D. E. (1994). Associated systems theory: A systematic approach to the cognitive representation of persons and events. In R. S. Wyer (Ed.) *Advances in social cognition: Vol. 7. Associated systems theory* (pp. 1–78). Hillsdale, NJ: Erlbaum.

Chambon, M., Droit-Volet, S., & Niedenthal, P.M. (2007). The effect of embodying the elderly on temporal perception. *Journal of Experimental Psychology, 44*, 672–677.

Cohen, C. E. (1981). Person categories and social perception: Testing some boundaries of the processing effects of prior knowledge. *Journal of Personality and Social Psychology, 40*, 441–452.

Collins, A. M., & Loftus, E. F. (1975). A spreading-activation theory of semantic processing. *Psychological Review, 82*, 407–428.

Damasio, A. R. (1989). The brain binds entities and events by multiregional activation from convergence zones. *Neural Computation, 1*, 123–132.

Damasio, A. R. (1994). *Descartes' error: Emotion, reason, and the human brain.* New York: Grosset/Putnam.

Decety, J., & Jackson, P. L. 2004. The functional architecture of human empathy. *Behavioral and Cognitive Neuroscience Reviews, 3*, 71–100.

Devine, P. G. (1989). Stereotypes and prejudice: Their automatic and controlled components. *Journal of Personality and Social Psychology, 56*, 5–18.

Dijksterhuis, A., & Bargh, J. A. (2001). The perception-behavior expressway: Automatic effects of social perception on social behavior. *Advances in Experimental Social Psychology, 33*, 1–40.

Dijksterhuis, A., Spears, R., & Lépinasse, V. (2001). Reflecting and deflecting stereotypes: Assimilation and contrast in impression formation and automatic behavior. *Journal of Experimental Social Psychology, 37*, 286–299.

Dovidio, J. F., & Gaertner, S. L. (1998). On the nature of contemporary prejudice: The causes, consequences and challenges of aversive racism. In S. T. Fiske & J. L. Eberhardt (Eds.), *Racism: The problem and the response* (pp. 3–32). Newbury Park, CA: Sage.

Drew, M. R., Fairhurst, S., Malapani, C., Horvitz, J. C., & Balsam, P. D. (2003). Effects of dopamine antagonists on the timing of two intervals. *Pharmacology Biochemistry and Behavior, 75*, 9–15.

Droit-Volet, S. (2003). Temporal experience and timing in children. In W. Meck (Ed.), *Functional and neural mechanisms of interval timing* (pp. 183–208). Boca Raton, FL: CRC Press.

Fazio, R. H., Jackson, J. R., Dunton, B. C., & Williams, C. J. (1995). Variability in automatic activation as an unobtrusive measure of racial attitudes: A bona fide pipeline? *Journal of Personality and Social Psychology, 69*, 1013–1027.

Ferguson, M. J., & Bargh, J. A. (2004). How social perception can automatically influence behavior. *Trends in Cognitive Sciences, 8*, 33–39.

Fiske, S. T. (1982). Schema-triggered affect: Applications to social perception. In M. S. Clark & S. T. Fiske (Eds.), *Cognition and affect: The 17th Annual Carnegie Symposium.* Hillsdale, NJ: Erlbaum.

Fodor, J. A. (1975). *The language of thought.* Cambridge, MA: Harvard University Press.

Gaertner, S. L., & McLaughlin, J. P. (1983). Racial stereotypes: Associations and ascriptions of positive and negative characteristics. *Social Psychology Quarterly, 46*, 23–30.

Gallese, V. (2003a). The roots of empathy: The shared manifold hypothesis and the neural basis of intersubjectivity. *Psychopathology, 36*, 71–180.

Gallese, V. (2003b). The manifold nature of interpersonal relations: The quest for a common mechanism. *Philosophical Transactions of the Royal Society of London B, 358,* 517–528.
Gibbon, J. (1977). Scalar expectancy theory and Weber's law in animal timing. *Psychological Review, 84,* 279–325.
Gibbon, J., Church, R. M., & Meck, W. H. (1984). Scalar timing in memory. In J. Gibbon & L. Allan (Eds.), *Timing and time perception* (pp. 57–78). New York: New York Academy of Sciences.
Glenberg, A. M. (1997). What memory is for. *Behavioral and Brain Sciences, 20,* 1–55.
Glenberg, A. M., & Kaschak, M. P. (2002). Grounding language in action. *Psychonomic Bulletin & Review, 9,* 558–565.
Goldstone, R. L., & Kersten, A. (2003). Concepts and categories. In A. F. Healy & R. W. Proctor (Eds.), *Comprehensive handbook of psychology, Volume 4: Experimental psychology* (pp. 591–621). New York: Wiley.
Goldstone, R. L., Medin, D. L., & Halberstadt, J. (1997). Similarity in context. *Memory & Cognition, 25,* 237–255.
Hastie, R. (1980). Memory for behavioral information that confirms or contradicts a personality impression. In R. Hastie, T. O. Ostrom, E. B. Ebbesen, R. S. Wyer, Jr., D. L. Hamilton, & D. E. Carlston. (Eds.), *Person memory: The cognitive basis of social perception* (pp. 155–177). Hillsdale, NJ: Erlbaum.
Jackson, P. L., & Decety, J. (2004). Motor cognition: A new paradigm to study self-other interactions. *Current Opinion in Neurobiology, 14,* 259–263.
James, W. (1890). *Principles of psychology.* New York: Holt.
Jennings, R. J., & van der Molen, M. W. (2002). Cardiac timing and the central regulation of action. *Psychological Research, 66,* 337–349.
Judd, C. M., & Park, B. (1993). Definition and assessment of accuracy in social stereotypes. *Psychological Review, 100,* 109–128.
Kan, I. P., Barsalou, L. W., Solomon, K. O., Minor, J. K., & Thompson-Schill, S. L. (2003). Role of mental imagery in a property verification task: fMRI evidence for perceptual representations of conceptual knowledge. *Cognitive Neuropsychology, 20,* 525–540.
Kashima, Y., & Kerekes, A. R. Z. (1994). A distributed memory model of averaging phenomena in person impression formation. *Journal of Experimental Social Psychology, 30,* 407–455.
Kawakami, K., Young, H., & Dovidio, J. F. (2002). Automatic stereotyping: Category, trait and behavioral activations. *Personality and Social Psychology Bulletin, 28,* 3–15.
Kellenbach, M. L., Brett, M., & Patterson, K. (2001). Large, colourful or noisy? Attribute- and modality-specific activations during retrieval of perceptual attribute knowledge. *Cognitive, Affective & Behavioral Neuroscience, 1*(3), 207–221.
Klatzky, A. L. et al. (1982).
Kosslyn, S. M. (1975). Information representation in visual images. *Cognitive Psychology, 7,* 341–370.
Kosslyn, S. M., and Pomerantz, J. R. (1977). Imagery, propositions, and the form of internal representations. *Cognitive Psychology, 9,* 52–76.
Kruschke, J. K. (2005). Category learning. In K. Lamberts and R. L. Goldstone (Eds.), *The handbook of cognition* (pp. 183–201). London: Sage.
Kunda, Z. (1999). *Social cognition: Making sense of people.* Cambridge, MA: MIT Press.
LaFrance, M., & Ickes, W. (1981). Posture mirroring and interactional involvement: Sex and sex typing effects. *Journal of Nonverbal Behavior, 5,* 139–154.
Lepore, L., & Brown, R. (1997). Category and stereotype activation: Is prejudice inevitable? *Journal of Personality and Social Psychology, 72,* 275–287.
Locke, J. (1979). *Essay concerning human understanding.* New York: Oxford University Press. (Original work published 1690.)

Logan, G. D. (2002). An instance theory of attention and memory. *Psychological Review, 109*, 376–400.
McClelland, J. L., & Rumelhart, D. E. (1985). Distributed memory and the representation of general and specific information. *Journal of Experimental Psychology: General, 114*, 159–197.
McClelland, J. L., McNaughton, B. L., and O'Reilly, R. C. (1995). Why there are complementary learning systems in the hippocampus and neocortex: Insights from the successes and failures of connectionist models of learning and memory *Psychological Review, 102*, 419–457.
Meck, W. (2003). *Functional and neural mechanisms of interval timing.* Boca Raton, FL: CRC Press.
Medin, D. L., & Schaffer, M. M. (1978). Context theory of classification learning. *Psychological Review, 85*, 207–238.
Mussweiler, T. (2006). Doing is for thinking! Stereotype activation by stereotypic movements. *Psychological Science, 17*, 17–21.
Newell, A., & Simon, H. A. (1972). *Human problem solving.* Englewood Cliffs, NJ: Prentice Hall.
Niedenthal, P. M., Barsalou, L. W., Ric, F., & Krauth-Gruber, S. (2005). Embodiment in the acquisition and use of emotion knowledge. In L. Feldman Barrett, P. M. Niedenthal, & P. Winkielman (Eds.), *Emotion: Conscious and unconscious* (pp. 21–50). New York: Guilford.
Niedenthal, P. M., Barsalou, L. W., Winkielman, P., Krauth-Gruber, S., & Ric, F. (2005). Embodiment in attitudes, social perception, and emotion. *Personality and Social Psychology Review, 9*, 184–211.
Niedenthal, P. M., Winkielman, P., Mondillon, L., & Vermeulen, N. (in press). Embodied emotion concepts. *Journal of Personality and Social Psychology.*
Nosofsky, R. M. (1986). Attention, similarity, and the identification–categorization relationship. *Journal of Experimental Psychology: General, 115*, 39–57.
Nosofsky, R. M. (1992). Exemplar-based approach to relating categorization, identification, and recognition. In F. G. Ashby (Ed.), *Multidimensional models of perception and cognition* (Scientific psychology series, pp. 363–393). Hillsdale, NJ: Lawrence Erlbaum Associates.
Nosofsky, R. M., & Palmeri, T. J. (1997). An exemplar-based random walk model of speeded classification. *Psychological Review, 104*(2), 266–300.
Pecher, D., Zeelenberg, R., & Barsalou, L. W. (2003). Verifying properties from different modalities for concepts produces switching costs. *Psychological Science, 14*, 119–124.
Pecher, D., Zeelenberg, R., & Barsalou, L. W. (2004). Sensorimotor simulations underlie conceptual representations: Modality-specific effects of prior activation. *Psychonomic Bulletin & Review, 11*, 164–167.
Piaget, J. (1929). *The child's conception of the world.* New York: Harcourt, Brace Jovanovich.
Posner, M. I., & Keele, S., (1968). On the genesis of abstract ideas. *Journal of Experimental Psychology, 77*, 353–363.
Pulvermüller, F., Shtyrov, Y., & Ilmoniemi, R. 2005: Brain signatures of meaning access in action word recognition. *Journal of Cognitive Neuroscience, 17*, 884–892.
Pylyshyn, Z. W. (1984). *Computation and cognition: Towards a foundation for cognitive science.* Cambridge, MA: MIT Press.
Roloff, M. E., & Berger, C. R. (Eds.). (1982). *Social cognition and communication.* Beverly Hills, CA: Sage.
Rumelhart, D. E. (1989). The architecture of mind: A connectionist approach. In M. Posner (Ed.), *Foundations of cognitive science* (pp. 133–160). Cambridge, MA: MIT Press.

Schubert, T. W. (2004). The power in your hand: Gender differences in bodily feedback from making a fist. *Personality and Social Psychology Bulletin, 30,* 757–769.

Shanks, D. R. (1997). Distributed representations and implicit knowledge: A brief introduction. In K. Lamberts and D. Shanks (Eds.), *Knowledge, concepts, and categories.* Cambridge, MA: MIT Press.

Simmons, K., & Barsalou, L. W. (2003). The similarity-in-topography principle: Reconciling theories of conceptual deficits. *Cognitive Neuropsychology, 20,* 451–486.

Smith, E. R. (1996). What do connectionism and social psychology offer each other? *Journal of Personality and Social Psychology, 70,* 893–912.

Smith, E. R. (1998). Mental representation and memory. In D. Gilbert, S. Fiske, & G. Lindzey (Eds.), *Handbook of social psychology* (4th ed., Vol. 1, pp. 391–445). New York: McGraw-Hill.

Smith, E. R., & DeCoster, J. (1998). Knowledge acquisition, accessibility, and use in person perception and stereotyping: Simulation with a recurrent connectionist network. *Journal of Personality and Social Psychology, 74,* 21–35.

Smith, E. R., & Zarate, M. A. (1992). Exemplar-based model of osical judgment. *Psychological Review, 99,* 3–21.

Solomon, K. O., & Barsalou, L. W. (2004). Perceptual simulation in property verification. *Memory & Cognition, 32,* 244–259.

Srull, T. K. (1981). Person memory: Some tests of associative storage and retrieval models. *Journal of Experimental Psychology: Human Learning and Memory, 7,* 440–463.

Srull, T. K., & Wyer, R. S., Jr. (1989). Person memory and judgment. *Psychological Review, 96,* 58–83.

Stangor, C., & Duan, C. (1991). Effects of multiple task demands upon memory for information about social groups. *Journal of Experimental Social Psychology, 27,* 357–378.

Stangor, C., & McMillan, D. (1992). Memory for expectancy-congruent and expectancy-incongruent information: A review of the social and social-developmental literatures. *Psychological Bulletin, 111,* 42–61.

Strack, F., & Deutsch, R. (2004). Reflective and impulsive determinants of social behavior *Personality and Social Psychology Review, 8,* 220–247.

Viviani, P. (2002). Motor competence in the perception of dynamic events: a tutorial. In W. Prinz & B. Hommel (Eds.), *Common mechanisms in perception and action: Attention and Performance XIX* (pp. 406–442). New York: Oxford University Press.

Wearden, J. H. (1991). Human performance on an analogue of an interval bisection task. *Quarterly Journal of Experimental Psychology, 43B,* 59–81.

Wegner, D. M., & Vallacher, R. R. (1977). *Implicit psychology: An introduction to social cognition.* New York: Oxford University Press.

Wheeler, S. C., & Petty, R. E. (2001). The effects of stereotype activation on behavior: A review of possible mechanisms. *Psychological Bulletin, 127,* 797–826.

Wyer, R. S., & Srull, T. K. (Eds.). (1984). *Handbook of social cognition.* Hillsdale, NJ: Erlbaum.

Zajonc, R. B., Adelmann, P. K., Murphy, S. T., & Niedenthal, P. M. (1987). Convergence in the physical appearance of spouses: An implication of the vascular theory of emotional efference. *Motivation and Emotion, 11,* 335–346.

Zajonc, R. B., & Markus, H. (1984). Affect and cognition: The hard interface. In C. Izard, J. Kagan, & R. B. Zajonc (Eds.), *Emotions, cognition and behavior* (pp. 73–102). Cambridge: Cambridge University Press.

Zajonc, R. B., & McIntosh, D. N. (1992). Emotions research: Some promising questions, some questionable promises. *Psychological Science, 3,* 70–74.

3

Unconscious, Conscious, and Metaconscious in Social Cognition

PIOTR WINKIELMAN and JONATHAN W. SCHOOLER

INTRODUCTION

Social cognition explains the mechanisms of social behavior using concepts and methods shared with related fields of cognitive psychology and cognitive science as well as new fields such as cognitive, social, and affective neuroscience. This approach led to remarkable progress in understanding social perception, memory, reasoning, emotion, and judgment and offered insights into real-world social issues, such as optimal decision making, stereotyping, and cultural differences (see other chapters, but especially 1, 5, and 14). We consider the role of consciousness in a variety of social cognition phenomena. In our contibution, we ask what people are conscious of, and not conscious of, during perception, memory, emotion, and decision making and how this matters for social interaction. We review several findings, but more important, we offer a fresh theoretical perspective on consciousness that differs from currently dominant views in social cognition. Our perspective is informed by recent developments in cognitive psychology, particularly in the area of metacognition, and draws on new discoveries in neurosciences.

We start with a few historical remarks, mostly to highlight that, over the years, psychology oscillated from viewing consciousness as indispensable to claiming it is unnecessary. We then discuss how to define consciousness and its possible functions and mechanisms. This gives us an opportunity to comment on some current debates in social cognition, including the automaticity of purposive behavior and sophistication of unconscious perception, thinking, and decision making. We then make a distinction critical for the remainder of our chapter among levels of awareness and review research on dissociations among mental events that are unconscious, conscious, and meta-aware. Reflecting the book's aims, throughout we discuss mechanisms of consciousness across different levels of explanation and include phenomena from different stages of social cognition, including perception, representation, memory, judgments, and decisions.

HISTORY

Reflecting its philosophical roots, early scientific psychology was fascinated with consciousness. In fact, one major goal was to accurately characterize conscious contents, which would establish a catalogue of basic mental elements that resembles in precision the Mendeleyev periodic table (Boring, 1953). The method of introspection assumed that critical elements of mental life (thoughts, feelings, volitions) are in principle consciously accessible. They might initially escape explicit attention, but with proper training of focus and reporting, researchers can capture most essential mental elements and discover lawful relations between them. An important assumption was that psychology should be fundamentally interested in "mental" events (i.e., content-bearing, intentional states) but not so much in nonmental events (e.g., associative chains, reflexes, physiological processes, etc.). Still, even the early psychologists admitted some role for unconscious processes. For example, Helmholtz famously proposed that vision is mediated by unconscious inferences, whereas James debated the role of habits and the subconscious (Kihlstrom, 2008). Behaviorism, and the ambition to make psychology "objective" and equal to other natural sciences, brought a disfavor for introspection and mentalistic concepts like consciousness. Along with this came the belief that behavior is ultimately under the control of the environment, and that somehow providing mechanistic explanations of behavior would make concepts like "consciousness" or "volition" superfluous (Kihlstrom, 2008). The situation started to change in the mid-1970s when cognitive psychologists revived the "black box" and began to tackle issues like controlled and automatic processing (Shiffrin & Schneider, 1977), attentional selection (Kahneman, 1973; Posner & Snyder, 1975), and unconscious perception (Marcel, 1983). Although few dared to speak its name, there was a growing recognition that consciousness might be "respectable, useful, and probably necessary" (Mandler, 1975, p. 229). Soon, the legitimacy of the topic was fully reestablished and now "everyone who is conscious, is studying consciousness" (Churchland, 2005, p. 46). Psychological journals routinely carry articles on consciousness, as do general journals such as *Science* and *Nature*, and there are journal outlets (e.g., *Consciousness and Cognition*) and serious annual conferences (*Association for Scientific Study of Consciousness*) exclusively dedicated to this topic. The enthusiasm is not only limited to psychology. The codiscoverer of DNA, Francis Crick, left genetics for neuroscience and declared consciousness the greatest puzzle of contemporary science. Subsequently, he even called the possibility of a biological account of consciousness *The Astonishing Hypothesis* (Crick, 1994). Indeed, some of the most interesting recent discoveries in neuroscience come from consciousness researchers (Edelman, 1989; Singer, 2000; Tononi, 2004). There is also exciting work in computer science on mechanistic, but not eliminative, explanations of consciousness and choice (e.g., Cleeremans, 2005; Hazy, Frank, & O'Reilly, 2007). And, philosophers try to bewitch the reader or outwit each other with book titles such as *Mystery of Consciousness, Consciousness Reconsidered, Reclaimed*, and even *Explained* (Zeeman, 2002).

It is encouraging that social cognition researchers have always been in the game, even providing some of the early impetus toward revival of interest in consciousness. Thus, an influential study showed that stimulus value can be enhanced via unconscious mere exposure (Kunst-Wilson & Zajonc, 1980). Another pioneering study showed that people's conscious beliefs about the causes of their own behavior can be at odds with actual causes (Nisbett & Wilson, 1977). Since then, there have been many influential studies of unconscious influences on social perception, affect, reasoning, judgment, and behavior. Ironically, much of the social cognition work on consciousness has always been aimed at showing its limits, if not unimportance (Bargh, 1989). This emphasis continues (Dijksterhuis & Nordgren, 2006; Wegner, 2002; Wilson, 2002), even as other disciplines progressively focus on understanding consciousness itself. Along with it comes fascination of social cognition with all things "implicit"—perception, learning, attitudes, self-esteem, self-concepts, stereotypes, partisanship, goals, and so on (Greenwald et al., 2002).[1] However, there have also been attempts to explore the limits of the unconscious mind (Baumeister, 2008; Kihlstrom, 2008; Greenwald, 1992).

DEFINITION AND DISTINCTIONS

But, what is *consciousness*? The term itself is quite slippery. The *Concise Oxford English Dictionary* lists two major meanings: (1) the state of being conscious and (2) one's awareness or perception of something. However, Webster's dictionary lists as many as five different definitions, and books on consciousness devote pages elucidating different meanings (e.g., Zeeman, 2002). Thus, it is useful to highlight different senses in which the term appears in psychological literature. This will also allow us to briefly comment on some debates in social cognition.

Conscious as "Awake and Mindful"

The word *conscious* can refer to a global state of an individual. One use of this word is similar to "awake" or "vigilant" as opposed to "asleep" or "comatose." The sleepy-vigilant dimension is typically investigated by neurologists, although some interesting social cognition studies showed that anesthetized patients form implicit, but not explicit, memory for events during the surgery (Kihlstrom, Schacter, Cork, Hurt, & Behr, 1990). Perhaps, a more relevant meaning of conscious as a description of a global state refers to a "mindful" as opposed to a "robot-like" dimension. In that sense, being conscious is the ability to have subjective experiences, wishes, desires, and complex thoughts and to perform flexible, self-initiated, purposeful behaviors. For example, patients in a persistent vegetative state (PVS) maintain regular sleep-wake cycles, respond to simple simulation (e.g., withdraw their hand from sharp objects), yet are not considered conscious and possessing of "personhood" because of their inability to make choices, process complex information, show flexible behavior, and initiate purposive actions (Laureys et al., 2002).[2] It is actually useful to contrast the above medical and legal view that consciousness is essential for personhood with the social cognition view that often minimizes the role of consciousness in complex thought, choice, and purposive behavior. Despite some radical "anticonsciousness" declarations (for samples, see Kihlstrom, 2008), we actually doubt that social cognition researchers seriously believe that there is little distinction between people and robots and would readily concede that only *some* goals or decisions are unconscious, and that only *sometimes* a sense of voluntary control is illusory. We return to this issue in this chapter.

Conscious as "Subjectively Experienced"

The second major meaning of the word *conscious* is in reference to the subjective status of a particular mental content (perception, thought, or feeling). Being conscious means being represented in subjective experience and, as a result, potentially available to report and to use in intentional control of behavior. It is in that sense that psychologists are interested in whether there are unconscious perceptions, memories, goals, attitudes, or emotions (Bargh, 1989; Greenwald, 1992; Winkielman & Berridge, 2004).

The interest in what makes certain mental content conscious and what makes it available for report and control binds together the research on consciousness with research on meta-cognition, for which the central effort is to uncover the relation between people's mental states and their beliefs about those mental states (Koriat, 2006). The meta-cognitive perspective, which guides much of our review in this chapter, highlights that mental content can stand in one of three relations to consciousness. First, mental content can be genuinely unconscious. One classic example comes from research on so-called blind-sight patients with damaged primary visual cortex (area V1 of the striate cortex) but intact subcortical visual pathways. These patients can discriminate simple visual information (e.g., location or shape) and use it in their motor pointing behavior without being able to verbally report on that discrimination (Weiskrantz, 1986). In that case, the mental representation (e.g., "x is a square") is genuinely unconscious—the patient truly does not know that he or she "knows" what shape was presented. Second, mental content could be "experientially conscious," existing in the ongoing experience without being reflected on. For example, preverbal infants are typically assumed to have conscious experiences (e.g., recognize and be happy to see their mother; feel pain, hunger, and pleasure) but limited meta-awareness. A less-speculative example comes from classic experiments on iconic memory, which showed that people are temporarily aware of a much larger amount of information presented in a visual matrix than they can spontaneously report (Sperling, 1960). Third, mental content can be "meta-conscious" (or "meta-aware") and be explicitly represented as a content of one's own consciousness (Schooler, 2001, 2002; Schooler, Ariely, & Loewenstein, 2003; Schooler & Schreiber, 2004). It is this type of consciousness that is typically assessed when an experimenter asks participants questions like, "How happy do you feel now? "Did you notice any briefly presented words?" or, "Did you pursue goal X in your behavior?"

FUNCTIONS OF CONSCIOUSNESS

A central assumption in social cognition is that mental information is represented on several levels. Accordingly, much research attention focuses on understanding how these different levels, or perhaps systems, relate to each other (Strack & Deutsch, 2004; Smith & DeCoster, 2000). So, what distinguishes unconscious, conscious, and metaconscious representation? This question touches on a more general problem of the purpose of consciousness—a problem that received a variety of functional and mechanistic answers in the psychological literature. In general, researchers have emphasized the idea that consciousness is associated with (a) special access to mental content and (b) special functions that can be performed on this content.

Conscious Access

Several theories posit that consciousness is a representational system characterized by special access to mental content. One useful framework is the global workspace theory, which proposes that consciousness functions to allow communication, transparency, and coordination between the many isolated, parallel subprocesses in the human mind (Baars, 1988). Consciousness constitutes a global workspace in which various local processes can "broadcast" their outcomes and talk to each other in a common "language" (more like a language of thought, rather than actual language). As a result, the previously independent and isolated local processes can coordinate, sequence, and structure their actions, thus helping the organism achieving its goals. For example, by representing tactile, visual, and auditory processes in a common matrix, global workspace allows novel cross-modal and cross-temporal connections (e.g., "The sequence of musical notes I just heard has the same order as the sequence of colored lights I saw before."). It also presumably helps us understand expressions such as "blue mood," "bitter cold," "sharp cheese," or "loud tie" (Ramachandran, 2004).[3] But, more important, this "global accessibility" of conscious representations makes them available for verbal report and for high-level processes such as conscious judgments, reasoning, and the planning and guiding of action.

But, what gives representations conscious or "global" access? Cognitive researchers often emphasize the role of "strength" (Cleeremans, 2005). The notion of strength captures the idea that representations require a certain stability and quality before they can enter working memory, where they can be actively maintained, and become accessible for potential report. One determinant of strength is activation, which in turn is determined by many factors, such as stimulus energy (longer presented items are more likely conscious than briefly presented items); familiarity (all things equal, more familiar items become conscious easier then less-familiar items); recency (more recent items are more likely to be conscious than older items); and so forth. Representational strength is also influenced by focused attention—a perceptual amplifier and selector of events (conscious and nonconscious) that fall into its scope. Thus, an objectively very weak stimulus can reach consciousness if it receives attentional processing, and there is little perceptual competition (Breitmeyer & Ogmen, 2006). Interestingly, recent research shows, somewhat paradoxically, that focused conscious attention may be necessary for some unconscious processes (Koch & Tsuchiya, 2007). For example, subliminal priming is enhanced by attentional cuing of location (Sumner, Tsai, Yu, & Nachev, 2006), and limbic responses are stronger if brief affective stimuli fall in the scope of focused attention (Pessoa, McKenna, Gutierrez, & Ungerleider, 2002). These observations may explain why so many successful subliminal priming paradigms in social cognition require that the subject is paying attention to a specific area on the screen (even if the prime remains invisible). It may also explain why many social cognitive studies on unconscious processes use "unobtrusive" rather than subliminal priming. In those studies, participants are exposed to stimuli in a definitely conscious, attended, and prolonged fashion (e.g., as a part of a sentence-unscrambling task or a crossword puzzle), with the "unconscious" element the relevance of the task to subsequent judgment or the importance of a particular stimulus dimension. In short, focused attention might be a precondition for many unconscious effects.

Another factor that modulates whether mental content is conscious has to do with anatomical and functional disconnection. Thus, a visual representation in previously mentioned blind-sight patients can be strong (it can drive pointing behavior) but remains unconscious because it is restricted to lower visual pathways (Weiskrantz, 1986). Similarly, habits (e.g., biking) may involve representations that are very robust, but unconscious, because they are only instantiated in the motor system (Cleeremans, 2005). A functional disconnection may occur when input is incoherent with the currently processed information. For example, a distinct, prolonged, unusual, and dynamic event (e.g., a gorilla slowly walking through a room of people passing balls to each other) can remain unconscious, even when participants "look" at the scene (Simons & Chabris, 1999). One explanation of this "blindness" is that the event is incompatible with the current mental model (i.e., generalized schema) of the situation or participants' current perceptual goals.

Finally, there is some exciting neuroscientific research on the mechanisms of conscious access. Some evidence suggests that consciousness represents a form of multiregional activation that is perhaps integrated by oscillatory activity (Singer, 2000; Tononi, 2004). For example, conscious perception of a stimulus is associated with a synchronous activation of higher associative cortices, particularly parietal, prefrontal, and anterior cingulate areas, whereas unconscious perception is associated only with a local activation (Dehaene, Changeux, Naccache, Sackur, & Sergent, 2006). Consistent with these ideas, clinical work has shown that the previously mentioned patients in a PVS (awake but unconscious) show only localized, modality-specific responses to stimuli, whereas patients in a minimally conscious state show coherent responses across multiple sensory and associative systems (Laureys et al., 2002).

Conscious Thinking

Some argue that consciousness enables higher-order, meaning-based, truth-value-preserving processing of information (Block, 1995; Searle, 1997). In contrast, the unconscious is restricted to a simpler, associative type of processing. This distinction resembles, although does not completely overlap, with "dual-process" theories in social cognition. For example, Strack and Deutsch (2004) suggested that social cognition is carried out by two systems: a reflective system that relies on knowledge about facts and values and an impulsive system based on associative links and motivational orientations. The differential information base on which the two systems rely determines the types of responses they engender. The reflective system, drawing on propositions about the world, leads to responses based on rational considerations. In contrast, the impulsive system, drawing on associations and impulses, leads to nonreasoned actions.

Does processing of meaning require consciousness? This question is a subject of long debate, which touches on tricky issues of the relation between semantic cognition and associationism (McClelland & Rogers, 2003). It is now widely accepted that subliminally presented pictures and words can activate related semantic and affective categories (Greenwald, Draine, & Abrams, 1996; Marcel, 1983). Even subliminally presented single digits can activate magnitude information (Dehaene et al., 2006). Thus, there is no doubt that complex content can be unconsciously activated across meaning dimension. However, the evidence for unconscious semantic *processing*, rather than automatic *activation*, is sparse. For example, unconscious priming responds to partial- rather than whole-word information, is not sensitive to basic operations like negations ("not," "un-," or "dis-"), and cannot process two-digit numbers (Abrams & Greenwald, 2000). One could wonder if these limitations arise because subliminal presentations afford very weak stimulus input. However, similar results hold when the input is conscious, and only conscious processing capacity is reduced. Thus, processing relational information such as negation ("no disease") or causality ("smoke causes fire") requires conscious capacity, whereas processing information about association does not (Deutsch, Gawronski, & Strack, 2006; Hummel & Holyoak, 2003). In a colorful demonstration of this point, DeWall, Baumeister, and Masicampo (2008) presented participants with a standard set of Graduate Record Examination (GRE) analytical problems and asked them to solve them under typical conditions or under cognitive load. Not surprisingly, loaded participants did much worse.

More generally, these findings highlight the difference between the position that many complex mental processes can be made to run automatically from the position that these processes do not require consciousness (i.e., never required it). To use an example, most adults can do the basic multiplication table automatically via associative recall (2 times 2 is 4). However, no one believes that the unconscious actually does multiplication. It simply means that highly trained operations become automatic over time and can eventually be performed by "dumb" associative retrieval (Logan, 1988; Rickard, 2005; Smith & DeCoster, 2000).[4]

The image of the "dumb unconscious" (Loftus & Klinger, 1992) has recently been challenged by claims of "unconscious thinking" (Dijksterjhuis, Bos, Nordgren, & van Baaren, 2006). For example, in one study, participants were quickly (although consciously) presented with a set of 12 positive and negative attributes each about four different cars (i.e., 48 attributes total, with one car having 75% positive attributes, two having 50% positive attributes, and one having 25% positive attributes). One group of participants (termed "conscious thinkers") made their decision after

4 min of deliberation and another group (termed "unconscious thinkers") after 4 min of engaging in a distracting anagram-solving task. Interestingly, the unconscious thinkers group was most likely to choose the "good" car, with the conscious group remaining at chance. For the authors, these results showed that unconscious thinking not only facilitates decisions but also might be better than conscious thinking. However, other interpretations are possible. First, it is not clear why distraction by anagrams eliminates conscious thought rather than simply reduces its amount. If so, perhaps the advantages of distraction occur because they help to prevent overthinking and encourage a reliance on more effective simple heuristics. In fact, when the best solution to the problem is simply to count the number of positive attributes, engaging in deeper processing that focuses on the attribute meaning might lead to suboptimal decision making (Gigerenzer & Goldstein, 1996). Accordingly, the benefits of unconscious thought may only apply to so-called linear integration problems, in which the attribute content either does not matter or can be consciously translated into attribute weights before unconscious "thought." Also, note that it is strange that giving people 4 min to think consciously about a simple choice produces only a chance response—after all, it is not that complicated to figure out that a car with 12 (75%) positive attributes is better than a car with 4 (25%) positive attributes. This suggests that the problem encountered by conscious thinkers may simply lie in confusion about the original attributes, perhaps because recall is susceptible to primacy or recency effects and interference by the intermediate task (Shanks, 2006). In short, while recent evidence does suggest some limitations to extensive deliberation, the degree to which this research implicates truly intelligent unconscious processing remains to be determined.

Conscious Control

Consciousness is associated not only with special access to mental content but also with special operations that can be performed on this content. Several of these operations fall under the umbrella name "control," thus linking consciousness to what cognitive scientists call "executive functions" (Norman & Shallice, 1986).[5] One aspect of control is selection. Thus, conscious content can be preferentially attended to and maintained in working memory or discarded if not needed. Another aspect of control is intentionality. Action can be deliberately started and stopped or can be delayed until appropriate conditions appear. Scheduling conflicts can be resolved, and new hierarchies can be established. Finally, with control comes flexibility. Thus, mental content can be used in adaptive, nonroutine ways, and old response chains can be broken and rearranged. This simple point was recently elegantly demonstrated in a study in which participants had to come up with novel titles, musical improvisations, or interesting drawings. Not surprisingly, participants under cognitive load produced repetitive, inflexible, and uninspiring works (Baumeister, Schmeichel, DeWall, & Vohs, 2007).

One interesting aspect of conscious control is its restricted capacity. Thus, only a few elements can be manipulated at a time; operations must be performed in a serial, rather than parallel fashion; and there are severe bottlenecks (Pashler, 1998). In fact, it is hard to be overwhelmed by the power of the unconscious given how many accidents are caused by people attempting to multitask (e.g., talking on the cell phone while driving; Levy, Pashler, & Boer, 2006), not to mention various social and physical disasters caused under the influence of various consciousness-impairing substances. Conscious operations also require effort and so are metabolically costly. As an illustration of this point, a recent series of studies has shown that manipulating an individual's blood glucose level affects mental control in basic tasks like the Stroop task, thought suppression, emotion regulation, attention control, or more social tasks like coping or helping (Gailliot et al., 2007). This is, of course, not terribly surprising given that measures of neuronal functioning, such as positron emission tomographic (PET) scanning, work by measuring glucose consumption in the brain, which is enhanced in mentally challenging tasks (Ward, 2006).

Of course, not all forms of control are conscious. The world is filled with mechanical devices, not only thermostats, that automatically check for a condition of a subordinate process and adjust its operation (Shinskey, 1979). The human body has many systems of complex control loops (e.g., homeostatic temperature and blood sugar mechanisms). Further, several "mental" processes automatically adjust their operation based on contextual conditions (Carver & Scheier, 1990). Thus, people unconsciously regulate eye movements to facilitate text processing (Reichle, Pollatsek, Fisher, & Rayner, 1998) and unconsciously adjust hand movements to capture the desired object (Triesch, Ballard, Hayhoe, & Sullivan, 2003). Finally, people are typically unaware of several aspects of control required for coherent speaking and writing.

In the domain of social cognition, there are many proposals that individuals engage in all kinds of automatic control (Fitzsimons & Bargh, 2004). One case is the pursuit of "unconscious goals." The evidence for this comes from studies in which individuals primed subliminally or unobtrusively with goal-related words (e.g., "cooperate," "achieve," "memorize") show corresponding adjustment in their behavior (e.g., show more helpful behavior, solve more problems, or remember more details). Further, they appear to be sensitive to conditions under which the goal is appropriate and track success at goal pursuit. These findings are interesting, but note that control explored in these studies is very different from control in research on executive functions. First, the unconscious goal paradigms rely on an unobtrusive activation of preformulated, standard goals, rather than formulation of novel goals. Second, those goals do not require participants to overcome a stronger alternative behavior (e.g., go against prepotent tendency), but operate when behavioral choices are already predetermined (participants can either cooperate or compete, with the likelihood of either action relatively equal). Third, the outcomes are fairly unimportant and do not require participants to reflect on the meaning or consequences of their actions. Accordingly, we suspect that many effects attributed to unconscious goals simply reflect influence of primes on interpretation of a vague experimental situation, including giving participants an idea of what and how much they are supposed to do (see Förster, Liberman, & Friedman, 2007, for discussion).[6] Finally, while unconscious goal activation clearly operates under some conditions, unconscious goals have yet to be shown to possess anything approaching the potency or flexibility of conscious goals.[7]

Indeed, in addition to offering a skewed perspective of the role of consciousness in mediating behaviors, the present trend toward attributing the bulk of human action to unconscious mechanisms may potentially have undesirable effects on people's self-regulatory ability. A study (Vohs & Schooler, 2008) exposed some participants to an excerpt from Francis Crick's *The Astonishing Hypothesis* that articulates the view that conscious control is an epiphenomenon, that is, that people lack any meaningful sort of free will. Compared to controls, participants exposed to the message that conscious control is illusory behaved more immorally on a passive cheating task. Moreover, their increased cheating was mediated by decreased belief in free will. In a second experiment, exposure to deterministic statements led participants to overpay themselves on a cognitive test relative to participants who were exposed to statements endorsing free will. Of course, such findings do not speak to the actual efficacy of conscious control. Nevertheless, they do raise concerns about the impact that a scientific dismissal of conscious control might have on the population at large and thus further highlight the importance of not overstating the degree to which science has shown consciousness to be impotent (Shariff, Schooler, & Vohs, 2008).

Metaconscious Monitoring

As we discussed, some forms of control might be automatized and unconscious, but others clearly involve consciousness. In fact, one form of control may require explicitly articulating the content of the conscious state to bring it into metaconsciousness. A good example is mind wandering (or "zoning out") during reading. Although we hope that readers have managed to keep their minds on our chapter as they have been reading it, we suspect that all readers have had the experience of suddenly realizing that, despite their best intentions and the fact that their eyes have continued to move across the page, they had no idea what they had been reading. Mind wandering suggests that the tacit monitoring systems failed to catch the mind's drifting and instead require a higher-level explicit monitoring process to take stock of the specific contents of thought and alert one to the fact that they have wandered off task. Schooler and colleagues have used the mind-wandering phenomenon to examine the function of meta-awareness in a domain in which mind wandering is antithetical to success (see Smallwood & Schooler, 2006, for a review). Specifically, Schooler, Reichle, and Halpern (2005) developed a paradigm to identify temporal lapses of meta-awareness during the attentionally demanding task of reading. In this research, participants read passages of text and indicated every time they caught their minds zoning out. They were then asked whether they had been aware that they had been zoning out prior to reporting it. In a second condition, participants were also probed intermittently and asked to indicate whether they had been zoning out at that moment. The results revealed that participants (a) frequently caught themselves zoning out during reading, (b) were still often caught zoning out by the probes, and (c) frequently reported that they had been unaware that they had been zoning out, particularly when they were caught by the probes. These findings demonstrate that individuals frequently lack meta-awareness of drifting off task, even when they are in a study in which they are specifically instructed to be vigilant for such lapses. In sum, explicit monitoring level (metaconsciousness) acts in effect like the pilot of an airplane. Although the autopilot system can handle mild adjustments due to normal shifts in wind and other conditions, when anything major occurs, the pilot is still needed to handle the situation. This second level of regulation has many more resources available to it, but because it draws on conscious processing, it is resource demanding and, as argued in this chapter, can even interfere with carrying out concurrent tasks. Thus, it is important to activate it only when needed as often the most effective performance may occur when individuals can smoothly operate without having to deliberately reflect on what they are doing.

DISSOCIATIONS BETWEEN LEVELS OF AWARENESS

The discussion so far suggests that at any given moment individuals' behavior reflects a variety of influences. There is the unconscious information, including various tacit monitoring processes that make routine adjustments. There is also information in their stream of consciousness (experiential consciousness). Periodically, however, the mind encounters situations that require more resource-dependent conscious monitoring process. In effect, it occurs anytime one explicitly attempts to answer the question, "What am I thinking or feeling?" Given that this answer represents a description of one's state, rather than the state itself, it offers individuals the opportunity to step out of the situation, which may be critical for many of the innovative behaviors of which individuals are capable. However, it also raises the possibility that in the re-description process individuals might get it wrong.

More specifically, there are three kinds of dissociations between levels of mental representation. There are *access dissociations,* in which a mental state occurs and has influence on behavior but is never directly accessed by consciousness. There are also two additional dissociations that follow from the claim that metaconsciousness involves the intermittent rerepresentation of the contents of consciousness (Schooler, 2002). *Temporal dissociations* occur when metaconsciousness temporarily fails to take stock of the current contents of thought (e.g., failing to notice that one is mind wandering during reading). *Translation dissociations* occur if the meta-representation process misrepresents the original experience. Such dissociations are particularly likely when one verbally reflects on nonverbal experiences or attempts to take stock of ambiguous experiences. Several interesting social cognitive phenomena illustrate these different dissociations.

Access Dissociations

An interesting dissociation occurs when a person is an affective state (as demonstrated by its impact on behavior, physiology, and cognition) without having conscious access to that state (see Winkielman, Berridge, & Wilbarger, 2005a, for comprehensive discussion). This idea of "unconscious affect" may seem initially strange, but note that, evolutionarily speaking, conscious representation of affect is a late achievement compared with the ability to respond affectively to relevant stimuli, which is presented in animals as simple as fish and reptiles. Accordingly, the basic affective neurocircuitry is contained in the subcortical brain and can operate even in the absence of cortex (Berridge, 2003). However, evolutionary and neuroscientific considerations can only be suggestive of unconscious affect in typical humans. Accordingly, Winkielman et al. (2005b) have tested this proposal in psychological studies aimed at dissociating the impact of simple affective stimuli on behavior from their impact on conscious feelings. For example, in one study participants were subliminally presented with a series of happy, neutral, or angry emotional facial expressions. Immediately after the subliminal affect induction, participants rated their conscious feelings and poured and consumed a novel drink. The results showed that the ratings of conscious feelings were unaffected by affective faces, even though the faces influenced consumption behavior, especially when participants were thirsty. Importantly, participants in those studies had no access to their affective reaction even when attending on-line to their feelings or even when they were told these feelings could bias their judgment (Winkielman, Zajonc, & Schwarz, 1997). Similarly, Förster (2003) found that manipulations of basic affective tendencies, via arm flexion versus arm extension, influence food intake without influencing conscious experience of moods. In sum, all these findings suggest that one can obtain genuine "access dissociation" between an underlying affective process and its conscious awareness.[8]

Temporal Dissociations

Sometimes, mental content is consciously experienced without being explicitly appraised in metaconsciousness. Temporal dissociations are illustrated by cases in which the induction of metaconsciousness causes one to assess aspects of experience that had previously eluded explicit appraisal. Several phenomena represent such dissociations.

Well-Being Appraisals We often fail to explicitly notice our own emotional states (e.g., sullenness, cheerfulness) until someone points them out to us. If we commonly lack metaconsciousness of affective states, then it follows that inducing continuous metaconsciousness of affect may alter that experience. Schooler et al. (2003) explored this issue by asking participants to report on-line happiness while listening to hedonically ambiguous music (Stravinsky). The results showed that continuous hedonic monitoring reduced individuals' postmusic ratings of happiness relative to a condition in which participants listened to music without monitoring. The fact that hedonic monitoring altered participants' experience suggests that by default individuals are, at most, only intermittently metaconscious of their affective state.

Automaticity Automatic behaviors are often assumed to be unconscious (Bargh, 1997; Jacoby, Yonelinas, & Jennings, 1997; Wood, Quinn, & Kashy, 2002). However, there is a peculiarity to this designation. Consider a person driving automatically while engaging in some secondary task (e.g., talking). Although such driving is compromised, one still experiences the road at some level. Thus, a more appropriate characterization of the consciousness of automatic behaviors may be that they are experienced but lack metaconsciousness, the latter only taking hold when individuals run into difficulty.

Unwanted Thoughts   Wegner (1994) suggested that individuals possess an implicit monitoring system that tracks unwanted thoughts (e.g., of a white bear) in order to veer away from them. But, what exactly is this system monitoring? Wegner suggests that it is monitoring the contents of preconsciousness (i.e., thoughts that are near, but below, the threshold of consciousness). However, another, and perhaps more intuitive possibility, is that system actually monitors the contents of consciousness itself. That is, perhaps individuals can consciously think about a white bear without explicitly realizing that they are doing so. In this case, the monitoring system can catch the unwanted thought and raise it to the level of meta-awareness, in effect saying: "There you go again, thinking about that unwanted thought." Recent evidence for this account comes from a study in which participants were asked to try not to think about a previous romantic relationship while reading or while simply sitting quietly (Fishman, Smallwood, & Schooler, 2006). As in standard unwanted thought paradigms, participants were asked to self-report every time they noticed an unwanted thought coming to mind. In addition, however, they were periodically randomly asked whether at that particular moment they were having the unwanted thought. The results revealed that participants frequently experienced "unnoticed unwanted thoughts" about their previous relationship that they experienced but failed to notice until they were probed. Further, these unnoticed unwanted thoughts were detrimental to participants' performance on a test of the reading material, suggesting again that they were conscious. Intriguingly, participants for whom the unwanted thoughts carried emotional weight (i.e., they still wished they were in the relationship) were less likely than participants who no longer wanted to be in the relationship to notice the thoughts themselves and more likely to be caught having the thought. This suggests that cognitive defenses do not banish disturbing thoughts to the unconscious but rather prevent us from reflecting on them (Schooler, 2001).

Translation Dissociations

The idea that metaconsciousness requires rerepresenting the contents of consciousness suggests that some information may become lost or distorted in the translation, as with any recoding process. The likelihood of noise entering the translation process may be particularly great when individuals (a) verbally reflect on inherently nonverbal experiences, (b) are motivated to misrepresent their experience, or (c) possess a lay theory that is inconsistent with their actual experience.

Verbal Reflection   There are some experiences that are inherently difficult to put into words: the structure of a face, the taste of a wine, complex tonalities of Stravinsky, the intuitions leading to insights. If individuals attempt to verbalize these inherently nonverbal and holistic experiences, the resulting rerepresentations may fail to do justice to the original experience. Schooler and Engstler-Schooler (1990) examined the effects of describing faces, which, because of their holistic nature, are notoriously difficult to commit to words. Participants viewed a face and subsequently either described it in detail or engaged in an unrelated verbal activity. When given a recognition test that included a different photograph of the target face, along with similar distractors, verbalization participants performed substantially worse than controls. This effect of verbalization, termed *verbal overshadowing*, has been found in variety of other domains of visual memory (Schooler, Fiore, & Brandimonte (1997), including colors (Schooler & Engstler-Schooler, 1990) and shapes (Brandimonte, Schooler, & Gabbino, 1997) as well as other modalities such as audition (Schooler et al., 1997) and taste (Melcher & Schooler, 1996). Similar disruptions resulting from verbal reflection have also been observed in various other domains hypothesized to rely on nonverbal cognition. Thinking aloud during problem solving can disrupt the intuitive processes associated with insight problem solving while having no effect on the logical processes associated with analytical problem solving (Schooler, Ohlsson, & Brooks, 1993). Verbally reflecting on the basis of affective judgments can interfere with quality of affective decision making, as assessed both by the opinions of experts (Wilson & Schooler, 1991) and by postchoice satisfaction (Wilson et al., 1993). Verbally articulating the basis of the match between analogical stories can reduce people's sensitivity to meaningful deep-structure relationships while increasing their emphasis on superficial surface-structure relationships (Sieck, Quinn, & Schooler, 1999). Of course, in many cases verbal analysis can be helpful. This occurs when experiences are readily translated into words, due either to the nature of the task (e.g., logical problem solving, Schooler et al., 1993) or individuals' unique verbal expertise (e.g., wine experts, Melcher & Schooler, 1996). However, our point here is that sometimes the very process of articulating experiences can result in translation dissociations, where meta-awareness misrepresents conscious content.

Motivation In some situations individuals may want to misrepresent their experiences to themselves. For example, homophobic individuals may not want to recognize when they are aroused by depictions of homosexual acts (Adams, Wright, & Lohr, 1996). That is, individuals may consciously experience the arousal but, because of their motivation, fail to become meta-aware of it (see also Lambie & Marcel, 2002). Our perspective also suggests a different view of repression. Freud argued that repression prevented unwanted feelings from coming to consciousness, but we would say that it primarily prevents such feelings from reaching meta-awareness (Schooler, 2002).

Faulty Theories Finally, translation dissociation can occur if individuals have a faulty theory about what they should be feeling in a particular situation, which then colors their appraisal of their actual experience. A compelling example of this comes from people's reports of their experience of catching a ball (McLeod, Reed, & Dienes, 2003). Most people believe that as they watch a ball, their eyes first rise and then go down following the trajectory of the ball. Indeed, this is the case when one watches someone else catch a ball. However, when people catch a ball themselves, they actually maintain the ball at precisely the same visual angle.

Nevertheless, when people who just caught a ball are asked what they experienced, they rely on their theory of experience rather than on what they actually did.

UNCONSCIOUS OR NOT METACONSCIOUS?

So, how can we empirically distinguish between processes that are genuinely unconscious or conscious but not meta-aware? This is tricky as a failure of verbal report could result from both an absence of an experience and an absence of meta-awareness. Distinguishing between these alternatives is not easy as the very same findings can often be reasonably construed from either perspective. For example, Winkielman and Berridge (2004) interpreted findings of indirect measures revealing unreported affective states as evidence for unconscious emotion, whereas Schooler and Schreiber (2004) interpreted the same types of data as suggesting affective experience without meta-awareness. At present, it is very difficult to distinguish between these two accounts; however, future studies may help to adjudicate between them. For example, if unreported states are indeed represented in consciousness, then in principle they should be influenced by manipulations targeting consciousness, such as cognitive load or explicit monitoring.

Experiences in the absence of meta-awareness can also be revealed retrospectively. For example, it is possible to catch conscious but not meta-aware states with the external probe procedure, which, as described, was successfully used in research on zoning out and unnoticed unwanted thoughts. In principle, similar strategies could be used in other paradigms. For example, perhaps individuals who fail to spontaneously report a goal (e.g., competition) could be caught consciously experiencing such goal states if probed at the right time. It may also be possible to refine individuals' ability to carefully scrutinize their prior state. For example, if individuals are experiencing something without meta-awareness at the time, then in principle it may be possible to have people later recall their old state when given some additional source of self-insight (e.g., mindfulness training) or by removing biases due to motivation. For example, individuals going through the breakup of a romantic relationship may retrospectively recognize past experiences of jealously or anger that had previously escaped meta-awareness. Of course, retrospective analyses have their own pitfalls as it is possible to infer states that may not have actually been experienced at the time (Joslyn & Schooler, 2006). However, if individuals are capable of retrospectively reporting states for which they lack a basis for inference (e.g., determining whether they were subject to subliminally presented mood manipulations), then the conclusion that the state was experienced seems reasonable. Ultimately, determination of whether unreported states are genuinely unconscious or experienced but not meta-aware will come down to an assessment of the preponderance of evidence in each case.

SUMMARY AND CONCLUSIONS

Our goal in this chapter was to offer a fresh perspective on consciousness in social cognition. We first highlighted that consciousness is currently seen as one of the key topics of contemporary science and contrasted this view to occasional dismissals of consciousness in social cognition. We then discussed what makes mental events conscious and highlighted the role of consciousness in complex thought and action. Finally, we distinguished among unconscious, conscious, and meta-aware events and discussed dissociations between different levels of representations, highlighting that seemingly unconscious events may simply be lacking in meta-awareness. In conclusion, clearly, there is much (if not most) that science still does not understand about consciousness. In fact, some believe that some of its critical features, like subjectivity, will always escape scientific scrutiny (Searle, 1997). On the other hand, there has also been remarkable progress in psychology, cognitive science, and neuroscience. We do not see this research as showing that consciousness is unimportant but rather as providing a more comprehensive understanding of its role in how we think, feel, and act. It is encouraging that the field of social cognition research has much to contribute to this objective.

ACKNOWLEDGMENT

We thank the book editors for inspiration, generous feedback, and incredible patience. Support was provided by a National Science Foundation (NSF) grant to P. W. (BCS-0350687) and a Social Sciences and Humanities Research Council of Canada (SHRCC) grant to J. S. This chapter greatly profited from discussions of these issues with Roy Baumeister, Kent Berridge, Patricia Churchland, Zoltan Dienes, Hal Pashler, V. S. Ramachandran, David Shanks, Jeanne Shinskey, and participants of the Cold Spring Harbor 2007 conference, New Frontiers in Studies of Nonconscious Processing.

NOTES

1. Some psychologists serve as empirical and theoretical "police" on more dramatic abilities attributed to the unconscious (Kihlstrom, 2008; Merikle & Reingold, 1998; Shanks, 2005, 2006).
2. North American readers will remember Terri Schiavo, who died in 2005. As a result of failing several neurological assessments, including tests for purposive behavior, she was declared unconscious, and her feeding tube was removed (Caplan, McCartney, & Sisti, 2006).
3. Note that cross-modal integration can be automatized into unconscious, suggesting that access in the global workspace might be only needed to initially connect novel sensations and responses. The famous McGurk effect illustrates not only the automatic influence of vision on speech perception but also the value of cross-modal integration for unity of conscious experience (McGurk & MacDonald, 1976).
4. A believer in the smart unconscious should attempt to solve a novel mathematical problem, like multiplying 87°65, under cognitive load or expose themselves to this problem before going to sleep to see if the unconscious provides an answer in the morning.
5. As Bargh (1989) pointed out, it is sometimes possible to dissociate consciousness and control.

6. In some "unconscious goal" paradigms, participants could actually be conscious of the goal but just confused about its source. As we discuss, there are also multiple ways in which goals could be conscious but not verbally reported because of temporal and translation dissociations.
7. Imagine the following experiment: Participants are in a room with both food and drink. Participants are first told once, consciously, that their goal is to eat. Next, participants are given an unconscious priming procedure with multiple words related to the goal of drinking. We predict that very few, if any participants, would behave in accordance with the more recent, but unconscious "goal" to drink.
8. The idea of "unconscious emotion" does not imply that conscious feelings are an unnecessary "icing on the emotional cake" (LeDoux, 1996). Conscious happiness, anxiety, anger, guilt, and sadness are critical in people's lives. Not only do they make life worth living (we would not pay much for a substance that makes us "unconsciously happy"), but also they are useful in judgments and decisions (Winkielman, Knutson, Paulus, & Trujillo, 2007). As with conscious and unconscious goals, future research may directly contrast the power of conscious and unconscious emotions.

REFERENCES

Abrams, R. L., & Greenwald, A. G. (2000). Parts outweigh the whole (word) in unconscious analysis of meaning. *Psychological Science, 11*, 118–124.

Adams, H. E., Wright, L. W., & Lohr, B. A. (1996). Is homophobia associated with homosexual arousal? *Journal of Abnormal Psychology, 105*, 440–445.

Baars, B. J. (1988). *A cognitive theory of consciousness*. Cambridge, England: Cambridge University Press.

Bargh, J. A. (1989). Conditional automaticity: Varieties of automatic influence in social perception and cognition. In J. S. Uleman & J. A. Bargh (Eds.), *Unintended thought* (pp. 3–51). New York: Guilford.

Bargh, J. A. (1997). Advances in social cognition. In R. S. Wyer, Jr. (Ed.), *The automaticity of everyday life* (pp. 1–61). Mahwah, NJ: Erlbaum.

Baumeister, R. F. (2008). Free will in scientific psychology. *Perspectives on Psychological Science, 3*, 14–19.

Baumeister, R. F., Schmeichel, B. J., DeWall, N., & Vohs, K.D. (2007). Is the conscious self a help, a hindrance, or an irrelevance to the creative process? In A.M. Columbus (Ed.) *Advances in psychology research* (vol. 53, pp. 137–152). New York: Nova.

Berridge, K. C. (2003). Comparing the emotional brain of humans and other animals. In R. J. Davidson, H. H. Goldsmith, & K. Scherer (Eds.), *Handbook of affective sciences* (pp. 25–51). New York: Oxford University Press.

Block, N. (1995). On a confusion about a function of consciousness. *Behavioral and Brain Sciences, 18*, 227–287.

Boring, E. G. (1953). A history of introspection. *Psychological Bulletin, 50*, 169–189.

Brandimonte, M. A., Schooler, J. W., & Gabbino, P. (1997). Attenuating verbal overshadowing through visual retrieval cues. *Journal of Experimental Psychology: Learning, Memory, and Cognition, 23*, 915–931.

Breitmeyer, B. G., & Ogmen, H. (2006). *Visual masking: Time slices through conscious and unconscious vision* (2nd ed.). New York: Oxford University Press.

Caplan, A., McCartney, J. J., & Sisti, D. (2006). *The case of Terri Schiavo: Ethics at the end of life*. Amherst, NY: Prometheus Books.

Carver, C. S., & Scheier, M. S. (1990). Origins and functions of positive and negative affect: A control-process view. *Psychological Review, 197*, 19–35.

Churchland, P. S. (2005, April 30). Brain wide shut. *New Scientist*, pp. 46–49.
Cleeremans, A. (2005). Computational correlates of consciousness. *Progress in Brain Research, 150*, 81–98.
Crick, F. (1994). *The astonishing hypothesis*. New York: Scribner's.
Dehaene, S., Changeux, J. P., Naccache, L., Sackur, J., & Sergent, C. (2006). Conscious, preconscious, and subliminal processing: A testable taxonomy. *Trends in Cognitive Sciences, 10*, 204–211.
Deutsch, R., Gawronski, B., & Strack, F. (2006). At the boundaries of automaticity: Negation as reflective operation. *Journal of Personality and Social Psychology, 91*, 385–405.
DeWall, C. N., Baumeister, R. F., & Masicampo, E. J. (2008). Evidence that logical reasoning depends on conscious processing. *Consciousness and Cognition, 17*, 628–645.
Dijksterhuis, A., Bos, M. W., Nordgren, L. F., & van Baaren, R. B. (2006). On making the right choice: The deliberation-without-attention effect. *Science, 311*, 1005–1007.
Dijksterhuis, A., & Nordgren, L. F. (2006). A theory of unconscious thought. *Perspectives on Psychological Science, 1*, 95–109.
Edelman. G. M. (1989). *The remembered present: A biological theory of consciousness*. New York: Basic Books.
Fishman, D., Smallwood, J., & Schooler, J. W. (2006). *Unwanted and meta-unknown*. Unpublished manuscript.
Fitzsimons, G. M., & Bargh, J. A (2004). Automatic self-regulation. In R. F. Baumeister & K. D. Vohs (Eds.), *Handbook of self-regulation: Research, theory and applications* (pp. 151–170). New York: Guilford Press.
Förster, J. (2003). The influence of approach and avoidance motor actions on food intake. *European Journal of Social Psychology, 33*, 339–350.
Förster, J., Liberman, N., & Friedman, R. (2007). Seven principles of automatic goal pursuit: A systematic approach to distinguishing goal priming from priming of non-goal constructs. *Personality and Social Psychology Review, 11*, 211–233.
Gailliot, M. T., Baumeister, R. F., DeWall, C. N., Maner, J. K., Plant, E. A., Tice, D. M., et al. (2007). Self-control relies on glucose as a limited energy source: Willpower is more than a metaphor. *Journal of Personality and Social Psychology, 92*, 325–336.
Gigerenzer, G., & Goldstein, D. (1996). Reasoning the fast and frugal way: Models of bounded rationality. *Psychological Review, 103*, 650–669.
Greenwald, A. G. (1992). New Look 3: Reclaiming unconscious cognition. *American Psychologist, 47*, 766–779.
Greenwald, A. G., Banaji, M. R., Rudman, L. A., Farnham, S. D., Nosek, B. A., & Mellott, D. S. (2002). A unified theory of implicit attitudes, stereotypes, self-esteem, and self-concept. *Psychological Review, 109*, 3–25.
Greenwald, A. G., Draine, S. C., & Abrams, R. L. (1996). Three cognitive markers of unconscious semantic activation. *Science, 273*, 1699–1702.
Hazy, T. E., Frank, M. J., & O'Reilly, R. C. (2007). Towards an executive without a homunculus: computational models of the prefrontal cortex/basal ganglia system. *Philosophical Transactions of the Royal Society B, 362*, 1601–1613.
Hummel, J. E., & Holyoak, K. J. (2003). A symbolic-connectionist theory of relational inference and generalization. *Psychological Review, 110*, 220–264.
Jacoby, L. L., Yonelinas, A. P., & Jennings, J. M. (1997). The relation between conscious and unconscious (automatic) influences: A declaration of independence. In J. C. Cohen & J. W. Schooler (Eds.), *Scientific approaches to consciousness* (pp. 13–48). Mahwah, NJ: Erlbaum.
Joslyn, S., & Schooler, J.W. (2006). Influences of the present on the past: The impact of interpretation on memory for abuse. In L. G. Nilsson & N. Ohta (Eds.), *Memory and society: Psychological perspectives*. New York: Psychology Press.
Kahneman, D. (1973). *Attention and effort*. Englewood Cliffs, NJ: Prentice-Hall.

Kihlstrom, J. F. (2008). The automaticity juggernaut—or, are we automatons after all? In J. Baer, J. C. Kaufman, & R. F. Baumeister (Eds.), *Psychology and free will* (pp. 155–180). New York: Oxford University Press.

Kihlstrom, J. F., Schacter, D. L., Cork, R. L., Hurt, C. A., & Behr, S. E. (1990). Implicit and explicit memory following surgical anesthesia, *Psychological Science, 1*, 303–306.

Koch, C., & Tsuchiya, N. (2007). Attention and consciousness: Two distinct brain processes. *Trends in Cognitive Science. 11*, 16–22.

Koriat, A. (2006). Metacognition and consciousness. In *Cambridge handbook of consciousness*. New York: Cambridge University Press.

Kunst-Wilson, W. R., & Zajonc, R. B. (1980). Affective discrimination of stimuli that cannot be recognized. *Science, 207*, 557–558.

Lambie, J. A., & Marcel, A. J. (2002). Consciousness and the varieties of emotion experience: A theoretical framework. *Psychological Review, 109*, 219–259.

Laureys, S., Faymonville, M. E., De Tiege, X., Peigneux, P., Berre, J., Moonen, G., et al. (2002). Brain function in the vegetative state. *Acta Neurologica Belgica, 102*, 177–185.

LeDoux, J. (1996). *The emotional brain: The mysterious underpinnings of emotional life*. New York: Simon and Schuster.

Levy, J., Pashler, H., & Boer, E. (2006). Central interference in driving: Is there any stopping the psychological refractory period? *Psychological Science, 17*, 228–235.

Loftus, E. F., & Klinger, M. R. (1992). Is the unconscious smart or dumb? *American Psychologist, 47*, 761–765.

Logan, G. D. (1988). Toward an instance theory of automatization. *Psychological Review, 95*, 492–527.

Mandler, G. (1975). Consciousness: Respectable, useful, and probably necessary. In R. Solso (Ed.), *Information processing and cognition: The Loyola symposium* (pp. 229–254). Hillsdale, NJ: Erlbaum.

Marcel, A. J. (1983). Conscious and unconscious perception: Experiments on visual masking and word recognition. *Cognitive Psychology, 15*, 197–237.

McClelland, J. L., & Rogers, T. T. (2003). The parallel distributed processing approach to semantic cognition. *Nature Reviews Neuroscience, 4*, 310–322.

McGurk, H., & MacDonald, J. (1976). Hearing lips and seeing voices. *Nature, 264*, 746–748.

McLeod, P., Reed, N., & Dienes, Z. (2003, July). *What implicit knowledge and motor skill: People do not know about how they catch a ball*. Paper presented at European Society of Philosophy and Psychology Congress 2003, Turin, Italy.

Melcher, J., & Schooler, J. W. (1996). The misremembrance of wines past: Verbal and perceptual expertise differentially mediate verbal overshadowing of taste. *The Journal of Memory and Language, 35*, 231–245.

Merikle, P. M., & Reingold, E. M. (1998). On demonstrating unconscious perception. *Journal of Experimental Psychology: General, 127*, 304–310.

Nisbett, R. E., & Wilson, D. S. (1977). Telling more than we can know: Verbal reports on mental processes. *Psychological Review, 84*, 231–253.

Norman, D. A., & Shallice, T. (1986). Attention to action: Willed and automatic control of behaviour. In R. J. Davidson, G. E. Schwartz, and D. Shapiro, D. (Eds.), *Consciousness and self-regulation: Advances in research and theory* (pp. 1–18). Plenum Press.

Pashler, H. E. (1998). *The psychology of attention*. Cambridge, MA: MIT Press.

Pessoa, L., McKenna, M., Gutierrez, E., & Ungerleider, L. G. (2002). Neural processing of emotional faces requires attention. *Proceedings of the National Academy of Sciences of the United States of America, 99*, 11458–11463.

Posner, M. I., & Snyder, C. R. R. (1975). Attention and cognitive control. In R. Solso (Ed.), *Information processing and cognition: The Loyola symposium*. Potomac, MD: Erlbaum.

Ramachandran, V. S. (2004). *A brief tour of human consciousness: From impostor poodles to purple numbers*. New York: Pearson Education.
Reichle, E., Pollatsek, A., Fisher, D. L., & Rayner, K. (1998). Toward a model of eye movement control in reading. *Psychological Review, 105,* 125–157.
Rickard, T. C. (2005). A revised identical elements model of arithmetic fact representation. *Journal of Experimental Psychology: Learning, Memory, and Cognition, 31,* 250–257.
Schooler, J. W. (2002). Re-representing consciousness: Dissociations between consciousness and meta-consciousness. *Trends in Cognitive Science, 6,* 339–344.
Schooler, J. W. (2001). Discovering memories in the light of meta-awareness. *The Journal of Aggression, Maltreatment and Trauma, 4,* 105–136.
Schooler, J. W., Ariely, D., & Loewenstein, G. (2003). The pursuit and assessment of happiness can be self-defeating. In I. Brocas and J. Carrillo (Eds.), *The psychology of economic decisions.* Oxford, England: Oxford University Press.
Schooler, J. W., & Engstler-Schooler, T. Y. (1990). Verbal overshadowing of visual memories: Some things are better left unsaid. *Cognitive Psychology, 17,* 36–71.
Schooler, J. W., Fiore, S. M., & Brandimonte, M. A. (1997). At a *loss* from words: Verbal overshadowing of perceptual memories. In D. L. Medin (Ed.), *The psychology of learning and motivation* (pp. 293–334). San Diego, CA: Academic Press.
Schooler, J. W., Ohlsson, S., & Brooks, K. (1993). Thoughts beyond words: When language overshadows insight. *Journal of Experimental Psychology: General, 122,* 166–183.
Schooler, J. W., Reichle, E. D., & Halpern, D. V. (2005). Zoning-out during reading: Evidence for dissociations between experience and meta-consciousness. In D. T. Levin (Ed.), *Thinking and seeing: Visual metacognition in adults and children* (pp. 204–226). Cambridge, MA: MIT Press.
Schooler, J., & Schreiber, C. A. (2004), Experience, meta-consciousness, and the paradox of introspection. *Journal of Consciousness Studies, 11*(7–8), 17–39.
Searle, J. (1997). *The mystery of consciousness.* New York: New York Review Press.
Shanks, D. R. (2005). Implicit learning. In K. Lamberts and R. Goldstone (Eds.), *Handbook of cognition* (pp. 202–220). London: Sage.
Shanks, D. R. (2006). Are complex choices better made unconsciously? *Science, 313,* p. 716.
Shariff, A. F., Schooler, J. W. and Vohs, K. D. (2008). The hazards of claiming to have solved the hard problem of free will. In J. Baer, J. C. Kaufman, & R. F. Baumeister (Eds.), *Psychology and free will* (pp. 181–204). New York: Oxford University Press.
Shiffrin, R. M., & Schneider, W. (1977). Controlled and automatic human information processing: II. Perceptual learning, automatic attending and a general theory. *Psychological Review, 84,* 127–190.
Shinskey, F. G. (1979). *Process control systems* (2nd ed.). New York: McGraw-Hill.
Sieck, W. R., Quinn, C. N., & Schooler, J. W. (1999). Justification effects on the judgment of analogy. *Memory and Cognition, 27,* 844–855.
Simons, D. J., & Chabris, C. F. (1999). Gorillas in our midst: Sustained inattentional blindness for dynamic events. *Perception, 28,* 1059–1074.
Singer, W. (2000). Phenomenal awareness and consciousness from a neurobiological perspective. In T. Metzinger (Ed.), *Neural correlates of consciousness: Empirical and conceptual questions* (pp. 121–138). Cambridge, MA: MIT Press.
Smallwood, J., & Schooler, J. W. (2006). The restless mind. *Psychological Bulletin, 132,* 946–958.
Smith, E. R., & DeCoster, J. (2000). Dual process models in social and cognitive psychology: Conceptual integration and links to underlying memory systems. *Personality and Social Psychology Review, 4,* 108–131.
Sperling, G. (1960). The information available in brief visual presentation, *Psychological Monographs, 74*(11), 1–29.

Strack, F., & Deutsch, R. (2004). Reflective and impulsive determinants of social behavior. *Personality and Social Psychology Review, 8,* 220–247.
Sumner, P., Tsai, P.-C., Yu, K., & Nachev, P. (2006). Attentional modulation of sensorimotor processes in the absence of perceptual awareness. *Proceedings of the National Academy of Sciences of the United States of America, 103,* 10520–10525.
Tononi, G. (2004). An information integration theory of consciousness. *BMC Neuroscience. 5,* 42.
Triesch, J., Ballard, D. H, Hayhoe, M. M., & Sullivan, B.T. (2003). What you see is what you need. *Journal of Vision, 3,* 86–94.
Vohs, K. D., & Schooler, J. W. (2008). The value of believing in free will: Encouraging a belief in determinism increases cheating. *Psychological Science, 19,* 49–54.
Ward, J. (2006). *The student's guide to cognitive neuroscience.* Hove, England: Psychology Press.
Wegner, D. M. (1994). Ironic processes of mental control. *Psychological Review, 101,* 34–52.
Wegner, D. M. (2002). *The illusion of conscious will.* Cambridge, MA: MIT Press.
Weiskrantz, L. (1986). *Blindsight: A case study and its implications.* Oxford, England: Oxford University Press.
Wilson, T. D. (2002). *Strangers to ourselves: Discovering the adaptive unconscious.* Cambridge, MA: Belknap Press of Harvard University Press.
Wilson, T. D., Lisle, D. J., Schooler, J. W., Hodges, S. D., Klaaren, K. J., & LaFleur, S. J. (1993). Introspecting about reasons can reduce post-choice satisfaction. *Personality and Social Psychology Bulletin, 19,* 331–339.
Wilson, T. D., & Schooler, J. W. (1991). Thinking too much: Introspection can reduce the quality of preferences and decisions. *Journal of Personality and Social Psychology, 60,* 181–192.
Winkielman, P., & Berridge, K. C. (2004). Unconscious emotion. *Current Directions in Psychological Science, 13,* 120–123.
Winkielman, P., Berridge, K. C., & Wilbarger, J. L. (2005a). Emotion, behavior, and conscious experience: Once more without feeling. In L. Feldman-Barrett, P. Niedenthal, & P. Winkielman (Eds.), *Emotion and consciousness.* New York: Guilford Press.
Winkielman, P., Berridge, K. C., & Wilbarger, J. L. (2005b). Unconscious affective reactions to masked happy versus angry faces influence consumption behavior and judgments of value. *Personality and Social Psychology Bulletin, 1,* 121–135.
Winkielman, P., Knutson, B., Paulus, M. P., & Trujillo, J. T. (2007). Affective influence on decisions: Moving towards the core mechanisms. *Review of General Psychology, 11,* 179–192.
Winkielman, P., Zajonc, R. B., & Schwarz, N. (1997). Subliminal affective priming resists attributional interventions. *Cognition and Emotion, 11,* 433–465.
Wood, W., Quinn, J., & Kashy, D. (2002). Habits in everyday life: Thought, emotion, and action. *Journal of Personality and Social Psychology, 83,* 1281–1297.
Zeeman, A. (2002). *Consciousness: A user's guide,* New Haven, CT: Yale University Press.

4

Conversational Inference
Social Cognition as Interactional Intelligence

DENIS HILTON

INTRODUCTION

The term *social cognition* has been used by psychologists to describe distinct objects of study. In one meaning, social cognition can be characterized as the application of cognitive psychology to understand how judgments are made about social objects (e.g., Fiske & Taylor, 1991). So, cognitive theories about category prototypes (Rosch & Mervis, 1975) were used to understand stereotypes about social groups (Cantor & Mischel, 1979; McCauley, Stitt, & Segal, 1980), and the distinction between automatic and controlled processing (Chaiken & Trope, 1999; Strack & Deutsch, 2004) has been used by social psychologists to better understand social judgment processes such as sentencing offenders in a criminal court (e.g., Englich, Mussweiler, & Strack, 2006). A related meaning of social cognition is the one used in developmental and comparative psychology research to characterize the ability to recognize that others have mental states such as intentions and beliefs ("theory of mind") and to adapt one's own behavior accordingly (e.g., Premack & Premack, 1995; Tomasello, Carpenter, Call, Behne, & Moll., 2005; Wimmer & Perner, 1983). Of course, the two kinds of social cognition are related—for example, developmental research into theory of mind bears much in common with attribution theory in social psychology (see Hilton, 2007; Malle, 2004, for reviews). What these approaches to social cognition share is that they deal with the cognitive processes that allow us to apprehend the social world, namely, the behaviors and characteristics of individuals and groups.

The research mentioned on inference and judgment processes in social psychology can be said to conform to an approach of "cognition of the social world." For example, much work demonstrates the importance of social content in understanding processes as (seemingly) diverse as motion perception and counterfactual reasoning. So, just as neuroscience work suggests that we have brain circuits specialized in detecting the kinds of movements that characterize self-propelled agents and that these circuits are used in the perception of intention and causality (Puce & Perrett, 2003), so work on counterfactual reasoning about event sequences suggests that we are disposed to find intentional actions very mutable (Girotto, Legrenzi, & Rizzo, 1991). Other work shows how the motivations of the perceiver may affect inference processes, whether these are to reduce cognitive dissonance, maintain a positive self-image of ourselves, or make upward or downward counterfactual inferences (e.g., Kunda, 1990; Roese & Olson, 1995).

In this chapter, I am concerned with a different sense of social cognition, namely, the social psychology of higher mental processes (Hilton & Slugoski, 2001; Slugoski & Hilton, 2001). In this view, social cognition informs the *process* of understanding itself through equipping individuals with the interactional intelligence that enables them to communicate with others through successful language use and understanding (Levinson, 1995, 2006). I present some recent thinking in linguistics to illustrate this perspective before returning to its implications for the psychology of reasoning and judgment.

Social Rationality and Interactional Intelligence: Effective Communication Design

If one were to design a protocol for communicating effectively with human beings, it seems quite likely that the result would look something like Grice's (1975) rules of communication. One reason is that human verbal communication has to transmit information across a communication bottleneck—the vocal channel. According to a rough estimation (Levinson, 2000), we can understand discourse four times faster than we can talk; that is, we can process information four times quicker in thought than we can encode it in words that are spoken serially. Just as telegraph operators would share a common codebook to share procedures for encoding and decoding what is explicitly transmitted across the low-transmission-capacity telegraph line, so we develop social conventions that make sure that both speaker and hearer share common understandings about how to interpret what is said verbally. These common understandings can be expressed in terms of Grice's assumption of cooperativeness and maxims of conversation that license shared understandings between the speaker and the hearer that go beyond what is explicitly said. For example, by the maxims of quantity, speakers are licensed not to mention information already shared with the hearer and are instead enjoined to focus on new information.

One of Grice's (1975) examples is illustrative of how these kinds of conversational inference processes allow mutual understanding and coordination:

> A: I am out of gas.
> B: There's a garage around the corner.

B could of course have said: "I guess that if you tell me you are out of gas, you do so for a reason, and you want me to help you. If you have no gas, you may need some, and if you want gas, you can get it at the garage around the corner." But, what B actually did say is just as much to the point as the conversational implicatures (speaker-intended inferences that are recovered by the hearer) allow him to economize on spelling out the whole chain of thought. The recovery of these conversational implicatures clearly requires reasoning, and indeed Grice (1975) speaks of the "calculation" of conversational implicatures. This reasoning combines information about the particular context of the utterance with general assumptions about the nature of conversation that follow from the assumption that interlocutors are cooperative and normally follow specific maxims of conversation that enjoin them to be truthful, informative, relevant, and clear.

Argument of the Chapter

Interactional intelligence in the form of knowledge of our own and others' goals and planning strategies is necessary for producing and understanding conversation (Levinson, 2000). The Gricean perspective presented in the preceding section gives a perspective of humankind as essentially sophisticated, aware, and rational, cooperatively respecting (and sometimes flouting) a communication contract with the other to achieve shared goals.

Nevertheless, while coordination of speaker and hearer perspectives can be achieved by conscious reasoning, this does not always have to be the case. Indeed, there are good arguments for considering that speaker-hearer coordination can be automated. I suggest that speaker-hearer coordination may be achieved through different pathways that reflect the distinction between automatic (System 1) and controlled (System 2) processing that has recently become familiar to psychologists (e.g., Evans & Over, 1996; Sloman, 2002; Stanovich & West, 2002; Strack & Deutsch, 2004). I therefore distinguish between automatic and controlled conversational inference and note the implications that this distinction has for the structure of language and for the way things can be put.

I then move to the speaker's perspective and show how different ways of framing the same thing have systematic effects on hearers' mental representations, preferences, and judgments. I conclude by examining the potential implications of the automatic versus controlled distinction for understanding the relationship between conversational inference and judgmental bias and the conditions under which conversational processes are likely to produce judgmental error or correct it.

AUTOMATIC VERSUS CONTROLLED CONVERSATIONAL INFERENCE

The dual-systems perspective invites a reconsideration of conversational rationality. Following Austin (1962), conversational rationality involves successful illocutionary uptake; that is, the hearer (H) must recognize what the speaker (S) meant by an utterance. In ordinary language philosophy, this process is assumed to involve a sophisticated process of intuitive reasoning, which includes conscious recognition of the speaker's intentions by the hearer. As formulated by Strawson (1964), who amended Grice's (1957) theory of linguistic communication (or "nonnatural meaning"), an illocutionary act must satisfy the following conditions: The speaker (S) intends:

> To produce by uttering x a certain response (r) in a hearer (H)
> That H shall recognize S's intention
> That H will recognize that S intended H to recognize his or her intention
> That this recognition will function as H's reason or part of the reason for his or her response

For example, in response to A's question, "Has Susan been working on the project today?" B's response, "She spent the afternoon watching birds," may be construed as intending that A recognize that he intends to suggest that Susan has *not* been working but does not wish to say so directly. Nevertheless, B wants A to recognize that B is still giving a relevant answer to A's question even if he is not answering it directly with "Yes," "No," or "I don't know," and that this information will legitimate any subsequent response by B. For example, if A knows that B is both his and Susan's boss, and A knows that B (like him) wants Susan to spend more time on the project in question, then successful illocutionary uptake would be shown by A if he then asks Susan to spend more time on the project.

While it is clear that sophisticated conscious reasoning of the kind described is necessary to achieve illocutionary uptake in human communication, some kinds of conversational coordination can occur outside of awareness. Thus, not all conversational implicatures are calculated on the basis of interpretations of the speaker's beliefs and intention in a given context. For example, Levinson (2000) argues that some *generalized* conversational implicatures (GCIs) are routinely and automatically made on the basis of the hearer's expectations about how language is normally used and not on the basis of the hearer's perceptions of the speaker's specific beliefs and intentions. For example, we can assume that cooperative speakers will follow the maxims of quantity and make the strongest statement that is relevant and compatible with what they know. Thus, regardless of context we can assume that if something is expressed the normal (unmarked) way, then we are to interpret it in a stereotypical fashion, and if it is said in an unusual (marked) way, then we are to interpret it as something nonstereotypic, as in the following examples:

> Unmarked: He lives in a house (a normal home).
> Marked: He lives in a manor (something older and grander than a normal home).
> Unmarked: She spent the afternoon watching birds (fly by).
> Marked: She spent the afternoon watching ducks (swimming).
> Unmarked: She met a professor at the university.
> Marked: She met the vice-chancellor at the university (the vice-chancellor is also a professor).

When unmarked terms are used, the hearer is entitled to suppose that the speaker is talking about a normal house, normal birds, or a normal professor, and that if the speaker had meant the hearer to think of a manor, ducks, or the university vice-chancellor, the speaker would have used the more specific marked terms. Such interpretations do not require inferences about this speaker's specific goals and beliefs; rather, they are based on general expectations about how language is used, whoever the particular speaker. In this respect, Levinson (2000) differs from those who believe that all conversational implicatures are calculated on the basis of perception of a particular speaker's intentions (Wilson & Sperber, 2004).

Generalized Versus Particular Conversational Implicature

Levinson (2000) argued that GCIs are routinized; that is, the hearer draws them automatically based on expectations about how language is generally used. He argued that these expectations can be expressed as *processing heuristics* and proposed that people use three when interpreting discourse; these three are summarized as follows:

Quantity 1: What is not said is not the case.
Quantity 2: What is simply described is stereotypically and specifically exemplified.
Manner: Marked description warns "marked situation."

Although the implicatures drawn by these heuristics are automatic, they are nevertheless *defeasible* as they can be cancelled by additional information given by the speaker. For example, implicatures that a situation is stereotypical consequent on the use of a simple, unmarked form can be cancelled by the addition of a marked description:

He went back to his house, in fact a beautiful old manor in the countryside.
She spent the afternoon watching birds, or rather, I should say, ducks.
She met a professor at the university, the vice-chancellor actually.

The difference between generalized and particular implicatures can be gauged by the following:

A: Has Susan been working on the project today?
B: She spent the afternoon watching birds.

Our calculation of the particular implicature conveyed by B's utterance will depend crucially on context: If we know that Susan is a zoologist, then we may think: "Aha—that means she worked hard today." If we know that she is a secretary, we may infer the opposite. But, the GCI remains unaffected by context: Unless we have reason to believe otherwise, we are entitled to assume she was watching birds that fly, not birds that swim. Note that we are likely to draw this inference even though it is irrelevant to A's question about Susan's work on the project, a sign that this kind of conversational implicature is automatic as it runs to completion without intentional control (Bargh, 1996).

Generalized Conversational Implicatures, Framing, and the Structure of the Logical Vocabulary

In addition to being routinized, Levinson (2000) argued that GCIs are so frequently called for that their pervasiveness influences the structure of the logical vocabulary itself. Following Horn (1989), he argued that such GCIs are triggered by logical particles that occupy the I-corner in Aristotle's square of opposition, where the A and I terms denote affirmatives (**AffI**rmo) and the E and O terms denote negations (n**EgO**). For example, he argued that *Some* routinely implicates *not all*, and only exceptionally is taken to implicate *possibly all*. Since *not all* is routinely understood as an implicature of *Some*, English has little need for a specific word such as *Nall* to occupy the O-corner in the square of opposition. Likewise, *sometimes* routinely implicates *not always*, which enables English to dispense with a specific word such as *nalways*.

A:	All	Always	Full	Necessary
E:	None	Never	Empty	Impossible
I:	Some	Sometimes	Not empty	Possible
O:	Not all	Not always	Not full	Possibly not

What is true of English seems to be true of most other languages, suggesting that these patterns are indeed universal.

Importantly, the contrast between the subcontraries (I and O terms) allows speakers to adopt opposing frames to describe the same event. For example, compare the following possible descriptions of the same state of affairs and the explanations they suggest:

Some of the boys went to the party because ...
Not all of the boys went to the party because ...

The girls sometimes went to the beach because ...
The girls didn't always go to the beach because ...

The water tank wasn't empty because ...
The water tank wasn't full because ...

It is possible that it will rain tomorrow because ...
It is possible that it will not rain tomorrow because ...

It is probable that the operation will succeed because ...
It is not certain that the operation will succeed because ...

Based on relevant research on quantifiers (Moxey & Sanford, 1993a, b; 2000) and probability expressions (Teigen & Brun, 2003), we can expect that explanations of unmarked events will focus reasons for the occurrence of the event in question (going to the party, going to the beach, the tank having some water, it raining tomorrow, the operation succeeding), whereas explanations of marked events will focus on reasons against the occurrence of that event (why some boys did not go to the party or the girls did not go to the beach, etc.).

Framing Conversational Inferences

Frames of this kind contain "pragmatic signals" about what a speaker considers interesting and important and are embedded in the vocabulary of language itself. Speakers, through the way they put things, can influence hearers' mental representations such that certain judgments "become" natural, solutions become clear, and choice options become preferable. Pragmatic signals are words or tools for structuring others' mental representations. All that is needed is that the hearer attends to what is said, and the hearer will automatically form a representation of what is explicitly mentioned (Gilbert, 1991; Johnson-Laird & Byrne, 2002). To use McKenzie's (2004) telling phrase, a frame can "leak" information about the speaker's beliefs about or attitudes toward a situation. For example, describing a glass as "half full" or "half empty" amounts to saying the same thing from a purely logical point of view. But, describing a glass as "half full" suggests that it was previously empty, whereas describing it as "half empty" suggests that it was previously full (Sher & McKenzie, 2006).

As an illustration of the power of the speaker's linguistic framing on the hearer's inference processes, consider the following examples from Majid, Sanford, and Pickering (2006), which show how seemingly innocent choices of vocabulary can have significant impact on the focus of causal explanations:

> Bill liked to visit Tom's Diner on his visits to town. Few other people liked to do the same.
> Bill liked to visit Tom's Diner on his visits to town. A few other people liked to do the same.

In the language of Kelley's (1967) covariational model of causal attribution, both descriptions suggest low consensus for Bill's behavior, which should lead to a person attribution to Bill (Hilton, 2007). This is indeed the pattern obtained by the first formulation, using the negative polarity quantifier *few*. But, the second formulation (using the positive polarity quantifier *a few*) prompts relatively more attributions to the stimulus (Tom's Diner) despite the fact that the two quantifiers are perceived to describe the same frequency of visits. Consequently, such different patterns of explanation cannot be readily accounted for by covariation-based models of causal explanation. Rather, a pragmatic explanation seems necessary that takes into account the way in which the hearer adopts the speaker-conveyed perspective on the event in question. Whereas the negative polarity quantifier emphasizes the set of people who are *unlike* Bill (thus emphasizing low consensus, leading to person attributions), the positive polarity quantifier emphasizes the set of people who are *like* Bill, thus emphasizing the consensus with his actions (thus creating "high" consensus, suggesting a stimulus attribution).

While unusual, abnormal events are likely to create surprises and trigger causal attribution processes (Hilton & Slugoski, 1986; Weiner, 1985), it seems that through framing speakers can exercise considerable control over what hearers will find surprising. Control of attention through adroit use of quantifiers can of course be exercised by experimenters writing vignettes for experimental subjects and journal readers. For example, Majid, Sanford, and Pickering (2006) noted that McArthur's (1972) classic experiment, which has been replicated innumerable times (Hilton, 2007), uses quantifier frames that favor the predictions of the Kelley (1967) analysis-of-variance (ANOVA) model (e.g., by using *few* rather than *a few* to present low-consensus information, as in the example). We move from considering how these framing processes can influence causal explanations for events that have already happened to how they can influence planning for and prediction of future events using conditional expressions.

FRAMING PLANS FOR DEALING WITH UNCERTAINTY

Humans are able to use language to evoke hypothetical states and discuss with others how best they are to be attained or avoided and thus jointly make plans to manage risk and uncertainty. For example, farmers would be able to use language to evoke a fort to defend their harvests during the winter from attack by brigands and through discussion to formulate plans for the construction of that fort (cf. Gärdenfors, 2003). Each could specialize in what he or she was good at: One could search for the wood, while another would smelt the nails, and yet another would assemble the components into a viable fortification. This division of labor would ensure efficiency in production, while effective communication would be necessary to make sure that each person did a job properly and in concert with others.

In such coordination, it will be useful to encourage some actions and discourage others. For example, the farmers in our example could advise each other on profitable courses of action: "There are a few usable trees in that wood over there" sounds like an encouragement to work in that wood, whereas "There are few usable trees in that forest over there" sounds like a discouragement from doing so. These quantifiers do more than just denote proportions; they also signal what activity the speaker favors. I examine how such pragmatic signals orient hearers to what the speaker considers to be interesting and important.

Pragmatic Signals: Utilities and the Framing of Conditional Instructions

In cooperative planning about how to manage uncertainty, a common task is to be able to communicate to others which courses of action are desirable opportunities that should be seized and which are undesirable risks fraught with danger. For example, deontic conditionals that tell people what they may or ought to do (permissions, advice, instructions, etc.) are judged felicitous when doing Q in the presence of P is judged to be more desirable than not doing Q in the presence of P (Over, Manktelow, & Hadjichristidis, 2004). For example, if a speaker considers that it is better to take a shower after a run than not, it will be judged felicitous for the speaker to say, *If you go for a run, then you must take a shower.*

Nevertheless, deontic conditionals can be framed in different ways depending on the utility structure in the context. Hilton, Kemmelmeier, and Bonnefon (2005) proposed a conversational action planning (CAP) model that shows how formulations of conditional instructions are adapted to assessments of the risks concomitant on putative courses of action. Consider the case of an airport security manager who has to give instructions to an operator about what to do when checking baggage that passes through the airport scanner. The manager may instruct the operator as follows: *If there is suspect baggage (P), then take it out (Q).* Using the terminology of signal detection theory, there are two kinds of correct responses here: a "hit" (the baggage is anomalous and is taken out for inspection; *P & does Q*) and a "correct rejection" (the baggage is innocuous, and left undisturbed; *notP & doesn't do Q*). There are also two kinds of error: a "miss" (the baggage is anomalous but is not taken out for inspection; *P & doesn't do Q*) and a "false alarm" (the baggage is innocuous but is nevertheless taken out for inspection; *notP & does Q*). Now, the mistake that is perceived as the most costly may depend on the context. For example, if the airport in question is under full alert because terrorist attacks have been threatened, the perceived cost of a miss is likely to be high. However, if the chief concern is not to keep business class passengers in a hurry waiting too long for fear of losing them as lucrative customers, then the perceived cost of a false alarm is likely to be high.

Pragmatic signals embedded in the formulation of conditionals enable speakers to transmit their preferences to hearers who do not know what those preferences are. Thus, Hilton et al. (2005, Experiment 3) showed that knowledge of differences in costs of misses and false alarms had a clear effect on how participants evaluated the effectiveness of conditional formulations for expressing a speaker's intention. When participants were placed in the role of a speaker (i.e., the boss) whose chief concern was to avoid misses, the classic *If P then do Q* form of the conditional was clearly preferred as most clearly expressing the speaker's intention, for example, *If the baggage is suspect, then take it out.* However, if the chief concern was to avoid a false alarm, then the explicit negative form *If not-P then don't do Q* was preferred, for example, *If the baggage is not suspect, then don't take it out.* In addition, concern to avoid a false alarm also led to increased preference for implicit negative forms such as *If and only if P then Q* and *Q only if P.*

But, do these different formulations lead to effective illocutionary pickup? That is, will hearers infer what it is they are supposed to do even if they do not know what the cost-benefit structure (defined by the relative costs of misses and false alarms) of the situation is? Hilton et al. (2005, Experiment 4) were then able to show that when participants were placed in role of a hearer (i.e., an employee) receiving an instruction, they indicated that they would behave in the way that would address the speaker's concerns. Thus, when told *If the baggage is suspect (P), then take it out (Q),* hearers interpret this as meaning that they must do Q when P is present but are free to decide what to do when P is not the case, thus avoiding misses (*P & not doing Q*). On the other hand, when told *If the baggage is not suspect (notP), then don't take it out (notQ),* participants in the role of a hearer assume that they are free to decide what to do when *P* is the case but must not take the baggage out (*not Q*) when *not P* is the case, thus avoiding false alarms (*notP & doing Q*). In this way, speakers are able to transmit their preferences to hearers under asymmetric information; that is, hearers do what the speakers want even when they do not explicitly know the speaker's utility matrix.

Framing Indicative Conditionals: The Rarity Principle

Whereas deontic conditionals are typically performative (advice, instructions, and warnings are given to bring about better states of affairs or at least stop things from deteriorating), indicative conditionals are constative, that is, they describe states of affairs and can be true or false. However, pragmatic concerns seem to govern the formulation of indicative conditionals in much the same way as they govern deontics. Building on the rarity principle of Oaksford and Chater (1994), McKenzie, Fereira, Mikkelsen, McDermott, and Skrable (2001) noted that the terms explicitly mentioned in conditional hypotheses are generally rare. For example, if one aims to test the hypothesis that a certain university is selective (i.e., accepts few students and rejects many), the conditional rule should focus on the few who are admitted, that is, say *If they get at least three Bs, then they will be admitted* rather than say *If they don't get at least three Bs, then they will be rejected*. But, if we are to test the hypothesis that the university in question is unselective (i.e., takes many students and rejects few), then we should say *If they don't get at least three Ds, then they will be rejected* rather than *If they get at least three Ds, then they will be accepted*. McKenzie et al. showed that participants did indeed choose to focus on the rarer cases in their formulations of the conditional rule. McKenzie et al. give a justification of participants' focus on rare events in terms of Bayesian hypothesis testing: By focusing on the rare instances, one has to search rather fewer exemplars to find disconfirmations.

These considerations suggest that there is no "neutral" way of expressing a logical proposition. Even the standard "If P then do Q" way of expressing a deontic conditional carries the implication the speaker thinks that Q is more desirable than notQ when P is the case, and avoiding misses (P & notQ) is more of a concern than avoiding false alarms (notP & Q). Likewise, the standard indicative conditional carries the implication that the speaker thinks Q is more probable than notQ when P is the case, Ps are rarer than notPs, and Qs are rarer than notQs. Consequently, whatever the choice of formulation, it will convey information about the speaker's beliefs and attitudes. Consequently, the best way to avoid framing effects is to provide both sides, even at the risk of Gricean redundancy.

Fleshing Out Frames: Making Explicit What Is Left Implicit

Tversky and Kahneman's (1981) Asian disease problem is justly renowned for its ability to demonstrate framing effects. Participants are asked to imagine that they have to choose between two plans to cope with a disease that will threaten the United States. When phrased in terms of lives saved, participants are told that Plan A will save 200 lives for sure, whereas Plan B will have a one third chance of saving 600 lives and a two thirds chance of saving none, participants prefer the sure gain associated with Plan A. But, when phrased in terms of lives lost, participants are told that under Plan A 400 will die for sure, whereas under Plan B there is a one third chance that no one will die and a two thirds chance that 600 people will die, more people chose the risky Plan B. This reversal of preferences due to the change in the description of the scenario is consistent with prospect theory (Kahneman & Tversky, 1979).

Jou, Shanteau, and Harris (1996) reasoned that an explanation for the presence of the framing effect would be the one-sided mental representations induced by the positive or negative frames. They then introduced a rationale that explained why Plan A would save a certain number of lives for sure, whereas Plan B was a risky choice. In each case, the decision maker had to manage the best use of a limited resource (e.g., a limited amount of vaccine) and consequently determine what trade-offs had to be made. In the limited resource conditions, no framing effects were observed as the majority participants uniformly preferred the sure option under both the gain and loss descriptions. Jou et al. then reasoned that this was due to greater availability of the reciprocal information in memory in the rationale condition: For example, if told that under Plan A 200 would be saved, the reciprocal information would be that 400 would die. A subsequent experiment indeed confirmed that the reciprocal information was indeed better recalled after an interpolated task in the rationale condition, indicating that it had been stored in the mental representation of the decision scenario.

Reframing Framing Effects

Jou et al.'s (1996) results reframe the framing effect by drawing attention to the effect of discourse frame on mental representation. Their analysis is consistent with psycholinguistic research on discourse comprehension and reasoning, which suggests that people first build mental representations of what is explicitly said and then "flesh out" out their mental models with complements (Jou et al.'s "reciprocal" information) during the reasoning process (Johnson-Laird & Byrne, 2002). For example, only when negations are introduced in a target conditional statement are complements automatically activated. For example, the statement, "If there is a vowel on one side (P), there is not an even number on the other (notQ)," prompts people to search for an even number (Q) on the Wason selection task (Evans, 1998). A related effect can be observed by contrasting the superior availability of complements in counterfactual conditionals, which carry the presupposition that the antecedent is false (and therefore its complement must be true) as compared to indicative conditionals (Byrne & Tasso, 1999). Finally, "partitive formulations," which clarify set–subset relations, have been shown to greatly facilitate Bayesian reasoning (Macchi, 1995, 2000). Macchi argued that these formulations lead participants to construct more complete mental representations of the information given, which facilitate solutions of the problem.

Frames can also be seen as persuasive devices. Related research by Van Buiten and Keren (2006) showed that people have clear intuitions about which frame to use in the Asian disease problem to persuade another. If one wants to induce another person to take Plan A (the sure thing), then one should use the gain frame;

one would use the loss frame if one wanted people to adopt Plan B (the risky option). If frames do indeed structure mental representations, then their influence will require further processing to be corrected. I turn now to a consideration of the role of automatic and controlled processes in conversational inference and their role in producing—or correcting—judgmental error.

CONVERSATIONAL INFERENCE AND JUDGMENTAL BIAS

Many researchers have argued that some of the more seemingly egregious "errors" of reasoning and judgment shown in experimental and survey research in fact can be explained in terms of participants' adherence to conversational assumptions (e.g., Bless, Strack, & Schwarz, 1993; Hilton, 1995; Hilton & Slugoski, 2000, 2001; Schwarz, 1994, 1996). For example, although Kahneman and Tversky (1973) may have presented base rate information *before* diagnostic information in the engineers-and-lawyers problem to put this information right "under the nose" of participants (and were astonished when participants did not use it), it turns out that participants who assumed conversational relevance in fact attached more significance to the *later* information (Krosnick, Li, & Lehman, 1990). Thus, the "underuse of base rate information" found in the original Kahneman and Tversky experiment can be attributed—at least in part—to conversational inference processes. Indeed, the point seems to have been taken by Kahneman and Frederick (2002), who accepted that certain studies on base rate fallacies and conjunction errors may have been "experimental flourishes" that implicitly used conversational processes to provide compelling demonstrations of effects.

In fact, Kahneman and Frederick's (2002) reformulation of the heuristics-and-biases research program allows connections to conversational pragmatics to be more clearly made. First, heuristic reasoning has been explicitly located as part of a question-answering process by which the addressee substitutes a *heuristic* attribute for which the addressee can compute an answer (e.g., the similarity between a target person and the person's prototype of a Parisian) for a *target* attribute that the addressee has been asked about but for which he or she does not know the answer (the probability that the person in question is indeed a Parisian). Second, it is argued that the reason that certain attributes, such as similarity, availability, recognition, or affective valence, are recruited to help produce answers about other attributes with which they are assumed to be correlated (such as probability, frequency, size, and utility) is that these heuristic attributes are easy for the human brain to compute, whereas the objective properties are unknown or require complex calculations. Finally, Kahneman and Frederick argued that the automatic nature of heuristics explains why people often use them anyway, even though they "know" rule-based reasoning processes that would enable them to calculate the correct answer.

The reformulation takes into account the development of the dual-systems perspective in psychology since the original studies on heuristics and biases (Tversky & Kahneman, 1974). In this kind of dual-process perspective, a natural question to pose is to identify the conditions under which one kind of processing will be favored over another. Kahneman and Frederick (2002) suggested that automatic System 1 processing will dominate unless System 2 is sufficiently alarmed by some anomaly to intervene and correct judgments; they wrote, "A judgment comes to mind and is not obviously mistaken: end of story" (p. 59). They used the difficulty of suppressing interference in the Stroop task to suggest that System 2 will be relatively weak in defending System 1 against errors and cite evidence suggesting that the impact of System 2 correctional processes is weakened by cognitive resource depletion.

Conversational Inference: Production of or Absolution from Error?

Kahneman and Frederick's sensitive discussion of conversational pragmatics—coupled with their reformulation of the theory of heuristics in terms of dual-process theory—invites a consideration of the role that automatic and controlled conversational inference processes may have in producing bias and error in judgment. While most research so far has used the conversational pragmatics perspective to absolve participants from the accusation of error, an alternative perspective is to argue that conversational inference processes can also produce judgmental errors (Levinson, 1995). For example, Krosnick et al.'s (1990) results can be used to support both points of view. Thus, the demonstration of order effects in use of base rate and diagnostic information can be argued to absolve participants of the charge of irrationality although showing that Kahneman and Tversky's original procedure led to overestimation of underuse of base rate information. But, the very fact that order of presentation influenced their judgments can itself also be argued to be a sign of irrationality—assuming that the statistical relevance of the base rate and individuating information does not change.

In fact, there is evidence (Slugoski & Wilson, 1998) that conversational skill (as measured by ability to correctly reconstruct the order of scrambled conversational exchanges) increases susceptibility to "error" on some tasks (e.g., confirmation bias on the Wason task, underuse of base rate information in the engineers-and-lawyers task, sensitivity to a leading question on an attributional inference task) but decreases it on others (conjunction fallacy, dilution effect, primacy effect in impression formation). The existence of such contradictory relationships invites a finer-grained analysis of the processes involved. I speculate now on how the distinction between automatic and controlled processes and close attention to what is meant by "correction" of judgments may help bring better understanding of the relation between conversational inference and judgment.

Automatic Error or Controlled Correction?

Research showed that the "leading questions" effect (Loftus & Palmer, 1974) is greatly attenuated when participants learn that the questions come from a potentially hostile source, such as a prosecution lawyer in a criminal trial (Dodd & Bradshaw, 1980). This research illustrated how conversational inference processes can be said to "correct" judgments in two distinct senses. First, deliberate processes may correct automatically produced judgments (cf. Keysar & O'Barr, 2002; Strack, Schwarz, Bless, Kübler, & Wänke, 1993). Thus, the leading questions (e.g., "How fast was the car going when it hit/crashed...") may be assumed to activate different schemata associated with each verb, which automatically influences the judgment of the car's speed. When the participant trusts the source (e.g., the experimenter, as in Loftus and Palmer's original procedure), no correction is made, and bias ensues. However, when the source is suspected of being manipulative, the judgment will then be adjusted by deliberative processes that take into account the intentions of the source ("Yes, but of course the prosecution lawyer would *want* me to say that …"). Second, the direction of the adjustment in this case is in the direction of the "correct," objective answer; judgmental correction thus leads to judgmental correctness. In this way, the conversational inference perspective allows human judgment to be absolved of error and viewed as more rational (cf. Hilton, 1995; Hilton & Slugoski, 2000; Lee, 2006).

However, correction of an initial judgment may conceivably *produce* error. An example suggested by Kahneman and Tversky (1982) concerns the "dilution effect" (Nisbett, Zukier, & Lemley, 1981), by which people inappropriately use nondiagnostic information (e.g., "Paul has blue eyes") to make inferences about a target characteristic (Paul's class grades). Kahneman and Tversky suggested that people feel obliged to use nondiagnostic information because it comes with a "guarantee" of conversational relevance. Consistent with their interpretation, the dilution effect is most likely to be present in high authoritarians, who are most likely to be sensitive to experimental demand effects (Slugoski & Noonan, 2004), but is attenuated when experimental demand is removed through the suspension of the assumption of conversational relevance (Tetlock, Lerner, & Boettger, 1996).

Let us note some important differences between the dilution effect and the leading questions paradigms. First, in the dilution paradigm there is no automatic association between the cue (blue eyes) and the target judgment (class grades); indeed, the nondiagnostic information was precisely selected on that basis. So, there is no initial automatic judgment to correct in this case. Second, the error of judgment seems to be produced by taking the conversational context into account, as if the experimental participants say to themselves, "Well, the experimenter wouldn't have given me all this information if he didn't expect me to use it." Having initially anchored on the correct judgment ("hmm, this stuff about his having blue eyes is no help here"), participants then appear to incorrectly adjust their response in the light of experimental demands. Here, judgmental correction would lead to judgmental error.

Distinguishing judgmental correction from making a correct judgment may give us a useful handle to address the question of how conversational inference processes can interact with processes of judgment. For example, pragmatic skill at controlled inferences may attenuate error on the dilution task as they correct for demand effects through evaluating the speaker's intentions. However, we may speculate that fluency at drawing automatic category-based inferences may increase "error" on the leading questions task as people are overly sensitive to the implications of the phrasing of the leading question ("crash" vs. "hit").

More generally, leading questions and judgmental anchors that activate automatic processes may be relatively impervious to conversational correction effects. For example, Englich et al. (2006) showed that high versus low anchors influenced sentence recommendations by experienced legal professionals, even when it was made clear that the anchor was irrelevant (because it came from a question posed by a journalist) or randomly determined (by a dice throw made by the judge himself or herself). This anchoring effect still persisted despite the fact that judges corrected for the fact that the demand was made by the prosecutor. Thus, consistent with Dodd and Bradshaw's (1980) findings, they gave overall lower sentences when the anchor—whether high or low—came from a prosecutor than from the judge's own dice throw.

CONCLUSIONS: WHAT HAVE WE LEARNED?

In this chapter, I have argued that both the structure and use of human language are adapted to key characteristics of human communication and thinking. The human logical vocabulary (e.g., quantifiers, conditionals) is not value neutral and emphasizes positive or negative aspects of a proposition or course of action depending on the speaker's interests and what aspects of a topic the speaker seeks to draw to the hearer's attention. I have suggested that these pragmatic signals have automatic effects on speakers' inference processes and serve either to encourage or discourage certain courses of action. Such framing can ensure coordination of speaker and hearer viewpoints without the hearer's conscious recognition of the speaker's intention—indeed, the speaker may not be aware of why he or she chose to frame a topic one way or another. Both the speaker's choice of frame and the hearer's responses to that frame may be driven by simple associative processes.

The use and automatic pickup of pragmatic signals by the hearer described can be distinguished from other kinds of conversational inference that cannot be achieved through simple associative processes. First, GCIs of the kind described by Levinson (2000) may be routinized, but they rely on higher-order assumptions about the nature of the conversational contract to make inferences about what is said (e.g., that *some* implicates *not all*). Second, the higher-level assumption of cooperativeness may be used to calculate implicatures from the speaker's flouting of the maxims (as when he does not answer a question directly). This manifests a different kind of conversational inference process than that described by the Gricean perspective in which hearers draw conversational inferences (e.g., implicatures) on the basis of perceptions of the speaker's intentions and expertise. This attributional perspective allows explanation of why many judgmental biases are attenuated, eliminated, and sometimes even induced by manipulations of experimental participants' perceptions of the source of information (Hilton, 1995; Hilton & Slugoski, 2000; see also Bless et al., 1993; Schwarz, 1994, 1996) and has provided an important qualification to the literature on bias and error in human judgment (Kahneman & Frederick, 2002).

However, pragmatic signals—like other discourse framing effects discussed in this chapter—appear to influence a hearer's judgment processes through making one aspect of a topic more salient than another in cognitive representations rather than through triggering attributional reasoning processes. I have suggested that this difference can be understood in terms of dual-systems theory—pragmatic signals and framing effects work through activating automatic comprehension processes, whereas Gricean attributional inference processes work through conscious recognition and pickup of the speaker's intentions.

In conclusion, one may wonder how pragmatic skill may influence conversationally driven attributional inference effects. For example, research shows that person-focused questions cause participants to make person-focused dispositional inferences (e.g., attributing nervous behavior to the target's anxious personality) unless they have cognitive resources available to correct their initial judgments (Gilbert, Pelham, & Krull, 1988), whereas situation-focused questions conversely lead them to make situational attributions (e.g., attributing nervous behavior to the anxiety-provoking nature of the situation) unless—again—cognitive resources are available to correct the initial judgment (Krull, 1993; Krull & Erickson, 1995). It may be that fluency in drawing category-based inferences may increase susceptibility to the (person vs. situation) focusing effects of the dispositional questions at the automatic inference stage, whereas awareness of (and dispositional resistance to) demand effects may lead to greater attenuation of priming effects at the controlled correction stage.

Why can it be so difficult to inhibit the effects of suggestion? One answer comes from the thoughts of Vygotsky (1962) and Luria (1959), who saw language as a means of social control and influence through its function as a "second signal system" that can, by associating responses to representations of objects rather than to the objects themselves, enable direction of human thought and behavior. While mentioning something is sufficient to orient a hearer to look at an object or perform an action, denying or forbidding something is a double-edged sword as the representation of that entity or action has to be activated before it can be negated (Wason, 1965). As we see next, developmental research showed that while simply mentioning a condition-action pair seems to be sufficient to excite that response in young children, inhibiting that condition-action pair is rather more difficult.

The Development of Negation

Luria (1959) recounted how children pass through three stages in associating conditions to actions. In the first stage, language orients children without their being able to make a stable connection between the condition and the response. When given an instruction of the kind, "When the light flashes, press the ball," younger children (aged around 2 years) orient toward the light when they hear, "When the light flashes," and immediately press the ball when they hear "press the ball." Although the words function as stimuli that trigger responses, the child does not yet represent this in a conditional relation. In a second stage, at about the age of 3 years, the child establishes the conditional connection but cannot inhibit it. As Luria wrote:

> A child at this age will as a rule make the required connexion without particular difficulty, and when the light flashes he will press the ball; however, he will be unable to stop the movements that have been triggered by speech and he will very soon begin to press the ball regardless of the signal, continuing involuntarily to repeat the previous movements. Even the repetition of

the instruction or the reinforcement of the inhibitory link which is hidden in it—even the request to "Press *only* when the light flashes" and "*Not to press* when there is no light"—all this turns out to be powerless to stop the motor excitation that has begun; on the contrary, this excitation is sometimes even *reinforced* by the inhibitory instructions.

In a modification of this procedure, children approximately 3.5 years of age were shown a red and a blue light and asked to press when the red light came on and not to press when the blue light came on. Despite attempting to control their responses, they would begin to press when the blue light came on and even assure the experimenter that the instructions were to press the ball in response to both signals. It seems that it is only at a later stage—around the age of 4.5 years—that children are able to inhibit their responses properly.

Conversational Inference and Informational Subtraction

Luria's developmental account is consistent with research on adults (e.g., Strack & Deutsch, 2004). Negation requires inhibition of an activated representation and does not always succeed, and there may even be "leakage," such as when the negated representation actually directs behavior (e.g., when children press a light when told not to or an adult swings a string in a straight line when told not to). However, adults are also able to routinely suppress activated—but irrelevant—information in conversational contexts. This is illustrated by the subtraction effect (Strack, Martin, & Schwarz, 1988), by which B interprets the word *family* to mean *not* including the man's wife in the following exchange:

> A: How is your wife?
> B: Not too good, I'm afraid.
> A: And how's your family?
> B: Oh, very well, thank you!

As Strack et al. showed, in a nonconversational context, activation of relevant information by a prior specific judgment will indeed be used in a subsequent general judgment on the same topic.

The example illustrates an intriguing gestalt switch in the perception of human inferential abilities. Whereas Hilton (1995; Hilton & Slugoski, 2001) used the subtraction effect to illustrate conversational inference, Kahneman and Frederick (2002) used the nonconversational context condition of Strack et al.'s (1988) study to illustrate the availability heuristic. Indeed, when the prior specific question is answered in a context that suggests that there is no conversational relation to the second, general question, then its influence indeed appears to "leak" and influence the judgment given in the second question. This gestalt switch illustrates the difference between information activation and conversational focus. In the example, the ability to recognize that activated information is irrelevant given conversational goals relies on higher-order knowledge of the rules of conversation (cf. Grice, 1975).

The directive function of speech analyzed by Vygotsky and Luria emphasizes how language can be used by others to control what we think. Much work on language and social cognition in social psychology has shown how different descriptions of the same thing or events can affect the categorizations of groups or attributions made for behavior. For example, Semin (2000) investigated ways in which vocabulary choice (e.g., type of verb used in a question) and linguistic focus (on the logical subject or object) can influence judgments of responsibility. This line of work examines how presuppositions carried by the choice of descriptions influence mental representations of an object, such as a person, or a social group (e.g., Maass, Salvi, Arcuri, & Semin, 1989). In particular, "abstract" or "concrete" descriptions of behavior may be used that convey more or less information about the actor performing that behavior (Semin & Fiedler, 1988).

The picture of the relation between social cognition and language given by our analysis of conversational implicature is somewhat different. Here, we assume cooperativeness between speakers and a mutual dedication to efficient exchange of information. It is social cognition that informs language through influencing its very structure and the way it is used. Although I have drawn attention to the ways in which much conversational inference is routinized, awareness of the other's intentions and beliefs nevertheless plays a central role. Indeed, as we have seen, it is this awareness of another's manipulative intentions that sometimes allows their effects to be resisted. As such, in an ideal Gricean conversation, the cognitive inferences that a hearer generates are the result of skilled cooperation with the speaker. Indeed, experimental evidence of cooperativeness is shown most clearly in tasks in which a speaker has to produce discourse destined for a hearer, such as when tailoring explanations to take into account the inquirer's state of knowledge (Slugoski, Lalljee, Lamb, & Ginsburg, 1993) or perceived interests (Norenzayan & Schwarz, 1999). It is quite possible that the kind of decentering needed for cooperative language production requires more conscious thought and explicit planning than does language understanding.

REFERENCES

Austin, J. L. (1962). *How to do things with words*. Oxford, England: Clarendon Press.

Bargh, J. A. (1996). Automaticity in social psychology. In E. T. Higgins & A. W. Kruglanski (Eds.), *Social psychology: Handbook of basic principles* (pp. 169–183). New York: Guilford Press.

Bless, H., Strack, F., & Schwarz, N. (1993). The informative function of research procedures: Bias and the logic of conversation. *European Journal of Social Psychology, 23*, 149–165.

Byrne, R. M., & Tasso, A. (1999). Deductions from factual, possible and counterfactual conditionals. *Memory and Cognition, 27*, 726–40.

Cantor, N., & Mischel, W. (1979). Prototypes in person perception. *Advances in Experimental Social Psychology, 12*, 3–52.

Chaiken, S., & Trope, Y. (Eds.). (1999). *Dual-process theories in social psychology*. New York: Guilford Press.

Dodd, D. H., & Bradshaw, J. M. (1980). Leading questions and memory: Pragmatic constraints. *Journal of Verbal Learning and Verbal Behavior, 19*, 695–704.

Englich, B., Mussweiler, T., & Strack, F. (2006). Playing dice with criminal sentences: The influence of irrelevant anchors on experts' judicial decision-making. *Personality and Social Psychology Bulletin, 32*, 188–200.

Evans, J. St. B. (1998). Matching bias in conditional reasoning: Do we understand it after 25 years? *Thinking and Reasoning, 4*, 45–82.

Evans, J. St. B. T., & Over, D. E. (1996). *Rationality and reasoning*. Hove, England: Psychology Press.

Fiske, S., & Taylor, S. E. (1991). *Social cognition* (2nd ed.). New York: McGraw-Hill.

Gärdenfors, P. (2003). *How homo became sapiens*. Oxford, England: Oxford University Press.

Gilbert, D. T. (1991). How mental systems believe. *American Psychologist, 46*, 107–119.

Gilbert, D. T., Pelham, B. W., & Krull, D. S. (1988). On cognitive busyness: When person perceivers meet persons perceived. *Journal of Personality and Social Psychology, 54*, 733–740.

Girotto, V., Legrenzi, P., & Rizzo, A. (1991). Event controllability in counterfactual thinking. *Acta Psychologica, 78*, 111–133.

Grice, H. P. (1957). Meaning. *Philosophical Review, 66*, 3, 377–388.

Grice, H. P. (1975). Logic and conversation. In P. Cole & J. L. Morgan (Eds.), *Syntax and semantics 3: Speech acts*. New York: Wiley.

Hilton, D. J. (1995). The social context of reasoning: Conversational inference and rational judgement. *Psychological Bulletin, 118*, 248–271.

Hilton, D. J. (2007). Causal explanation: From social perception to knowledge-based attribution. In A. Kruglanski & E. T. Higgins (Eds.), *Social psychology: Handbook of basic principles* (2nd ed., pp. 232–253). New York: Guilford Press.

Hilton, D. J., & Slugoski, B. R. (1986). Knowledge-based causal attribution: The abnormal conditions focus model. *Psychological Review, 93*, 75–88.

Hilton, D. J., & Slugoski, B. R. (2000). Discourse processes and rational inference: Judgment and decision-making in a social context. In T. Connolly, H. Arkes & K. Hammond (Eds.). *Judgment and decision-making: A Reader.* (2nd edition). Cambridge: Cambridge University Press.

Hilton, D. J., & Slugoski, B. R. (2001). The conversational perspective in reasoning and explanation. In A. Tesser & N. Schwarz (Eds.), *Blackwell handbook of social psychology: Vol. 1: Intrapersonal processes* (pp. 181–206). Oxford, England: Blackwell.

Hilton, D. J., Kemmelmeier, M., & Bonnefon, J. F. (2005). Putting *ifs* to work: Goal-based relevance in conditional directives. *Journal of Experimental Psychology: General, 134*, 388–405.

Horn, L. R. (1989). *A natural history of negation*. Chicago: University of Chicago Press.

Johnson-Laird, P. N., & Byrne, R. M. J. (2002). Conditionals: A theory of meaning, pragmatics, and inference. *Psychological Review, 109*, 646–678.

Jou, J., Shanteau, J., & Harris, R. J. (1996). An information-processing view of framing effects: The role of causal schemas in decision-making. *Memory & Cognition, 24*, 1–15.

Kahneman, D., & Frederick, S. (2002). Representativeness revisited: Attribute substitution in intuitive judgment. In T. Gilovich, D. Griffin, & D. Kahneman (Eds.), *Heuristics and biases: The psychology of intuitive judgement* (pp. 49–81). Cambridge, England: Cambridge University Press.

Kahneman, D., & Tversky, A. (1972). Subjective probability: A judgment of representativeness. *Cognitive Psychology, 3*, 430–454.

Kahneman, D., & Tversky, A. (1973). On the psychology of prediction. *Psychological Review, 80*, 237–251.

Kahneman, D., & Tversky, A. (1979). Prospect theory: An analysis of decision under risk. *Econometrica, 47*, 263–291.

Kahneman, D. E., & Tversky, A. (1982). On the study of statistical intuitions. *Cognition, 11*, 123–141.

Kelley, H. H. (1967). Attribution in social psychology. In *Nebraska Symposium on Motivation, 15*, 192–238.

Keysar, B., & O'Barr, D. J. (2002). Self-anchoring in conversation: When language users do not do what they "should." In T. Gilovich, D. Griffin, & D. Kahneman (Eds.), *Heuristics and biases: The psychology of intuitive judgement* (pp. 150–166). Cambridge, England: Cambridge University Press.

Krosnick, J. A., Li, F., & Lehman, D. R. (1990). Conversational conventions, order of information acquisition, and the effect of base rates and individuating information on social judgments. *Journal of Personality and Social Psychology, 59*, 1140–1152.

Krull, D. S. (1993). Does the grist change the mill? The effect of the perceiver's inferential goal on the process of social inference. *Personality and Social Psychology Bulletin, 19*, 340–348.

Krull, D. S., & Erickson, D. J. (1995). Judging situations: On the effortful process of taking dispositional information into account. *Social Cognition, 13*, 417–438.

Kunda, Z. (1990). The case for motivated reasoning. *Psychological Bulletin, 108*, 480–498.

Lee, C. J. (2006). Gricean charity: The Gricean turn in psychology. *Philosophy of the Social Sciences, 36*, 193–218.

Levinson, S. C. (1995). Interactional biases in human thinking. In E. Goody (Ed.), *Social intelligence and interaction*. Cambridge, England: Cambridge University Press.

Levinson, S. C. (2000). *Presumptive meanings: The theory of generalized conversational implicature*. Cambridge, MA: MIT Press.

Levinson, S. C. (2006). On the human "interaction engine." In N. Enfield and S. C. Levinson (Eds.), *Roots of human sociality: Culture, cognition and human interaction* (pp. 39–69). Oxford, England: Berg.

Loftus, E., & Palmer, J. C. (1974). Reconstruction of automobile destruction. *Journal of Verbal Learning and Verbal Behavior, 13*, 585–589.

Luria, A. R. (1959). The directive function of speech in development and dissolution, part I. *Word, 15*, 341–352.

Maass, A., Salvi, D., Arcuri, L., & Semin, G. (1989). Language use in intergroup contexts. The linguistic intergroup bias. *Journal of Personality and Social Psychology, 57*, 981–993.

Macchi, L. (1995). Pragmatic aspects of the base-rate fallacy. *Quarterly Journal of Experimental Psychology, 48A*, 188–207.

Macchi, L. (2000). Partitive formulation of information in probabilistic problems: Beyond heuristics and frequency format explanations. *Organizational Behavior and Human Decision Processes, 82*, 217–236.

Majid, A., Sanford, A. J., & Pickering, M. J. (2006) Covariation and quantifier polarity: What determines causal attribution in vignettes? *Cognition, 99*, 35–51.

Malle, B. F. (2004). *How the mind explains behavior: Folk explanations, meaning and social interaction*. Cambridge, MA: MIT Press.

McArthur, L. A. (1972). The how and what of why: Some determinants and consequences of causal attributions. *Journal of Personality and Social Psychology, 22*, 171–193.

McCauley, C., Stitt, C. L., & Segal, M. (1980). Stereotyping: From prejudice to prediction. *Psychological Bulletin, 87*, 195–208.

McKenzie, C. R. M. (2004). Framing effects in inference tasks—and why they're normatively defensible. *Memory & Cognition, 32*, 874–885.

McKenzie, C. R. M., Fereira, V. S., Mikkelsen, L. A., McDermott, K. J., & Skrable, R. P. (2001). Do conditional hypotheses target rare events? *Organizational Behavior and Human Decision Processes, 35*, 291–309.

Moxey, L. M., & Sanford, A. J. (1993a). *Communicating quantities: A psychological perspective.* Hove, England: Erlbaum.

Moxey, L. M., & Sanford, A. J. (1993b). Prior expectation and the interpretation of natural language quantifiers. *European Journal of Cognitive Psychology, 5*, 73–91.

Moxey, L. M., & Sanford, A. J. (2000). Communicating quantities: A review of psycholinguistic evidence of how expressions determine perspectives. *Applied Cognitive Psychology, 14*, 237–255.

Nisbett, R. E., Zukier, H., & Lemley, R. H. (1981). The dilution effect: Nondiagnostic information. *Cognitive Psychology, 13*, 248–277.

Norenzayan, A., & Schwarz, N. (1999). Telling what they want to know: Participants tailor causal attributions to researchers' interests. *European Journal of Social Psychology, 29*, 1011–1020.

Oaksford, M., & Chater, N. (1994). A rational analysis of the selection task as optimal data selection. *Psychological Review, 101*, 608–631.

Over, D. E., Manktelow, K. I., & Hadjichristidis, C. (2004). Conditions for the acceptance of deontic conditionals. *Canadian Journal of Experimental Psychology, 58*, 96–105.

Premack, D., & Premack, A. (1995). Intention as a psychological cause. In D. Sperber, D. Premack, & A. J. Premack (Eds.), *Causal cognition: A multidisciplinary debate* (pp. 185–199). Oxford, England: Clarendon Press.

Puce, A., & Perrett, D. (2003). Electrophysiology and brain imaging of biological motion. In C. Frith & D. Wolpert (Eds.), *The neuroscience of social interaction* (pp. 1–21). Oxford, England: Oxford University Press.

Roese, N. J., & Olson, J. M. (1995). Functions of counterfactual thinking. In N. J. Roese & J. M. Olson (Eds.), *What might have been: The social psychology of counterfactual thinking* (pp 169–197). Mahwah, NJ: Erlbaum.

Rosch, E., & Mervis, C. B. (1975). Family resemblances: Studies in the internal structure of categories. *Cognitive Psychology, 7*, 573–605.

Schwarz, N. (1994). Judgment in a social context: biases, shortcomings and the logic of conversation. *Advances in Experimental Social Psychology, 26*, 123–162.

Schwarz, N. (1996). *Cognition and communication: Judgmental biases, research methods and the logic of conversation.* Mahwah, NJ: Erlbaum.

Semin, G. R. (2000). Language as a cognitive and behavioral structuring resource: Question-answer exchanges. *European Review of Social Psychology, 11*, 75–104.

Semin, G., & Fiedler, K. (1988). The cognitive functions of linguistic categories in describing persons: Social cognition and language. *Journal of Personality and Social Psychology, 54*, 558–568.

Sher, S., & McKenzie, C. R. M. (2006). Information leakage from logically equivalent frames. *Cognition, 101*, 467–494.

Sloman, S. A. (2002). Two systems of reasoning. In T. Gilovich, D. Griffin, & D. Kahneman (Eds.), *Heuristics and biases: The psychology of intuitive judgement* (pp. 379–396). Cambridge, England: Cambridge University Press.

Slugoski, B. R., & Wilson, A. E. (1998). Contribution of conversational skills to the production of judgmental errors. *European Journal of Social Psychology, 28*, 575-601.

Slugoski, B. R., Lalljee, M. G., Lamb, R., & Ginsburg, J. (1993). Attribution in conversational context: Effect of mutual knowledge on explanation-giving. *European Journal of Social Psychology, 23*, 219–238.

Slugoski, B. R., & Noonan, K. (2004). *Compliance bias in the use of non-diagnostic information.* Paper presented at the 5th International Conference on Thinking, University of Leuven, Belgium, July 2004.

Slugoski, B. R., & Hilton, D. J. (2001). Conversation. In W. P. Robinson & H. Giles (Eds.), *Handbook of language and social psychology* (2nd ed., pp. 193–220). Chichester, England: Wiley.

Stanovich, K. E., & West, R. F. (2002). Individual differences in reasoning. In T. Gilovich, D. Griffin, & D. Kahneman (Eds.), *Heuristics and biases: The psychology of intuitive judgement* (pp. 421–440). Cambridge, England: Cambridge University Press.

Strack, F., & Deutsch, R. (2004). Reflective and impulsive determinants of human behavior. *Personality and Social Psychology Review, 8,* 220–247.

Strack, F., Martin, L. L., & Schwarz, N. L. (1988). Priming and communication: The social determinants of information use in judgments of life-satisfaction. *European Journal of Social Psychology, 18,* 429–442.

Strack, F., Schwarz, N., Bless, H., Kubler, A., & Wänke, M. (1993). Awareness of the Influence as a determinant of assimilation versus contrast. *European Journal of Social Psychology, 23,* 53–62.

Strawson, P. F. (1964). Intention and convention in speech acts. *Philosophical Review, 73,* 439–460.

Teigen, K. H., & Brun, W. (2003). Verbal probabilities: A question of frame? *Journal of Behavioral Decision Making, 16,* 53–72.

Tetlock, P. E., Lerner, J., & Boettger, R. (1996). The dilution effect: Judgmental bias or conversational convention or a bit of both? *European Journal of Social Psychology, 26,* 914–934.

Tversky, A., & Kahneman, D. (1974). Judgment under uncertainty: Heuristics and biases. *Science, 185,* 1124–1131.

Tversky, A., & Kahneman, D. (1981). The framing of decisions and the psychology of choice. *Science, 211,* 453–458.

Tomasello, M., Carpenter, M., Call, J., Behne, J., & Moll, H. (2005). Understanding and sharing intentions: The origins of cultural cognition. *Behavioral and Brain Sciences, 28,* 675–691.

Van Buiten, M., & Keren, G. (2006). *Speaker-listener incompatibility: Joint and separate processing in risky choice framing.* Unpublished manuscript.

Vygotsky, L. S. (1962). *Thought and language.* Cambridge, MA: MIT Press.

Wason, P. C. (1965). The contexts of plausible denial. *Journal of Verbal Learning and Verbal Behavior, 4,* 7–11.

Weiner, B. (1985). "Spontaneous" causal thinking. *Psychological Bulletin, 109,* 74–84.

Wilson, D., & Sperber, D. (2004). Relevance theory. In G. Ward & L. Horn (Eds.), *Handbook of pragmatics* (pp. 607–632). Oxford, England: Blackwell.

Wimmer, H., & Perner, J. (1983). Beliefs about beliefs. Representation and constraining function of wrong beliefs in young children's understanding of deception. *Cognition, 13,* 103–128.

5

Induction
From Simple Categorization to Higher-Order Inference Problems

KLAUS FIEDLER AND HENNING PLESSNER

INTRODUCTION

A ll cognitive information processing involves an interplay of both deductive and inductive processes. The deductive "top-down" part is basically knowledge-driven, drawing on schemas, categories, scripts, and higher-order knowledge structures, like semantic networks or autobiographical memory. The inductive or "bottom-up" component is stimulus-driven. In reality, cognitive tasks vary greatly in the relative extent to which they call for inductive and deductive operations. However, every single cognitive process involves a genuine interaction of both aspects. On one hand, there is no purely data-driven, merely inductive processing. Even the most primitive act of perception or learning does not take place on a *tabula rasa*, but is subject to the top-down constraints of prior knowledge, Gestalts, and preparedness to perceive or learn some patterns better than others (Garcia & Koelling, 1966; Gibson, 1979). On the other hand, deductive inferences do not proceed in an empty sphere; they are triggered by stimuli and task affordances. Reading involves decoding letters (inductive) as well as inferences from semantic, orthographic, and phonetic knowledge (deductive). Getting acquainted with people requires assessing their utterances, interests, and expressions (inductive) but at the same time draws on cultural norms, group stereotypes, and expectations derived from former acquaintanceship (deductive).

Nevertheless, having acknowledged the co-existence of deduction and induction as complementary aspects of the same cognitive processes, separating induction analytically, as a distinct chapter topic, is both sensible and useful. There is wide consensus about the paradigms to be called "inductive," such as category learning, conditioning, rule extraction, or correlation assessment and hypothesis testing. The common denominator is that these inductive tasks call for the cognitive assessment of empirical observations, whereas deductive tasks can be solved by logical or analogical rules alone (cf. Evans, 1982; Klauer, Musch, & Naumer, 2000; Krauss & Wang, 2003).

The present chapter is confined to inductive-statistic problems that call for probabilistic inferences under uncertainty. We refrain from including similarity-based or analogical inferences as well as the huge literature on causal inference, although the sections devoted to contingency are closely related to causal attribution.

A Taxonomy of Inductive Processes

How can the domain of induction be organized conceptually? The following taxonomy (cf. Fiedler & Plessner, 2006) affords a framework for understanding the structural relations between induction tasks. The most elementary task, to start with, is categorization.

Categorization involves the inference that an observed stimulus object or person belongs to an object class, category, or group. This inference, expressed with a certain probability or confidence level, is mediated by one or more attributes or "cues" that define category membership. Thus, in eyewitness identification, the confidence with which a suspect is categorized, based on facial cues, as identical to the perpetrator is estimated to be 80%.

Discrimination is the second inductive task level in the hierarchy, conceived as a comparison, or competition, of two (or more) possible categorizations. A stimulus object or person has to be classified as belonging to one of two (or more) competing categories. Under uncertainty, a probability scale can again be used to quantify the discriminating inference. For example, the witness may indicate her confidence of correctly discriminating between the actual perpetrator and an innocent suspect to be 90%.

Contingency tasks, in turn, can be conceived as comparisons between discrimination tasks. If a contingency exists then the probability of discriminating objects on a criterion attribute changes as a function of their categorization on another predictor attribute. Thus, the tendency to identify a suspect as the (alleged) perpetrator, rather than discarding him as a foil, may be contingent on the similarity of the suspect to the original perpetrator.

At the highest level, *higher-order contingency* problems involve comparisons of contingencies, just as contingencies involve comparisons of discrimination tasks and discrimination involves comparisons of elementary categorizations. In our example, the degree to which the discrimination of perpetrator and foil is dependent on similarity is itself moderated by the method of presenting the lineup (i.e., the contingency should be stronger given simultaneous raather than successive presentation; Wells, 2001).

Although seemingly complex and hard to understand, this upper-most level of induction is at the heart of the most real problems, and social cognition research paradigms. Just as higher-order cognition in Piaget's (1963) developmental psychology begins at the operational level, when children understand that the volume of a glass depends on both diameter and height, higher-order social cognition begins when individuals realize that behavior depends on both dispositions and situational constraints (Ross & Nisbett, 1991; Gilbert & Malone, 1995). Thus, higher-order contingency inferences are involved in the correspondence bias (trait-behavior contingency moderated by situation), discounting in attribution (cause-effect relation reduced by presence of second cause), or in dilemma games (depending on both short-term payoffs and long-term strategy). Higher-order contingency tasks are common in dual-process approaches (Strack & Deutsch, 2004) as well as in the ecological approach advocated in the present chapter, which calls for the joint consideration of both cognitive and environmental factors underlying social behavior (Denrell, 2005; Fiedler, 2007).

Chapter Scope and Organization

To fit a volume in a series called Frontiers in Social Cognition, this chapter deviates from a conventional handbook review in two respects. First, we concentrate on recent evidence that we feel deserves the name "frontiers," placing an emphasis on recent evidence about realistic induction problems of the contingency and higher-order contingency type, while giving less attention to well-known categorization and discrimination tasks. Second, we concentrate on "frontiers" in those areas in which we have ourselves witnessed the progress through our own research.

We start with an overview of recent findings from the more basic categorization and discrimination paradigms. Some exciting developments in these areas have led to new theoretical accounts of prominent effects and cognitive illusions. Little room will be given to the mere repetition of common-sense textbook knowledge on heuristics and biases.

Then, two major sections will be devoted to inductive inferences of contingencies and higher-order contingencies. The findings reviewed in all three sections will converge in a threefold theoretical message: (1) Probabilistic inferences, even in complex environments and under extreme cognitive load, are often remarkably accurate, relative to the sample of stimulus information given. (2) However, in spite of this impressive accuracy, serious illusions and shortcomings result from people's "myopia" for the logic of inductive inferences: the asymmetry of inferences, the regression trap, and insensitivity to sampling biases. (3) Moreover, what appears to be "logical," "rational," or "normative" at first sight often turns out to be problematic upon closer inspection. Normative standards are hard to defend, while seemingly strong violations of rationality may be functional. Our final conclusions will address the adaptive value and the possible evolutionary origins of biases and shortcomings of induction, and we point out some challenging lines of future research.

RECENT RESEARCH AND THEORIZING IN BASIC INDUCTION PARADIGMS

Let us now turn to the basic induction paradigms, categorization and discrimination. Although each paradigm provides its own empirical highlights, there is much convergence in the theoretical messages, which often diverge from traditional theories of inductive judgments and decisions under uncertainty. Whereas traditional accounts of biases and shortcomings emphasize capacity limitations and insufficient motivation, or heuristic as opposed to systematic processing, many findings reviewed in this chapter point to alternative causes, residing in ecological structures, stimulus sampling biases, and inadequate normative models.

Categorization

Inductive judgments in the context of categorization tasks are the traditional home domain of the huge research program on heuristics and biases (Kahneman. Slovic, & Tversky, 1982; Gilovich, Griffin, & Kahneman, 2002). Judgments of the likelihood that an object belongs to a category are supposed to depend on the category's representativeness (Kahneman & Tversky, 1972) or the availability of relevant evidence in memory (Schwarz et al., 1991; Tversky & Kahneman, 1973).[1] In social cognition, the accessibility of categories is considered a chief explanatory construct (Dijksterhuis & van Knippenberg, 1996; Higgins, 1996). To account for persisting stereotypes or prejudice, the concept of chronic accessibility was introduced (Bargh et al., 1986). Stereotype change is conceived as an attempt to decrease the accessibility of stereotypical categories while at the same time increasing the accessibility of super-ordinate categories that unify people from different groups (Dovidio et al., 2005). As every person is a member of multiple categories, their relative accessibility is manipulated for cross-categorization and re-categorization (Hewstone, Rubin, & Willis, 2002).

Plausible and familiar as these approaches may appear, they hardly provide a sufficient account of inductive inferences, for several reasons.

First, many critical empirical tests did not provide support for availability and other heuristics. For instance, Tversky and Kahneman's (1974) famous demonstration that the letter "k" is erroneously judged to appear more often in the first than in the third position, allegedly reflecting the enhanced availability of words starting with "k," could not be replicated in a systematic study covering all letters of the alphabet (Sedlmeier, Hertwig, & Gigerenzer, 1998). The discrepancy was shown to reflect a stimulus-sampling problem (i.e., intuitively selecting stimuli that confirm the hypothesis in the researcher's mind), which is also apparent in research on other biases, particularly overconfidence (Juslin, 1994; Juslin, Winman, & Olsson, 2000; Sedlmeier et al., 1998).

Second, the availability account contradicts the implication of another basic finding, namely, that inductive judgments tend to ignore base rates. However, any assessment of a category's availability entails a base rate.

Third, in many priming experiments, increasing the accessibility of a category through priming did not yield an assimilation effect (i.e., increased likelihood of the primed category) but a contrast effect (Schwarz & Bless, 1992; Strack, Schwarz, Bless, Kübler, & Wänke, 1993).

Similarly, the common notion that base rates are overridden by the representativeness heuristic hardly rests on safe empirical ground. Again, the famous demonstrations of base-rate neglect were not corroborated in recent research showing that, under some conditions, judges are amazingly good at assessing and utilizing base rates (e.g., Fiedler, Brinkmann, Betsch, & Wild, 2000; Gigerenzer, 1991; Hasher & Zacks, 1984; Plessner, Hartmann, Hohmann, & Zimmermann, 2001). This is particularly the case when the probability of serially observed stimulus events has to be judged in inductive task settings (rather than verbally stated statistics problems), or when statistical problems are presented in an intelligible format (Gigerenzer, 1991). By using cardinal frequencies rather than probabilities, for instance, the conjunction fallacy can be eliminated (Fiedler, 1988; Hertwig & Gigerenzer, 1999).

Sensitivity to category frequencies is evident in learning and conditioning (Domjan, 2003), word frequency estimates (Hasher & Zacks, 1984), or a teacher's ability to keep track of student performance. In a simulated-classroom paradigm (Fiedler, Walther, Freytag, & Plessner, 2002), participants had to assess the rate of 16 students' correct versus incorrect answers to knowledge questions in 8 different disciplines (making 16 x 8 = 128 ability estimates). In addition, they had to assess the same students' motivation (i.e., frequency of raising hands). In spite of the enormous load and complexity of the task, the estimates were remarkably accurate. They were even able to detect changes in students' ability parameters from one lesson to another (Fiedler & Walther, 2004; see also Jussim & Eccles, 1992).

Such evidence is not compatible with the notion of restricted capacity or motivation—a pessimistic premise that does not apply to many real-world induction tasks. Research on the recognition heuristic (Goldstein & Gigerenzer, 2002) shows impressively that organisms are highly sensitive at classifying stimuli as "old" (cf. Zajonc, 1980), and the fluency heuristic highlights the sensitivity for category frequencies (Schooler & Hertwig, 2005).

However, whereas generalized claims about capacity constraints as the major cause of impairment appear unwarranted, inductive inferences do produce systematic error and bias. Often the same experiments provide testimony for both accuracy and inaccuracy, although the obtained errors and biases do not reflect shallow and mindless processing. Rather, they may result from over-generalized induction rules leading to accurate inferences most of the time.

One universal source of error, reflecting such a valid induction rule, lies in the regressive nature of all judgments of frequency and probability. High frequencies tend to be underestimated whereas low frequencies tend to be overestimated (Fiedler, 1996; Greene, 1984; Sedlmeier & Gigerenzer, 1997). Regressing judgments to actual frequencies yields regression slopes less than 1. No cognitive bias has to be postulated to account for this rule. Although regression reflects unsystematic error, due to unreliability, rather than a systematic bias, applying the regression rule to real problems can nevertheless lead to biased judgments.

For another general rule, inductive judgments are contingent on samples. For example, when estimating danger or risk, the entire population of all prior occurrences of the risk category is unknown. The best "proxy" for risk judgment is the proportion of the critical event in the sample at hand—as long as the sample is unbiased and representative of the universe, this proxy will inform accurate estimates. However, if the sample happens to be biased, the same rule will lead to erroneous inferences, however accurately it is applied to the sample data.

Recent sampling approaches (see Fiedler & Juslin, 2005) highlight that inductive biases can often result from unbiased cognitive operations applied to biased stimulus samples. This initial sampling bias may not reflect the judge's own selective memory but the selective manner in which the environment supplies judges with relevant information. For instance, pleasant and positive information is typically more available in the social environment (advertising, social interaction etc.), because a normal sampling rule says that an information search is continued when it is pleasant but truncated when it is unpleasant (Denrell, 2005). Likewise, larger samples are supplied about oneself than about others, about one's own in-group or culture than others (Fiedler & Walther, 2004). Accordingly, judgments often exhibit a general positivity bias, and a self-serving bias or in-group-serving bias in particular.

Sampling models provide excellent approximations of inductive judgment biases in various paradigms, such as overconfidence (Klayman et al., 1999), hindsight bias (Winman & Juslin, 2005), base-rate neglect (Fiedler et al., 2000), or biases in meta-cognitive judgments (Koriat, Fiedler, & Bjork, 2006). For instance, people overestimate the association frequency from "cheese" to "cheddar" in the sample because the outcome, cheddar, biases the sampling of information about the stimulus, cheese. Such a sampling bias is analogous to the impact of selective accessibility in producing anchoring effects (Mussweiler & Strack, 1999; Strack & Mussweiler, 1997). When comparing a medium-size target stimulus (e.g., the river Main) to a large alternative (e.g., Mississippi), the sample of epistemic cues used to represent the target will let the target appear larger than when comparing it to a small creek.

Discrimination

The prominent phenomenon of overconfidence reflects to a large degree a sampling bias in the researcher's stimulus selection. In a typical experiment, judges have to provide forced-choice responses to binary knowledge questions (Which city is larger in population size, San Antonio or San Diego?), which is by definition a discrimination task. Judges then indicate the confidence of being correct on a percentage scale. Across many trials, the actual percentage of being correct at a certain confidence level turns out to be lower (e.g., 65%) than the indicated confidence (e.g., 80%). This finding has been shown to mainly reflect a selective sample of knowledge tasks rather than a bias in the judges' minds. If items are sampled representatively from a universe (e.g., all American cities over 200,000), confidence judgments turn out to be quite well calibrated (Juslin et al., 2000).

The most prominent model of the cognitive process applied to such probability choices or paired comparisons is probabilistic mental models (PMM) theory (Gigerenzer, Hoffrage, & Kleinbölting, 1991). Accordingly, the two objects are compared on various successive cue dimensions. The first cue is always the recognition cue. If recognition discriminates between the two objects (e.g., San Diego recognized, San Antonio not), then the recognized one will be considered more probable (e.g., leading to higher population-size estimates). If the recognition cue does not discriminate, then the next cue will be considered (e.g., presence of an airport), and so forth, until one cue is found that discriminates between the objects.

Such a process is clearly heuristic in nature, relying on only one cue at a time, rather than integrating all cues systematically. However, single-cue heuristics have been shown to produce accurate judgments and often even to outperform exhaustive strategies (Gigerenzer & Goldstein, 1996). To be sure, such single-cue strategies may produce systematic biases. A stereotype cue, for instance, may be salient and discriminatory, but wrong. Gender mimics to predict talent in science (Spelke, 2005), familiarity may wrongly suggest truth (Begg, Anas, & Farinacci, 1992), or avoiding eye contact may be a mistaken cue to lie detection (Zuckerman, DePaulo, & Rosenthal, 1981). Nevertheless, the induction rule per se—relying on experience-based cues—is not flawed or inferior to cue-based inferences in such prestigious areas as medical diagnosis, expert judgments (Goldberg, 1970), or scientific validity judgments (Mynatt, Doherty, & Tweney, 1977), supposed to reflect systematic rather than heuristic processes.

An alternative to using abstract cue rules is to base inferences on exemplar-based memories (Juslin, Olsson, & Olsson, 2002; Nosofsky & Johansen, 2000). Thus, inferences of population size may be based on memory for other cities that resemble the target city. Research by Juslin et al. (2002) shows that dichotomous discrimination tasks (large vs. small) induce exemplar-based strategies, whereas continuous tasks solicit rule-based strategies.

Discrimination is the home domain of signal-detection analysis (Swets, Dawes, & Monahan, 2000)—one of the most valuable methods that psychology has ever developed. In such diverse domains as medical diagnosis, lie detection, face recognition, or guilt judgment in the courtroom, signal-detection analysis affords a statistical model for diagnosing cognitive processes. In particular, discrimination proper can be set apart from response tendencies. For example, a problem in eyewitness identification is a too lenient response criterion, leading to many correct identifications, but also to many false alarms (Malpass & Devine, 1981; Wells, 2001). A more conservative response strategy (i.e., identifying a suspect only when the match is very strong) can result in better performance when the false rate decreases more than the hit rate. However, crucially, such a performance increase would merely reflect an altered response strategy rather than a genuine improvement in the witness's memory. Signal-detection analysis highlights this important distinction, showing that high motivation or payoff can reduce performance by inducing a lenient, over-motivated response criterion.

Statistical tools like signal-detection analysis or Bayesian calculus also serve to point out the limits and the relativity of the normative models and tests. For instance, the lenient response criterion built into an HIV test yields too many positive results, a highly inflated false-alarm rate. As Swets et al. (2000) have shown, only about 1 out of 7 people with a positive result on an HIV screening test actually have the virus, given the currently used biochemical test.[2] Introducing a more conservative criterion would greatly change the test results without changing the nature of the HIV test proper.

Contingency

According to the taxonomy, a contingency task involves the relation between two discrimination tasks, such as capturing the prevalence of an outcome (e.g., good performance) under two different conditions (e.g., given students from different classes). The ability to detect and estimate contingencies between dichotomous variables or, more generally, correlations between all kinds of variables,[3] constitutes a chief module of adaptive intelligence (Inhelder & Piaget, 1958). It allows us to predict future events from past observations and to gain control over the physical and social environment. At a basic associative level, we learn correlations between signals and their meaning, between behaviors and reinforcements. At higher levels, we assess relations between groups and their attributes, or scientific laws linking symptoms to diseases. Correctly assessed contingencies enable us to avoid danger and to achieve environmental control. Impaired contingency assessment leads to wrong predictions, erroneous decisions, and maladaptive behavior.

Illusory correlations A large body of research is concerned with distorted contingency assessments, commonly referred to as illusory correlations (for a review, see Fiedler, 2000b). Subjective contingency judgments often deviate from the objectively existing contingency between two variables (cf. Chapman & Chapman, 1967, 1969; Crocker, 1981). In social psychology, illusory correlations are applied to the development and maintenance of stereotypes (e.g., Hamilton & Rose, 1980), defined as (illusory) correlations between groups and stereotypical attributes. We will discuss three distinct types of illusory correlations.

The huge evidence for typically rather strong illusory correlations in many different areas suggests that people lack the basic ability to assess environmental contingencies. However, such a pessimistic conclusion would be premature and presumably wrong. There is sufficient evidence to demonstrate that, under auspicious conditions, people are remarkably accurate in assessing correlations between two or more variables even in complex and demanding problem situations (e.g., Fiedler, Walther, Freytag, & Plessner, 2002; McKenzie, 1994; Plessner et al., 2001). Serious biases are peculiar to specific problem structures and contents, which have been the preferred focus of researchers motivated to demonstrate errors and biases rather than accuracy and well-calibrated judgments (Krueger & Funder, 2004). However, before we turn to the counter-evidence that exists for accurate inferences, let us first consider the three major classes of illusory correlations, namely, expectancy-based illusory correlations, illusions arising from the inequality of positive and negative information, and illusory correlations resulting from skewed frequency distributions.

Expectancy-based illusory correlations Expectancies derived from general world knowledge exert a strong impact on cognitive inferences, causing potential error and bias when expectancies are transferred to new task environments (Olson, Roese, & Zanna, 1996). The top-down impact of prior expectancy is apparent in basic perception and categorization (Bruner & Postman, 1949; Higgins, Rholes, & Jones, 1977) as well as achievement evaluation in the classroom

(Rosenthal, 1968) and decision making in sports (Plessner, 1999; Plessner & Haar, 2006). The same top-down bias has been shown in countless experiments on correlation assessment. People believe they see the correlations they expect; that is, subjectively assessed contingencies tend to be distorted toward the sign and size of the expected contingency (e.g., Berndsen, Van der Pligt, Spears, & McGarty, 1996; Chapman & Chapman, 1967, 1969; Hamilton & Rose, 1980; Spears, Eiser, & van der Pligt, 1987).

To explain such expectancy-based illusory correlations, a processing advantage of expectancy-congruent over expectancy-incongruent information has been proposed (Hamilton, 1981). However, this cannot be the whole story because other evidence suggests superior memory for expectancy-incongruent information (Stangor & McMillan, 1992).

Another theoretical problem is that correlation expectancies are often confounded by the similarity that holds between the variables, or their semantic meaning (Fiedler, 2000b; Plessner, Freytag, & Fiedler, 2000; Shweder, 1982). Similarity between two concepts can be understood as the overlap of the cues defining the concepts (Medin, Goldstone, & Genter, 1993; Tversky, 1977). For example, participants in a study by Plessner et al. (2000) had to learn two novel concepts pertaining to a fictitious painter called "Greve" and a fictitious artistic style called "Wenturalism." Both concepts were defined by a set of three visual cues characterizing the paintings. These defining cue sets overlapped in one experimental condition, such that part of the cues indentifying the painter Greve was also indicative of the Wenturalism style. In another condition, the cues did not overlap. The expectancy of a positive versus negative contingency was manipulated orthogonally to the similarity (based on cue overlap). Later on, a series of paintings was presented in which the correlation between style (Wenturalism vs. other) and painter (Greve vs. other) was zero. Subsequent contingency judgments exhibited two main effects, for expectancy induction as well as for similarity, highlighting the logical independence. By analogy, many illusory correlations that are commonly attributed to expectancies may reflect the confounded influence of similarity.

Illusory correlations arising from the inequality of present versus absent features Another class of illusory correlations originates in the unequal weighting of observations belonging to different cells of the contingency table, referring to present versus absent information (e.g., Allan & Jenkins, 1983, Jenkins & Ward, 1965; Wasserman et al., 1993). Kao and Wassermann (1993) asked their participants to assess a fertilizer's value in promoting an unknown plant to bloom. They were presented with information about the frequencies of all four combinations of the effect (blooming or not) and the cause (fertilizer given or not). Participants saw a positive correlation between blooming and fertilizing if the *absolute* frequency of fertilizer/blooming was higher than the frequency of fertilizer/no-blooming, even when the *relative* frequency of blooming was the same in the presence as in the absence of the fertilizer. For a cognitive-process explanation of this often-replicated finding, it is assumed that present features are given more weight than absent features (e.g., feature-positive effect; Newman, Wolff,

& Hearst, 1980). This unequal weighting of positive and negative variable levels most likely occurs during early stages of perception or encoding, but later stages of retrieval and judgment formation may also involve selective weighting.

Illusory correlations resulting from skewed frequency distributions
Selective attention is also biased toward rare and distinctive stimuli, as evident in the so-called von Restorff (1933) effect. Because infrequent stimuli are outstanding and salient, they can have a memory advantage (Taylor & Fiske, 1978). Indeed, such a memory advantage ascribed to rare and distinctive events was long considered as the origin of the third major type of illusory correlations, which arose in a seminal study of Hamilton and Gifford (1976). Participants were presented with 26 behaviors of group A and 13 behaviors of group B. As the ratio of positive to negative behaviors was the same for both groups (18+ / 8– in group A and 9+ / 4– in group B), the objective correlation was zero. Nevertheless, a systematic bias towards a more favorable impression of the large group A than of the small group B was evident in frequency estimates, trait ratings, and in the cued-recall of behavior-group associations. This seminal finding suggests that a challenging ordinary-memory account for the discrimination against minorities turned out to be robust and replicable (Mullen & Johnson, 1990).

Infrequency-based illusory correlations have been commonly explained in terms of the distinctiveness and the alleged memory advantage of the rarest event combination, negative behaviors by the minority, which highlight the negative aspects of the minority (cf. Hamilton & Sherman, 1989). However, no evidence for a memory advantage of the rarest event combination was obtained in several experiments using signal detection analysis (Fiedler, Russer, & Gramm, 1993) or multinomial modeling (Klauer & Meiser, 2000) to measure memory appropriately. An alternative explanation, which is parsimonious and consistent with most data, is in terms of a simple induction rule: learning increases with the number of trials. As twice as many trials are available for the majority than the minority, the prevailing positivity is more apparent in the former than the latter group (Fiedler, 1991, 1996).

A simple connectionist simulation model called BIAS (Brunswikian Induction Algorithm for Social Inference; Fiedler, 1996) corroborates this alternative explanation, showing that the number of learning trials alone is sufficient to produce the Hamilton-Gifford effect. Moreover, BIAS can simulate all three classes of illusory correlations within the same integrative framework (Fiedler, 2000b), showing how biases can reflect constraints imposed by the learning environment on ordinary cognitive processes of learning and memory.

Sample size and contingency assessment
Within such a cognitive-ecological approach, we are confronted with novel and counter-intuitive findings that do not fit the common meta-theory explaining biases as due to "merely" heuristic cognitive strategies. The cognitive-ecological approach highlights the fact that, under specific conditions, less can be more. Small samples of information (i.e., "heuristic" processing) can lead to more sensitive contingency detection than large samples (attributed to "systematic" or "exhaustive" processing).

Such a reversal of the law of large numbers, which was first demonstrated by Kareev (2000), can be derived from statistical sampling theory. Under specific conditions, the contingencies observed in small samples are likely to be stronger than in large samples drawn from the same population. This is because the left skew of the sampling distribution of correlation coefficients (i.e., the predominance of exaggerated correlations when repeated samples are drawn from a population) increases with decreasing sample size. In accordance with this ingenious model, Kareev (1995) found that people with an impaired working memory span (restricting the size of the effective samples) actually outperform people with higher memory capacity in contingency detection. The cognitive-ecological framework also clarifies the limits of the small-sample advantage, which only holds for qualitative choice tasks as opposed to quantitative estimations (cf. Fiedler & Kareev, 2006).

HIGHER-ORDER INDUCTIVE COGNITION PROBLEMS

Higher-order cognitive induction tasks have been defined as tasks in which two or more contingencies compete for the explanation of an event or behavior. Their structure is related to Piaget's (1963) marker of operational intelligence. Young children at a pre-operational level of cognitive development understand that the height of a glass determines the amount of water one can pour in it. To live up to the operational level, they have to overcome centration on a single correlation and realize that volume is jointly correlated with both height and diameter of the glass. The quantitative degree to which volume increases with height depends on the diameter. Such problems that call for an understanding of two (or more) competing contingencies are the topic of the present section and the major focus of this chapter.

By all Piagetian criteria, the modal participant in a social cognition experiment has not reached the level of operative intelligence. The fundamental attribution bias, for a prominent example, seems to testify to people's inability, or unwillingness, to take more than one determinant of behavior into account. They typically attribute behaviors to internal traits or dispositions within the person, disregarding external causes in the situation. Had they overcome this centration, they ought to understand that the power of situations can moderate and override the power of traits, for instance, when virtually everybody shows aggression (Haney & Zimbardo, 1976), or that some situations render trait explanations non-viable (Jones & Harris, 1967), as when an aggression is staged or performed on instruction. However, social inferences are often conspicuously blind for this level of induction.

Studying higher-order induction therefore affords a major challenge to social cognition research. Understanding why most people—across cultures (Miyamoto & Kitayama, 2002) and education—fail on such higher-order induction tasks is of theoretical and applied interest. Studies of these markers of operative intelligence have obvious implications for legal decision making, education, consumer behavior, social justice, and conflict resolution.

Apart from such applied issues, higher-order contingency problems are also crucial for theories of social cognition. Again, the typical theory context, within which the fundamental attribution error and related phenomena have been treated, is the heuristics and biases approach (Kahneman et al., 1982; Gilovich et al., 2002) and the dual-process approach (Chaiken & Trope, 1999). Within both frameworks, the failure to meet the level of operative intelligence on many tasks of realistic complexity is attributed to restricted cognitive and motivational resources. For the full mental capacity to be mobilized, individuals have to be prompted or motivated to engage in systematic rather than heuristic processing (Chaiken, 1987). Only through such a shift in processing mode can the accuracy and efficiency of inferences be expected to increase, particularly on complex induction problems that call for the simultaneous consideration of two or more contingencies.

The message to be conveyed in the present review diverges from this prevailing view. Many findings demonstrate, impressively, that mastery of higher-order induction problems may not be a matter of restricted capacity or motivation, but that the obstacles lying in the way of solving such problems are of a different nature.

Discounting and Augmentation

In attribution research, higher-order contingency tasks underlie the principles of discounting and augmentation (Kelley, 1973; McClure, 1998; Morris & Larrick, 1995). According to Kelley's (1973) original formulation, the causal impact attributed to one cause that covaries with an effect decreases (i.e., is partially discounted) if another cause is shown to covary with the effect too. Discounting occurs when the secondary cause correlates with the effect in the same direction as the primary cause, providing an alternative account. In contrast, augmentation occurs when the secondary cause's correlation with the effect is opposite to the primary cause's correlation, which produces the effect in spite of the counteracting influence. Thus, given two causes of academic achievement, student ability and task difficulty, the perceived causal impact of high student ability is augmented when a difficult task inhibits performance, but student ability is discounted when an easy task facilitates success.

Note that such a primitive, unrefined version of the discounting rule, which is merely sensitive to the presence of another cause, falls short of Piaget's criterion of operative intelligence. A full understanding of the joint influence of two factors (e.g., the multiplicative influence of height and diameter) requires the individual not to discount, but to understand the specific interaction (e.g., recognizing that the increase of volume with height *increases* with increasing diameter). Thus, upon closer inspection, discounting prevents the individual from understanding interacting causes. Discounting is only adequate when two (or more) mutually exclusive causes compete for an exclusive one-factor explanation of an effect.

In reality, however, the interplay of two or more causes can take different forms, which may not call for discounting (Figure 5.1). In the simplest case, two causes may exert independent, additive influences. Thus, an aggressive trait and an aggressive environment (such as TV) may independently facilitate violent behavior; manipulating one factor may leave the impact of the other factor unchanged. Discounting only makes sense when a precise quantitative model exists that already predicts a ceiling effect due to one cause, leaving no latitude for the impact of a second cause.

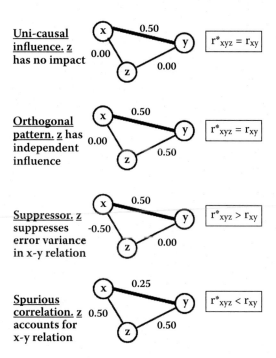

Figure 5.1 Different tri-variate relationships by which a secondary factor z can mediate, moderate, or combine additively with the impact of a primary causal factor x on an effect y.

Alternatively, the two causes might be correlated or redundant, reflecting (in part) the same common variance. Both trait aggression and violent TV consumption may reflect the same social background. In such a case, the presence of one cause entails, rather than excludes, the other cause to some degree. Correlated causes may call for a mediational model, such that the impact of one cause is mediated by the second cause (e.g., trait aggression → violent TV consumption → imitation of aggressive behaviors). Discounting a mediator would obscure the process, and maybe the spurious nature of, the original cause.

Related but in a way opposite to a mediator effect is a suppressor effect, which is also incompatible with discounting. Whereas a mediator captures that part of variance of a cause that is related to the effect, a suppressor serves to bind the error variance in the cause that is unrelated to the effect. For instance, the trait "energetic" may bind the positive aspects of aggressiveness that are not turned into destruction, but into constructive achievement.

Last but not least, the secondary cause may be a moderator. The impact of a primary cause may change with the levels of the moderator cause. Trait aggressiveness may lead to manifest aggression against low-status persons, but not against high-status persons. Discounting the role of the moderator, social status, would mean to miss a crucial point.

This discussion purports to illustrate that higher-order inductive reasoning problems are indeed very difficult, even for highly intelligent people. The evidence to be reviewed in this section suggests that normatively correct solutions to such problems often do not exist. It is only logical that motivation and cognitive involvement—the major remedies of dual-process approaches—cannot undo the inherent difficulty of such problems. Let us first elaborate on this important point by considering Simpson's (1951) paradox, a problem structure that calls for a mental covariance analysis (Schaller & O'Brien, 1992).

Simpson's paradox Simpson's paradox is at work when, say, there is clear-cut evidence that men are on average more aggressive than women but, when a distinction between two situation types is introduced, competitive and communal settings, and the impact of different situations is partialled out, it turns out that within both settings, male aggression is at most equal, or even lower, than female aggression. In other words, male aggression prevails at aggregate level (across situations), whereas female aggression prevails at the level of specific situations. Such a seeming paradox is possible when men engage in more competitive settings and women engage in more communal settings, and when in general aggression is much more common in competitive than in communal settings. In Figure 5.1, this corresponds to a spurious correlation, in which the secondary cause (settings) accounts for the apparent influence of the primary cause (gender) on the effect (aggression).

One of the most studied Simpson's paradox is the allegedly higher academic success of male than female students (Fiedler, Walther, Freytag, & Nickel, 2002; Schaller, 1992). Participants are presented with information showing that female applicants (e.g., for two graduate programs, or different universities) are more likely rejected than male applicants. However, on closer inspection it becomes evident that, within both graduate programs or universities, females are actually more successful than males. Figure 5.2 shows how this is possible. The rejection rate is much higher in Program B than A; as more women apply for B whereas more men apply for the easier Program A, the difference between programs can account for the alleged male advantage.

Participants have a hard time solving Simpson's paradox. In the version depicted here, they would typically report higher success rates for men, reflecting discrimination against women. Only under exceptional conditions were respondents found to "solve" Simpson's paradox: when an appropriate mental model was available

	Total +	Total −		University A +	University A −		University B +	University B −
Men	19	13	=	17	7	+	2	6
Women	13	19		7	1		6	18

Figure 5.2 Illustration of Simpson's paradox: Although across universities female applicants are more often rejected than male applicants, females are more successful within both universities, A and B.

(Waldmann & Hagmayer, 2001), or when they were motivated to see a female advantage. In a study by Schaller (1992), female participants with a feminist motive reported that "in fact" females have outperformed male applicants. However, "solving" the paradox here means to switch over from seeing a male advantage to seeing a female advantage, rather than gaining insight into the problem structure.

Mastery of the full induction problem would involve more than a motivated switch from one bias to the opposite. A convincing solution would consist in demonstrating that judges recognize that two opposing tendencies exist at the same time. Women are both less successful and more successful, depending on the level of analysis. Fiedler, Walther, Freytag, and Nickel (2002) called for separate estimates of female and male rejection rates, across contexts or within contexts. Hardly anybody saw the double message in the data, even though most judges did realize the overall difference (favoring males), the fact that most females (males) applied for B (A), and that the rejection rate for B was much higher than for A. Even when they were endowed with strong and plausible causal models (i.e., the hypothesis that women strive for higher goals), when the motivation was enhanced, and when the exposure time was increased, there was little improvement.

The only factor that finally helped judges to overcome the inductive reasoning barrier was the temporal presentation mode. As long as the primary cause, gender, was presented prior to the secondary cause, University A versus B, the rejection rate was explained as a function of gender, and the crucial role of the context factor (universities) was overlooked. Only when the context factor was presented first on every trial (i.e., indicating the university before the gender of the applicant) did the judges get the double message. Convergent evidence for the crucial role of temporal organization of the stimulus information comes from another recent investigation, using different problem contents (Fiedler, Walther, Freytag, & Stryczek, 2002). Together, these findings suggest that performance on complex inductive tasks depends more on environmental fit (presentation format) than on motivation.

This interpretation is consistent with Gigerenzer and colleagues' emphasis on presentation format (Gigerenzer et al., 1991; Gigerenzer & Hoffrage, 1995). Furthermore, given that no single normatively correct solution exists, the failure of processing motivation to improve performance is not surprising. Simpson's paradox highlights the insight that partial correlation is no more valid, or closer to reality, than a zero-order correlation. In other words, the truth is not that "in actuality" women are better than men, when controlling for unequal difficulty levels of University A and B. Rather than assuming that the different prestige or rejection rate of universities explains why women fail more often, it is also possible that the higher rejection rate reflects the higher proportion of women applying for B. Thus, whether the context factor constitutes an alternative account of the apparent gender difference—calling for discounting—or only mediates a genuine gender effect—rendering discounting inadequate—cannot be decided statistically. Rather, a mental model is necessary to figure out which factor plays the leading causal role.

Competing correlations This important point is also central for Trope's (1986) approach to correspondent inference and the fundamental attribution error. When aggressive behavior occurs in an aggressive situation, suggesting an external cause, the dominant attribution to an internal trait may not decrease (discounting), but may actually increase. This is because in an early stage of attribution, the aggressive situation facilitates the identification of an otherwise ambiguous behavior as aggressive. In a later stage of cognitive processing, though, when the nature of the behavior is clearly identified and alternative causes compete for its explanation, pointing to the aggressive nature of the situation may serve to discount the causal impact of the trait. Again, the temporal pragmatics of the stimulus presentation determines the outcome of an induction conflict. Simply increasing the motivation or monetary reward will hardly undo the two-fold role played by the secondary, situational cause, to identify the primary cause but also to suggest an alternative explanation.

Strictly speaking, the aggression proneness of an aggressive situation, which facilitates the identification of an aggressive trait in Trope's (1986) framework, was not observed statistically, or inductively, but derived deductively from world knowledge. However, a conceptually similar task was constructed in a genuine induction experiment by Fiedler, Walther, and Nickel (1999). Participants were asked to imagine being a manager of a variety show who is to hire a multi-talented entertainer. Each trial of the stimulus series involved some positive (+) or negative (–) performance of one of five applicants (Filipo, Leandro, Angelo, Salvatore, Francesco) in one of five disciplines (dancing, joking, singing, voices, magical tricks). Performance always covaried with entertainers; the number of positive outcomes for the five entertainers was 1, 2, 3, 4, 5, respectively. This covariation suggests an internal causal attribution to differences between persons. However, in different experimental conditions, performance was either also correlated with the secondary factor, disciplines (with the five disciplines producing 1, 2, 3, 4, 5 + outcomes) or uncorrelated (all five disciplines producing 3 + outcomes). Figure 5.3 shows the stimulus patterns used for these two conditions. Classical attribution theory predicts a clear-cut entertainer attribution in the single-covariate condition, but a less clear-cut (discounted) entertainer attribution in the double-covariate condition, in which performance differences can be as plausibly attributed to disciplines as to entertainers.

However, given such a complex pattern, identifying the differences between entertainers is not an easy task, so that an entertainer attribution may profit from any factor that facilitates the assessment of the entertainer-performance covariance. Indeed, this primary cause is more easily identified in the double-covariate than in the single-covariate condition. Identification is facilitated when performance not only covaries with entertainers but at the same time with disciplines in a highly regular fashion, such that the best entertainer masters all disciplines, the second best only four, the third-ranking entertainer three, the fourth entertainer two, and the worst entertainer succeeds only at the easiest discipline. In the double-covariate condition, then, when both the ability of entertainers and the difficulty of disciplines can be represented on the same joint scale, the focal relation between entertainers and performance was assessed more successfully, producing more entertainer attributions than in the single-covariate condition. These results are at variance with classical attribution theory's discounting principle, but in line with Trope's (1986; Trope & Liberman, 1993) more refined model.

Disciplines

Entertainers

	Dancing	Joking	Singing	Voices	Magical Tricks	
Filipo	+	+	+	+	+	5
Leandro	+	+	+	+	−	4
Angelo	+	+	+	−	−	3
Salvatore	+	+	−	−	−	2
Francesco	+	−	−	−	−	1
	5	4	3	2	1	

(a)

	Dancing	Joking	Singing	Voices	Magical Tricks	
Filipo	+	+	+	+	+	5
Leandro	+	+	−	+	+	4
Angelo	+	−	+	+	−	3
Salvatore	−	+	−	−	+	2
Francesco	−	−	+	−	−	1
	3	3	3	3	3	

(b)

Figure 5.3 Illustration of an effect (+ vs. − performance outcome) that covaries with only one causal factor (entertainers) or with two causal factors (entertainers and disciplines) in different experimental conditions used by Fiedler et al. (1999).

Other experiments within this paradigm demonstrate, as in Simpson's paradox, that when an effect covaries to the same degree with two causes, entertainers and disciplines, the induction conflict cannot be solved statistically. Again, whether performance differences are attributed to entertainers or to disciplines depends on the task ecology, that is, on whether the attention focus during stimulus presentation is on persons or tasks as the primary factor.

These findings corroborate the notion that inductive reasoning is by no means a sole function of statistical information. Neither Simpson's paradox nor other higher-order induction problems can be disambiguated on the basis of statistical frequencies alone. Instead, inductive inferences rely heavily on other factors residing in the ecological context. One important non-statistical source is spatial-temporal contiguity, that is, how close to each other stimulus elements are presented in time and space. For instance, when presenting one causal covariation in close contiguity while dispersing and hiding another covariation between many distracting events, the former gets an ecological advantage. Another source is intensional information (as opposed to extensional), that is, whether a cause somehow fits the format or Gestalt of an effect.

An experiment by Fiedler and Stroehm (1986) may illustrate the joint influence of all three sources of inductive inference, extensional (i.e., statistical), intensional, and contiguity. Participants were presented with a video-taped discussion among three discussants, A, B, and C, and instructed to figure out differences in the frequency of agreement between all three pairs of discussants, AB, AC, and BC. Objectively, AB and AC agreed equally often (i.e., on 10 out of 18 topics), whereas BC agreed less often (6). However, the statistically equivalent pairs, AB and AC, varied in terms of contiguity and intensional information, in different experimental conditions. Contiguity was manipulated by letting one pair agree more often in close temporal succession, whereas the other pair's agreement was often interrupted by an interspersed utterance of the third person. Intensional information was manipulated by letting two people use either the same key words when agreeing on a topic or using different key words. As predicted, judges were generally quite sensitive to statistical information, but the same statistical agreement rate was judged to be higher when contiguity was high, and when intensional relatedness was high.

While statistical information has been the focus of thousands of induction studies on subjective probability in categorization, discrimination, contingency assessment, and higher-order reasoning, the role of contiguity and intensional information has been rarely studied. This neglect of non-statistical sources of inductive inference—both in terms of empirical evidence and conceptual groundwork—stands in sharp contrast to the ecological reality. Well-adapted organisms often have to draw inductive decisions in the absence of large statistical samples, on the basis of one or two observations. Contiguity and intensional relatedness are much more important for adaptive behavior in such situations than frequency distributions.

Ecological correlations and pseudocontingencies

The importance of the ecological input format, in which complex inductive problems are presented, and the ambiguity of statistical indices, is highlighted by the long-known but widely neglected notion of ecological correlations (Robinson, 1950). The size and even the sign of a correlation between two variables can depend dramatically on the unit of analysis, or aggregation level. For example, the correlation between race and illiteracy across individual persons in the United States is negligible. However, when the same correlation is computed between the proportion of Blacks and the proportion of illiterates per region or district, the resulting coefficient will be extremely high. In this special case of a higher-order induction problem, then, the third variable, which moderates the focal correlation, is the level of analysis or "zooming factor" with which ecologies are assessed. Again, the insight to be gained says that statistic-immanent factors—such as sample size, or capacity of data included in an analysis—cannot solve the higher-order contingency problem. Rather, one has to face the puzzle that different levels of analysis yield completely different contingencies. An ecological model, or standpoint, has to be taken to disambiguate the question of what the "real" correlation is (e.g., between race and education, price and quality, or smoking and lung cancer).

The cognitive-psychological analog of ecological correlations has been recently investigated by Fiedler and Freytag (2004), who coined the term pseudocontingencies for a cognitive illusion that reflects the confusion of different aggregation levels. In this new experimental paradigm, participants learn about the base rates of two attributes in different groups or ecologies. For instance, teachers observe that in one subgroup of students the base rate of highly motivated students is high and base rate of high-ability students is also high, whereas in another subgroup the base rates for high-motivation and high-ability students is low. From this alignment of two high base rates in one group and two low base rates in the other group, or one might say from this correlation between base rates at group level, the teacher infers that motivation and ability are correlated across individual students. Thus, when they have to predict or evaluate the performance of individual students with respect to both motivation (frequency of raising hands) and ability (frequency of correct responses), based on a longer period of observing all students in a class, their judgments of both aspects correlate positively, even when the actual correlation at the level of individual students has been exactly zero (Fiedler, Freytag, & Unkelbach, 2007).

Logically, this is a category mistake. The high base rate of highly motivated and high-ability students in one subgroup, along with mostly unmotivated and unable students in the other subgroup, does not imply a correlation at the level of individual students. It is possible that in the former subgroup the high ability trend is mainly due to the less motivated minority, just as in the latter subgroup, the lack of ability may be mainly due to the minority of low-motivation students. However, there is a pervasive tendency for inductive judgments at one level (students) to be influenced by rules that hold at a superordinate level (groups).

Other prominent examples of pseudocontingency illusions would be the inference that the correlation between price and quality of consumer products, which may hold at the level of markets or brands, also holds for individual products, or the illusion in psychological research that findings based on group averages can be used to explain individual behavior. Pseudocontingencies have been shown to generalize across situations in which the genuine individual correlations are available or not, in which the sign of correlation at different levels is the same or different, and across different numbers of groups or ecologies. As a general rule, the strength of the illusion, which is typically rather strong, does not decrease with the participant's cognitive capacity or motivation. On the contrary, more careful processing or motivated participation increases the illusion because the base-rate differences are more likely to be detected when motivation and cognitive capacity are high, rather than low.

Again, analogous to the conclusions drawn from the other paradigms, it has to be acknowledged that pseudocontingency illusions are not a matter of low capacity or low processing motivation. They can hardly be understood within the traditional dual-process framework, or the old heuristics and biases framework, according to which deeper processing is the major remedy against illusions. Rather, pseudocontingencies, like the other higher-order induction tasks, call for an analysis of the ecological conditions under which contingencies have to be learned in reality. Very often, the format in which the environment provides information about two variables (e.g., students' motivation and ability) does not permit teachers to compute contingencies properly, because joint observations of both variables are rarely available, and motivation and ability observations are detached in time and context and mixed up with countless observations pertaining to other variables and contexts. In such a learning environment, assessing category base rates rather than individuating frequencies may be a highly efficient encoding strategy, leading to correct predictions at both category level and individual level on many occasions. Only when the aggregation level used for judgments and decisions differs from the natural aggregation level used for learning and encoding will pseudocontingencies produce erroneous results. This insight is analogous to most cognitive and perceptual illusions, which are functional under their original learning conditions and misleading only when they are carried over to different task conditions.

CONCLUSIONS

To recapitulate, our perspective on the frontiers of induction research relied on a hierarchical taxonomy of induction tasks, ranging from categorization at the most elementary level to discrimination, contingency, and higher-level contingency problems at the most complex level. Although less familiar and less prominently represented in the literature than the other three paradigms, higher-order contingency tasks are of particular interest to major theories of social cognition, such as attribution, dual-process approaches, hybrid models of attitudes, or multiple group memberships. These higher-order induction tasks have been the major focus of the present chapter, drawing on such paradigms as Simpson's paradox or pseudocontingencies. However, we have also reviewed distinct highlights of the remaining three induction paradigms: new evidence on heuristics and biases in simple categorization tasks, insights from signal-detection analyses of discrimination tasks, and the surprising accuracy of contingency assessment based on minimal information.

Despite these distinct topics, convergent insights have been gained from recent research in all four induction paradigms. Most importantly, perhaps, as the research interest has shifted from hunting biases and mental shortcomings to serious attempts to understand the processes and limitations of cognitive illusions, the viability of seemingly obvious normative models has been called into question.

Logical or statistical models are now understood as a similarly severe problem as the bounded rationality of the human mind.

All four paradigms highlight the impossibility of a normative model that offers a globally correct solution to induction problems. With regard to categorization, the true probability that I become the victim of a car accident is undetermined, because the normatively correct reference set required to calculate the probability is arbitrary. After all, I belong to an indefinite number of risk-relevant categories—such as gender, age, profession, geographic residence, a category for driving experience, for type of car, and so forth *ad infinitum*. Therefore, there is an indefinite number of ways to calculate the "true probability," based on all kinds of category subsets. In discrimination, similarly, although the signal-detection model affords a powerful analytical tool, the utility function required to determine benefits and costs associated with hits and false alarms is indeterminate. In the contingency paradigm, too, different statistical models offer different measures of the "true" contingency that holds in an environment (Kareev & Fiedler, 2006). And finally, Simpson's paradox and other higher-order induction problems underscore the insight that different or even opposite realities may exist, for which no normative model can provide a single correct solution.

The common interpretation of bounded rationality—that inductive inference biases reflect the individual's resource limitations—cannot explain many findings that testify to accurate categorization, discrimination, and contingency assessment, even in complex task settings, under cognitive load, and with impoverished input information. This is not to deny the existence of cognitive biases and illusions. What has changed, however, is the theoretical accounts of the causes and learning history of inference mistakes. Many failures arise when accuracy motivation is very high, mental capacity is neither restricted nor depleted, and when judges prove to be very sensitive to the stimulus input proper. However, in spite of such accurate and unbiased processing of the stimulus data, judges fail to recognize that the stimulus sample itself is biased. This selective ability to see the data clearly but to miss the story behind it has been called meta-cognitive myopia (Fiedler, 2000a; Fiedler & Wänke, 2004).

Meta-cognitive myopia offers a plausible account for biases in various induction paradigms, such as overconfidence (Juslin, 1994), the hindsight bias (Winman & Juslin, 2005), anchoring effects (Mussweiler & Strack, 1999), false alarms in medical diagnosis (Swets et al., 2000), or inflated correlations perceived in self-terminated samples (Fiedler & Kareev, 2006). Myopia for the deep structure of the stimulus samples is particularly relevant to the higher-order contingency tasks that have been the focus of this chapter.

ACKNOWLEDGMENTS

The research underlying the present chapter was supported by various grants from the Deutsche Forschungsgemeinschaft to both authors. Helpful comments by Peter Freytag, Tobias Vogel, and Christian Unkelbach are gratefully acknowledged.

NOTES

1. The simulation heuristic (Kahneman & Tversky, 1982) can be considered a variant of availability, with an emphasis on active generation of "new" evidence as distinguished from retrieval of "original" information.
2. As explained by Swets et al. (2000), the lenient criterion of HIV tests reflects the fact that the norm distribution is biased towards risk groups (drug addicts; homosexuals).
3. The term "contingency" usually refers to a correlation between two dichotomous variables, represented as a 2 x 2 table of the frequency distribution of all four combinations of the 2 x 2 variable levels. From these four cell frequencies (a, b, c, d), the contingency can be calculated, either as a symmetrical phi-coefficient, $\Phi = (ad - bc) / \sqrt{ab + cd + ac + bd}$, or as a directional delta-coefficient, $\Delta = (a / a + b) - (c / c + d)$. The symmetrical φ coefficient is the geometric mean of the two Δ coefficients that can be computed from the comparisons of rows and columns, respectively, of a 2 x 2 table. Most examples used in this chapter refer to the contingencies between dichotomous variables, but the theoretical arguments generalize to correlations between continuous variables.

REFERENCES

Allan, L. G., & Jenkins, H. M. (1983). The effect of representations of binary variables on judgment of influence. *Learning and Motivation, 14*, 381–405.

Bargh, J. A., Bond, R. N., Lombardi, W. J., & Tota, M. E. (1986). The additive nature of chronic and temporary sources of construct accessibility. *Journal of Personality and Social Psychology, 50*, 869–878.

Begg, I., Anas, A., & Farinacci, S. (1992). Dissociation of processes in belief: Source recollection, statement familiarity, and the illusion of truth. *Journal of Experimental Psychology: General, 121*, 446–458.

Berndsen, M., Van der Pligt, J., Spears, R., & McGarty, C. (1996). Expectation-based and data-based illusory correlation: the effects of confirming versus disconfirming evidence. *European Journal of Social Psychology, 17*, 899–913.

Bruner, J. S., & Postman, L. J. (1949). On the perception of incongruity: A paradigm. *Journal of Personality, 18*, 206–223.

Chaiken, S. (1987). The heuristic model of persuasion. In M. P. Zanna, J. M. Olson, & P. C. Herman (Eds.), *Social influence: The Ontario Symposium* (Vol. 5, pp. 3–39). Hillsdale, NJ: Lawrence Erlbaum.

Chaiken, S., & Trope, Y. (1999). *Dual-process theories in social psychology*. New York: Guilford Press.

Chapman, L. J., & Chapman, J. P. (1967). Genesis of popular but erroneous diagnostic observations. *Journal of Abnormal Psychology, 72*, 193–204.

Chapman, L. J., & Chapman, J. P. (1969). Illusory correlation as an obstacle to the use of valid psychodiagnostic signs. *Journal of Abnormal Psychology, 74*, 271–280.

Crocker, J. (1981). Judgment of covariation by social perceivers. *Psychological Bulletin, 90*, 272–292.

Denrell, J. (2005). Why most people disapprove of me: Experience sampling in impression formation. *Psychological Review, 112*, 951–978.

Dijksterhuis, A., & van Knippenberg, A. (1996). The knife that cuts both ways: Facilitated and inhibited access to traits as a result of stereotype activation. *Journal of Experimental Social Psychology, 32*, 271–288.

Domjan, M. (2003). *The principles of learning and behavior* (5th ed.). Belmont, CA: Wadsworth.
Dovidio, J. F., Gaertner, S. L., Hodson, G., Houlette, M., & Johnson, K. M. (2005). Social Inclusion and Exclusion: Recategorization and the perception of Intergroup Boundaries. In D. Abrams, J. M. Marques, & M. A. Hogg (Eds.), *The social psychology of inclusion and exclusion* (pp. 246 – 264). Philadelphia, PA: Psychology Press.
Evans, J. St. B. T. (1982). *Psychology of deductive reasoning.* London, UK: Routledge and Kegan Paul.
Fiedler, K. (1988). The dependence of the conjunction fallacy on subtle linguistic factors. *Psychological Research, 50,* 123–129.
Fiedler, K. (1991). The tricky nature of skewed frequency tables: An information loss account of distinctiveness-based illusory correlations. *Journal of Personality and Social Psychology, 60,* 24–36.
Fiedler, K. (1996). Explaining and simulating judgment biases as an aggregation phenomenon in probabilistic, multiple-cue environments. *Psychological Review, 103,* 193–214.
Fiedler, K. (2000a). Beware of samples! A cognitive–ecological sampling approach to judgment biases. *Psychological Review, 107,* 659–676.
Fiedler, K. (2000b). Illusory correlations: A simple associative algorithm provides a convergent account of seemingly divergent paradigms. *Review of General Psychology, 4,* 25–58.
Fiedler, K. (2007). Information ecology and the explanation of social cognition and behavior. In E.T. Higgins & A. Kruglanski (Eds.), *Social psychology. Handbook of basic principles* (pp. 176-200). New York: Guilford.
Fiedler, K., Brinkmann, B., Betsch, R., & Wild, B. (2000). A sampling approach to biases in conditional probability judgments: Beyond baserate neglect and statistical format. *Journal of Experimental Psychology: General, 129,* 1–20.
Fiedler, K., & Freytag, P. (2004). Pseudocontingencies. *Journal of Personality and Social Psychology, 87,* 453–467.
Fiedler, K., Freytag, P., & Unkelbach, C. (2007). Pseudocontingencies in a simulated classroom. *Journal of Personality and Social Psychology, 92,* 665-667.
Fiedler, K., & Juslin, P. (Eds.). (2005). *In the beginning there is a sample: Information sampling as a key to understand adaptive cognition.* New York: Cambridge University Press.
Fiedler, K., & Kareev, Y. (2006). Does decision quality (always) increase with the size of information samples? Some vicissitudes in applying the law of large numbers. *Journal of Experimental Psychology: Learning, Memory & Cognition, 32,* 883–903.
Fiedler, K., & Plessner, H. (2006). Induktives Schließen: Umgang mit Wahrscheinlichkeiten. In J. Funke (Ed.), *Enzyklopädie der Psychologie Band C/II/8: Denken und Problemlösen* (pp. 265–328). Göttingen: Hogrefe.
Fiedler, K., Russer, S., & Gramm, K. (1993). Illusory correlations and memory performance. *Journal of Experimental Social Psychology, 29,* 111–136.
Fiedler, K., & Stroehm, W. (1986). The use of statistical, spatial-temporal, and intensional information in judgments of contingency. *European Journal of Social Psychology, 16,* 385–398.
Fiedler, K., & Wänke, M. (2004). On the vicissitudes of cultural and evolutionary approaches to social cognition: The case of meta-cognitive myopia. *Journal of Cultural and Evolutionary Psychology, 2,* 23–42.
Fiedler, K., & Walther, E. (2004). *Stereotyping as inductive hypothesis testing.* New York: Psychology Press.
Fiedler, K., Walther, E., Freytag, P., & Nickel, S. (2002). Inductive Reasoning and Judgment Interference: Experiments on Simpson's Paradox. *Personality and Social Psychology Bulletin, 29,* 14–27.

Fiedler, K., Walther, E., Freytag, P., & Plessner, H. (2002). Judgment biases in a simulated classroom — A cognitive-environmental approach. *Organizational Behavior and Human Decision Processes, 88,* 527–561.

Fiedler, K., Walther, E., Freytag, P., & Stryczek, E. (2002). Playing mating games in foreign cultures: A conceptual framework and an experimental paradigm for inductive trivariate inference. *Journal of Experimental Social Psychology, 38,* 14–30.

Fiedler, K., Walther, E., & Nickel, S. (1999). Covariation-based attribution: On the ability to assess multiple covariates of an effect. *Personality and Social Psychology Bulletin, 25,* 607–622.

Garcia, J., & Koelling, R. A. (1966). A relation of cue to consequence in avoidance learning. *Psychonomic Society, 4,* 123–124.

Gibson, J. J. (1979). *The ecological approach to visual perception.* Boston, MA: Houghton Mifflin.

Gigerenzer, G. (1991). How to make cognitive illusions disappear. *European Review of Social Psychology, 2,* 83–115.

Gigerenzer, G., & Goldstein, D. G. (1996). Reasoning the fast and frugal way: Models of bounded rationality. *Psychological Review, 103,* 650–669.

Gigerenzer, G., & Hoffrage, U. (1995). How to improve Bayesian reasoning without instruction: Frequency formats. *Psychological Review, 102,* 684–704.

Gigerenzer, G., Hoffrage, U., & Kleinbölting, H. (1991). Probabilistic mental models: A Brunswikian theory of confidence. *Psychological Review, 98,* 506–528.

Gilbert, D. T., & Malone, P. S. (1995). The correspondence bias. *Psychological Bulletin, 117,* 21–38.

Gilovich, T., Griffin, D., & Kahneman, D. (Eds.) (2002). *Heuristics and biases: The psychology of intuitive judgment.* New York: Cambridge University Press.

Goldberg, L. R. (1970). Man versus model of man: A rationale, plus some evidence, for a method of improving on clinical inferences. *Psychological Bulletin, 73,* 422–432.

Goldstein, D. G., & Gigerenzer, G. (2002). Models of ecological rationality: The recognition heuristic. *Psychological Review, 109,* 75–90.

Greene, R.L. (1984). Incidental learning of event frequencies. *Memory and Cognition, 12,* 90–95.

Hamilton, D. L. (1981). Illusory correlations as a basis for stereotyping. In D. L. Hamilton (Ed.), *Cognitive processes in stereotyping and intergroup behavior* (pp. 115–144). Hillsdale, N.J.: Lawrence Erlbaum.

Hamilton, D. L., & Gifford, R. K. (1976). Illusory correlation in interpersonal perception: A cognitive basis of stereotypic judgments. *Journal of Experimental Social Psychology, 12,* 392–407.

Hamilton, D. L., & Rose, T. (1980). Illusory correlation and the maintenance of stereotypic beliefs. *Journal of Personality and Social Psychology, 39,* 832–845.

Hamilton, D. L., & Sherman, S. J. (1989). Illusory correlations: Implications for stereotype theory and research. In D. Bar-Tal, C. F. Graumann, A. W. Kruglanski, & W. Stroebe (Eds.). *Stereotype and prejudice: Changing conceptions* (pp. 59–82). New York: Springer.

Haney, C., & Zimbardo, P. G. (1976). Social roles and role-playing: Observations from the Stanford prison study. In E. P. Hollander & R. G. Hunt (Eds.), *Current perspectives in social psychology* (4th ed., pp. 266–274). New York: Oxford University Press.

Hasher, L., & Zacks, R. T. (1984). Automatic processing of fundamental information: The case of frequency of occurrence. *American Psychologist, 39,* 1372–1388.

Hertwig, R., & Gigerenzer, G. (1999). The "conjunction fallacy" revisited: How intelligent inferences look like reasoning errors. *Journal of Behavioral Decision Making, 12,* 275–305.

Hewstone, M., Rubin, M., & Willis, H. (2002). Intergroup bias. *Annual Review of Psychology, 53,* 575–604.
Higgins, E.T. (1996). Knowledge application: Accessibility, applicability, and salience. In E.T. Higgins & A.W. Kruglanski (Eds.), *Social psychology: Handbook of basic principles* (pp. 133–168). New York: Guilford Press.
Higgins, E.T., Rholes, W.S., & Jones, C.R. (1977). Category accessibility and impression formation. *Journal of Experimental Social Psychology, 13,* 141–154.
Inhelder, B., & Piaget, J. (1958). *The growth of logical thinking from childhood to adolescence.* New York: Basic Books.
Jenkins, H. M., & Ward, W. C. (1965). Judgment of contingency between responses and outcomes. *Psychological Monographs, 79*(1,Whole No. 594).
Jones, E. E., & Harris, V. A. (1967). The attribution of attitudes. *Journal of Experimental Social Psychology, 3,* 1–24.
Juslin, P. (1994). The overconfidence phenomenon as a consequence of informal experimenter-guided selection of almanac items. *Organizational Behavior and Human Decision Processes, 57,* 226–246.
Juslin, P., Olsson, H., & Olsson, A.-C. (2002). Exemplar effects in categorization and multiple-cue judgments. *Journal of Experimental Psychology: General, 132,* 133–156.
Juslin, P., Winman, A., & Olsson, H. (2000). Naive empiricism and dogmatism in confidence research: A critical examination of the hard-easy effect. *Psychological Review, 107,* 384–396.
Jussim, L., & Eccles, J. S. (1992). Teacher expectations II: Construction and reflection of student achievement. *Journal of Personality and Social Psychology, 63,* 947–961.
Kahneman, D., Slovic, P., & Tversky, A. (Eds.) (1982). *Judgment under uncertainty: Heuristics and biases.* Cambridge, UK: Cambridge University Press.
Kahneman, D., & Tversky, A. (1972) Subjective probability: A judgment of representativeness. *Cognitive Psychology, 3,* 430–451.
Kahneman, D., & Tversky, A. (1982). The simulation heuristic. In D. Kahneman, P. Slovic, & A. Tversky (Eds.), *Judgment under uncertainty: Heuristics and biases* (pp. 201–208). Cambridge, England: Cambridge University Press.
Kao, S. -F., & Wasserman, E. A. (1993). Assessment of an information integration account of contingency judgment with examination of subjective cell importance and method of information presentation. *Journal of Experimental Psychology: Learning, Memory, and Cognition, 19,* 1363–1386.
Kareev, Y. (1995). Through a narrow window: Working memory capacity and the detection of covariation. *Cognition, 56,* 263–269.
Kareev, Y. (2000). Seven (indeed, plus minus two) and the detection of correlation. *Psychological Review, 107,* 397–402.
Kareev, Y., & Fiedler, K. (2006). Nonproportional sampling and the amplification of correlations. *Psychological Science, 17,* 715–720.
Kelley, H.H. (1973). The process of causal attribution. *American Psychologist, 28,* 107–128.
Klauer, K. C., & Meiser, T. (2000). A source-monitoring analysis of illusory correlations. *Personality and Social Psychology Bulletin, 26,* 1074–1093.
Klauer, K. C., Musch, J., & Naumer, B. (2000). On belief bias in syllogistic reasoning. *Psychological Review, 107,* 852–884.
Klayman, J., Soll, J. B., González-Vallejo, C., & Barlas, S. (1999). Overconfidence: It depends on how, what, and whom you ask. *Organizational Behavior and Human Decision Processes, 79,* 216–247.
Koriat, A., Fiedler, K., & Bjork, R. A. (2006). The inflation of conditional predictions. *Journal of Experimental Psychology: General, 135,* 429–447.

Krauss, S., & Wang, X. T. (2003). The psychology of the Monty Hall Problem: Discovering psychological mechanism for solving a tenacious brain teaser. *Journal of Experimental Psychology: General, 132,* 3–22.

Krueger, J. I., & Funder, D. C. (2004). Towards a balanced social psychology: Causes, consequences, and cures for the problem-seeking approach to social behavior and cognition. *Behavioral and Brain Sciences, 27,* 313–327.

Malpass, R.S., & Devine, P.G. (1981). Eyewitness identification: Lineup instructions and the absence of the offender. *Journal of Applied Psychology, 66,* 482–489.

McClure, J. (1998). Discounting causes of behavior: Are two reasons better than one? *Journal of Personality and Social Psychology, 74,* 7–20.

McKenzie, C. R. M. (1994). The accuracy of intuitive judgment strategies: Covariation assessment and Bayesian inference. *Cognitive Psychology, 26,* 209–239.

Medin, D. L., Goldstone, R. L., & Genter, D. (1993). Respects for similarity. *Psychological Review, 100,* 254–278.

Miyamoto, Y., & Kitayama, S. (2002). Cultural variation in correspondence bias: The critical role of attitude diagnosticity of socially constrained behavior. *Journal of Personality and Social Psychology, 83,* 1239–1248.

Morris, M.W., & Larrick, R.P. (1995). When one cause casts doubt on another: A normative analysis of discounting in causal attribution. *Psychological Review, 102,* 331–335.

Mullen, B., & Johnson, C. (1990). Distinctiveness-based illusory correlations and stereotyping: A meta-analytic integration. *British Journal of Social Psychology, 29,* 11–28.

Mussweiler, T., & Strack, F. (1999). Hypothesis-consistent testing and semantic priming in the anchoring paradigm: A selective accessibility model. *Journal of Experimental Social Psychology, 35,* 136–164.

Mynatt, C.R., Doherty, M.E., & Tweney, R.D. (1977). Confirmation bias in a simulated research environment: An experimental study of scientific inference. *Quarterly Journal of Experimental Psychology, 29,* 85–95.

Newman, J., Wolff, W. T., & Hearst, E. (1980). The feature-positive effect in adult human subjects. *Journal of Experimental Psychology: Human Learning and Memory, 6,* 630–650.

Nosofsky, R.M., & Johansen, M.K. (2000). Exemplar-based accounts of "multiple-system" phenomena in perceptual categorization. *Psychonomic Bulletin and Review, 7,* 375–402.

Olson, J. M., Roese, N., & Zanna, M. P. (1996). Expectancies. In E. T. Higgins & A. W. Kruglanski (Eds.), *Social psychology: Handbook of basic principles* (pp. 211–238). New York: Guilford Press.

Piaget, J. (1963). *The psychology of intelligence.* New York: Routledge.

Plessner, H. (1999). Expectation biases in gymnastics judging. *Journal of Sport and Exercise Psychology, 21,* 131–144.

Plessner, H., Freytag, P., & Fiedler, K. (2000). Expectancy-effects without expectancies: Illusory correlations based on cue-overlap. *European Journal of Social Psychology, 30,* 837–851.

Plessner, H., & Haar, T. (2006). Sports performance judgments from a social cognitive perspective. *Psychology of Sport and Exercise, 7,* 555-575.

Plessner, H., Hartmann, C., Hohmann, N., & Zimmermann, I. (2001). Achtung Stichprobe! Der Einfluss der Informationsgewinnung auf die Bewertung sportlicher Leistungen. *Psychologie und Sport, 8,* 91–100.

Robinson, W. S. (1950). Ecological correlations and the behavior of individuals. *American Sociological Review, 15,* 351–357.

Rosenthal, R. (1968). Self-fulfilling prophecy. *Psychology Today, 2,* 46–51.

Ross, L., & Nisbett, R. E. (1991). *The person and the situation: Perspectives of social psychology.* New York: McGraw-Hill.

Schaller, M. (1992). Sample size, aggregation, and statistical reasoning in social inference. *Journal of Experimental Social Psychology, 28,* 65–85.

Schaller, M., & O'Brien, M. (1992). "Intuitive analysis of covariance" and group stereotype formation. *Personality and Social Psychology Bulletin, 18,* 776–785.

Schooler, L., & Hertwig, R. (2005). How forgetting aids heuristic inference. *Psychological Review, 112,* 610–628.

Schwarz, N., & Bless, H. (1992). Constructing reality and its alternatives: An inclusion/exclusion model of assimilation and contrast effects in social judgment. In H. Martin & A. Tesser (Eds.). *The construction of social judgment* (pp. 217–245). Hillsdale, NJ: Lawrence Erlbaum.

Schwarz, N., Bless, H., Strack, F., Klumpp, G., Rittenauer-Schatka, H., & Simons, A. (1991). Ease of retrieval as information: Another look at the availability heuristic. *Journal of Personality and Social Psychology, 61,* 195–202.

Sedlmeier, P., Hertwig, R., & Gigerenzer, G. (1998). Are judgments of the positional frequencies of letters systematically biased due to availability? *Journal of Experimental Psychology: Learning, Memory, and Cognition, 24,* 754–770.

Sedlmeier, P., & Gigerenzer, G. (1997). Intuitions about sample size: The empirical law of large numbers. *Journal of Behavioral Decision Making, 10,* 33–51.

Shweder, R. A. (1982). Fact and artifact in trait perception: The systematic distortion hypothesis. In B. A. Maher, & B. Maher (Eds.), *Progress in personality research* (Vol. 2, pp. 65–101). New York: Academic Press.

Simpson, E. H. (1951). The interpretation of interaction in contingency tables. *Journal of the Royal Statistical Society, Ser, B, 13,* 238–241.

Spears, R., Eiser, J. R., & Van der Pligt, J. (1987). Further evidence for expectation-based illusory correlations. *European Journal of Social Psychology, 17,* 253–258.

Spelke, E.S. (2005). Sex differences in intrinsic aptitude for mathematics and science? *American Psychologist, 60,* 950–958.

Stangor, C., & McMillan, D. (1992). Memory for expectancy-congruent and expectancy-incongruent information: A review of the social and social developmental literatures. *Psychological Bulletin, 111,* 42–61.

Strack, F., & Deutsch, R. (2004). Reflective and impulsive determinants of social behavior. *Personality and Social Psychology Review, 8,* 220–247.

Strack, F., & Mussweiler, T. (1997). Explaining the enigmatic anchoring effect: Mechanisms of selective accessibility. *Journal of Personality and Social Psychology, 73,* 437–446.

Strack, F., Schwarz, N., Bless, H., Kübler, A., & Wänke, M. (1993). Awareness of the influence as a determinant of assimilation versus contrast. *European Journal of Social Psychology, 23,* 53–62.

Swets, J., Dawes, R.M., & Monahan, J. (2000). Psychological science can improve diagnostic decisions. *Psychological Science in the Public Interest, 1,* Whole No. 1.

Taylor, S. E., & Fiske, S. T. (1978). Salience, attention, and attribution: Top of the head phenomena. In L. Berkowitz (Ed.). *Advances in experimental social psychology* (Vol. 11, pp. 249–288). New York: Academic Press.

Trope, Y. (1986). Identification and inference processes in dispositional attribution. *Psychological Review, 93,* 239–257.

Trope, Y., & Liberman, A. (1993). The use of trait conceptions to identify other people's behavior and to draw inferences about their personalities. *Personality and Social Psychology Bulletin, 19,* 553–562.

Tversky, A. (1977). Features of similarity. *Psychological Review, 84,* 327–352.

Tversky, A., & Kahneman, D. (1974). Judgment under uncertainty: Heuristics and biases. *Science, 185,* 1124–1131.

Tversky, A., & Kahneman, D. (1973). Availability: A heuristic for judging frequency and probability. *Cognitive Psychology, 5,* 207–232.

von Restorff, H. (1933). Über die Wirkung von Bereichsbildungen im Spurenfeld. *Psychologische Forschung, 18,* 299–342.

Waldmann, M. R., & Hagmayer, Y. (2001). Estimating causal strength: The role of structural knowledge and processing effort. *Cognition, 82,* 27–58.

Wasserman, E. A., Elek, S. M., Chatlosh, D. L., & Baker, A. G. (1993). Rating causal relations: Role of probability in judgments of response-outcome contingency. *Journal of Experimental Psychology: Learning, Memory, and Cognition, 19,* 174–188.

Wells, G. L. (2001). Eyewitness lineups: Data, theory, and policy. *Psychology, Public Policy, and Law, 7,* 791–801.

Winman, A., & Juslin, P. (2005). "I'm m/n Confident that I'm Correct": Confidence in foresight and hindsight as a sampling probability. In K. Fiedler & P. Juslin (Eds.), *In the beginning there is a sample: Information sampling as a key to understand adaptive cognition* (pp. 409–439). New York: Cambridge University Press.

Zajonc, R. B. (1980). Feeling and thinking: Preferences need no inferences. *American Psychologist, 35,* 151–175.

Zuckerman, M., DePaulo, B. M., & Rosenthal, R. (1981). Verbal and nonverbal communication of deception. *Advances in Experimental Social Psychology, 14,* 1–57.

6

Mental Construal in Social Judgment

NORBERT SCHWARZ

INTRODUCTION

A classic hallmark of the social psychological analysis of human behavior is the emphasis on the power of situations: Whereas laypersons commonly explain others' behavior by reference to their dispositions, social psychologists documented that situational influences dwarf the influence of individuals' dispositions (for a review, see Ross & Nisbett, 1991). A second hallmark of social psychological analysis emphasizes that people do not respond to the situation per se but to the situation *as they see it*. Hence, understanding the mental processes underlying people's construction of the world in which they live is a core task of social psychology. Over the last three decades, this task has been tackled within the theoretical framework of social cognition research. This chapter reviews the key lessons learned.

Mental representations are based on information that comes to mind at a given point in time. What comes to mind can be a function of haphazard influences as well as of the person's goals and numerous other variables relevant to daily action. The first section addresses these variables and introduces principles of accessibility and situated cognition. However, knowing what comes to mind is not enough to predict a person's judgment. Instead, the same piece of accessible information can have opposite effects on judgment, depending on how it is used. The second section discusses issues of information use and the emergence of assimilation and contrast effects. In addition, the implications of accessible information may be qualified by metacognitive experiences that accompany the thought process, and people may sometimes rely on their feelings instead of any descriptive information about the target of judgment. These issues are touched on in the third section and addressed in more detail by Bless and colleagues (chapter 8, this volume). Finally, the chapter concludes with a discussion of the conditions under which mental construals assessed at one point in time are likely to predict behavior at a later time.

WHAT COMES TO MIND

A core principle of social cognition theorizing holds that our mental construals of the world are based on the information that is most accessible at the time (for a review, see Higgins, 1996). Social cognition experiments illustrate this accessibility principle by bringing information to mind that might otherwise not be considered. In daily life, however, the information that is most likely to come to mind is meaningfully related to the person's goals and current situation. Both aspects are addressed in turn.

The Accessibility Principle

The principle that mental construals are based on the information that is most accessible at the time applies to how we make sense of new information as well as to how we form judgments based on information retrieved from memory.

Making Sense of New Information Suppose you learn that whenever my friend Donald starts something new, he is well aware that he will excel at it. Do you admire Donald for his confidence, or do you despise him for being so conceited? As a classic experiment by Higgins, Rholes, and Jones (1977; see also Srull & Wyer, 1979) demonstrated, your reaction may have little to do with Donald. Specifically, Higgins and colleagues had participants learn a number of trait concepts as part of an allegedly unrelated experiment before they exposed them to a story about Donald. Participants' impressions of Donald depended on the trait rendered accessible by the preceding task: They interpreted his behavior as confident (and likable) when exposed to the concept "confident" but as conceited (and dislikable) when exposed to the concept "conceited." This and related findings (see Higgins, 1998; Wyer & Srull, 1989) illustrate that we interpret new information in terms of the first applicable concept that comes to mind—and which concept that is, is often a function of haphazard influences. Not surprisingly, such trait-priming effects are not observed when the behavior is unambiguous and hence does not allow the application of different concepts (e.g., Higgins et al., 1977).

More important, people only rely on the concept that comes to mind when they perceive it as their response to the new information. In most cases, the sheer fact that something comes to mind is sufficient to suggest that it is relevant to what we are thinking about—or why else would it come to mind now? Higgins (1998) refers to this assumption as the "aboutness" principle. When people are aware that "conceited" may only come to mind because it was part of an earlier task, they are unlikely to draw on this concept in forming an impression. Accordingly, trait-priming effects are not observed when people are reminded of the earlier trait-priming task (Strack, Schwarz, Bless, Kübler, & Wänke, 1993) or when the task is sufficiently blatant to make people aware of its possible influence (Martin, 1986). In these cases, people may attempt to correct for the perceived influence. Because it is difficult to determine what one's judgment would have been without the perceived influence, correction attempts often result in overcorrection, that is, judgments that are biased in the opposite direction (e.g., Martin, 1986; Strack et al., 1993; for reviews, see Strack & Hannover, 1996; Wilson & Brekke, 1994).

Memory-Based Judgments The accessibility principle also holds for memory-based judgments. When people are asked to form a judgment, they rarely, if ever, retrieve all information that may be relevant to it. Instead, they truncate the search process as soon as enough information has come to mind to form a judgment with sufficient certainty (e.g., Bodenhausen & Wyer, 1987). Accordingly, the information that is most accessible in memory, and hence comes to mind most easily, exerts a disproportionate influence.

For example, Schwarz, Strack, and Mai (1991; see also Strack, Martin, & Schwarz, 1988) asked survey respondents to report their marital satisfaction and their general life satisfaction in different question orders. When the general life satisfaction question was asked first, it correlated with marital satisfaction, $r = .32$. Reversing the question order, however, increased this correlation to $r = .67$. This reflects that the marital satisfaction question brought marriage-related information to mind that respondents drew on in forming a representation of their lives in general. This increase in correlation was attenuated to $r = .43$ when questions about three different life domains (job, leisure time, and marriage) preceded the general question, thus bringing a more diverse range of information to mind. Parallel influences were observed in the mean reports. Happily married respondents reported higher, and unhappily married respondents reported lower, general life satisfaction when their attention was drawn to their marriage by the preceding question. In short, respondents did not review myriad different aspects of their lives to arrive at a judgment. Instead, they relied on the information that came to mind most easily, namely, the information brought to mind by a preceding question (for a more extensive review of related findings, see Schwarz & Bohner, 2001).

Many other characteristics of the judgment task can exert a similar influence. For example, Schkade and Kahneman (1997) asked students living in the Midwest of the United States if they would be happier living in California? One salient feature that distinguishes the Midwest from California is the climate, and not surprisingly, Midwesterners believed that life would be better in sunny California—much as Californians believed that life would be worse in the Midwest. Yet, a comparison of students' actual life satisfaction revealed no difference between California and the Midwest. Again, respondents focused on the most accessible feature, namely, the salient difference in climate, at the expense of other information—missing that many other aspects of life would remain very similar. Thus, our tendency to truncate the search process early and to focus on the most accessible information can give rise to profound *focusing illusions*, leading us to overestimate the relevance of whatever we focus on.

Temporary Versus Chronic Accessibility   In the examples, information was rendered *temporarily* accessible by a preceding task or by characteristics of the question asked. In daily life, other haphazard influences, like exposure to the news (e.g., Iyengar, 1987), have been found to have similar effects. In addition, information can be chronically accessible and may come to mind independent of contextual influences (for a review, see Higgins, 1996). For example, persons who are newly married or who go through a divorce may always consider marriage-related information when evaluating their lives, and persons who are preoccupied with confidence may apply this concept independent of a preceding priming task. In general, temporarily accessible information is the source of context effects in judgment, whereas chronically accessible information lends judgments some context-independent stability (see Schwarz & Bohner, 2001).

Situated Cognition

At first glance, one may wonder how people make it through the day when their thought processes are as profoundly shaped by haphazard influences as the above examples illustrate. One answer is that the context sensitivity of human cognition is more adaptive in daily life than many social cognition experiments suggest. In daily life, the information brought to mind by a given context is indeed often relevant to the person's current situation, thus facilitating adequately contextualized responses. As William James (1890, p. 333) observed more than a century ago, "My thinking is first and last and always for the sake of my doing." From this perspective, human cognition stands in the service of action. To serve action, cognition needs to be responsive to our goals and to the immediate social and physical environment in which we pursue them. This pragmatic, motivated, and situated nature of cognition has recently received increased attention (for reviews, see Barsalou, 2005; Smith & Semin, 2004).

Situated Concepts   Cognitive psychologists have long assumed that we acquire knowledge about a category (say, "chairs") by abstracting it from the exemplars we encounter (living room chairs, office chairs, airplane chairs, etc.). The resulting representation of the category chairs is typically thought of as a list of the shared core features of the exemplars. Recent research indicated, however, that such abstract and context invariant knowledge is not what is most accessible in a given situation. Instead, which features are most likely to come to mind depends on whether we think about chairs in the context of a living room or of an airplane (for a review, see Yeh & Barsalou, in press). Social psychological research reiterates this theme. The same face of a young African American elicits a more positive response when shown in the context of a church scene than when shown in the context of a street corner scene (Wittenbrink, Judd, & Park, 2001). In both cases, the context influences which attributes of the general category (chairs, African Americans) come to mind and are used in forming a representation of the target. This context sensitivity of accessible knowledge facilitates meaningful interaction with the environment (and results in counterintuitive effects when an arbitrary context is introduced in experiments).

Levels of Construal Human actions can be represented at many different levels of abstraction—from "having dinner" to the component acts of "ordering," "being served," and so on, to the even lower-level representation of using the utensils. The level of representation chosen is usually the one that is most functional in the present context. When all goes smoothly, higher-level representations (having dinner) are fine, but when obstacles are encountered, say in the form of a dull knife, attention shifts to the lower level—and after dinner, the knife may only be remembered when it caused a problem. Numerous variables can influence at which level of abstraction an activity is represented, as some examples may illustrate. In all cases, the relevant variables can be conceptualized as bearing on the person's goal-directed actions.

As seen in the example, attention shifts to lower levels, resulting in a more fine-grained representation when people encounter a problem (see Wegner & Vallacher, 1986, for a review). However, a concrete problem is not always needed, and more remote problem signals have been found to exert a similar influence. For example, we usually feel good when things are going smoothly and bad when things are going wrong. Hence, negative affect can serve as a generic problem signal, and people in a sad mood attend more to the specifics at hand, form more fine-grained categories, and encode and recall information at a lower level of abstraction (for a review, see Schwarz & Clore, 2007). Similar shifts in processing strategy have been observed for affective environmental cues and presenting information on paper of an upbeat red or depressed blue hue is sufficient to affect people's processing strategies (Soldat, Sinclair, & Mark, 1997). Throughout, such findings illustrate that mental processes are tuned to meet situational requirements.

If cognition stands in the service of action, we may also assume that temporally proximal actions (e.g., what we plan to do tomorrow) are represented at a more detailed level than temporally distant actions (e.g., what we plan to do next year). An impressive program of research by Trope, Liberman, and colleagues supports this prediction (for a review, see Trope, Liberman, & Wakslak, 2007). Not surprisingly, people's decisions are more likely to be based on their general goals than on a consideration of specific means and ends when the act is in the distant rather than the near future—after all, the specifics of the distant future are still uncertain. However, people also categorize objects associated with an event into fewer and broader categories when the event is in the distant rather than the near future (e.g., Liberman, Sagristano, & Trope, 2002), indicating that the influence of temporal distance on the level of construal extends beyond the consideration of means and ends.

Similarly, perceivers use more generalized, abstract concepts when describing and predicting temporally distant behaviors (Nussbaum, Trope, & Liberman, 2003). Again, such changes in the level of construal are likely to support goal-directed action.

Summary

As this selective review illustrates, the mental representations we form of the world are highly context dependent. We rarely consider all information that may be relevant and instead rely on the subset that is most accessible at the time. In daily life, this is often adaptive because what comes to mind is likely to reflect our goals and the situation in which we pursue them. Similarly, the representation's level of abstraction is often tuned to our current needs. However, this flexible, situated nature of human cognition also opens the door for many haphazard influences, as numerous social cognition experiments illustrate. Next, we turn to the judgment processes for which accessible information serves as input.

INFORMATION USE: CONSTRUCTING TARGETS AND STANDARDS

How accessible information influences a judgment depends on how it is used. Evaluative judgments that are based on features of the target (rather than on the perceiver's affective response, addressed in another section) require two mental representations: a representation of the target and a representation of a standard against which the target is evaluated (Schwarz & Bless, 1992a, in press). Information that is used in forming a representation of the target results in *assimilation effects*; that is, the inclusion of positive (negative) information results in a more positive (negative) judgment. Accordingly, the happy participants in Schwarz, Strack, and Mai's (1991) marital satisfaction-life satisfaction experiment reported higher, and the unhappily married participants lower, general life satisfaction when their marriage was brought to mind through a preceding question. Conversely, information that is used in forming a representation results in a *contrast effect*; that is, more positive (negative) information results in a more positive (negative) standard, against which the target is evaluated less (more) favorably. Compared to one's wonderful marriage, for example, one's modest job may seem even less attractive. Hence, the *same* piece of accessible information can have opposite effects, depending on how it is used.

The variables that influence the use of information have been conceptualized in Schwarz and Bless's (1992a, 2007) inclusion/exclusion model. The model assumes that perceivers tacitly ask themselves three questions, which serve as filters that channel information use: Why does it come to mind? Does it bear on the target? Is it conversationally appropriate to use this information? .

Why Does It Come to Mind?

The first filter is: "Am I only thinking of this information because it was brought to mind due to some irrelevant influence?" If so, the accessible information is not used in forming a representation of the target, as already discussed. Accordingly, awareness of the priming episode, for example, undermines use of the primed information, resulting in contrast effects (e.g., Lombardi, Higgins, & Bargh, 1987; Martin, 1986; Strack et al., 1993).

Does It Bear on the Target?

When the information passes this first test, the second filter is, "Does this information represent a feature of the target?" This decision is subject to myriad variables known to influence categorization processes (for reviews, see Schwarz & Bless, 1992a, 2007).

Category Structure   One of these variables is the categorical relationship between the contextual information and the target of judgment. As an example, consider the impact of political scandals on judgments of the trustworthiness of politicians. Not surprisingly, thinking about a politician who was involved in a scandal, say Richard Nixon, decreases trust in American politicians in general. This reflects that the exemplar is included in the representation formed of the superordinate category "American politicians." If the trustworthiness question pertains to a specific politician, however, say Bill Clinton, the primed exemplar cannot be included in the representation formed of the target—after all, Clinton is not Nixon. In this case, Richard Nixon may serve as a standard of comparison, relative to which Bill Clinton seems very trustworthy. An experiment with German exemplars confirmed these predictions (Schwarz & Bless, 1992b): Thinking about a politician who was involved in a scandal decreased the trustworthiness of politicians in general but increased the trustworthiness of every specific exemplar assessed. Similarly, Konrath and Schwarz (2005) observed that the increased accessibility of Martin Luther King Jr. during the MLK holiday exerted a positive influence on judgments of African Americans in general (a superordinate category) but a negative influence on judgments of other specific African American leaders.

In general, the same information is likely to result in assimilation effects in the evaluation of superordinate target categories (which allow for the inclusion of all information pertaining to subordinate categories) but in contrast effects in the evaluation of lateral target categories (which are mutually exclusive). Accordingly, the previous discussion of levels of construal also bears on the emergence of assimilation and contrast effects: Construals at lower levels of abstraction result in narrower categories, which are more likely to give rise to contrast effects.

Category Boundaries   How we categorize a given piece of information further depends on the salience of category boundaries. For example, Strack, Schwarz, and Gschneidinger (1985) asked participants to recall a positive or negative life event that happened either recently or several years ago. When the event was recent, participants were more satisfied with their lives after recalling a positive rather than negative event, whereas the opposite pattern was obtained for distant events. This reflects that recent events could be included in the representation of the target category "my life now," whereas the distant events could not and hence served as a standard of comparison. In follow-up experiments (reviewed in Schwarz & Strack, 1999), freshmen were asked during their first month at college to recall a positive or negative life event that happened "during the last 2 years." Replicating the earlier findings, these recent events resulted in assimilation effects on current life satisfaction. Other freshmen were given the same task except for a small addition to the instructions: They were asked to recall a positive or negative event that happened "during the last 2 years, that is, before you came to the university." This addition emphasized a category boundary that invited them to chunk the stream of life into their high school time and college time. As expected, they now reported lower current life satisfaction after recalling a positive rather than negative "high school" event. In combination, these findings illustrate that the same information can make life look good or bad, depending on how it is used. Hence, today's source of misery can always become tomorrow's source of happiness—provided that you chunk the stream of life in the right way (Schwarz & Strack, 2007).

Feature Overlap Another general determinant of categorization is feature overlap: A given stimulus is more likely to be assigned to a given category the more it shares category features. For example, Herr, Sherman, and Fazio (1983; see also Herr, 1986) observed assimilation effects when a target stimulus was rated in the context of moderate stimuli but contrast effects when it was rated in the context of extreme stimuli. They concluded that "to the extent that a comparison of features of the activated category and the target stimulus results in matching or overlap, a judgment of category membership should occur" (Herr, 1986, p. 1107), eliciting an assimilation effect. If the overlap is insufficient, on the other hand, thus constituting an exclusion relationship, "the priming exemplars serve as standards of comparison" (Herr, 1986, p. 1107), resulting in a contrast effect. Findings of this type converge on the conclusion that "distinct" information (low feature overlap) elicits contrast effects, whereas "nondistinct" information (high feature overlap) elicits assimilation effects, as Stapel and colleagues observed in numerous experiments (e.g., Stapel & Koomen, 2000; Stapel & Winkielman, 1998).

Summary In sum, *any* variable that influences the categorization of information can determine whether a given piece of information is included in the representation of the target, giving rise to assimilation effects or, in the representation of the standard, giving rise to contrast effects (for extended reviews, see Biernat, 2005; Schwarz & Bless, 2007). As reviewed in this chapter, research into situated cognition identified numerous variables that influence at which level of detail we mentally represent the world, that is, whether we form broad or narrow categories. These variables, from goals to moods and temporal distance, are also likely to influence how a given piece of information is used and hence whether it results in assimilation or contrast effects in evaluative judgment. This possibility provides a promising avenue for further research.

Conversational Norms

The third and final filter pertains to the norms of conversational conduct that govern information use in conversations: "Is it conversationally appropriate to use this information?" Conversational norms prohibit redundancy and invite speakers to provide information that is new to the recipient rather than information that the recipient already has (for a review, see Schwarz, 1994). Hence, highly accessible information is not used when it violates this conversational norm, again resulting in contrast effects (e.g., Schwarz, Strack, and Mai, 1991; Strack et al., 1988).

Information that passes all three tests is included in the representation formed of the target and results in assimilation effects. Information that fails any one of these tests is excluded from the representation formed of the target but may be used in forming a representation of the standard, resulting in contrast effects.

The Size of Assimilation and Contrast Effects

In addition to specifying the mental construal processes underlying the emergence of assimilation and contrast effects, the inclusion/exclusion model (Schwarz & Bless, 1992a, 2007) also predicts the size of these effects. As already seen in the discussion of Schwarz, Strack, and Mai's (1991) marital satisfaction study, the impact of marital satisfaction on general life satisfaction decreased as a broader range of information about respondents' lives was brought to mind. This observation illustrates the *set size principle*, which determines the size of context effects: The impact of a given piece of information decreases with the amount and extremity of other information that is used in forming the respective representation. Hence, a given piece of temporarily (e.g., Bless, Igou, Schwarz, & Wänke, 2000) or chronically (e.g. Wänke, Bless, & Schwarz, 1998) accessible information results in smaller assimilation or contrast effects the more other information is used to construct a mental representation of the target or the standard, respectively. Bless, Schwarz, and Wänke (2003) provided a more detailed discussion of these processes.

Summary

As this selective review illustrates, how we see the world does not only depend on which information comes to mind at a given point in time—it also depends on how we use this information. The same piece of information elicits an assimilation effect when it is used to form a mental representation of the target but a contrast effect when it is used to form a mental representation of the standard. Hence, merely thinking of a positive life event, for example, does not guarantee a positive outlook—in fact, last year's exciting vacation may only make our daily routines look more dreadful (Schwarz & Strack, 2006). The general variables underlying information use are reasonably well understood (for a review, see Schwarz & Bless, 2007), although much more will be learned as we increasingly understand how people's goals, and the obstacles they encounter, shape the mental representations they form in daily life.

EXPERIENTIAL INFORMATION

So far, this chapter has focused on declarative information about the object of judgment and addressed which information is likely to come to mind and how it is used. However, thinking is accompanied by a variety of subjective experiences, and these experiences can serve as a source of information in their own right. This section discusses what people learn from subjective experiences, like the ease or difficulty with which they can bring some information to mind or their emotional responses to what they think about. While a detailed review of the interplay of feeling and thinking is beyond the scope of this chapter, some examples can highlight the role of experiential information in mental construal (see Schwarz & Clore, 2007, for a comprehensive discussion).

Metacognitive Experiences

As every reader knows from personal experience, recalling information or generating reasons for a course of action can be experienced as easy or difficult. These *accessibility experiences* are informative in their own right and can qualify the conclusions drawn from what comes to mind. Hence, we need to consider accessible thought content (what comes to mind) as well as subjective accessibility experiences (how easily it comes to mind) in predicting a person's judgments.

Based on what comes to mind, we would expect, for example, that people judge themselves as more assertive after recalling many rather than few examples of their own assertive behavior. Yet, recalling many examples is often experienced as difficult, and this difficulty suggests that there may not be that many examples after all. Hence, Schwarz, Bless, Strack, Klumpp, Rittenauer-Schatka, and Simons (1991) observed that participants judged themselves as less assertive after recalling many rather than few examples of assertive behavior, in contrast to what accessible thought content would suggest. In general, judgments are only consistent with the implications of accessible content when recall or thought generation is experienced as easy, but are opposite to the implications of accessible content when recall or thought generation is experienced as difficult. Finally, accessibility experiences exert no influence when their informational value for the judgment at hand is discredited; in this case, people discount the experience and turn to accessible content as the most diagnostic source of information. For example, when participants in the Schwarz, Bless et al. (1991) study were told that background music played to them may interfere with their recall task, they discounted the experienced difficulty and reported higher assertiveness after recalling many rather than few assertive behaviors, thus reversing the otherwise observed pattern. Bless, Keller, and Igou (chapter 8, this volume) and Schwarz (2004) reviewed this literature and discussed its implications.

Similarly, new information, like a text we read or a picture we see, can be easy or difficult to process. This experience of high or low *processing fluency* can again serve as input into a variety of judgments (for reviews, see Reber, Schwarz, & Winkielman, 2004; Schwarz, 2004). Of particular interest to social psychologists is that high processing fluency feeds into judgments of familiarity, truth, and liking.

Familiar information is usually easier to process than unfamiliar information. Hence, people often infer from ease of processing that the presented information is familiar—even when fluent processing results merely from presentation variables like long exposure times, good figure-ground contrast, an easy-to-read print font, or preceding semantic primes. One consequence of this feeling of familiarity is erroneous recognition of new information as previously seen (for a review, see Kelley & Rhodes, 2002). Another consequence is that fluently processed information is more likely to be accepted as true—the feeling of familiarity suggests that one has heard this before, so there is probably something to it. Simply printing a statement like "Orsono is a city in Chile" in a color that makes it easy rather than difficult to read against a colored background is enough to increase its acceptance as true (Reber & Schwarz, 1999). Similarly, substantively equivalent statements are more likely to be judged true when they are presented in a rhyming rather than nonrhyming form (McGlone & Tofighbakhsh, 2000); that "birds of a feather flock together" is certainly true—but "birds of a feather flock conjointly" just does not have that ring of truth to it.

In addition, fluent processing is experienced as affectively positive, as captured by psychophysiological measures (Winkielman & Cacioppo, 2001). Like other sources of positive affect, discussed next, the positive affective response elicited by high processing fluency gives rise to more positive judgments of liking, beauty, and preference (see Reber et al., 2004, for a review).

Affective Response

Instead of basing their judgments on the mental representation formed of the target, people can simplify the judgment process by consulting their apparent affective response to the target, essentially asking themselves, "How do I feel about this?" (for reviews, see Pham, 2004; Schwarz & Clore, 2007). When their feelings are indeed elicited by the target, they provide diagnostic information, making this a useful heuristic. Unfortunately, however, we have only one window on our experience and may misread feelings that are due to another source as our apparent response to the target. This gives rise to more positive judgments when people are in happy rather than sad mood unless the informational value of the mood for the judgment at hand is called into question (Schwarz & Clore, 1983). For the same reason, the positive affect associated with fluent processing results in more positive evaluations of fluently processed targets (Reber et al., 2004).

Finally, specific emotions provide information that goes beyond the global positive/negative valence information provided by moods. Which information emotions provide can be derived from their underlying appraisal patterns (Ellsworth & Scherer, 2003; Ortony, Clore, & Collins, 1988). Sadness, for example, signals a loss or lack of reward that is not attributed to the causal action of another agent; when it is attributed to the causal action of another agent, it gives rise to anger. Accordingly, sadness and anger inform us not only about a loss but also about its likely cause, giving rise to different attributions in judgment studies (e.g., Keltner, Ellsworth, & Edwards, 1993).

Implications

As these examples illustrate, experiential information can play an important role in mental construal. First, metacognitive experiences can qualify the implications of accessible declarative information. Finding it difficult to recall many assertive behaviors, we may conclude that there are not many; finding it easy to process a statement, we may conclude that it seems familiar and is probably true. Second, specific emotions can inform us about features of the current situation. Feeling angry rather than sad in light of a loss implies that the loss was caused by the actions of another person, or else we would not be so angry. Such affect-based attributions may become part of the mental representation of what happened, exerting an influence after the affect dissipated. Third, as seen in the section on situated cognition, feelings that signal a benign or problematic situation can influence our processing style and determine at which level of detail a situation is represented (Schwarz, 2002). Finally, by asking ourselves, "How do I feel about this?" we may arrive at evaluative judgments without any detailed review of the features of the target, relying on our feelings rather than our mental representation of the target as the crucial input, thus dissociating the attributes of the target from its evaluation.

FROM JUDGMENT TO BEHAVIOR

As the reviewed research indicates, our mental representations of the world are situated and highly context dependent—and so are the judgments based on these representations. The same mental construal logic applies to people's behavioral decisions. People respond to objects, situations, and people as they see them—and how they see them is subject to contextual influences. It is therefore not surprising that psychologists' attempts to predict people's behavior in a specific situation from their general attitudes, reported in a different situation, have met with limited success (for a review, see Eagly & Chaiken, 1993). From a mental construal perspective, judgments formed at Time 1 are only likely to predict behavior at Time 2 when the judgment and the behavioral decision are based on similar mental representations. This *matching principle* (Lord & Lepper, 1999; Schwarz & Bohner, 2001) provides a parsimonious conceptualization of core findings of the extensive literature on attitude-behavior consistency.

First, illustrating the general matching principle, judgment and behavior are likely to be consistent when the temporary representation formed of the target at the time of judgment matches the temporary representation formed at the time of behavior. For example, Ramsey, Lord, Wallace, and Pugh (1994) observed that participants' attitude judgments toward former substance abusers were a better predictor of their behavior toward an exemplar when the description of the exemplar matched rather than mismatched participants' representation of the group, as assessed 2 weeks earlier. Because many exemplars provide a poor match with our general representation of the category to which they belong, it is difficult to predict behaviors toward exemplars from judgments about the category, resulting in the usually observed low judgment-behavior relationship.

Second, suppose that the attitude judgment is based on respondents' mood at the time of judgment (Schwarz & Clore, 2007). In this case, we may be hard put to detect any judgment-behavior consistency unless respondents happen to be in the same mood in the behavioral situation, and the behavior is inconsequential, thus rendering one's apparent affective response sufficient for a decision. Moreover, any other difference in processing motivation at the time of judgment and behavior is similarly likely to decrease the judgment-behavior relationship (e.g., Blessum,

Lord, & Sia, 1998). When asked in a consumer survey how much we like a Volvo, for example, we are likely to draw on fewer features of the Volvo than when pondering whether to actually buy one, thus increasing the likelihood of mismatches between the two representations. In a similar vein, Wilson and his colleagues (for a review, see Wilson & Hodges, 1992) observed that writing an essay that justifies one's attitude judgment can undermine the judgment-behavior relationship—in writing the essay, participants draw on many aspects they may not consider in the behavioral situation, thus reducing the match between the relevant representations.

Third, as Millar and Tesser (1992) noted, we engage in some behaviors for their instrumental value in reaching a goal and in other behaviors for the pleasures they provide. If so, judgments should be a better predictor of instrumental behaviors when the judgment is based on a consideration of the behavior's instrumental implications rather than hedonic implications. But judgments based on our hedonic assessments of the behavior should be an excellent predictor for consummatory behaviors, that is, behaviors we engage in for enjoyment. An elegant series of studies confirmed this variant of the general matching hypothesis (see Millar & Tesser, 1992).

Fourth, numerous studies have shown that judgment-behavior consistency is higher when the individual has direct behavioral experience with the target (for a review, see Fazio & Zanna, 1981). For example, Regan and Fazio (1977) observed that participants' evaluations of a set of puzzles were better predictors of how much time they spent on each puzzle in a subsequent free play period when their ratings were based on prior behavioral experience than when they were not. Presumably, the behavioral experience resulted in a temporary representation that provided a better match with participants' experiences during the free play period.

Fifth, judgment-behavior consistency is likely to be higher when individuals take the context in which the behavior is to be performed into account when they form a judgment. In most cases, however, evaluative judgments are assessed without mentally instantiating the relevant context, resulting in low judgment-behavior consistency. Hence, evaluations assessed in a "cold" state (e.g., attitudes toward condom use assessed in a research setting) are poor predictors of actual behavior in a "hot" state, like a romantic encounter (for a review, see Loewenstein & Schkade, 1999).

Finally, the matching assumption also explains why some measurement procedures are more likely to identify judgment-behavior consistency than others. As Fishbein and Ajzen (1975) demonstrated, we are more likely to observe judgment-behavior consistency when we use multiple behavioral criteria rather than a single criterion. In terms of the preceding discussion, an aggregation across multiple behaviors or multiple situations increases the likelihood that some matches are included in the assessment. Moreover, judgment-behavior consistency increases the better the judgment task matches the behavioral criterion. For example, respondents' evaluation of "donating money to the Democratic party" is a better predictor of this particular behavior than their general evaluation of the Democratic party per se. Such matches between the judgment task and the target behavior again increase the likelihood that both responses are based on similar representations.

In combination, these examples illustrate that evaluative judgments at Time 1 are only likely to predict behavior at Time 2 when the judgment and the behavioral decision are based on similar mental representations. If so, however, we may hesitate to conclude that some preexisting stable attitude plays a causal role in the behavioral decision. Instead, the observed relationship may be rather spurious, reflecting that the evaluative judgment and the behavioral decision are based on similar representations (see Schwarz & Bohner, 2001; Schwarz, 2007, for a more detailed discussion).

REFERENCES

Barsalou, L. W. (2005). Situated conceptualization. In H. Cohen & C. Lefebvre (Eds.), *Handbook of categorization in cognitive science* (pp. 619–650). Amsterdam: Elsevier.

Biernat, M. (2005). *Standards and expectancies.* New York: Psychology Press.

Bless, H., Igou, E. R. Schwarz, N., & Wänke, M. (2000). Reducing context effects by adding context information: The direction and size of context effects in political judgment. *Personality and Social Psychology Bulletin, 26,* 1036–1045.

Bless, H., Schwarz, N., Bodenhausen, G. V., & Thiel, L. (2001). Personalized versus generalized benefits of stereotype disconfirmation: Tradeoffs in the evaluation of atypical exemplars and their social groups. *Journal of Experimental Social Psychology, 37,* 386–397.

Bless, H., Schwarz, N., & Wänke, M. (2003). The size of context effects in social judgment. In J. P. Forgas, K. D. Williams, & W. von Hippel (Eds.), *Social judgments: Implicit and explicit processes* (pp. 180–197). Cambridge, England: Cambridge University Press.

Blessum, K. A., Lord, C. G., & Sia, T. L. (1998). Cognitive load and positive mood reduce typicality effects in attitude-behavior consistency. *Personality and Social Psychology Bulletin, 24,* 496–504.

Bodenhausen, G. V., & Wyer, R. S. (1987). Social cognition and social reality: Information acquisition and use in the laboratory and the real world. In H. J. Hippler, N. Schwarz, & S. Sudman (Eds.), *Social information processing and survey methodology* (pp. 6–41). New York: Springer-Verlag.

Eagly, A. H., & Chaiken, S. (1993). *The psychology of attitudes.* Fort Worth, TX: Harcourt Brace Jovanovich.

Ellsworth, P. C., & Scherer, K. R. (2003). Appraisal processes in emotion. In R. J. Davidson, K. R. Scherer, & H. H. Goldsmith (Eds.), *Handbook of affective sciences* (pp. 572–595). New York: Oxford University Press.

Fazio, R. H., & Zanna, M. P. (1981). Direct experience and attitude-behavior consistency. *Advances in Experimental Social Psychology, 14,* 161–202.

Fishbein, M., & Ajzen, I. (1975). *Belief, attitude, intention, and behavior: An introduction to theory and research.* Reading, MA: Addison-Wesley.

Herr, P. M. (1986). Consequences of priming: Judgment and behavior. *Journal of Personality and Social Psychology, 51,* 1106–1115.

Herr, P. M., Sherman, S. J., & Fazio, R. H. (1983). On the consequences of priming: Assimilation and contrast effects. *Journal of Experimental Social Psychology, 19,* 323–340.

Higgins, E. T. (1996). Knowledge activation: Accessibility, applicability, and salience. In E. T. Higgins & A. W. Kruglanski (Eds.), *Social psychology: Handbook of basic principles* (pp. 133–168). New York: Guilford Press.

Higgins, E. T. (1998). The aboutness principle: A pervasive influence on human inference. *Social Cognition, 16,* 173–198.

Higgins, E. T., Rholes, W. S., & Jones, C. R. (1977). Category accessibility and impression formation. *Journal of Experimental Social Psychology, 13,* 141–154.

Iyengar, S. (1987). Television news and citizens' explanations of national affairs. *American Political Science Review, 81,* 815–831.

James, W. (1890). *The principles of psychology* (Vol. 2). New York: Henry Holt.

Kelley, C. M., & Rhodes, M. G. (2002). Making sense and nonsense of experience: Attributions in memory and judgment. *The Psychology of Learning and Motivation, 41,* 293–320.

Keltner, D., Ellsworth, P., & Edwards, K. (1993). Beyond simple pessimism: Effects of sadness and anger on social perception. *Journal of Personality and Social Psychology, 64,* 740–752.

Konrath, S., & Schwarz, N. (2005, January). *MLK Day and attitude change: Liking the group more but specific exemplars less.* Paper presented at the meeting of the Society for Personality and Social Psychology, New Orleans.

Liberman, N., Sagristano, M., & Trope, Y. (2002). The effect of temporal distance on level of mental construal. *Journal of Experimental Social Psychology, 38,* 523–534.

Loewenstein, G., & Schkade, D. (1999). Wouldn't it be nice?: Predicting future feelings. In D. Kahneman, E. Diener, & N. Schwarz (Eds.), *Well-being: The foundations of hedonic psychology* (pp. 85–101). New York: Russell-Sage.

Lombardi, W. J., Higgins, E. T., & Bargh, J. A. (1987). The role of consciousness in priming effects on categorization: Assimilation and contrast as a function of awareness of the priming task. *Personality and Social Psychology Bulletin, 13,* 411–429.

Lord, C. G., & Lepper, M. R. (1999). Attitude representation theory. *Advances in Experimental Social Psychology, 31,* 265–343.

Martin, L. L. (1986). Set/reset: Use and disuse of concepts in impression formation. *Journal of Personality and Social Psychology, 51,* 493–504.

McGlone, M. S., & Tofighbakhsh, J. (2000). Birds of a feather flock conjointly (?): Rhyme as reason in aphorisms. *Psychological Science, 11,* 424–428.

Millar, M. G., & Tesser, A. (1992). The role of beliefs and feelings in guiding behavior: The mismatch model. In L. L. Martin & A. Tesser (Eds.), *The construction of social judgments* (pp. 277–300). Mahwah, NJ: Erlbaum.

Nussbaum, S., Trope, Y., & Liberman, N. (2003). Creeping dispositionism: The temporal dynamics of behavior prediction. *Journal of Personality and Social Psychology, 84,* 485–497.

Ortony, A., Clore, G. L., & Collins, A. (1988). *The cognitive structure of emotions.* New York: Cambridge University Press.

Pham, M. T. (2004). The logic of feeling. *Journal of Consumer Psychology, 14,* 360–369.

Ramsey, S. L., Lord, C. G., Wallace, D. S., & Pugh, M. A. (1994). The role of subtypes in attitudes towards superordinate social categories. *British Journal of Social Psychology, 33,* 387–403.

Reber, R., & Schwarz, N. (1999). Effects of perceptual fluency on judgments of truth. *Consciousness and Cognition, 8,* 338–342.

Reber, R., Schwarz, N., & Winkielman, P. (2004). Processing fluency and aesthetic pleasure: Is beauty in the perceiver's processing experience? *Personality and Social Psychology Review, 8,* 364–382.

Regan, D. T., & Fazio, R. H. (1977). On the consistency between attitudes and behaviors: Look to the method of attitude formation. *Journal of Experimental Social Psychology, 13,* 28–45.

Ross, L., & Nisbett, R. E. (1991). *The person and the situation.* New York: McGraw-Hill.

Schkade, D. A., & Kahneman, D. (1997). Does living in California make people happy? A focusing illusion in judgments of life satisfaction. *Psychological Science, 9,* 340–346.

Schwarz, N. (1994). Judgment in a social context: Biases, shortcomings, and the logic of conversation. *Advances in Experimental Social Psychology, 26,* 123–162.

Schwarz, N. (2002). Situated cognition and the wisdom of feelings: Cognitive tuning. In L. Feldman Barrett & P. Salovey (Eds.), *The wisdom in feelings* (pp. 144–166). New York: Guilford.

Schwarz, N. (2004). Meta-cognitive experiences in consumer judgment and decision making. *Journal of Consumer Psychology, 14,* 332–348.

Schwarz, N. (2007). Attitude construction: Evaluation in context. *Social Cognnition, 25,* 638–656.

Schwarz, N., & Bless, H. (1992a). Constructing reality and its alternatives: Assimilation and contrast effects in social judgment. In L. L. Martin & A. Tesser (Eds.), *The construction of social judgments* (pp. 217–245). Hillsdale, NJ: Erlbaum.

Schwarz, N., & Bless, H. (1992b). Scandals and the public's trust in politicians: Assimilation and contrast effects. *Personality and Social Psychology Bulletin, 18,* 574–579.

Schwarz, N., & Bless, H. (2007). Mental construal processes: The inclusion/exclusion model. In D. A. Stapel & J. Suls (Eds.), *Assimilation and contrast in social psychology* (pp. 119–141). Philadelphia: Psychology Press.

Schwarz, N., Bless, H., Strack, F., Klumpp, G., Rittenauer-Schatka, H., & Simons, A. (1991). Ease of retrieval as information: Another look at the availability heuristic. *Journal of Personality and Social Psychology, 61,* 195–202.

Schwarz, N., & Bohner, G. (2001). The construction of attitudes. In A. Tesser & N. Schwarz (Eds.), *Blackwell handbook of social psychology: Intraindividual processes* (pp. 436–457). Oxford, England: Blackwell.

Schwarz, N., & Clore, G. L. (1983). Mood, misattribution, and judgments of well-being: Informative and directive functions of affective states. *Journal of Personality and Social Psychology, 45,* 513–523.

Schwarz, N., & Clore, G. L. (2007). Feelings and phenomenal experiences. In E. T. Higgins & A. Kruglanski (Eds.), *Social psychology. Handbook of basic principles* (2nd ed., pp. 385–407). New York: Guilford.

Schwarz, N., & Strack, F. (1999). Reports of subjective well-being: Judgmental processes and their methodological implications. In D. Kahneman, E. Diener, & N. Schwarz (Eds.), *Well-being: The foundations of hedonic psychology* (pp. 61–84). New York: Russell-Sage.

Schwarz, N., & Strack, F. (2007). Thinking about your life: Healthy lessons from social cognition. In K. van den Bos, M. Hewstone, M. Stroebe, H. Schut, & J. de Wit (Eds.), *The scope of social psychology: Theory and applications* (pp. 121–136). Philadelphia: Psychology Press.

Schwarz, N., Strack, F., & Mai, H. P. (1991). Assimilation and contrast effects in part-whole question sequences: A conversational logic analysis. *Public Opinion Quarterly, 55,* 3–23.

Smith, E. R., & Semin, G. R. (2004). Socially situated cognition: Cognition in its social context. *Advances in Experimental Social Psychology, 36,* 53–117.

Soldat, A. S., Sinclair, R. C., & Mark, M. M. (1997). Color as an environmental processing cue: External affective cues can directly affect processing strategy without affecting mood. *Social Cognition, 15,* 55–71.

Srull, T. K., & Wyer, R. S. (1979). The role of category accessibility in the interpretation of information about persons. *Journal of Personality and Social Psychology, 38,* 841–856.

Stapel, D. A., & Koomen, W. (2000). Distinctness of others, mutability of selves: Their impact on self-evaluations. *Journal of Personality and Social Psychology, 79,* 1068–1087.

Stapel, D. A., & Winkielman, P. (1998). Assimilation and contrast as a function of context-target similarity, distinctness, and dimensional relevance. *Personality and Social Psychology Bulletin, 24*, 634–646.
Strack, F., & Hannover, B. (1996). Awareness of influence as a precondition for implementing correctional goals. In P. M. Gollwitzer & J. A. Bargh (Eds.), *The psychology of action: Linking cognition and motivation to behavior* (pp. 579–596). New York: Guilford Press.
Strack, F., Martin, L. L., & Schwarz, N. (1988). Priming and communication: The social determinants of information use in judgments of life-satisfaction. *European Journal of Social Psychology, 18*, 429–442.
Strack, F., Schwarz, N., Bless, H., Kübler, A., & Wänke, M. (1993). Awareness of the influence as a determinant of assimilation versus contrast. *European Journal of Social Psychology, 23*, 53–62.
Strack, F., Schwarz, N., & Gschneidinger, E. (1985). Happiness and reminiscing: The role of time perspective, mood, and mode of thinking. *Journal of Personality and Social Psychology, 49*, 1460–1469.
Trope, Y., & Liberman, N. (2003). Temporal construal. *Psychological Review, 110*, 403–421.
Trope, Y., Liberman, N., & Wakslak, D. (2007). Construal levels and psychological distance: Effects on representation, prediction, evaluation, and behavior. *Journal of Consumer Psychology, 17*, 83–95.
Wänke, M., Bless, H., & Schwarz, N. (1998). Contrast and assimilation in product line extensions: Context is not destiny. *Journal of Consumer Psychology, 7*, 299–322.
Wegner, D. M., & Vallacher, R. R. (1986). Action identification. In R. M. Sorrentino & E. T. Higgins (Eds.), *Handbook of motivation and cognition: Foundations of social behavior* (pp. 550–582). New York: Guilford Press.
Wilson, T. D., & Brekke, N. (1994). Mental contamination and mental correction: Unwanted influences on judgments and evaluations. *Psychological Bulletin, 116*, 117–142.
Wilson, T. D., & Hodges, S. D. (1992). Attitudes as temporary constructions. In L. L. Martin & A. Tesser (Eds.), *The construction of social judgments* (pp. 37–65). Hillsdale, NJ: Erlbaum.
Winkielman, P. & Cacioppo, J. T. (2001). Mind at ease puts a smile on the face: Psychophysiological evidence that processing facilitation leads to positive affect. *Journal of Personality and Social Psychology, 81*, 989–1000.
Wittenbrink, B., Judd, C. M., & Park, B. (2001). Spontaneous prejudice in context: Variability in automatically activated attitudes. *Journal of Personality and Social Psychology, 81*, 815–827.
Wyer, R. S., & Srull, T. K. (1989). *Memory and cognition in its social context*. Hillsdale, NJ: Erlbaum.
Yeh, W., & Barsalou, L. W. (2006). The situated nature of concepts. *American Journal of Psychology, 119*, 349–384.

7

Comparison

THOMAS MUSSWEILER

INTRODUCTION

Everything is relative. In line with this truism, few psychological processes play as central a role in as many psychological phenomena as comparisons. Whenever information is perceived, processed, or evaluated, it is compared to a salient context, norm, or standard. Already the perception of a physical object involves a comparison with a pertinent standard (Helson, 1964). The perceived size of a target circle, for example, critically depends on whether the target is surrounded by a set of large or small circles, as is evident in the classic Ebbinghaus illusion (Coren & Enns, 1993). Similarly, the perceived weight of a target object depends on whether it is presented with a set of heavy or light objects (Brown, 1954). The perception and evaluation of social targets are equally comparative in nature. The perceived hostility of a target person, for example, depends on whether this person is evaluated in comparison to a set of hostile or nonhostile persons (Herr, 1986). In much the same way, whether we see a social issue as important (Sherman, Ahlm, Berman, & Lynn, 1978), a trial judge as lenient (Higgins & Stangor, 1988), or ourselves as competent (Morse & Gergen, 1970) all depend on whether these targets are compared to high or low standards.

UBIQUITY AND ROBUSTNESS OF COMPARISON

This fundamental tendency toward comparative information processing is particularly apparent in social psychological research. Comparisons play a fundamental role in many core social psychological areas, such as attitudes (Eiser, 1990; Hovland & Sherif, 1952; Sherif & Hovland, 1961), stereotyping (Biernat, 2003; Biernat & Manis, 1994), person perception (Herr, 1986; Higgins & Lurie, 1983), decision making (Kahneman & Miller, 1986; Sherman, Houston, & Eddy, 1999;

Tversky & Kahneman, 1974), affect (Higgins, 1987), and the self (Festinger, 1954; Higgins, Strauman, & Klein, 1986; Miller & Prentice, 1996). In all of these domains, it has been suggested—and demonstrated—that people's psychological reactions are shaped by the comparisons they make. Social judgments, for one, are typically made by comparing the target entity to a particular standard (Eiser, 1990; Mussweiler, 2003). For instance, people judge the attitudes of others by comparing them to their own (Hovland & Sherif, 1953); they judge other people by comparing them to a salient stereotype (Biernat, 2003), a particularly accessible other (Herr, 1986), or themselves (Dunning & Hayes, 1996); and they judge themselves by comparing to others (Festinger, 1954). In much the same way, peoples' affective reactions depend on how their outcomes and achievements compare to salient norms (Higgins, 1987), and people's behavior depends on how they compare with salient standards (Mussweiler & Strack, 2000a; Seta 1982). Comparison thus appears to be a truly ubiquitous psychological process that contributes to a broad variety of social psychological phenomena.

People's tendency to compare is not only ubiquitous but also remarkably robust. Comparisons are engaged even if they are not explicitly requested. When processing information about another person, for example, people spontaneously compare this person to themselves (Dunning & Hayes, 1996). Similarly, when processing information about themselves, people spontaneously compare themselves to another person (Festinger, 1954; Mussweiler & Rüter, 2003). Recent evidence suggests that this tendency to make spontaneous comparisons when processing information about a given target goes so far that people even use comparison standards of whom they are not aware because they were presented subliminally (Mussweiler & Englich, 2005; Mussweiler, Rüter, & Epstude, 2004a; Stapel & Blanton, 2004).

In addition, the leaning toward comparative processing is so robust that comparisons are even engaged with standards that—from a normative perspective—are unlikely to provide useful information about the target. Abundant research has demonstrated that even standards that are clearly irrelevant because they were selected at random are used for comparison. The most prominent example for this use of random comparison standards is given by research on judgmental anchoring (Tversky & Kahneman, 1974). Participants who are asked to estimate the percentage of African nations in the United Nations, for example, make use of a salient numeric standard (e.g., 65%) even if this standard has merely been determined by spinning a wheel of fortune (Tversky & Kahneman, 1974). In fact, even judges who are experienced experts in the critical domain are influenced by such randomly determined comparison standards—even if judges themselves readily evaluate these standards as irrelevant (Englich, Mussweiler, & Strack, 2006).

Why is people's reliance on comparisons so ubiquitous and robust? A first reason is that much of the information we process pertains to dimensions that are inherently comparative. Judging a given circle as large or a person as hostile implies that these targets are larger or more hostile than a pertinent norm or standard (Huttenlocher & Higgins, 1971). To successfully interpret incoming information that is to be processed and to successfully communicate the processing outcome on such inherently comparative dimensions, judges have to relate target information to the inferred reference norm of their communication partner. The information

"Donald is a hostile person," for example, has quite different implications if the pope or Adolf Hitler are the implicit comparison standards.

Empirical evidence supports this assumption and demonstrates that judges do indeed tune into the inferred reference norms of their communication partners (Clark & Schober, 1992; Schwarz, 1994; Strack & Martin, 1987) when processing and communicating information. For example, judges may use a given range of possible extensions of the target to infer whether the same information indicates a high or a low standing on the critical dimension. In one study illustrating this possibility, for example, medical doctors inferred that having a specific symptom twice a week reflected a less-severe medical condition if this frequency were presented in a range of higher frequencies rather than in a range of lower frequencies (Schwarz, Bless, Bohner, Harlacher, & Kellenbenz, 1991). As seems to be the case in this example, judges may use a given comparison context to infer the meaning of incoming information. In much the same way, people may also use a given comparison context when communicating information themselves. More specifically, judges may infer the range of extensions of the target that their communication partner is likely to use when interpreting this information (Ostrom & Upshaw, 1968) and relate their communication to this range. As a consequence, identical target extensions may be communicated in different ways. In one study, for example, the identical target weight of 90 g was described as lighter if it was presented in the context of a set of heavier weights than if no such context was given (Brown, 1954). These findings suggest that judges compare a given target extension to an inferred reference norm when processing incoming information and when communicating processing outcomes.

In light of the fact that much of the information people process is inherently relative in nature, such comparisons appear to be both a logical and a conversational necessity. Only if judges compare incoming information to the pertinent norm may they be able to successfully interpret and communicate information.

In addition, comparisons may be so ubiquitous because they allow processing information in a more efficient manner than more absolute modes of information processing (Mussweiler & Epstude, 2008). People as cognitive misers (Taylor, 1981) typically have to resort to information-processing strategies that save their limited cognitive capacities. Comparative information processing appears to be one general and widely applicable psychological mechanism that serves this resource-preserving goal. More specifically, comparisons may act as an all-purpose heuristic because they limit the range of information that has to be considered to evaluate or judge a given object. Rather than considering the whole array of potentially judgment-relevant knowledge that is required for more absolute modes of information processing, comparative information processing allows judges to focus on the subset of this knowledge that is immediately relevant for the engaged comparison. Evaluating their athletic ability in an absolute manner, for example, in principle requires judges to retrieve and integrate all the information that has some implications about their athletic abilities. In marked contrast, evaluating their athletic abilities relative to a salient comparison standard, such as their tennis partner or the like, allows them to focus on only the information that is required for the comparison. It may, for example, be sufficient to bring to mind that the tennis partner has won 98 of the last 100 matches to come to the conclusion that one is not particularly athletic. This informational focusing effect of comparisons appears to render comparative information processing relatively efficient.

Consistent with this reasoning, a series of studies has demonstrated that comparative information processing does indeed have efficiency advantages (Mussweiler & Epstude, 2008). In these studies, inducing participants to rely more heavily on comparisons when processing information allowed them to be more efficient in making a critical series of judgments. These efficiency advantages of comparative information processing were apparent in the fact that the critical judgments were made faster and that more residual capacity was left for a secondary task. In fact, the efficiency advantages of comparisons are also apparent on an electrocortical level, as a recent electroencephalographic (EEG) study demonstrated (Keil, Mussweiler, & Epstude, 2006). Participants who were induced to process information in a more comparative manner showed smaller changes in the lower alpha-band—a pattern that is closely associated with less mental effort.

Taken together, this research suggests that people's tendency to engage in comparisons is strikingly ubiquitous and robust, and that this is the case because of the logical, conversational, and efficiency requirements of information processing. If comparisons play as crucial a role in social information processing as this evidence suggests, then at least six critical questions emerge. With what do people compare? That is, what are the psychological mechanisms that underlie standard selection? Once a standard has been determined, what specific features of the comparison target and the standard are taken into account? And, how is the actual comparison of these features carried out? What are the psychological mechanisms that underlie comparisons? Finally, what are the consequences of comparison? How do comparisons shape people's psychological reactions?

STANDARD SELECTION

The process of standard selection critically influences a comparison because it determines the referent that is used for comparison. Standard selection sets the informational stage for the ensuing comparison and its consequences. What are the psychological mechanisms that operate at this influential stage of the comparison process? What mechanisms influence the selection of a standard?

A first mechanism that may induce judges to select a particular standard for the comparison process is conversational inference (Grice, 1975; Schwarz, 1994). People typically expect their communicational counterparts to be maximally informative in asking their questions. Thus, if a particular standard is explicitly or implicitly mentioned in an inquiry that triggers a comparison process, this standard is likely to be taken into consideration. Much of the research on judgmental anchoring (Tversky & Kahneman, 1974; for reviews, see Chapman & Johnson, 2002; Mussweiler, Englich, & Strack, 2004; Mussweiler & Strack, 1999) provides an example for this conversational route to standard selection. In particular, implicitly provided anchors that are of clear relevance for the estimate to be made (Northcraft & Neale, 1987) may exert their assimilative effect through this mechanism. In the absence of a randomized procedure of anchor selection, it is reasonable for participants to interpret relevant anchors as a hint to the actual value. More generally, conversational inferences may be the basis of anchoring effects found in many natural settings because there anchors are not selected at random and usually are of clear relevance to the judgment at hand. However, conversational inferences are not limited to relevant anchors that are deduced from the judgmental context. Such inferences may also be applied when explicitly provided anchors were not selected at random (e.g., Plous, 1989; Wright & Anderson, 1989). In the absence of a randomized procedure of anchor selection, participants are likely to infer that the actual value is not too far removed from the anchor value provided by the experimenter. For example, participants who are asked whether the chances of a nuclear war between the United States and the Soviet Union are greater or smaller than 90% (Plous, 1989) may assume that the actual probability is close to the anchor value and respond accordingly.

Alternatively, judges may select a particular standard because it is highly accessible in memory. In searching for a relevant standard of comparison, the higher the accessibility of any standard, the more likely it is to come to mind, and the higher the chances are that it will be selected. The most direct demonstrations for this influence of accessibility on standard selection are provided by studies using priming procedures to examine the consequences of comparison processes on judgment (e.g., Herr, 1986; Wilson, Houston, Etling, & Brekke, 1996). In one study (Herr, 1986), for example, increasing the accessibility of hostile (e.g., Adolf Hitler) versus peaceful (Pope John Paul) celebrities by inducing participants to find these names in a word search puzzle influenced judgments about the hostility of an ambiguously described target person. In another study (Wilson et al., 1996), increasing the accessibility of a specific range of numbers by inducing judges to copy 5 pages of numbers in this range influenced a subsequent numeric estimate (i.e., the number of students who will get cancer in the next 40 years). These findings attest that judges are particularly likely to select a given standard for comparison if this standard is easily accessible in memory, even if the source of accessibility is extraneous to the critical judgment.

In addition, standard selection may also be driven by efficiency considerations. The necessity to save scarce cognitive resources permeates any facet of social information processing and is thus also likely to play a role in standard selection. People who are stingy with their scarce resources when processing social information in general (Taylor, 1981) are also likely to be so when selecting comparison standards. One of the main tools that is applied to simplify complex tasks and to consequently make them more efficient is the application of routines (e.g., Aarts & Dijksterhuis, 2000; Betsch, Haberstroh, Glöckner, Haar, & Fiedler, 2001; Verplanken & Aarts, 1999). *Routines* are solutions that are closely associated with a particular task due to extensive repetition. Relying on routines frees cognitive capacities as is, for example, apparent in the fact that people resort more readily to their decision routines under suboptimal conditions (Betsch, Fiedler, & Brinkmann, 1998).

In much the same way, routines can also be applied to simplify otherwise complex standard selection processes. Instead of engaging in an arduous standard selection task, people may simply compare a given target with those standards that are routinely used for comparison. The development of such a routine would thereby depend on the frequency of prior use of the routine standard. The more often a particular standard has been used, the stronger it would be associated with the judgment task and the more likely one engages in further comparisons with this standard. If I always compare with my best friend during self-evaluation, for example, then this friend will become a routine standard that is typically used for self-evaluation (Mussweiler & Rüter, 2003). The same would be true for any other standard that is often used for self-evaluation, such as one's partner, sibling, neighbor, and so on. In this respect, routine standards enable people to skip a standard selection process altogether and still engage in comparative self-evaluation. Consistent with these assumptions, it has been demonstrated that judges do indeed often resort to the use of routine standards. For example, people spontaneously activate information about their best friends when evaluating themselves (Mussweiler & Rüter, 2003). They compare this standard information to themselves (Rüter & Mussweiler, 2005), which is more efficient than comparing to a nonroutine standard (Rüter & Mussweiler, 2008). Thus, people may generally rely on a particular standard simply because they have frequently done so in the past.

In addition to these general principles of conversational inference, knowledge accessibility, and routine formation, the standard selection process may also be guided by normative concerns about selecting a relevant or diagnostic standard. This concern has been a particularly prominent notion in the literature on self-evaluative comparisons (Wood, 1989). More specifically, this literature emphasizes the importance of target-standard similarity for selection processes. Here, normative theoretical accounts formulating what people should do to obtain diagnostic information via social comparison (e.g., Festinger, 1954; Goethals & Darley, 1977; Wheeler, Martin, & Suls, 1997) have acknowledged the diagnostic advantages of comparisons with standards that are similar on the critical dimension (Festinger, 1954) or on attributes related to this dimension (Goethals & Darley, 1977) (for a discussion of the limitations of both notions, see Miller & Prentice, 1996).

Empirical evidence generally confirms the central role ascribed to similarity by these theoretical formulations. Both types of similarity—similarity on a critical dimension and similarity on related dimensions—appear to exert powerful effects on the selection of social comparison standards. For example, participants who receive feedback about their performance in a given task and who are given the opportunity to see the scores of other participants tend to select comparison standards who have similar performance (e.g., Gruder, 1971; Wheeler, 1966), thus demonstrating that similarity on the critical dimension itself influences standard selection. Similarity of related attributes has also been shown to be important in standard selection (Miller, 1982, 1984; Suls, Gaes, & Gastorf, 1979; Suls, Gastorf, & Lawhon, 1978; Wheeler, Koestner, & Driver, 1982; Zanna, Goethals, & Hill, 1975). For example, participants have been found to compare their own task performance to others who had similar practice with the task when practice was related to performance but not when it was unrelated (Wheeler et al., 1982). These findings suggest that the process of selecting a social comparison standard is indeed heavily influenced by similarity between the comparison target and the standard, as was originally proposed by Festinger (1954). Notably, this influential role of similarity is likely to extend beyond the realm of self-evaluative comparisons. In fact, norm theory (Kahneman & Miller, 1986) suggests that it may well be the driving force behind the recruitment of norms and standards in any domain, such as decision making, attitudes, and person perception.

In all, this discussion indicates that the process of standard selection may be influenced by conversational, cognitive, and normative factors.

FEATURAL FOCUS

Selecting a particular standard for comparison, however, still does not provide one with concrete referent information with which to compare the target. At least in the realm of social judgment, most standards are sufficiently complex and multifaceted so that a comparison can potentially focus on a multitude of characteristics. Once you have selected your best friend as a standard of comparison for evaluating your athletic abilities, for example, you could potentially base the comparison on any ability that is related to athletics. Which characteristics should the ensuing comparison be based on? Should you focus on your tennis and running skills or on your soccer and swimming skills? Thus, after selecting a particular standard, judges still have to determine the specific featural focus of the comparison.

The cognitive literature on similarity comparisons (Gentner, 1983; Gentner & Markman, 1994, 1997; Markman & Gentner, 1993, 1996; Medin, Goldstone, & Gentner, 1993; Ritov, 2000; Tversky, 1977) has closely examined what featural focus judges have during a comparison and which particular aspects of the target and the standard form the basis of a comparison. The process of determining the featural focus of a comparison is akin to the process of determining the similarity of two objects. Just as similarity comparisons require judges to identify the specific features with respect to which similarity is to be assessed, comparisons in general require judges to identify the critical features that carry weight in the comparison. For similarity comparisons, Tversky's (1977) seminal feature-matching model implies that comparisons involve a process of matching features or attributes of the target and the comparison standard and weighing the resulting number of shared and unshared features. From this theoretical perspective, the individual attributes of the target and the standard are seen as the core constituents of the comparison process. This feature-matching process has been demonstrated as crucial for assessments of similarity (Srull & Gaelick, 1983; Tversky, 1977; Tversky & Gati, 1978) as well as decisions of choice (Houston & Sherman, 1995; Houston, Sherman, & Baker, 1989; Sherman et al., 1999).

More recent conceptualizations emphasize the importance of relational structures between these individual attributes (Gentner, 1983; Gentner & Markman, 1994, 1997; Markman & Gentner, 1993, 1996; Medin et al., 1993). The basic assumption of such a structure-mapping approach to similarity comparison is that in comparing two objects, people are influenced not merely by sets of separate properties, but also by how the properties are interrelated within the standard and the target. There is considerable research demonstrating that people first determine a general relational structure among individual properties that is shared by the target and the standard of the comparison and then primarily base their comparison on properties that are related to the shared or alignable relational structure. That is, the comparison focuses primarily on alignable features. From this perspective, the impact of individual attributes on similarity judgments critically depends on their role in the overall alignable structure.

The central role relational structures play in similarity comparisons is illustrated by a study (Markman & Gentner, 1993) in which participants compared two rugs that depicted a number of different objects (e.g., an octagon and an oval) that were arranged in a similar symmetric relation. The target and the standard of the comparison thus consisted of a number of different objects that were related to one another by their position in the overall symmetry of the rug. The participants' task was to identify the object on the standard rug that corresponded to an identified target object (an oval in the middle of the left side) on the target rug. The target and the standard rug were constructed such that for the target object an object correspondence as well as a structure correspondence existed on the standard rug. The object correspondence was a highly similar object (i.e., another oval) that appeared in a different position on the standard rug. The structure correspondence was a different object (an octagon) that appeared in the same position as the target object (i.e., in the middle of the right side). If the structural relations among the individual objects do indeed play a crucial role in comparison, then judges should primarily focus on the structure rather than the object correspondence. This was indeed the case. Participants who judged the similarity of both rugs were more likely to identify the octagon that appeared in the same position as the target oval as the corresponding object. These findings indicate that structural correspondences play a core role in similarity comparisons.

This perspective on similarity comparison is supported by a host of empirical findings (for an overview, see Gentner & Markman, 1997). For one, judges typically consider facts that are related to the shared alignable structure to be more central to the comparison than facts that are not related to this structure (e.g., Clement & Gentner, 1991). Thus, commonalities related to the alignable structure are more salient than those that are unrelated. The same appears to be true for differences (Gentner & Markman, 1994; Markman & Gentner, 1996). When asked to list differences, people tend to list alignable differences—differences related to the common structure—rather than nonalignable (unrelated) differences. Furthermore, explicit judgments of similarity are more strongly influenced by the existence of alignable differences than by differences not related to the common structure (Markman & Gentner, 1996), suggesting that alignable attributes weigh more heavily in similarity judgments. All in all, these findings stress the importance shared relational structures among individual features play during the comparison process. To compare two objects, judges appear to first establish a relational structure that is shared by the target and the standard and then make the comparison along this alignable structure by focusing on those attributes that are related to the structure.

In summary, the processes of selecting a standard and determining the featural focus of the comparison critically influence the outcome of comparisons in that they set the stage for the subsequent comparison process. In particular, they determine which aspects of the comparison target will be taken into account during the comparison and will consequently become accessible. The process of standard selection may be guided by at least four fundamental principles. Judges are likely to select standards that are suggested by conversational inferences that are highly accessible, that may be efficiently determined because they are used routinely, and that promise to be the most diagnostic standards because they are similar to the judgmental target. When a standard has been selected, the specific featural focus of the comparison is likely to be determined by processes of feature matching and structural alignment. Once a comparison standard has been selected and the critical features of the target and the standard have been identified, the actual comparison has to be carried out.

COMPARISON MECHANISMS

I have proposed a selective accessibility model that describes the psychological mechanisms that are involved in carrying out a comparison (Mussweiler, 2003). This model takes an informational perspective on the comparison process. It assumes that to compare a given target to a specific standard, judges have to obtain specific judgment-relevant information about the target and the standard that allows them to evaluate both entities relative to one another. This specific knowledge is best obtained by an active search for judgment-relevant information through processes of hypothesis testing in which judges relate their stored knowledge regarding the target to the judgmental task at hand (Trope & Liberman, 1996). Such hypothesis-testing processes are often selective in that they focus on one single hypothesis that is then evaluated against a specific criterion (Sanbonmatsu, Posavac, Kardes, & Mantel, 1998; see also Klayman & Ha, 1987; Trope & Liberman, 1996). Rather than engaging in an exhaustive comparative test of all plausible hypotheses, judges often limit themselves to the test of a single focal hypothesis. In light of this tendency toward selective hypothesis testing, the critical question is which concrete hypothesis will be tested.

In principle, two hypotheses can be distinguished. Judges can either test the possibility that the target is similar to the standard or they can test the possibility that the target is dissimilar from the standard. Which of these hypotheses is tested depends on the overall perceived similarity of the target and the standard. As an initial step in the selective accessibility mechanism, judges engage in a quick holistic assessment of target and standard (Smith, Shoben, & Rips, 1974) in which they briefly consider a small number of salient features (e.g., category membership, salient characteristics) to determine whether both are generally similar or dissimilar. The outcome of this screening is a broad assessment of similarity. Although such an assessment is by itself too general to be used as the basis for target evaluation, it is sufficient to determine the specific nature of the hypothesis that is then tested. The hypothesis-testing mechanism thus focuses on the possibility that is suggested by the initial holistic assessment. If this assessment indicates that the target is generally similar to the standard, judges will engage in a process of similarity testing and test the hypothesis that the target is similar to the standard. If the initial assessment indicates that the target is dissimilar from the standard, however, judges will engage in a process of dissimilarity testing and test the hypothesis that the target is dissimilar from the standard.

Notably, because judges typically select standards that are similar to a given target (Festinger, 1954) and because they initially establish a common ground on which they compare target and standard (Gentner & Markman, 1994), similarity testing constitutes the default comparison mechanism. In fact, comparisons are often characterized by an initial focus on similarities (Chapman & Johnson, 1999; Lockwood & Kunda, 1997), so that dissimilarity testing is more of an exception that is primarily carried out when salient characteristics clearly indicate target-standard dissimilarity.

The critical initial assessment of target-standard similarity constitutes a quick holistic screening of features that are salient, are easy to process, and have immediate implications for target-standard similarity. Two features that fulfill these criteria are category membership and standard extremity. Similarity testing, for example, is more likely to be engaged for standards that belong to the same category as the standard (Mussweiler & Bodenhausen, 2002) and whose standing on the judgmental dimension is moderate rather than extreme (Mussweiler, Rüter, & Epstude, 2004a, 2004b). In addition, the motivational underpinnings of the comparison situation may influence the outcome of this initial assessment. For example, if judges are motivated to keep a positive self-image when confronted with a low standard, they may focus more on the ways in which they are different from this standard and consequently engage in dissimilarity testing.

The literature on hypothesis testing further suggests that once a hypothesis is selected, it is often tested by focusing on hypothesis-consistent evidence (Klayman & Ha, 1987; Snyder & Swann, 1978; Trope & Bassok, 1982; Trope & Liberman, 1996). Applied to the case of hypothesis testing in comparative information processing, this suggests that judges selectively generate information that is consistent with the focal hypothesis of the comparison. If judges test the hypothesis that the target is similar to the standard, for example, they will do so by selectively searching for standard-consistent target knowledge—evidence indicating that the target's standing on the judgmental dimension is indeed similar to that of the standard. If judges test the hypothesis that the target is dissimilar from the standard, however, they do so by selectively searching for standard-inconsistent target knowledge—evidence indicating that the target's standing differs from that of the standard. This selectivity in the acquisition of judgment-relevant knowledge about the target has clear informational consequences. The mechanism of similarity testing selectively increases the accessibility of standard-consistent target knowledge, whereas dissimilarity testing selectively increases the accessibility of standard-inconsistent target knowledge. This selective accessibility effect constitutes the core informational consequence of comparison (see Figure 7.1).

To the extent that the target knowledge that became accessible during the comparison forms the basis for subsequent judgments, feelings, and behaviors, these psychological reactions will reflect the implications of this knowledge. If standard-consistent target knowledge forms the basis, then judgment, feeling, and behavior are assimilated toward the standard. If standard-inconsistent knowledge forms the basis, then judgment, feeling, and behavior are contrasted away from the standard. This suggests that the default consequence of similarity testing is assimilation, whereas dissimilarity testing typically leads to contrast.

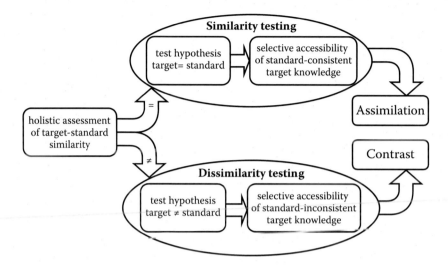

Figure 7.1 The selective accessibility mechanism (from Mussweiler, 2003).

This perspective on the psychological mechanisms that underlie comparisons and the consequences they produce is supported by a large body of empirical evidence (for more detailed discussions, see Mussweiler, 2007, in press). First, it has been demonstrated that, in carrying out a comparison, judges do indeed selectively focus on and activate a specific subset of target knowledge (Mussweiler & Strack, 2000a, 2000b; Strack & Mussweiler, 1997). As is suggested by the selective accessibility framework, judges focus on standard-consistent knowledge about the comparison target if similarities between target and standard are in the foreground. One supporting study (Mussweiler & Bodenhausen, 2002) made use of the fact that, in the context of spontaneous social comparison, similarity testing is more likely to occur if the self and the standard belong to the same social category, whereas dissimilarity testing is more likely if both belong to different categories. If these alternative selective accessibility mechanisms are indeed engaged, then social comparisons with intracategorical versus extracategorcial standards should render divergent sets of standard-consistent versus standard-inconsistent self-knowledge accessible. This was indeed the case, in a variant of a lexical decision task (Dijksterhuis et al., 1998)—a standard measure of knowledge accessibility—standard-consistent self-knowledge (i.e., knowledge indicating that oneself is fairly neat after a comparison with a neat standard) was more accessible after a spontaneous comparison with an in-group member (i.e., same gender) than after a comparison with an out-group member (i.e., different gender). Using standard extremity as a moderator for similarity versus dissimilarity testing, this finding was conceptually replicated by Smeesters and Mandel (2006). Building on previous studies demonstrating that exposure to moderate context stimuli leads to judgmental assimilation, whereas exposure to extreme stimuli leads to contrast (Herr, 1986; Mussweiler, Rüter, & Epstude, 2004a, 2004b), these researchers demonstrated that exposure to moderately thin versus heavy models renders standard-consistent self-knowledge accessible. Exposure to extremely thin versus heavy models, however, renders standard-inconsistent self-knowledge accessible. These studies demonstrated that, in carrying out a comparison, judges do indeed selectively focus on a specific subset of target knowledge. Standard-consistent knowledge becomes more accessible in situations that promote similarity testing, whereas standard-inconsistent knowledge becomes more accessible in situations that promote dissimilarity testing.

Notably, the selective accessibility consequences of comparisons are fairly ubiquitous and robust and have been demonstrated to result from different types of comparison. No matter whether judges were explicitly asked to compare the target to the standard (Mussweiler & Strack, 2000a, 2000b), whether the standard was made accessible in the judgmental situation (Mussweiler & Bodenhausen, 2002; Smeesters & Mandel, 2006), or whether it was subliminally presented (Mussweiler & Englich, 2005) the accessibility of a specific subset of target knowledge was selectively increased.

COMPARISON CONSEQUENCES

Comparisons influence peoples' judgments and affective reactions, as well as their behavior. How people evaluate a given target, how they feel, and how they behave very much depends on the type of comparison process in which they engaged. For all of these psychological reactions, assimilation is more likely to result under conditions that foster similarity testing, whereas contrast occurs under conditions that foster dissimilarity testing. The informational focus judges take during the comparison—whether they focus on similarities or differences—thus determines whether their judgmental, affective, and behavioral reactions are assimilated toward or contrasted away from a standard.

In the realm of judgmental comparison consequences, direct support for the critical effect judges' informational focus has on the direction of comparison consequences stems from a series of studies that manipulated participants' informational focus during a comparison with the help of a procedural priming task (Mussweiler, 2001). Here, it was demonstrated that participants who were procedurally primed to focus on similarities during a social comparison task assimilated their self-evaluations toward the standard. Participants who were procedurally primed to focus on differences, however, contrasted their self-evaluations away from the standard (Mussweiler, 2001).

Extending this initial work on judgmental comparison consequences, more recent evidence shows similar effects in the realm of affect and behavior. Epstude and Mussweiler (2008), for example, demonstrated that whether participants' affective state was assimilated toward or contrasted away from the affective state of another person depended on a focus on similarities versus differences. In one study, these different comparison foci were induced with the help of a procedural priming technique (Mussweiler, 2001). In a priming task, participants were given sketches of two scenes and were asked to list either all the similarities or all the differences they could find between these scenes. In either case, searching for similarities or differences sets participants' minds on this processing style, so that they search for the same type of information in the subsequent experimental task. That is, searching for similarities in the priming task induces a similarity focus, whereas searching for differences induces a dissimilarity focus. In the experimental task, participants were then exposed to a series of faces with either emotionally positive or emotionally negative expressions and then made to indicate how they felt themselves. Participants who were primed on similarity testing felt better after exposure to faces with an emotionally positive expression than after exposure to faces with an emotionally negative expression. This is an assimilation effect. For participants who were primed on dissimilarity testing, however, the reverse pattern occurred, which corresponds to a contrast effect.

In much the same way, behavioral comparison consequences depend on whether participants are induced to focus on similarities or differences. Specifically, it has been demonstrated that participants who are induced to focus on similarities assimilate their behavior toward a set of context stimuli, whereas participants who are induced to focus on differences contrast their behavior away from the exact same stimuli (Haddock, Macrae, & Fleck, 2002; see also Schubert & Häfner, 2003). More specifically, judges who focused on similarities among a set of supermodels behaved unintelligently. That is, they assimilated their behavior toward the behavior that is stereotypically associated with supermodels (an assimilation effect). Judges who focused on differences between the models, however, behaved more intelligently and thus contrasted their behavior away from the context stimuli. Taken together, these findings demonstrate that influences on judgment, affect, and behavior critically depend on the type of comparison process in which judges engage. If they focus on similarities and engage in similarity testing, judgments, affective reactions, and behavior are assimilated toward a standard. If they focus on differences and engage in dissimilarity testing, however, these psychological reactions are contrasted away from the pertinent standard.

CONCLUSION

Comparison constitutes a strikingly ubiquitous psychological process. Whenever people process information, when they perceive, evaluate, feel about, or behave toward a particular target, do they compare it to a salient norm or standard? In fact, comparisons contribute to many core aspects of social psychological theory and research. Person perception, stereotyping, self-evaluation, attitudinal judgments—to name a few—all involve comparison processes. In light of this ubiquity of comparative information processing, it seems particularly important to pay close attention to the psychological mechanisms that underlie comparisons. A firm understanding of how people select a particular standard, how they determine what information to consider, and how they carry out the actual comparison may also enrich our understanding of those phenomena that are shaped by comparisons. Such a comparison perspective may help to integrate a diverse set of classic and recent findings in social psychology—and beyond.

ACKNOWLEDGMENT

The research described in this chapter was supported by a grant from the German Research Foundation (DFG). I would like to thank the members of the Würzburg Social Cognition Group and those of Social Cognition Cologne for stimulating discussions of this work.

REFERENCES

Aarts, H., & Dijksterhuis, A. (2000). Habits as knowledge structures: Automaticity in goal directed behavior. *Journal of Personality and Social Psychology, 78*, 53–63.

Betsch, T., Fiedler, K., & Brinkmann, J. (1998). Behavioral routines in decision making: The effects of novelty in task presentation and time pressure on routine maintenance and deviation. *European Journal of Social Psychology, 28*, 861–878.

Betsch, T., Haberstroh, S., Glöckner, A., Haar, T., & Fiedler, K. (2001). The effects of routine strength on adaptation and information search in recurrent decision making. *Organizational Behavior and Human Decision Processes, 84*, 23–53.

Biernat, M. (2003). Toward a broader view of social stereotyping. *American Psychologist, 58*, 1019–1027.

Biernat, M., & Manis, M. (1994). Shifting standards and stereotype-based judgments. *Journal of Personality and Social Psychology, 66*, 5–20.

Brown, D. R. (1954). Stimulus-similarity and the anchoring of subjective scales. *American Journal of Psychology, 66*, 199–214.

Chapman, G. B., & Johnson, E. J. (1999). Anchoring, activation, and the construction of values. *Organizational Behavior and Human Decision Processes, 79*, 1–39.

Chapman, G. B., & Johnson, E. J. (2002). Incorporating the irrelevant: Anchors in judgment of belief and value. In T. Gilovich, D. Griffin, & D. Kahneman (Eds.), *Heuristics and biases: The psychology of intuitive judgment* (pp. 120–138). Cambridge, England: Cambridge University Press.

Clark, H. H., & Schober, M. F. (1992). Asking questions and influencing answers. In J. M. Tanur (Ed.), *Questions about questions: Inquiries into the cognitive bases of surveys* (pp. 15–47). New York: Russell Sage.

Clement, C. A., & Gentner, D. (1991). Systematicity as a selection constraint in analogical mapping. *Cognitive Science, 15*, 89–132.

Coren, S., & Enns, J. T. (1993). Size contrast as a function of conceptual similarity between test and inducers. *Perception and Psychophysics, 54*, 579–588.

Dijksterhuis, A., Spears, R., Postmes, T., Stapel, D. A., Koomen, W., van Knippenberg, A., et al. (1998). Seeing one thing and doing another: Contrast effects in automatic behavior. *Journal of Personality and Social Psychology, 75*, 862–871.

Dunning, D., & Hayes, A. F. (1996). Evidence of egocentric comparison in social judgment. *Journal of Personality and Social Psychology, 71*, 213–229.

Eiser, J. R. (1990). *Social judgment*. Milton Keynes, England: Open University.

Englich, B., Mussweiler, T., & Strack, F. (2006). Playing dice with criminal sentences: The influence of irrelevant anchors on experts' judicial decision making. *Personality and Social Psychology Bulletin, 32*, 188–200.

Epstude, K., & Mussweiler, T. (2008). *What you feel is how you compare. How comparisons influence the social induction of affect.* Manuscript under review.

Festinger, L. (1954). A theory of social comparison processes. *Human Relations, 7*, 117–140.

Gentner, D. (1983). Structure-mapping: A theoretical framework for analogy. *Cognitive Science, 7*, 155–170.
Gentner, D., & Markman, A. B. (1994). Structural alignment in comparison: No difference without similarity. *Psychological Science, 5*, 152–158.
Gentner, D., & Markman, A. B. (1997). Structure mapping in analogy and similarity. *American Psychologist, 52*, 45–56.
Goethals, G. R., & Darley, J. M. (1977). Social comparison theory: An attributional approach. In J. M. Suls & R. L. Miller (Eds.), *Social comparison processes: Theoretical and empirical perspectives* (pp. 259–278). Washington, DC: Hemisphere.
Grice, H. P. (1975). Logic and conversation. In P. Cole & J. L. Morgan (Eds.), *Syntax and semantics 3: Speech acts* (pp. 41–58). New York: Academic Press.
Gruder, C. L. (1971). Determinants of social comparison choices. *Journal of Experimental Social Psychology, 7*, 473–489.
Haddock, G., Macrae, C. N., & Fleck, S. (2002). Syrian science and smart supermodels: On the when and how of perception-behavior effects. *Social Cognition, 20*, 469–479.
Helson, H. (1964). *Adaptation level theory: An experimental and systematic approach to behavior*. New York: Harper.
Herr, P. M. (1986). Consequences of priming: Judgment and behavior. *Journal of Personality and Social Psychology, 51*, 1106–1115.
Higgins, E. T. (1987). Self-discrepancy: A theory relating self and affect. *Psychological Review, 94*, 319–340.
Higgins, E. T., & Lurie, L. (1983). Context, categorization, and recall: The "change-of-standard" effect. *Cognitive Psychology, 15*, 525–547.
Higgins, E. T., & Stangor, C. (1988). A "change-of-standard" perspective on the relations among context, judgment, and memory. *Journal of Personality and Social Psychology, 54*, 181–192.
Higgins, E. T., Strauman, T., & Klein, R. (1986). Standards and the process of self-evaluation: Multiple affects from multiple stages. In R. M. Sorrentino & E. T. Higgins (Eds.), *Handbook of motivation and cognition: Foundations of social behavior* (pp. 23–63). Chichester, England: Wiley.
Houston, D. A., & Sherman, S. J. (1995) Cancellation and focus: The role of shared and unique features in the choice process. *Journal of Experimental Social Psychology, 25*, 357–378.
Houston, D. A., Sherman, S. J., & Baker, S. M. (1989). The influence of unique features and direction of comparison on preferences. *Journal of Experimental Social Psychology, 25*, 121–141.
Hovland, C. I., & Sherif, M. (1952). Judgmental phenomena and scales of attitude measurement: Item displacement in Thurstone scales. *Journal of Abnormal and Social Psychology, 47*, 822–832.
Huttenlocher, J., & Higgins, E. T. (1971). Adjectives, comparatives, and syllogisms. *Psychological Review, 78*, 487—504.
Kahneman, D., & Miller, D. T. (1986). Norm theory: Comparing reality to its alternatives. *Psychological Review, 93*, 136–153.
Keil, A., Mussweiler, T., & Epstude, K. (2006). Alpha-band activity reflects reduction of mental effort in a comparison task: A source space analysis. *Brain research, 1121*, 117–127.
Klayman, J., & Ha, Y.-W. (1987). Confirmation, disconfirmation, and information in hypotheses testing. *Psychological Review, 94*, 211–228.
Lockwood, P., & Kunda, Z. (1997). Superstars and me: Predicting the impact of role models on the self. *Journal of Personality and Social Psychology, 73*, 91–103.
Markman, A. D., & Gentner, D. (1993). Structural alignment during similarity comparisons. *Cognitive Psychology, 25*, 431–467.

Markman, A. D., & Gentner, D. (1996). Commonalities and differences in similarity comparisons. *Memory & Cognition, 24*, 235–249.

Medin, D. L., Goldstone, R. L., & Gentner, D. (1993). Respects for similarity. *Psychological Review, 100*, 254–278.

Miller, C. T. (1982). The role of performance-related similarity in social comparison of abilities: A test of the related attributes hypothesis. *Journal of Experimental Social Psychology, 18*, 513–523.

Miller, C. T. (1984). Self-schemas, gender, and social comparison: A clarification of the related attributes hypothesis. *Journal of Personality and Social Psychology, 46*, 1222–1228.

Miller, D. T., & Prentice, D. A. (1996). The construction of social norms and standards. In E. T. Higgins and A. W. Kruglanski (Eds.), *Social psychology: Handbook of basic principles* (pp. 799–829). New York: Guilford Press.

Morse, S., & Gergen, K. J. (1970). Social comparison, self-consistency, and the concept of self. *Journal of Personality and Social Psychology, 16*, 148–156.

Mussweiler, T. (2001). "Seek and ye shall find": Antecedents of assimilation and contrast in social comparison. *European Journal of Social Psychology, 31*, 499–509.

Mussweiler, T. (2003). Comparison processes in social judgment: Mechanisms and consequences. *Psychological Review, 110*, 472–489.

Mussweiler, T. (2007). Assimilation and contrast as comparison consequences: A selective accessibility model. In D. A. Stapel & J. Suls (Eds.), *Assimilation and contrast* (pp. 165–185). New York: Psychology Press.

Mussweiler, T., & Bodenhausen, G. (2002). I know you are but what am I? Self-evaluative consequences of judging ingroup and outgroup members. *Journal of Personality and Social Psychology, 82*, 19–32.

Mussweiler, T., & Englich, B. (2005). Subliminal anchoring: Judgmental consequences and underlying mechanisms. *Organizational Behavior and Human Decision Processes, 98*, 133–143.

Mussweiler, T., Englich, B., & Strack, F. (2004). Anchoring effect. In R. Pohl (Ed.), *Cognitive illusions—A handbook on fallacies and biases in thinking, judgment, and memory* (pp. 183—200). London: Psychology Press.

Mussweiler, T., & Epstude, K. (2008). *Relatively fast! Efficiency advantages of comparative thinking.* Manuscript submitted for publication.

Mussweiler, T., & Rüter, K. (2003). What friends are for! The use of routine standards in social comparison. *Journal of Personality and Social Psychology, 85*, 467–481.

Mussweiler, T., Rüter, K., & Epstude, K. (2004a). The man who wasn't there: Subliminal social comparison standards influence self-evaluation. *Journal of Experimental Social Psychology, 40*, 689–696.

Mussweiler, T., Rüter, K., & Epstude, K. (2004b). The ups and downs of social comparison: Mechanisms of assimilation and contrast. *Journal of Personality and Social Psychology, 87*, 832–844.

Mussweiler, T., & Strack, F. (2000a). The "relative self": Informational and judgmental consequences of comparative self-evaluation. *Journal of Personality and Social Psychology, 79*, 23–38.

Mussweiler, T., & Strack, F. (2000b). The use of category and exemplar knowledge in the solution of anchoring tasks. *Journal of Personality and Social Psychology, 78*, 1038–1052.

Northcraft, G. B., & Neale, M. A. (1987). Experts, amateurs, and real estate: An anchoring-and-adjustment perspective on property pricing decisions. *Organizational Behavior and Human Decision Processes, 39*, 84–97.

Ostrom, T. M., & Upshaw, H. S. (1968). Psychological perspectives and attitude change. In A. G. Greenwald, T. C. Brock, & T. M. Ostrom (Eds.), *Psychological foundations of attitudes* (pp. 217–242). New York: Academic Press.

Plous, S. (1989). Thinking the unthinkable: The effects of anchoring on likelihood estimates of nuclear war. *Journal of Applied Social Psychology, 19*, 67–91.

Ritov, I. (2000). The role of expectations in comparisons. *Psychological Review, 107*, 345–357.

Rüter, K., & Mussweiler, K. (2005). Bonds of friendship—Comparative self-evaluations evoke the use of routine standards. *Social Cognition, 23*, 137–160.

Rüter, K., & Mussweiler, T. (2008). *Practice effects in social comparisons with routine standards.* Manuscript submitted for publication.

Sanbonmatsu, D. M., Posavac, S. S., Kardes, F. R., & Mantel, S P. (1998). Selective hypothesis testing. *Psychonomic Bulletin and Review, 5*, 197–220.

Schwarz, N. (1994). Judgment in social context: Biases, shortcomings, and the logic of conversation. In M. P. Zanna (Ed.), *Advances in experimental social psychology* (pp. 125–162). San Diego, CA: Academic Press.

Schwarz, N., Bless, H., Bohner, G., Harlacher, U., & Kellenbenz, M. (1991). Response scales as frames of reference: The impact of frequency range on diagnostic judgment. *Applied Cognitive Psychology, 5*, 37–50.

Schubert, T. W., & Häfner, M. (2003). Contrast from social stereotypes in automatic behavior. *Journal of Experimental Social Psychology, 39*, 577–584.

Seta, J. J. (1982). The impact of comparison processes on coactors' task performance. *Journal of Personality and Social Psychology, 42*, 281–291.

Sherif, M., & Hovland, C. I. (1953). Judgmental phenomena and scales of attitude measurement: Placement of items with individual choice of number of categories. *Journal of Abnormal and Social Psychology, 48*, 135–141.

Sherif, M., & Hovland, C. I. (1961). *Social judgment: Assimilation contrast in communication and attitude change.* New Haven, CT: Yale University Press.

Sherman, S. J., Ahlm, D., Berman, L., & Lynn, S. (1978). Contrast effects and their relationship to subsequent behavior. *Journal of Experimental Social Psychology, 14*, 340–350.

Sherman, S. J., Houston, D. A., & Eddy, D. (1999). Cancellation and focus: A feature-matching model of choice. In W. Stroebe & M. Hewstone (Eds.), *European review of social psychology* (Vol. 10, pp. 169–197). Chichester, England: Wiley.

Smeesters, D., & Mandel, N. (2006). Positive and negative media effects on the self. *Journal of Consumer Research, 22*, 576–582.

Smith, E. E., Shoben, E. J, & Rips, L. J. (1974). Structure and process in semantic memory: A featural model for semantic decisions. *Psychological Review, 81*, 214–241.

Snyder, M., & Swann, W. B. (1978). Hypothesis-testing processes in social interaction. *Journal of Personality and Social Psychology, 36*, 1202–1212.

Srull, T. K., & Gaelick, L. (1983). General principles and individual differences in the self as a habitual reference point: An examination of self-other judgments of similarity. *Social Cognition, 2*, 108–121.

Stapel, D. A., & Blanton, H. (2004). From seeing to being: Subliminal social comparisons affect implicit and explicit self-evaluations. *Journal of Personality and Social Psychology, 87*, 468–481.

Strack, F., & Martin, L. L. (1987). Thinking, judging, and communicating: A process account of context effects in attitude surveys. In H. J. Hippler, N. Schwarz, & S. Sudman (Eds.), *Social information processing and survey methodology* (pp. 123–148). New York: Springer.

Strack, F., & Mussweiler, T. (1997). Explaining the enigmatic anchoring effect: Mechanisms of selective accessibility. *Journal of Personality and Social Psychology, 73*, 437–446.

Suls, J., Gaes, G., & Gastorf, J. W. (1979). Evaluating a sex-related ability: Comparison with same-, opposite-, and combined-sex norms. *Journal of Research in Personality, 13,* 294–304.

Suls, J., Gastorf, J. W., Lawhon, J. (1978). Social comparison choices for evaluating a sex- and age-related ability. *Personality and Social Psychology Bulletin, 4,* 102–105.

Taylor, S. E. (1981). The interface of cognitive and social psychology. In J. Harvey (Ed.), *Cognition, social behavior, and the environment* (pp. 182–211). Hillsdale, NJ: Erlbaum.

Trope, Y., & Bassok, M. (1982). Confirmatory and diagnostic strategies in social information gathering. *Journal of Personality and Social Psychology, 43,* 22–34.

Trope, Y., & Liberman, A. (1996). Social hypothesis testing: Cognitive and motivational factors. In E. T. Higgins, & A. W. Kruglanski (Eds.), *Social psychology: Handbook of basic principles* (pp. 239–270). New York: Guilford Press.

Tversky, A. (1977). Features of similarity. *Psychological Review, 84,* 327–352.

Tversky, A., & Gati, I. (1978). Studies in similarity. In E. Rosen & B. B. Lloyd (Eds.), *Cognition and categorization* (pp. 79–98). Hillsdale, NJ: Erlbaum.

Tversky, A., & Kahneman, D. (1974). Judgment under uncertainty: Heuristics and biases. *Science, 185,* 1124–1130.

Verplanken, B., Aarts, H. (1999). Habit, attitude, and planned behavior: Is habit an empty construct or an interesting case of goal-directed automaticity. In W. Stroebe & M. Hewstone (Eds.), *European review of social psychology* (Vol. 10, pp. 101–134). Chichester, England: Wiley.

Wheeler, L. (1966). Motivation as a determinant of upward comparison. *Journal of Experimental Social Psychology, 2* (Suppl. 1), 27–31.

Wheeler, L., Koestner, R., & Driver, R. E. (1982). Related attributes in choice of comparison others. *Journal of Experimental Social Psychology, 18,* 489–500.

Wheeler, L., Martin, R., Suls, J. (1997). The proxy model of social comparison for self-assessment of ability. *Personality and Social Psychology Review, 1,* 54–61.

Wilson, T. D., Houston, C., Etling, K. M., & Brekke, N. (1996). A new look at anchoring effects: Basic anchoring and its antecedents. *Journal of Experimental Psychology: General, 4,* 387-402.

Wood, J. V. (1989). Theory and research concerning social comparisons of personal attributes. *Psychological Bulletin, 106,* 231–248.

Wright, W. F., & Anderson, U. (1989). Effects of situation familiarity and financial incentives on use of the anchoring and adjustment heuristics for probabiliy assessment. *Organizational Behavior and Human Decision Processes, 44,* 68–82.

Zanna, M. P., Goethals, G. R., & Hill, J. F. (1975). Evaluating a sex-related ability: Social comparison with similar others and standard setters. *Journal of Experimental Social Psychology, 11,* 86–93.

8

Metacognition

HERBERT BLESS, JOHANNES KELLER, and ERIC R. IGOU

INTRODUCTION

*I*t seems almost like a truism that when individuals make sense of their social environment, form judgments, and plan behaviors, they use the information that comes to mind. And, the kind of information that comes to mind is a function of accessibility. In this respect, individuals' judgments reflect the accessibility of concepts at the time of judgment. These concepts can be either chronically or temporarily accessible (cf. Förster & Liberman, 2007; Higgins, 1996), and the underlying mechanisms rely heavily on automatic processes in the form of a spreading activation from one activated concept to other associated concepts and inhibition patterns.

One may argue that reliance on what comes to mind is a reasonable principle. In fact, it is very likely that information that comes to mind is actually relevant: The activation is the result either of the recency principle, suggesting that the activated information has something to do with the present situation, or of the frequency principle, suggesting that the activated information is often used and is therefore important for the individual in general. Thus, individuals could rely on a sort of autopilot by relying blindly on the activated information, in this case on highly automatized processes. They would then simply need to integrate the activated information, rely on the activated concepts when interpreting a social situation, or perform the behavior that is most accessible in a given situation. From this perspective, the automaticity aspect of accessibility would do most of the work, with little else needed. From such a perspective, judgments and behaviors would shift toward the implications of the (automatically) activated information. Priming positive material would result in more positive judgments, whereas priming negative material would result in more negative judgments. For example, having just thought about a scandal-ridden politician should result in more negative judgments about politicians in general (Schwarz & Bless, 1992a).

A blind reliance on the autopilot, however, comes with some problems. While the information that comes to mind is relevant in many—perhaps even most—cases, this relevance cannot necessarily be taken for granted all the time. First, a concept may come to mind because it was activated in a prior but unrelated situation. Although no longer relevant, the activation decays only slowly, thus leaving the concept with a heightened accessibility. In this case, relevance and accessibility drift apart. Second, information may be considered relevant although not representative (see Schwarz & Bless, 1992a) for the judgmental target. While the notion of relevance pertains primarily to the relation between the priming episode and the judgmental situation, representativeness pertains primarily to the relation between the primed concept and the judgmental target. Third, specific concepts may be intentionally activated by communicators who want to influence their recipients (e.g., "This is the best product available"). To avoid unwanted influence from activated information on their judgment, recipients need to make sure that they do not simply rely on the information activated by the communicator.

In all these cases, individuals would have good reason to protect themselves against the assimilative impact of the activated information. Of course, there may be various ways to achieve such protection. We propose that one powerful tool is the use of metacognitive strategies. We argue that individuals apply naïve theories concerning their cognitive processes to determine whether and how to use activated information (for other approaches holding similar assumptions, see, e.g., Wilson & Brekke, 1994; Wilson, Gilbert, & Wheatley, 1998). Such naïve theories on how judgments and behaviors could be affected by activated information serve as a basis for individuals' "decisions" on whether and how to use activated information. If the respective information is perceived as not representative for the target, naïve theories are likely to limit the direct assimilative impact of activated information and thus guide individuals to alternative judgmental processes. In such cases, individuals resort instead to alternative judgmental processes. In line with prior research, we suggest that the naïve theories underlying those alternative processes serve at least three functions: First, they provide the basis for detecting potential contamination; second, they serve as guidelines that influence how individuals deal with the activated information, that is, how they use this information; third, they allow for additional inferences and judgments. We examine these issues and in doing so address the role of such naïve theories with respect to the potential impact on judgment and decision making from (a) activated declarative knowledge, (b) feelings, and (c) recollective memory experiences.

We assume that naïve metacognitive theories can be located on different levels of abstraction. On the most abstract level, individuals hold a general naïve theoretical assumption that nonrepresentative or irrelevant information may potentially bias their judgmental processes. On an intermediate level, individuals hold more concrete assumptions or naïve theories concerning when and why a distinct piece of information may be considered nonrepresentative and hence a potential source of bias in their judgmental process. Finally, on a concrete level, individuals hold assumptions about exactly how a piece of information or specific contextual factors might exert a biasing impact on their judgments and what type of judgmental strategy may be most appropriate to prevent a biasing influence.

METACOGNITIVE NAÏVE THEORIES AND THE USE OF DECLARATIVE KNOWLEDGE

A general assumption about human information processing holds that individuals cannot process all potentially relevant pieces of information and therefore truncate their search for information. As a result of this truncation, only the most accessible information will be used, although other, less-accessible information would be equally or even more applicable. As mentioned, accessibility often goes along with relevance, and the accessibility mechanism therefore leads to appropriate judgments in many—if not most—situations. However, the relevance of the activated information cannot be taken for granted in each and every situation. Consequently, since individuals are motivated to form unbiased judgments, they need to make sure that the activated subset of information is not biased. In other words, they need to make sure that the activated subset of information is relevant and representative of the whole set of potentially relevant pieces of information. For example, imagine a personnel manager interviewing an applicant. The applicant's name, Oliver, reminds him of an excellent employee he hired 2 years ago; in other words, the name *Oliver* activates the concept of excellence. Given that the first name is unlikely to be related to the applicant's actual performance later, the interviewer would be well advised not to rely on the currently activated concept of excellence in making his hiring decision.

To protect themselves against unwanted influences from activated declarative knowledge, individuals must recognize the possibility that they might be affected by such unwanted influences as a first step. Since such a potential unwanted influence is hardly observable in a direct way, individuals need other ways to detect it. Along with other approaches (e.g., Strack, 1992; Wegener, Petty, & Dunn, 1998; Wilson & Brekke, 1994), we argue that individuals solve this task by drawing inferences on the basis of their naïve theories about the functioning of their mind. We propose that one such naïve metacognitive theory holds that judgments are likely to be assimilated toward activated information unless activated information obviously serves as a standard of comparison (although we readily acknowledge the importance of the fact that individuals hold naïve metacognitive theories about contrast effects [see Wegener & Petty, 1997], we refrain from further elaborating on this issue given the scope of the present chapter). Consequently, individuals need to differentiate between activated information that appropriately influences their judgments and activated information that might do so inappropriately. We argue that, in this process, individuals will again rely on their metacognitive knowledge. The relevant metacognitive knowledge holds that accessible declarative knowledge can inappropriately influence judgments (a) when the information comes to mind independent of the judgmental target, (b) when the information is not representative of the judgmental target, or (c) when communication rules that guide the interpretation of the situation indicate that the use of the accessible information is inadequate. These three aspects that individuals need to check to avoid inappropriate informational influences are core elements of the inclusion/exclusion model proposed by Schwarz and Bless (1992a, in press; Bless & Schwarz, 1998; see also Schwarz, chapter 6, this volume).

The inclusion/exclusion model holds that individuals who form a judgment about a target need to retrieve some cognitive representation of it in a first step. In addition, they need to determine some standard of comparison against which the target is evaluated (Kahneman & Miller, 1986). Both the representation of the target and of the comparison standard are in part context dependent, and these representations include chronically as well as temporarily accessible information (Higgins, 1996). The specific impact of accessible information depends on how it is used. Information that is included in the representation formed about the target results in assimilation effects. If the respective information is not included in the representation formed about the target but excluded, it may be used in constructing a standard of comparison, which in turn results in contrast effects (for details, see Schwarz & Bless, 1992a, in press). The inclusion/exclusion model describes three filter rules that parallel these considerations. Individuals will exclude accessible information from the representation of a target (a) when they believe that this information was brought to mind by some irrelevant influence, (b) when the information is not considered representative of the target, or (c) when its (repeated) use would violate conversational norms.

Substantial empirical evidence supports the notion that individuals exclude information on the basis of the three filter rules. In other words, individuals scrutinize activated information on the basis of their naïve metacognitive theories. One of these midlevel metacognitive theories holds that inappropriately activated information may contaminate social judgments. Accordingly, individuals try to avoid an influence when they believe that the activated information was brought to mind by some irrelevant influence. This assumption can nicely be demonstrated in priming experiments. In priming experiments, participants are typically taking part in two ostensibly unrelated studies, in which the priming is disguised in the "first" study, and the impact of the priming is assessed in the second "unrelated" study, often with a different experimenter in a different location. Relying on such a paradigm, Lombardi, Higgins, and Bargh (1987) demonstrated that when individuals became aware of a (unrelated) priming procedure, they no longer relied on the activated concepts to interpret a subsequent situation. Going beyond this correlational evidence, Strack, Schwarz, Bless, Kübler, & Wänke (1993) primed either positive or negative concepts, presented the description of a target person, and experimentally manipulated participants' attention to a priming procedure. When individuals' attention was not directed toward the subtle priming procedure, judgments reflected the implications of the activated primes (assimilation); that is, priming applicable positive concepts resulted in more positive evaluations than priming negative concepts. However, when individuals' attention was directed at the priming procedure, judgments reflected contrast effects; that is, priming positive concepts resulted in more negative evaluations than priming negative concepts (see also Martin, 1986, for directing individuals' attention indirectly by applying a subtle or a blatant priming procedure).

This finding can be attributed to individuals' motivation to avoid the unwanted influences from activated information. The perception of potential bias and the resulting attempt to avoid the influence by excluding the activated information (or by other means; see section on Alternative Shielding Strategies) necessarily required metacognitive knowledge about the potential influence. Without such metacognitive knowledge, no attempt to counteract the activated but irrelevant information would have been possible. In this respect, metacognitive theories provide a shield against the unwanted influences from activated information.

It follows from what has been said that individuals' metacognitive theories hold that information that is not representative for the judgmental target may contaminate judgment. Consequently, individuals should try to avoid an unwanted influence if they believe that the information is not representative for the target. For example, in one exemplary study, Bless and Schwarz (1998) activated a very positively evaluated politician and assessed how this specific politician affected the evaluation of the superordinate category, his political party. Participants were provided with an ostensible knowledge test, and the questions were varied so that answering the questions correctly resulted in a categorization of the politician. With this procedure, participants were thus subtly led to categorize the politician as either typical for his party (due to long-term membership) or as standing apart from his party. When the positively evaluated politician was perceived as typical, the evaluation of the party increased (assimilation). When the politician was perceived as atypical, the party evaluation decreased (contrast). Again, this finding can be attributed to individuals' motivation to avoid potentially biasing influences from activated information. Participants presumably followed a metacognitive theory according to which nonrepresentative information leads to biased judgments. They counteracted the potential influence and excluded the information from their mental representation of the target (i.e., the political party). Again, individuals seemed to apply a strategy to protect against the unwanted influences from activated information that was based on a metacognitive theory.

Numerous variables may influence individuals' decisions about whether a piece of information is representative for the judgmental target. For example, information may be perceived as nonrepresentative and consequently as exerting an inappropriate influence on judgment if it is perceived as falling outside the boundaries of a relevant target category (cf. Strack, Schwarz, & Gschneidinger, 1985) or, in a related vein, if an insufficient feature overlap with the judgmental target is detected (Herr, 1986; Herr, Sherman, & Fazio, 1983). In addition, variables that pertain to the category structure may affect the perceived representativeness and as a consequence assimilation and contrast effects (e.g., Bless, Igou, Schwarz, & Wänke, 2000; Schwarz & Bless, 1992b; Stapel & Schwarz, 1998). In all cases, the perception of the nonrepresentativeness of activated information eliminates the otherwise observed assimilation effects and in turn elicits contrast effects (for an experimental test of the role of perceived typicality, see Bless & Wänke, 2000; for reviews, see Schwarz & Bless, 1992a, 2007; Martin, Strack, & Stapel, 2001).

Important implications can be drawn from these findings about numerous everyday settings. In person perception, for example, individuals often want their judgments to be unbiased by the stereotype about the social group to which the target belongs (see, e.g., Macrae & Bodenhausen, 2000). Because the stereotype and related stereotypic information are likely to be automatically activated once the target is assigned to the category (Devine, 1989; however, see also Lepore & Brown, 1997), individuals striving for uncontaminated judgments need to shield themselves against the impact of the activated stereotypic information. Again, they can do so on the basis of their metacognitive theory that information should be representative to be used in constructing the representation of the judgmental target. If the target person is perceived as atypical, individuals are likely to exclude the activated stereotypic information from the mental representation of the target, and according to the inclusion/exclusion model described, this will result in contrast effects.

Empirical evidence for these assumptions was reported by Bless and colleagues (Bless, Schwarz, Bodenhausen, & Thiel, 2001). In these studies, all participants received the same description of a target person. Perceived typicality was manipulated by asking different questions about the description so that participants' responses implied either typicality (i.e., the target was representative for the social group) or not. When participants perceived the target as typical, the classic stereotyping effect (assimilation of the person's evaluation toward the stereotype) was obtained. However, a different picture emerged when participants perceived the target as atypical. In line with the naïve theory that nonrepresentative information may influence judgments inappropriately, participants attempted to avoid the impact of the stereotypic information. Presumably, they did so by excluding the stereotypic information from the representation of the target person, which in turn resulted in contrast effects. Individuals' metacognitive theory concerning the inappropriate influence from nonrepresentative information thus eliminated the assimilative stereotyping effect (see also Devine's [1989] assumption that awareness is a prerequisite for shielding).

Interestingly, a successful shielding on the level of person perception seems to be accompanied by opposite effects on the level of stereotype change. Whereas judging a target as atypical with respect to a social category resulted in less stereotyping of the target person, it increased the stereotypic perception of the superordinate social category. The exception (the atypical target person) reinforced the belief in the rule (the stereotype; see also Kunda & Oleson, 1997, for similar contrast effects in this respect). It is obvious that participants, by applying their metacognitive knowledge, eliminated not only the assimilative impact of the stereotype on the target person, but also the impact of the deviant target person on the evaluation of the social category. Interestingly, the perception of the atypicality of a target person has been demonstrated as less likely if situational constraints limit individuals' processing resources (Yzerbyt, Coull, & Rocher, 1999). We return to this issue in this chapter.

The assumption that individuals exclude activated information if they do not consider this information (a) relevant or (b) representative is at the heart of the outlined inclusion/exclusion model. The activated information has to pass these two filters. In addition, the model assumes a third filter that pertains to norms of conversational conduct that govern information use in conversations. Although activated information may be considered relevant and representative on an intrapersonal level, it is likely to be excluded when its repeated use would violate conversational norms of nonredundancy. In complying with such conversational norms, individuals may perceive some activated information as not representative or relevant to their ongoing communication. For example, when asked, "How is your family?" one would not include one's spouse if this information has just been given as a response to the preceding question, "How is your spouse?" By relying on such information, individuals would bias their communication—and in turn the recipients' interpretation—and they will therefore exclude it (e.g., Schwarz, Strack, & Mai, 1991; for a review, see Schwarz, 1996). Note that this third filter is grounded on assumptions concerning *inter*personal communication processes rather than on metacognitive assumptions regarding *intra*personal cognitive processes.

Alternative Shielding Strategies

We outlined the exclusion mechanism as one possible way of dealing with perceived unwanted influences from activated information. We readily acknowledge that other alternative processes have been proposed and have received considerable empirical substantiation. Various accounts (e.g., Strack & Hannover, 1996; Wegener & Petty, 1995, 1997) are based on the general assumption that individuals apply correction processes to eliminate the unwanted influence from activated information. These models hold that individuals do in fact compute a judgment that includes the potentially contaminating information and in a second step correct for the assumed unwanted influence. Empirical evidence for these assumptions has been obtained most prominently within the flexible correction model proposed by Wegener and Petty (1995, 1997). Not surprisingly, Wegener and colleagues (1998) explicitly linked their model to metacognition and to individuals' naïve theories about the biasing impact of context information.

One possible way of reconciling the different assumptions in the inclusion/exclusion model and the flexible correction model about the shielding strategies that individuals may apply in forming their judgments might be to look at the timing of when a potential contamination of the judgmental process is perceived. Perhaps a flexible correction is most likely when an unwanted influence is perceived after the judgment has already been made. In contrast, an exclusion mechanism seems most likely when an unwanted influence is perceived prior to judgment formation. Note that the flexible correction model requires individuals to hold assumptions about the direction and size of a potential bias. Since much of the research addressing the flexible correction assumption has revealed contrast effects, the flexible correction approach needs to assume that individuals usually overestimate the impact of unwanted influences to account for these findings.

Besides inclusion/exclusion and the flexible correction, other shielding strategies have been proposed. For example, Martin and colleagues (Martin, 1986; Martin, Seta, & Crelia, 1990) proposed that when perceiving a potential bias due to activated information, individuals "reset" the primed information. As this process might also eliminate information that is indeed relevant and representative, it may in turn result in contrast effects. Whereas the inclusion/exclusion model holds that nonrepresentative information may be used for constructing a standard of comparison, the set/reset model does not entail such an assumption.

Cognitive Requirements

The various mechanisms that are applied to shield the judgmental process from unwanted influences of activated information share some basic requirements. First, they require screening and detection of the potential unwanted bias. Second, the additional processes that go beyond a default use of the unwanted information take up capacity. How much additional capacity is necessary depends on the demands of the underlying mechanisms (exclusion, flexible correction, reset, etc.). Because both the screening and the additional processes are likely to demand cognitive resources, it is no surprise that contrast effects resulting from the described shielding mechanisms have been demonstrated as most likely when processing capacity and processing motivation are high (Martin & Achee, 1992; Meyers-Levy & Tybout, 1997).

METACOGNITIVE NAÏVE THEORIES AND THE RELIANCE ON FEELINGS

We discussed how individuals can shield themselves against the unwanted impact of activated declarative knowledge on the basis of their metacognitive naïve theories. Declarative knowledge, however, is not the only information that enters into human judgment and decision making. The processing of declarative knowledge is in many cases accompanied by subjective experiences (Bless & Forgas, 2000; Clore, 1992; Schwarz, 1998; Schwarz & Clore, 1996). These subjective experiences include affective feelings and cognitive feelings and can themselves serve as a basis for social judgments. Thus, they can exert an impact that is, at least partly, independent of the declarative knowledge. Often, such a reliance on subjective experiences is highly justified, for example, when individuals use their current mood to evaluate the likeability of a person they have been talking to for an hour. In this case, the feeling state presumably results from the interaction with the target person and reflects as a sort of summary of the perceiver's thoughts and evaluations ("I feel good because of this person") and can thus provide a solid basis for judgment—in other words, the feeling is representative for the judgmental target.

Similar to declarative knowledge being considered relevant by default, feeling states are often attributed by default to the current situation and to the current judgmental object and are thus seen as relevant for the judgment. However, the link between the experienced feeling and its origin is often unclear. Feelings are often diffuse, work in the background, and are frequently not the focus of an individual's attention. As a consequence, feelings may sometimes not be attributed to their correct source. Under such conditions, however, relying on the feeling could result in an unwanted influence on the individuals' judgments. For example, a target person may be evaluated rather negatively simply because the judge was in a negative mood due to some unrelated event prior to encountering the target person. Given the robust impact of feelings on human judgment and decision making and given the diffuse nature of feelings and their often-unclear origin, individuals would be well advised to shield themselves against unwanted influences from their feelings. We argue that in this respect, individuals—similar to the unwanted influence of declarative knowledge—rely on their metacognitive naïve theories. In the next section, we address this issue, in turn, for affective and cognitive feelings.

Affective Feelings

Schwarz and Clore (1983) proposed that individuals use their current affective state as a source of information for their judgments. Instead of relying on an elaboration of declarative knowledge about the relevant judgmental object, individuals may ask themselves, "How do I feel about it?" and use this feeling as the basis of their judgment (see Schwarz & Clore, 1996). In a now-classic experiment, Schwarz and Clore (1983) interviewed participants on the telephone on either a sunny or a rainy day and assessed participants' current mood and their life satisfaction. Not surprisingly, participants were happier on a sunny day. More important, they reported more satisfaction with their life in general on a sunny day. To demonstrate that individuals relied on the "How do I feel about it?" heuristic (rather than on the activated content), Schwarz and Clore introduced additional experimental conditions in which the informational value of the present mood state was manipulated. Some of the participants were made aware of the weather (and thus indirectly about the weather as a cause of their current mood). In this case, the impact of the current mood on judgments of life satisfaction in general was reduced. Presumably, participants became aware of the fact that their mood might inappropriately influence their judgments about their life in general—or, in other words, participants realized that mood was no longer representative for the judgmental object and therefore no longer used it (see the comments on the representativeness of declarative knowledge). Interestingly, similar effects have been documented for the impact of mood on processing strategies (Sinclair, Mark, & Clore, 1994).

This evidence suggests that individuals cease to rely on their affective state as a source of information when the informational value of the affective state is called into question, that is, when the affective state is considered not representative. Note that these conclusions require that individuals hold naïve metacognitive theories about how affective states may influence their judgments. Only this metacognitive background knowledge allows them to switch to alternative processes, which in turn attenuates the unwanted impact of their current mood state.

Cognitive Feelings

The impact of feelings on social judgment and decision making is not restricted to affective feelings (such as happy, sad, or angry moods). On the contrary, cognitive feelings have been shown to have a pronounced impact on individuals' information processing, as well. Cognitive feelings comprise a spectrum of phenomena like the feeling of knowing (e.g., Koriat, 1993; Nelson, Leonesio, Landwehr, & Narens, 1986), the feeling of familiarity (Jacoby, Kelley, Brown, & Jasechko, 1989), or the experienced ease of retrieval (Schwarz, 1998; Tversky & Kahneman, 1973). Many of these phenomena are implicitly or explicitly based on the experienced fluency of information processing, that is, on the experienced ease with which cognitive processes can be performed (e.g., encoding or retrieval; for a discussion see Schwarz, 2004).

One of these cognitive feelings pertains to the experienced ease of retrieval. Tversky and Kahneman (1973) proposed that judgments are based on the "ease with which instances or associations could be brought to mind" (p. 208). Note that this assumption implies an influence of the experienced ease independent, or at least partly independent, of the activated content, that is, the activated declarative knowledge. Interestingly, in many situations the activated content and the experienced ease of retrieval have very similar implications (see Schwarz, 1998; Taylor, 1982). Consider, for example, a person retrieving arguments in favor of a particular position. It is very likely the person will retrieve more arguments (content) the easier it is to retrieve arguments (ease of retrieval).

A methodological paradigm to disentangle activated declarative knowledge (content) and the experienced ease of retrieval was proposed by Schwarz, Bless et al., (1991). In one of their studies, participants were asked to recall either 6 or 12 examples of assertive behaviors, after which they rated their own assertiveness. Pretests had demonstrated that participants could retrieve 6 behaviors easily, whereas recalling 12 behaviors was perceived as difficult. Within this paradigm, the impact of ease and content can be disentangled, and conflicting predictions can be tested. If individuals base their judgment on the content that comes to mind, they should rate themselves as more assertive the more information they recall, that is, in the condition in which 12 rather than 6 assertive behaviors are accessible. Conversely, if individuals base their judgment on the ease with which the content comes to mind, they should rate themselves as more assertive when the relevant pieces of information come to mind easily, that is, when they recall 6 (easy) rather than 12 (difficult) assertive behaviors. The results of a series of studies supported the latter explanation (for additional evidence, conceptual replications, and extensions, see Dijksterhuis, Macrae, & Haddock, 1999; Fishbach, Igou, & Kruglanski, 2005; Greifeneder & Bless, 2007; Keller & Bless, 2005; Rothman & Schwarz, 1998; Stepper & Strack, 1993; Wänke, Bless, & Biller, 1996; for overviews, see Schwarz, 1998, 2004).

The findings obtained in the studies mentioned reflect a reliable effect of the experienced ease of retrieval on a wide spectrum of social judgments. Presumably, relying on the experienced ease often results in fairly good judgments. After all, in many situations the ease of retrieval reflects, for example, that many instances are stored in memory. For instance, a lazy student will easily elicit many memories of bad performance. However, there are also situations in which the feeling does not reflect the amount of information stored in memory but is the result of some other determinant For example, information may be easily retrieved when it is vivid or when it has just been used in a prior situation. In such situations, the feeling of ease is no longer representative for the judgmental target and may thus bias individuals' judgments. We argue that—similar to declarative knowledge and affective feelings—individuals can shield themselves against unwanted influences from their cognitive feelings by using their naïve metacognitive theories about the impact of cognitive feelings on judgments and decisions.

The question of whether individuals are inevitably influenced by the experienced ease of retrieval or whether they can shield themselves against a potentially unwanted influence has been addressed in a number of studies. In these studies, individuals were informed that their experienced ease of retrieval might stem from some source that accompanied the retrieval process and not from the retrieval processes itself (and thus from the amount of information stored in memory). For example, individuals were informed that the retrieval task was made easier or more difficult by music that was played during the retrieval (Schwarz, Bless et al., 1991) or by special arrangements in the answer format (Greifeneder & Bless, 2005; Ruder & Bless, 2003; Wänke, Schwarz, & Bless, 1995; for applications of this logic to the ease/difficulty to suppress thoughts, see Förster & Liberman, 2001, 2007). Across these various studies, individuals were able to avoid the impact of their feelings. When the experienced ease was perceived as nondiagnostic, that is, as not representative for the judgmental target, individuals' judgments did not reflect the experienced ease of retrieval. Instead, individuals resorted to the activated content; that is, judgments reflected the activated declarative knowledge. Note that these conclusions again require that individuals hold naïve metacognitive theories about how their cognitive feelings affect judgmental processes. Their metacognitive background knowledge allows them to switch to alternative judgmental processes.

We focused on the experienced ease of retrieval as one variant of cognitive subjective experiences. Given the scope of this chapter, we refrain from elaborating on other fluency experiences in detail. However, we argue that fairly similar considerations apply to the impact of other fluency experiences. In this respect, perceptual fluency (e.g., Bornstein & D'Agostino, 1994; Whittlesea, 1993; Zajonc, 2000) as it is perceived during the encoding of stimuli can be interpreted as akin to the fluency at retrieval (for overviews, see Reber, Schwarz, & Winkielman, 2004, or Jacoby, Kelley, & Dywan, 1989). In line with this assumption, Bornstein and D'Agostino (1994) as well as Van den Bergh and Vrana (1998) reported findings documenting an impact of attributional processes in judgmental situations for which perceptual fluency was involved (i.e., a reduced impact of perceptual fluency when participants became aware that it may reflect the influence of an unrelated variable) that parallels the impact of attributional processes as documented in studies involving ease-of-retrieval manipulations (cf. Schwarz, Bless et al., 1991).

Cognitive Requirements

The discussion reflects that when individuals form social judgments, they often rely on their affective and cognitive feelings as a source of information. As is the case with activated declarative knowledge, these feelings are often, but not always, representative of the judgmental target. If they are perceived as not representative, individuals can make efforts to shield themselves against their unwanted impact and can resort to alternative judgmental strategies. Most probably, the screening and detection of the potential unwanted bias and the application of alternative judgmental strategies involve certain requirements. First, to screen for and detect potential biasing influences, individuals need a naïve theory concerning the potential influence of their feelings, as well as a naïve theory regarding when this impact is unwanted. One may speculate that because of the diffuse nature of feelings, detecting a potential bias is more difficult in this case than it is with declarative knowledge, although no direct evidence pertaining to this assumption is available so far. In fact, in the misattribution studies reported, participants were rather directly made aware of the nonrepresentative source of their feeling state. However, it should be noted that although the experimental instructions increased the awareness of a potential source of the feeling, the instructions did not refer to a potential impact of the feeling on the judgment or even a direction of the impact. For example, when investigating the impact of mood on general subjective well-being, Schwarz and Clore (1983) directed individuals' attention toward the weather; however, no direct statement about the weather influencing mood or general well-being was presented. Second, after having detected an unwanted influence of their feelings, individuals need to resort to an alternative judgmental process. Given that judgments based on feelings are often considered simplifying heuristics requiring few resources, it is very likely that the alternative judgmental process requires additional cognitive resources. In line with this assumption, Siemer and Reisenzein (1998) demonstrated that individuals relied more heavily on the How do I feel about it? heuristic when the situational circumstances reduced processing capacity. Parallel findings are available with respect to cognitive feelings in the form of ease of retrieval. The impact of the experienced ease of retrieval on social judgments was most pronounced when processing capacity (Greifeneder & Bless, 2007) or processing motivation was decreased (Rothman & Schwarz, 1998; however, see also Tormala, Petty, & Briñol, 2002).

METACOGNITIVE NAÏVE THEORIES ABOUT MEMORY

We addressed how individuals use their metacognitive naïve theories about the impact of declarative knowledge and feelings to shield themselves against unwanted influences from these sources of information. In this section, we extend our discussion to individuals' recollections of prior occurrences and to individuals' metacognitive theories about memory processes.

Let us assume, for example, that a person is asked whether she saw a blue Volkswagen parked in front of her house on the previous day. At first glance, individuals' response strategy in such situations seems straightforward. They try to retrieve the event from memory, and if they can retrieve it, that is, in the presence of a recollective experience, they affirm the occurrence of the event in question. In the absence of a recollective experience, they deny the occurrence of the event. However, a second look reveals a more complicated picture. Neither the absence nor the presence of a recollective experience is diagnostic in itself and may require additional interpretation on the basis of metacognitive processes.

Absence of a Recollective Experience
The absence of a recollective experience may either reflect that the stimulus in question has not been presented

or, alternatively, that the stimulus has been presented but its presentation cannot be remembered. In the latter case, the absence of the recollective experiences would not be representative for the response, "No, the event did not occur," thus exerting an unwanted influence on individuals' responses. We argue that individuals can reduce the potential impact of this unwanted influence on the basis of naïve metacognitive theories they hold about memory processes.

What assumptions might individuals have about memory processes and the absence of recollective experiences? Their naïve theories could hold that the absence of a recollective experience is not diagnostic (in other words, is not representative) when this absence might be caused by conditions that are independent of the prior occurrence of the stimulus. This should be the case, for example, when the encoding or the retrieval conditions are suboptimal or when the stimulus in question is nonsalient. For example, the absence of a recollection is less diagnostic when nonsalient routine behaviors are to be recalled (e.g., whether one watched the news on TV last Monday) compared to recalling a salient event (whether one attended a Rolling Stones concert last Monday). In such cases, individuals should be less likely to rely solely on their (nonrepresentative) recollective experience but should resort to other strategies. Other strategies could, for example, reflect random guessing, reasoning about the objective likelihood of a particular event, or attempts to pick up even subtle cues of the situation that imply the occurrence or nonoccurrence. We will return to this possibility.

In a series of studies, Strack and Bless (1994) addressed the considerations discussed. In one of these studies, participants were presented with 30 slides that all showed objects of the category "tools" (e.g., hammer, screwdriver) and with 4 slides of nontools (e.g., flowers, a book), each of which belonged to a unique category. As a result of this presentation format, the tool items were nonsalient, whereas the nontool items were highly salient. In a subsequent recognition test, participants' recognition of the targets was close to perfect; that is, independent of the experimental conditions, participants correctly reported that the targets were part of the presentation set. The main focus, however, was on the distractor items for which participants could not have a recollective experience. Salient distractors (e.g., a telephone) were correctly rejected, and additional judgments indicated that these rejections were made with high confidence. The results suggest that this confidence was based on the application of metacognitive inferences ("If this item had been presented, I would surely remember it"). For nonsalient items, however, individuals presumably hold other naïve theories. Here, the absence of a recollective experience is not very diagnostic—after all, nonsalient items have a high chance of not being remembered ("A pair of pliers could have been among all those tools"). Since this reduces the diagnosticity of the absence of a recollective experience, individuals resorted to other strategies in forming their recognition judgments—in this case resulting in a (false) recognition of the nonsalient distractors.

One possible interpretation of these findings holds that individuals differentially relied on their recollective experience based on their metacognitive knowledge about memory, in this case about the likelihood of remembering salient versus nonsalient stimuli. When their theories implied that the absence of a recollective experience could be due to aspects that were independent of a prior presentation of the stimulus, individuals relied less on this experience. In other words, if the absence of a recollective experience was considered less representative, individuals realized the potential bias that may arise from relying on this experience and resorted to alternative response strategies.

Of course, the logic outlined can be applied to other metacognitive assumptions. Another very reasonable naïve theory would hold that the absence of a recollective experience is not very diagnostic if the items were encoded under suboptimal conditions (e.g., short presentation latencies). Data reported by Strack and Bless (1994) support this notion. Individuals were less likely to rely on the absence of a recollective experience when they perceived the encoding conditions to be suboptimal—presumably because under these conditions, the absence of a recollective experience was considered not representative.

One could easily add other variables that have been demonstrated to affect memory performance (e.g., self-reference, retrieval conditions, interval between encoding and retrieval, mood congruity, etc.). It should be noted that for the described mechanism itself, it is not important whether individuals' naïve theories are correct. The only requirement is that individuals believe in them. Förster and Strack (1998) convincingly demonstrated this by inducing beliefs that certain conditions (e.g., listening to music) exerted either an inhibiting or a facilitating effect on memory performance. Parallel to the findings of Strack and Bless, participants were more (less) likely to reject a distractor item if they believed that the music had facilitated (inhibited) the encoding of that item.

Presence of a Memory Trace Along with the empirical evidence reported by Strack and Bless (1994), we have focused here on the absence of a recollective experience. Note, however, that similar considerations can be applied to the presence of a memory trace. Again, the presence of a recollective experience per se is not completely diagnostic. The recollection may, for example, result from subsequent information (Loftus, 1975) or from the event having been merely imagined (Johnson & Raye, 1981). If individuals are aware of these alternatives, they may be hesitant to use the presence of a memory trace as a representative source of information. In that case, it is likely that individuals will resort to alternative judgment strategies (for a discussion, see Bless & Strack, 1998; Strack & Förster, 1998).

It is important to point out that resorting to alternative response strategies does not necessarily imply more accurate judgments or less bias in general. As discussed, participants in the studies reported by Strack and Bless were likely to resort to alternative judgmental strategies when they considered the absence of a recollective experience as nondiagnostic. Interestingly, in this research participants resorted to a reliance on context cues embedded in the recognition test. Strack and Bless (1994) argued that instead of relying on the absence of the recollective experience, participants based their judgments on subtle presuppositions that were embedded in the questions. Specifically, participants were more likely to falsely recognize a distractor stimulus when the questions were asked with the definite versus the indefinite article ("Did you see the [a] car?"). Thus, because they resorted to an alternative judgmental strategy, participants became the "victim" of the impact of the presupposition embedded in the wording of the question (see Loftus, 1979).

We speculate that with respect to processing requirements, considerations similar to those outlined apply here as well—although to the best of our knowledge, no direct evidence of this exists at this time. Specifically, we would expect that the fewer the processing resources that are available to scrutinize and detect the potential nondiagnosticity of the recollective experience, the more likely individuals will be to rely on the absence of their recollective experiences.

CONCLUSIONS

We elaborated on the important role that individuals' naïve metacognitive theories play in social cognition. We suggested that declarative knowledge, affective and cognitive feelings, as well as memory experiences that come to mind in a given situation are usually very relevant for judgments required in a given situation. However, in some cases the feelings and information may come to mind even though they are not relevant or representative for the current judgmental task and may consequently bias individuals' judgments. We proposed that individuals can engage in efforts to control for such unwanted influences by relying on their metacognitive knowledge.

We argue that in a general or abstract form this metacognitive knowledge holds that if information that comes to mind is not representative for the judgmental target, it may inappropriately bias judgments. On a medium level, individuals will hold more specific assumptions about why information could be considered not relevant or not representative. For example, declarative knowledge could be considered not representative because it was not elicited by the judgmental situation. Feelings could be perceived as not representative because they are not attributed to the judgmental target, and the absence of recollective experiences could be treated as not representative when situational constraints are perceived as the source of impaired memory performance. On an even more specific level, individuals can hold very concrete assumptions, for example, that noise during the encoding of stimuli may cause later absence of a recollective experience. Drawing on such abstract, midlevel, or concrete naïve metacognitive theories, individuals will try to avoid unwanted influences on their judgments and resort to alternative judgmental strategies.

Presumably, the two steps, awareness of the unwanted influence and resorting to alternative judgmental strategies, are associated with various processing requirements. First, it is necessary that the relevant metacognitive knowledge is not only available but also accessible in the judgment situation. Moreover, this step requires sufficient motivation (Wegener & Petty, 1995) to form unbiased judgments and the capacity to detect potentially biasing influences. Not surprisingly, the available evidence so far suggests that shielding against biasing influences of activated declarative knowledge and feelings is most likely to occur when processing resources are unconstrained and processing motivation is high (e.g., Martin et al., 1990; Rothman & Schwarz, 1998; see also Yzerbyt, Coull, & Rocher, 1999, for evidence that detecting atypical, nonrepresentative information requires substantial cognitive resources). Besides motivation and capacity, other variables may also influence the likelihood of perceiving an unwanted influence from activated information. In this respect, it has been suggested that awareness of an irrelevant influence is more likely when the contextual information is externally presented (e.g., by an experimenter) rather than generated by participants themselves (e.g., Mussweiler & Neumann, 2000).

Second, for individuals to resort to alternative judgmental strategies, such alternatives must be available. These alternative strategies may differ, and which alternative eventually serves as a substitute depends on a number of aspects, including accessibility. Moreover, given that individuals very often initially prefer less-taxing judgmental processes (e.g., Fiske & Neuberg, 1990), it is likely that following an alternative processing strategy requires more processing than pursuing the initial attempt. Note, however, that this may not be true in every case. For example, instead of relying on activated declarative knowledge (because this knowledge may exert an unwanted influence), individuals may resort to their feeling as a basis of their judgment—a process that would presumably require fewer cognitive resources.

Do these considerations regarding the interplay of activated information and metacognitive processes imply the existence of a homunculus—an inner being inside the brain that is supervising our cognitive activities? In this respect, one may assume that the judgment about the representativeness of information is again influenced by activated information and metacognitive knowledge about how to use this information and so forth. We refrain from proposing a homunculus perspective. In fact, in most cases activated declarative knowledge is relevant for the judgment, and affective and cognitive feelings most often do result from the judgmental target. Thus, it is very reasonable that individuals use the activated information by default. Note that an exclusion of activated information from the judgmental process is presumably much less likely in everyday situations than one would expect on the basis of the experimental findings. In experimental settings, researchers, for very good reasons, try to disentangle the activation of knowledge from the judgment situation, the induction of an affective feeling from the judgmental target, or the experienced ease of retrieval from the activated content. In natural situations, such diversions are clearly less likely. In addition, general motivational variables may influence the reliance on the most accessible information. For example, individuals low in need for closure (cf. Kruglanski, 2004) will be less likely to rely on the most accessible information as a basis of a judgment.

Are judgments that directly or indirectly result from the attempt to avoid an unwanted influence more accurate—in other words, does the application of metacognitive knowledge improve judgments? Leaving aside the obvious problems in defining judgmental accuracy, the accuracy question is not addressed by our arguments. The accuracy of judgments depends on several aspects that are independent of the outlined mechanisms. The first aspect pertains to the question of whether the exclusion of activated information is justified. This may depend in part on the accuracy of the naïve metacognitive theories and on the appropriateness of their application in a given situation. If individuals' metacognitive assumptions are correct, and if their use is adequate, accuracy may be improved.

The second aspect pertains to the alternative judgment processes to which individuals resort. It may well be that an alternative processing strategy is associated with an even larger bias than the initial one. If this bias is not detected, accuracy is unlikely to be improved. This aspect is reflected, for example, in the fact that attempts to avoid assimilation effects often result in contrast effects (see also the bias due to presuppositions as a consequence of not relying on recollective experiences in the research reported by Strack & Bless, 1994). Note that the accuracy of the metacognitive theories is independent of the potential bias resulting from the application of alternative processing strategies.

In sum, the outlined considerations strongly suggest that individuals do not have to base their judgments invariably on the activated information in the form of declarative knowledge, affective and cognitive feelings, or recollective experiences. The accessibility of these sources of information is just one—perhaps often overestimated—side of the coin. We argue that the other, complementary side of the same coin is how the activated information is used. We suppose that this aspect deserves particular attention, and that in this respect individuals' naïve metacognitive theories play a very important role in understanding human judgments and decision making.

REFERENCES

Bless, H., & Forgas, J. P. (Eds.). (2000). *The message within. The role of subjective experience in social cognition and behaviour*. Philadelphia: Psychology Press.

Bless, H., Igou, E. R., Schwarz, N., & Wänke, M. (2000). Reducing context effects by adding context information: The direction and size of context effects in political judgment. *Personality and Social Psychology Bulletin, 26*, 1036–1045.

Bless, H., & Schwarz, N. (1998). Context effects in political judgment: Assimilation and contrast as a function of categorization processes. *European Journal of Social Psychology, 28*, 159–172.

Bless, H., Schwarz, N., Bodenhausen, G. V., & Thiel, L. (2001). Personalized versus generalized benefits of stereotype disconfirmation: Tradeoffs in the evaluation of atypical exemplars and their social groups. *Journal of Experimental Social Psychology, 37*, 386–397.

Bless, H., & Strack, F. (1998). Social influence on memory: Evidence and speculations. In V. Yzerbyt, G. Lories, & B. Dardenne (Eds.), *Metacognition: cognitive and social dimensions* (pp. 90–106). Thousand Oaks, CA: Sage.

Bless, H., & Wänke, M. (2000). Can the same information be typical and atypical? How perceived typicality moderates assimilation and contrast in evaluative judgments. *Personality and Social Psychology Bulletin, 26*, 306–314.

Bornstein, R. F., & D'Agostino, P. R. (1994). The attribution and discounting of perceptual fluency: Preliminary tests of a perceptual fluency/attributional model of the mere exposure effect. *Social Cognition, 12*, 103–128.

Clore, G. L. (1992), Cognitive phenomenology: Feelings and the construction of judgment. In L. L. Martin & A. Tesser (Eds.), *The construction of social judgment* (pp. 133–164). Hillsdale, NJ: Erlbaum.

Devine, P. G. (1989). Stereotypes and prejudice: Their automatic and controlled components. *Journal of Personality and Social Psychology, 56*, 5–18.

Dijksterhuis, A., Macrae, C. N., & Haddock, G. (1999). When recollective experiences matter: Subjective ease of retrieval and stereotyping. *Personality and Social Psychology Bulletin, 25*, 760–768.

Fishbach, A., Igou, E. R., & Kruglanski, A. W. (2005). A unimodel account for the ease of retrieval effect. Unpublished manuscript.

Fiske, S. T., & Neuberg, S. L. (1990). A continuum of impression formation from category-based to individuating processing: Influences of information and motivation on attention and interpretation. *Advances in Experimental Social Psychology, 23*, 1–74.

Förster, J., & Liberman, N. (2001). The role of attribution of motivation in producing post-suppressional rebound. *Journal of Personality and Social Psychology, 81*, 377–390.

Förster, J., & Liberman, N. (2005). A motivational model of post-suppressional rebound. *European Review of Social Psychology, 15*, 1–32.

Förster, J., & Liberman, N. (2007). Knowledge activation. In E. T. Higgins & A. W. Kruglanski (Eds.), *Social psychology: Handbook of basic principles* (2nd ed.; pp. 201–231). New York: Guilford Press.

Förster, J., & Strack, F. (1998). Subjective theories about encoding may influence recognition: Judgmental regulation in human memory. *Social Cognition, 16*, 78–92.

Greifeneder, R., & Bless, H. (2007). Relying on accessible content versus accessibility experiences: The case of processing capacity. *Social Cognition, 25*, 853–881.

Herr, P. M. (1986). Consequences of priming: Judgment and behavior. *Journal of Personality and Social Psychology, 51*, 1106–1115.

Herr, P. M., Sherman, S. J., & Fazio, R. H. (1983). On the consequences of priming: Assimilation and contrast effects. *Journal of Experimental Social Psychology, 19*, 323–340.

Higgins, E. T. (1996). Knowledge activation: Accessibility, applicability, and salience. In E. T. Higgins & A. W. Kruglanski (Eds.), *Social psychology: Handbook of basic principles* (pp. 133–168). New York: Guilford Press.

Jacoby, L. L., Kelley, C. M., Brown, J., & Jasechko, J. (1989), Becoming famous overnight: Limits of the ability to avoid unconscious influences of the past. *Journal of Personality and Social Psychology, 56*, 326–338.

Jacoby, L. L., Kelley, C. M., & Dywan, J. (1989). Memory attributions. In H. L. Roediger & F. I. M. Craik (Eds.), *Varieties of memory and consciousness: Essays in honour of Endel Tulving* (pp. 391–422). Hillsdale, NJ: Erlbaum.

Johnson, M. K., & Raye, C. L. (1981). Reality monitoring. *Psychological Review, 88*, 67–85.

Kahneman, D., & Miller, D. (1986). Norm theory: Comparing reality to its alternatives. *Psychological Review, 93*, 136–153.

Keller, J., & Bless, H. (2005) When negative expectancies turn into negative performance: The role of ease of retrieval. *Journal of Experimental Social Psychology, 41*, 535–541.

Koriat, A. (1993), How do we know what we know? The accessibility model of the feeling of knowing, *Psychological Review, 100*, 609–639.

Kruglanski, A. W. (2004). *The psychology of closed mindedness*. New York: Psychology Press.

Kunda, Z., & Oleson, K.C. (1997). When exceptions prove the rule: How extremity of deviance determines the impact of deviant examples on stereotypes. *Journal of Personality and Social Psychology, 72*, 965–979.

Lepore, L., & Brown, R. (1997). Category and stereotype activation: Is prejudice inevitable? *Journal of Personality and Social Psychology, 72*, 275–287.

Loftus, E. F. (1975). Leading questions and the eyewitness report. *Cognitive Psychology, 7*, 560–572.

Loftus, E. F. (1979). *Eyewitness testimony*. Cambridge, MA: Harvard University Press.

Lombardi, W. J., Higgins, E. T., & Bargh, J. A. (1987). The role of consciousness in priming effects on categorization: Assimilation and contrast as a function of awareness of the priming task. *Personality and Social Psychology Bulletin, 13,* 411–429.

Macrae, C. N., & Bodenhausen, G. V. (2000). Social cognition: Thinking categorically about others. *Annual Review of Psychology, 51,* 93–120.

Martin, L. L. (1986). Set/reset: The use and disuse of concepts in impression formation. *Journal of Personality and Social Psychology, 51,* 493–504.

Martin, L. L., & Achee, J. W. (1992). Beyond accessibility: The role of processing objectives in judgment. In L. L. Martin & A. Tesser (Eds.), *The construction of social judgments* (pp. 195–216). Hillsdale, NJ: Erlbaum.

Martin, L. L., Seta, J. J., & Crelia, R. (1990). Assimilation and contrast as a function of people's willingness and ability to expend effort in forming an impression. *Journal of Personality and Social Psychology, 59,* 27–37.

Martin, L. L., Strack, F., & Stapel, D. A. (2001). How the mind moves: Knowledge accessibility and the fine-tuning of the cognitive system. In A. Tesser & N. Schwarz (Eds.), *Blackwell handbook of social psychology: Intrapersonal processes* (pp. 236–256). Oxford, England: Blackwell.

Meyers-Levy, J., & Tybout, A. M. (1997). Context effects at encoding and judgment in consumption settings: The role of cognitive resources. *Journal of Consumer Research, 24,* 1–14.

Mussweiler, T., & Neumann, R. (2000). Sources of mental contamination: Comparing the effects of selfgenerated versus externally provided primes. *Journal of Experimental Social Psychology, 36,* 194–206.

Nelson, T. O., Leonesio, R. J., Landwehr, R. F., & Narens, L. (1986), A comparison of three predictors of an individual's memory performance: The individual's feeling of knowing versus the normative feeling of knowing versus base-rate item difficulty. *Journal of Experimental Psychology: Learning, Memory, and Cognition, 12,* 279–287.

Reber, R., Schwarz, N., & Winkielman, P. (2004). Processing fluency and aesthetic pleasure: Is beauty in the perceiver's processing experience? *Personality and Social Psychology Review, 8,* 364–382.

Rothman, A. J., & Schwarz, N. (1998). Constructing perceptions of vulnerability: Personal relevance and the use of experiential information in health judgments. *Personality and Social Psychology Bulletin, 24,* 1053–1064.

Ruder, M., & Bless, H. (2003). Mood and the reliance on the ease of retrieval heuristic. *Journal of Personality and Social Psychology, 85,* 20–32.

Schwarz, N. (1990). Feelings as information: Informational and motivational functions of affective states. In R. M. Sorrentino & E. T. Higgins (Eds.), *Handbook of motivation and cognition: Foundations of social behavior* (Vol. 2, pp. 527–561). New York: Guilford Press.

Schwarz, N. (1996). *Cognition and communication: Judgmental biases, research methods, and the logic of conversation.* Hillsdale, NJ: Erlbaum.

Schwarz, N. (1998). Accessible content and accessibility experiences: The interplay of declarative and experiential information in judgment. *Personality and Social Psychology Review, 2,* 87–99.

Schwarz, N. (2004). Meta-cognitive experiences in consumer judgment and decision making. *Journal of Consumer Psychology, 14,* 332–348.

Schwarz, N., & Bless, H. (1992a). Constructing reality and its alternatives: An inclusion/exclusion model of assimilation and contrast effects in social judgment. In L. L. Martin & A. Tesser (Eds.), *The construction of social judgment* (pp. 217–245). Hillsdale, NJ: Erlbaum.

Schwarz, N., & Bless, H. (1992b). Scandals and the public's trust in politicians: Assimilation and contrast effects. *Personality and Social Psychology Bulletin, 18,* 574–579.

Schwarz, N., & Bless, H. (2007). Mental construal processes. The inclusion/exclusion model. In D. A. Stapel & J. Suls (Eds.), *Assimilation and contrast in social psychology* (pp. 119–141). New York: Psychology Press.

Schwarz, N., Bless, H., Strack, F., Klumpp, G., Rittenauer-Schatka, H., & Simons, A. (1991). Ease of retrieval as information: Another look at the availability heuristic. *Journal of Personality and Social Psychology, 61*, 195–202.

Schwarz, N., & Clore, G.L. (1983). Mood, misattribution, and judgments of well-being: Informative and directive functions of affective states. *Journal of Personality and Social Psychology, 45*, 513–523.

Schwarz, N., & Clore, G. L. (1996). Feelings and phenomenal experiences. In E. T. Higgins & A. Kruglanski (Eds.), *Social psychology: A handbook of basic principles* (pp. 433–465). New York: Guilford Press.

Schwarz, N., Strack, F., & Mai, H. P. (1991). Assimilation and contrast effects in part-whole question sequences: A conversational logic analysis. *Public Opinion Quarterly, 55*, 3–23.

Siemer, M., & Reisenzein, R. (1998). Effects of mood on evaluative judgments: Influence of reduced processing capacity and mood salience. *Cognition and Emotion, 12*, 783–805.

Sinclair, R. C., Mark, M. M., & Clore, G. L. (1994). Mood-related persuasion depends on misattributions. *Social Cognition, 12*, 309–326.

Stapel, D. A., & Schwarz, N. (1998). The Republican who did not want to become president: An inclusion/exclusion analysis of Colin Powell's impact on evaluations of the Republican Party and Bob Dole. *Personality and Social Psychology Bulletin, 24*, 690–698.

Stepper, S., & Strack, F. (1993). Proprioceptive determinants of emotional and nonemotional feelings. *Journal of Personality and Social Psychology, 64*, 211–220.

Strack, F. (1992). The different routes to social judgments: Experiential versus informational strategies. In L. L. Martin & A. Tesser (Eds.), *The construction of social judgment* (pp. 249–275). Hillsdale, NJ: Erlbaum.

Strack, F., & Bless, H. (1994). Memory for non-occurrences: Metacognitive and presuppositional strategies. *Journal of Memory and Language, 33*, 203–217.

Strack, F., & Förster, J. (1998). Self-reflection and recognition: The role of metacognitive knowledge in the attribution of recollective experience. *Personality and Social Psychology Review, 2*, 111–123

Strack, F., & Hannover, B. (1996). Awareness of influence as a precondition for implementing correctional goals. In P. Gollwitzer & J. A. Bargh (Eds.), *The psychology of action: Linking cognition and motivation to behavior* (pp. 579–595). New York: Guilford Press.

Strack, F., Schwarz, N., Bless, H., Kübler, A., & Wänke, M. (1993). Awareness of the influence as a determinant of assimilation versus contrast. *European Journal of Social Psychology, 23*, 53–62.

Strack, F., Schwarz, N., & Gschneidinger, E. (1985). Happiness and reminiscing: The role of time perspective, mood, and mode of thinking. *Journal of Personality and Social Psychology, 49*, 1460–1469.

Taylor, S. E. (1982), The availability bias in the social perception and interaction. In D. Kahneman, P. Slocic, & A. Tversky (Eds.), *Judgment under uncertainty: Heuristics and biases* (pp. 190–200). Cambridge, England: Cambridge University Press.

Tormala, Z. L., Petty, R. E., & Briñol, P. (2002). Ease of retrieval effects in persuasion: A self-validation analysis. *Personality and Social Psychology Bulletin, 28*, 1700–1712.

Tversky, A., & Kahneman, D. (1973), Availability: A heuristic for judging frequency and probability. *Cognitive Psychology, 5*, 207–232.

Van den Bergh, O., & Vrana, S. R. (1998). Repetition and boredom in a perceptual fluency/attributional model of affective judgments. *Cognition and Emotion, 12*, 533–553.

Wänke, M., Bless, H., & Biller, B. (1996). Subjective experience versus content of information in the construction of attitude judgments. *Personality and Social Psychology Bulletin, 22*, 1105–1113.

Wänke, M., Schwarz, N., & Bless, H. (1995), The availability heuristic revisited: Experienced ease of retrieval in mundane frequency estimates. *Acta Psychologica, 89*, 83–90.

Wegener, D. T., & Petty, R. E. (1995). Flexible correction processes in social judgment: The role of naive theories in corrections for perceived bias. *Journal of Personality and Social Psychology, 68*, 36–51.

Wegener, D. T., & Petty, R. E. (1997). The flexible correction model: The role of naïve theories of bias in bias correction. In M. P. Zanna (Ed.), *Advances in experimental social psychology* (Vol. 29, pp. 141–208). Mahwah, NJ: Erlbaum.

Wegener, D. T., Petty, R. E., & Dunn, M. (1998). The metacognition of bias correction: Naive theories of bias and the flexible correction model. In V. Yzerbyt, G. Lories, & B. Dardenne (Eds.), *Metacognition: Cognitive and social dimensions* (pp. 202–227). London: Sage.

Whittlesea, B. W. A. (1993). Illusions of familiarity. *Journal of Expermental Psychology: Learning, Memory & Cognition, 19*, 1235–1253.

Wilson, T. D., & Brekke, N. (1994). Mental contamination and mental correction: Unwanted influences on judgments and evaluations. *Psychological Bulletin, 116*, 117–142.

Wilson, T. D., Gilbert, D. T., & Wheatley, T. (1998). Protecting our minds: The role of lay beliefs. In V. Yzerbyt, G. Lories, & B. Dardenne (Eds.), *Metacognition: Cognitive and social dimensions* (pp. 171–201). New York: Sage.

Yzerbyt, V. Y., Coull, A., & Rocher, S. J. (1999). Fencing off the deviant: The role of cognitive resources in the maintenance of stereotypes. *Journal of Personality and Social Psychology, 77*, 449–462.

Zajonc, R. B. (2000). Feeling and thinking: Closing the debate over the independence of affect: In J. P. Forgas (Ed.), *Feeling and thinking: The role of affect in social cognition* (pp. 31–58.). New York: Cambridge University Press.

9

Intuition

FRITZ STRACK and ROLAND DEUTSCH

APPROACHING INTUITION

Intuition in Everyday Language

The term *intuition* has its history outside of psychology. Specifically, there is wide popular agreement that intuition is an important quality of human judgments. Intuitive judgments are seen as a capacity to reach insights on ways that are "more direct," "based on feelings," and "effortless" (Myers, 2002). In addition, people have an immediate sense of validity that is associated with the judgment. Wherever they come from, people trust their "gut feelings" more than the outcome of complex inferences. Although intuition is an idea that everybody appears to understand (at least intuitively), the meaning of intuition as a scientific concept is less clear.

Intuition in Psychological Research

In psychology, the empirical study of intuition can be found in the domains of judgment and decision making and cognitive and personality psychology. Although not under the label of intuition, decision researchers (e.g., Tversky & Kahneman, 1974) have studied simplifying rules ("heuristics") that come to bear under internal and external conditions that prevent people from applying normative principles under suboptimal conditions, like high complexity, time pressure, distraction, low motivation, or little knowledge (e.g., Gigerenzer & Todd, 1999). In the domain of cognitive psychology, research on implicit memory and learning suggest that people may acquire and use relatively complex knowledge without being able to verbalize its content (e.g., Berry & Dienes, 1993; Cleeremans, Destrebecqz, & Boyer, 1998). Among personality psychologists, Seymour Epstein and his colleagues (1991;

Epstein, Pacini, Denes-Raj, & Heier, 1996) have proposed a theory of the self from which he derived an intuitive thinking style as a person characteristic.

When intuition was studied as a topic of its own, psychologists have pointed at a multitude of meanings (Epstein, 2007) and have focused their research on different aspects. Yet, most of them included two components: Intuition is described as effortless and as occurring with little awareness of the underlying process (e.g., Bruner, 1960; Hammond, 1996; Hogarth, 2005; Kahneman & Frederick, 2002; Lieberman, 2000). Other criteria are the acquisition through personal experience and practice (Epstein, 2007; Lieberman, 2000) and a dominance of cognitive feelings and affect (Kahneman & Frederick, 2002; Loewenstein, Weber, Hsee, & Welch, 2001). Also, intuition is seen to be based on a holistic assessment of the situation (e.g., Hogarth, 2005). All of those characteristics point at a simplifying function that allows people to arrive at judgments under suboptimal circumstances.

At the same time, such simplifying procedures are often based on people's subjective experiences to arrive at various decisions (e.g., Schwarz, chapter 6, this volume). In this case, it is possible that the accompanying feelings may provide an immediate hint that the decision is correct. Thus, intuitive judgments can be described by both the simplifying processes and their accompanying subjective experiences or feelings. While psychologists' attention is directed on the underlying processes, people's phenomenal experiences are in the focus of the everyday understanding of intuition.

Under the label of intuition, we describe simplifying procedures that are more likely to be used under specific circumstances that prevent people from engaging in effortful cognitive activities. This may be driven either by a characteristic of the task and its context (like complexity or time pressure) or by a lack of motivation. As a consequence, judgments will gain an intuitive component that may vary in degree.

For example, a person may be asked at a party to estimate the proportion of divorced people in his or her country. Clearly, the best way of generating a judgment would be to consult the official statistics. If this is not possible or too tedious, given the casual interest in the matter, the person may draw a sample and extrapolate the proportion in the population from the number of divorces among personal acquaintances. Alternatively, the person may rely on what is reported in the news and infer that frequent reports on divorced actors or politicians reflect a high number of divorces in the general population.

However, there are other strategies at simplifying this judgment that draw on the people's experiences while generating a judgment. Specifically, feelings may be elicited and used as a basis for the judgments. These feelings may be affective in nature and simplify judgments that involve evaluations. Thus, a judgment about the effect of divorce on people's happiness may depend on how thinking about divorce may make people feel. That is, an unpleasant feeling will be likely to be used to make the judgment more negative. For judgments of frequency or probability, feelings of ease may play an important role. In the present case, people may use their experienced effort (or ease) as a basis for the judgment. Specifically, they may be more likely to infer a low proportion of divorces if it feels difficult to come up with instances; conversely, higher estimates will be provided if it feels easy to execute the task.

Thus, the intuitive simplification of judgments may occur in different ways. First, it may be achieved by employing "external" cues that afford shortcuts to the decision. Second, people may rely on "internal" cues while executing the task. In both cases, judges may pursue goals other than that of generating an accurate judgment. For example, they may be concerned about being fast or about spending too much effort. However, there is also the possibility that simplifying cues (particularly internal ones) may be seen as more diagnostic. We illustrate the different ways of adding intuitive components to a judgment by reporting some empirical findings.

INTUITION BY SHORTCUTS

Following Brunswik's (1956) seminal analysis of judgment and perception, a person's external and internal environment typically offers multiple cues that correlate with a judged criterion to varying degrees (*cue validity*). These cues in turn influence a person's judgment or perceptions to varying degrees (*cue utilization*) and may be more or less easy to process. Using relatively valid and easy-to-process cues is a viable means for simplifying judgments.

External Shortcuts

Psychology has little to say about the number and validity of external cues in a given situation. Correlations between external cues and judgmental criteria are greatly determined by the specific environment or culture. Take, for example, a cue that has received some experimental attention in recent years: the presence or absence of a major league soccer club in German cities. Interestingly, this cue is a good predictor of which of two German cities is larger (Gigerenzer & Goldstein, 1996). However, the cue validity may depend on the sociological and economic structures in Germany. It is easily conceivable that in other societies, no such correlation or even a reversed relationship would occur.

Although psychology cannot predict a priori which stimuli can serve as cues, research has established a wealth of external cues that humans use for a multitude of judgments and decisions. Such external cues vary along several dimensions, such as whether they can be found in the social or nonsocial world, their validity, how easy to process they are, or how frequently they occur in the environment (cf. Kruglanski, Erb, Spiegel, & Pierro, 2003). In what follows, we briefly describe some important social and nonsocial external cues.

Social psychology has identified numerous social cues that are frequently used to simplify judgment and decision making. Probably the most powerful external social cues are related to basic social categories, such as gender, age, ethnic background, or socioeconomic status. When motivation or capacity for thorough processing of individuating information is low, people show a propensity to base their judgments about individuals on group membership cues and thereby rely on stereotypic knowledge (e.g., Bodenhausen, 1990; Bodenhausen & Hugenberg, chapter 1, this volume; Brewer, Dull, & Lui, 1981). Presumably, stereotype-related cues have at least some validity in some cases (Judd & Park, 1993). But, in many cases they are relatively inaccurate, and people often maintain a belief in their validity even in the face of disconfirming information (Brewer et al., 1981; Taylor, 1981). At the same time, basic social categories are easily detectable, and stereotypic knowledge is activated on their perception in a very efficient manner (Devine, 1989). Hence, stereotypic cues may have at least some subjective validity and may often be used because of their ease of processing.

Besides cues signaling membership in basic social categories, other easy-to-process features of persons were demonstrated to influence a variety of judgments. In persuasive settings, various features of the communicators determined the outcome of persuasive attempts (Petty & Wegener, 1999). Expert, trustworthy, likable, attractive, powerful, and famous communicators seemed to be more persuasive, especially if the recipient had little motivation or cognitive capacity to process the message (Maio & Haddock, 2007).

Social consensus cues have powerful effects on many judgmental processes. In general, social consensus has a strong normative and informative power (Asch, 1956; Deutsch & Gerard, 1955; Festinger, 1954; Kruglanski & Mackie, 1990). Using others' behavior as a guide can be a powerful heuristic for animals (Hutchinson & Gigerenzer, 2005), and various studies have shown that social consensus cues can affect how much humans publicly or privately endorse or like opinions, objects, or behaviors (Martin & Hewstone, 2003).

Facial expressions and gestures serve as cues to infer inner states of other people. In their seminal research, Ekman and colleagues (e.g., Ekman, 1999; Ekman & Friesen, 1971) established that facial expressions provide relatively reliable information about emotions. Facial expressions are valid cues even across cultures, although there is evidence for culture-specific aspects of emotion expression (Elfenbein & Ambady, 2003). When judging the truthfulness of other persons, observers consistently use cues such as speed of talking or the use of illustrating gestures (e.g., Frank & Ekman, 2004), some of which may indeed correlate with truthfulness in many cultures (e.g., Ekman & O'Sullivan, 2005).

Generally, inferring other's intentions is an important social-cognitive task for humans and primates (Tomasello, Carpenter, Call, Behne, & Moll, 2005). Although coming to valid inferences about the causes of other's behaviors may be a very demanding task (Kelley, 1967), psychologists have identified a number of environmental cues that social perceivers may use to simplify this task. For example, evidence suggests that social perceivers exploit simple motion cues to infer intentions (Barrett, Todd, Miller, & Blythe, 2005; Blakemore & Decety, 2001). Research participants of Barrett et al. (2005) were able to discriminate between six intentions with remarkable accuracy by merely observing very abstract representations of movements of two alleged interaction partners. Motion cues seem to be so powerful that they result in intention inferences even with nonsocial objects, such as triangles (Heider & Simmel, 1944; Zogmaister, 2004).

Besides external social cues, a variety of nonsocial external cues have attracted the attention of researchers. Although nonsocial in nature, some of them were primarily studied in social realms. For instance, the scarcity of a commodity has been shown to be a powerful cue to value (Ditto & Jemmott, 1989), which is frequently used by advertisers and salespeople (Cialdini, 1993) to exert social influence. Generally, positive objects or attributes that are hard to obtain are perceived to be more desirable than when they are easy to obtain (Ditto & Jemmott, 1989; Gosling, Ko, Mannarelli, & Morris, 2002; Litwin, 1966).

In the realm of persuasion, the length of messages serves as a cue to message validity, especially when recipients are low in accuracy motivation or cognitive capacity (Petty & Cacioppo, 1986). In consumer psychology, brand names are interpreted as cues, which may (or may not) correlate with attributes of the individual product (e.g., Maheswaran, Mackie, & Chaiken, 1992). Research by Yeung and Soman (2007) suggests that consumers sometimes base their evaluation of services on their mere duration.

Another line of research has focused on heuristics rules of thumb that people may use to select and integrate cues (e.g., Gigerenzer & Goldstein, 1996; Gigerenzer, Hoffrage, & Kleinbölting, 1991). One remarkable finding resulting from this research is that often using only one or a few cues results in equally or even more accurate judgments than basing a judgment on numerous cues at a time. Simple decision rules such as the take-the-best heuristic (Gigerenzer & Goldstein, 1996) may have a quite general validity. Yet, their validity may be greatly influenced by the particular environment and the cues it provides (Hogarth & Karelaia, 2006, 2007).

Mediators of External Cue Effects How exactly do external cues bring about their effects? Obviously, people may directly base their judgments on external cues. For instance, people may consciously reason that high consensus on an opinion may indicate that the opinion is true. Or, people may consciously infer that long arguments are usually better arguments. Reflective processing of external cues of this kind best resembles what Kahneman and Frederick (2002) labeled *heuristic processing*. Such processing is not holistic but selective in that one or a few easy-to-process cues are used as substitutes for more effortful processing.

Besides heuristic processing, external cues often have more indirect effects on judgments. For example, the attractiveness of a communicator may elicit positive feelings, which then in turn may tune further processing to be less accurate (Schwarz, Bless, & Bohner, 1991). Another example is consensus information, which may result in biased message processing in the direction of the majority opinion (Erb, Bohner, Schmälzle, & Rank, 1998). In essence, external cues often cause inner responses, which may then influence further judgmental process. Such processes are discussed in greater detail in the next section.

Internal Shortcuts

Like their external counterparts, internal cues can also be correlated with a criterion of the judgment (Brunswik, 1956). For example, we may be aware of recalling a lot of information about a particular topic. This experience may be used for further inferences. For example, we may conclude that we are knowledgeable about the area, or that the exemplar in question exists in a high frequency. These "accessibility experiences" (e.g., Schwarz & Clore, 2007) are based on the outcome of recall from memory and are often accompanied by experiences that emerge as a function of the psychological process. For example, the process of recall may be experienced as effortful. Typically, this would be akin to other feelings that accompany many human activities. We feel locomotion, pressure, heat, effort, pain, and other experiential qualities. These feelings can be described on the dimensions of valence and intensity. They may guide our behaviors very efficiently and without much effort. For example, the feeling of unpleasant heat will cause us to immediately retreat from its origin or to eliminate its source.

At the same time, such feelings may provide a basis for people's decisions not only about the stimulus that has caused the feeling but also about the perceivers themselves. Thus, an intense pain may be used to assess the heat of an object. At the same time, it may serve to judge one's own sensitivity, particularly if another person reports a less-painful experience.

Next, we describe how judgments may be influenced by subjective experiences, even if people do not know their source. Moreover, we argue that feelings may be produced by mental activities and used to simplify judgments.

Affective Experiences Most important, people's moods may simplify their judgments. That is, how they feel may help them evaluate different targets, including themselves. For example, people were found more likely to expect a movie to be funny if they were in a positive mood (Pham, 2004). Also, in a positive mood, they judged themselves to be happier with their life (Schwarz & Clore, 1983, 1988). It is important to note that, unlike emotions, moods are highly malleable to be used because their source is not immediately available to the person. As a consequence, moods that are elicited by irrelevant sources may influence unrelated judgments. For example, good weather conditions (Schwarz & Clore, 1983), a success of the national soccer team (Schwarz, Strack, Kommer, & Wagner, 1987), or a pleasant room (Schwarz et al., 1987) may equally influence evaluations of one's life. Similarly, Johnson and Tversky (1983) have found that negative mood induced by reading about a particular negative event increased people's assessments of risk for a series of entirely different events. At the same time, this lack of awareness about the origin allows for unwanted influences. For example, a customer may come to like a particular product simply because she has a positive "gut feeling." The possibility that this feeling may have been strategically elicited by sources other than the product may not be noted, and its influence on the judgment will be unlikely to be corrected (e.g., Strack & Hannover, 1996).

Things are somewhat different for specific emotions. Such experiences also facilitate judgments and decisions. Feeling anxious, for example, may cause negative evaluations of the origin and may automatically elicit behaviors of withdrawal. At the same time, the representation of an emotion typically includes its source. As a consequence, the judgmental effect of emotion should not generalize across valence but across the specific content and implications. Thus, although anger and fear share the same (negative) valence, they have different judgmental and behavioral implications. Because their source is included in the representation, emotions are less malleable by the contexts than moods. That is, emotional influences can be expected to be less likely to cause misattributions (e.g., Schwarz & Clore, 2007). Conversely, because the source of emotions can be easily recognized as unrelated to an irrelevant target, it is easier to correct their influence on a judgment.

Bodily Sensations Other inputs on judgments may come from bodily sensations. As activations of both the autonomic and the central nervous system are related to emotions (Russell, 1980), it is likely that the resulting sensations may by themselves enter into the judgment. Most important, perhaps, autonomic arousal is an experience that serves as an ingredient of emotions. For example, Schachter and Singer (1962) found that arousal may fuel emotions that even have a different valence, like anger and enjoyment. In a related vein, Zillmann (1983) demonstrated that arousal may "transfer" from one emotion to another, even if their valence differs. For example, arousal that originates from aggression may facilitate subsequent erotic attraction (Zillmann, 1989). Not surprisingly, arousal can be misattributed (Zanna & Cooper, 1976), and its transfer to specific emotions depends on a sufficient temporal dissociation from the original source (Zillmann, 1978).

The second type of bodily sensations comes from the central nervous system that controls voluntary muscle contractions. In particular, muscles from the face are linked to specific emotions. Most important, the zygomaticus and the corrugator muscle are involved in smiling and frowning, facial expressions of joy and anger (e.g., Ekman, 1999). Moreover, a large body of research (e.g., Laird, 2007) has shown that facial expressions exert an impact on people's feelings and emotions. Theories that account for this influence propose two underlying mechanisms. One (James, 1894) assumes that the bodily action is the origin of the emotion; the other (Darwin, 1872) holds that the appropriate bodily action merely intensifies the emotion that is elicited by a different stimulus. In both cases, bodily actions exert a causal influence that has been investigated in a series of experiments. Ekman, Levenson, and Friesen (1983) had participants pose different facial expressions and found changes both in the experience of the emotions and in autonomic reactions. In a related vein, Laird (e.g., 1974) had participants contract the corrugator by pointing at the muscle without actually referring to the concept of smiling. Even in this situation, the induced muscle contraction intensified judgments of funniness. However, all of these procedures do not rule out a mediating process that is not the mechanism that James and Darwin had in mind. Specifically, with these procedures it is possible that people engage in a process of self-perception (Bem, 1967) and infer their emotional state from their bodily expression. The result of such an inference, however, does not necessarily possess the phenomenal quality of a feeling and may also be inferred from other people's expressions. Thus, to demonstrate the direct impact of facial expressions, it was necessary to prevent participants from recognizing the actual nature of the facial action. We (Strack, Martin, & Stepper, 1988) were able to do this by having participants execute a task that would activate either the zygomaticus muscle or its antagonist. Specifically, we had people hold a pen either between their teeth (which elicits a smile) or their protruded lips (which prevents a smile) while they were reading cartoons. As a result, the cartoons were rated as funnier in the teeth condition than in the lips condition.

Comparable results were obtained for body postures. In a study by Stepper and Strack (1993), participants were unobtrusively induced to adopt either an upright or a slumped posture while they received feedback about their result in a task they had previously accomplished. As a consequence of the induced posture, participants who had received above-average feedback reported to be prouder if they had been induced to adopt an upright as compared to a slumped position.

Cognitive Feelings Another type of experience is not readily tied to a particular valence. It emerges from the way information is processed. Specifically, the ease of the processing is represented in a feeling that can be used for further processing. In one of the earliest studies on this issue, Schwarz, Bless, Strack et al. (1991) had participants recall past behaviors while changing the difficulty with which these memories could be generated. This was achieved by simply varying the number of episodes (6 or 12) that had to be retrieved. The dependent variable was the inference that they drew on the basis of their retrieval. As a result, people assigned themselves more of the characteristics (in this case, assertiveness) that were implied by the behavior if recall was easy as opposed to difficult. It is important to note that this finding stands in stark contrast to other notions (e.g., Stapel & Spears, 1996) that would assume the amount of behavioral information would be the basis for trait inferences. In fact, other studies (Rothman & Schwarz, 1998) showed that both types of information may be used depending on the importance of the judgment. That is, if the judgment was important, people were more likely to use the implications of the recalled information and were therefore more influenced if the higher number of episodes had to be recalled. However, when importance was low, the impact of the recalled information was greater in the "easy" (few recalled episodes) than in the "difficult" (many recalled episodes) condition.

The flexibility in the use of the feeling also becomes apparent in the fact that its impact depends on its perceived source. That is, if the experience is attributed to an irrelevant source, it will not become a basis of the judgment (Schwarz, Bless, Strack et al., 1991; Wänke, Schwarz, & Bless, 1995).

The ease with which information is recalled from memory is related to the concept of fluency that was studied in cognitive psychology (e.g., Whittlesea, Jacoby, & Girard, 1990; Wippich, 1994; Witherspoon & Allan, 1985). Various experiments have shown that the ease of processing affects judgments of all kinds.

In our own research (e.g., Bolte & Goschke, 2005; Topolinski & Strack, in press), we found judgments of coherence to be influenced by the fluency with which readers were able to process a set of three words that were either semantically related by a superordinate concept (e.g., "salt," "sand," and "wave" are related by the concept "sea") or not. Specifically, we found that participants who had not explicitly identified the existing commonality were able to indicate if the words were related. This was even the case if they were not asked to search for the common associate but merely to read the words (Topolinski & Strack, 2008).

The question arises if fluency is represented as an experience and if this experience has a particular quality. In fact, evidence exists that fluency is linked to positive affect (Winkielman & Cacioppo, 2001; but see also Unkelbach, 2006). In other words, it feels good if things go easy. If this is the case, the opposite causal direction should also obtain. In other words, people may use their positive affect as an indication that easy processing is possible, that is, that there exists a common associate. This was, in fact, the case. If participants were primed with a smiling (as opposed to a frowning) face, they were more likely to arrive at a judgment of coherence. The same was true if the words of the triad had a positive (as opposed to a negative) valence. Additional evidence comes from our finding that the valence of the words contributed to the perceived coherence. That is, if the triad was made up of positive words, people were more likely to see it as more coherent than when it was made up of negative words.

These findings suggest that people's cognitive functioning may be represented in subjective feelings that may themselves become a basis for various judgments. This pertains not only to judgments of semantic coherence but also to loudness (e.g., Jacoby, Allan, Collins, & Larwill, 1988), clarity (e.g., Whittlesea et al., 1990), or duration (e.g., Witherspoon & Allan, 1985), familiarity (e.g., Whittlesea, 1993), typicality (Schwarz, 1998), fame (Jacoby, Kelley, Brown, & Jasechko, 1989; Jacoby, Woloshyn, & Kelley, 1989), and even truth (e.g., Begg, Anas, & Farinacci, 1992; Reber & Schwarz, 1999).

Like other feelings, they are bodily expressed and can be influenced by adopting the appropriate expressions. For example, we (Topolinski, Likowski, Weyers, & Strack, in press) have found that the processing of semantically incoherent triads was more likely to cause contractions of the corrugator muscle (involved in anger) than coherent triads. Demonstrating the reverse causal direction, Strack and Neumann (2000) found that inducing participants to contract the corrugator led to judgments of less fame. Presumably, this was the case because judgments of fame may be based on the pleasant feeling of ease that is created by familiarity (Jacoby, Kelley et al., 1989; Jacoby, Woloshyn et al., 1989), while furrowing the brow creates an unpleasant feeling of effort.

In summary, these findings show that human judgments can be facilitated by the use of subjective experiences. These experiences differ in their malleability, and the judgments differ in their evaluative component. That is, some judgments are attitudinal in the sense that they imply an evaluation of a target. Other judgments are factual in that they assign a nonevaluative characteristic. For all types of judgments, subjective experiences may play a role not only by facilitating them but also by creating a specific phenomenal state. Thus, they combine both characteristics that are typically associated with intuition: They ease the judgment, and they render it a particular feeling quality.

A Special Case: Self-Perception One source of input that it is difficult to assign to the internal-external dichotomy is that of self-perception. This mechanism goes back to Bem (1967), who argued that under special conditions, people infer their attitudes from their own behavior. In this case, the person is in the same position as an outside observer who has no privileged access to others' internal states. At the same time, however, behavior produces proprioceptive cues that are internally perceived and may cause subjective experiences. Thus, one's own behavior may exert its impact on judgments through both the external and the internal cues it produces. However, it is possible to prevent it from operating as an external information by avoiding its categorization. In other words, people can draw inference from their (and others') behavior only to the degree that the behavior has a certain meaning, that is, that it is categorized. If such a categorization is suppressed, an impact is more likely to be caused by internal cues. This was experimentally demonstrated in a series of studies by Strack and his collaborators (Martin, Harlow, & Strack, 1992; Stepper & Strack, 1993; Strack et al., 1988; Strack & Neumann, 2000). Also, people may draw inferences from the experienced difficulty of a decision. Specifically, Liberman and Förster (2004; see also Förster & Liberman, 2001) have shown that the difficulty that is experienced during decision making may serve as a cue for making further inferences about the attractiveness of decision alternatives.

A MODEL FOR INTUITIVE JUDGMENTS

The brief review of the literature suggests that numerous psychological mechanisms may be involved in simplifying judgments to varying degrees. It appears therefore inappropriate to categorize judgments as either intuitive or nonintuitive. Instead, intuition may be better conceived as a property of judgmental processes that is gradual in nature. Consequently, most judgments will have both intuitive and nonintuitive components. This multifaceted conception implies that cognitive theories of intuition have to be relatively complex. Specifically, such theories will have to aim at describing processes underlying external and internal shortcuts and to capture how they interactively determine judgment and decision making.

There have been attempts to reconstruct simplifying processes in judgment and decision making as a function of two interacting mental systems that follow different operational characteristics (e.g., Epstein & Pacini, 1999; Hogarth, 2005; Kahneman & Frederick, 2002; Lieberman, 2000; Sloman, 1996). Correspondingly, social psychologists have proposed dual-system models to explain simplifying processes in person perception, persuasion, or attribution (e.g., Lieberman, 2003; Smith & DeCoster, 2000; Strack & Deutsch, 2004). Despite that dual-system models were developed in different branches of psychology such as personality (e.g., Epstein, 1994), judgment and decision making (e.g., Hogarth, 2005; Kahneman & Frederick, 2002), and social psychology (e.g., Lieberman, 2000), they share a remarkable number of basic assumptions. At the same time, they differ in various aspects and draw on different literatures to support their assumptions.

In the remainder of this chapter, we present a social-cognition perspective on how dual-system models can explain more or less simple varieties of judgment and decision making. Instead of discussing a number of existing models in parallel (for a synopsis, see Smith & DeCoster, 2000), we use the reflective-impulsive model (RIM; Strack & Deutsch, 2004) of social behavior as a prototype (see also Deutsch & Strack, 2007) because it applies to both decision making and behavior.

Overview Over the Reflective Impulsive Model

Based on the assumption that human behavior is determined by at least two forces, the RIM invokes two processing systems that follow different operational principles (see Figure 9.1). Related to many other models of judgments and decision making (e.g., Epstein, 1991, 1994; Lieberman, 2000; Smith & DeCoster, 1999,

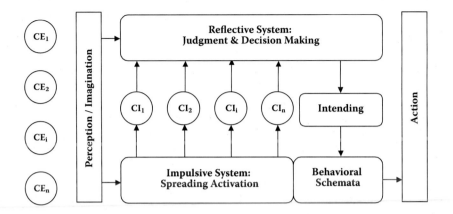

Figure 9.1 Schematic description of judgment and decision making in the reflective-impulsive model (RIM). CE, environmental cues; CI, internal cues generated by the impulsive system (e.g., feelings, conceptual activation). (From Deutsch & Strack, 2007.)

2000), the reflective system (RS) is assumed to generate judgments and decisions by creating and transforming knowledge. At the same time, the impulsive system (IS) operates by associative mechanisms. Specifically, the IS determines behavior by linking learned cues to behavioral schemata (Schmidt, 1975). Activation is assumed to spread efficiently and independent of intentions. This occurs in a parallel fashion in which perceptual features of the situation are integrated.

The RS has features that are complementary to the IS and serve different goals. It generates a representation of what is activated in the IS and may fulfill executive functions, such as overcoming habitual responses or compiling action plans in new situations (Lieberman, Gaunt, Gilbert, & Trope, 2002). The RS needs cognitive resources, and its operations, which are based on a few, distinct symbolic representations are slower than those of the IS. Actions are elicited as a consequence of decisions, which in turn activate behavioral schemata through a process of intending (Gollwitzer, 1999). This mechanism automatically reactivates behavioral schemata that correspond with the decision and directs attention toward stimuli that are relevant for the implementation of the decision.

Two Routes to Judgments

Deviating from other two-process models (e.g., Kahneman, & Frederick, 2005), the RIM assumes that all judgments and decisions are exclusively generated in the RS, which operates in a controlled fashion. At the same time, cues from the environment may influence explicit judgments and decisions. This may occur in two different ways (see Figure 9.1). First, the RS may select certain cues and integrate them directly into a judgment, like estimating the price of a product based on the brand, its advertised price, or data from consumer reports. This route to judgments is best applicable to those phenomena described in the section on external shortcuts.

In addition, external cues trigger internal responses of the IS, of which the most important ones are the activation of concepts, affective and nonaffective feelings, and behavioral tendencies. These internal cues can be represented in the RS and enter into the formation of judgments. For instance, perceiving subtle cues of a smile may automatically elicit positive feelings. Alternatively, seeing a member of a stereotyped group may activate negative personality traits (Devine, 1989, see also Bodenhausen and Hugenberg, this volume). Just as environmental cues, internal cues may also enter into judgmental processes in the RS. A situation may be judged as dangerous because it elicits feelings of anxiety (Loewenstein et al., 2001); a person may be regarded as dishonest because the concept *dishonest* keeps popping into one's mind during the person's presence. We may like another person just because we automatically imitate her smiles (e.g., Chartrand & Bargh, 1999). This route to judgments is best applicable to those phenomena described in the section on internal shortcuts. Compared to external cues, internal cues are assumed to be processed more easily because they largely represent automatic responses of the IS, such as readily interpretable feelings, accessible concepts, or perceivable behavioral tendencies. Thus, environmental cues can either directly or indirectly (i.e., mediated by organismic responses) enter into judgments.

Cue Selection

If all judgments and decisions are allocated in the RS, what are their determinants? The RIM assumes that this depends on motivation and cognitive capacity. Generally, the RS is assumed to choose those cues that (a) serve best the current goal (like accurate judgments or coming to a particular conclusion; cf. Kruglanski et al., 2003) and (b) are compatible with the available cognitive resources. How the IS responds depends on the associations that were created through learning and on the momentary accessibility based on recent activation. However, accessibility is also influenced by motivational processes in the IS and RS. They are important for judgments and decisions because they influence the generation of internal cues. Specifically, people's active reflection, their basic needs, and their general motivational orientation are assumed to determine what will come to mind. That is, intensively coping with an issue will selectively activate the information that is being considered. Also, distinct need states will increase the accessibility of information about ways of need satisfaction (e.g., Bruner, 1947). Finally, a general orientation toward approach or avoidance will selectively increase the activation potential for positive or negative information. The exact operation of these mechanisms is discussed elsewhere more thoroughly (e.g., Deutsch & Strack, 2007; Strack & Deutsch, 2004).

CONCLUSION

Using the RIM as a conceptual orientation allows a new understanding of intuition that deviates from the notion that intuitive judgments are generated by a separate system of information processing or are the result of unique cognitive operations. Instead, it assumes that intuitive judgments are cut from the same cognitive cloth as their nonintuitive counterparts. While they are not distinct by the processes that generate them, intuitive judgments differ in terms of their informational bases. Specifically, such judgments use cues that are less complex, which can be found either in the environment or as an internal response to the environment, such as affective and nonaffective feelings, conceptual activation, and behavioral responses. Importantly, the dual-system perspective advanced here suggests that various and potentially very different processes generate the simplifying cues that may feed into judgments. Subsuming them under the label of intuition is certainly useful. At the same time, the mechanisms that bring about internal cues may follow different psychological rules. An important task for future research is to further expand our knowledge on how exactly these processes are similar or different and how they interactively may influence judgments and decisions.

Judgments based on internal cues typically possess those features that are ascribed to intuition, such as being formed with little effort, low process awareness, being based on personal experience, or being based on feelings. As we have argued, however, some of these features can also be absent in judgments based on internal cues. Thus, according to the RIM, intuition as defined by common criteria represents a subset of a broader range of indirect cue effects mediated by responses of the IS.

REFERENCES

Asch, S. E. (1956). Studies of independence and conformity: A minority of one against a unanimous majority. *Psychological Monographs: General and Applied, 70*(9), 1–70.

Barrett, H. C., Todd, P. M., Miller, G. F., & Blythe, P. W. (2005). Accurate judgments of intention from motion cues alone: A cross-cultural study. *Evolution and Human Behavior, 26*, 313–331.

Begg, I. M., Anas, A., & Farinacci, S. (1992). Dissociation of processes in belief: Source recollection, statement familiarity, and the illusion of truth. *Journal of Experimental Psychology: General, 121*, 446–458.

Bem, D. J. (1967). An alternative interpretation of cognitive dissonance phenomena. *Psychological Review, 73*, 183–200.

Berry, D. C., & Dienes, Z. (1993). *Implicit Learning: Theoretical and Empirical Issues.* Hillsdale, NJ: Erlbaum.

Blakemore, S. J., & Decety, J. (2001). From the perception of action to the understanding of intention. *Nature Reviews Neuroscience, 2*, 561–567.

Bodenhausen, G. V. (1990). Second-guessing the jury: Stereotypic and hindsight biases in perceptions of court cases. *Journal of Applied Social Psychology, 20*, 1112–1121.

Bolte, A., & Goschke, T. (2005). On the speed of intuition: Intuitive judgments of semantic coherence under different response deadlines. *Memory & Cognition, 33*, 1248–1255.

Brewer, M. B., Dull, V., & Lui, L. (1981). Perceptions of the elderly: Stereotypes as prototypes. *Journal of Personality and Social Psychology, 41*, 656–670.

Bruner, J. S. (1947). Value and need as organizing factors in perception. *The Journal of Abnormal and Social Psychology, 42*, 33–44.

Bruner, J. S. (1960). *The process of education.* Cambridge, MA: Harvard University Press.

Brunswik, E. (1956). *Perception and the representative design of psychological experiments* (2nd ed.). Berkeley: University of California Press.

Chartrand, T. L., & Bargh, J. A. (1999). The chameleon effect: The perception behavior link in social perception. *Journal of Personality and Social Psychology, 76,* 893–910.

Cialdini, R. B. (1993). *Influence. Science and practice* (3rd ed.). New York: Harper Collins.

Cleeremans, A., Destrebecqz, A., & Boyer, M. (1998). Implicit learning: News from the front. *Trends in Cognitive Sciences, 2–10,* 406–416.

Darwin, C. (1872). *The expression of the emotions in man and animals.* New York: Appleton.

Deutsch, M., & Gerard, H.B. (1955). A study of normative and informational social influences upon individual judgment. *The Journal of Abnormal and Social Psychology, 51,* 629–636.

Deutsch, R., & Strack, F. (2007). Variants of judgment and decision-making: A dual-system analysis. In H. Plessner, C. Betsch & T. Betsch (Eds.), *A new look on intuition in judgment and decision making.* Mahwah, NJ: Erlbaum.

Devine, P. G. (1989). Stereotypes and prejudice: Their automatic and controlled components. *Journal of Personality and Social Psychology, 56,* 5–18.

Ditto, P. H., & Jemmott, J. B. (1989). From rarity to evaluative extremity: Effects of prevalence information on evaluations of positive and negative characteristics. *Journal of Personality and Social Psychology, 57,* 16–26.

Ekman, P. (1999). Facial expressions. In M. J. Power & T. Dalgleish, (Eds.), *Handbook of cognition and emotion* (pp. 301–320). New York: Wiley.

Ekman, P., & Friesen, W. V. (1971). Constants across cultures in the face and emotion. *Journal of Personality and Social Psychology, 17,* 124–129.

Ekman, P., Levenson, R. W., & Friesen, W. V. (1983). Autonomic nervous system activity distinguishes among emotions. *Science, 221,* 1208–1210.

Ekman, P., & O'Sullivan, M. (2005). From flawed self-assessment to blatant whoppers: The utility of voluntary and involuntary behavior in detecting deception. *Behavioral Sciences and the Law, 24,* 673–686.

Elfenbein, H. A., & Ambady, N. (2003). Universals and cultural differences in recognizing emotions of a different cultural group. *Current Directions in Psychological Science, 12,* 159–164.

Epstein, S. (1991). Cognitive-experiential self-theory: An integrative theory of personality. In R. Curtis (Ed.), *The relational self: Theoretical convergences in psychoanalysis and social psychology* (pp. 111–137). New York: Guilford Press.

Epstein, S. (1994). Integration of the cognitive and the psychodynamic unconscious. *American Psychologist, 49,* 709–724.

Epstein, S. (2007). Intuition from the perspective of cognitive-experiential self-theory. In H. Plessner, C. Betsch, & T. Betsch (Eds.), *Intuition in judgment and decision making* (pp. 23–38). Mahwah, NJ: Erlbaum.

Epstein, S., & Pacini, R. (1999). Some basic issues regarding dual-process theories from the perspective of cognitive-experiential self-theory. In Y. Trope & S. Chaiken (Eds.), *Dual-process theories in social psychology* (pp. 462–482). New York: Guilford Press.

Epstein, S., Pacini, R., Denes-Raj, V., & Heier, H. (1996). Individual differences in intuitive-experiential and analytical-rational thinking styles. *Journal of Personality and Social Psychology, 71,* 390–405.

Erb, H. P., Bohner, G., Schmälzle, K., & Rank, S. (1998). Beyond conflict and discrepancy: Cognitive bias in minority and majority influence. *Personality and Social Psychology Bulletin, 24,* 620–633.

Festinger, L. (1954). A theory of social comparison processes. *Human Relations, 7,* 117–140.

Förster, J., & Liberman, N. (2001). The role of attribution of motivation in producing post-suppressional rebound. *Journal of Personality and Social Psychology, 81,* 377–390.

Frank, M. G., & Ekman, P. (2004). Appearing truthful generalizes across different deception situations. *Journal of Personality and Social Psychology, 86,* 486–495.

Gigerenzer, G., & Goldstein, D. G. (1996). Reasoning the fast and frugal way: Models of bounded rationality. *Psychological Review, 103,* 650–669.

Gigerenzer, G., Hoffrage, U., & Kleinbölting, H. (1991). Probabilistic mental models: A Brunswikian theory of confidence. *Psychological Review, 98,* 506–528.

Gigerenzer, G., & Todd, P. M. (1999). Fast and frugal heuristics: The adaptive toolbox. In G. Gigerenzer & P. M. Todd (Eds.), *The ABC Research Group: Simple heuristics that make us smart* (pp. 3–34). New York: Oxford University Press.

Gollwitzer, P.M. (1999). Implementation intentions. Strong effects of simple plans. *American Psychologist, 54,* 493–503.

Gosling, S. D., Ko, S. J., Mannarelli, T., & Morris, M. E. (2002). A room with a cue: Personality judgments based on offices and bedrooms. *Journal of Personality and Social Psychology, 82,* 379–398.

Hammond, K. R. (1996). *Human judgment and social policy: Irreducible uncertainty, inevitable error, unavoidable injustice.* New York: Oxford University Press.

Heider, F., & Simmel, M. (1944). An experimental study of apparent behavior. *American Journal of Psychology, 57,* 243–259.

Hogarth, R. M. (2005). Deciding analytically or trusting your intuition? The advantages and disadvantages of analytic and intuitive thought. In T. Betsch & S. Haberstroh (Eds.), *The routines of decision making* (pp. 67–82). Mahwah, NJ: Erlbaum.

Hogarth, R. M., & Karelaia, N. (2006). "Take-the-best" and other simple strategies: Why and when they work "well" with binary cues. *Theory and Decision, 61,* 205–249.

Hogarth, R. M., & Karelaia, N. (2007). Heuristic and linear models of judgment: Matching rules and environments. *Psychological Review, 114,* 733–758.

Hutchinson, J. M. C., & Gigerenzer, G. (2005). Simple heuristics and rules of thumb: Where psychologists and behavioral biologists might meet. *Behavioural Processes, 69,* 97–124.

Jacoby, L. L., Allan, L. G., Collins, J. C., & Larwill, L. K. (1988). Memory influences subjective experience: Noise judgments. *Journal of Experimental Psychology: Learning, Memory, and Cognition, 14,* 240–247.

Jacoby, L. L., Kelley, C., Brown, J., & Jasechko, J. (1989). Becoming famous overnight: Limits on the ability to avoid unconscious influences of the past. *Journal of Personality and Social Psychology, 56,* 326–338.

Jacoby, L. L., Woloshyn, V., & Kelley, C. (1989). Becoming famous without being recognized: Unconscious influences of memory produced by dividing attention. *Journal of Experimental Psychology: General, 118,* 115–125.

James, W. (1894). Discussion: The physical basis of emotion. *Psychological Review, 1,* 516–529.

Johnson, E. J., & Tversky, A. (1983). Affect, generalization, and the perception of risk. *Journal of Personality and Social Psychology, 45,* 20–31.

Judd, C., & Park, B. (1993). Definition and assessment of accuracy in social stereotypes. *Psychological Review, 100,* 109–128.

Kahneman, D., & Frederick, S. (2002). Representativeness revisited: Attribute substitution in intuitive judgment. In T. Gilovich, D. Griffin, & D. Kahneman (Eds.), *Heuristics and biases: The psychology of intuitive judgment* (pp. 49–81). New York: Cambridge University Press.

Kahneman, D., & Frederick, S. (2005). A model of heuristic judgment. In R. G. Morrison & K. J. Holyoak (Eds.), *The Cambridge handbook of thinking and reasoning* (pp. 267–293). New York: Cambridge University Press.

Kelley, H. H. (1967). Attribution theory in social psychology. In D. Levine (Ed.), *Nebraska symposium on motivation* (pp. 192–238). Lincoln: University of Nebraska Press.

Kruglanski, A. W., Erb, H. P., Spiegel, S., & Pierro, A. (2003). The parametric unimodel of human judgment: A fanfare to the common thinker. In L. G. Aspinwall & U. M. Staudinger (Eds.), *A psychology of human strengths: Perspectives on an emerging field* (pp. 197–210). Washington, DC: APA.

Kruglanski, A. W., & Mackie, D. M. (1990). Majority and minority influence: A judgmental process analysis. In W. Stroebe & M. Hewstone (Eds.), *European review of social psychology* (pp. 229–261). Chichester, England: Wiley.

Laird, J. D. (1974). Self-attribution of emotion: The effects of expressive behavior on the quality of emotional experience. *Journal of Personality and Social Psychology, 29,* 475–486.

Laird, J. D. (2007). *Feelings: The perception of self.* New York: Oxford University Press.

Liberman, N., & Förster, J. (2004). Motivation and construct accessibility. In J. P. Forgas, K. D. Williams, & S. M. Laham (Eds.), *Social motivation: Conscious and unconscious processes* (pp. 228-248). Cambridge, MA: Cambridge University Press.

Lieberman, M. D. (2000). Intuition: A social-cognitive neuroscience approach. *Psychological Bulletin, 126,* 109–137.

Lieberman, M. D. (2003). Reflective and reflexive judgment processes: A social cognitive neuroscience approach. In J. P. Forgas, K. R. Williams, & W. von Hippel (Eds.), *Social judgments: Implicit and explicit processes* (pp. 44–67). New York: Cambridge University Press.

Lieberman, M. D., Gaunt, R., Gilbert, D. T., & Trope, Y. (2002). Reflection and reflexion: A social cognitive neuroscience approach to attributional inference. In M. Zanna (Ed.), *Advances in experimental social psychology* (Vol. 34, pp. 199–249). New York: Academic Press.

Litwin, G. H. (1966). Achievement motivation, expectancy of success, and risk-taking behavior. In J. W. Atkinson & N. T. Feather (Eds.), *A theory of achievement behavior* (pp. 103–115). New York: Wiley.

Loewenstein, G. F., Weber, E. U., Hsee, C. K., & Welch, N. (2001). Risk as feelings. *Psychological Bulletin, 122,* 267–286.

Maheswaran, D., Mackie, D. M., & Chaiken, S. (1992). Brand name as a heuristic cue: The effects of task importance and expectancy confirmation on consumer judgments. *Journal of Consumer Psychology, 1,* 317–336.

Maio, G. R., & Haddock, G. (2007). Attitude change. In A. W. Kruglanski & E. T. Higgins (Eds.), *Social psychology: Handbook of basic principles* (2nd ed., pp. 565–586). New York: Guilford.

Martin, L. L., Harlow, T. F., & Strack, F. (1992). The role of bodily sensations in the evaluation of social events. *Personality and Social Psychology Bulletin, 18,* 412–419.

Martin, R., & Hewstone, M. (2003). Social influence. In M. Hogg & J. Cooper (Eds.), *Sage handbook of social psychology* (pp. 347–366). London: Sage.

Myers, D. G. (2002). *Intuition: Its powers and perils.* New Haven, CT: Yale University Press.

Petty, R. E., & Cacioppo, J. T. (1986). The elaboration-likelihood model of persuasion. In L. Berkowitz (Ed.), *Advances in experimental social psychology* (pp. 124–206). Orlando, FL: Academic Press.

Petty, R. E., & Wegener, D. T. (1999). The elaboration likelihood model: Current status and controversies. In S. Chaiken & Y. Trope (Eds.), *Dual process theories in social psychology* (pp. 41–72). New York: Guilford Press.

Pham, M. T. (2004). The logic of feeling. *Journal of Consumer Psychology, 14,* 360–369.

Reber, R., & Schwarz, N. (1999). Effects of perceptual fluency on judgments of truth. *Consciousness and Cognition, 8,* 338–342.
Rothman, A. J., & Schwarz, N. (1998). Constructing perceptions of vulnerability: Personal relevance and the use of experiential information in health judgments. *Personality and Social Psychology Bulletin, 24,* 1053–1064.
Russell, J. A. (1980). A circumplex model of affect. *Journal of Personality and Social Psychology, 39,* 1161–1178.
Schachter, S., & Singer, J. (1962). Cognitive, social, and physiological determinants of emotional state. *Psychological Review, 69,* 379–399.
Schmidt, R. A. (1975). A schema theory of discrete motor skill learning. *Psychological Review, 82,* 225–260.
Schwarz, N. (1998). Accessible content and accessibility experiences: The interplay of declarative and experiential information in judgment. *Personality and Social Psychology Bulletin, 2,* 87–99.
Schwarz, N., Bless, H., & Bohner, G. (1991). Mood and persuasion: Affective states influence the processing of persuasive communications. *Advances in Experimental Social Psychology, 24,* 161–199.
Schwarz, N., Bless, H., Strack, F., Klumpp, G., Rittenauer-Schatka, H., & Simons, A. (1991). Ease of retrieval as information: Another look at the availability heuristic. *Journal of Personality and Social Psychology, 61,* 195–202.
Schwarz, N., & Clore, G. L. (1983). Mood, misattribution, and judgments of well-being: Informative and directive functions of affective states. *Journal of Personality and Social Psychology, 45,* 513–523.
Schwarz, N., & Clore, G. L. (1988). How do I feel about it? Informative functions of affective states. In K. Fiedler & J. P. Forgas (Eds.), *Affect, cognition, and social behavior* (pp. 44–62). Toronto: Hogrefe International.
Schwarz, N., & Clore, G. L. (2007). Feelings and phenomenal experiences. In E. T. Higgins & A. Kruglanski (Eds.), *Social psychology. Handbook of basic principles* (2nd ed., pp. 385–407). New York: Guilford.
Schwarz, N., Strack, F., Kommer, D., & Wagner, D. (1987). Soccer, rooms, and the quality of your life: Mood effects on judgments of satisfaction with life in general and with specific domains. *European Journal of Social Psychology, 17,* 69–79.
Sloman, S. A. (1996). The empirical case for two systems of reasoning. *Psychological Bulletin, 119,* 3–22.
Smith, E. R., & DeCoster, J. (1999). Associative and rule-based processing: A connectionist interpretation of dual process models. In S. Chaiken & Y. Trope (Eds.), *Dual-process theories in social psychology* (pp. 323–338). New York: Guilford Press.
Smith, E. R., & DeCoster, J. (2000). Dual process models in social and cognitive psychology: Conceptual integration and links to underlying memory systems. *Personality and Social Psychology Review, 4,* 108–131.
Stapel, D. A., & Spears, R. (1996). Event accessibility and context effects in causal inference: Judgment of a different order. *Personality and Social Psychology Bulletin, 22,* 979–992.
Stepper, S., & Strack, F. (1993). Proprioceptive determinants of emotional and noncmotional feelings. *Journal of Personality and Social Psychology, 64,* 211–220.
Strack, F., & Deutsch, R. (2004). Reflective and impulsive determinants of social behavior. *Personality and Social Psychology Review, 8,* 220–247.
Strack, F., & Hannover, B. (1996). Awareness of influence as a precondition for implementing correctional goals. In P. M. Gollwitzer & J. A. Bargh (Eds.), *The psychology of action: Linking cognition and motivation to behavior* (pp. 579–596). New York: Guilford Press.

Strack, F., Martin, L. L., & Stepper, S. (1988). Inhibiting and facilitating conditions of the human smile: A nonobtrusive test of the facial feedback hypothesis. *Journal of Personality and Social Psychology, 54,* 768–777.

Strack, F., & Neumann, R. (2000). Furrowing the brow may undermine perceived fame: The role of facial feedback in judgments of celebrity. *Personality and Social Psychology Bulletin, 26,* 762–768.

Taylor, S. E. (1981). The interface of cognitive and social psychology. In J. Harvey (Ed.), *Cognition, social behavior, and the environment* (pp. 189–211). Hillsdale, NJ: Erlbaum.

Tomasello, M., Carpenter, M., Call, J., Behne, T., & Moll, H. (2005). Understanding and sharing intentions: The origins of cultural cognition. *Behavioral and Brain Sciences, 28,* 675–735.

Topolinski, S., & Strack, F. (in press). The analysis of intuition: Processing fluency, and affect in judgments of semantic coherence. *Cognition and Emotion.*

Topolinski, S., Likowski, K. U., Weyers, P., & Strack, F. (in press). The face of fluency: Semantic coherence automatically elicits a specific pattern of facial muscle reactions. *Cognition and Emotion.*

Topolinski, S., & Strack, F. (2008). Where there's a will—there's no intuition: The unintentional basis of semantic coherence judgments. *Journal of Memory and Language, 58*(4), 1032–1048.

Tversky, A., & Kahneman, D. (1974). Judgment under uncertainty: heuristics and biases. Biases in judgments reveal some heuristics of thinking under uncertainty. *Science, 185,* 1124–1131.

Unkelbach, C. (2006). The learned interpretation of cognitive fluency. *Psychological Science, 17,* 339–345.

Wänke, M., Schwarz, N., & Bless, H. (1995). The availability heuristic revisited: Experienced ease of retrieval in mundane frequency estimates. *Acta Psychologica, 89,* 83–90.

Whittlesea, B. W. A. (1993). Illusions of familiarity. *Journal of Experimental Psychology: Learning, Memory, and Cognition, 19,* 1235–1253.

Whittlesea, B. W. A., Jacoby, L. L., & Girard, K. (1990). Illusions of immediate memory: Evidence of an attributional basis for feelings of familiarity and perceptual quality. *Journal of Memory and Language, 29,* 716–732.

Winkielman, P., & Cacioppo, J. T. (2001) Mind at ease puts a smile on the face. Psychophysiological evidence that processing facilitation elicits positive affect. *Journal of Personality and Social Psychology, 81,* 989–1000.

Wippich, W. (1994). Intuition in the context of implicit memory. *Psychological Research, 56,* 104–109.

Witherspoon, D., & Allan, L. G. (1985). The effects of a prior presentation on temporal judgments in a perceptual identification task. *Memory & Cognition, 13,* 103–111.

Yeung, C., & Soman, D. (2007). The duration heuristic. *Journal of Consumer Research, 34,* 315–326.

Zanna, M. P., & Cooper, J. (1976). Dissonance and the attribution process. In J. H. Harvey, W. J. Ickes, & R. F. Kidd (Eds.), *New directions in attribution research* (pp. 199–217). Hillsdale, NJ: Erlbaum.

Zillmann, D. (1978). Attribution and misattribution of excitatory reactions. In J. H. Harvey, W. Ickes, & R. F. Kidd (Eds.), *New directions in attribution research* (pp. 335–368). New York: Wiley.

Zillmann, D. (1983). Transfer of excitation in emotional behavior. In J. T. Cacioppo & R. E. Petty (Eds.), *Social psychophysiology: A sourcebook,* (pp. 215–240). New York: Guilford Press.

Zillmann, D. (1989). Aggression and sex: Independent and joint operations. In A. Manstead & H. Wagner (Eds.), *Handbook of social psychophysiology* (pp. 229–259). Oxford, England: Wiley.

Zogmaister, C. (2004). Memoria implicita ed esperienze sociali/Implicit memory and social experience. *Giornale Italiano di Psicologia, 31,* 467–493.

10

Spontaneous Evaluations

KARL CHRISTOPH KLAUER

INTRODUCTION

*E*valuations play an important role in determining human behavior. It is rare that an object or event is completely neutral rather than endowed with a certain valence (Osgood, Suci, & Tannenbaum, 1957); even unfamiliar objects can be quickly and consistently evaluated (Duckworth, Bargh, Garcia, & Chaiken, 2002). Objects that are liked tend to be approached, whereas disliked objects are avoided or rejected. Evaluations color other judgments (Cooper, 1981) and influence social interactions (Curtis & Miller, 1986), consumer choices, and many other aspects of everyday life. Emotion theories often put evaluations at the heart of emotions (e.g., Ortony, Clore, & Collins, 1988). The contemporary definition of *attitudes* as "likes and dislikes" (Bem, 1970, p. 14) equates attitudes and evaluations.

Social psychologists have long been interested in evaluation as a psychological dimension broadly characterized as good versus bad, positive versus negative, traditionally operationalized by means of rating measures such as the semantic differential (Osgood et al., 1957). Data from such measures have been used to address a broad range of issues bearing on human interactions, such as impression formation, information integration, implicit personality theory, the dimensionality and structure of the evaluative space, attitude-behavior consistency, context dependency of evaluations, and many others. In recent years, reaction-time paradigms have been adapted from cognitive psychology, prompting a new focus on spontaneous evaluations that are typically made in a few hundreds of milliseconds, sometimes in the absence of the respondents' awareness.

MEASURES OF SPONTANEOUS EVALUATION

One of the earliest such paradigms is based on sequential priming (Neely, 1991). A priming effect occurs when the processing of a target stimulus is influenced by a preceding stimulus on the basis of a particular relationship between prime and target. For instance, the processing of the word *doctor* may be facilitated by the prime *nurse* on the basis of a nonevaluative associative relationship. Priming effects based on associative and nonevaluative semantic relationships are called *semantic-priming effects*. So-called evaluative priming focuses on evaluative relationships between primes and targets (Fazio, Sanbonmatsu, Powell, & Kardes, 1986). In each trial of an evaluative-priming paradigm, a positive or negative target (e.g., sunshine) is preceded by a prime of the same valence (e.g., priest) or of the opposite valence (e.g., death). Respondents' task is usually to decide whether the target denotes something positive or negative. An *evaluative-priming effect* is defined as an interaction of prime valence and target valence such that the decision on the target occurs faster and more accurately when prime and target share the same valence relative to when both have opposite valences. Conversely, direction and size of priming effects are indicators of prime evaluation (Wittenbrink, 2007).

Another measure of spontaneous evaluation is the widely used implicit association test (IAT; Greenwald, McGhee, & Schwartz, 1998). The IAT involves two tasks, a concept task, in which exemplars of two target concepts (e.g., flowers and insects) are to be classified according to their category membership, and an attribute task, in which stimuli are to be classified with respect to a pair of attribute categories (e.g., as either positive or negative). In the critical phases of the IAT procedure, both tasks are to be performed in alternation, and they are mapped onto the same response keys, which can be done in two different ways: For example, flowers and positive stimuli can share one of the two response keys and insects and negative stimuli the other one. Another possibility is that flowers and negative stimuli share the same response key and insects and positive stimuli the other one. The former response mapping usually leads to better performance than the latter. The mapping that leads to faster and more accurate responding is called the *compatible mapping*, the other one the incompatible mapping. The performance difference between the two kinds of mappings is called the IAT effect.

The IAT rests on the assumption that it is easier to make the same behavioral response to concepts and attributes that are strongly associated than to concepts and attributes that are weakly associated. In this view, direction and size of the IAT effect indicate the relative association strengths between the target concepts and attributes. There are a number of related procedures, such as the extrinsic affective Simon task (EAST; De Houwer, 2003a), the go/no go association task (Nosek & Banaji, 2001), and an affective-priming paradigm by Payne, Cheng, Govorun, and Stewart (2005).

These procedures tap fast evaluative processes with a time course of a few hundreds of milliseconds that often occur without, and sometimes against, the respondents' intentions. They have been found particularly useful in socially sensitive domains (such as racial issues, criminal behavior, addictions, etc.). Respondents holding attitudes that are socially undesirable or even sanctioned may be reluctant to reveal their attitudes in traditional self-report measures, but it may be more difficult for respondents to edit their responses to conceal their attitudes in measures of spontaneous evaluation. This idea is supported by two lines of evidence: A number of studies have shown that people low in motivation to control open expressions of undesirable attitudes show stronger correlations between measures of spontaneous evaluation and self-report measures than people high in such motivation, presumably because the latter distort the self-report measures intentionally but are less able to do so for the measures of spontaneous evaluation (e.g., Dunton & Fazio, 1997). A couple of studies have directly addressed the fakeability of the IAT (Banse, Seise, & Zerbes, 2001; Egloff & Schmukle, 2002), demonstrating that instructions to fake the IAT have little effect. On the other hand, Fiedler and Blümke (2005) showed that faking is possible for participants with a minimal amount of IAT experience.

SPONTANEOUS EVALUATION AND SELF-REPORT OF EVALUATIONS

The advent of these procedures also raised a couple of theoretical questions: What is the nature of the fast evaluative processes underlying these procedures, and how do these processes relate to the traditional self-report measures of evaluations? One idea that has driven research on spontaneous evaluations is that they tap stored evaluations automatically without any deliberation (Wittenbrink, 2007). One possibility is that a stored evaluation is an integral part of the evaluated object's representation in memory (e.g., Wyer & Gordon, 1983); another possibility is that it is stored as an association between the object and its evaluation in memory (e.g., Fazio et al., 1986). When the associative link is strong, the evaluation is highly accessible and will come to mind very quickly and perhaps automatically as soon as the object is encountered. This point of view therefore agrees well with the fast evaluative processes observed in evaluative priming and related measures of spontaneous evaluation.

Self-report measures, on the other hand, have long been known to be relatively context dependent or, to use a recently popular term, malleable, suggesting that evaluative judgments are in part constructed on the spot, a process that is influenced by the information that is available at the time of the judgment but also by the respondents' current goals, feelings, mood states, reflections, and deliberations (Schwarz & Bohner, 2001). For example, self-reports of attitudes can be profoundly influenced by minor changes in question wording, question format, or question order. As a motivational example, one's evaluation of a glass of water is likely to differ quite a bit before and after spending a day without water in the desert. Many of the context effects reflect the respondent's deliberations and inferences at the time of judgment. Wilson, Lindsey, and Schooler (2000) argued that construction of an evaluative judgment requires time, cognitive capacity, and effort.

The simple and attractive distinction between automatic access to well-learned evaluative associations in measures of spontaneous evaluation and context-dependent and effortful constructions of evaluative judgments in self-report has however been questioned by recent findings demonstrating that even fast evaluative processes can depend on a variety of contextual influences (Blair, 2002). Considerable evidence has now accrued suggesting that measures of spontaneous evaluation are sensitive to (a) the presentation, whether real or imagined, of exemplars; (b) recently activated task sets; and (c) currently active goals and other contextual factors.

As an example of the influence of exemplars, Dasgupta and Greenwald (2001) found that exposure to admired black persons and disliked white persons versus disliked black persons and admired white persons had an impact on prejudice scores in a black-versus-white race IAT.

Regarding the influence of recently activated tasks sets, Olson and Fazio (2003) used black and white faces as primes in an evaluative priming paradigm; participants either expected a later recognition test for the face primes or they were asked to make a mental tally of the numbers of black and white faces presented. When the task set involving the categorization of primes as black versus white was active, priming effects indicated more negative evaluations of black relative to white faces than when participants merely tried to remember the faces for a later recognition test. Similarly, Mitchell, Nosek, and Banaji (2003) found more positive evaluations of black athletes than of white politicians in an attitude IAT when the concept task was to discriminate athletes from politicians and the reverse pattern when the concept task was to discriminate black from white persons.

Considering finally currently activated goals, Sherman, Presson, Chassin, Rose, and Koch (2003) found that nicotine deprivation temporarily influenced cigarette smokers' responses to cigarettes in a priming task, and Ferguson and Bargh (2004) found that thirsty participants showed more positivity toward goal-relevant stimuli (e.g., juice, water) than nonthirsty participants in evaluative priming.

For some of these studies, it may be a question of perspective whether a contextual influence on fast evaluative processes is really implied. For example, Wittenbrink, Judd, and Park (2001) found more negativity toward black face primes relative to white face primes when the faces were embedded in the picture of a dilapidated street corner, but no differences between black and white faces when these were embedded in a church scene. It seems to be a matter of perspective whether this is considered a context effect on spontaneous evaluation. On the one hand, if the white and black faces are seen as primes, the picture context moderated their priming effects, and this moderation was indeed what Wittenbrink et al. (2001) were interested in for theoretical reasons. On the other hand, if the different pictures are seen as primes, the results merely indicate that church pictures are evaluated generally more positive and pictures of a dilapidated street corner with black persons more negative than street pictures with white persons.

Similarly, Gawronski, Deutsch, and Seidel (2005) found that an evaluative context moderated priming effects. Specifically, their findings suggest that presenting two prime words in succession in an evaluative-priming paradigm moderates the effect of the second prime on the target: When the first and second prime word were evaluatively consistent (i.e., both positive or both negative), the evaluative-priming effect engendered by the second prime was smaller than when first and second prime words were evaluatively inconsistent (i.e., one of them positive, the other one negative). This three-way interaction between consistency of first and second prime word, second prime valence, and target valence was interpreted as the crucial bit of evidence for an effect of the first prime on the perception of the second prime, more precisely as a contrastive rather than additive effect so that a mismatch in valence between the two primes made the valence of the second prime word more salient and thereby more impactful. The three-way interaction is, however, mathematically identical to a two-way interaction between first prime valence and target valence, that is, to a priming effect engendered by the first prime that is independent of the priming effect caused by the second prime and additively superimposed on it. Note that when this priming effect for the first prime is computed, it is found to be reversed in direction, which is somewhat unusual but not unheard of (e.g., Glaser & Banaji, 1999; Wentura & Rothermund, 2003). In this alternative view, the priming effect by the second prime is not in any way affected or moderated by the first prime. Bargh (1999) raised similar points for earlier studies.

MALLEABILITY AND CONTROLLABILITY OF SPONTANEOUS EVALUATIONS

Findings of context influences are interesting and surprising to the extent to which the measures of spontaneous evaluation reveal automatic evaluations rather than strategically controlled constructions. However, different researchers mean different things when they characterize processes as automatic, and there is a tendency to decompose the concept of automaticity into several features, such as unintentional, uncontrolled, goal independent, resource independent, and so forth, that do not necessarily have to cooccur. Moors and De Houwer (2006) argued that the core feature that is necessary for a process to be automatic is that it is what they call partially autonomous, corresponding roughly to what Logan and Cowan (1984) call ballistic and Bargh (1992) autonomous: A process that once started continues and runs to completion independently of goals to modify, alter, or stop it. Thus, the lack of controllability with respect to these goals is a minimal feature at the heart of the automaticity concept.

What is the evidence for partial autonomy? As mentioned, IAT effects can be faked, suggesting that the effects are not partially autonomous. Evidence regarding evaluative priming is largely indirect and drawn by analogy from findings in the semantic-priming literature.

For example, in semantic priming participants exhibit larger priming effects if the list of trials contains a high rather than low proportion of associatively related prime-target pairs. This so-called relatedness proportion effect is usually attributed to the strategical use of primes to generate expectations for likely targets (Neely, 1991). The interval between the onset of the prime and the onset of the target in sequential priming paradigms is called the *stimulus onset asynchrony* (SOA). Interestingly, the relatedness proportion effect occurs reliably only for rather long SOAs, suggesting that semantic priming with short SOA below 300 ms cannot be so controlled and may be partially autonomous. In evaluative priming, when the proportion of evaluatively consistent prime-target pairs (i.e., pairs in which prime and target are both positive or both negative) is varied, an analogous so-called consistency proportion effect is found such that larger priming effects are observed as the consistency proportion is increased. Interestingly, the consistency proportion effect is found with short SOAs (Klauer, Roßnagel, & Musch, 1997) and even with simultaneous presentation of prime and target (Musch & Klauer, 1997), suggesting by analogy with the just-reviewed semantic-priming literature that participants can exert some control over their priming effects even at short SOAs. It is, however, possible that the consistency proportion effects do not rely on consciously controlled strategies but reflect covariational learning of a more implicit kind.

Another frequent reference in the literature discussing the automaticity of automatic evaluations is a semantic-priming study by Neely (1977). In that study, there were four types of prime stimuli: neutral primes (the letter string XXX) and the prime words *bird*, *body*, and *building*. Participants were told that the prime word *bird* would usually be followed by an exemplar of a bird such as robin as target, whereas the prime word *body* would usually be followed by the name of a part of a building such as door, and the prime word *building* by the name of a part of the body such as arm. For *body* and *building*, participants were thus instructed to expect a semantically unrelated target from the category *building* and *body*, respectively. In two thirds of the trials, primes and targets actually conformed to this expectation, but there were also trials in which targets unexpectedly stemmed from the category *bird* or the prime category itself. Participants could and did use the instructed expectations to facilitate their responses when SOA was long (2000 ms), but at a short SOA (250 ms) priming effects were observed only as a function of semantic relatedness: Thus, *bird* primed robin, *body* primed arm, and *building* door. This suggests that at short SOAs strategic expectancies do not influence priming effects, and that at such SOAs priming effects are automatic. This is a bit puzzling as the prime words were visible and clearly recognizable at short SOAs. Nothing really prevented participants from taking all the time they needed, short SOA or not, to generate an expectation for the target on the basis of the prime word. It may, however, be more effortful to do this sufficiently fast to influence the decision on the target when SOA is short, and participants may be unwilling to expend that effort. Or, it may simply be unnatural or inefficient to continue thinking strategically about the prime word when the imperative target stimuli is already on the screen and can be analyzed directly, whereas it may be natural to fill the long pause between prime and target presentation at long SOAs with such thoughts.

Sarah Teige-Mocigemba and I recently tested the possibility of strategic responding in evaluative priming using a short SOA (275 ms) and a design adapted from the original study by Neely (1977). Positive and negative pictures were used as primes and positive and negative words as targets. Specifically, there were a negative and a positive prime, which we called shift primes. Shift primes were followed by targets of the opposite valence in two thirds of trials. Two additional primes, one positive and one negative, were followed by targets of the same valence in two thirds of trials. There were three groups (one experimental, two control groups) with different instructions. Members of the experimental group and the first control group were told that they would earn 2 Euro cents for each correct response that was given while the target was visible on the screen (that is, within 800 ms). Members of the experimental group, but not of the control groups, were also informed that shift primes were usually followed by targets of the opposite valence, and that they could use this fact to maximize their overall payoff. Members of the first control group did not obtain instructions about the prime words. Members of the second control group were told that they would receive 3 Euro cents for correct responses in trials with shift primes and 1 Euro cent for correct responses in other trials. This control group is perhaps a more appropriate control than the first because attention is drawn to the shift primes by the instructions, like in the experimental group. Results were clear-cut: Significant priming effects emerged for shift primes as well as for nonshift primes except for shift primes in the experimental group, for which the priming effects were eliminated and in part reversed. Thus, given sufficient motivation to alter priming effects strategically, it is possible to do so even for short SOAs and under considerable time pressure; remember that participants had to respond within 800 ms to add to their payoff. These results suggest that priming effects are not partially autonomous.

Although the strategy to counteract the prime influence is simple (prepare for a target of the opposite valence of the prime), it is nevertheless plausible that participants do not as frequently engage in such strategies to counteract the prime influence as they do in self-report. Note on the other hand that the studies mentioned on motivation to control prejudice do not help to make this point. People with high motivation to control prejudice may show smaller correlations between measures of spontaneous evaluation and self-report measures because they conceal their attitudes on self-report measures, on the measures of spontaneous evaluation, or on both, but with different results.

ACCOUNTING FOR MALLEABILITY: CONNECTIONIST AND EXEMPLAR-BASED MODELS

Assuming nevertheless that little control is typically exerted over fast evaluative processes, the malleability of fast evaluative processes poses a problem for the view that such processes tap stable memory traces (Blair, 2002), represented perhaps as associative links in long-term memory that are the products of long learning histories (e.g., Greenwald & Banaji, 1995; Wilson et al., 2000). One possible move in this situation is to appeal to connectionist models (e.g., Blair, 2002; Ferguson & Bargh, 2004; Gawronski, Strack, & Bodenhausen, in press). In such models, there are nodes and links between nodes as in traditional associative memory models, but these nodes and links do not correspond to specific concepts or experiences. Rather, concepts and experiences are stored in the pattern of weights and activations distributed over all nodes and links, with different memories superimposed on each other. Link weights are usually assumed to be modified through learning processes, and they regulate the flow of activation through the network. Connectionist models thus share the concept of spreading activation with traditional models of associative networks. Depending on the link structure that is assumed for the network, some connectionist models have the ability to settle into an overall pattern of activation that best fits the current input (including contextual stimuli) and the stored representation in a process that is sometimes called parallel constraint satisfaction. Connectionist models do not explicitly represent associations; nevertheless, their behavior can mimic that of a model in which associative links exist between concepts. At the same time, the class of models is so flexible that it allows for contextual influences of various kinds either through context-induced changes in the link weights or through the process of constraint satisfaction in the flow of activation when contextual stimuli and experiential states serve as input to the model (see Smith, 1996, for examples). In fact, connectionist models with hidden layers of nodes are very powerful computing machines, and unless restrictions are specified for the link structure, the learning rule, and the model's learning history, it may always be possible to explain given empirical findings by suitable connectionist models in a post hoc fashion. For example, Gawronski et al. (in press) drew a distinction between associative evaluations and effortful reflections such that the former are based on a connectionist model whereas the latter also invoke reasoning by logical rules that concern propositions and their truth values. However, connectionist models can also mimic the behavior of systems obeying so-called hard constraints such as logical rules or the laws of probability (Gigerenzer & Regier, 1996).

It is perhaps worthwhile to see how far one can get in explaining fast evaluative processes with simpler models. Connectionist models get rid of the notion of associations. Associations are not explicitly represented; instead they are an emergent quality of certain connectionist models given suitable learning histories. Connectionist models still preserve the idea of spreading activation and in fact build a powerful computer out of the flow of activation in complicated network structures. Is it possible also to get rid of the notion of spreading activation?

Consider a simple exemplar-based model of categorization and memory along the lines of models by Hintzman (1984, 1986, 1988), Smith (1991), and Smith and Zárate (1992). In such a model, memory traces correspond to objects and experiences as encoded in specific real or imagined encounters. Every stimulus that is encountered is recorded in long-term memory. The perceiver is assumed to be sensitive to a large number of stimulus properties or features, some based on sensory information, others based on abstractions and inferences made at the time of encoding. Each stimulus is encoded as a vector of binary features taking the values of -1 and 1. The value zero can also be stored, meaning that the value of a particular feature is indeterminate. Different groups of features encode different aspects of the encountered object or person that were observed or inferred at the time of the encounter, such as categorizations of it, individuating information that was noticed, evaluations that were made, the perceiver's motivational state, other stimuli that were present in the encounter, and so forth. Note in particular that evaluations are thereby an integral part of those memory traces for which an evaluation was made and encoded at the time of encounter. In sum, the memory store consists of a collection of independent memory traces that are not related by associative links or superimposed on each other or in any other sense interdependent. Each memory trace has a strength or activation level that is subject to decay, starting from an initially high level, implying that recently encoded exemplars will be associated with stronger memory traces than less recently encountered exemplars.

Memory is probed with vectors of the same format as that of memory traces. For example, when the task is to evaluate the word *sunshine*, a memory probe will be formed encoding an initial lexical identification of that word, leaving evaluative features unset and equal to zero. The memory probe then accesses each of the memory traces stored in memory (in a parallel process). Each trace is thereby activated to an extent that is a nonlinear, increasing function of the trace's similarity to the probe and the trace's initial activation level. This produces a memory response called an echo with two properties, intensity and content. The intensity is the sum of the traces' activation levels, whereas the content is the summed content of all memory traces, each weighted by its activation level. The echo content itself thus has the same format as a memory trace, although its features can take any real value as weighted sums of the binary trace features. Note that the model has the property to complete incomplete probe patterns: Features that were indeterminate in the probe vector will be filled on the basis of the subset of similar traces with determinate feature values. Pattern completion is often seen as the hallmark of the above-discussed connectionist models and the principle of parallel constraint satisfaction.

Intensity serves as a kind of familiarity signal: High values mean that many or recent experiences similar to the memory probe reside in memory; intensity therefore governs judgments based on familiarity, such as old-new recognition and lexical decisions in which words have to be discriminated from nonwords, whereas echo content governs semantic categorizations (such as whether the memory probe is positive or negative in affective connotation). For example, the memory echo produced by the word *sunshine* is a weighted average of memory traces involving features similar to the stimulus sunshine. In many such traces, a positive evaluation will have been present in the original encounter and will therefore be stored in the evaluative features. This means that the echo content's evaluative features will also be dominated by positive rather than negative features, leading to a positive evaluation of the word. Even novel stimuli (Duckworth et al., 2002) will produce an echo content with evaluative features typically different from zero and can therefore be evaluated nonneutrally.

More specifically, the model explains spontaneous evaluations as a three-step procedure: A memory probe is formed first. An echo is then produced by accessing memory with this probe, and finally echo content or intensity is used to arrive at a decision or judgment. Note that the model does not encode associations explicitly, and there is no mechanism of spreading activation. How does it then explain evaluative and other kinds of priming or IAT effects? Considering evaluative priming and the IAT effect, there are prominent models of the mechanisms underlying these effects that do not appeal to associative links or spreading activation. For example, Klauer and Musch (2003) and others (De Houwer, 2003b; Wentura & Rothermund, 2003) have argued that evaluative priming results in large part from synergy and conflict between the evaluative responses to prime and target derived separately and independently from each other. Similarly, regarding the IAT, there are process models of it that assume that the effects are caused by spontaneous evaluations of the stimuli encountered (Mierke & Klauer, 2001, 2003) without invoking associative links or spreading activation. All that is required in these models is that the different presented stimuli are evaluated spontaneously, eliciting response tendencies that concur or conflict with responses demanded by the respondents' task. This is well within the scope of explanation of the exemplar-based model.

Considering traditional associative priming, one prominent account (e.g., Ratcliff & McKoon, 1994) assumes that semantic priming arises from the way the memory probe is constructed in lexical decisions. Specifically, according to Ratcliff and McKoon, a compound memory probe is formed that contains identifying features of both prime and target. This will yield high echo intensity, that is, high feelings of familiarity, to the extent to which memory traces that contain identifying features of both prime and target are frequent or recent. In particular, there should be many such traces for associated primes and targets almost by definition of the word *association*. High echo intensity entails a fast and accurate lexical decision, explaining facilitatory effects of associative prime-target relatedness without associative links or spread of activation. The exemplar-based model thereby mimics associative links as an emergent quality; association is encoded as frequent cooccurrence of prime and target features across the set of stored exemplars.

Effects of context can enter into the evaluative process in three ways: (a) through recently encoded exemplars; (b) by the way the memory probe is set up; and (c) by differential weights for relevant dimensions in the computation of similarity between probe and memory traces (Smith & Zárate, 1992).

Recently encoded exemplars obtain special weight in the memory echo because their decay has not progressed as far as that of older traces, explaining effects of actual or imagined exposures to exemplars on spontaneous evaluation (e.g., Dasgupta & Greenwald, 2001).

Regarding the construction of the memory probe, there is considerable flexibility in how a memory probe is formed in a given situation. For example, current motivational or emotional mood states might be encoded as part of the memory probe so that the echo will be based on a subset of traces encoding previous situations with similar experiential states, explaining motivational and emotional context effects (e.g., Ferguson & Bargh, 2004; Sherman et al., 2003). Another example of context effects mediated by probe construction is the mentioned compound-cue account of semantic priming.

Finally, it has been argued that attentional factors at the time of memory retrieval can determine the weight of different dimensions or, more precisely, of different groups of features encoding such dimensions in computing the similarity of trace and memory probes (Smith & Zárate, 1992). This explains readily why recently activated task sets have a strong impact on fast evaluative processes. For example, if a black versus white racial dimension is salient, evaluation of given stimuli will be based on a subset of memory traces that are similar to the probe stimuli in terms of race. Conversely, if professions (politician vs. athlete) are salient, evaluation will be based on a subset of memory traces that are similar to the probe stimuli in terms of profession, accounting for the fact that the same stimuli (e.g., black athletes and white politicians) can receive very disparate spontaneous evaluations as a function of a concurrent categorization task focusing on either race or professions (Mitchell et al., 2003; see also Olson & Fazio, 2003). Smith and

Zárate (1992) also explain how motivational and goal-related factors can influence spontaneous evaluations via this route.

Consider as a final and somewhat tentative application a surprising set of findings by Gawronski and Bodenhausen (2005). In their Study 2, participants asked to generate 3 disliked African Americans showed larger evaluative-priming effects than participants asked to generate 10 disliked exemplars, indicating more negative evaluation of the prime word *black* relative to *white* given fewer exemplars. Conversely, generation of 3 disliked exemplars led to less priming by stereotypical relatedness for the prime words *black* relative to *white* in a lexical decision task than generation of 10 disliked exemplars. Thus, evaluative and stereotype priming showed opposite effects of the number of generated exemplars.

Consider first evaluative priming. According to the exemplar-based model, recent exemplars, including self-generated ones, have special weight in the fast evaluation of stimuli. Thus, the evaluative response to the prime word *black* is strongly influenced by the most recently generated exemplars of African Americans. This explains the effect observed in evaluative priming if it is assumed that the 3 disliked African Americans generated first are more strongly negative than those generated later (e.g., than the last 3) when 10 exemplars have to be generated. Unfortunately, there are no data on the evaluation of the generated exemplars in the work of Gawronski and Bodenhausen (2005), so that evaluating the assumption will probably require new data. Alternatively, the effect is also obtained if participants reflect on the perceived difficulty to generate many exemplars as they attempt to generate as many as 10 exemplars, inferring that there are not many disliked African Americans and mitigating negative evaluations of that category (Schwarz, 1998).

On the other hand, the stereotype-priming effect in lexical decisions is readily explained by compound cueing that is assumed to drive lexical decisions in sequential priming paradigms (Ratcliff & McKoon, 1994): The compound memory probe encodes both features identifying the prime (e.g., black) and the target (e.g., lazy). An especially high echo intensity, entailing a fast lexical decision, will occur if a recent African American exemplar was encoded in terms of race (black) and the particular target (lazy). When there are 10 recent exemplars, the likelihood is greater that for at least one of these the combination of black race and any particular, stereotypically related target trait such as lazy was explicitly encoded than if there are only 3 recent exemplars. This explains larger stereotype priming when 10 rather than 3 exemplars were generated.

In summary, the principles of memory encoding and retrieval may be sufficient to account for most of the effects surrounding fast evaluative processes and their context dependency. There appears to be little need for elaborate assumptions about the structure of the memory representation or for the computational power of spreading activation in connectionist networks.

EVIDENCE AGAINST EXEMPLAR-BASED MODELS

What kind of data would be inconsistent with exemplar-based models? Perhaps the most radical difference between exemplar-based and connectionist models is that the former are based on separate and independent memory traces, whereas all memory traces are superimposed and maximally interdependent in connectionist models. This interdependency means that changing or replacing one memory trace has the potential to change other traces in connectionist models but not in exemplar-based models. Consistency theories such as dissonance theory or cognitive balance postulate that changes in one element stored in memory can under certain circumstances propagate to result in changes in other elements. For example, learning that a person A holds a positive view of another person B will usually lead to a positive evaluation of person B. But, given additional information leading to a negative evaluation of person A, person A's sympathy for person B should give rise to a negative evaluation of person B according to balance theory. If both pieces of information (person A holds a positive view of person B, and there are reasons to dislike person A) are given in unrelated contexts, making it likely that no conscious connection is made between the two pieces at the time of encoding, the two pieces of information should be laid down as separate memory traces. In an exemplar-based model, cognitive balance, that is, a negative evaluation of person B, should then not result in measures of spontaneous evaluation.

Gawronski, Walther, and Blank (2005; see also Gawronski & Strack, 2004) found that indeed cognitive balance was obtained in measures of spontaneous evaluation only if all relevant information was already present at the time of encoding (and therefore probably not encoded separately), but additive effects of the separate pieces of information were obtained if the pieces of information were presented in a temporal sequence that made their conscious integration and balancing less likely at the times of encoding.

Another domain in which it might be promising to look for interactive effects is evaluative conditioning (De Houwer, Thomas, & Baeyens, 2001). In evaluative conditioning, an initially neutral conditioned stimulus (e.g., the picture of a neutrally evaluated person) is repeatedly paired with a valued stimulus (e.g., a picture of a liked person). In subsequent ratings and measures of spontaneous evaluation, the conditioned stimulus acquires some of the valence of the valued stimulus. Evaluative conditioning per se naturally flows from the exemplar-based model: Each trial of the conditioning phase is laid down as a memory trace comprising identifying features of both conditioned and valued stimulus, including evaluative features evoked by the latter. These memory traces and evaluative features are later activated when memory is probed with the conditioned stimulus.

Two phenomena, so-called postacquisition revaluation and to a lesser extent so-called sensory preconditioning, have the potential to disconfirm exemplar-based models in favor of models postulating interdependency of memory traces such as connectionist models. In postacquisition revaluation, the valued stimulus is revalued after the conditioning phase. For example, a positively evaluated picture of a person might be revalued by providing a negative personality description of that person after the conditioning phase. Baeyens, Eelen, Van den Bergh, and Crombez (1992) found that the revaluation shifted not only the valence of the valued stimulus, but also that of the conditioned stimulus previously paired with it. Assuming that the conditioning trials and the revaluation information are stored in separate memory traces, their integration as implied by revaluation is not consistent with an exemplar-based model. In particular, probing memory with the conditioned stimulus should not strongly activate memory traces of the revaluation phase. It might therefore be worthwhile to test for postacquisition revaluation with paradigms that make it more likely that a conscious and intentional integration of the separate bits of information is not made during the revaluation phase or at the time of judgment. For example, measures of spontaneous evaluation might be used and revaluation phase and conditioning phase might be separated temporally and psychologically through appropriate cover stories.

In the studies by Gawronski, Walther et al. (2005), a phenomenon similar to revaluation was in fact observed. Participants first read about positive or negative sentiments of neutral and unfamiliar source individuals for equally neutral and unfamiliar target individuals in what is analogous to a conditioning phase. Negative or positive information on the different source individuals was then presented in what is similar to a revaluation phase. Spontaneous evaluation of the target individuals was measured and found to be an additive function of both kinds of information: Liked targets received more positive evaluations than disliked targets, and target individuals initially paired with positive sources received more positive evaluations than target individuals paired with negative sources.

The main effect of the sources' sentiments for the targets (like vs. dislike) is easy to account for by the exemplar-based model by means of the principles discussed. The effect of source valence, however, is more difficult to explain if it is assumed that the evaluative information about the source is encoded in memory independently of the target individuals. If so, the evaluative source information should not be activated strongly when memory is later probed with the target individuals in spontaneous evaluation.

On the other hand, it is likely in the Gawronski, Walther et al. (2005) design that encountering the source in the revaluation phase leads to spontaneous memory retrieval of identifying features of at least some of the target individuals for whom the source showed sentiments. To put it more simply, the source individual is remembered and in part defined as the person who expressed sentiments about target individuals A, B, C, and so on; there is after all little other information that characterizes the source at this point. If memory traces of the revaluation phase include these activated target features along with the features identifying the source and its new evaluation, a later test of spontaneous evaluation for a given target individual would also activate such memory traces of the source-revaluation phase, accounting for the effect of source valence on target evaluation.

In sensory preconditioning, there are two conditioned stimuli A and B, which are frequently presented together in a preconditioning phase. This is followed by a conditioning phase involving only one of the conditioned stimuli, say B. In the subsequent test phase, ratings for the other conditioned stimulus A undergo a shift in the direction of the valued stimulus paired with conditioned stimulus B, although A itself was never directly paired with the valued stimulus (Hammerl & Grabitz, 1996; Walther, 2002). Like postacquisition revaluation, sensory preconditioning appears to imply an integration of separate memory traces outside the scope of an exemplar-based model of spontaneous evaluation. It is likely, however, that after sensory preconditioning, conditioned stimulus B evokes features of stimulus A due to their recent frequent pairing. Hence, the presence of conditioned stimulus B in the conditioning trials would lead to the spontaneous retrieval of features of stimulus A from memory, which would then enter into the memory trace that is formed of the conditioning trial. In other words, the separate bits of information learned in the preconditioning phase and in the conditioning phase proper may already be integrated at the time of encoding in the conditioning phase.

A FINAL CAVEAT: TASK VARIABLES NOT RELATED TO SPONTANEOUS EVALUATIONS

Measures of spontaneous evaluation typically rely on indirect influences of evaluations on task performance. For example, in evaluative priming, the task is to evaluate target words as fast and accurately as possible; performance in that task is of interest only to the extent to which it is influenced by prime evaluations. Task performance is, however, a function of many variables. Unless a complete model specifies how these variables interact in shaping task performance, there is the danger that measures of spontaneous evaluations in part reflect the operation of task variables other than the spontaneous evaluation (e.g., Gawronski & Bodenhausen, 2007).

In this section, two such variables are briefly highlighted that seem particularly likely to contaminate measures of spontaneous evaluations, namely, strategic speed-accuracy settings and central-executive functions. Any speeded task requires a decision on the part of the participant about how much emphasis is to be placed on accurate responding versus fast responding. Assuming that task-relevant information accrues over time, response thresholds can be chosen conservatively, leading to relatively slow responses that are based on much information and therefore likely to be accurate. Conversely, more risky response criteria can be set, leading to faster responses based on less information and entailing a larger risk of errors. Speed-accuracy settings are a function of many situational and person-specific variables, including age, general intelligence, motivational focus, instructions, and so forth, and they are likely to distort priming measures both in the latency domain as well as in the error domain. Wentura and Rothermund (2003) considered the effects of speed-accuracy instructions on evaluative priming and even surmised that there may be qualitative changes in the processes underlying evaluative priming, leading under some circumstances to reversed priming effects given a strong emphasis on accuracy. They presented first data supporting this point of view. For the IAT, the potential influence of differential speed-accuracy settings was discussed by Brendl, Markman, and Messner (2001).

Task performance in speeded tasks also depends on central-executive capacity (Payne, 2005). Priming effects and IAT effects derived from such tasks are likely to be a function of central-executive factors as well, given that both involve the screening out of distracting information (i.e., of the prime influence in priming and of misleading evaluations in the inconsistent phase of IATs). Inhibition of distracting elements is one function of the central executive according to current conceptualizations (e.g., Miyake et al., 2000). The ability to inhibit distracting associations is part of a model of errors in the IAT by Conrey, Sherman, Gawronski, Hugenberg, and Groom (2005). Klauer and Mierke (2005) reported experimental evidence for inhibition of evaluations in IATs, and Chee, Sriram, Soon, and Lee (2000) also suggested that inhibitory processes play a role in IAT responses on the basis of brain-imaging data. Payne (2005) reported a significant correlation between a central-executive measure of the ability to inhibit distracting stimuli based on the so-called antisaccade task and a prejudice IAT but did not obtain a significant correlation with prejudice scores based on evaluative priming. However, work on Stroop and flanker tasks that probably rely on similar principles of response conflict and synergy as evaluative priming (Klauer & Musch, 2003) suggests that a lack of central-executive capacity should also increase priming effects (Kane & Engle, 2003; Lavie, Hirst, De Fockert, & Viding, 2004).

Note in particular that context effects on measures of spontaneous evaluation can also be mediated by these task variables, speed-accuracy settings, and central-executive capacity rather than being effects on the evaluations themselves.

CONCLUSIONS

In this chapter, I argued that measures of spontaneous evaluation are not partially autonomous, the minimal feature defining automaticity. Nevertheless, it seems plausible that respondents do not regularly engage in the control strategies that counteract and alter priming and IAT effects. Inasmuch as this assumption is true, context effects on measures of spontaneous evaluations question the attractive idea that these measures tap stable associative evaluations residing in long-term memory. An exemplar-based model was sketched that seems to deal with many of the phenomena of spontaneous evaluation, including priming and context effects, and that does not require the assumption of associative links or the powerful notion of spreading activation and parallel constraint satisfaction embodied by connectionist models. This means that the current data on spontaneous evaluation may not be strong enough to rule out either family of models. Exemplar-based models, but not connectionist models, would be difficult to reconcile with interactive effects of separately encoded bits of evaluative information as postulated in cognitive-balance theory and other consistency theories, but the evidence to date seems to suggest that interactive effects occur only when conscious reflection on, and integration of, the separate bits of information occurs at the time of encoding or at the time of judgment. It would be helpful to specify connectionist models, their link structure, learning rule, and learning history, to the point at which testable and potentially falsifiable predictions also can be derived from them.

Spontaneous evaluations are recruited by task sets that are compiled in response to the instructions on the tasks defining the measures of spontaneous evaluation. The task sets recruit additional processes and strategic settings, such as speed-accuracy settings and central-executive functions, in a way that is likely to contaminate measures of spontaneous evaluation to some extent. Factoring out these processes probably requires a model that explicitly specifies the interaction of speed-accuracy settings, executive functions, and spontaneous evaluations in determining task performance in terms of both errors and latencies (to capture speed-accuracy trade-offs) and at the level of the individual respondent.

REFERENCES

Baeyens, F., Eelen, P., Van den Bergh, O., & Crombez, G. (1992). The content of learning in human evaluative conditioning: Acquired valence is sensitive to US-revaluation. *Learning and Motivation, 23,* 200–224.

Banse, R., Seise, J., & Zerbes, N. (2001). Implicit attitudes towards homosexuality: Reliability, validity, and controllability of the IAT. *Zeitschrift für Experimentelle Psychologie, 48,* 145–160.

Bargh, J. A. (1992). The ecology of automaticity. Toward establishing the conditions needed to produce automatic effects. *American Journal of Psychology, 105,* 181–199.

Bargh, J. A. (1999). The cognitive monster: The case against controllability of automatic stereotype effects. In S. Chaiken & Y. Trope (Eds.), *Dual process theories in social psychology* (pp. 361–382). New York: Guilford Press.

Bem, D. J. (1970). *Belief, attitudes, and human affairs.* Belmont, CA: Brooks/Cole.

Blair, I. V. (2002). The malleability of automatic stereotypes and prejudice. *Personality and Social Psychology Review, 6,* 242–261.

Brendl, C. M., Markman, A. B., & Messner, C. (2001). How do indirect measures of evaluation work? Evaluating the inference of prejudice in the implicit association test. *Journal of Personality and Social Psychology, 81,* 760–773.

Chee, M. W. L., Sriram, N., Soon, C. S., & Lee, K. M. (2000). Dorsolateral prefrontal cortex and the implicit association of concepts and attributes. *NeuroReport, 2,* 135–140.

Conrey, F. R., Sherman, J. W., Gawronski, B., Hugenberg, K., & Groom, C. (2005). Separating multiple processes in implicit social cognition: The Quad-model of implicit task performance. *Journal of Personality and Social Psychology, 89,* 469–487.

Cooper, W. H. (1981). Ubiquitous halo. *Psychological Bulletin, 90,* 218–244.

Curtis, R. C., & Miller, K. (1986). Believing another likes or dislikes you: Behaviors making the belief come true. *Journal of Personality and Social Psychology, 51,* 284–290.

Dasgupta, N., & Greenwald, A. G. (2001). On the malleability of automatic attitudes: Combating automatic prejudice with images of admired and disliked individuals. *Journal of Personality and Social Psychology, 81,* 800–814.

De Houwer, J. (2003a). The extrinsic affective Simon task. *Experimental Psychology, 50,* 77–85.

De Houwer, J. (2003b). A structural analysis of indirect measures of attitudes. In J. Musch & K. C. Klauer (Eds.), *The psychology of evaluation: Affective processes in cognition and emotion* (pp. 219–244). Mahwah, NJ: Erlbaum.

De Houwer, J., Thomas, S., & Baeyens, F. (2001) Associative learning of likes and dislikes: A review of 25 years of research on human evaluative conditioning. *Psychological Bulletin, 127,* 853–869.

Duckworth, K. L., Bargh, J. A., Garcia, M., & Chaiken, S. (2002). The automatic evaluation of novel stimuli. *Psychological Science, 13,* 513–519.

Dunton, B. C., & Fazio, R. H. (1997). An individual difference measure of motivation to control prejudiced reactions. *Personality and Social Psychology Bulletin, 23,* 316–326.

Egloff, B., & Schmukle, S. C. (2002). Predictive validity of an implicit association test for assessing anxiety. *Journal of Personality and Social Psychology, 83,* 1441–1455.

Fazio, R. H., Sanbonmatsu, D. M., Powell, M. C., & Kardes, F. R. (1986). On the automatic activation of attitudes. *Journal of Personality and Social Psychology, 50,* 229–238.

Ferguson, M. J., & Bargh, J. A. (2004). Liking is for doing: The effects of goal pursuit on automatic evaluation. *Journal of Personality and Social Psychology, 87*, 557–572.

Fiedler, K., & Blümke, M. (2005). Faking the IAT: Aided and unaided response control on the implicit association test. *Basic and Applied Social Psychology, 27*, 307–316.

Gawronski, B., & Bodenhausen, G. V. (2005). Accessibility effects on implicit social cognition: The role of knowledge activation and retrieval experiences. *Journal of Personality and Social Psychology, 89*, 672–685.

Gawronski, B., & Bodenhausen, G. V. (2007). What do we know about implicit attitude measures and what do we have to learn? In B. Wittenbrink & N. Schwarz (Eds.), *Implicit measures of attitudes: Procedures and controversies* (pp. 265–286). New York: Guilford Press.

Gawronski, B., Deutsch, R., & Seidel, O. (2005). Contextual influences on implicit evaluation: A test of additive versus contrastive effects of evaluative context stimuli in affective priming. *Personality and Social Psychology Bulletin, 31*, 1226–1236.

Gawronski, B., & Strack, F. (2004). On the propositional nature of cognitive consistency: Dissonance changes explicit, but not implicit attitudes. *Journal of Experimental Social Psychology, 40*, 535–542.

Gawronski, B., Strack, F., & Bodenhausen, G. V. (in press). Attitudes and cognitive consistency: The role of associative and propositional processes. To appear in R. E. Petty, R. H. Fazio, & P. Briñol (Eds.), *Attitudes: Insights from the new wave of implicit measures*. Mahwah, NJ: Erlbaum.

Gawronski, B., Walther, E., & Blank, H. (2005). Cognitive consistency and the formation of interpersonal attitudes: Cognitive balance affects the encoding of social information. *Journal of Experimental Social Psychology, 41*, 618–626.

Gigerenzer, G., & Regier, T. (1996). How do we tell an association from a rule? Comment on Sloman (1996). *Psychological Bulletin, 119*, 23–26.

Glaser, J., & Banaji, M. R. (1999). When fair is foul and foul is fair: Reverse priming in automatic evaluation. *Journal of Personality and Social Psychology, 77*, 669–687.

Greenwald, A. G., & Banaji, M. R. (1995). Implicit social cognition: Attitudes, self-esteem, and stereotypes. *Psychological Review, 102*, 4–27.

Greenwald, A. G., McGhee, D. E., & Schwartz, J. L. K. (1998). Measuring individual differences in implicit cognition: The implicit association test. *Journal of Personality and Social Psychology, 74*, 1464–1480.

Hammerl, M., & Grabitz, H.-J. (1996). Human evaluative conditioning without experiencing a valued event. *Learning and Motivation, 27*, 278–293.

Hintzman, D. L. (1984). MINERVA 2: A simulation model of human memory. *Behavior Research Methods and Instrumentation, 16*, 96–101.

Hintzman, D. L. (1986). "Schema abstraction" in a multiple-trace memory model. *Psychological Review, 93*, 411–428.

Hintzman, D. L. (1988). Judgments of frequency and recognition memory in a multiple-trace memory model. *Psychological Review, 95*, 528–551.

Kane, M. J., & Engle, R. W. (2003). Working memory capacity and the control of attention: The contributions of goal neglect, response competition, and task set to Stroop interference. *Journal of Experimental Psychology: General, 132*, 47–70.

Klauer, K. C., & Mierke, J. (2005). Task-set inertia, attitude accessibility, and compatibility-order effects: New evidence for a task-set switching account of the implicit association test effect. *Personality and Social Psychology Bulletin, 31*, 208–217.

Klauer, K. C., & Musch, J. (2003). Affective priming: Findings and theories. In J. Musch & K. C. Klauer (Eds.), *The psychology of evaluation: Affective processes in cognition and emotion* (pp. 7–50). Mahwah, NJ: Erlbaum.

Klauer, K. C., Roßnagel, C., & Musch, J. (1997). List-context effects in evaluative priming. *Journal of Experimental Psychology: Learning, Memory, and Cognition, 23*, 246–255.
Lavie, N., Hirst, A., De Fockert, J. W., & Viding, E. (2004) Load theory of selective attention and cognitive control. *Journal of Experimental Psychology: General, 133*, 339–354.
Logan, G., & Cowan, W. B. (1984). On the ability to inhibit thought and action: A theory of an act to control. *Psychological Review, 91*, 295–327.
Mierke, J., & Klauer, K. C. (2001). Implicit association measurement with the IAT. Evidence for effects of executive control processes. *Zeitschrift für Experimentelle Psychologie, 48*, 107–122.
Mierke, J., & Klauer, K. C. (2003). Method-specific variance in the implicit association test. *Journal of Personality and Social Psychology, 85*, 1180–1192.
Mitchell, J. P., Nosek, B. A., & Banaji, M. R. (2003). Contextual variations in implicit evaluations. *Journal of Experimental Psychology: General, 132*, 455–469.
Miyake, A., Friedman, N. P., Emerson, M. J., Witzki, A. H., Howerter, A., & Wager, T. D. (2000). The unity and diversity of executive functions and their contributions to complex "frontal lobe" tasks: A latent variable analyses. *Cognitive Psychology, 41*, 49–100.
Moors, A., & De Houwer, J. (2006). Automaticity: A conceptual and theoretical analysis. *Psychological Bulletin, 132*, 297–326.
Musch, J., & Klauer, K. C. (1997). Der Anteilseffekt beim affektiven Priming: Replikation und Bewertung einer theoretischen Erklärung [The consistency proportion effect in affective priming: Replication and evaluation of a theoretical account]. *Zeitschrift für Experimentelle Psychologie, 44*, 266–292.
Neely, J. H. (1977). Semantic priming and retrieval from lexical memory: Roles of inhibitionless spreading activation and limited-capacity attention. *Journal of Experimental Psychology: General, 106*, 226–254.
Neely, J. H. (1991). Semantic priming effects in visual word recognition: A selective review of current findings and theories. In D. Besner & G. W. Humphreys (Eds.), *Basic processes in reading: Visual word recognition* (pp. 264–336). Hillsdale, NJ: Erlbaum.
Nosek, B. A., & Banaji, M. R. (2001). The go/no-go association task. *Social Cognition, 19*, 161–176.
Olson, M. A., & Fazio, R. H. (2003). Relations between implicit measures of prejudice: What are we measuring? *Psychological Science, 14*, 36–39.
Ortony, A., Clore, G., & Collins, A. (1988). *The cognitive structures of emotions.* Cambridge, MA: Cambridge Press.
Osgood, C. E., Suci, G. J., & Tannenbaum, P. H. (1957). *The measurement of meaning.* Urbana: University of Illinois Press.
Payne, K. B. (2005). Conceptualizing control in social cognition: How executive functioning modulates the expression of automatic stereotyping. *Journal of Personality and Social Psychology, 89*, 488–503.
Payne, B. K., Cheng, C. M., Govorun, O., & Stewart, B. (2005). An inkblot for attitudes: Affect misattribution as implicit measurement. *Journal of Personality and Social Psychology, 89*, 277–293.
Ratcliff, R., & McKoon, G. (1994). Retrieving information from memory: Spreading-activation theories versus compound-cue theories. *Psychological Review, 101*, 177–184.
Schwarz, N. (1998). Accessible content and accessibility experiences: The interplay of declarative and experiential information in judgment. *Personality and Social Psychology Review, 2*, 87–99.

Schwarz, N., & Bohner, G. (2001). The construction of attitudes. In A. Tesser & N. Schwarz (Eds.), *Blackwell handbook of social psychology: Intraindividual processes* (Vol. 1, pp. 436–457). Oxford, England: Blackwell.

Sherman, S. J., Presson, C. C., Chassin, L., Rose, J., & Koch, K. (2003). Implicit and explicit attitudes toward cigarette smoking: The effects of context and motivation. *Journal of Social and Clinical Psychology, 22,* 13–39.

Smith, E. R. (1991). Illusory correlation in a simulated exemplar-based memory. *Journal of Experimental Social Psychology, 27,* 107–123.

Smith, E. R. (1996). What do connectionism and social psychology offer each other? *Journal of Personality and Social Psychology, 70,* 893–912.

Smith, E. R., & Zárate, M. A. (1992). Exemplar-based model of social judgment. *Psychological Review, 99,* 3–21.

Walther, E. (2002). Guilty by mere association: Evaluative conditioning and the spreading attitude effect. *Journal of Personality and Social Psychology, 82,* 919–934.

Wentura, D., & Rothermund, K. (2003). The "meddling-in" of affective information: A general model of automatic evaluation. In J. Musch and K. C. Klauer (Eds.), *The psychology of evaluation: Affective processes in cognition and emotion* (pp. 51–86). Mahwah, NJ: Erlbaum.

Wilson, T. D., Lindsey, S., & Schooler, T. Y. (2000). A model of dual attitudes. *Psychological Review, 107,* 101–126.

Wittenbrink, B. (2007). Measuring attitudes through priming. In B. Wittenbrink & N. Schwarz (Eds.), *Implicit measures of attitudes: Procedures and controversies* (pp. 17–58). New York: Guilford Press.

Wittenbrink, B., Judd, C. M., & Park, B. (2001). Spontaneous prejudice in context: Variability in automatically activated attitudes. *Journal of Personality and Social Psychology, 81,* 815–827.

Wyer, R. S., & Gordon, S. E. (1983). The cognitive representation of social information. In R. S. Wyer & T. K. Srull (Eds.), *Handbook of social cognition* (Vol. 2, pp. 73–150). Hillsdale, NJ: Erlbaum.

11

Emotion

ROLAND NEUMANN

INTRODUCTION

To denote affective states, we use many different terms, such as emotions, moods, affect, feelings, and more. Feelings can be conceived of as the broadest concept that includes affective and nonaffective feelings. Both emotions and moods are affective feelings, while feelings that are neither pleasant nor unpleasant, such as boredom or familiarity, are nonaffective feelings (Clore, 1992).

Moods can be conceived of as feelings that are either pleasant or unpleasant (affective feeling). The object of the mood state is not necessarily known. In contrast, emotions always refer to an object: We are proud of a praiseworthy action, or we get angry at the action of someone else.

Although it may be argued that moods and emotions are different in some respects, they nevertheless share important features, such as the affective feeling state. There is some recent debate about whether both moods and emotions might have the same underlying affective feeling state (Neumann, Seibt, & Strack, 2001; Siemer & Reisenzein, 1998). Russell (2003) argued that core affect states, describable within a two-dimensional space whose axes are pleasantness and arousal, underlie both emotions and moods. Changes of core affect can be, but do not necessarily have to be, attributed to some object. This claim is supported by evidence showing that emotions are intensified or dampened by preceding mood states, which suggests that the underlying feeling state is the same (Neumann et al., 2001; Siemer & Reisenzein, 1998). Moreover, the fact that the object of an emotion is not remembered after some delay supports the idea that core affect is partly independent of attribution processes.

Emotions consist of several components, such as feelings, nonverbal expressions, autonomic changes, and instrumental actions. Several definitions of emotion take into account the idea that some coherence among these components of emotions is necessary. According to Scherer (1990), emotions can be conceived of as sequences of related, synchronized changes in the states of all subsystems. Evidence for the coherence of the components, however, is mixed (Lang, 1993; Mauss, Levenson, McCarter, Wilhelm, & Gross, 2005; Reisenzein, 2000; Russell, 2003). Many studies showed a rather low correlation among the components of emotion (Lang, 1993). Reisenzein observed a medium-size correlation between the intensity of the feeling of surprise and the expressive component of surprise. In a similar vein, Mauss et al. showed a medium-size correlation between the feeling component of humor responses and the expressive component. The physiological response, however, was weakly correlated with both the feeling component and the expressive component. Moreover, no correlation was obtained among the feeling component, the expressive component, and the physiological component for the emotion of sadness.

Thus, emotions are at least not always characterized by a close coherence among the components. These findings direct the focus of attention to the question of what triggers the coherence among the components of emotion and which mechanisms are responsible for the dissociation of the components. For example, display rules activated in a specific situation can decrease the coherence between the expressive component and the feeling component.

ELICITATION OF MOODS

As pointed out, moods and emotions share the affective feelings component but are different in object relatedness, duration, and intensity. If we focus on mechanisms that elicit moods and emotions, it is not surprising that processes that lead to emotions might also trigger moods. For example, being informed of a high score after participating in an intelligence test elicits pride in most persons. Given that emotions can be prolonged into moods, it is likely that after some time the object of the feeling of pride is no longer the focus of attention. Thus, the appraisal processes that elicit emotions are also able to induce mood states. That motivational factors might indeed contribute to the elicitation of moods can be illustrated with the Velten technique, a procedure often used in experimental studies to induce mood states (Velten, 1968). A positive mood is induced when sentences such as "I am happy" are repeated, and a negative mood is induced by sentences such as "I am sad." Niedenthal has shown that successful mood induction by the Velten technique depends on self-referential processing. That is, sentences such as "I am happy" were successful in inducing a happy mood but not those sentences in the third person, such as "He is happy." This research supports the idea that the mechanisms that induce moods are similar to those that elicit emotions.

However, since we are concerned with appraisal processes in more detail, we need to consider possible factors that exclusively trigger moods and not emotions. There has been some debate regarding whether psychoactive drugs can induce emotions. Lazarus (1991) conceded that it is yet unknown whether drugs have an impact on appraisal processes and thereby change emotional response. Moods can be elicited by physiological changes such as hypoglycemia (Gold, MacLeod, Frier,

& Deary, 1995). However, whether these mood changes occur in the absence of appraisal processes will need to be demonstrated in future research. Yet unknown are mechanisms that mediate the influence of more distal factors such as climate (Keller, Fredrickson, & Ybarra, 2005), emotional expressions of interaction partners (Monahan, Murphy, & Zajonc, 2000; Neumann & Strack, 2000b), autobiographical memories, and music (Gaver & Mandler, 1987; Scherer & Zentner, 2001).

STRUCTURAL APPROACHES TO THE ELICITATION OF EMOTIONS: PHYSIOLOGICAL APPROACHES

Since the seminal writings of William James (1890) and Charles Darwin (1872/1965), emotions have been regarded as closely related to behavior, emotional expression, and physiological processes. According to James (1890), emotional experiences can be conceived of as a perception of the physiological and behavioral changes in a person that occur in response to a situation (such as for example running away from a bear). A similar position was advanced by Charles Darwin (1872/1965), who proposed that the intensity of emotions was influenced by emotional expressions and behavior. In contrast to James, Darwin (1872/1965) was convinced that emotional expression could not elicit the full-blown emotional episode but had an impact exclusively on the intensity of emotions. From his point of view, the interpretation of a situation triggers an emotion and the expressive behavior can either dampen or intensify the emotional experience.

The influence of emotional expressions on emotional experiences was investigated in the so-called facial-, postural-, or vocal feedback hypothesis. In actuality, there seems to be more evidence for the effect of motor responses on emotional intensity than for the claim that motor response by itself can trigger full blown emotions. First, several studies show that motor feedback alone is insufficient to induce emotions. For example, in one study either an upright or a slumped body position was induced (Stepper & Strack, 1993). Participants were required to fill out an alleged intelligence test and received either moderate or above-average feedback irrespective of their performance. Those who received an above-average feedback in an upright rather than in a slumped position experienced more pride. Importantly, however, the manipulation of the posture had no effect on those who received average feedback about their achievement. In order to feel proud it is therefore not sufficient to adopt an upright posture. Rather, it is necessary that individuals attribute a positive outcome to their own efforts (Weiner, 1986). Additional support for the assumption that motor feedback exerts an influence on the intensity of emotions comes from research showing that the influence of a specific muscle contraction is not restricted to the corresponding emotion but can influence other emotions as well. For example, contractions of the corrugator muscle intensify feelings of anger and feelings of sadness (Larsen, Kasimatis, & Frey, 1992) as well as non-affective feelings such as those of mental effort (Stepper & Strack, 1993; Strack & Neumann, 2000). Thus, in line with Winton's (1986) proposal, motor feedback seems to influence the intensity rather than the quality of the emotional response.

Accordingly, these findings tend to support the position that motor feedback exerts an influence on intensity of emotions (Darwin 1872/1965) rather than James' claim that motor feedback is sufficient to induce a full blown emotion. The influence on intensity of emotions is achieved by the facilitation of congruent evaluative information processing by motor responses (Neumann & Strack, 2000a).

The Somatic-Marker-Theory (Damasio, 1994) can be regarded as a modern variant of the James-Lange Theory. According to the Somatic-Marker-Approach, automatic physiological responses directly influence decision-making. In one experiment participants with and without prefrontal damage were required to perform a gambling task in which self-reported and physiological responses were recorded (Bechara, Damasio, Tranel, & Damasio, 1997). It was observed that normal participants began to choose advantageously before they detected a strategy in the game whereas prefrontal patients choose disadvantageously. Interestingly, anticipatory skin conductance responses were ascertained for risky choices in normal participants but not in patients. The authors suggested that nondeclarative knowledge about emotional events is automatically and non-consciously activated in response to situations and this nondeclarative knowledge in turn provides input for evaluation and decision making. Batson, Engel, and Fridell (1999) examined whether false feedback about physiological processes was sufficient to influence affect-based decisions. In this study, participants received alleged feedback about their arousal while listening to audiotapes describing situations threatening two values, freedom, and equality. Subsequent decisions which involved these values favored whichever value had received stronger feedback. Thus, the perception of a somatic change is more important than actual somatic changes for influencing decision making.

The Somatic-Marker-Approach demonstrates that emotions are adaptive because they can provide an advantage in helping us to arrive at decisions in complex situations. However, one might doubt that emotions are always functional (Parrott, 1995), since whether emotions are functional or not might depend on the situation. This idea was recently tested in a study where a less conservative gambling strategy was more advantageous (Shiv, Loewenstein, Bechara, Damasio, & Damasio, 2006). In this study patients with lesions in the prefrontal cortex invested in 84 percent of the rounds and earned more money than normal participants who invested in just 58 percent of the rounds. So it is not always advantageous to use somatic markers as a basis for decision making. Normal persons are risk averse and therefore judge more conservatively than those with prefrontal lesions. Whether it is advantageous to use emotions as a basis of decision making thus depends on the nature of the task.

STRUCTURAL APPROACHES TO THE ELICITATION OF EMOTIONS: COGNITIVE APPROACHES

To explain why people respond differently to the same emotion-eliciting event and why slight changes in a situation can have a dramatic impact on emotional response, it has been posited that emotions stem from at least a minimum of cognitive processing. According to appraisal theories, emotions arise from the evaluation of the significance of one's circumstances. Thus, different emotions emerge from repeatedly evaluating the implications of encountered situations for one's well-being (Lazarus, 1991). If, for example, a situation is interpreted as being beneficial for one's needs or goals, positive emotions such as joy or pride should emerge.

According to Ortony, Clore, and Collins (1988), different emotions emerge from valenced reactions to aspects of objects, to actions of agents, and to consequences of events. If one focuses on an event, one can be pleased or displeased about the outcome of the event, and emotions such as hope, fear, relief, disappointment, happiness, and sadness may result. To be pleased or displeased about an event presupposes that goals are involved. If one focuses on an action, one can approve or disapprove of the action, and emotions such as pride, admiration, shame, or reproach would result. The origin of these emotions is the appraisal of action with respect to one's standards. Finally, one can focus on an object and like or dislike the attributes of the object. In this case, emotions such as love, hate, or disgust emerge. The liking or disliking itself stems from the appraisal of objects with respect to tastes or attitudes.

Weiner (1986) proposed that the quality of emotions is shaped by inferences concerning the perceived causes of an outcome. In his approach, emotions emerge from a temporal sequence of three different processes. As in appraisal approaches, initially the success or failure of an outcome is evaluated. Second, individuals will search for a cause only if the outcome is evaluated as negative or unexpected. In a third step, this cause can be classified regarding its (a) locus, (b) stability, and (c) controllability. The classification of an outcome along these attributional dimensions determines which emotion is evoked. For example, attributing a negative outcome to another person's efforts triggers the feeling of anger, whereas feelings of guilt follow from the perception that a negative outcome is caused by one's own efforts.

Roseman, Antoniou, and Jose (1996) presented an approach that tries to predict the quality of emotions as a function of both cognitive and motivational processes. Similar to other appraisal accounts, this approach suggests that emotions are determined by dimensions including whether something is caused by an event or person and whether the outcome is positive or negative, certain or uncertain. Going beyond other approaches, Roseman et al. (1996) suggested that the current motivational state determines the quality of emotions as well. More specifically, the model states that, for example, being in an appetitive motivational state leads to emotions such as pride, while being in an aversive state results in relief.

Because support for appraisal approaches comes mainly from correlational studies that do not allow us to test whether appraisal processes exert a causal influence on emotions, it is conceivable that consistencies between appraisal dimensions and quality of emotional response are due to the fact that they reflect folk theories about emotions (Parkinson & Manstead, 1992). Experimental studies showing that appraisal dimensions exert an influence on the elicitation of qualitatively distinct emotions are rare. In one such study, participants tried to repeatedly execute either internal or external attributions before being exposed to an ambiguous negative event (Neumann, 2000). In line with Weiner's approach, it was observed that participants being confronted with an ambiguous negative event experienced anger rather than guilt when they had repeatedly performed external attributions (Neumann, 2000). These findings support the assumption that attributions exert a causal influence on emotions.

Roseman and Evdokas (2004) provided another experimental test of appraisal approaches. To induce an appetitive state, participants in this study were told that, of the two participating groups, their group would get a pleasant taste afterward instead of no taste. To induce an aversive motivation, participants were informed that they were to be in the group that would get an unpleasant taste afterward instead of no taste. In addition, the outcome probability was manipulated as a second and independent appraisal dimension. Therefore, half of the participants were informed that they would definitely be in the condition to which they had previously been assigned. The other half were informed that they would be in the opposite condition (no taste instead of a pleasant or unpleasant taste). It turns out that joy was more a consequence of appetitive than of aversive motivational states. Moreover, being in an aversive motivational state led to relief rather than to joy (see also Strauman & Higgins, 1987). Thus, motivational states exert specific influences on the quality of the elicited emotion.

Motivational processes do not only play a role in appraisal models of emotions. Strauman and Higgins (1987) proposed that the quality of emotions is a function of the perceived discrepancy between different instances of the self. Two kinds of discrepancies can emerge: Discrepancies between the ideal self (attributes that someone wishes or hopes to possess) and the actual self and discrepancies between the ought-self (attributes that someone feels a duty or obligation to possess) and the actual self. These types of discrepancy can lead to different emotions: Discrepancies between the ideal and the actual self lead to syndromes of dejection (sadness, low arousal), whereas discrepancies between actual and ought-self lead to syndromes of agitation (nervousness, increased arousal). These assumptions were supported in a study in which participants were primed with either discrepancies with their ideal self or discrepancies with their ought-self. In line with expectations, participants responded with sadness and decreased arousal to discrepancies with their ideal self and with nervousness and increased arousal to discrepancies with their ought-self.

PROCEDURAL APPROACHES TO THE ELICITATION OF EMOTIONS

Appraisal approaches were mainly concerned with specifying the cognitive structures and contents that trigger emotions. The interest in procedural aspects of emotion elicitation increased in response to the Zajonc-Lazarus debate (Lazarus, 1984; Zajonc, 1980, 1984). Several authors proposed that appraisal processes proceeded by and large automatically and without conscious control (Lazarus, 1991; Leventhal & Scherer, 1987). Others suggested that new information had to be generated in a more effortful process to elicit full-blown emotions (Weiner, 1986). Based on these arguments, it seems somewhat plausible to assume that emotions do not hinge on either automatic or controlled processes, but both possibilities might exist. Depending on the emotion-eliciting event and on experiences stored in memory, at least some emotions, such as fear, disgust, anger, and sadness, might be generated by either automatic or deliberate processes or by both.

In recent years, several dual-processing models in emotion were developed. The most influential dual-process model was developed by LeDoux (1996). This model distinguishes two different neurophysiological structures that generate fear responses: On the so-called high road, information about the fear stimulus is processed by the thalamus and the neocortex before a behavioral response is generated in the amygdala. However, LeDoux discovered the so-called low road, which is a direct pathway between the thalamus and the amygdala. This low road allows quicker transmission of information than the high road. The disadvantage, however, is that the information about the fearful stimulus is only superficially processed in the thalamus. Thus, although the response to a stimulus is generated faster, which might be adaptive since the information is superficially processed in the thalamus, this route of information processing is more error prone than the high road across the neocortex. LeDoux conducted studies in which rats were fear conditioned to a tone. Avoidance responses were observed also in rats in which lesions were induced in the connection between thalamus and neocortex. Thus, although the fear stimulus could no longer be processed by the neocortex, a fast avoidance response was observed. This suggests that (a) the neocortex is not necessary to generate fear responses and (b) there is an alternative pathway between the thalamus and amygdala. Research found evidence for this dual-processing model in humans (Adolphs, 1999). However, it is yet unknown whether the model can be applied to other emotions such as happiness, anger, or sadness. Moreover, it is unclear if the direct pathway is able to trigger just a motor response or the feeling component of fear as well.

Leventhal and Scherer (1987) distinguished three different forms of emotion processing. First, sensorimotor processes can be regarded as the most primitive form of processing. The authors assumed that immediate motor responses and emotional responses are generated by a simple feature detection process in response to simple patterns in the environment, such as loud or abrupt noises. On this level of information processing, individuals need no prior experience with the stimulus pattern to generate the response. On a second level, emotions emerge from the activation of acquired schemata. Thus, stimulus configurations such as height or narrowness can trigger fear. The more similar a stimulus configuration is to the represented prototype of the situation, the stronger is the elicited emotional response. The process by which emotions are generated on both the sensorimotor and schematic levels is relatively inflexible and automatic. Leventhal and Scherer suggested that conceptual processing can also elicit emotions in a more flexible and deliberate form of information processing. Conceptual processing hinges on propositionally organized memory structures. The distinction between schematic and conceptual processing is a cornerstone of many modern dual-processing approaches in emotion.

In their dual-processing approach, Clore and Ortony (2000) distinguished among associative and rule-based processes that generate emotions. Associative processing is conceived of as a memory-based mechanism. On encountering an action, object, or event, prior stored affective, physiological, and behavioral responses are activated. Rule-based processing relies instead on sensory input. Emotional responses depend on bottom-up processes that allow for a more context-sensitive and flexible form of reasoning.

Among the dual-processing models, there exists a consensus to distinguish both more automatic and more deliberate forms of emotion elicitation. There is some preliminary evidence that automatic and controlled processes can have a differential impact on other components of emotion. A study by Egloff, Wilhelm, Neubauer, Mauss, and Gross (2002) showed that heart rate and blood pressure during a speech stressor task are better predicted by an implicit measure of anxiety than by an explicit measure of anxiety. Given the dissociation often observed between physiological and cognitive components of emotion (Lang, 1993; Mauss et al., 2005; Reisenzein, 2000), these findings suggest that different processes may be responsible for each component. Thus, dissociations among the components of emotion might be due to dissociations among automatic and controlled processes. Future research will show whether we are justified in assuming that emotions are elicited by two entirely different types of processing or whether one mechanism is more likely. For a more extensive review of dual-processing approaches to emotions, see the work of Smith and Neumann (2005).

AFFECT REGULATION

Since Darwin, emotions have been regarded as adaptive systems that enhance assimilation to the environment and accelerate beneficial behavioral responses. Emotions exert pressure to reorganize the priority of one's actions. For example, fear might protect an individual by provoking avoidance behavior. However, what may be adaptive from a short-term perspective can be maladaptive in the long run. For example, in the short term, it might seem effective to avoid an examination to reduce the fear of exams, but from a long-term perspective, the negative consequences of avoiding the exam would prevail.

Thus, acting immediately on urges that are elicited by emotions might often be maladaptive. To avoid indulging emotional urges, people develop strategies to change their emotions, such as becoming distracted, avoiding situations, and thinking of positive outcomes. Acting appropriately in social situations sometimes requires that people try to share the negative emotions of others and thereby worsen their own well-being. *Emotion regulation* refers to attempts individuals make to influence which emotions they have, when they have them, and how these emotions are experienced and expressed (Gross, Richards, & John, 2006). Thus, emotion regulation involves both the upregulation of an emotion (if one wants to improve his or her affect) as well as the downregulation (if one wants to assimilate to a sad person).

The consequences of emotion regulation depend on the timing of the regulating strategy across the process of the unfolding of the emotional response. Gross (1998) distinguished strategies that have an impact either before or after the emotion is fully activated. *Antecedent-focused* strategies refer to strategies employed before the emotions are elicited, such as situation selection, situation modification, attention deployment, and cognitive change. *Response-focused strategies* refer to ways to modify emotional responses when they are already elicited. An example is hiding one's emotions.

One form of antecedent-focused strategy is *cognitive reappraisal*, which refers to changes in construing a potential emotion-eliciting event in a way that changes its emotional impact. The fact that it is possible to change physiological and experiential responses to emotion-eliciting situations was one reason for assuming that emotions are elicited by the cognitive interpretation of the situation and not by the situation itself (Lazarus, 1984). Several studies had shown that changing the interpretation of a distressing film decreases the intensity of emotional responses to that film (Gross, 1998; Koriat, Melkman, Averill, & Lazarus, 1972; Lazarus, Opton, Nomikos, & Rankin, 1965; Speisman, Lazarus, Mordkoff, & Davison, 1964). According to these studies, two different strategies can change the intensity of elicited stressful emotions: First, people can deny the reality of an emotion-eliciting situation. For example, one could assume that the information about a sad event hinges on fiction rather than on fact. In that case, the intensity of the sadness would be diminished. Such influences can be accounted for by assuming that emotions hinge on propositions that are believed to be true (e.g., Reisenzein, 1998).

A second form of antecedent-focused emotion regulation refers to a way of thinking: Trying to think analytically about an emotion-eliciting event should lower the intensity of the emotional response. Evidence for the assumption that an abstract or analytical way of thinking can reduce negative affect comes from studies by Strack, Schwarz, and Gschneidinger (1985). In these studies, participants were instructed to remember a sad event in either a vivid and detailed manner (what has happened) or in a rather abstract manner (why it happened). A mood state was induced by the remembered event only if it was remembered in a vivid and detailed manner. As a related strategy, the physical or temporal distance to an emotion-eliciting event can be changed. This implies that the emotion-eliciting event is represented in a metaphorical manner by which changing the distance between the eliciting event and the self changes its importance for oneself and therefore the motivational relevance (Fujita, Henderson, Eng, Trope, & Liberman, 2006).

The interactive effectiveness of both antecedent-focused regulation strategies was examined in a study by Kross, Ayduk, and Mischel (2005). In this study, participants were instructed to remember an anger-eliciting event from a self-distanced or self-involved perspective and to think about the event in either an abstract or a concrete way. They found that self-distanced processing reduced emotional response only if it was combined with an abstract way of processing.

A completely different strategy for regulating emotions is attempting to suppress already elicited emotional expressions. Thus, in contrast to the strategies reported so far, the strategy to suppress an already elicited emotion implies that some components of the emotional response are activated. This response-focused strategy leads to heightened physiological responses (Gross, 1998) and weaker memory for the details of the situation during which one is trying to suppress one's emotional expression. The memory impairment is due to the fact that suppression of one's emotional expression is taxing and therefore requires additional cognitive capacity, which is then not available for encoding (Richards & Gross, 1999).

Förster and Strack (1996) showed that encoding positive information is facilitated by nodding, while encoding negative information is facilitated by shaking one's head. This suggests that memory impairments are decreased when encoding congruent information and increased when encoding information incongruent with the facial expression in which people are actually engaging. The strategy of hiding one's emotion has consequences not only for physiological responses and memory, but also for disrupting social interaction and inhibiting relationship formation (Butler et al., 2003). This is at least in part due to the contagious effect of emotion suppression.

THE PERCEPTION AND COMMUNICATION OF EMOTIONS

Communication can be conceived of as the fundamental precondition for social cohesion and the development of social relationships. Specifically, the communication of emotions and their underlying motivational states contributes to establishing and retaining relationships. Emotions can be expressed by verbal and nonverbal communication. What exactly is communicated by facial display is still under debate. According to Darwin (1872/1965), the similarities of nonverbal emotional expressions in humans and animals are due to the same evolutionary origin. Thus, facial displays can be conceived of as direct action of the nervous system, and emotions possess a tendency to express themselves in vocal, facial, or postural expressions. Nevertheless, this tendency can be suppressed by voluntary effort. Given that facial displays are an immediate readout of the nervous system that humans share at least in part with other mammals, Darwin (1872/1965) suggested that there should be a number of emotions that are similarly encoded and decoded in every culture.

Ekman and Friesen (1975) found support for the thesis that at least six emotions (happiness, sadness, fear, disgust, anger, and surprise) are similarly expressed and detected in different cultures all over the world. Much less is known about universals of posture or vocal expression. Scherer (1984) conducted some research showing that, at least for anger, fear, and sadness, there exist universals in the vocal expression of emotions. Moreover, Atkinson, Dittrich, Gemmell, and Young (2004) observed that body movements of basic emotions can be detected even if presented with a point-light picture (a limited display consisting only of the notion of points corresponding to the joints of a target person).

Based on Darwin's model, Ekman and Friesen (1975) proposed that facial displays are a function of underlying emotions and display rules. Display rules can be conceived of as norms that determine when it is appropriate or inappropriate to express an emotion. In this approach, facial displays are not automatically influenced by underlying emotions. Rather, emotional expressions are qualified, modulated, or masked by communicative intent. Fridlund (1991) presented a contrasting view in assuming that displays of emotion serve exclusively communicative functions and do not provide any information about underlying emotions. Does that mean that emotions have no influence on facial displays?

To answer the question, Hess, Banse, and Kappas (1995) conducted a study in which participants watched a comedy show with a friend, with an unfamiliar person, or alone. It turned out that both the emotion and the social intent had an influence on the facial expression. That social intent had an influence on facial display is evident from the finding that smiles were more intense when the film was watched with a friend. Assuming that processes that contribute to the elicitation of an emotion refer to an interaction of situational aspects and motivational demands, facial displays can be conceived of as action tendencies (Frijda & Tcherkassof, 1997). Such speculations are in line with neurophysiological research, showing that facial displays are associated with two different neural structures that are believed to be involved in the generation of approach and avoidance responses (Davidson, Ekman, Saron, Senulis, & Friesen, 1990). Left frontal lobe electroencephalographic (EEG) activity, which is associated with an approach orientation, was observed during smiling. Conversely, a consistent pattern of activity in the right frontal lobe emerged during frowning.

Based on dual-processing models (Chaiken & Trope, 1999), it is reasonable to assume that emotions trigger more automatic responses of the facial muscles, whereas display rules require more effortful strategies. In line with this reasoning, it has been shown that contractions of the zygomaticus muscle were facilitated in response to pictures of flowers, whereas contractions of the corrugator were facilitated in response to pictures of snakes (Dimberg, Thunberg, & Grunedal, 2002). Further support for the link between facial displays and evaluative processes comes from a study by Neumann, Hess, Schulz, and Alpers (2005), which found that the processing of positive words facilitated smiling, and the processing of negative words facilitated frowning. In sum, although there are voluntary influences on facial display, evaluative processes are faster in influencing expressions.

We now turn to the question of how perceivers absorb the information included in emotional expressions. Obviously, catching the emotions of other persons around us might be especially important for adaptation to our environment (Buck & Ginsburg, 1991). That, for example, an overlooked threat in the environment can be detected in the facial display of other witnesses is an imminent advantage, and not only for toddlers. Given that the expression of other persons' emotions might possess significance for adaptation to our environment, one might speculate that humans are prepared to grasp the meaning of emotional expressions without much inferential effort.

In reality, the processes underlying decoding of nonverbal behavior are different from those for the comprehension of language. That is, the interpretation of nonverbal cues is much more efficient (Gilbert, Pelham, & Krull, 1988) and proceeds outside awareness (Dimberg, Thunberg, & Elmehed, 2000). On the other hand, judgments about another person's emotion have been shown to be highly context dependent (Trope, 1986). For example, the smile of a friend might have a different meaning than the smile of an enemy. Moreover, tears can express joy at a wedding ceremony or sadness at a funeral. Trope (1986) pointed out that two different processes contribute to such dispositional inferences: identification, which can be conceived of as an automatic process that ties the behavior to the observed person, and a more controlled process that takes the situation into account.

Based on this insight, Buck and Ginsburg (1991) developed a model for the communication of emotions. Specifically, they distinguished between voluntary and spontaneous communication. Spontaneous communication is biologically determined, and the meaning of the display does not have to be learned. Voluntary communication uses culturally shared symbols that bear an arbitrary relationship to the referent. Both sender and receiver must share a similar language for symbolic communication to be successful. Spontaneous communication is not propositional in that by definition it cannot be false. The fact that emotions might be automatically exchanged by this communication system is addressed in more detail in the section about contagion.

However, from an evolutionary point of view, all communicated emotions might not be equally important. Some emotions are assumed to have a special status in capturing other persons' attention. Fear and anger especially are important interpersonal signals that convey information about social status in hierarchically structured cultures. Hansen and Hansen (1988) found support for the thesis that attention is automatically captured by angry faces. In their study, participants were exposed to matrices of emotional expressions with the task of finding either similar or discrepant emotions. They observed faster detection of a discrepant angry face among happy faces than vice versa. This effect was replicated using sad faces as a contrasting category (Öhman, Flykt, & Esteves, 2001). Thus, evolutionary significant threat stimuli such as anger are automatically detected.

Whether one automatically responds to another person's emotional expression might also be due to the relationship to this person. Interacting with a significant other person or with a person who resembles the significant other (Andersen & Chen, 2002) might automatically trigger specific aspects of the relational self that can mediate automatic affective responses. Evidence for this assumption comes from a study in which students were subliminally primed with the frowning face of their advisor or the smiling face of an unfamiliar person (Baldwin, Carrell, & Lopez, 1990). After the subliminal exposure to the disapproving face of the advisor, students judged their research ideas to be more negative than after the face of the smiling unfamiliar other. In a second study, Catholic and non-Catholic students were exposed to the subliminal presentation of the frowning face of the pope or the frowning face of an unfamiliar person. Only Catholic participants judged their self-concept to be more negative after the presentation of the frowning face of the pope. No effect was obtained for the subliminal presentation of the unfamiliar other and for non-Catholic participants. These findings can be interpreted as evidence that relational schemata are activated by significant others, and that self-evaluation is automatically triggered in response to the facial expression of a significant other.

EMPATHY

In many approaches to emotion, emotions are conceived of as a response to circumstances that have an impact on one's own concerns (e.g., Lazarus, 1991). Emotions, however, also arise if someone else's concerns are at stake. Thus, one can be pleased or displeased about an event that is desirable or undesirable for someone else, with emotions such as pride, joy, pity, gloating, or resentment resulting (Ortony et al.,

1988). Moreover, being able to imagine how someone else would evaluate one's behavior is an important prerequisite of emotions such as pride and shame.

The ability to see a situation or outcome from the role or perspective (Underwood & Moore, 1982) of another person has often been condensed in the concept of empathy. The concept of empathy goes back to Lipps (1907), who conceived of it as a process of projecting oneself into the objects of perception. Thus, empathy blurs the distinction between self and object, and empathy is thus conceived of as a self-other merging (Batson, Sager, & Garst 1997). *Empathy* refers to the attempt by one self-aware self to comprehend unjudgmentally the positive and negative experiences of another self (Wispé, 1986). The mechanisms underlying empathy, such as role or perspective taking, are not yet well understood.

In addition to the more effortful strategies to see a situation from the role or perspective of another person, Hoffman (1984) conceptualized a more automatic form of empathy. Sometimes, individuals simply "catch" another's emotion without knowing the source of their empathetic response. This form of empathy was defined as "primitive emotional contagion" (Hatfield, Cacioppo, & Rapson, 1992). This primitive emotional contagion is assumed to consist of two processes: the spontaneous imitation of another person's emotional expression and the feeling induced by the motor feedback from the imitation.

MIMICRY

The tendency to unintentionally imitate the behavior of observed others is seen as a basis for various forms of social behavior, such as affiliation, rapport, emotional contagion, or prosocial behavior, and whether it exists in primates has also been discussed (Preston & de Waal, 2002). Lipps (1907) was among the first to propose that empathy hinges on the urge to unintentionally imitate others. Modern approaches use the term *motor mimicry* to refer to the tendency to automatically imitate the behavior of others (Bavelas et al., 1987). Individuals mimic gestures and postures (LaFrance, 1979), tone of voice, speech (Bernieri, 1988; Condon & Ogston, 1966), and facial displays of interaction partners (Meltzoff & Moore, 1977; Scheflen, 1964; Vaughan & Lanzetta, 1980).

In an experimental demonstration of motor mimicry, participants interacted with a confederate who smiled, shook her foot, or touched her face (Chartrand & Bargh, 1999). Although not required to empathize with the confederate, participants spontaneously imitated these behaviors. Further research has shown that the tendency to mimic interaction partners is enhanced by dispositional empathy (Chartrand & Bargh, 1999), high self-monitoring (Cheng & Chartrand, 2003), an interdependent self-construal (van Baaren, Maddux, Chartrand, de Bouter, & van Knippenberg, 2003), context dependency (Van Baaren, Horgan, & Chartrand, 2004), and the goal to affiliate (Lakin & Chartrand, 2003).

Derived from the ideomotor theory (James, 1890), motor mimicry is assumed to be due to the fact that both the perception and generation of behavior use impart the same representational format (Prinz, 1990). Thus, the generation of a specific behavior is facilitated while watching another person performing the same behavior.

Imitation emerges even if the eliciting facial display was not consciously recognized. This was shown in a study in which participants' electromyographic responses to the subliminal presentation of angry and smiling faces were recorded (Dimberg et al., 2000). Higher activation across the corrugator muscle was assessed after being exposed to an angry face, whereas higher activation across the zygomaticus muscle was obtained after being exposed to a smiling face. Based on these findings, it is likely that certain classes of behavior, such as facial displays of emotion, elicit the urge to spontaneously mimic these behaviors.

Motor mimicry has been assumed to have several consequences. One consequence is that imitation increases mutual liking and affiliation. Lakin and Chartrand (2003) have shown that the goal to affiliate with another person increases nonconscious mimicry. In their study, participants were primed with either affiliation-related words or neutral words. Afterward, they interacted with a confederate, who either shook her foot or touched her face. It turned out that the goal to affiliate augmented nonconscious mimicry of these gestures. Lakin and Chartrand interpreted these findings as indication that participants used mimicry as a means of affiliating with the interaction partner. The affiliative tendency is not restricted to the person being imitated. In an alleged marketing study, participants were required to verbally describe advertisements (Van Baaren, Holland, Kawakami, & van Knippenberg, 2004). While they did so, the body orientation and position of extremities of half of them were mimicked by the experimenter. The participants who were imitated were more likely to pick up a pen that was dropped accidentally by the experimenter. In a second experiment, the procedure was the same except that a new experimenter was introduced. Those participants who were imitated by a first experimenter were more likely to help the second experimenter who dropped a pen accidentally. Thus, helping was more likely after being mimicked, regardless of whether the person being mimicked and the person being helped were identical or not. Yet, the behavioral consequences of motor mimicry are not restricted to prosocial behavior. In a field study, waitresses either repeated customers' orders or replied with "okay" (Van Baaren, Holland, Steenaerts, & van Knippenberg, 2003). Repeating customers' orders increased the tip for the waitress from 52% to 78%. Together, these findings suggest that an important function of motor mimicry is to increase interpersonal closeness and mutual liking.

CONTAGION

Going one step further, emotional expressions might not only be spontaneously imitated; the imitation itself might have consequences for the affective feelings of the imitating person. Motor mimicry therefore might be the first part of a mediating mechanism of emotional contagion. The second part consists of the feedback process following the imitative behavior that induces a congruent feeling. To give an example, the sight of a smiling face or the tone of a happy voice will involuntarily elicit the same motor response in the recipient, which feeds into the corresponding emotion. Many studies have tried to collect evidence for emotional contagion. For example, it is relatively easy to demonstrate that laughter is contagious either alone (Provine, 1992) or in combination with comedies (Bush, Barr, McHugo,

& Lanzetta, 1989; Cupchik & Leventhal, 1974; Leventhal & Cupchik, 1975; Nosanchuk & Lightstone, 1974). That emotional contagion is actually mediated by motor mimicry was suggested by a study in which participants were exposed to films (Laird et al., 1994). For example, in a short sequence from the film *Crocodile Dundee*, a crocodile suddenly appeared beside the fearful face of a woman. While watching these sequences, participants were asked to display either the same or an incongruent facial expression. Consistent with a motor mimicry approach to emotional contagion, participants' emotions matched those of the target person only if they displayed a congruent facial expression. In this study, however, it is still possible that participants responded to the emotional situation instead of the fearful face of the woman.

To examine if exposure to vocal expression of emotions is sufficient to trigger emotional contagion, a study was conducted in which the vocal expression of emotions was subtly manipulated (Neumann & Strack, 2000b). More specifically, participants in an alleged study on text comprehension listened to an abstract philosophical text. This text was spoken in a happy, neutral, or sad voice. Participants listening to the happy voice were in a better mood afterward than those who listened to the neutral voice or to the sad voice. In addition, no evidence was obtained that more specific emotions were induced. That a mood state instead of an emotion was induced by the subtle manipulation of vocal expression makes sense if one assumes that emotional contagion might represent a feeling state whose object is not necessarily known. Are these effects due to the imitation of the vocal expression? To answer this question, participants were required to repeat the talk they were listening to on audiophones (Neumann & Strack, 2000b). These repetitions were then presented to another group of participants, who were required to judge the target person's emotion. It turned out that those who repeated the text spoken in a happy voice were judged to be happier than those who repeated the sad version. Thus, in line with approaches assuming that we spontaneously imitate the prosody of those to whom we are listening, it was found that the vocal emotional expression of others was spontaneously imitated. In sum, these findings provide the first evidence for emotional contagion. Listening to another person's vocal expression is sufficient to induce a congruent mood state in the listener.

THE INFLUENCE OF AFFECT ON MEMORY, JUDGMENT, AND PROCESSING

It is part of our everyday knowledge that emotions influence how we see the world: Love leads to a rose-colored view or makes us blind, whereas feeling down leads to a negative view. Thus, one's own emotions and moods have an impact on all steps of information processing. The two major approaches to this issue, the associative network model and the feeling-as-information model, are briefly described.

Based on associative network approaches to memory, it has been proposed that affect and cognition represent nodes in a network that is linked by associations (Bower, 1981). Given that the activation spreads from an affective node to cognitive nodes in the network, an affective state should automatically activate congruent thoughts and ideas in memory. Thus, positive moods and emotions should increase the activation of positive cognitive contents so that they come to mind more easily, whereas negative moods and emotion should spontaneously activate negative cognitive contents.

The implication for perception is that affect can influence perception in a mood-congruent manner. That is, in a positive mood the perception of positive content in the perceptual field is facilitated. These predictions are supported by findings showing that attention is attracted by affect-congruent details (Bower, 1981), and that more time is required to read affect-congruent contents (Forgas, 1995). Moreover, ambiguous information is interpreted in an affect-congruent manner (Martin, Seta, & Crelia, 1990). Further implications of this approach refer to the effect of affect on memory. The first implication is that whenever the affect state at encoding is congruent with the affect state at decoding, recall should be better. This relationship is called *state-dependent memory*. A second implication is called *mood-congruency effect* and refers to the assumption that affect activates congruent cognitive nodes in the associative network. The empirical support for state-dependent memory is weak (Bower & Mayer, 1985). It has been speculated that the intensity of mood states and the constructiveness of the underlying processes might play a role in state-dependent memory.

Mood congruency has been shown to be a much more reliable phenomenon (Blaney, 1986). It has been repeatedly demonstrated that positive contents are more likely to be recalled in a positive mood than in a negative mood, whereas negative contents are better recalled in a sad mood (Blaney, 1986). Mood-congruent recall has been most reliably demonstrated in autobiographical memory (Blaney, 1986). This might be due to the fact that more associations exist for autobiographical contents, and that the affect-congruency effect increases as a function of the constructiveness of the underlying process (Forgas, 1995). One might object that it is unlikely that positive mood influences all positive contents in memory and negative mood all negative contents. Niedenthal and Setterlund (1994) therefore proposed that the influence of affect on perception is more specific. According to their approach, emotions rather than moods influence perception. To test this idea, Niedenthal and Setterlund induced happy or sad feelings in participants before they performed a lexical decision task. The task involved words that are related to happy, positive (happy unrelated), sad, negative (sad unrelated), and neutral emotional states. It turned out that emotions facilitated lexical decision about words specifically related to participants' emotional states. However, effects of emotion on perception of valence-congruent stimuli were not observed. In another study, participants made judgments about facial expressions of emotion more quickly when the expression of the faces matched the participants' emotion. This suggests that the perception of emotions is facilitated in an emotion-congruent manner. Future research will have to show whether such a lack of specificity is partly responsible for the unreliable findings in the research on mood congruency.

Somewhat different predictions for the influence of affective responses on judgments arise from the feeling-as-information approach (Schwarz & Clore, 1983). Individuals may use their affective response to a target as a basis of judgment. Instead of exerting effort to retrieve information about the object being judged, the immediate affective response to the target can be a useful source for the judgment. For example, it is unlikely that individuals try to retrieve all information about a dish before they come to a decision. Rather, the decision can be simplified by asking, "How do I feel about it?" Such a mechanism allows for the possibility that the current feelings actually do not stem from reasoning about the target object but from other sources. Thus, the current feeling might stem from several origins or from preexisting affective responses. According to the feeling-of-information approach, the impact of feelings on judgments should depend on the informational value of the affective response. In line with this prediction, Schwarz and Clore observed that the influence of mood on judgments of life satisfaction was eliminated when participants attributed their current feelings to causes that are irrelevant for the judgment at hand. Participants uttered higher life satisfaction and better mood in a telephone survey when called on sunny rather than on rainy days. This influence was eliminated, however, when the attention of the interviewed participants was directed to the weather.

In a study by Keltner, Locke, and Audrain (1993), participants framed the causes of their negative feelings in either general or specific terms. Consistent with the feeling-of-information approach, participants who framed their feelings in more general terms used this feeling to judge their general life satisfaction. However, no such effect was obtained for those who framed the causes of their feelings in specific terms. Moreover, the impact of negative feelings on judgments of personal satisfaction is increased if the feeling is attributed to self-referential rather than to situational causes. In such cases, the current feeling is judged to be more representative for the judgment at hand (Strack, 1992).

Unlike moods, emotions have localized effects on judgments and possess a more specific informational value. This assumption is supported by a series of experiments in which participants were required to imagine hypothetical situations that elicit either anger or sadness (Keltner, Ellsworth, & Edwards, 1993). It turned out that sad participants perceived situationally caused events as more likely than angry participants did. Angry participants, in contrast, perceived events caused by humans as more likely than sad participants did. In sum, these findings support the assumption that feelings possess an informational value for evaluative judgments. Moreover, the informational value of emotions is more specific than the informational value of moods. Importantly, the feeling-as-information approach differs from the associative network approach in several respects: Whereas for the associative network approach activation should spread between moods and cognitive contents, no such reciprocal influence is postulated for the feeling-as-information approach. In fact, there is some evidence for the independence of activated cognitive contents and affective feelings (e.g., Innes-Ker & Niedenthal, 2002; Johnson & Tversky, 1983). Moreover, the associative network approach but not the feeling-as-information approach predicts mood-congruent influences on perception. As was outlined in more detail, there is ample evidence for the influence of moods and emotions on perception.

The feeling-as-information approach has proven to be useful in explaining mechanisms underlying anticipation of affective responses in future or self-reports about affective responses in the past (Robinson & Clore, 2002; Wilson & Gilbert,

2005). Actually having an emotional experience is much different from trying to reexperience an emotion or just thinking that one is having an emotional experience (Robinson & Clore, 2002). Feelings cannot be stored in memory. They are states that change from moment to moment. Thus, answers about prior feelings are not necessarily based on the feeling itself but on episodic memory or theories about one's own emotional responding. For example, whereas on-line emotional experience is sensitive to the duration of a negative or positive event, retrospective emotion reports are not. Evidence for this assumption comes from a study in which participants were exposed to pleasant and aversive film clips (Fredrickson & Kahneman, 1993). Although the effect of the duration of the film on the global retrospective evaluation was small, the peak affect rating and the final rating obtained on-line explained the considerable variance in retrospective global evaluation. Accordingly, retrospective evaluations of emotional responses seem to be determined by salient episodes that can be retrieved from memory.

Similar distortions appear if individuals anticipate affective responses in the future. For example, the holiday trip to a tropical island might turn out to be quite boring after a few days because the weather did not change at all, and the hotel is lousy. When thinking about affective response to future events, people often oversimplify their feelings. In a series of studies, participants were required to describe affective events in either the near or distant future (Trope & Liberman, 2003). A repeated finding in these studies was that events in the distant future were typically described exclusively on the basis of acknowledging the valence of the event. However, descriptions of near events were characterized by a much more moderate affective response and by more reasoning about how the anticipated event could be reached (Trope & Liberman, 2003). Thus, a source of misprediction is that individuals fail to take into account that their actual feeling in the real situation is determined by factors other than the focused one. Although humans have access to internal states such as feelings, they do not have access to the processes that contribute to these feelings (Nisbett & Wilson, 1977).

THE INFLUENCE ON PROCESSING STRATEGIES

So far, we have reported evidence that moods influence the contents of information processing. Affective states, however, exert an impact on processing strategies as well. That is, whether information is processed in a heuristic or more systematic manner is triggered by affective states. According to Schwarz and Bless (1991), affective states possess the function of informing the individual about states of the world. A positive mood state provides information that the situation is safe, and that the situation facilitates goal attainment. Negative moods, in contrast, signal that the current situation is problematic and requires an intervention. If an intervention is required, effective action is facilitated by a systematic, detail-oriented, resource-dependent processing strategy (Schwarz & Bless, 1991). If, however, a positive mood signals that the situation is safe, it is not necessary to deplete cognitive resources, and taking a risk might be acceptable in the pursuit of one's goal. Accordingly, one can use simple heuristics to process information and rely on long-established knowledge that has been successfully used in the past. As an alternative explanation, Ellis and Ashbrook (1988) suggested that dysphoric affective states limit attentional resources because these feelings trigger intrusive thoughts.

In a direct test between these two approaches, participants in different affective states were exposed to a restaurant story while working on a secondary motor task (Bless et al., 1996). It turned out that happy participants made more intrusion errors and performed better on a secondary task than sad participants. This suggests that happy mood increases reliance on general knowledge, and this increase is due to the reduced processing of schema-consistent information. These findings are incompatible with a view that dysphoric affective states reduce the attentional resources (Ellis & Ashbrook, 1988).

Further support for the feeling-as-information approach (Schwarz & Bless, 1991) comes from a study by Gasper and Clore (2002) in which participants were required to judge the similarity of geometrical shapes. These shapes (e.g., triangles) were made of smaller geometrical figures (e.g., squares). The task was to judge which of the two figures (e.g., the triangle made of squares or the square made of triangles) was more similar to a target figure. Derived from the affect-as-information approach, both happy and sad moods promote attention to either general or local information.

In this study, individuals in a negative mood were less likely than individuals in a positive or neutral mood to use the global shape as a basis for similarity judgments. This suggests that individuals are tuned to process information in a more detail-oriented manner if individuals are in a sad rather than in a happy mood. However, further research demonstrated that the influence of moods on global or detailed processing was apparent only if the mood was deemed representative for the similarity judgments (Gasper & Clore, 2002). If in contrast an affective response is deemed irrelevant to the current task, the effect of moods on the level of focus disappears.

In sum, evidence in the reported research suggests that mood exerts an influence not only on the valence of the processed information but also on the processing level. Apparently, sad mood triggers a more systematic, careful, and detail-oriented way of information processing, whereas happy individuals rely on their general knowledge and process information in a more heuristic manner.

REFERENCES

Adolphs, R. (1999). Social cognition and the human brain. *Trends in Cognitive Sciences, 3,* 469–479.

Andersen, S. M., & Chen, S. (2002). The relational self: An interpersonal social-cognitive theory. *Psychological Review, 109,* 619–645.

Atkinson, A. P., Dittrich, W. H., Gemmell, A. J., & Young, A. W. (2004). Emotion perception from dynamic and static body expressions in point light and full-light displays. *Perception, 33,* 717–746.

Baldwin, M. W., Carrell, S. E., & Lopez, D. F. (1990). Priming relationship schemas: My advisor and the Pope are watching me from the back of my mind. *Journal of Experimental Social Psychology, 26,* 435–454.

Batson, C. D., Engel, C. L., & Fridell, S. R. (1999). Value judgments: Testing the somatic-marker hypothesis using false physiological feedback. *Personality and Social Psychology Bulletin, 8,* 1021–1032.

Batson, C. D., Sager, K., & Garst, E. (1997). Is empathy-induced helping due to self-other merging? *Journal of Personality and Social Psychology, 73,* 495–509.

Bavelas, J. B., Black, A., Lemery, C. R., & Mullett, J. (1987). Motor mimicry as primitive empathy. In N. Eisenberg & J. Strayer (Eds.). *Empathy and its development* (pp. 317–338). Cambridge, UK: Cambridge University Press.

Bechara, A., Damasio, H., Tranel, D., & Damasio, A.(1997). Deciding advantageously before knowing the advantageous strategy. *Science, 275,* 1293–1294.

Bernieri, F. J. (1988). Coordinated movement and rapport in teacher-student interactions. *Journal of Nonverbal Behavior, 12,* 120–138.

Blaney, P. H. (1986). Affect and memory: A review. *Psychological Bulletin, 99,* 229–246.

Bless, H., Clore, G. L., Schwarz, N., Golisano, V., Rabe, C., & Wölk, M. (1996). Mood and the use of scripts: Does being in a happy mood really lead to mindlessness? *Journal of Personality and Social Psychology, 71,* 665–679.

Bower, G. H. (1981). Mood and memory. *American Psychologist, 36,* 129–148.

Bower, G. H., & Mayer, J. D. (1985). Failure to replicate mood-dependent retrieval. *Bulletin of the Psychonomic Society, 23,* 39–42.

Buck, R., & Ginsburg, B. (1991). Emotional communication and altruism: The communicative gene hypothesis. In M. Clark (Ed.), *Altruism. Review of personality and social psychology* (Vol. 11, pp. 149–175). Newbury Park, CA: Sage.

Bush, L. K., Barr, C. L., McHugo, G. J., & Lanzetta, J. (1989). The effects of facial control and facial mimicry on subjective reactions to comedy routines. *Motivation and Emotion, 13,* 31–52.

Butler, E. A., Egloff, B., Wilhelm, F. H., Smith, N. C., Erickson, E. A., & Gross, J. J. (2003). The social consequences of expressive suppression. *Emotion, 3,* 48–67.

Chaiken, S., & Trope, Y. (1999). *Dual process theories in social psychology.* New York: Guilford.

Chartrand, T. L., & Bargh, J. A. (1999). The chameleon effect: The perception-behavior link and social interaction. *Journal of Personality and Social Psychology, 76,* 893–910.

Cheng, C. M., & Chartrand, T. L. (2003). Self-monitoring without awareness: Using mimicry as a nonconscious affiliation strategy. *Journal of Personality and Social Psychology, 85,* 1170–1179.

Clore, G. L. (1992). Cognitive phenomenology: Feelings and the construction of judgment. In L. L. Martin & A. Tesser (Eds.), *The construction of social judgments* (pp. 133–163). Mahwah, NJ: Erlbaum.

Clore, G. L., & Ortony, A. (2000). Cognition in emotion: Always, sometimes, or never? In L. Nadel, R. Lane, & G. L. Ahern (Eds.), *The cognitive neuroscience of emotion* (pp. 24–61). New York: Oxford University Press.

Condon, W. S., & Ogston, W. D. (1966). Sound film analysis of normal and pathological behavior patterns. *Journal of Nervous and Mental Disease, 143,* 338–347.

Cupchik, G. C., & Leventhal, H. (1974). Consistency between expressive behavior and the elevation of humorous stimuli: The role of sex and self-observation. *Journal of Personality and Social Psychology, 30,* 429–442.

Damasio, A. (1994). *Descartes' error.* New York: Putnam.

Darwin, C. (1965). *The expression of emotion in man and animals.* New York: Philosophical Library. (Original work published 1872)

Davidson, R. J., Ekman, P., Saron, C. D., Senulis, J. A., & Friesen, W. V. (1990). Approach-withdrawal and cerebral asymmetry: emotional expression and brain physiology. *Journal of Personality and Social Psychology, 58,* 330-341.

Dimberg, U., Thunberg, M., & Elmehed, K. (2000). Unconscious facial reactions to emotional facial expressions. *Psychological Science, 11,* 86–89.
Dimberg, U., Thunberg, M., & Grunedal, S. (2002). Facial reactions to emotional stimuli: Automatically controlled emotional responses. *Cognition & Emotion, 16,* 449–472.
Egloff, B., Wilhelm, F. H., Neubauer, D. H., Mauss, I. B., & Gross, J. J. (2002). Implicit anxiety measure predicts cardiovascular reactivity to an evaluated speaking task. *Emotion, 2,* 3–11.
Ekman, P., & Friesen, W. V. (1975). *Unmasking the face. A guide to recognizing emotions from facial clues.* Englewood Cliffs, NJ: Prentice-Hall.
Ellis, H. C., & Ashbrook, P. W. (1988). Resource allocation model of the effects of depressed mood states on memory. In K. Fiedler & J. Forgas (Eds.), *Affect, cognition, and social behavior* (pp. 25–43). Gottingen, Germany: Hogrefe.
Forgas, J. P. (1995). Mood and judgment: The affect infusion model (AIM). *Psychological Bulletin, 117,* 39–66.
Förster, J., & Strack, F. (1996). Influence of overt head movements on memory for valenced words: A case of conceptual-motor compatibility. *Journal of Personality and Social Psychology, 71,* 421–430.
Fredrickson, B. L., & Kahneman, D. (1993). Duration neglect in retrospective evaluations of affective episodes. *Journal of Personality and Social Psychology, 65,* 45–55.
Fridlund, A. J. (1991). Sociality of solitary smiling: Potentiation by an implicit audience. *Journal of Personality and Social Psychology, 60,* 229–240.
Frijda, N. H., & Tcherkassof, A. (1997). In J. A. Russell & J. M. Fernández-Dols (Eds.), *The psychology of facial expression* (pp. 78–102). New York: Cambridge University Press.
Fujita, K., Henderson, M., Eng, J., Trope, Y., & Liberman, N. (2006). Spatial distance and mental construal of social events. *Psychological Science, 17,* 278–282.
Gasper, K., & Clore, G. L. (2002). Attending to the big picture: Mood and global versus local processing of visual information. *Psychological Science, 13,* 33–39.
Gaver, W. W., & Mandler, G. (1987). Play it again, Sam: On liking music. *Cognition and Emotion, 1,* 259–282.
Gilbert, D. T., Pelham, B. W., & Krull, D. S. (1988). On cognitive busyness: When person perceivers meet persons perceived. *Journal of Personality and Social Psychology, 54,* 733–740.
Gold, A. E., MacLeod, K. M., Frier, B. M., & Deary, I. J. (1995). Changes in mood during acute hypoglycemia in healthy participants. *Journal of Personality and Social Psychology, 68,* 498–504.
Gross, J. J. (1998). Antecedent- and response-focused emotion regulation: Divergent consequences for experience, expression, and physiology. *Journal of Personality and Social Psychology, 74,* 224–237.
Gross, J. J., Richards, J. M., & John, O. P. (2006). Emotion regulation in everyday life. In D. K. Snyder, J. A. Simpson, & J. N. Hughes (Eds.), *Emotion regulation in families: Pathways to dysfunction and health* (pp. 13–35). Washington, DC: American Psychological Association.
Hansen, C. H., & Hansen, R. D. (1988). Finding the face in the crowd: An anger superiority effect. *Journal of Personality and Social Psychology, 54,* 917–924.
Hatfield, E., Cacioppo, J. T., & Rapson, R. L. (1992). Primitive emotional contagion. In M. S. Clark (Ed.), *Emotion and social behavior* (pp. 151–177). Thousand Oaks, CA: Sage.
Hess, U., Banse, R., & Kappas, A. (1995). The intensity of facial expression is determined by underlying affective state and social situation. *Journal of Personality and Social Psychology, 69,* 280–288.
Hoffman, M. L. (1984). Interaction of affect and cognition in empathy. In C. Izard, J. Kagan, & R. Zajonc (Eds.), *Emotions, cognition and behavior* (pp. 103–131). New York: Cambridge University Press.

Innes-Ker, A., & Niedenthal, P. M. (2002). Emotion concepts and emotional states in social judgment and categorization. *Journal of Personality and Social Psychology, 83,* 804–816.

James, W. (1890). *Principles of psychology.* New York: Holt.

Johnson, E. J., & Tversky, A. (1983). Affect, generalization, and the perception of risk. *Journal of Personality and Social Psychology, 45,* 20–31.

Keller, M. C., Fredrickson, B. L., & Ybarra, O. (2005). A warm heart and a clear head: The contingent effects of weather on mood and cognition. *Psychological Science, 16,* 724–731.

Keltner, D., Ellsworth, P. C., & Edwards, K. (1993). Beyond simple pessimism: Effects of sadness and anger on social perception. *Journal of Personality and Social Psychology, 64,* 740–752.

Keltner, D., Locke, K. D., & Audrain, I.C. (1993). The influence of attributions on the relevance of negative feelings to satisfaction. *Personality and Social Psychology Bulletin, 19,* 1–29.

Koriat, A., Melkman, R., Averill, J. R., & Lazarus, R. S. (1972). The self-control of emotional reactions to a stressful film. *Journal of Personality, 40,* 601–619.

Kross, E., Ayduk, O., & Mischel, W. (2005). When asking "why" does not hurt: Distinguishing rumination from reflective processing of negative emotions. *Psychological Science, 16,* 709–715.

LaFrance, M. (1979). Nonverbal synchrony and rapport: Analysis by the cross-lag panel technique. *Social Psychology Quarterly, 42,* 66–70.

Laird, J. D., Alibozak, T., Davainis, D., Deignan, K., Fontanella, K., Hong, J., et al. (1994). Individual differences in the effects of spontaneous mimicry on emotional contagion. *Motivation and Emotion, 18,* 231–247.

Lakin, J. L., & Chartrand, T. L. (2003). Using nonconscious behavioral mimicry to create affiliation and rapport. *Psychological Science, 14,* 334–339.

Lang, P. J. (1993). The three-system approach to emotion: Philosophical and theoretical problems. In N. Birbamer & A. Ohman (Eds.), *The structure of emotion: Psychophysiological, cognitive, and clinical aspects* (pp. 18–30). Seattle: Hogrefe & Huber.

Larsen, R. J., Kasimatis, M., & Frey, K. (1992). Facilitating the furrowed brow: An unobtrusive test of the facial feedback hypothesis applied to unpleasant affect. *Cognition & Emotion, 6,* 321–338.

Lazarus, R. S. (1984). On the primacy of cognition. *American Psychologist, 39,* 124–129.

Lazarus, R. S. (1991). Progress on a cognitive-motivation-relational theory of emotion. *American Psychologist, 46,* 819-834.

Lazarus, R. S., Opton, E., Nomikos, M. S., & Rankin, N. O. (1965). The principle of short-circuiting of threat: Further evidence. *Journal of Personality, 33,* 307–316.

LeDoux, J. (1996). *The emotional brain: The mysterious underpinnings of emotional life.* New York: Simon and Schuster.

Leventhal, H., & Cupchik, G. C. (1975). The informational and facilitative effects of an audience upon expression and the evaluation of humorous stimuli. *Journal of Experimental Social Psychology, 11,* 363–380.

Leventhal, H., & Scherer, K. (1987). The relationship of emotion to cognition: A functional approach to a semantic controversy. *Cognition & Emotion, 1,* 3–28.

Lipps, T. (1907). Das Wissen von fremden Ichen. *Psychologische Untersuchungen, 1,* 694–722.

Martin, L. L., Seta, J. J., & Crelia, R. A. (1990). Assimilation and contrast as a function of people's willingness and ability to expend effort in forming an impression. *Journal of Personality and Social Psychology, 59,* 27–37.

Mauss, I. B., Levenson, R. W., McCarter, L., Wilhelm, F. H., & Gross, J. J. (2005). The tie that binds? Coherence among emotion experience, behavior, and physiology. *Emotion, 5,* 175–190.

Meltzoff, A. N., & Moore, M. K. (1977). Imitation of facial and manual gestures by human neonates. *Science, 198,* 75–78.

Monahan, J. L., Murphy, S. T., & Zajonc, R. B. (2000). Subliminal mere exposure: Specific, general, and diffuse effects. *Psychological Science, 11,* 462–466.

Neumann, R. (2000). The causal influences of attributions on emotions: A procedural priming approach. *Psychological Science, 11,* 179–182.

Neumann, R., Hess, M., Schulz, S., & Alpers, G. (2005). Automatic behavioral responses to valence: Evidence that facial action is facilitated by evaluative processing. *Cognition and Emotion, 19,* 499–519.

Neumann, R., & Strack, F. (2000a). Approach and avoidance: The influence of proprioceptive and exteroceptive cues on encoding of affective information. *Journal of Personality and Social Psychology, 79,* 39–48.

Neumann, R., & Strack, F. (2000b). "Mood contagion". The automatic transfer of mood between persons. *Journal of Personality and Social Psychology, 79,* 211–223.

Neumann, R., Seibt, B., & Strack, F. (2001). The influence of mood on the intensity of emotional responses: Disentangling feeling and knowing. *Cognition & Emotion, 15,* 725–747.

Niedenthal, P. M., & Setterlund, M. B. (1994). Emotion congruence in perception. *Personality and Social Psychology Bulletin, 20,* 401–411.

Nisbett, R., & Wilson, T. (1977). Telling more than we can know: Verbal reports on mental processes. *Psychological Review, 84,* 231–259.

Nosanchuk, T. A., & Lightstone, J. (1974). Canned laughter and public and private conformity. *Journal of Personality and Social Psychology, 29,* 153–156.

Öhman, A., Flykt, A., & Esteves, F. (2001). Emotion drives attention: Detecting the snake in the grass. *Journal of Experimental Psychology: General, 130,* 466–478.

Ortony, A., Clore, G. L., & Collins, A. (1988). *The cognitive structure of emotions.* Cambridge, England: Cambridge University Press.

Parkinson, B., & Manstead, A. S. R. (1992). Appraisal as a cause of emotion. In M. Clark (Ed.), *Emotion. Review of personality and social psychology* (Vol. 13, pp. 122–149). Newbury Park, CA: Sage.

Parrott, W. G. (1995). But emotions are sometimes irrational. *Psychological Inquiry, 6,* 230–232.

Preston, S. D., & de Waal, F. B. M. (2002). Empathy: Its ultimate and proximate bases. *Behavioral and Brain Sciences, 25,* 1–71.

Prinz, W. (1990). A common coding approach to perception and action. In O. Neumann & W. Prinz (Eds.), *Relationships between perception and action* (pp. 167–201). Berlin: Springer.

Provine, R. R. (1992). Contagious laughter: Laughter is a sufficient stimulus for laughs and smiles. *Bulletin of the Psychonomic Society, 30,* 1–4.

Reisenzein, R. (1998). Outlines of a theory of emotions as metarepresentational states of mind. In A. H. Fischer (Ed.), *ISRE'98. Proceedings of the 10th Conference of the International Society for Research on Emotions* (pp. 186–191). Amsterdam: Faculty of Psychology.

Reisenzein, R. (2000). Exploring the strength of association between the components of emotion syndromes: The case of surprise. *Cognition & Emotion, 14,* 1–38.

Richards, J. M., & Gross, J. J. (1999). Composure at any cost? The cognitive consequences of emotion suppression. *Personality and Social Psychology Bulletin, 25,* 1033–1044.

Robinson, M. D., & Clore, G. L. (2002). Belief and feeling: Evidence for an accessibility model of emotional self-report. *Psychological Bulletin, 128,* 934–960.

Roseman, I. J., Antoniou, A. A., & Jose, P. E. (1996). Appraisal determinants of emotions: Constructing a more accurate and comprehensive theory. *Cognition and Emotion, 10,* 241–278.

Roseman, I. J., & Evdokas, A. (2004). Appraisals cause experienced emotions: Experimental evidence. *Cognition & Emotion, 18,* 1–28.

Russell, J. A. (2003). Core affect and the psychological construction of emotion. *Psychological Review, 110,* 145–172.

Scheflen, A. E. (1964). The significance of posture in communication systems. *Psychiatry, 27,* 316–331.

Scherer, K. R. (1984). State of the art in vocal communication: A partial view. In A. Wolfgang (Ed.), *Nonverbal behavior: Perspectives, applications, intercultural insights* (pp. 41–73). Lewiston, NY: Hogrefe and Huber.

Scherer, K. R. (1990). Theorien und aktuelle Probleme der Emotionspsychologie. In K. R. Scherer (Ed.), *Psychologie der Emotionen. Enzyklopädie der Psychologie* (pp. 1–38). Göttingen, Germany: Hogrefe.

Scherer, K. R., & Zentner, M. R. (2001). Emotional effects of music: Production rules. In P. N. Juslin & J. A. Sloboda (Eds.), *Music and emotion: Theory and research* (pp. 361–392). New York: Oxford University Press.

Schwarz, N., & Bless, H. (1991). Happy and mindless, but sad and smart? The impact of affective states on analytic reasoning. In J. Forgas (Ed.), *Emotion and social judgments* (pp. 55–71). Oxford, England: Pergamon.

Schwarz, N., & Clore, G. L. (1983). Mood, misattribution, and judgments of well-being: Informative and directive functions of affective states. *Journal of Personality and Social Psychology, 45,* 513–523.

Shiv, B., Loewenstein, G., Bechara, A., Damasio, H., & Damasio, A. R. (2006). Investment behavior and the dark side of emotion. *Psychological Science, 16,* 435–439.

Siemer, M., & Reisenzein, R. (1998). Effects of mood on evaluative judgements: Influence of reduced processing capacity and mood salience. *Cognition & Emotion, 12,* 783–805.

Smith, E. R., & Neumann, R. (2005). Emotion processes considered from the perspective of dual-process models. In L. Feldman Barrett, P. M. Niedenthal, & P. Winkielman (Eds.), *Emotion and consciousness* (pp. 287–311). New York: Guilford Press.

Speisman, J. C., Lazarus, R. S., Mordkoff, A., & Davison, L. (1964). Experimental reduction of stress based on ego-defense theory. *Journal of Abnormal and Social Psychology, 68,* 367–380.

Stepper, S., & Strack, F. (1993). Proprioceptive determinants of emotional and nonemotional feelings. *Journal of Personality and Social Psychology, 64,* 211–220.

Strack, F. (1992). The different routes to social judgments: Experiential versus informational strategies. In L. L. Martin & A. Tesser (Eds.), *The construction of social judgment* (pp. 249–275). Hillsdale, NJ: Erlbaum.

Strack, F., & Neumann, R. (2000). Furrowing the brow may undermine perceived fame: The role of facial feedback in judgments of celebrity. *Personality and Social Psychology Bulletin, 26,* 762–768.

Strack, F., Schwarz, N., & Gschneidinger, E. (1985). Happiness and reminiscing: The role of time perspective, affect, and mode of thinking. *Journal of Personality and Social Psychology, 47,* 1460–1469.

Strauman, T. J., & Higgins, E. T. (1987). Automatic activation of self-discrepancies and emotional syndromes: When cognitive structures influence affect. *Journal of Personality and Social Psychology, 53,* 1004–1014.

Trope, Y. (1986). Identification and inferential processes in dispositional attribution. *Psychological Review, 93,* 239–257.

Trope, Y., & Liberman, N. (2003). Temporal construal. *Psychological Review, 110,* 401–421.

Underwood, B., & Moore, B. (1982). Perspective-taking and altruism. *Psychological Bulletin, 91,* 143–173.

Van Baaren, R. B., Holland, R. W., Kawakami, K., & van Knippenberg, A. (2004). Mimicry and pro-social behavior. *Psychological Science, 15,* 71–74.

Van Baaren, R. B., Holland, R. W., Steenaerts, B., & van Knippenberg, A. (2003) Mimicry for money: Behavioral consequences of imitator. *Journal of Social Psychology, 39,* 393–398.

Van Baaren, R. B., Horgan, T. G., & Chartrand, T. L. (2004). The forest, the trees, and the chameleon: Context dependence and mimicry. *Journal of Personality and Social Psychology, 86,* 453–459.

Van Baaren, R. B., Maddux, W. W., Chartrand, T. L., de Bouter, C., & van Knippenberg, A. (2003). It takes two to mimic: Behavioral consequences of self-construals. *Journal of Personality and Social Psychology, 84,* 1093–1102.

Vaughan, K. B., & Lanzetta, J. T. (1980). Vicarious instigation and conditioning of facial expressive and autonomic responses to a model's expressive display of pain. *Journal of Personality and Social Psychology, 38,* 909–923.

Velten, E. (1968). A laboratory task for the induction of mood states. *Behavioral Research and Therapy, 6,* 473–482.

Weiner, B. (1986). Attribution, emotion, and action. In R. M. Sorrentino & E. T. Higgins (Eds.), *Handbook of motivation and cognition: Foundations of social behavior* (pp. 281–312). New York: Guilford Press.

Wilson, T. D., & Gilbert, D. T. (2005). Affective forecasting: Knowing what to want. *Current Directions in Psychological Science, 14,* 131–134.

Winton, W. M. (1986). The role of facial response in self-reports of emotion: A critique of Laird. *Journal of Personality and Social Psychology, 50,* 808–812.

Wispé, L. (1986). The distinction between sympathy and empathy: To call forth a concept, a word is needed. *Journal of Personality and Social Psychology, 50,* 314–321.

Zajonc, R. B. (1980). Feeling and thinking: Preferences need no inferences. *American Psychologist, 35,* 151–175.

Zajonc, R. B. (1984). On the primacy of affect. *American Psychologist, 39,* 117–123.

12

A Social-Cognitive Perspective on Automatic Self-Regulation
The Relevance of Goals in the Information-Processing Sequence

JENS FÖRSTER and MARKUS DENZLER

AUTOMATIC SELF-REGULATION

People self-regulate. They resist temptations, cope with negative situations, and avoid undesired end states. Both self-regulation and self-control can describe people's capacity to strive for desired end states. Notably, self-regulation can be defined in a variety of ways (see, e.g., Baumeister & Vohs, 2004): In a nutshell, traditional research on self-regulation attempted to explain situations in which people delay gratification, resist temptation, or more generally, suppress dominant responses to fulfill higher-order goals. When a social cognition researcher talks about self-regulation, however, typically included in the definition is basic research on goal pursuit (Fitzsimons & Bargh, 2004). On the one hand, this broadening of the field may come at the cost of specificity, but from a social cognition perspective this change in definition may be justified by two arguments. First, any goal-related behavior is based on a discrepancy between a person's actual and a person's desired self (Higgins, 1987), which causes an unpleasant state the person would like to change (see Lewin, 1926). If all goal-related behavior starts with self-discrepancy, a situation in which a person attempts to resist a temptation is just a special case of goal pursuit, and basic cognitive and motivational principles may be identified that underlie a multitude of situations, including self-control, striving for desired end states, and goal conflict, to name a few. Recent research made enormous progress to understand the very nature of self-discrepancies (see Higgins, 1987).

Second, one may then argue that self-control is different from goal pursuit because it involves conscious and effortful processes, whereas goal pursuit can be "automatic." For this reason, self-control usually comprises conscious processes and self-regulation of both automatic and controlled processes (see Baumeister, Schmeichel, & Vohs, 2007). We think that one major contribution of social cognition theories is—beyond their focus on underlying cognitive mechanisms—their strong focus on automatic processes. Based on this research, we apply a sharper distinction between self-regulation and self-control. We use the term self-control for controlled processes (see Carver & Scheier, 1998; Metcalfe & Mischel, 1999) and the term (automatic) self-regulation exclusively for automatic self-regulatory processes (see Bargh & Chartrand, 1999; Fitzsimons & Bargh, 2004). Because research on conscious self-control has been summarized elsewhere, in this chapter we mainly focus on self-regulation and its interaction with information processing, the psychology of self-discrepancies, and automatic goal pursuit. More specifically, we focus on how information processing serves automatic self-regulation and how self-regulation affects cognition. We first outline the importance of goals in the information-processing sequence. Subsequently, we discuss how and when goals can be activated automatically and which kinds of desired end states exist.

HOW DOES MOTIVATION AFFECT INFORMATION PROCESSING?

In the following, we summarize research showing how goals affect the information-processing sequence. First, we focus on accessibility as a core principle of information processing that affects all stages of the sequence. Afterward, we present some research illustrating how goals affect the different stages of information processing.

Accessibility from Concepts and Goals

Classic experiments show that information activated (i.e., made accessible) in one phase of the experiment influences perception, cognitive operations such as making inferences and decision making, memory, and behavior in a second phase (for reviews, see Förster & Liberman, 2007; Higgins, 1996). For example, studies showed that when participants read about concepts such as "adventurous" in one phase of the experiment, they judged an unrelated target person who is later presented in an allegedly unrelated phase of the experiment as more positive than participants who were formerly exposed to concepts such as "reckless" (Higgins, Rholes, & Jones, 1977). Such priming effects occur out of awareness, happen unintentionally, and do not need many mental resources: They are called *automatic effects*. It is suggested that memory consists of semantic networks (Collins & Loftus, 1975), and that as a result, activation of one memory node (e.g., a weapon) activates related nodes (e.g., aggression), thus increasing accessibility of the entire network. Accessible concepts are then used as a foundation for further judgments and behavior. On the basis of such memory models, in their goal systems theory (GST) Kruglanski and colleagues (Kruglanski, 1996; Kruglanski et al., 2002) argued that goals and means, like concepts, can be stored in memory, that they can build functional networks in which goals are linked with other goals and means, and that they can be activated out of awareness (Bargh & Ferguson, 2000).

According to GST, means prime goals (bottom up) and goals prime means (top down). As a consequence, lexical decision times for means are faster if an associated goal is primed (Kruglanski et al., 2002; Shah & Kruglanski, 2000) as well as being faster for a goal if relevant and specific means are primed (Shah & Kruglanski, 2003). Notably, subliminal priming procedures were used in many experiments to show unconscious effects of goals and means on accessibility. Such unconscious facilitation or accessibility of means is said to be functional since it prepares for a relevant action without much thinking (Gollwitzer, 1996; Liberman & Förster, 2005). Beyond means, links between semantic constructs and goals exist (Ach, 1935). For example, Förster, Liberman, and Higgins (2005) showed that if people were asked to search for a word like "glasses" within a series of pictures, lexical decision times for associations such as "reading" or "sun" increased.

The similarity between semantic priming and goal priming calls for an analysis distinguishing between the two: Are they the same, and do they have the same implications? In a recent analysis, principles derived from self-regulation research were identified that help to distinguish between goal priming and semantic priming (Förster, Liberman, & Friedman, 2007).

First, goal-priming effects involve value: They affect value or are affected by value. For example, when we need to find a needle to fix a button on our shirt, the value of the needle increases. Priming the mere semantic construct of "loose button" with no goal involved would presumably activate "needle," but it would not increase the value of this associate. Seibt, Häfner, and Deutsch (2007), for example, showed that the valence of food was more positive for food-deprived participants than for nondeprived participants, demonstrating that the need to eat changes the value of means to goal fulfillment (food). It has also been shown that goal-related concepts may lose value after goal fulfillment (Ferguson & Bargh, 2004). Thus, the value of the needle would drop after the button was fixed successfully. Furthermore, it has been shown that goal priming depends on importance (i.e., the value) of the goal. For example, people who need money are more easily primed with descriptions of another person making money than those that do not need money (so-called goal contagion; see Aarts, Gollwitzer, & Hassin, 2004). Presumably, important needs and goals prepare for higher activation of self-relevant goals.

A second principle of motivation is that it decreases after goal attainment, and research showed that after participants were primed with a goal (e.g., find a sequence of glasses and scissors among a series of pictures), they showed decreased accessibility of goal-related concepts after goal fulfillment (Denzler, Förster, & Liberman, 2008; Förster et al., 2005; see also Marsh, Hicks, & Bink, 1998; Marsh, Hicks, & Bryan, 1999). According to semantic-priming principles, goal fulfillment would constitute a recent activation of a memory node, and an increase rather than a decrease of accessibility would be predicted (Higgins, 1996). In semantic priming, the more frequently and the more recently you activate a memory node, the higher its accessibility. Importantly, if accessibility is inhibited after goal fulfillment (e.g., if the priming phase leads to some feeling of goal completion), it will not affect social judgments any more and would not even produce contrast effects. This has been shown recently: Uncompleted priming tasks lead to assimilation effects, whereas completed priming tasks lead to inhibition or contrast (Liberman, Förster, & Higgins; 2007).

The third principle is based on the fact that motivation increases toward the goal (Förster, Higgins, & Idson, 1998; Miller, 1944). Research showed that, similarly, accessibility of goal-related concepts (measured via lexical decision tasks) increases the closer people are to the goal (Förster et al., 2005). This has implications for the duration of priming effects since as long as the goal has not been fulfilled accessibility is high, whereas semantic-priming effects fade away rather quickly (see Bargh & Barndollar, 1996).

The fourth principle is the expectancy value function (EXV), which shows that motivation is a product of expectancy and value (see Fishbein & Ajzen, 1974). Studies of priming goals showed that accessibility of goal-related concepts is dependent on EXV; for example, when the expectancy of finding a target was high and participants expected a high reward for finding it, accessibility of goal-related concepts increased, whereas if either the reward or the expectancy of finding the target was low, no priming took place (Förster et al., 2005).

To sum, the four principles include instrumental value and change of value due to distance to the goal and goal fulfillment; they further point to the importance of the expectancy value interaction. Instrumental value is subject to changes in the situation and, consequently, representations of goals and their associates also change. So, if you need a needle to be prepared for a concert since your favorite shirt lacks a button, needle and concert become associated; however, both this association and its value fade after goal attainment. If a priming study reflects instrumental value, then it most likely involves goal priming.

The fifth and sixth principles encompass lateral and hierarchical inhibition or "goal shielding." To enable successful completion of one goal, the self-regulatory system needs to put other simultaneously active goals on hold. Within the context of GST, as mentioned, it could be shown that when goals were subliminally primed, reaction times to competing goals were slowed relative to reaction times to control goals that were not competing. This suggests that the mere activation of a goal automatically suppresses the accessibility of goals that stand to interfere with its pursuit (Shah, Friedman, & Kruglanski, 2002). GST allows for inhibitory links between competing goals, which lead to decreased accessibility for distracting goals (e.g., studying vs. partying) and help people concentrate on their goals. A specific case of such goal shielding is resistance to temptations. Research by Fishbach, Friedman, and Kruglanski (2003) convincingly demonstrated that when situationally enticed to pursue short-term goals representing temptations (e.g., subliminally priming temptation-related words such as "sex" or "drugs"), some people immediately activate superordinate goals (e.g., "bible" or "academic achievement"), which is then reflected in faster lexical decisions on words related to the higher-order goals.[1] Those higher-order goals then inhibit temptation-related associates and thus help to control behavior. In general, lateral and hierarchical inhibitory mechanisms seem to help the organism to focus on information that is conducive to goal pursuit, to activate appropriate means without much effort, and to understand the situation faster and in a better way.

The seventh principle is that goal priming is affected by equifinality and multifinality. Equifinality reflects the fact that sometimes individuals may have multiple means of achieving the same goal (Kruglanski et al., 2002). For example, it is possible to fix a button with glue or by giving the shirt to a tailor. It is also possible that the same means serves more than one goal: One can use a needle to sew, to extract a thorn from one's hand, or to affix a note to a bulletin board. This is the case of multifinality. As discussed, GST predicts that goals and means are linked, and that one can elicit the other. It also predicts that the extent to which a goal activates a given means is inversely related to the number of means that are connected to that goal. Likewise, it is anticipated that the extent to which a means activates a goal is inversely related to the number of goals that are connected to that means. Consistently, research showed that the greater the uniqueness of the goal-means connection (i.e., the less equifinality it possesses), the more accessible was a means listed (as indicated by speeded lexical decision time) after it was primed with the corresponding goal.

In sum, the last three principles point to the functional structure of goal networks, reflecting the instrumental relations between goals. These relations form a network comprised of hierarchies of subordinate and superordinate goals, a network that may or may not correspond to associative or semantic networks. For example, the link between "needle" and "button" possibly reflects both a cognitive association as well as a goal-network relation. However, if "needle" is connected to "concert" because my favorite concert shirt lacks a button, then a goal is probably driving this process.

For social cognition researchers, it is important that accessibility produced by goals follows different principles than semantic priming. Decay rates as well as activation and inhibition follow different rules. It is thus important to know what has been activated, a goal or a concept. Research also points to a different representational format for goals compared to mere semantic networks. We now continue by summarizing findings reflecting the operation of goals on social cognition, some of which may be caused by accessible goals and goal-related constructs as well. Since research on "motivated social cognition" (Kruglanski, 1996) exploded over the last decade, this summary can by no means be exhaustive.

How Self-Regulation Affects the Steps of Information Processing

Perception, Attention, and Encoding
People selectively encode information that helps them pursue their goals, thereby preparing the mental system to take appropriate and efficient actions. Moreover, our mental system protects us by filtering out self-threatening information. We first focus on the contents of the information that is more easily processed and then describe how self-regulation influences the way people perceive the world.

Discrepancies between actual states and desired end states should motivate and prepare the perceptual system to perceive and pay attention to relevant stimuli. In a study by Lazarus, Yousem, and Arenberg (1953), participants had to recognize objects in tachistoscopically presented pictures: Some of the pictures contained food objects, others nonfood objects. Food-deprived participants recognized the food-related objects better than nondeprived participants (see also Aarts, Dijksterhuis, & De Vries; 2001). Thus, it seems that discrepancies due to unfulfilled needs lead to a processing advantage for goal-relevant objects, preparing the organism for reducing these (Bruner, 1957).

In the social domain, goals enhance encoding of self-relevant information. To give a prominent example, the "cocktail party phenomenon" reflects the fact that even in cases of background noise, mentioning one's name is a better attention getter than information not related to the self (Cherry, 1953). Other research shows the superiority of self-referent information independent from one's name (for a review, see Symons & Johnson, 1997). In the seminal study by Rogers, Kuiper, and Kirker (1977), participants encoded information better if it was framed in relation to the self ("Does the word describe you or not?") compared to, for example, a structural frame ("Is the size of the word the same as the sample given?"). This encoding strategy then led to better recall for words under the self-referent frame than the structural frame. It is suggested that the superiority of self-referent information is functional because it enhances goal pursuit by gaining relevant information about oneself (Banaji & Prentice, 1994; Kunda, 1990).

One could argue that valence (i.e., whether an event is good or bad) is always dependent on one's needs and goals, and thus valenced information should have a general processing advantage over neutral information. Results showed that this is the case; furthermore, negative information is better encoded than positive information (e.g., Hansen & Hansen, 1988; Rothermund, Wentura, & Bak, 2001). From a functional perspective, valenced cues may automatically trigger approach or avoidance behavior (Förster, 2004), which helps the organism start the appropriate reaction without much thinking. Moreover, it seems functional that, overall, negative or potentially threatening information receives more attention than positive information. To give an example, Pratto and John (1991) showed that participants in a Stroop task paradigm needed longer to name the color of negative trait words than positive ones, demonstrating that negative information does automatically attract attention.

Clearly, such a finding is at odds with the hedonic principle. After all, high accessibility of negative thoughts is related to depression (Bargh & Tota, 1988). Yet another line of research (e.g., Allport, 1993) questions the notion of a general negativity processing advantage. From a functional perspective, people should especially focus on such negative events that they can deal with or that they have under control. Consistently, Brandstädter, Voss, and Rothermund (2004) were able to demonstrate that negative information possesses a perceptual advantage over neutral information *only* when the result of the negative information can be controlled and thus when the organism can prevent the consequences that follow from the negative information. Without such action implication, negative information does not possess such a perceptual advantage. Beyond the fact that by such a mechanism the organism would be shielded against negative information, this could point to an energy-saving mechanism since attention and further investment of resources is avoided when problematic events cannot be changed anyway.

Information violating one's expectancies (e.g., stereotypes) can be threatening. One could argue that disconfirming an important belief about a certain group (e.g., a sexist who is told a woman likes wrestling) would pose a threat to one's efficient self-regulation (Förster, Higgins, & Strack, 2000). After all, people hold such theories about the world partly to understand it better and to have a predictable environment. Defensive mechanisms on such attacks to self-control include ignoring the event, if possible, or resolving the inconsistency (e.g., Hastie, 1980; Wyer & Srull, 1986). Förster et al. (2000) argued that if inconsistent information is a threat and cannot be ignored, individuals will become vigilant and scrutinize the threatening object. As a result, vigilance will cause better encoding of the threatening information *and* its context since to prepare an appropriate response to a threatening object it is important to know where the threat originates. Using measures sensitive to source memory, the authors found that information inconsistent with gender stereotypes was encoded and thus remembered better by participants for whom such discrepancy was highly relevant (i.e., who were sexists) and for whom security was a concern (i.e., who had a chronic prevention focus). Thus, faced with a threat to their worldview, participants' vigilance increased and biased encoding, presumably to better deal with the threat.

Beyond selective encoding concerning different sorts of content, motivation affects the way we perceive the world. For example, while looking at a bunch of trees one may perceive the trees or the forest. Whereas the former is called a local-processing style, the latter reflects a global-processing style (Navon, 1977). According to Derryberry and Tucker (1994), approach versus avoidance motivation can broaden or narrow the focus of attention. In line with this theory, it has been shown that under aversive motivational states such as anxiety or stress, people perceive the component features of stimuli better than the global form (Easterbrook, 1959; Tyler & Tucker, 1982). Gasper and Clore (2002) showed that situationally induced good mood broadened perception in participants, whereas bad mood narrowed it. Such "cognitive tuning" (Schwarz & Bless, 1991) could be a preparation for appropriate responses: Whereas in situations of danger scrutinizing the details of the surroundings may be useful, in positive situations focusing on the entire gestalt of an event may help efficient goal pursuit (Fredrickson, 2001).

Förster, Friedman, Özelsel, and Denzler (2006) found that experiencing mood is not necessary to produce such effects. They replicated cognitive tuning effects with rudimentary cues of promotion (gaining rewards) versus prevention (seeking security) focus (Higgins, 1997). In one experiment, participants worked on a maze task eliciting the respective foci (Friedman & Förster, 2001, Experiment 3). In the promotion motivation condition, participants had to lead a cartoon mouse from the center of the maze to the exit, where a piece of cheese was located, thus priming a mental process of "seeking reward"; in the prevention condition, participants led the cartoon mouse through the same maze, but this time helped it escape from an owl, representing "gaining security." Using a reaction time paradigm assessing whether participants better attend to the global gestalt of letters made of small letters or to the details (the small letters that constitute the big letters; see Navon, 1977), it could be shown that participants primed with the promotion maze were faster in identifying global letters than participants primed with the prevention maze, who were faster in identifying local letters (see also Förster & Higgins, 2005). To sum, certain inner affective states or cues signaling security or growth immediately tune people's cognition toward efficient ways of solving problems, enhancing goal pursuit.

Retrieval Encoding is strongly related to retrieval: As a rule, what receives more attention is better encoded and retrieved. However, since memory is constructive, at the time of retrieval biases may occur; these biases are often self-serving or related to further goal pursuit. In the following, we focus especially on research using memory paradigms that are sensitive to processes occurring at retrieval.

Goals guide retrieval. In a classic experiment by Anderson and Pichert (1978), a story about two boys being truant was read by participants according to the perspective of either a burglar or a person interested in buying a home. After recalling the story once, participants were directed to shift perspectives and then recall the story again. Results showed that, on the second recall, participants recalled significantly more information important to the second perspective that had been unimportant to the first one. They also recalled less information unimportant to the second perspective that had been important to the first one. Results showed the operation of biased memory due to different goals at the time of retrieval.

Moreover, mood repair or mood maintenance goals may bias memory of positive and negative events. For example, people in a bad mood seem to remember more positive information because it enhances their self-esteem. Most prominently, Isen (1985) argued that people focus on positive events or focus attention away from negative events to maintain or regain positive mood. Forgas (1995) argued that such effects take place when people have access to information related to personal goals or motives (e.g., to regulate mood states), whereas mood congruency effects (people encode negative information while they are in negative affective states) occur when more heuristic processing styles are adopted. This assumption was supported by Förster and Strack (1996), who showed that encoding of valence-compatible information needs fewer cognitive resources than valence-incompatible information. Furthermore, Rusting and DeHart (2000) showed that reminding people of mood repair strategies by telling them that "sometimes even when bad things happen, they ultimately have positive consequences" (positive reappraisal) led to more positive recall when in a negative mood compared to participants who were not reminded of such strategies. The authors also showed that such effects are pronounced in individuals chronically using negative mood regulation strategies.

In the domain of autobiographic memory, positivity biases emerge (for a review, see Taylor & Brown, 1988). To give one prominent example, Sanitoso, Kunda, and Fong (1990) gave participants the information that either extraversion or introversion was associated with professional success; participants were then asked to explain why this might be the case. When later asked to remember relevant autobiographic behavior, participants were faster in describing situations of introversion or extraversion depending on whether such traits had been previously described as leading to success. It seems that people, presumably to maintain their good mood, focus on positive self-relevant information while remembering and defend against information that threatens their self-esteem.

In an effort to unravel the cognitive fabric of self-defense, Sedikides and Gregg (2003) proposed the mnemic neglect model; it suggests that the organism's tendency to avoid potential threat to the self leads to poor recall of information that constitutes a threat to the self. In the typical paradigm, Sedikides and Green (2000) presented a list to participants with behaviors describing a person who was either the self or a hypothetical acquaintance. The behaviors were either negative or positive, and either pertained to central self-concepts like "trustworthiness" or to peripheral self-concepts like "modesty." The authors found that individuals remember negative information that is central to the self-concept worse when it is self-referent compared to other referent. Green, Sedikides, and Gregg (2007) further demonstrated failure to replicate the effects with a recognition task which used accuracy measures (d') indicating that negative information was still recognized, while in the same study results on a free-recall task replicated mnestic neglect effects. These results suggest that negative information is well encoded (as reflected in good d') but suppressed at retrieval when participants are asked to remember it freely. Obviously, the typical defense mechanism breaks down at retrieval when people are exposed to threatening information that still sits in the back of their mind. Notably, mnemic neglect only happens for information that is uncontrollable (Green, Pinter, & Sedikides, 2005). This parallels findings by Brandstädter et al. (2004), mentioned here regarding encoding: The organism seems to inhibit information that cannot be changed anyway at both encoding and retrieval. Presumably, this saves resources and shields the organism from negative experiences.

Beyond the content of information, research has shown that goals affect *quantity* of information recalled. Kruglanski (1996; Kruglanski & Webster, 1996) argued that people differ in their need for closure (a desire for a firm answer and an aversion toward ambiguity), and that people with a high need for closure remember less information because they are satisfied with recalling only the most accessible information and invest less effort in attempting to retrieve all information. Accordingly, Sanbonmatsu and Fazio (1990) showed that when participants were asked to judge a store for which they received information in a previous phase of the experiment, participants with high need for closure recalled highly accessible information and left out important but less-accessible information, whereas participants low in need for closure took both highly and less-accessible information into account. To sum, amount and quality of retrieved information depend on self-regulatory mechanisms such as people's goals and needs. We now turn to how the use of information is influenced by motivation.

Information Use and Thinking Research consistently demonstrates that individuals in negative relative to positive moods process persuasive messages more systematically (e.g., Bless, Bohner, Schwarz, & Strack, 1990) and are less likely to rely on effort-saving, albeit error-prone, rules of thumb in domains such as person perception (e.g., Bodenhausen, 1993), statistical inference (e.g., Sinclair & Mark, 1995), and logical reasoning (e.g., Isen, Means, Patrick, & Nowicki, 1982).

To explain this effect, a number of theories have been developed to account for how mood states have an impact on cognition and action (see Martin & Clore, 2001, for a review); these are, among others, the feelings-as-information (FAI) model developed by Schwarz, Clore, and Bless (see, e.g., Schwarz & Bless, 1991; Schwarz & Clore, 1996) and the mood-as-input (MAI) model by Martin (2001). Essentially, FAI proposes that mood states serve to inform individuals about the nature of their current situation. Positive moods thus signal that the situation is safe, suggesting to the individual that effort is unnecessary unless specifically required by other ongoing goals or directives; negative moods instead signal that the current situation is problematic, suggesting to the individual that effort is required to assess and remedy this adverse state of affairs. Within the framework of the MAI model, the information conveyed by positive and negative moods can lead to either increments or decrements in processing effort, depending on which "stop rule" is adopted during task engagement. When provided with enjoyment-based stop rules (i.e., stop when you no longer feel like continuing), Martin and his colleagues (e.g., Martin & Stoner, 1996) have found that participants in positive moods misattribute their pleasant feelings to task enjoyment and exert more effort than those in negative moods, who misattribute their unpleasant feelings to a lack of task enjoyment. Likewise, when they are provided with performance-based stop rules (i.e., stop when you think it is a good time to stop), individuals in positive moods misattribute their pleasant feelings to having made adequate progress on the task and thereby withdraw processing effort sooner than participants in negative moods, who misattribute their unpleasant feelings to having failed to make adequate progress.

Both models point to important self-regulatory mechanisms that do not contradict each other. Whereas the FAI model shows how people naturally draw inferences from mood states to prepare for appropriate behavior (e.g., threat signal: be systematic), the MAI model shows what happens when instructions such as other goals or situational demands (i.e., stop rules) are salient. In general, people seem to spontaneously infer appropriate action from their mood. As noted, the notion of cognitive tuning has been applied to affective signals that do not elicit mood (see Friedman & Förster, 2008). Friedman and Förster (2001) suggested and showed that subtle cues of a promotion versus a prevention focus led to analytic or algorithmic versus heuristic and creative thinking styles. Thus, on elicitation of affective cues, the organism seems to immediately adopt certain ways of information processing.

In the domain of "motivated inferences," it was further shown that inferences and conclusions are highly affected by motivation. Because relevant research programs have been summarized elsewhere (Kruglanski, 1996; Kunda, 1999), we only briefly examine some influences of self-regulatory mechanisms on inferences and biases.

Dissonance from behavior-attitude discrepancy (you smoke, but you know it will kill you) is said to cause unpleasant arousal that people may want to reduce (Festinger, 1957). People reduce dissonance by, for example, changing their behavior (quit smoking) or their attitudes ("research on smoking is biased"). Challenges were advanced by researchers who showed that arousal is sometimes not elicited by dissonance, and thus purely cognitive mechanisms of self perception can produce the results (see Bem, 1967). However, further research showed that, in those cases in which dissonance actually leads to high arousal, there are attempts to reduce dissonance by changing behavior or attitudes (Zanna & Cooper, 1976).

Steele and Liu (1983) argued that an important aspect of dissonance stems from the threat to the self inherent in a given consistency, and that self-affirming thoughts reduce dissonance effects. They demonstrated that reminding people of valued aspects of themselves (e.g., reminding economists of economics) in a domain unrelated to the contents of the dissonance-provoking event reduced dissonance effects. Unfortunately, another source of self-affirmation is derogating others (Fein & Spencer, 1997), which according to research also reduces dissonance. These are only some examples to show how arousal reduction can change attitudes.

Another prominent phenomenon is self-enhancement in attributions and inference making, which is said to improve a person's mood (Taylor & Brown, 1988) and might actually work as a self-fulfilling prophecy, eventually enhancing well-being and improving performance. Researchers demonstrated stronger self serving biases after failure feedback (Dunning, Leuenberger, & Sherman, 1995). Moreover, individuals construe future events more positively if they are self-relevant; for example, people expecting that somebody would be their partner in a dating experiment liked him or her better than the other alternatives (Berscheid, Graziano, Monson, & Dermer, 1976). This also works for strangers for whom no expectancies could be established, showing that motivational explanations (people want to cooperate with nice people) seem to be more valid than cognitive ones (people expect a partner to be nice).

Attributions of failure in group settings are also biased by self-defensive mechanisms. Attributing failure in interactions to others and success to oneself was, for example, shown to be mediated by the degree to which participants' self-esteem was involved in the experimental task (Miller, 1976). Self-enhancement biases have been shown to be limited by the individual's knowledge about the situation. When traits are clearly defined (such as punctuality), when their self-evaluation of ambiguous traits is based on clearly defined criteria, or when counterevidence cannot be dismissed (see Dunning, Meyerowitz, & Holzberg, 1989), people's ability to draw desired conclusions is constrained.

Moreover, it has been shown that the effort in making a judgment depends on goals. Schaller (1992) found that spurious correlations are better detected if they are unfavorable; Lord, Ross, and Lepper (1979) showed that flaws in a study showing counterattitudinal arguments were more likely to be detected than proattitudinal arguments. As a conceptual framework, Kruglanski and Webster (1996) developed their need for closure theory, stating that it matters whether people have a need for closure (want to arrive at a conclusion) as opposed to avoidance of closure. Accuracy goals, which have been shown to generally improve decision making and inferences (for exceptions, see, e.g., Wilson & Schooler, 1991) lead to closure avoidance, whereas cognitive load, for example, leads to high need for closure. It has been shown that high need for closure leads to more pronounced correspondence biases, primacy effects in impression formation, prejudiced evaluations of essays, and less anchoring on irrelevant values (for a review, see Kruglanski, 1996). Gollwitzer and his colleagues also showed that accuracy goals can be elicited by deliberative mind-sets (when people are in the process of making a decision) as opposed to implementation mind-sets (when people focus on thoughts and actions to attain an outcome). In an extensive research program, Gollwitzer and his cooperators showed that in deliberative mind-sets people are less likely to think that they have control over uncontrollable events (Gollwitzer & Kinney, 1989) and biased self-perceptions, such as the better-than-average effect in self-ascription of desirable skills and the unlikelihood of unfavorable events occurring to oneself (disease and divorce; Taylor & Gollwitzer, 1995).

To summarize, this research shows that, depending on what goals they have, people either prefer self-flattering information or confrontation with useful but unfavorable events. It seems that goals of accuracy and mood maintenance or mood repair change from situation to situation, reflecting the fact that people can have more realistic perceptions about themselves but not every day at any time. In the next section, we discuss the automaticity of goal striving and self-regulatory attempts.

HOW (CONSCIOUSLY) ARE WE STRIVING?

Psychological concepts defining goals and self-regulation such as "goal pursuit," "intentions," or "impulse control," action control," or "thought control" inherently contain some notion of consciousness. Accordingly, classic theories assume that goal adoption is accompanied by a conscious decision, and that goal striving (i.e., the initiation and maintenance of goal-directed action) is characterized by intent and conscious monitoring (e.g., Ajzen, 1991; Bandura, 1986; Deci & Ryan 1985; Locke & Latham, 1990). However, quite recently researchers applied knowledge gained from priming research in social judgments to goals and behavior. In concert with researchers in the domain of self-control, they claimed that part of people's self-regulation and goal pursuit occurs outside the individual's awareness (see Bargh, Gollwitzer, Lee-Chai, Barndollar, & Trötschel, 2001; Baumeister & Vohs, 2003; Carver & Scheier, 1998; Chartrand & Bargh, 1996; Förster et al., 2007; Kruglanski et al., 2002; Kuhl, 1996; Moskowitz, Li, & Kirk, 2004). The study by Fishbach et al. (2003) is one example. To reiterate, the study showed that people who were highly motivated can automatically resist temptations (e.g., eating a cake) because as soon as they encounter tempting stimuli, they are automatically reminded of higher goals (such as dieting), and the accessibility of temptations is inhibited.

The notion of automaticity in self-regulation, however, deserves a more finely grained analysis as human behavior is usually based on both automatic and more conscious processes. Let us briefly examine whether self-regulation fits the criteria of Bargh's (1994) notion of automaticity, namely, whether people are *unaware* of the cues facilitating self-regulation, whether the initiation of the process is *unintentional* (control over startup), whether the ongoing process is *controllable* (e.g., can be stopped), and whether it is *efficient* (demands few cognitive resources). The self-regulation sequence, the attempt to approach desired end states or to reach a goal, has been broken down into three psychological components (e.g., Baumeister & Vohs, 2003): (a) setting and activating a goal or desired end state, (b) engaging in appropriate behaviors to obtain one's goals, and (c) monitoring progress toward a goal. Research suggests that at least the first two stages involve some automatic processes.

Establishing and Activating a Goal

Although establishing a goal is a conscious process, goals once set can be activated out of awareness by subliminal priming procedures (e.g., Shah & Kruglanski, 2003). Furthermore, people can chronically activate certain goals and not be aware of why they decided to start a certain sort of action (e.g., Moskowitz, Gollwitzer, Wasel, & Schaal, 1999). Custers and Aarts (2005) also showed that the value of a goal can change out of awareness. They conditioned activities with positive and negative words that were not related to the content of the goal and found that positive affect increased strength of goal pursuit. Thus, a part of the establishment and activation of goals can happen unintentionally, efficiently, and out of awareness. It has not been tested yet, but once elicited, behavior could potentially be stopped when people become aware of what they are doing (i.e., when they are "meta-conscious"; see Winkielman & Schooler, chapter 3, this volume), and thus only three criteria of automatic processes may apply to so-called automatic goal pursuit.[2]

Engaging in Goal-Appropriate Behavior

With respect to the engagement in appropriate behaviors, it has been shown that implementation intentions (i.e., plans for future tasks such as "in situation X, I will do Y"; Gollwitzer; 1993) can be stored in memory and are activated outside of awareness in relevant situations on presentation of goal-related cues (see Gollwitzer, 1990). Furthermore, as described, activation of a goal leads to higher accessibility of means (Kruglanski et al., 2002), thus preparing the individual to solve the problem at hand sufficiently and with little awareness. To give an example, experiments showed that if people are reminded of a library, they unintentionally lower their voice (Aarts & Dijksterhuis, 2000). Furthermore, it has been shown that such automaticity lowers ego depletion (i.e., when self-control exerted in one task leads to lower self-control in a subsequent one; Vohs & Baumeister, 2004), demonstrating its efficiency. If people pursue goals using appropriate means, this "feels right," as Higgins (2000) argued, and such feelings are elicited even when people are not aware of such a fit.

Monitoring Progress Toward the Goal

It is less clear whether people can track the distance to a goal unconsciously. In Carver and Scheier's (1998) cybernetic model, proceduralized control loops are assumed (see also Winkielman & Schooler, chapter 3, this volume); however, it is questionable whether the actual computation of distance between actual and desired end states can occur without any awareness involved. The calculation affords a statement about the actual (e.g., "I passed kilometer 33 of the marathon"; "I repeated the basic grammar for my Dutch class") and the desired state (e.g., "42.2 km"; "I would like to speak fluently") as well as a computation of the relation between them ("42.2 − 33 = 12.2 km"; "I don't really speak well enough"); in the end, a decision follows regarding which action should be taken (e.g., save energy and then sprint, or give up, etc.; take additional lessons, change the study program, etc.) or whether the desired end state should be adjusted (e.g., marathons are not so important; speaking fluently is unrealistic). It seems unlikely that such calculation can occur out of awareness. Of course, proceduralization can occur. The commuter with a daily train trip from his or her house to the office might track the discrepancy at any place on the way using fewer resources by way of effortlessly noticing informative cues with respect to distance than a novice, who would have to read signs and listen carefully to announcements. However, presumably no actual calculation is needed in such cases since the calculation process is replaced by stored knowledge. As we know that $2 + 2 = 4$, the commuter may know that station X means "close" or "1 min more" and may activate certain routine behaviors such as putting on a coat. Thus, for the commuter, the calculation process is simply replaced by activation of appropriate knowledge and behavior (see Winkielman & Schooler, chapter 3, this volume).

Yet, people can unconsciously increase certain types of motivation the closer they are to a goal. In a study by Förster et al. (1998), participants showed an automatic increase in approach motivation when they focused on gains or had a chronic promotion focus on ideals, whereas a constant increase in avoidance motivation resulted when participants focused on losses or had a chronic prevention focus. Regulatory focus theory predicts that a promotion focus on positive outcomes is related to eager approach strategies, whereas a prevention focus is related to vigilant avoidance strategies (Higgins, 1997). In the actual experiment, participants worked on a set of anagrams while their approach and avoidance strength was subtly measured with an on-line measurement. It was found that specific increases in motivation occurred out of participants' awareness. The results suggest that the use of strategies and thus the investment of specific resources automatically increases the closer one is to the goal (Lewin, 1951; Miller, 1944).

In summary, research using social cognition paradigms and theories looked at the organism's capacity to efficiently prepare action and to automatically pursue goals without much thought or awareness. But, what is the exact content of such a goal or people's "desired" end state?

WHAT ARE WE STRIVING FOR?

Generally, people's desired end state is a positive experience (as a result of successful goal pursuit), with negative experiences (as a result of failure to attain a goal) constituting undesired end states. However, even though the general idea of a "hedonic principle" (e.g., Atkinson, 1964; Festinger, 1957; Heider, 1958; Mowrer, 1960, to name a few) is true on a very general level of analysis, it has been qualified by recent theories that criticized the lack of specificity of such a principle.

Prominently, Higgins (1997) in his regulatory focus theory (RFT), pointed out that the hedonic principle is silent on the *kind* of positive end states that motivate people. Higgins and his colleagues showed that people focusing on prevention goals of security and safety or who experience an actual-ought discrepancy, compared to people focusing on promotion goals of growth and nurturance or who experience an actual-ideal discrepancy, differ with respect to their emotional experiences as well as in their strategies to approach or avoid (for reviews, see Förster & Werth, in press; Higgins & Molden, 2003).

For example, it has been shown that people in a prevention focus on loss and nonloss experience quiescence-related emotions after they have attained security, whereas people in a promotion focus on gains and nongains experienced cheerfulness-related emotions after they have attained an ideal (see Idson, Liberman, & Higgins, 2000). Note that promotion and prevention focus both represent desired end states, leading to qualitatively different emotions. Thus, regulatory foci, beyond the hedonic principle, predict the emotional quality of goal attainment. This could also mean that people with different foci strive for different emotional states. A person in a promotion focus may strive for a happy emotional state, and then a relaxed or calm state on goal fulfillment may be not enough for the person, whereas a person in a prevention focus may feel good when calm and relaxed.

The RFT also makes original predictions with respect to approach versus avoidance motivation; whereas the hedonic principle predicts a close relationship between approach motivation and desired end states and avoidance and undesired end states (see, e.g., Miller, 1944), RFT can predict avoidance behavior toward desired end states. According to Higgins (1997), people with a prevention focus aiming at positive end states may vigilantly avoid certain events (e.g., a runner trying to concentrate on not turning his head in order to win the race), whereas people with a promotion focus may eagerly approach certain events (e.g., a runner fixating the goal in order to win the race). For example, Higgins, Roney, Crowe, and Hymes (1994) showed that people with a prevention focus used more avoidance strategies when they wanted to have friends (i.e., a desired end state) compared to people with a promotion focus who used more approach strategies. The hedonic principle is silent on such results.

From a different perspective, the hedonic principle has problems in explaining why people in certain situations prefer working on serious compared to funny tasks. Based on the aforementioned FAI accounts (e.g., Schwarz & Clore, 1996), Friedman, Förster, and Denzler (2007) suggested that positive moods signal to individuals that they are safe, motivating them to take advantage of this presumed safety by seeking stimulation and incentives, whereas negative moods signal to individuals that there are problems at hand, motivating them to solve them. To maintain their moods, for a task that is primarily construed as fun, individuals in a positive mood should invest more energy in the tasks, thereby demonstrating enhanced performance. The problem signal elicited by negative moods, however, should motivate those in such states to attempt to solve problems. The authors predicted and found that bad mood and framing the task as "serious" and good mood and framing the task as "silly" both enhanced performance compared to all other conditions (good mood and serious framing; bad mood and silly framing).

An alternative hedonic model by Wegener and Petty (1994) predicts that positive and negative affective states signal which reinforcement contingencies are currently in force. It is suggested that people in positive moods would prefer engaging in hedonically positive tasks because it is presumed that the majority of other available activities will make them feel worse. In contrast, for individuals in negative affective states, it is presumed that virtually any available activity will make them feel better; as a consequence, people in negative moods should invest processing effort in both relatively uplifting and depressing tasks. The latter was not the case in the studies of Friedman et al. (2007), in which participants in bad moods invested more effort in the serious than the funny task.

In sum, one of the principles taken most for granted, namely, the hedonic principle, needs to be qualified by various psychological variables to predict behavior in specific situations. People can strategically pursue desired end states using both approach (in case they have a promotion focus on growth) and avoidance (in case they have a prevention focus on security) strategies, and they can at times be interested in less-pleasant tasks (if the situation prepares them for solving problems in a serious way). It is important that future research further investigate the nature of desired end states.

FINAL REMARKS

We aimed to summarize research showing the relevance of goals and automatic self-regulation with respect to the information-processing sequence. Such endeavors enhance our understanding of what drives people's perception of other people and situations, their representations, the changes in their cognitive operations, as well as their selective recall and forgetfulness—all of which ultimately shape their behavior. It seems that recent research has focused mainly on the question of whether and which aspects of self-regulation are conscious and which can be automatized, thereby overlooking other interesting aspects of goal activation. Furthermore, the notion that automatic goal pursuit is beneficial has been overly stressed: If goal pursuit operates like a proceduralized routine, then mistakes due to automatic goal pursuit should occur. From this perspective, automatic regulation shares some similarities with heuristics or habits; it is triggered by systematic changes in the individual or by external cues of the situation and with little effort successfully guides decision and behavior. However, it can also systematically lead to problems because it may contain a generalized routine that is not sufficiently suited and fine grained for a particular situation. For example, it might be less than efficient if, on hearing "cake," an automatic avoidance reaction would always result—even though such a general behavioral routine might overall be beneficial; when the cake is low in calories or the body actually needs food, such an avoidance reaction would be a "mistake." It is noteworthy that the classic research in heuristics has been focused on mistakes, whereas the modern automatic goal approach focuses on the benefits. Maybe both disciplines could learn from each other.

Some fundamental questions have as yet been underinvestigated. For example, we have just begun to understand the nature of such basic principles as "desired end states" and "value" (Higgins, 2006). Furthermore, little research has been done to apply the knowledge gained to interpersonal research designs. To give an example, our feelings not only send important signals to us, but also our emotions affect others (see Fischer & Manstead, 2008), and goals may be imposed or activated by other people (see Aarts et al., 2004).

NOTES

1. For a more detailed discussion of why the effects cannot be explained by semantic fan effects, see Förster et al. (2007).
2. To reiterate, not all experiments claiming automatic goal pursuit may actually reflect the activation of goals; rather, some experiments may reflect semantic priming or concept-behavior links (see Prinz, 1990). An attempt to distinguish between automatic goal priming and semantic priming was made by Förster et al. (2007), as reported here.

REFERENCES

Aarts, H., & Dijksterhuis, A. (2000). The automatic activation of goal-directed behavior: The case of travel habit. *Journal of Environmental Psychology, 20,* 75–82.

Aarts, H., Dijksterhuis, A., & De Vries, P. (2001). On the psychology of drinking: Being thirsty and perceptually ready. *British Journal of Psychology, 92,* 631–642.

Aarts, H., Gollwitzer, P. M., & Hassin, R. R. (2004). Goal contagion: Perceiving is for pursuing. *Journal of Personality and Social Psychology, 87,* 23–37.

Ach, N. (1935). Analyse des Willens. In E. Abderhalden (Ed.), *Handbuch der biologischen Arbeitsmethoden, Bd. VI.* (pp. 1–460), Berlin: Urban & Schwarzenberg.

Ajzen, I. (1991). The theory of planned behavior. *Organizational Behavior and Human Decision Processes, 50,* 179–211.

Allport, A. (1993). Attention and control: Have we been asking the wrong questions? A critical review of 25 years. In D. E. Meyer & S. Kornblum (Eds.), *Attention and performance 14: Synergies in experimental psychology, artificial intelligence, and cognitive neuroscience* (pp. 183–218). Cambridge, MA: MIT Press.

Anderson, R. C., & Pichert, J. W. (1978). Recall of previously unrecallable information following a shift in perspective. *Journal of Verbal Learning & Verbal Behavior, 17,* 1–12.

Atkinson, J. W. (1964). *An introduction to motivation.* Princeton, NJ: Van Nostrand.

Banaji, M. R., & Prentice, D. A. (1994). The self in social contexts. *Annual Review of Psychology, 45,* 297–332.

Bandura, A. (1986). From thought to action: Mechanisms of personal agency. *New Zealand Journal of Psychology, 15,* 1–17.

Bargh, J. A. (1994). The four horsemen of automaticity: Awareness, intention, efficiency, and control in social cognition. In R. S. Wyer & T. K. Srull (Eds.), *Handbook of social cognition* (pp. 1–40). Hillsdale, NJ: Erlbaum.

Bargh, J. A., & Barndollar, K. (1996). Automaticity in action: The unconscious as repository of chronic goals and motives. In P. M. Gollwitzer & J. A. Bargh (Eds.), *The psychology of action: Linking cognition and motivation to behavior* (pp. 457–481). New York: Guilford.

Bargh, J. A., & Chartrand, T. L. (1999). The unbearable automaticity of being. *American Psychologist, 54,* 462–479.

Bargh, J. A., & Ferguson, M. J. (2000). Beyond behaviorism: On the automaticity of higher mental processes. *Psychological Bulletin, 126,* 925–945.

Bargh, J. A., Gollwitzer, P. M., Lee-Chai, A., Barndollar, K., & Trötschel, R. (2001). The automated will: Nonconscious activation and pursuit of behavioral goals. *Journal of Personality and Social Psychology, 81,* 1014–1027.

Bargh, J. A., & Tota, M. E. (1988). Context-dependent automatic processing in depression: Accessibility of negative constructs with regard to self but not others. *Journal of Personality and Social Psychology, 54,* 925–939.

Baumeister, R. F., Schmeichel, B. J., and Vohs, K. D. (2007). Self-regulation and the executive function: The self as controlling agent. In A. W. Kruglanski & E. T. Higgins (Eds.), *Social psychology: Handbook of basic principles* (2nd ed., pp. 516–539). New York: Guilford Press.

Baumeister, R. F., & Vohs, K. D. (2003). Willpower, choice, and self-control. In G. Loewenstein, D. Read, & R. Baumeister (Eds.), *Time and decision: Economic and psychological perspectives on intertemporal choice* (pp. 201–216). New York: Russell Sage Foundation.

Baumeister, R. F., & Vohs, K. D. (2004). *Handbook of self-regulation: Research, theory, and applications.* New York: Guilford Press.

Bem, D. J. (1967). Self-perception: An alternative interpretation of cognitive dissonance phenomena. *Psychological Review, 74,* 183–200.

Berscheid, E., Graziano, W., Monson, T., & Dermer, M. (1976). Outcome dependency: Attention, attribution, and attraction. *Journal of Personality and Social Psychology, 34,* 978–989.

Bless, H., Bohner, G., Schwarz, N., & Strack, F. (1990). Mood and persuasion: A cognitive response analysis. *Personality and Social Psychology Bulletin, 16,* 331–345.

Bodenhausen, G. V. (1993). Emotions, arousal, and stereotypic judgments: A heuristic model of affect and stereotyping. In D. M. Mackie & D. L. Hamilton (Eds.), *Affect, cognition, and stereotyping: Interactive processes in group perception* (pp. 13–37). San Diego, CA: Academic Press.

Brandtstädter, J., Voss, A., & Rothermund, K. (2004). Perception of danger signals: The role of control. *Experimental Psychology, 51,* 24–32.

Bruner, J. S. (1957). On perceptual readiness. *Psychological Review, 64,* 123–152.

Carver, C. S., & Scheier, M. F. (1998). *On the self-regulation of behavior.* New York: Cambridge University Press.

Chartrand, T. L., & Bargh, J. A. (1996). Automatic activation of social information processing goals: Nonconscious priming reproduces effects of explicit conscious instructions. *Journal of Personality and Social Psychology, 71,* 464–478.

Cherry, E. C. (1953). Some experiments on the recognition of speech, with one and with two ears. *Journal of the Acoustical Society of America, 25,* 975–979.

Collins, A. M., & Loftus, E. F. (1975). A spreading activation theory of semantic processing. *Psychological Review, 82,* 407–428.

Custers, R., & Aarts, H. (2005). Positive affect as implicit motivator: On the nonconscious operation of behavioral goals. *Journal of Personality and Social Psychology, 89,* 129–142.

Deci, E. L., & Ryan, R. M. (1985). The general causality orientations scale: Self-determination in personality. *Journal of Research in Personality, 19,* 109–134.

Denzler, M., Förster, J., & Liberman, N. (2008). How goal-fulfillment decreases aggression. *Journal of Experimental Social Psychology.*

Derryberry, D., & Tucker, D. M. (1994). Motivating the focus of attention. In P. M. Niedenthal & S. Kitayama (Eds.), *Heart's eye: Emotional influences in perception and attention* (pp. 167–196). New York: Academic Press.

Dunning, D., Leuenberger, A., & Sherman, D. A. (1995). A new look at motivated inference: Are self-serving theories of success a product of motivational forces? *Journal of Personality and Social Psychology, 69,* 58–68.

Dunning, D., Meyerowitz, J. A., & Holzberg, A. D. (1989). Ambiguity and self-evaluation: The role of idiosyncratic trait definitions in self-serving assessments of ability. *Journal of Personality and Social Psychology, 57,* 1082–1090.

Easterbrook, J. A. (1959). The effect of emotion on cue utilization and the organization of behavior. *Psychological Review, 66,* 183–201.

Fein, S., & Spencer, S. J. (1997). Prejudice as self-image maintenance: Affirming the self through derogating others. *Journal of Personality and Social Psychology, 73*, 31–44.
Ferguson, M. J., & Bargh, J. A. (2004). Liking is for doing: The effects of goal pursuit on automatic evaluation. *Journal of Personality and Social Psychology, 87*, 557–572.
Festinger, L. (1957). *A theory of cognitive dissonance*. Oxford, England: Row, Peterson.
Fischer, A. & Manstead, A. (2008). Social functions of emotions. In M. Lewis, J. Haviland-Jones, & F. Barrett (Eds.), *Handbook of emotions* (3rd ed., pp. 456–470). New York: Guilford Press.
Fishbach, A., Friedman, R. S., & Kruglanski, A. W. (2003). Leading us not into temptation: Momentary allurements elicit overriding goal activation. *Journal of Personality and Social Psychology, 79*, 493–506.
Fishbein, M., & Ajzen, I. (1974). Attitudes toward objects as predictors of single and multiple behavioral criteria. *Psychological Review, 81*, 59–74.
Fitzsimons, G. M., & Bargh, J. A. (2004). Automatic self-regulation. In R. F. Baumeister & K. D. Vohs (Eds.), *Handbook of self-regulation* (pp. 151–170). New York: Guilford Press.
Forgas, J. P. (1995). Mood and judgment: The affect infusion model (AIM). *Psychological Bulletin, 117*, 39–66.
Förster, J. (2004). How body feedback influences consumers' evaluations of products. *Journal of Consumer Psychology, 14*, 416–426.
Förster, J., Friedman, R. S., Özelsel, A., & Denzler, M. (2006). Enactment of approach and avoidance behavior influences the scope of perceptual and conceptual attention. *Journal of Experimental Social Psychology, 42*, 133–146.
Förster, J., & Higgins, E. T. (2005). How global versus local perception fits regulatory focus. *Psychological Science, 16*, 631–636.
Förster, J., Higgins, E. T., & Idson, L. C. (1998). Approach and avoidance strength during goal attainment: Regulatory focus and the "goal looms larger" effect. *Journal of Personality and Social Psychology, 75*, 1115–1131.
Förster, J., Higgins, E. T., & Strack, F. (2000). When stereotype disconfirmation is a personal threat: How prejudice and prevention focus moderate incongruency effects. *Social Cognition, 18*, 178–197.
Förster, J., & Liberman, N. (2007). Knowledge activation. In E. T. Higgins & A. W. Kruglanski (Eds.), *Social psychology: Handbook of basic principles* (2nd ed., pp. 201–231). New York: Guilford Press.
Förster, J., Liberman, N., & Friedman, R. S. (2007). Seven principles of goal activation: A systematic approach to distinguishing goal priming from priming of non-goal constructs. *Personality and Social Psychology Review, 11*, 211–233.
Förster, J., Liberman, N., & Higgins, E. T. (2005). Accessibility from active and fulfilled goals. *Journal of Experimental Social Psychology, 41*, 220–239.
Förster, J., & Strack, F. (1996). Influence of overt head movements on memory for valenced words: A case of conceptual-motor compatibility. *Journal of Personality and Social Psychology, 71*, 421–430.
Förster, J., & Werth, L. (in press). Regulatory focus: Classic findings and new directions. In G. Moskowitz & H. Grant (Eds.), *The psychology of goals*.
Fredrickson, B. L. (2001). The role of positive emotions in positive psychology: The broaden-and-built theory of positive emotions. *American Psychologist, 56*, 218–226.
Friedman, R., & Förster, J. (2001). The effects of promotion and prevention cues on creativity. *Journal of Personality and Social Psychology, 81*, 1001–1013.
Friedman, R., & Förster, J. (2008). Activation and measurement of motivational states. In A. Elliott (Ed.), *Handbook of approach and avoidance motivation* (pp. 235–246). Mahwah, NJ: Erlbaum.
Friedman, R., Förster, J., & Denzler, M. (2007). Interactive effects of mood and task framing on creative generation. *Creativity Research Journal, 19*, 141–162.

Gasper, K., & Clore, G. (2002). Attending to the big picture: Mood and global versus local processing of visual information. *Psychological Science, 13*, 34–40.
Gollwitzer, P. M. (1990). Action phases and mindsets. In R. M. Sorrentino & E. T. Higgins (Eds.), *Handbook of motivation and cognition* (pp. 53–92). New York: Guilford Press.
Gollwitzer, P. M. (1993). Goal achievement: the role of intentions. *European Review of Social Psychology, 4*, 141–185.
Gollwitzer, P. M. (1996). The volitional benefits of planning. In P. M. Gollwitzer & J. A. Bargh (Eds.), *The psychology of action* (pp. 287–312), New York: Guilford Press.
Gollwitzer, P. M., & Kinney, R. F. (1989). Effects of deliberative and implemental mind-sets on illusion of control. *Journal of Personality and Social Psychology, 56*, 531–542.
Green, J. D., Pinter, B., & Sedikides, C. (2005). Mnemic neglect and self-threat: Trait modifiability moderates self-protection. *European Journal of Social Psychology, 35*, 225–235.
Green, J. D., Sedikides, C., & Gregg, A. P. (2007). Forgotten but not gone: The recall and recognition of self-threatening memories. *Journal of Experimental Social Psychology, 44*, 547–561.
Hansen, C. H., & Hansen, R. D. (1988). Finding the face in the crowd: An anger superiority effect. *Journal of Personality and Social Psychology, 54*, 917–924.
Hastie, R. (1980). *Person memory: The cognitive basis of social perception.* Hillsdale, NJ: Erlbaum.
Heider, F. (1958). *The psychology of interpersonal relations.* New York: Wiley.
Higgins, E. T. (1987). Self-discrepancy: A theory relating self and affect. *Psychological Review, 3*, 319–340.
Higgins, E. T. (1996). Knowledge activation: Accessibility, applicability and salience. In E. T. Higgins & A. W. Kruglanski (Eds.), *Social psychology: Handbook of basic principles* (pp. 133–168). New York: Guilford Press.
Higgins, E. T. (1997). Beyond pleasure and pain. *American Psychologist, 52*, 1280–1300.
Higgins, E. T. (2000). Making a good decision: Value from fit. *American Psychologist, 55*, 1217–1230.
Higgins, E. T. (2006). Value from hedonic experience and engagement. *Psychological Review, 113*, 439–460.
Higgins, E. T., & Molden, D. C. (2003). How strategies for making judgments and decisions affect cognition: Motivated cognition revisited. In G. V. Bodenhausen & A. J. Lambert (Eds.), *Foundations of social cognition: A Festschrift in honor of Robert S. Wyer, Jr.* (pp. 211–235). Mahwah, NJ: Erlbaum.
Higgins, E. T., Rholes, W. S., & Jones, C. R. (1977). Category accessibility and impression formation. *Journal of Experimental Social Psychology, 13*, 141–154.
Higgins, E. T., Roney, C. J. R., Crowe, E., & Hymes, C. (1994). Ideal versus ought predilections for approach and avoidance distinct self-regulatory systems. *Journal of Personality and Social Psychology, 66*, 276–286.
Idson, L. C., Liberman, N., & Higgins, E. T. (2000). Imagining how you'd feel: The role of motivational experiences from regulatory fit. *Personality and Social Psychology Bulletin, 30*, 926–937.
Isen, A. M. (1985). Asymmetry of happiness and sadness in effects on memory in normal college students: Comment on Hasher, Rose, Zacks, Sanft, and Doren. *Journal of Experimental Psychology, 114*, 388–391.
Isen, A. M., Means, B., Patrick, R., & Nowicki, G. (1982). Some factors influencing decision-making strategy and risk-taking. In M. S. Clark & S. T. Fiske (Eds.), *Affect and cognition: The 17th Annual Carnegie Symposium on Cognition* (pp. 243–262). Hillsdale, NJ: Erlbaum.

Kruglanski, A. W. (1996). Motivated social cognition: Principles of the interface. In E. T. Higgins & A. W. Kruglanski (Eds.), *Social psychology: Handbook of basic principles* (pp. 493–520). New York: Guilford Press.

Kruglanski, A. W., Shah, J. Y., Fishbach, A., Friedman, R., Chun, W., & Sleeth-Keppler, D. (2002). A theory of goal systems. In M. P. Zanna (Ed.), *Advances in experimental social psychology* (Vol. 34, pp. 331–378). San Diego, CA: Academic Press.

Kruglanski, A. W., & Webster, D. M. (1996). Motivated closing of the mind: "Seizing" and "freezing." *Psychological Review, 103,* 263–283.

Kuhl, J. (1996). Who controls whom when "I control myself"? *Psychological Inquiry, 7,* 61–68.

Kunda, Z. (1990). The case for motivated reasoning. *Psychological Bulletin, 108,* 480–498.

Kunda, Z. (1999). *Social cognition: Making sense of people.* Cambridge, MA: MIT Press.

Lazarus, R. S., Yousem, H., & Arenberg, D. (1953). Hunger and perception. *Journal of Personality, 21,* 312–328.

Lewin, K. (1926). *Vorsatz, Wille und Bedürfnis: mit Vorbemerkungen über die psychischen Kräfte und Energien und die Struktur der Seele.* Berlin: Springer.

Lewin, K. (1951). *Field theory in social science: Selected theoretical papers.* New York: Harper and Row.

Liberman, N., & Förster, J. (2005). Motivation and construct accessibility. In J. P. Forgas, K. D. Kipling, & S. M. Laham (Eds.), *Social motivation: Conscious and unconscious processes (Sydney Symposium of Social Psychology)* (pp. 228–248). Cambridge, England: Cambridge University Press.

Liberman, N., Förster, J., & Higgins, E. T. (2007). Completed versus interrupted priming: Reduced accessibility from post-fulfillment inhibition. *Journal of Experimental Social Psychology, 43,* 258–264.

Locke, E. A., & Latham, G. P. (1990). *A theory of goal setting and task performance.* Englewood Cliffs, NJ: Prentice-Hall.

Lord, C. G., Ross, L., & Lepper, M. R. (1979). Biased assimilation and attitude polarization: The effects of prior theories on subsequently considered evidence. *Journal of Personality and Social Psychology, 37,* 2098–2109.

Marsh, R. L., Hicks, J. L., & Bink, M. L. (1998). Activation of completed, uncompleted and partially completed intentions. *Journal of Experimental Psychology: Learning, Memory and Cognition, 24,* 350–361.

Marsh, R. L., Hicks, J. L., & Bryan, E. S. (1999). The activation of unrelated and canceled intentions. *Memory and Cognition, 27,* 320–327.

Martin, L. L. (2001). Mood as input: A configural view of mood effects. In L. L. Martin & G. L. Clore (Eds.), *Theories of mood and cognition: A user's guidebook* (pp. 135–157). Mahwah, NJ: Erlbaum.

Martin, L. L., & Clore, G. L. (2001). *Theories of mood and cognition: A user's guidebook.* Mahwah, NJ: Erlbaum.

Martin, L. L., & Stoner, P. (1996). Mood as input: What we think about how we feel determines how we think. In L. L. Martin & A. Tesser (Eds.), *Striving and feeling: Interactions among goals, affect, and self-regulation* (pp. 279–301). Hillsdale, NJ: Erlbaum.

Metcalfe, J., & Mischel, W. (1999). A hot/cool system analysis of delay of gratification: Dynamics of willpower. *Psychological Review, 106,* 3–19.

Miller, N. E. (1944). Experimental studies of conflict. In J. McV. Hunt (Ed.), *Personality and behavior disorders* (Vol. 1, pp. 431–465). New York: Ronald Press.

Miller, N. E. (1976). Learning, stress, and psychosomatic symptoms. *Acta Neurobiologiae Experimentalis, 36,* 141–156.

Moskowitz, G. B., Gollwitzer, P. M., Wasel, W., & Schaal, B. (1999). Preconscious control of stereotype activation through chronic egalitarian goals. *Journal of Personality and Social Psychology, 77,* 167–184.

Moskowitz, G. B., Li, P., & Kirk, E. R. (2004). The implicit volition model: On the preconscious regulation of temporarily adopted goals. In M. P. Zanna (Ed.), *Advances in experimental social psychology* (Vol. 36, pp. 317–404). New York: Academic Press.

Mowrer, O. H. (1960). *Learning theory and behavior.* Hoboken, NJ: Wiley.

Navon, D. (1977). Forest before trees: The precedence of global features in visual perception. *Cognitive Psychology, 9*, 353–383.

Pratto, F., & John, O. P. (1991). Automatic vigilance: The attention-grabbing power of negative social information. *Journal of Personality and Social Psychology, 61*, 380–391.

Prinz, W. (1990). A common coding approach to perception and action. In O. Neumann & W. Prinz (Eds.), *Relationships between perception and action* (pp. 167–201). Heidelberg: Springer.

Rogers, T. B., Kuiper, N. A., & Kirker, W. S. (1977). Self-reference and the encoding of personal information. *Journal of Personality and Social Psychology, 35*, 677–688.

Rothermund, K., Wentura, D., & Bak, P. M. (2001). Automatic attention to stimuli signaling chances and dangers: Moderating effects of positive and negative goal and action contexts. *Cognition & Emotion, 15*, 231–248.

Rusting, C. L., & DeHart, T. (2000). Retrieving positive memories to regulate negative mood: Consequences for mood-congruent memory. *Journal of Personality and Social Psychology, 78*, 737–752.

Sanbonmatsu, D. M., & Fazio, R. H. (1990). The role of attitudes in memory-based decision making. *Journal of Personality and Social Psychology, 59*, 614–622.

Sanitoso, R., Kunda, Z., & Fong, G. (1990). Motivated recruitment of autobiographical memories. *Journal of Personality and Social Psychology, 57*, 229–241.

Schaller, M. (1992). In-group favoritism and statistical reasoning in social inference: Implications for formation and maintenance of group stereotypes. *Journal of Personality and Social Psychology, 63*, 61–74.

Schwarz, N., & Bless, H. (1991). Happy and mindless, but sad and smart? The impact of affective states on analytic reasoning. In J. Forgas (Ed.), *Emotion and social judgments* (pp. 55–71). Oxford, England: Pergamon.

Schwarz, N., & Clore, G. L. (1996). Feelings and phenomenal experiences. In E. T. Higgins & A. W. Kruglanski (Eds.), *Social psychology: Handbook of basic principles* (pp. 433–465). New York: Guilford Press.

Sedikides, C., & Green, J. D. (2000). The rocky road from affect to attentional focus. In H. Bless & J. P. Forges (Eds.), *The message within: The role of subjective experience in social cognition and behavior* (pp. 203–215). New York: Psychology Press.

Sedikides, C., & Gregg, A. P. (2003). Portraits of the self. In M. Hogg & J. Cooper (Eds.), *The Sage handbook of social psychology* (pp. 110–138). London: Sage.

Seibt, B., Häfner, M., & Deutsch, R. (2007). Prepared to eat: How immediate affective and motivational responses to food cues are influenced by food deprivation. *European Journal of Social Psychology, 37*, 359–379.

Shah, J. Y., Friedman, R., & Kruglanski, A. W. (2002). Forgetting all else: On the antecedents and consequences of goal shielding. *Journal of Personality and Social Psychology, 83*, 1261–1280.

Shah, J. Y., & Kruglanski, A. W. (2000). Aspects of goal networks: Implications for self-regulation. In M. Boekaerts, P. R. Pintrich, & M. Zeidner (Eds.), *Handbook of self regulation* (pp. 85–110). San Diego, CA: Academic Press.

Shah, J. Y., & Kruglanski, A. W. (2003). When opportunity knocks: Bottom-up priming of goals by means and its effects on self-regulation. *Journal of Personality and Social Psychology, 84*, 1109–1122.

Sinclair, R. C., & Mark, M. M. (1995). The effects of mood state on judgmental accuracy: Processing strategy as a mechanism. *Cognition & Emotion, 9*, 417–438.

Steele, C. M., & Liu, T. J. (1983). Dissonance processes as self-affirmation. *Journal of Personality and Social Psychology, 45*, 5–19.

Symons, C. S., & Johnson, B. T. (1997). The self-reference effect in memory: A meta-analysis. *Psychological Bulletin, 121*, 371–394.

Taylor, S. E., & Brown, J. D. (1988). Illusion and well-being: A social psychological perspective on mental health. *Psychological Bulletin, 103*, 193–210.

Taylor, S. E., & Gollwitzer, P. M. (1995). The effects of mindsets on positive illusions. *Journal of Personality and Social Psychology, 69*, 213–226.

Tyler, S. K., & Tucker, D. M. (1982). Anxiety and perceptual structure: Individual differences in neuropsychological function. *Journal of Abnormal Psychology, 91*, 210–220.

Vohs, K. D., & Baumeister, R. F. (2004). Ego-depletion, self-control, and choice. In J. Greenberg, S. L. Koole, & T. Pyszczynski (Eds.), *Handbook of experimental existential psychology* (pp. 398–410). New York: Guilford Press.

Wegener, D. T., & Petty, R. E. (1994). Mood management across affective states: The hedonic contingency hypothesis. *Journal of Personality and Social Psychology, 66*, 1034–1048.

Wilson, T. D., & Schooler, J. W. (1991). Thinking too much: Introspection can reduce the quality of preferences and decisions. *Journal of Personality and Social Psychology, 60*, 181–192.

Wyer, R. S., & Srull, T. K. (1986). Human cognition in its social context. *Psychological Review, 93*, 322–359.

Zanna, M., & Cooper, J. (1976). Dissonance and the attribution process. In J. Harvey, W. Ickes, & R. Kidd (Eds.), *New directions in attribution research* (pp. 199–217). Hillsdale, NJ: Erlbaum.

13

Language and Social Cognition

GÜN R. SEMIN

LANGUAGE AND SOCIAL COGNITION

This chapter addresses the classic puzzle of the relationship between language and cognition from a social psychological point of view. The two central questions driving this field are as follows: Does language influence, shape, or perhaps even determine human cognitive activities?' For the flip side of the coin, do cognitive processes affect language? This classic problem has occupied a prominent position in human intellectual history and has an intellectual heritage that was shaped by a number of eminent scholars (e.g., Boas, 1949; Sapir, 1951; von Humboldt, 1843; Whorf, 1956). This question has also featured in social psychology, increasingly so over the last 10 to 20 years, largely due to the formulation of language-related research questions that made the language-cognition interface more amenable to systematic investigation.

This chapter constitutes an appraisal of these developments, as well as their origins, and is organized in three sections. The first outlines a traditional and a functional look at language and cognition. These perspectives shape the different ways of looking at the very same phenomena in this field. The main body of the research on language and social cognition is presented in the second section through these two lenses. Notably, this section includes only research that has explicitly addressed the language-social cognition interface. The concluding section explores some of the implications of a functional view of language.

META-THEORETICAL ASSUMPTIONS ABOUT THE LANGUAGE-COGNITION INTERFACE

Two contrasting perspectives have driven the research on the language and cognition interface. One can be referred to as a traditional approach to language, which still informs much research in social cognition. In this view, language is a disembodied structure and is examined from an individual perspective. The critical question revolves around the mutual influence between language and social cognition as a dilemma of two "inner representational" systems rather than language as an instrument for communication. Language is distanced from real time and is regarded as a tool for representation and computation. Similarly, social cognition refers to individual processes—encoding, representing, thinking, retrieving, and so on. For instance, if two cultures linguistically code the color spectrum differently, do they then perceive and represent colors incommensurably or not (cf. Özgen, 2004)? Not surprisingly, thinking of language and cognition in this way leads to the fascinating and classic issues that have occupied many scholars about the relationship between language and cognition and their mutual influence.

The traditional view dismisses the inherently variable processes that characterize the adaptive flexibility of cognition as a property that emerges in the interaction between the organism and the social environment (Smith & Semin, 2004), sensorimotor activity (e.g., Pulvermüller, 2007), and the use of language as a tool to extend cognition in real or imagined communicative contexts. The alternative way of looking at this relationship is a functional one by considering the language-cognition interface in a "language use" context. In this functional view, language is treated as a tool and a means to extend cognition in the implementation of action (e.g., Semin, 2000b, 2001). This particular take on the relationship between language and cognition assigns different roles to language and cognition. Language becomes the tool by means of which cognition is implemented in action. I elaborate on these two approaches since they inform the review of the literature presented in the second section of this chapter.

The Traditional Perspective

In the traditional perspective, language is regarded as a set of "rules" that are "virtual and outside of time" (Ricoeur, 1955). Language is considered in the abstract, "without a subject," and not as a tool that is strategically used in situated action. This lens presents language as an extra-individual and systematic set of abstract properties. Language has a life of its own. Consequently, it is "subjectless," "timeless," and disembodied. This assumption enables the examination of language in terms of the relationships between its specific properties in detached abstraction (e.g., lexical semantics, grammatical categories, word order). The treatment that cognition receives in this perspective is comparable. Cognitive processes are also thought of in a disembodied, timeless, and subjectless manner. Given these assumptions, the interface between language and social cognition becomes an investigation of the interaction between two different representational modules. This viewpoint has informed the discussion of the linguistic relativity debate (Whorf, 1956) in psychology (Brown & Lenneberg, 1954; Lenneberg, 1953; Lenneberg & Roberts, 1956). The paradigmatic feature of this agenda was how categorization influences cognitive processes (e.g., Hardin & Banaji, 1993; Hoffman, Lau & Johnson, 1986; Hunt & Agnoli, 1991).

The Functional Perspective

A different way of looking at this interface is to look at the complementary relationship between language and cognition and their respective functions. If cognition is not detached thought but adaptively successful interaction (James, 1890, p. 333) with other agents and with the world (Smith & Semin, 2004), then an inevitable question is how this cognition "happens." For cognition to happen, it has to be "coupled" with an external entity in a two-way interaction (Clark & Chalmers, 1997). Among humans, this process of coupling takes place chiefly, but not only (Semin, 2007), by language. This coupling with external reality is achieved by using language as a tool (see also the 1979 work of Bakhtin as cited in Wertsch, 1984; Mead, 1934; Vygotsky, 1978, 1981; Wertsch, 1991, 1994), which extends cognition by enabling adaptive social interaction (Semin, 1998, 2000a). In this view, language does not constitute a mirror of our inner states but is a complement to them. It serves as a tool whose role is to extend cognition in ways that onboard devices cannot.

Language, very much like other tools (e.g., a pair of scissors) is a device that has evolved to meet the dual demands involved in solving a problem by adapting to the features or properties of a particular task (e.g., cutting a piece of paper) as well as the constitutional features of human capabilities and body (e.g., the shape of the hand). This dual adaptation of tools gives capabilities or powers to do things that we do not have by nature. The distinctive feature of any tool, as in the case of a pair of scissors, is the way it has been engineered; the sharp blades, the way the blades are pivoted, the rings on the blades constitute a remarkable achievement in terms of facilitating the interface or the coupling between the human constitution and the human goal. The distinctive feature of any device is that it is embodied (Semin & Smith, 2008). Tools are shaped by the constraints of the human biological constitution on the one hand and the types of adaptation that the tasks at hand require on the other. This way of looking at language takes it from the exclusively representational perspective and grounds it into an embodied framework. Consequently, "(t)he fundamental function of words is to bring about changes in the speaker's environment and linguistic understanding consists in a grasp of these causal relations" (Gauker, 1990, p. 44). Thus, all a language user needs to know is how to use language to achieve a particular goal (Semin, 2006). Language is a tool that facilitates communication by interfacing speakers and receivers and has evolved such that it is optimally adapted to the basic computational capacities of the human brain as well as the sensorimotor capabilities of both speakers and receivers. Language has therefore evolved with three adaptive constraints: communication, representing aspects of reality, and finally the sensorimotor functions of humans. In such a functional perspective, language becomes a tool at the service of cognition by extending cognition.

OVERVIEW: THE PROPERTIES AND FUNCTIONS OF INTERPERSONAL VERBS

I now turn to a selection of research areas to illustrate the two perspectives on language. First, I review the literature on interpersonal verbs, which probably has the richest research tradition in social psychology, an area that is anchored in the representational tradition. How the very same phenomena acquire a different complexion in a functional perspective is discussed in the following section. The classic issue of how stereotypes are communicated (cf. Maass, 1999) and transmitted is discussed next. This research review concludes with an overview of the language-based implicit measurement of preferences and prejudices (cf. Semin, 2006; Vargas, Sekaquaptewa, & von Hippel, 2007).

The Traditional Perspective

How do transitive verbs that describe interpersonal events (e.g., to help, to cheat, to respect, to surprise) influence cognition? This field, addressed within a traditional view, has examined the types of systematic inferences that interpersonal verbs convey. This question has a long-forgotten tradition that preceded the entire research field on language and cognition in social psychology. It originated in research on "inductive logic" and the discovery that interpersonal verbs exerted a powerful and systematic influence on generalizations (Gilson & Abelson, 1965), followed by a systematic research program on the inferential properties of interpersonal verbs (e.g., Abelson & Kanouse, 1966; the 1969 work of Cohen as cited in McArthur, 1972; Gilson & Abelson, 1965; Kanouse, 1972; McArthur, 1972; Paquette, 1970, as cited in McArthur, 1972, p. 177). The question was: Do interpersonal verbs function as implicit quantifiers, and if so, are there any systematic differences between action and state verbs (SVs)? For instance, Kanouse (1972) examined the role of implicit quantifiers in a recall paradigm. The stimulus sentences were designed to control for verb type (state vs. action) and valence (positive vs. negative). In addition, these sentences were factorially combined with four qualifiers ("all," "most," "some," and "one or two"). Participants were shown all the stimulus sentences in the first trial. They were then presented with the first two words on each stimulus sentence (subject and verb) and responded by writing the entire sentence on an answer sheet. They were then shown the correct stimulus sentence. This was repeated seven times. The dependent variable was the correct recall of the sentences presented on individual cards. The predicted interaction effect was confirmed. Sentences with SVs were remembered correctly more frequently when paired with large object quantifiers but less frequently when paired with small quantifiers. Furthermore, sentences with action verbs were recalled more correctly when paired with small quantifiers and less well when paired with large quantifiers. Similarly, the interaction between verb valence and quantifier type was also supported in the predicted direction—for verbs with a positive valence, recall was better for smaller quantifiers, whereas the reverse was true for verbs with negative valences.

Some 11 years later, Brown and Fish (1983) addressed the same problem with a somewhat different question: How do interpersonal verbs influence causal inference? This question was cast in the then-prevailing attribution theoretical zeitgeist. They demonstrated that verbs referring to visible actions (to help, to hit, to cheat, etc.) lead predominantly to the inference that the event represented in a simple sentence was caused by the sentence subject, namely, "David" in a sentence such as "David punches John." In contrast, verbs that refer to psychological-affective states (to dislike, to trust, to respect, to hate, etc.) were shown to give rise to the inference that the sentence object (i.e., to John in "David dislikes John") was the causal origin of the event. Their major contribution was introducing a systematic way to differentiate between different verb classes (action vs. SVs) by examining the semantic roles (see Chafe, 1970; Fillmore, 1968, 1971) associated with the sentence subject and object (noun predicates). This permitted them to advance independent linguistic criteria for classifying verbs objectively, namely, criteria that are independent from the predicted outcomes, and thereby avoiding circularity between verb categorization and inference types. For a group of verbs that have to do with overt and observable actions such as help, disagree, cheat, the relevant semantic roles are that of agent and patient. The *agent role* refers to somebody who causes or instigates an action. The *patient role* refers to somebody who is undergoing change. In the case of verbs of *state* (like, hate, trust), the relevant roles are those of *stimulus* and *experiencer*. The stimulus role refers to the originator of the experience and the latter role to the person who has a specific experience.

Brown and Fish (1983) showed, in repeated demonstrations, that sentences with action verbs lead to stronger causal attributions to the sentence subject (agent), and sentences with SVs lead to stronger causal attributions to the sentence object (stimulus). Their account of how these inferences were mediated relied on a "causal schema" hypothesis (Brown & Van Kleeck, 1989; Van Kleeck, Hillger, & Brown, 1988). According to this hypothesis, implicit causality is a universal of human thought (see Brown, 1986; Brown & Fish, 1983, p. 271). Accordingly, agent-patient and experiencer-stimulus schema are elicited by action and SVs, respectively. A sentence with an action verb (e.g., "John helps David") activates an agent-patient schema, whereas a SV sentence (e.g., "John likes David") elicits an experiencer-stimulus schema. According to this model, a sentence verb primes a lexical entry in memory. This lexical entry is assumed to include a syntactical class (verb) along with its subclass (action or state). This leads to accessing of the semantic roles and the assignment of relative causal weights. These schemata are further coupled to attribution theoretical principles of consensus and distinctiveness, by which the agent-patient schema is associated with a low consensus-low distinctiveness schema, whereas the experiencer-stimulus schema is associated with a high consensus-high distinctiveness schema. Therefore, sentences with action verbs are easily generalized to other objects or patients, whereas sentences with SVs are more easily generalized across subjects or experiencers (see also Rudolph & Försterling, 1997). The underlying assumption is that one can equate verb-mediated implicit causality with dispositional inferences that are drawn from these simple sentences.

Brown and Fish's (1983) contribution, in contrast to the program generated by Abelson, has stimulated considerable discussion about the processes driving inferences from sentences with different interpersonal verbs. I briefly survey these without going into much detail of the actual research. One of the early explorations was driven by the "morphological" hypothesis. The argument here is that the verb-derived adjective—namely, whether it is subject (e.g., John helps David. John is helpful.) or object referent (John likes David. David is likable.)—mediates the causal inference (e.g., Hoffman & Tchir, 1990; Holtgraves & Raymond, 1995; Semin & Marsman, 1994). Overall, the evidence on the morphological hypothesis can be regarded as mixed.

An alternative account is the so-called antecedent-consequent event structure account of implicit causality (Au, 1986; Fiedler & Semin, 1988). According to this view, implicit causality is mediated by the imagined context of a stimulus sentence that is elicited by the question to disambiguate a stimulus sentence. Briefly, the argument is that when participants are asked to generate sentences about what they think the event is that preceded a stimulus sentence constructed with an action verb (antecedent), then the subject in the stimulus sentence is referred to more frequently. In the case of SVs, references to the stimulus sentence object are more likely to occur in the antecedent sentence. Precisely the reverse is predicted for sentences that are generated about consequent events, namely, those events that are likely to occur after the event described in the stimulus sentence. Now, the prediction is that events following stimulus sentences with action verbs are expected to contain more references to the stimulus object. The data provide reasonable but not entirely convincing evidence particularly for the consequences of action verbs and for the antecedents of SVs (cf. Semin & Fiedler, 1992, p. 64; see also Franco & Arcuri, 1990). Research that is closely related although preceding this approach is also to be found in linguistics; the goal was to show that verbs carry semantic information about implicit causes (e.g., Garvey & Caramazza, 1974; Garvey, Caramazza, & Yates, 1974/1975). According to Caramazza and his colleagues, verbs induce cause, by which some other factors, such as status or gender, moderate this inference (see also Caramazza, Grober, Garvey, & Yates, 1977; Ehrlich, 1980; Vonk, 1985a, 1985b; Vonk & Noordman, 1991).

A further account has been advanced by Gilovich and Regan (1986), who proposed a "volitional model" to explain implicit causality. They drew attention to the asymmetries in volition inherent in the semantic roles of agent-patient versus stimulus-experiencer. Whereas actions are under the volitional control of agents, experiences are under the control of stimuli. According to them, this volitional asymmetry contributes to the differential elicitation of the semantic role schemata proposed by Brown and Fish (1983). Kasoff and Lee (1993) advanced an "implicit salience" argument to explain how causal inferences are mediated by interpersonal verbs. According to this view, "sentences that describe interpersonal events evoke mental representations in which subjects and objects differ in salience" (p. 878). Thus, people are more likely to attribute causality to the more salient object rather than the less-salient one, for which they produce correlational evidence.

A number of studies have focused on the role played by verbs in text comprehension within the broader context of discourse models (e.g., Garnham & Oakhill, 1985; Garnham, Oakhill, & Cruttenden, 1992; Garnham, Traxler, Oakhill, & Gernsbacher, 1996; Greene & McKoon, 1994; McKoon, Greene, & Ratcliff, 1993). This research focuses on the causal relations implied by verbs, which is an important factor in the comprehension of narratives. This entire research field, which revolves on different types of assumed mediating processes, presents a set of paradoxes addressed next.

The Paradoxes

The research on interpersonal verbs suggests that the very same verb categories systematically influence (a) inductive and deductive generalizations; (b) implicit quantifiers; (c) implicit causality; (d) dispositional inferences (Semin & Fiedler, 1988); (e) salience judgments; (f) judgments of the temporal duration of events (e.g., Maass, Salvi, Arcuri, & Semin, 1989); (g) judgments of affective states (Semin & Fiedler, 1991, 1992); (h) verifiability judgments (Semin & Fiedler, 1988); (i) judgments of volitional control; (j) antecedent-consequent contexts; and more.

The different explanations that are offered reduce the phenomena to a determinate relationship between verb type and an inference that automatically and autonomously activates a cognitive inference. How can it be that a verb by its own force activates an inference process? If all of the systematic inferences noted above were automatic and autonomous and were to be coactivated, then the sheer cognitive load that this would introduce would in all likelihood bring the "cognitive apparatus" to a grinding halt.

While implicit causality is given an epistemically privileged position, there is no specific or a priori theoretical or empirical reason to privilege implicit causality over any other correlated inferences that have been demonstrated. Moreover, there is evidence that dispositional inferences are orthogonal to implicit causality (e.g., Semin & Marsman, 1994). Indeed, some of the evidence using recall paradigms suggests that if anything, then a dispositional inference rather than implicit causality may be the spontaneous or privileged one (Holtgraves & Raymond, 1995; Semin & Marsman, 2000). While the standard for theory testing is to pit one explanation against another in a critical experiment, this field has been driven by evidence that is supportive of specific inference patterns, and a critical test is impossible because of the correlational nature of the evidence.

The Nature of the Impasse and Toward a Resolution: Functions of Language and Their Implications

It would appear that despite the wealth of findings, a proper explanation of what happens when people read a simple "subject-verb-object" sentence has been somewhat elusive. First, there is no evidence that interpersonal verbs (in their own right and without the experimental context provided by instructions and questions) elicit, cue in, or activate any particular inference process. Second, there is no reason to assume that interpersonal verbs privilege a particular inference (e.g., causality) over another. Finally, there is no evidence to date of any process mediating the path from language to inference. I argue that these issues are a result of using a representational framework. This is not to deny the verity of the data.

The tacit treatment of language and cognition as inner representational systems rather than at the service of adaptive interaction with the world renders the puzzle of inferential processes an individually centered one. Language and cognition are assumed to "happen" within an individual. Language and cognitive processes remain timeless and subjectless, thus disembodied. This perspective is consequently not informed about a communicative or interpersonal context and the chief function that language serves. In the functional view, language is for use, and in general terms language use is a "design process" that extends (is the result of) cognitive and motivation processes of a speaker with a view to affect the focus of the attention of a listener to some aspect of social, physical, or psychological reality. In other words, language is used in a communicative context with a view to structure the cognitions of an addressee. Obviously, this is an interactive process and not unidirectional (see Figure 13.1). Seen this way, cognition can refer to (a) processes that contribute to how a speaker shapes a communicative act (production processes), (b) those processes that contribute to how a communicative act (a message) is received by an addressee (comprehension processes), and (c) the entirety of communication itself, namely independent of the individual productions, as a regulator of joint action (see Hutchins, 1996).

What are the implications of these considerations for the puzzle posed by the diverse inferences drawn from interpersonal verbs? One way of looking at this research is to situate the stimulus sentences and the question (dependent variable, DV) in a communicative context. The experimenter introduces a task by asking a question (DV) that is designed to draw attention to a specific aspect of an event (stimulus sentence, e.g., "A sailor *likes* [*goes to*] classical music concerts"). The function of the experimenter's question is simply to focus the participant's answer to a specific aspect (e.g., who caused the event = implicit causality; How likely is it that sailors like music concerts? = inductive generalization; How likely is it that the sailor will like the Pergolesi's "Stabat Mater"? = deductive generalization, and so on). Thus, given the very same event (stimulus sentence), the DV functions as an attention-driving device, and the subject is "compelled" by the rules of conversation (Grice, 1975) to oblige to the social contract that is issued by giving the

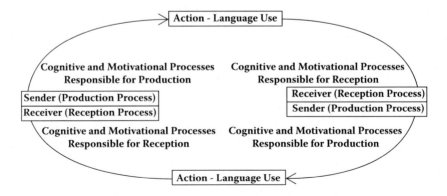

Figure 13.1   The interface between psychological processes and language.

"appropriate" answer. The appropriate answer is driven by the conventional cognitive properties of interpersonal verbs (e.g., Semin & Fiedler, 1988), and these are not determinate because language is not a determinate tool. As von Humboldt has (1836/1999) observed, language "makes infinite use of finite media" (p. 70) whose "synthesis creates something that is not present *per se* in any of the associated constituents" (p. 67).

While the above considerations remain thought experiments, there is research that has investigated the attention-driving or thematic-focusing function of interpersonal verbs (action and SVs) in experimentally situated contexts. The two types of interpersonal verbs function as structural devices that differentially focus attention (Stapel & Semin, 2007) on either the sentence subject or object in the question. This function of interpersonal verbs is what has been termed by some (e.g., Kay, 1996) "perspectivization" or "topicalization" (Fillmore, 1968). This attention-driving function of interpersonal verbs and their psychological implications have been examined in an experimentally induced communication paradigm termed the question-answer paradigm (QAP; Semin, 2000b). Semin, Rubini, and Fiedler (1995) systematically manipulated the verb in question formulation and examined whether verb types (action vs. SVs) systematically bias a target's answer as well as the implications of this answer (cf. De Poot & Semin, 1995; Rubini & Kruglanski, 1997; Semin & De Poot, 1997a, 1997b). The research by Semin et al. (1995) indicated that questions formulated with action verbs (e.g., "to help," "to write") cue the logical subject of a question as the causal origin of answers. Questions formulated with SVs (e.g., "to love" or "to like") cue the logical *object* of a question as the causal origin for answers. Thus, if asked such a simple and mundane question as, "Why do you *own* a dog?" (using an action verb), participants are prompted to respond by referring to themselves (the subject of the question) as the causal agent in the answer, such as by stating "Because *I* enjoy the companionship that dogs provide." If one is asked "Why do you like dogs?," however, one is prompted to respond by referring to the object itself, such as, "Because *dogs* are good companions" (e.g., Semin & De Poot, 1997b). Furthermore, the abstractness level of questions was also shown to influence the abstractness level of the answers (cf. Semin, 2000b, for a review). Thus, more abstractly formulated questions tend to elicit more abstract answers.

Interestingly, Rubini and Kruglanski (1997) set out to investigate the further implications of such differences in abstractness not only for how such verbs steer thematic focus but also the implications of dialogue sessions controlled over experiments for perceived interpersonal proximity and distance. They did so by examining if individuals had the impression that they disclosed more about themselves when asked questions formulated with action verbs (concrete) as opposed to state verbs (abstract) as well as examining the moderating role of need for closure. In their first experiment designed to investigate these issues, Rubini and Kruglanski (1997) had participants under high (vs. low) need for closure (operationalized via ambient noise) rank order questions from a list in terms of their likelihood of using them in a real interview. It was found that participants under noise (vs. no noise) assigned higher ranks to questions characterized by higher (vs. lower) level of abstractness. In a follow-up study, questions selected by participants under high (vs. low) need for closure were found to elicit more abstract answers from respondents and ones focused more on the logical object (vs. subject) of the question. In addition, respondents reported that they felt less friendly toward the interviewer whose questions were more (vs. less) abstract. These results suggest that the permanence tendency induced by the need for nonspecific closure influences the level of linguistic abstractness, which affects the nature of the social relationship between conversation partners.

This part of the research review contrasted two different approaches to the language-cognition interface. The former approach, about social cognition and language, paradoxically individual centered and thus nonsocial, has examined the interface taking place in the "mind" of the person. The latter, a functional one, treats language as an attention-driving device in an interpersonal context. While the traditional approach to this specific field has yielded a wealth of findings, the very nature of the findings gives rise to internal inconsistencies and paradoxes. The functional approach casting language as an extension of cognition in a communicative context has the advantage of not only situating the diversity of findings in specifiable communication contexts but also embedding the research questions in a broader social context and investigating its social psychological consequences, as for instance in the case of how social proximity and distance are mediated by verb choice (e.g., Rubini & Kruglanski, 1997).

The next and final example is how cognitive and motivational processes shape stereotype communication. Similar to the extended vision ranging from language use to social psychological consequences, this research has also investigated the full cycle extending from psychological factors influencing language use, to the impact of such messages on recipients, as well as how the inferences recipients make contribute to the regulation of social relationships. This section is introduced with a model of interpersonal language, which provides the research that is reported with the relevant grounding.

REPRESENTING, COMMUNICATING, AND TRANSMITTING STEREOTYPES IN COMMUNICATION: THE PSYCHOLOGICAL PROCESSES SHAPING STRATEGIC LANGUAGE USE AND ITS IMPLICATIONS

In the following, a model of the cognitive properties of interpersonal language is presented that has been important to ground the influential work on strategic language use in the research conceived by Anne Maass (cf. 1999 for a review) on how stereotypes are communicated and transmitted.

The Linguistic Category Model

An informed analysis of the linguistic devices that are used to communicate about social events requires an analysis of the distinctive properties of such devices. What are the distinctive interpersonal lexical units that are available, and are there systematic properties that they share in differing degrees? Any social event can be represented in a number of different ways with a number of different linguistic devices that give different nuances to the aspect of the reality to which we would like to draw the listener's attention. Concretely, this means to draw attention to specific aspects of the physical, psychological, and social environment in communication (e.g., an event by which David's fist connects with John's jaw). To do so, the speaker has a variety of options in terms of the devices that can be used to draw attention to the very same reality (e.g., "He punched John"; "He hurt John"; "He hates John"; "He is aggressive"). The choice of a specific verbal representation gives shape to a communicative act (utterance) that directs attention to a specific aspect of reality. Accordingly, different linguistic devices (e.g., punch, hurt, hate, aggressive) serve different perceptual functions.

Knowing the distinctive cognitive properties of different devices is important because this facilitates our understanding of which devices people choose to represent a specific event in communication rather than others. Moreover, comparing the properties of potentially available devices with those that are chosen could inform us about the psychological processes that drive the distinctive selection of linguistic tools over others. The linguistic category model (LCM; Semin, 2000a; Semin & Fiedler, 1988, 1991) was designed to reveal the distinctive properties of the different linguistic tools in the domain of interpersonal language. It is a classificatory approach that covers interpersonal (transitive) verbs that are tools used to describe actions (help, punch, cheat, surprise) or psychological states (love, hate, abhor) and adjectives and nouns that are employed to characterize persons (e.g., extroverted, helpful, religious).

The LCM furnishes the means by which it is possible to identify the nuances of how people use interpersonal terms and thus is informative about how verbal behavior is driven strategically by psychological processes and communication constraints. The LCM furnishes this information by providing a systematic model of the cognitive properties that are peculiar to the linguistic terms (verbs, adjectives, and nouns) in the interpersonal domain. In this model, a distinction is made between five different categories of interpersonal terms, namely, descriptive action verbs (DAVs), interpretative action verbs (IAVs), state action verbs (SAVs), SVs, and adjectives (cf. Semin & Fiedler, 1991).

The DAVs are the most concrete terms and are used to convey a description of a single, observable event and preserve perceptual features of the event (e.g., "A punches B," whereby punching is always achieved by means of a fist). Similarly, the second category (IAVs) describes specific observable events. However, these verbs are more abstract in that they refer to a general class of behaviors and do not preserve the perceptual features of an action (e.g., "A hurts B").

The next two categories, SAVs and SVs, refer to psychological states, while DAVs and IAVs do not. SAVs refer to the affective consequences of actions that are not specified any further (to amaze, surprise, bore, thrill, etc.) but can be supplied when asked (e.g., "Why was she surprised?"). The next category (SVs) typically describes an unobservable emotional state and not a specific event (e.g., "A hates B"). SAVs refer to states that are caused by the observable action of an agent and describe the "emotional consequences" of this action on a patient (surprise, bore, thrill). SVs refer to unobservable states (love, hate, despise).

Finally, adjectives (e.g., "A is aggressive") constitute the last and most abstract category. These generalize across specific events and objects and describe only the subject. They show a low contextual dependence and a high conceptual interdependence in their use. In other words, the use of adjectives is governed by abstract, semantic relations rather than by the contingencies of contextual factors. The opposite is true for action verbs (e.g., Semin & Fiedler, 1988; Semin & Greenslade, 1985). The most concrete terms retain a reference to the contextual and situated features of an event.

A general property across these categories is the dimension of abstractness-concreteness of interpersonal predicates and has been operationalized in terms of a number of different inferential features or properties. Some of these inferential properties are (a) how enduring the characteristic is of the sentence subject; (b) the ease and difficulty of confirming and disconfirming statements constructed with these predicates; (c) the temporal duration of an interpersonal event depicted by these terms; (d) how informative the sentence is about situational pressures or circumstances; and (e) the likelihood of an event reoccurring at a future point in time (Maass et al., 1989; Semin & Fiedler, 1988; Semin & Greenslade, 1985; Semin & Marsman, 1994). These variables have been shown to form a concrete-abstract dimension on which the four categories of the LCM (Semin & Fiedler, 1988) are ordered systematically. DAVs (hit, kiss) constitute the most concrete category. IAVs (help, cheat) are more abstract. SVs (like, abhor) follow next, and adjectives (friendly, helpful) are the most abstract predicates. Thus, one can determine how abstractly or concretely people represent an event in conversation. For example, the very same event can be described as somebody *hitting* a person, *hurting* a person (actions), *hating* a person (state), or simply as being *aggressive* (adjective).

It is important to note that the properties by which abstractness-concreteness has been operationalized are generic to the entire predicate classes represented in the LCM. The types of meanings or implications as defined by the distinctive inferential properties of the LCM are different from the more conventional study of meaning, namely, semantics. The more conventional approaches in linguistics are the study of meaning in terms of semantic fields, semantic relations, or the analysis of lexical items in terms of semantic features to investigate the semantic component of a grammar's organization. While semantic fields are concerned with how vocabulary is organized into domains or areas within which lexical items interrelate, semantic or sense relations address relationships such as synonymity (e.g., affable, amiable, friendly) and antonymity (e.g., friendly vs. unfriendly, good vs. bad). The inferential properties identified by the LCM are not domain specific (e.g., economic exchange words, such as give, take, buy, sell, etc.) or expressed in terms of interrelationships between the surface properties of terms (e.g., semantic overlap between terms that constitute codefining properties of the meanings, such as the semantic overlap between terms such as friendly, talkative, extroverted). One may refer to the meaning domain identified by the LCM as meta-semantic since the inferential properties apply across semantic fields.

The Communication of Stereotypes: Their Psychological Propellers and Implications

Stereotypes are the emergent results of socially situated interactions between individuals rather than a product that resides within the head of an individual, an idea whose roots can be dated in Lippman's (1922) famous metaphor of "pictures in the head." The research on strategic language use and stereotypes, initiated by Anne Maass and her colleagues, has the most direct bearing on the relationship between psychological processes (cognitive and motivational) and language as a tool to extend these processes in the public domain, namely, communication.

The linguistic intergroup bias (LIB; Maass & Arcuri, 1992; Maass, Milesi, Zabbini, & Stahlberg, 1995; Maass et al., 1989; Maass & Stahlberg, 1993) involves a strategy for individuals to describe positive in-group and negative out-group behaviors in relatively abstract terms, implying that the behavior is due to enduring dispositions or the actor's stable characteristics. Conversely, negative in-group and positive out-group behaviors are typically described in relatively concrete terms, implying the incidental or situational specificity of the behavior and hence an external attribution of the behavior.

Two mechanisms have been postulated to account for these systematic differences that people display when they are talking about positive and negative out- and in-group behaviors. One possible mechanism of the LIB could be motivational (Maass, 1999; Maass et al., 1989), having to do with the fact that abstract descriptions of positive in-group behaviors and of negative out-group behaviors portray the in-group in favorable and the out-group in unfavorable terms, implying that these behaviors are due to enduring characteristics. Similarly, concrete depictions of negative in-group behaviors minimize their significance as evidence for corresponding group characteristics, as do concrete depictions of positive out-group behaviors. In other words, those linguistic (and conceptual) tendencies serve to protect the perception that the in-group is superior to the out-group. Another mechanism to account for these patterns of language use is provided by a cognitive or expectancy account that states that expected behaviors are described with abstract language and unexpected behaviors by the use of concrete predicates (e.g., Rubini & Semin, 1994). Both processes appear to be operative depending on the motivational circumstances under which the strategic language is produced (Maass, 1999; Maass et al., 1995). This mechanism has been termed the linguistic expectancy bias (LEB; Wigboldus, Semin, & Spears, 2000).

The research on the LIB/LEB extends the language social cognition interface by showing precisely how both cognitive and motivational processes systematically influence language as a tool that renders these processes as action. Indeed, subsequent research investigating the impact of these messages on third parties has shown that third parties draw the implications for which the messages are designed (Werkman, Wigboldus, & Semin, 1999; Wigboldus et al., 2000). Extending this line of thinking, and building on their earlier work (2003), Douglas and Sutton showed that linguistic choices implicitly convey to listeners of messages the type of relationship that holds between the producers of such messages and the targets of their message (Douglas & Sutton, 2006).

The communication cycle between psychological processes, message production, and message impact is closed in a series of studies reported by Reitsma-van Rooijen, Semin, and van Leeuwen (2007). Similar to the findings reported by Rubini and Kruglanski (1997), Reitsma-van Rooijen et al. (2007) showed in an entirely different context that abstract messages about positive behaviors and concrete messages about negative behaviors produced perceived social proximity. In contrast, receiving concrete messages about positive behaviors and abstract messages about negative behaviors led to judgments of social distance to the sender of the message.

Again, these studies take the language-cognition interface outside the boundaries of the individual "mind" and investigate the effects of psychological processes on strategic language use in the first instance. How do, more broadly conceived now, cognitive and motivational processes influence the language people use when producing utterances? The step that comes after this is to investigate the impact of such messages. This can be done in a number of ways, as reported in this chapter. How do uninvolved participants decipher what is in a message in contrast to involved participants whose doings are talked about. How do they react to such senders? More important, how does language use, as reviewed in this section, contribute to the regulation of social behavior? This is the central mission that in my view emerges from the research reviewed here, namely, it is not only the contribution of a functional take on language and psychological processes or how they lead to a translation of the very same classic puzzles into contextually situated problems that open increasingly broader research challenges. The central mission that emerges is interfacing psychological processes within a communication context with a view toward developing a better understanding of the regulation of social behavior.

CONCLUDING WORDS: THE ATTENTIONAL CONSEQUENCES OF LANGUAGE USE

One of the main functional arguments that has emerged in considering the theme of this chapter, namely, relationship between language and cognition, is the role that language plays in extending cognition into action. A related driving corollary in this context is the attention-driving function of language. Language directs people's attention and perceptual focus, and different linguistic devices direct attention to different aspects of reality. This is an idea that is also at the core of Whorf's (1956, p. 221) linguistic relativity hypothesis, which suggests that the use of different "grammars" directs people to different types of observations and evaluation of events. But, what is distinctive about this assumption is that the focus is on the content of attention driving, which is more about associations and specific topics, themes, or beliefs. Moreover, the entire process is supposed to be played out in a person's head. The perspective presented here suggests that the attention-driving function of language is always played out in a communicative context (real or imagined), and that such functions of language may be much broader and not merely caught in specific semantic domains, such as the types of lexical categories that are available to describe persons in English and Chinese (e.g., Hoffman, Lau, & Johnson, 1986); the domain of language responsible for spatial locations (Majid, Bowerman, Kita, Haun, & Levinson, 2004); variations in the availability of basic color terms across a diversity of linguistic communities (e.g., Berlin & Kay, 1969); differences between languages in gender marking (e.g., English vs. Turkish) or pronoun drop (e.g., Kashima & Kashima, 2003); or lexical categorizations of emotional states (Semin, Görts, Nandram, & Semin-Goossens, 2002). Notably, all these cultural differences are domain specific and can be seen as culturally marked manners by which attention is driven to specific aspects of the social, physical, and psychological reality.

If, however, language is an attention-driving device, then it may be the case that specific linguistic devices, such as the meta-semantic linguistic categories identified by the LCM (Semin & Fiedler, 1988), are functionally organized to drive attention in a generic fashion. Indeed, there is recent evidence suggesting that this is the case. Stapel and Semin (2007) used the LCM (Semin, 2000a, 2000b; Semin & Fiedler, 1988, 1991) as a conceptual framework to investigate the hypothesis that different linguistic devices within a language may have generic, meta-semantic effects on cognition. In their studies, Stapel and Semin (2007) focused on the abstractness-concreteness dimension and suggested that if concrete terms such as action verbs ("John punched David") are used predominantly in situated contexts and refer to the specific details of a social event, then their obvious function—aside from providing a semantic representation of the event—is to draw attention to the situated, local features of the event. At the other end, abstract terms such as adjectives detract from any transient situated features of an event and direct global focus ("John is aggressive").

These authors hypothesized that different predicates are likely to direct attention to different features of an object. Notably, the research question is not about specific semantic categories (e.g., freedom fighter) and its semantic associates. It is about meta-semantic features of interpersonal language. Stapel and Semin (2007) hypothesized that concrete terms (e.g., action verbs) are more likely to direct attention to the local properties and details of an object, whereas abstract terms (e.g., adjectives) are more likely to draw attention to the global properties of an object. These hypotheses were examined in four experiments utilizing an "unrelated tasks" paradigm. Participants either used or were exposed to abstract predicates (adjectives) versus concrete predicates (action verbs). Next, in an ostensibly unrelated second task, they were asked to complete one or more dependent measures. In the first experiment, participants used the linguistic categories in a spontaneous narrative, or they were subtly primed with these categories supraliminally (Experiments 2 and 3) or subliminally (Experiment 4). The impact of language on cognition was examined using a variety of dependent measures. These were self-report (Experiments 1 and 4), Kimchi and Palmer's (1982) perceptual global-specific focus task (Experiments 1 and 4), Isen and Daubman's (1984) categorical inclusiveness task (Experiment 2), and Kitayama, Duffy, Kawamura, and Larsen's (2003) framed line test (Experiment 3). Consistently across all four experiments and all dependent variables, the authors showed that abstract predicates induced a global perceptual focus, while concrete predicates induced a local perceptual focus.

The results of these experiments have far-reaching implications for the general debate on the linguistic relativity debate, which has always focused on specific semantic domains, such as color (e.g., Özgen, 2004), space (e.g., Majid et al., 2004), and gender (e.g., Stahlberg, Sczesny, & Braun, 2001), to name a few, predominantly in studies comparing different linguistic communities. The research reported by Stapel and Semin opens an entirely different way of looking at the language cognition interface that is made possible by taking a functional approach to language. The new look advanced in this research on the way language influences cognition is made possible by taking a use perspective. Such a perspective on language provides new insights into age-old problems. One implication is that the research by Stapel and Semin supplies the "missing link" in the culture-language-perception interface and scaffolds the relationship between cultural differences and the attention-driving function of language. This scaffold is supported by the following comparisons: First, meta-semantic features of language are demonstrated to drive attention to different features of a stimulus environment. Second, cultural differences in the relative use of the meta-semantic categories are likely to give rise to differences in the way the stimulus environment is perceived. This would suggest that a culture that is more likely to use concrete language would also be more likely to attend to contextual (local) features of a stimulus compared to cultures that use a more abstract language. Indeed, there is comparative research showing that interdependent cultures have a preference for concrete language use relative to independent cultures (e.g., Maass, Karasawa, Politi, & Suga, 2006; Semin et al., 2002). Speculatively, one could then predict that participants from interdependent cultures with a preference for concrete language use (e.g., Japan) will make more errors in a perceptual task, such as the absolute version of the framed line task, compared to participants from a culture that is independent and uses more abstract language habitually (e.g., Americans). Indeed, Kitayama et al. (2003) showed these perceptual differences for participants coming from the respective cultures.

This is the type of generalization that can be advanced by taking a functional view of the puzzle and extending the implications of such a perspective not only for one broad problem such as the regulation of social interaction as I discussed, but also the other age-old problem of the language-cognition interface from a cultural perspective. In concluding, it should be noted that these are only the early yields of a functional perspective, and the invitations that such a perspective is extending are entirely new windows on age-old problems that have kept many scholars busy.

ACKNOWLEDGMENT

This work was supported by the Royal Netherlands Academy of Arts and Sciences (ISK/4583/PAH). I would like to express my gratitude to Anna Clark and Jens Förster for their constructive input.

REFERENCES

Abelson, R. P., & Kanouse, D. E. (1966). Subjective acceptance of verbal generalizations. In S. Feldman (Ed.), *Cognitive consistency: Motivational antecedents and behavioral consequents* (pp. 171–197). New York: Academic Press.

Au, T. K. (1986). A verb is worth a thousand words: The causes and consequences of interpersonal events implicit in language. *Journal of Memory and Language, 25*, 104–122.

Berlin, B., & Kay, P. (1969). *Basic color terms: Their universality and evolution.* Berkeley, CA: University of California Press.

Boas, F. (1949). *Race, language, and culture.* New York: Macmillan.

Brown, R. (1986). Linguistic relativity. In S. Hulse & B. F. Green (Eds.), *One hundred years of psychological research in America: G. S. Hall and the John Hopkins tradition* (pp. 241–276). Baltimore, MD: John Hopkins University Press.

Brown, R., & Fish, D. (1983). The psychological causality implicit in language. *Cognition, 14*, 233–274.

Brown, R., & Lenneberg, E. H. (1954). A study in language and cognition. *Journal of Abnormal and Social Psychology, 49*, 454–462.

Brown, R., & Van Kleeck, M. H. (1989). Enough said: Three principles of explanation. *Journal of Personality and Social Psychology, 57*, 590–604.

Caramazza, A., Grober, E., Garvey, C., & Yates, J. (1977). Comprehension of anaphoric pronouns. *Journal of Verbal Learning and Verbal Behavior, 16*, 601–609.

Chafe, W. I. (1970). *Meaning and the structure of language.* Chicago: University of Chicago Press.

Clark, A., & Chalmers, R. (1997). The extended mind. *Analysis, 58*, 7–19.

De Poot, C., & Semin, G. R. (1995). Pick your verbs with care when you formulate a question! *Journal of Language and Social Psychology, 14*, 351–368.

Douglas, K. M., & Sutton, R. M. (2003). Effects of communication goals and expectancies on language abstraction. *Journal of Personality and Social Psychology, 84*, 682–696.

Douglas, K. M., & Sutton, R. M. (2006). When what you say about others says something about you: Language abstraction and inferences about describer's attitudes and goals. *Journal of Experimental Social Psychology, 42*, 500–508.

Ehrlich, K. (1980). Comprehension of pronouns. *Quarterly Journal of Experimental Psychology, 32*, 247–255.

Fiedler, K., & Semin, G. R. (1988). On the causal information conveyed by different interpersonal verbs: The role of implicit sentence context. *Social Cognition, 6*, 21–39.

Fillmore, C. J. (1968). The case for case. In E. Bach and R. G. Harms (Eds.), *Universals in linguistic theory* (pp. 1–87). New York: Holt, Rinehart and Winston.

Fillmore, C. J. (1971). Verbs of judging: An exercise in semantic description. In C. J. Fillmore & D. T. Langendoen (Eds.), *Studies in linguistic semantics* (pp. 273–296). New York: Holt, Rinehart and Winston.

Franco, F., & Arcuri, L. (1990). Effect of semantic valence on implicit causality of verbs. *British Journal of Social Psychology, 29*, 161–170.

Garnham, A., & Oakhill, J. (1985). On-line resolution of anaphoric pronouns: Effects of inference making and verb semantics. *British Journal of Psychology, 76*, 385–393.

Garnham, A., Oakhill, J., & Cruttenden, H. (1992). The role of implicit causality and gender cue in the interpretation of pronouns. *Language and Cognitive Processes, 7*, 231–255.

Garnham, A., Traxler, M., Oakhill, J., & Gernsbacher, M. A. (1996). The locus of implicit causality effects in comprehension. *Journal of Memory and Language, 35*, 517–543.

Garvey, C., & Caramazza, A. (1974). Implicit causality in verbs. *Linguistic Inquiry, 5*, 459–464.

Gauker, C. (1990). How to learn language like a chimpanzee. *Philosophical Psychology, 3,* 31–53.
Gilovich, T., & Regan, D. (1986). The actor and the experiencer: Divergent patterns of causal attribution. *Social Cognition, 4,* 342–352.
Gilson, C., & Abelson, R. P. (1965). The subjective use of inductive evidence. *Journal of Personality and Social Psychology, 2,* 301–310.
Greene, S. B., & McKoon, G. (1994). *Initiating/reacting verbs and the accessibility of discourse referents.* Unpublished master's thesis, Princeton University.
Grice, H. P. (1975). Logic and conversation. In P. Cole & J. Morgan (Eds.), Syntax and semantics (pp. 41–58). New York: Academic Press.
Hardin, C., & Banaji, M. R. (1993). The influence of language on thought. *Social Cognition, 11,* 277-308.
Hoffman, C., & Tchir, M. A. (1990). Interpersonal verbs and dispositional adjectives: The psychology of causality embodied in language. *Journal of Personality and Social Psychology, 58,* 765–778.
Hoffman, C., Lau, I. J., & Johnson, D. R. (1986). The linguistic relativity of person cognition. *Journal of Personality & Social Psychology, 51,* 1097–1105.
Holtgraves, T. M., & Raymond, S. (1995). Implicit causality and memory: Evidence for a priming model. *Personality and Social Psychology Bulletin, 21,* 5–12.
Hunt, E., & Agnoli, F. (1991). The Whorfian hypothesis: A cognitive psychology perspective, *Psychological Review, 98,* 377–389.
Hutchins, E. (1996). *Cognition in the wild.* Cambridge, MA: MIT Press.
Isen, A. M., & Daubman, K. A. (1984). The influence of affect on categorization. *Journal of Personality and Social Psychology, 47,* 1206–1217.
James, W. (1890). *Psychology.* New York: Holt.
Kanouse, D. E. (1972). Verbs as implicit quantifiers. *Journal of Verbal Learning and Verbal Behavior. 11,* 141–147.
Kashima, Y., & Kashima, E. S. (2003). Individualism, GNP, climate, and pronoun drop: Is individualism determined by affluence and climate, or does language use play a role? *Journal of Cross-Cultural Psychology, 34,* 125–134.
Kasoff, J., & Lee, J. Y. (1993). Implicit causality as implicit salience. *Journal of Personality and Social Psychology, 65,* 877–891.
Kay, P. (1996). Inter-speaker relativity. In J. J. Gumpertz & S. C. Levinson (Eds.), *Rethinking linguistic relativity* (pp. 97–114). Cambridge, MA: Cambridge University Press.
Kimchi, R., & Palmer, S. E. (1982). Form and texture in hierarchically constructed patterns. *Journal of Experimental Psychology: Human Perception and Performance, 8,* 521–535.
Kitayama, S., Duffy, S., Kawamura, T., & Larsen, J. T. (2003). Perceiving an object and its context in different cultures. *Psychological Science, 14,* 201–207.
Lenneberg, E. H. (1953). Cognition in ethnolinguistics. *Language, 29,* 463–471.
Lenneberg, E. H., & Roberts, J. M. (1956). The language of experience: A study in methodology. *International Journal of American Linguistics. 22* (part 2, Memoir 13).
Lippman, W. (1922). *Public opinion.* New York: Harcourt Brace.
Maass, A. (1999). Linguistic intergroup boas: Stereotype perpetuation through language. In M. P. Zanna (Ed.), *Advances in experimental social psychology* (vol. 11; pp. 79–122). California: Academic Press.
Maass, A., & Stahlberg, D. (1993, September). *The linguistic intergroup bias: The role of differential expectancies and in-group protective motivation.* Paper presented at the conference of EAESP, Lisbon.
Maass, A., & Arcuri, L. (1992). The role of language in the persistence of stereotypes. In G. Semin and K. Fiedler (Eds.), *Language, interaction and social cognition* (pp. 129–43). Newbury Park, CA: Sage.

Maass, A., Karasawa, M., Politi, F., & Suga, S. (2006). Do verbs and adjectives play different roles in different cultures? A cross-linguistic analysis of person representation. *Journal of Personality and Social Psychology, 90*, 734–750.

Maass, A., Milesi, A., Zabbini, S., & Stahlberg, D. (1995). The linguistic intergroup bias: Differential expectancies or in-group protection? *Journal of Personality and Social Psychology, 68*, 116–126.

Maass, A., Salvi, D., Arcuri, L., & Semin, G. (1989). Language use in intergroup contexts: The linguistic intergroup bias. *Journal of Personality and Social Psychology, 57*, 981–993.

Majid, A., Bowerman, M., Kita, S., Haun, D. B. M., & Levinson, S. C. (2004). Can language restructure cognition? The case for space. *Trends in Cognitive Sciences, 8*, 108–114.

McArthur, L. A. (1972). The how and what of why: Some determinants and consequences of causal attribution. *Journal of Personality and Social Psychology, 22*, 171–193.

McKoon, G., Greene, S. B., & Ratcliff, R. (1993). Discourse models, pronoun resolution, and the implicit causality of verbs. *Journal of Experimental Psychology: Learning, Memory, and Cognition, 19*, 1040–1052.

Mead, G. H. (1934). *The social psychology of George Herbert Mead.* Chicago: University of Chicago Press.

Özgen, E. (2004). Language, learning, and color perception. *Current Directions in Psychological Science, 13*, 95–98.

Paquette, P. (1970). Unpublished research. (Cited in McArthur 1972, p. 177).

Pulvermüller, F. (2007). Action-perception circuits as brain mechanisms of semantic grounding and embodiment. In G. R. Semin & E. R. Smith (Eds.), *Embodied grounding: Neural, affective, cognitive and social perspectives.* New York: Cambridge University Press.

Reitsma-van Rooijen, M., Semin, G. R., & van Leeuwen, E. (2007). The effects of linguistic abstraction on interpersonal distance. *European Journal of Social Psychology, 37*, 817–823.

Ricoeur, P. (1955). The model of the text: Meaningful action considered as text. *Social Research, 38*, 530–547.

Rubini, M., & Kruglanski, A.W. (1997). Brief encounters ending in estrangement: Motivated language use and interpersonal rapport in the question-answer paradigm. *Journal of Personality and Social Psychology, 72*, 1047–1060.

Rubini, M., & Semin, G. R. (1994). Language use in the context of congruent and incongruent in group behaviors. *British Journal of Social Psychology, 33*, 355–362.

Rudolph, U., & Försterling, F. (1997). The psychological causality implicit in verbs: A review. *Psychological Bulletin, 121*, 192–218.

Sapir, E. (1951). *Selected writings of Edward Sapir in language, culture, and personality.* D. G. Mandelbaum (Ed.). Berkeley: California University Press.

Semin, G. R. (1998). Cognition, language. and communication. In S. R. Fussell & R. J. Kreuz (Eds.), *Social and cognitive psychological approaches to interpersonal communication* (pp. 229–257). Hillsdale, NJ: Erlbaum.

Semin, G. R. (2000a). Agenda 2000: Communication: Language as an implementational device for cognition. *European Journal of Social Psychology, 30*, 595–612.

Semin, G. R. (2000b). Language as a cognitive and behavioral structuring resource: Question-answer exchanges. In W. Stroebe & M. Hewstone (Eds.), *European review of social psychology* (pp. 75–104). Chichester, England: Wiley.

Semin, G. R. (2001). Language and social cognition. In A. Tesser & N. Schwarz (Eds.), *Handbook of social psychology, intraindividual processes* (Vol. 1, pp. 159–180). Oxford, England: Blackwell.

Semin, G. R. (2006). Modeling the architecture of linguistic behavior: Linguistic compositionality, automaticity, and control. *Psychological Inquiry, 17*, 246–255.

Semin, G. R. (2007). Grounding communication: Synchrony. In A. Kruglanski & E. T. Higgins (Eds.), *Social psychology: Handbook of basic principles* (2nd edition; pp. 630–649). New York: Guilford Press.

Semin, G. R., & De Poot, C. J. (1997a). Bringing partiality to light: Question wording and choice as indicators of bias. *Social Cognition, 15*, 91–106.

Semin, G. R., & De Poot, C. J. (1997b). The question-answer paradigm: You might regret not noticing how a question is worded. *Journal of Personality and Social Psychology, 73*, 472–480.

Semin, G. R., & Fiedler, K. (1988). The cognitive functions of linguistic categories in describing persons: Social cognition and language. *Journal of Personality and Social Psychology, 54*, 558–568.

Semin, G. R., & Fiedler, K. (1991). The linguistic category model, its bases, applications and range. In W. Stroebe & M. Hewstone (Eds.), *European review of social psychology* (Vol. 2, pp. 1–30). Chichester, England: Wiley.

Semin, G. R., & Fiedler, K. (1992).The configuration of social interaction in interpersonal terms. In G. R. Semin & K. Fiedler (Eds.), *Language, interaction and social cognition* (pp. 82–97). London, Thousand Oaks, CA: Sage.

Semin, G. R., Görts, C., Nandram, S., & Semin-Goossens, A. (2002). Cultural perspectives on the linguistic representation of emotion and emotion events. *Cognition and Emotion, 16*, 11–28.

Semin, G. R., & Greenslade, L. (1985). Differential contributions of linguistic factors to memory based ratings: Systematizing the systematic distortion hypothesis. *Journal of Personality and Social Psychology, 49*, 1713–1723.

Semin, G. R., & Marsman, G. (1994). On the information mediated by interpersonal verbs: Event precipitation, dispositional inference and implicit causality. *Journal of Personality and Social Psychology, 67*, 836–849.

Semin, G. R., & Marsman, G. J. (2000). The mnemonic functions of interpersonal verbs: Spontaneous trait inferences. *Social Cognition, 18*, 75–96.

Semin, G. R., Rubini, M., & Fiedler, K. (1995). The answer is in the question: The effect of verb causality on locus of explanation. *Personality and Social Psychology Bulletin, 21*, 834–841.

Semin, G. R., & Smith, E. R. (Eds.) (2008) *Embodied grounding: Social, cognitive, affective, and neuroscientific approaches*. New York: Cambridge University Press.

Smith, E. R., & Semin, G. R. (2004). Socially situated cognition: Cognition in its social context. *Advances in Experimental Social Psychology, 36*, 53–117.

Stahlberg, D., Sczesny, S., & Braun, F. (2001). Name your favorite musician: Effects of masculine generics and of their alternatives in German. *Journal of Language and Social Psychology, 20*, 464–469.

Stapel, D., & Semin, G. R. (2007). The magic spell of language: linguistic categories and their perceptual consequences. *Journal of Personality and Social Psychology, 93*, 23–33.

Van Kleeck, M. H., Hillger, L. A., & Brown, R. (1988). Pitting verbal schemas against information variables in attribution. *Social Cognition, 6*, 89–106.

Vargas, P. T., Sekaquaptewa, D., & von Hippel, W. (2007) Armed only with paper and pencil: "Low-tech" measures of implicit attitudes. In N. Schwarz & B. Wittenbrink (Eds.), *Implicit measures of attitudes* (pp. 103–124). New York: Guilford Press.

Von Humboldt, W. (1999). *Linguistic variability and intellectual development*. (G. C. Buck & F. Raven, Trans.) Baltimore, MD: University of Miami Press. (Original work published 1836.)

Von Humboldt, W. (1843). Über das Entstehen der grammatischen Formen und deren Einfluß auf die Ideenentwicklung. In *Gesammelte Werke* (Vol. 3, pp. 269–306). Berlin: Reimer.

Vonk, W. (1985a). The immediacy of inferences in the understanding of pronouns. In G. Rickheit & H. Strohner (Eds.), *Inferences in text processing* (pp. 205–218). New York: North Holland.

Vonk, W. (1985b). On the purpose of reading and the immediacy of text processing. In R. Groner, G. W. Cronkie, & C. Menz (Eds.), *Eye movements and human information processing* (pp. 207–215). New York: North Holland.

Vonk, W., & Noorman, L. G. M. (1991). Inferentieprocessen bij lezen. In A. J. W. M. Thomassen, L. G. M. Noordman, & P. A. T. M. Elring (Eds.), *Lezen en begrijpen: De psychologie van het leesproces* (pp. 37–48). Amsterdam: Swets & Zeitlinger.

Vygotsky, L. S. (1978). *Mind in society. The development of higher psychological processes*. In M. Cole, V. J. Steiner, & S. Scribner (Eds.). Cambridge, MA: Harvard University Press.

Vygotsky, L. S. (1981). The instrumental method in psychology. In J. V. Wertsch (Ed.), *The concept of activity in Soviet psychology* (pp. 196–227). Armonk, NY: Sharpe.

Werkman, W. M., Wigboldus, D. H., & Semin, G. R. (1999). Children's communication of the Linguistic Intergroup Bias and its impact upon cognitive inferences. *European Journal of Social Psychology, 29*, 95-104.

Wertsch, J. (1984). The zone of proximal development: Some conceptual issues. In B. Rogoff & J. Wertsch (Eds.). *Children's learning in the zone of proximal development: New directions for child development* (pp. 7–18). San Francisco, CA: Jossey-Bass.

Wertsch, J. V. (1991). *Voices of the mind: A sociocultural approach to mediated action*. Cambridge, MA: Harvard University Press.

Wertsch, J. V. (1994). The primacy of mediated action in socio-cultural studies. *Mind, Culture, and Activity, 1*, 202–208.

Whorf, B. L. (1956). *Language, thought, and reality*. Cambridge, MA: MIT Press.

Wigboldus, D., Semin, G. R., & Spears, R. (2000). How do we communicate stereotypes? Linguistic bases and inferential consequences. *Journal of Personality and Social Psychology, 78*, 5–18.

14

Culture and Social Cognition in Human Interaction

BETTINA HANNOVER and ULRICH KÜHNEN

INTRODUCTION

This book investigates the fundamental cognitive processes that underlie social interaction. Many cognitive and social psychologists talk about "fundamental processes" as if they were universally uniform, thus independent of culture. Yet, this assumption seems questionable if one takes into account that the vast majority of what is known in psychology has been found in experiments conducted by Western, individualist researchers with Western, individualist college students as participants. In this chapter, we explore the extent to which even fundamental cognitive processes involved in social interaction are influenced and shaped by the individual's cultural background.

We open our chapter by characterizing a few basic positions around which the debates on the relation of culture and cognition have been led. Since social interaction critically depends on how individuals interpret other persons and the situations they are in, we will then show that already the subjective construal of the person and the situation differs between cultures. Finally, we describe how these differences affect social interaction.

Universalism Versus Relativism

It is a widely shared, sometimes implicit, yet often openly expressed basic assumption that psychological research must identify the basic and fundamental mechanisms of the human mind—mechanisms that all humans share. This universalist position does not reject cultural variation in psychological functioning right away. Rather, according to this view psychological research must focus on the universals underlying the apparent variability: While the basic processes of the human mind are regarded as universally uniform, cultural variability in thinking is traced back to the fact that these processes are applied to different contexts and contents in different cultures.

This perspective differs substantially in basic assumptions from the relativist one within which researchers seek to advance an understanding of the person in a historical and sociocultural context, thus ultimately discarding the possibility of comparing basic aspects of the human mind across cultures. The aim of this approach is to understand how mind and culture define and build on each other in specific contexts (Adamopoulos & Lonner, 2001).

Stability Versus Flexibility

Many cross-cultural researchers treat culture as a stable interindividual difference: A given person comes, for example, either from a collectivist or an individualist society, with culture-specific socialization processes having a profound impact on the individual's psychological functioning. Interestingly, this is somewhat at odds with the fundamental insight from social psychology that, irrespective of past experiences, the present social context influences our ways of thinking importantly. Of course, social psychologists have never denied that there are interindividual differences, but in many cases they have tried to trace these differences back to the person being exposed to different social contexts for a long time. Consequently, to understand the source of interindividual differences, one needs to understand how the present social context influences individual behavior and judgment. In summary, while cross-cultural psychologists typically investigate the consequences of interindividual differences, many social psychologists try to identify the antecedents of these differences.

Social Cognition: An Integration?

We believe that the social cognition perspective advanced in this book can contribute to resolve some aspects of the controversies that we have addressed. One of the central assumptions of this paradigm is the idea that human thinking, feeling, and action are profoundly influenced by existing knowledge that is accessible from memory in a given situation. Which knowledge becomes accessible in a given moment is due to chronic and temporary activation (Förster & Liberman, 2007; Higgins, 1996). Thus, interindividual and intraindividual variability can be traced back to the same principle: Judgments, feeling, and behavior are influenced by knowledge structures accessible in a given moment. Within this view, culture is understood as a chronic source of activation of certain pieces of knowledge, with the chronic accessibility of the respective concepts increasing with each activation. This line of argumentation has an important implication for investigating the interplay of culture and cognition: If cross-cultural variability in a given psychological domain can indeed be traced back to specific knowledge aspects being chronically more accessible for the members of one culture as compared to another, then experimentally increasing the accessibility of this knowledge structure for one group of research participants but not for another should result in analogous differences, as the cross-cultural comparison has revealed. By doing so, hypotheses about the causal impact of certain knowledge aspects being accessible can be experimentally tested. Therefore, in this chapter we review both chronic cross-cultural differences as well as experimental studies in which these knowledge structures have been temporarily primed.

CULTURE-SPECIFIC CONSTRUALS OF PERSON, SELF, AND THE SOCIAL SITUATION

In his groundbreaking research project, Hofstede (1980) analyzed value and belief surveys from employees of an international company from more than 70 countries. From this, he derived four dimensions on which cultures differ from one another: power distance (extent to which the less-powerful individual in a society considers inequality normal and accepts it); individualism (extent to which individuals consider personal goals more important than in-group goals); uncertainty avoidance (extent to which a culture's members feel threatened by unstructured situations and thus implement strict codes of behavior); and masculinity (extent to which social roles for men and women differ from each other). Each nation can be calibrated on these four key dimensions (Schimmack, Oishi, & Diener, 2005; however, see also Oyserman, Coon, & Kemmelmeier, 2002). The dimensions are usable not only for describing culture on a national level but also for calibrating cultures at the level of organizations or of ethnic, social, and occupational communities. The most important reason why Hofstede's work had such a strong impact on social psychology is, however, that the dimensions are relevant not only for describing social systems but also for describing the individual since a culture's members *experience* their culture on these dimensions. Hofstede thus offered a way of studying culture without running into the methodological and conceptual problems that had previously contributed to the reluctance of scholars committed to the empirical-experimental research paradigm to engage in doing cross-cultural studies, like confounded variables that are almost impossible to exclude when studying culture by comparing countries or not knowing on which level of abstraction to define culture (van der Vijver & Leung, 2000).

Culture-Specific Personality Patterns and Self-Construals

From the four key dimensions of culture as described by Hofstede (1980), within social psychology the individualism dimension most strongly stimulated empirical research. Individualism is opposed by collectivism, which describes cultures in which the individual gives priority to in-group goals. Hofstede's approach of defining cultures via its members' subjective experience of the social system preceded the emergence of Triandis's (1995, 2002) concept of personality patterns in individualistic versus collectivistic cultures and of Markus and Kitayama's (1991) concept of the self in independent versus interdependent cultures. Triandis differentiated idiocentristic and allocentristic personality patterns. Idiocentrism is characterized by the person defining himself or herself via own preferences, needs, and rights, mainly motivated by pursuing personal goals. In contrast, the allocentristic personality pattern describes individuals who view themselves primarily as members of their in-groups, such as their family, company, or nation. They subordinate personal goals to group goals and are most strongly motivated by duties and norms imposed by their collective.

Similarly, Markus and Kitayama (1991) distinguished between two ways in which people may construe their selves. While the independent self is primarily defined by characteristics that distinguish the person from others, like traits, attitudes, or abilities, the interdependent self incorporates elements of the social world, such as close relationships, contexts for behavior, important roles, and group memberships.

Triandis (2002) as well as Markus and Kitayama (1991) have linked their differentiations to a culture's degree of individualism versus collectivism. According to Triandis, allocentrism describes the personality attributes typically found in Eastern, collectivist cultures. In contrast, *idiocentrism* refers to personality attributes found among members of Western, individualistic cultures. Triandis (1995, 2002) focused on macro-level factors, such as ecology, form of economy, population density, standard of living, or child-rearing patterns that establish a culture's position on the individualism-collectivism continuum. A culture's degree of individualism-collectivism in turn influences the development of idiocentristic versus allocentristic personalities, evident in people's way of thinking, behaving, and experiencing of emotions.

In comparison, Markus and Kitayama (1991) put more emphasis on meso-level factors moderating culture's influence on the construal of its members' selves. They called these factors *selfways* and suggested that they comprise norms or imperatives a person has to fulfill to be or to become a good person within his or her culture (Markus, Mullally, & Kitayama, 1997). In cultures with dominating independent selfways, people most likely develop an independent self, that is, they learn to define themselves via personal attributes that distinguish them from others. In cultures with dominating interdependent selfways, people acquire interdependent self-construals, which means that they tend to define themselves primarily by their interconnectedness with others.

Culture-Specific Concepts of Personal Agency

A culture's degree of individualism versus collectivism also seems to have an impact on agency concepts held by its members. Acquiring a sense of agency can be considered a universal human task. However, while traditionally psychologists have used the terms *autonomy* and *agency* interchangeably, there is a growing understanding that different *cultures* encourage the development of different implicit theories of agency, implying that many popular theories in psychology may rest on too narrow Western models of agency.

As one of the first, Joan Miller (2003) questioned whether attempts to fulfill social obligations in fact impede personal growth and the development of an authentic sense of self and raised doubts whether we act with agency only if we create our life on our own terms and not by living up to society's expectations. Consistent with these considerations, Morris, Menon, and Ames (2001) reported evidence according to which Western cultures conceptualize agency as a property of the individual, whereas Eastern cultures see the group (or nonhuman actors like deities or fate) as the origin of agency. Kitayama and Uchida (2004) introduced the notion of interdependent agency: They assumed that while members of Western, individualist cultures construe personal agency in reference to privately held attitudes, preferences, and judgments, members of Eastern, collectivist cultures define personal agency in reference to attitudes, preferences, and expectations held by relevant others. As a result, Westerners experience agency as fully detached from their social surroundings, whereas Easterners experience it as interdependent with others in their social surroundings.

Culture-Specific Concepts of the Social Situation

Coinciding with culture-specific construals of person and self, people have perceptions and cognitive representations of the social situation that reflect the salient characteristics of their culture. Kitayama, Markus, Matsumoto, and Norasakkunkit (1997) assumed that an apparently identical social situation may have different meanings for members of different cultures. For instance, while in individualistic cultures people shall consider situations that offer a chance to engage in self-enhancement as particularly self-relevant, in collectivistic cultures failure situations have particular importance because they are highly diagnostic about where a person has failed to meet his or her reference group's expectations. The authors provided American and Japanese students with a total of 400 situations and asked them to indicate whether they considered them relevant to their self-esteem. As expected, while Americans more likely chose success situations than failure situations as relevant, the opposite was true for Japanese. Also, Americans judged success situations as having a stronger impact on their self-esteem than failure situations. In contrast, Japanese assumed that the failure situations would have a stronger negative impact on their self-esteem than the success situations would increase it. These results support the assumption that a culture's individualism or collectivism influences the way in which its members collectively elaborate and comprehend definitions of social situations.

CULTURAL SOCIAL COGNITION UNDERLYING SOCIAL INTERACTION

The construal of the person and the self as well as the construal of the social situation shape the nature and outcome of social interaction in many ways. In this section, we review empirical evidence for cultural variation in self-evaluation and regulation, social perception, and direct social interaction.

Self-Evaluation and Self-Regulation

Both the differentiation in personality patterns (Triandis, 2005) and the differentiation between independent and interdependent selves (Markus & Kitayama, 1991) have strongly stimulated empirical research, with the findings attesting to the value of this differentiation for explaining cross-cultural variations in self-enhancement, self-esteem, self-presentation, and self-regulation. Some of the empirical studies illustrating this are reported next.

Culture-Dependent Variations in Self-Enhancement, Self-Esteem, and Self-Presentation

Psychologists have always assumed that striving to feel good about oneself is a universal force behind human behavior. This assumption is the topic of some debate, however, since first evidence was provided that people from collectivistic cultures report lower self-esteem and psychological well-being than Westerners (e.g., Diener, Diener, & Diener, 1995; Kitayama et al., 1997). Similarly, self-enhancing biases were found to be elusive in studies conducted within collectivistic cultures (e.g., Brown, 2003; Heine, 2003).

Four different explanations for these cross-cultural differences can be distinguished: (a) The self-enhancement motive is less pronounced or nonexistent in collectivistic cultures. (b) Individualistic cultures encourage the expression of the self-enhancement motive, whereas collectivistic cultures reinforce modest self-presentations, such that the differences in reported self-esteem and affect are due to different self-presentation strategies. (c) Depending on culture, the self-enhancement motive expresses itself by different means or under different circumstances. (d) Depending on culture, people self-enhance on different dimensions, with conventional scales or measures tapping individualistic dimensions only.

Concerning the first explanation, to test the notion that the strengths of the self-enhancement motive vary cross culturally, several studies investigated whether self-enhancement biases are differently related to self-esteem or well-being in Western versus Eastern cultures: If self-enhancement is universally psychologically beneficial, it should have positive effects on self-esteem and well-being irrespective of the person's surrounding culture. In support of this assumption, Kurman (2003) found that *self-enhancement* measures were significantly and positively related to *self-esteem* and to indices of well-being in samples from both collectivistic and individualistic cultures. Similarly, Kobayashi and Brown (2003) found in the Japanese as well as in the American culture that people with high self-esteem displayed stronger self-enhancement biases than people with low self-esteem. The correspondence between self-enhancement and self-esteem found by Kurman (2003) and Kobayashi and Brown (2003) suggests that the self-enhancement motive operates irrespective of culture.

For the second explanation of these cross-cultural differences, from the concept of selfways (Markus et al., 1997) it can be inferred that independents should be very much concerned with expressing positively valenced internal attributes, while interdependents are attuned to identifying personal shortcomings and to presenting themselves in a modest manner. To scrutinize self-presentation strategies that may be responsible for the cross-cultural differences in reported self-esteem and in self-enhancement biases, some studies made use of the differentiation between implicit and explicit self-esteem. Implicit measures tap automatic, nonconscious evaluations of the self that become apparent in spontaneous reactions to self-relevant stimuli, for instance, letters contained in one's name. While self-representation goals may guide people's self-description on explicit measures, implicit measures can be interpreted as unaffected by self-presentation strategies.

Kitayama and Karasawa (1997) presented first evidence for positive implicit self-esteem in Japanese. Positive feelings attached to the self became evident in their Japanese participants when they demonstrated a liking for letters included in their personal names and numbers corresponding to month and day of their birthday, significantly more than for the remaining letters or numbers. Differentiating participants within culture according to their self-construal as independent or interdependent, Pöhlmann, Hannover, Kühnen, and Birkner (2002) found interdependents to report lower self-esteem on an explicit measure but no difference between the two self-construal groups when self-esteem was measured implicitly via the letter-liking technique. Hannover, Birkner, and Pöhlmann (2006) went one step further and manipulated self-esteem in independent and interdependent participants via a priming of self-knowledge that was either consistent or inconsistent with the ideal independent self (consisting of autonomous and context-independent self-knowledge) or the ideal interdependent self (consisting of social and context-dependent self-knowledge). On both explicit and implicit self-esteem measures, participants with independent construal indicated higher self-esteem following a priming of autonomous or context-independent knowledge than after a priming of social or context-dependent knowledge. The opposite pattern was observed in participants with interdependent construal.

Results of these studies suggest that self-liking and self-enhancement motives prevail, irrespective of a person's surrounding culture and irrespective of a person's self as independent or interdependent. However, the motives only become obvious once restrictions that normally discourage their expression in collectivistic cultures or in interdependents are loosened or eliminated, for instance, when a subtle priming is used to manipulate self-esteem or when implicit measures are used that tap automatic, nonconscious evaluations of the self.

Regarding the third explanation, this explanation assumes that individualists and collectivists self-enhance by different means or under different situational circumstances. Some studies suggest that collectivists use others to indirectly boost their self-esteem. Comparing Japanese versus Asian Canadian and European Canadian college students, Endo, Heine, and Lehman (2000) found that while all three groups viewed their own relationships with best friend, closest family member, and romantic partner as more positive than those of their peers, only Japanese judged themselves more negatively than the different relationship partners. Possibly, by enhancing others with whom they are interconnected, collectivists indirectly express appreciation for themselves: They describe themselves positively while viewing themselves through others' lenses.

Takata (2003) found that one crucial determinant of whether *self-enhancement* occurs is the quality of the interpersonal relationship in a given situation. Takata gave students false feedback on an ostensible performance test. Specifically, they received information about their personal performance and about the scores obtained by others. The information was provided in such a manner that it would be difficult for participants to find out whether they had performed better or worse than the average person. Japanese tended to be *self*-critical, so that they incorrectly concluded that they had done worse than average when they were under a competition-free situation and when they felt some affective bonds to others. However, if the situation was competitive with others to whom they were not affectively related, they engaged in *self-enhancement* as much as American participants.

In summarizing, this explanation suggests that the striving to self-enhance is a universal principle that, depending on culture, expresses itself through different means (upgrading self versus others) and depending on the quality of the interpersonal relationship constituting the social situation.

The final explanation assumes that people self-enhance on those dimensions that are imposed as particularly important by their surrounding culture. Hence, while the motive for self-enhancement may be universally valid, according to culture there is variation in what makes people feel good about themselves or which aspects of their personality people consider particularly important and positive.

While in individualistic cultures people gain self-esteem from being unique, from achieving highly, and from outperforming others, in collectivistic cultures self-esteem mainly rests on the quality of one's interpersonal relations. Consistently, Pöhlmann et al. (2002) found implicit self-esteem in participants with independent self-construal to be more positive the higher they rated their personal abilities, whereas interdependents' self-esteem increased along with participants' opinion of the quality of their personal relationships. Similarly, Sedikides, Gaertner, and Toguchi (2003) found that independents and Americans self-enhance on autonomous traits (e.g., "unconstrained") and behaviors (e.g., "engage in open conflict with your group"), whereas interdependents and Japanese self-enhance on social traits (e.g., "agreeable") and behaviors (e.g., "follow the rules by which your group operates"). Self-enhancement was mediated by attribute importance such that independents regarded autonomous self-attributes as particularly important, whereas interdependents considered social self-attributes to be the most important.

Results of these studies suggest that while finding and confirming positive internal attributes of the self are the most important basis of a person's self-worth among independents, being positively interconnected with others is the prominent source from which self-esteem arises for interdependents.

Culture-Dependent Variations in Self-Regulation A central interindividual difference variable in self-regulation is the self-regulatory focus. Whereas some people focus on promotion (i.e., on gains and ideals), others pursue prevention goals: They try to avoid losses and to fulfill obligations imposed on them by others (Higgins, 1997). Lee, Aaker, and Gardner (2000) have linked regulatory focus to culture. They suggested that independency goals such as being positively different from others are more consistent with the self-regulatory pattern of promotion entailing the pursuit of gains and aspiration toward ideals. In contrast, the interdependency goals of fitting in and maintaining interconnectedness with others are more consistent with the self-regulatory focus of prevention entailing concerns of avoidance of losses and the fulfillment of obligations. Lee et al. (2000) provided participants with scenarios that either contained promotion-framed information emphasizing potential gains (e.g., "If you pick Alternative A, you will keep $400 worth of prizes") or prevention-framed information emphasizing potential losses (e.g., "If you pick Alternative A, you will have to give up $800 worth of prizes"). Independents perceived promotion-framed scenarios more important than prevention-framed ones, whereas the opposite applied to interdependents. In an additional study, Lee et al. (2000) replicated these findings using independence-interdependence not as a chronically accessible person variable but as a situationally accessible context variable. These findings are consistent with the notion that self-regulatory focus varies according to self-construal. Whereas the independent person focuses on his or her capabilities and on potential gains, to outperform others or to achieve positive distinctiveness from others, the interdependent person is attuned to not making mistakes to fulfill obligations imposed by others and thus focuses on negative self-aspects and on possible losses.

The Social Perceiver: How We Think About Ourselves Influences How We Think in General

The Self and Social Information Processing A variety of differences between the members of different cultural backgrounds can consistently be traced back to their members defining the self either in independent or interdependent terms. While the individual construal of the self is a result of being socialized in either individualistic or collectivistic societies, the self in turn shapes the ways in which we think, feel, and interact with others. This assumption was first put forward by Markus and Kitayama (1991), who proposed that the way identity is formed mediates the impact of culture on cognition. Yet, the exact mechanisms by which both kinds of self-construal affect information processing have only begun to be understood. In our own work, we have proposed the semantic-procedural-interface (SPI) model of the self, which aims at describing these mechanisms in more detail (e.g., Hannover & Kühnen, 2004; Hannover, Pöhlmann, Roeder, Springer, & Kühnen, 2005; Kühnen, Hannover, & Schubert, 2001). The model suggests to distinguish two such mechanisms.

One mechanism refers to the different semantic content areas from which independent and interdependent self-construals arise, being autonomous or respectively social. The most frequently used self-knowledge is most likely applied when processing newly incoming information. Accordingly, this information can be expected to be assimilated toward autonomous contents to the extent that autonomous self-knowledge is chronically accessible and toward social contents to the extent that social self-knowledge is chronically accessible for that particular person. In our model, we refer to this as the *semantic application mechanism*.

To illustrate this mechanism, in a study by Olvermann, Metz-Göckel, Hannover, and Pöhlmann (2004), participants with either independent or interdependent self-construal were asked to freely describe seven ambiguous pictures taken from a projective measure of motivation. As predicted by the SPI model's semantic application mechanism, independents assimilated the ambiguous information contained in the stimulus material toward the contents of accessible independent self-knowledge: They used categories indicating personal goals to achieve success and independency ("achievement motives") more frequently than did interdependents. In contrast, interdependents' interpretations of the ambiguous stimulus material were assimilated toward the contents of accessible interdependent self-knowledge: They used descriptions indicative of personal goals to affiliate with others ("affiliation motives") more frequently than independents.

In addition to the semantic application mechanism, the SPI model proposes that interdependent and independent self-construals promote different procedural modes of thinking. This is expected to be the case because both types of self-knowledge differ not only with respect to their semantic content but also with respect to their degree of context dependency. In particular, in cultures fostering independence, individuals tend to behave consistently across situations and over time, that is, to be the same irrespective of the social situation. We therefore assume that what predominates in independent construal is self-knowledge that describes the person irrespective of any qualifying contextual circumstances. Such *context-independent self-knowledge* is represented independently of mental representations of particular social contexts (e.g., "I am yielding, regardless of contextual circumstances"). In contrast, in cultures that foster interdependent selfways people are trying to adjust their behavior to changing contexts, thus achieving the cultural mandate of being interrelated with others and meeting their expectations. We therefore expect self-knowledge that is represented beneath the mental representation of particular social contexts or particular other persons to dominate in the interdependent construal. Such *context-dependent self-knowledge* describes the person as part of a particular social context (e.g., "I am yielding toward my daughter Louise, but I am demanding toward my coworkers"). In our SPI model, we assume that the cognitive information-processing style coinciding with the activation of autonomous self-knowledge is context independent. In contrast, the activation of social self-knowledge is expected to induce a context-dependent mode of thinking. The SPI model refers to this as the *procedural application mechanism*.

We have found empirical evidence from cross-cultural studies as well as from experimental priming studies that access to independent or interdependent self-knowledge respectively fosters context-independent or context-dependent information processing (for a review, see Hannover & Kühnen, 2004). For instance, in a series of studies, Kühnen, Hannover, and Schubert (2001) primed independent or interdependent self-knowledge and used semantic-free dependent variables that were sensitive for the degree of context dependency of accessible knowledge only. One such variable is the capability to discern simple figures from more complex geometrical patterns into which they are embedded, a task that is achieved more quickly the more context independently a person processes the material. Supporting the SPI model's assumption, we found (a) that individualist culture members outperformed collectivist ones on this test (Kühnen, Hannover, & Schubert, 2001), and (b) that a priming of independent self-knowledge (participants were asked to think about what makes them different from their family and friends; in the interdependency-priming condition, participants had to think about what they have in common with family and friends; Trafimow, Triandis, & Goto, 1991) facilitated identifying the embedded figures (Kühnen, Hannover, Roeder, et al., 2001).

Similarly, Masuda and Nisbett (2001) found that collectivists are more likely to bind objects perceptually to the surrounding background and are subsequently better in spontaneously recalling background information than individualists are. Conceptually equivalent findings have been obtained by Kühnen and Oyserman (2002), who primed either independent (participants had to circle all pronouns in a short text, most of which represented the independent self, such as "I" or "mine"; Gardner, Gabriel, & Lee, 1999) or interdependent self-knowledge (pronouns mostly referred to the interdependent self: "we," "our," etc.; Gardner et al.) before giving participants a memory task. Participants had to encode a picture showing a square frame including 28 simple items, such as a house or a moon. Next, the stimulus material was taken away, and participants were asked to write down in each cell which items had been presented at the respective spot. Participants did not know that they would have to recall not only the objects they had seen, but also exactly where in the context of the original picture the respective item had been located.

Interdependence-primed participants (rather than independence-primed ones) were expected to process the stimulus material in a context-dependent way by relating the objects to the context in which they were presented. If so, these participants should be more likely to recall this incidentally encoded contextual information. This hypothesis was supported in that interdependence-primed participants recalled more items at their old position than independence-primed participants.

Together, these studies showed that independent and interdependent self-knowledge affects information processing via both the semantic and the procedural application mechanisms. As described in this chapter, the two mechanisms may in turn influence social interaction.

Attribution: Perception of the Acting Person Many tendencies in social perceivers' judgments about the acting person are traceable to implicit theories of causality that are acquired from socialization and hence differ cross culturally. Analyzing extensive ethnographic and psychological data from different cultures, Choi, Nisbett, and Norenzayan (1999) found that, irrespective of culture, people are very likely to engage in dispositional explanations. Culture-specific differences only exist in that (a) Easterners have a more holistic concept of the person embedded in a social context, (b) Easterners conceive of dispositions as more malleable, and (c) Easterners consider the context of behavior more important and therefore are more likely to also engage in situational attributions. As a result, while members of Western independence cultures prefer dispositional explanations of behavior, members of Eastern interdependence cultures apply both dispositional and situational explanations.

These conclusions are consistent with the results of Chiu, Hong, and Dweck (1997), who found that people's tendency to use traits as the basic unit of analysis in social perception is generalizable across cultures. Chiu et al. scrutinized the origin of this tendency and were able to show that the extent to which individuals use trait-relevant information to make future behavioral predictions or to make inferences from behavior is dependent on the extent to which they conceive of traits as malleable. Thus, Easterners' conception of traits as more malleable may explain why they show weaker lay dispositionalism than Westerners.

In a widely recognized article, Nisbett, Peng, Choi, and Norenzayan (2001) embedded cross-cultural differences in attributional inferences to what they called culture-specific "systems of thought." While Easterners think holistically, attending to the entire field and assigning causality to it, Westerners engage in more analytic thinking: To understand behavior, they focus their attention on the focal information and apply rules, such as formal logic. Nisbett et al. (2001) suggested that analytic versus holistic thinking is embedded in different naïve metaphysical systems, that is, that the two cognitive processes are traceable to different epistemological theories.

Going beyond the suggestion that lay theories may guide people's attributions, other studies have raised the question whether culture's influence extends to automatic aspects of the attribution process. In an endeavor to disentangle culture's influence on automatic and controlled mechanisms of attributional inferences, Lieberman, Jarcho, and Obayashi (2005) hypothesized that Easterners and Westerners would not differ in their automatic attributions but only show different controlled corrections. They suggested that the attribution process starts with an inferential goal that can either be dispositional (e.g., "What is this person like?") or situational (e.g., "What is this situation like?"), with these goals activating a corresponding automatic inference process. Subsequently, if the person has enough cognitive capacity and is motivated, a theory-driven controlled correction process can be initiated, as a result of which the person takes constraint information into account.

Lieberman et al. (2005) made use of the fact that people who are cognitively busy do not have the capacity to engage in inferential correction. Their findings showed that when under cognitive load, attributions did not differ between Easterners and Westerners. In contrast, while not under cognitive load, culture-specific attributional theories guiding controlled correction processes became obvious. Specifically, Easterners applied a situational attributional theory when correcting an automatic attribution (no matter if the content of the constraint information should have promoted stronger dispositional inferences or stronger situational inferences), while Westerners corrected their attributions according to the normative rules of inference (augmentation vs. discounting). As a result, Easterners showed weaker dispositional and stronger situational attributions than Westerners.

From Perception to Behavior

Cultural influences on social behavior are manifold and vary along a continuum of complexity, starting from uncontrollable, presumably unintentional processes, to motivated and highly complex issues such as communication.

Automatic Processes Involved in Social Interaction
By far, not all components of social interaction are consciously controlled and intentional. In fact, if individuals were to make deliberate decisions about each and every potentially

relevant act, social interaction would be virtually impossible. Automatic processes facilitate social interaction. One of these phenomena is *mimicry,* that is, the spontaneous behavioral imitation of others in the social context, for example, by unintentionally taking similar body positions, language styles, gestures, or mimicking. Van Baaren, Maddux, Chartrand, de Bouter, and van Knippenberg (2003) predicted that since the tendency to mimic others is an unrecognized influence of the social context, this tendency might be increased by the context-dependent processing mode coinciding with the accessibility of interdependent self-knowledge. To test this assumption, after being primed for independent or interdependent self-knowledge, their research participants interacted with a confederate on an irrelevant listening task during which the confederate played with a pen. The participants' behavior was coded with regard to the extent to which they mimicked the confederate's behavior. As expected, participants in the interdependent-self prime condition mimicked more than those in the independent-self prime condition. In another study, van Baaren et al. (2003) found parallel results in a cross-cultural investigation: Collectivist (i.e., Asian) participants were more likely to mimic the experimenter's behavior than were individualist (i.e., American) research participants.

Another unobtrusive influence on social interaction is the personal distance individuals prefer. While some early studies provided episodic evidence that individualism is associated with a need for greater personal space than collectivism (e.g., Watson, 1970), Holland, Roeder, van Baaren, Brandt, and Hannover (2004) experimentally tested the causal impact that independence versus interdependence of the self may have on behavior conducive to interpersonal proximity. They found that, compared to control participants, participants who were primed with the independent (or personal) self sat farther away from where they anticipated another person would sit in a waiting room than participants primed with the interdependent (or social) self. In another study, the authors found that chronic self-construal of participants predicted the seating distance in dyadic settings: Greater independence was associated with greater spatial distance during the interaction. Together, the studies provided evidence that self-construal activation automatically influences interpersonal behavior as reflected in the actual distance between the self and others.

Motivated Behavior   While interacting with others, we are driven by certain motives and goals. Related to the study of culture-dependent variations in agency concepts, we have come to an understanding that, depending on culture, individuals may be driven by different forces: While people from individualistic *cultures* are intrinsically motivated to the extent that they perceive their behaviors as self-initiated and aim for the achievement of personal goals, people from collectivistic cultures are more motivated the more they perceive their actions as in accordance with the expectations of others and as serving the attainment of the collective's goals.

Support for these assumptions comes from studies by Iyengar and Lepper (1999). They questioned the notion that provision of choice is universally linked to an increased level of intrinsic motivation: Whereas for independents exerting choice provides an opportunity to express unique internal attributes and to pursue personal preference fulfillment, for interdependents contexts offering choice may be less rewarding because they might be perceived as imperatives to identify choices that are in accordance with others' expectations. Hence, for interdependents, having to choose may even pose a threat because their personal preferences could prove to diverge from those of their reference group, and they might therefore prefer to accept choices expressed by others.

Iyengar and Lepper (1999) asked Anglo American and Asian American grade-school children to solve anagrams. While in one experimental condition children could choose the anagrams they were to try resolving, in a different condition they were told that the category of anagrams they had been given had been chosen for them by their mothers. Results showed that in the personal choice condition, Anglos outperformed Asians, whereas in the mom choice condition Asians performed better than Anglos. During a free-play period following participation in the personal choice condition, Anglos spent more time on the anagrams than Asians. In contrast, following participation in the mom condition, Asians spent more time on the anagrams during a free-play period than Anglos. These findings suggest that the link between the provision of choice and intrinsic motivation is not universally applicable but bound to individualistic cultures.

Communication Communication is at the heart of social interaction. The way the members of different cultures communicate varies in many ways. Most obviously, they communicate differently because they use different languages. However, not only *what* is typically said in a given context varies between cultures, but also the *way* in which messages are typically conveyed. Hall (1976) differentiated high-context cultures from low-context cultures according to particular features of language use. A low-context culture is one in which the intended message is largely conveyed directly and in openly spoken words. High-context cultures, on the other hand, communicate more indirectly; meaning is conveyed implicitly and has to be inferred by the listener on the basis of past experience with the speaker, the setting of that particular communication, and other contextual cues. Hall classified numerous cultures according to these categories. A later reanalysis of his findings by Gudykunst, Ting-Toomey, and Chua (1988) showed that those societies that Hall had classified as high-context cultures were, according to Hofstede's differentiation, collectivistic ones, and the low-context cultures were individualistic ones.

To more directly investigate the relation between individualism-collectivism and communication style, Gudykunst, Gao, and Franklyn-Stokes (1996) constructed a self-report measurement of low-context versus high-context communication and differentiated eight relevant aspects: the ability to infer others' meaning, the use of direct versus ambiguous communication, interpersonal sensibility, use of dramatic communication, use of feelings to guide behavior, openness in discourse, precision, and positive perception of silence. In addition, Gudykunst et al. measured the participants' self-construal as either independent or interdependent. The results showed that interdependence of the self positively predicted sensitivity and negatively predicted favorable attitudes toward silence. Independent self-construals, however, positively predicted use of dramatic, open, and precise communication.

In sum, self-construals were found to mediate the high-context versus low-context styles of communication of individualistic versus collectivistic cultures.

As described, one important feature of high-context communication is to be attentive to the intended meaning of a speaker's utterance, even if this is not openly expressed—thus, in a way, to "read others' minds." Haberstroh, Oyserman, Schwarz, Kühnen, and Ji (2002) argued that collectivists might accomplish the goal of reading others' minds by paying closer attention to principles of cooperative conversational conduct, for instance, the rule that speakers should provide information that is new to the recipient rather than reiterate information that the recipient already has. To test this assumption, Haberstroh et al. asked research participants two partially redundant questions, one question pertaining to a specific aspect of the participants' lives (i.e., satisfaction with their academic life) and a general question, which also included the specific aspects (i.e., general life satisfaction). If the specific question is asked before the general one, answering the latter one as if it were primarily pertaining to the same life domain (i.e., academic life satisfaction) as the first question would violate the nonredundancy norm. Thus, the closer participants pay attention to this norm, the lower their answers to the two questions should correlate. As predicted, Haberstroh et al. in a first study found lower correlations between the two answers for interdependence-primed participants than independence-primed ones. In a second study, this finding was conceptually replicated with participants from either an individualist (Germany) or a collectivist (China) cultural background. Together, these results showed that if interdependent self-knowledge is accessible (due to a person's collectivist background or due to situational priming), participants are more likely to infer the pragmatic meaning of a speaker's utterance by monitoring its preceding context than if independent self-knowledge prevails.

SUMMARY AND OUTLOOK

Today, it almost seems like a truism to us that cultural patterns should lead people to attach different meanings to social situations and to view others and themselves through different lenses, such that social interaction varies considerably across cultures. If we look back through time, however, we realize that it was only recently that social psychologists came to agree with each other about the notion that the individual can only be understood if studied as an integral member of a given cultural system and not as an isolated entity. Even though Tajfel (1972) had already criticized social psychology in the early 1970s for not taking cultural influences on behavior into account, mainstream research did not reflect culture's relevance until the mid-1980s. At the time, the social cognition paradigm emerged, integrating social psychology issues—like culture—into the paradigm of information processing (Strack, 1988).

In this chapter, we argued that with the ascent of the social cognition paradigm cross-cultural research reached a qualitatively new stage. In applying research tools from cognitive psychology to the study of the social situation, the social cognition paradigm lends itself to go beyond only describing cross-cultural differences in social interaction by providing overarching principles of explanation of a culture's influence on its members. One of the central assumptions of the social cognition paradigm is that human thinking, feeling, and action are profoundly influenced by existing knowledge that is accessible from memory in a given situation. In our chapter, we offered both studies from cross-cultural research and from experimental research supporting the notion that social interaction within a given cultural context is influenced by mental construals people have about the social situation, the person, and the self, with the accessibility of these knowledge structures dependent on the frequency of activation that varies according to culture.

For the different phases of the social interaction process, we highlighted empirical evidence that cultural differences are mediated by chronically accessible mental categories. We started out with the self and the social perceiver as the protagonists constituting a social interaction context. Cross-cultural variations in the processing of social information and in the construal of the acting person were traced back to the more frequent use either of knowledge structures that contain autonomous contents and are not bound to any particular social context (in independence or individualist cultures) or of knowledge structures that consist of social contents and are bound to a particular context (in interdependence or collectivist cultures). Via the semantic and the procedural application mechanisms described in the SPI model (e.g., Hannover & Kühnen, 2004; Kühnen, Hannover, & Schubert, 2001), the accessibility of knowledge of one kind or the other has an impact on social interaction. As a result, automatic behavior like mimicry or regulation of interpersonal distance, motivated behavior and decision making, and communication patterns differ depending on the cultural context within which the behavior is enacted. While cultures differ with respect to the frequency with which they chronically activate either autonomous and context-independent knowledge structures or social and context-dependent ones, there is also variation within cultures—and even within individuals—due to factors influencing the situational accessibility of knowledge of one kind or the other. Hence, the social cognition paradigm opened the arena to test culture on its causal impact on individuals in the context of social interactions.

REFERENCES

Adamopoulos, J., & Lonner, W. J. (2001). Culture at a crossroad: Historical perspectives and theoretical analysis. In D. Matsumoto (Ed.), *The handbook of culture and psychology* (pp. 11–34). New York: Oxford University Press.

Brown, J. (2003). The self-enhancement motive in collectivistic cultures. The rumors of my death have been greatly exaggerated. *Journal of Cross-Cultural Psychology, 34*, 603–605.

Chiu, C., Hong, Y., & Dweck. C. (1997). Lay dispositionism and implicit theories of personality. *Journal of Personality and Social Psychology, 73*, 19–30.

Choi, I., Nisbett, R. E., & Norenzayan, A. (1999). Causal attribution across cultures: Variation and universality. *Psychological Bulletin, 1*, 47–63.

Diener, E., Diener, M., & Diener, C. (1995). Factors predicting the subjective well-being of nations. *Journal of Personality and Social Psychology, 69*, 851–865.

Endo, Y., Heine, S., & Lehman, D. (2000). Culture and positive illusions in close relationships: How my relationships are better than yours. *Personality and Social Psychology Bulletin, 26*, 1571–1586.

Förster, J. & Liberman, N. (2007). Knowledge activation. In A. W. Kruglanski & E. T. Higgins (Eds.), *Social psychology: Handbook of basic principles* (2nd ed., pp. 201–231). New York: Guilford Press.

Gardner, W., Gabriel, S., & Lee, A. (1999). "I" value freedom but "we" value relationships: Self-construal priming mirrors cultural differences in judgment. *Psychological Science, 10*, 321–326.

Gudykunst, W. B., Gao, G., & Franklyn-Stokes, A. (1996). Self-monitoring and concern for social appropriateness in China and England. In J. Pandey, D. Sinha, & D. P. Bhawuk (Eds.), *Asian contributions to cross-cultural psychology* (pp. 255–267). New Delhi: Sage.

Gudykunst, W. B., Ting-Toomey, S., & Chua, E. (1988). *Culture and interpersonal communication*. Newbury Park, CA: Sage.

Haberstroh, S., Oyserman, D., Schwarz, N., Kühnen, U., & Ji, L. (2002). Is the interdependent self a better communicator than the independent self? Self-construal and the observation of conversational norms. *Journal of Experimental Social Psychology 38*, 323–329.

Hall, E. T. (1976). *Beyond Culture*. New York: Doubleday.

Hannover, B., Birkner, N., & Pöhlmann, C. (2006). Self-discrepancy and self-esteem in people with independent or interdependent self-construal. *European Journal of Social Psychology, 36*, 119–133.

Hannover, B., & Kühnen, U. (2004). Culture, context, and cognition: The semantic procedural interface model of the self. *European Review of Social Psychology, 15*, 297–333.

Hannover, B., Pöhlmann, C., Roeder, U., Springer, A., & Kühnen, U. (2005). Eine erweiterte Version des Semantisch-Prozeduralen Interface-Modells des Selbst: Funktion des mentalen Interface und Implikationen des Modells für motivierte Prozesse [An updated version of the semantic procedural interface model of the self: Mental interface and the model's implications for motivated cognition]. *Psychologische Rundschau, 56*, 99–112.

Heine, S. (2003). Making sense of East Asian self-enhancement. *Journal of Cross Cultural Psychology, 34*, 596–602.

Higgins, E. T. (1996). Knowledge activation: Accessibility, applicability, and salience. In E. T. Higgins & A. W. Kruglanski (Eds.), *Social psychology: Handbook of basic principles* (pp. 133–168). New York: Guilford Press.

Higgins, E. T. (1997). Beyond pleasure and pain. *American Psychologist, 52*, 1280–1300.

Hofstede, G. (1980). *Culture's consequences: Intentional differences in work-related values*. Beverly Hills, CA: Sage.

Holland, R., Roeder, U., van Baaren, R., Brandt, A., & Hannover, B. (2004). Don't stand so close to me: The effects of self-construal on interpersonal closeness. *Psychological Science, 15*, 237–242.

Iyengar, S., & Lepper, M. (1999). Rethinking the value of choice: A cultural perspective on intrinsic motivation. *Journal of Personality and Social Psychology, 76*, 349–366.

Kitayama, S., & Karasawa, M. (1997). Implicit self-esteem in Japan: Name letters and birthday numbers. *Personality and Social Psychology Bulletin, 23*, 736–742.

Kitayama, S., Markus, H. R., Matsumoto, H., & Norasakkunkit, V. (1997). Individual and collective processes in the construction of the self: Self-enhancement in the United States and self-criticism in Japan. *Journal of Personality and Social Psychology, 72*, 1245–1267.

Kitayama, S., & Uchida, Y. (2004). Interdependent agency: An alternative system for action. In R. Sorrentino, D. Cohen, J. M. Olson, & M. P. Zanna (Eds.), *Culture and social behavior: The Ontario Symposium* (Vol. 10, pp. 134–164). Mahwah, NJ: Erlbaum.

Kobayashi, C., & Brown, J. (2003). Self-esteem and self-enhancement in Japan and America. *Journal of Cross-Cultural Psychology, 34*, 567–580.

Kühnen, U., Hannover, B., Roeder, U., Schubert, B., Shah, A., Upmeyer, A., et al. (2001). Cross-cultural variations in identifying embedded figures: Comparisons from the US, Germany, Russia, and Malaysia. *Journal of Cross Cultural Psychology, 32*, 365–371.

Kühnen, U., Hannover, B., & Schubert, B. (2001). The semantic-procedural interface model of the self. The role of self-knowledge for context-dependent versus context-independent modes of thinking. *Journal of Personality and Social Psychology, 80*, 397–409.

Kühnen, U., & Oyserman, D. (2002). Thinking about the self influences thinking in general: Cognitive consequences of salient self-concept. *Journal of Experimental Social Psychology, 38*, 492–499.

Kurman, J. (2003). Why is self-enhancement low in certain collectivist cultures? An investigation of two competing explanations. *Journal of Cross-Cultural Psychology, 34*, 496–520.

Lee, A., Aaker, J., & Gardner, W. (2000). The pleasures and pains of distinct self-construals: The role of interdependence in regulatory focus. *Journal of Personality and Social Psychology, 78*, 1122–1134.

Lieberman, M., Jarcho, J., & Obayashi, J. (2005). Attributional inference across cultures: Similar automatic attributions and different controlled corrections. *Personality and Social Psychology Bulletin, 31*, 889–901.

Markus, H., & Kitayama, S. (1991). Culture and the self: Implications for cognition, emotion, and motivation. *Psychological Review, 98*, 224–253.

Markus, H. R., Mullally, P., & Kitayama, S. (1997). Selfways: Diversity in modes of cultural participation. In U. Neisser & D. A. Jopling (Eds.), *The conceptual self in context: Culture, experience, self-understanding* (pp. 13–61). Cambridge, England: Cambridge University Press.

Masuda, T., & Nisbett, R. E. (2001). Attending holistically versus analytically: Comparing the context sensitivity of Japanese and Americans. *Journal of Personality and Social Psychology, 81*, 922–934.

Miller, J. G. (2003). Culture and agency: Implications for psychological theories of motivation and social development. In V. Murphy-Berman & J. Berman (Eds.), *Cross-cultural differences in perspectives on the self* (pp. 76–116). Lincoln: University of Nebraska Press.

Morris, M., Menon, D., & Ames, D. (2001). Culturally conferred conceptions of agency: A key to social perception of persons, groups, and other actors. *Personality and Social Psychology Review, 5*, 169–182.

Nisbett, R. E., Peng, K., Choi, I., & Norenzayan, A. (2001). Culture and systems of thought. *Psychological Review, 108*, 291–310.

Olvermann, R., Metz-Göckel, H., Hannover, B., & Pöhlmann, C. (2004). Motivinhalte und Handlungs-versus Lageorientierung bei independenten oder interdependenten Personen. *Zeitschrift für Differentielle und Diagnostische Psychologie, 25*(2), 87–103.

Oyserman, D., Coon, H. M., & Kemmelmeier, M. (2002). Rethinking individualism and collectivism: Evaluation of theoretical assumptions and meta-analyses. *Psychological Bulletin, 128*, 3–71.

Pöhlmann, C., Hannover, B., Kühnen, U., & Birkner, N. (2002). Independente und interdependente Selbstkonzepte als Determinanten des Selbstwerts. [Independent and interdependent self-construals as determinants of self-esteem]. *Zeitschrift für Sozialpsychologie, 33*, 111–121.

Schimmack, U., Oishi, S., & Diener, E. (2005). Individualism: A valid and important dimension of cultural differences between nations. *Personality and Social Psychology Review, 9*, 17–31.

Sedikides, C., Gaertner, L., & Toguchi, Y. (2003). Pancultural self-enhancement. *Journal of Personality and Social Psychology, 84*, 60–79.

Strack, F. (1988). Social cognition: Sozialpsychologie innerhalb des Paradigmas der Informationsverarbeitung [Social cognition: Social psychology within the paradigm of information processing]. *Psychologische Rundschau, 39*, 72–82.

Tajfel, H. (1972). Experiments in a vacuum. In J. Israel & H. Triandis (Eds.), *The context of social psychology A critical assessment* (pp. 69–119). London: Academic Press.

Takata, T. (2003). Self-enhancement and self-criticism in Japanese culture. An experimental analysis. *Journal of Cross-Cultural Psychology, 34*, 542–551.

Trafimow, D., Triandis, H. C., & Goto, S. G. (1991). Some tests of the distinction between the private self and the collective self. *Journal of Personality and Social Psychology, 60*, 649–655.

Triandis, H. C. (1995). *Individualism and collectivism.* New York: McGraw-Hill.

Triandis, H. C. (2002). Cultural influences on personality. *Annual Review of Personality, 53*, 133–160.

Trandis, H. C. (2005). Issues in individualism and collectivism research. In R. Sorrentino & D. Cohen (Eds.), *Culture and social behavior: The Ontario Symposium* (Vol. 10, pp. 207–215). Mahwah, NJ: Erlbaum.

van Baaren, R. B., Maddux, W. W., Chartrand, T. L., de Bouter, C., & van Knippenberg, A. (2003). It takes two to mimic: Behavioral consequences of self-construals. *Journal of Personality and Social Psychology, 84*, 1093–1102.

van der Vijver, F., & Leung, K. (2000). Methodological issues in psychological research on culture. *Journal of Cross Cultural Psychology, 31*, 33–51.

Watson, O. M. (1970). *Proxemic behaviour.* Paris: Mouton.

Author Index

A

Aaker, J., 298, **308**
Aarts, H., 15, 16, **18**, 143, **152, 156,** 247, 250, 257, 260, **261, 262**
Abderhalden, E., **261**
Abelson, R.P., 272, 273, **285, 286**
Abrams, D., 115
Abrams, R.L., 55, **65, 66**
Ach, N., 247, **261**
Achee, J.W., 164, **175**
Adamopoulos, J., 292, **306**
Adams, H.E., 62, **65**
Adelmann, P.K., 38, **47**
Adolphs, R., 225, **237**
Agnoli, F., 271, **286**
Ahern, G.L., **238**
Ahlm, D., 139, **155**
Ajzen, I., 133, **134,** 248, 256, **261, 263**
Alibozak, T., **240**
Allan, L.G., **44,** 101, **114,** 186, 187, 193, 196
Allen, C., **18**
Allport, A., 250, **261**
Alpers, G., 229, **241**
Ambady, N., 3, 6, **18,** 182, **192**
Ames, D., 295, **308**
Anas, A., 99, **114,** 187, **191**
Andersen, S.M., 230, **237**
Anderson, J.R., 26, **43**
Anderson, N.H., 31, **43**
Anderson, R.C., 252, **261**
Anderson, U., 143, **156**
Antoniou, A.A., 223, **242**
Arcuri, L., 88, **90,** 274, 275, 281, **285,** 286, 287
Arenberg, D., 250, **265**
Ariely, D., 52, **68**
Asch, S., 9, **17,** 182, **191**
Ashbrook, P.W., 237, **239**
Aspinwall, L.G., **194**
Atkinson, A.P., 228, **237**
Atkinson, J.W., **194,** 258, **261**
Au, T.K., **285**
Audrain, I.C., 235, **240**

Austin, J.L., 73, **88**
Averill, J.R., 227, **240**
Ayduk, O., 227, **240**

B

Bach, E., **285**
Baer, J., **67, 68**
Baeyens, F., 210, **214**
Bak, P.M., 250, **266**
Baker, A.G., **120**
Baker, S.M., 145, **153**
Bakhtin, M.M., 271
Balcetis, E., 13, **17**
Baldwin, M.W., 230, **237**
Ballard, D.H., 57, **69**
Balsam, P.D., 38, **44**
Banaji, M.R., **66,** 200, 202, 203, 205, **215, 216,** 250, **261,** 271, **286**
Bandura, A., 256, **261**
Banse, R., 201, **214,** 228, **239**
Barbey, A., 24, 36, **43**
Bargh, J.A., 16, **17, 18,** 36, 37, **43, 44,** 51, 52, 57, 60, 64, **65, 66,** 76, **88,** 96, **114,** 126, **135, 136,** 160, **175, 176,** 190, **192, 195,** 199, 202, 203, 205, 208, **214, 215,** 231, **238,** 245, 246, 247, 248, 250, 256, **261, 262, 263, 264**
Barlas, S., **117**
Barndollar, K., 248, 256, **261**
Baron, R.M., 9, **20**
Barr, C.L., 232, **238**
Barrett, F., **263**
Barrett, H.C., 182, **191**
Barsalou, L.W., viii, xiii, 23, 24, 25, 28, 29, 31, 32, 33, 34, 35, 36, 40, 41, **43, 45, 46, 47,** 124, **134, 137**
Bar-Tal, D., **116**
Bassok, M., 148, **156**
Batson, C.D., 222, 231, **238**
Baumeister, R.F., 51, 55, 56, 64, **65, 66, 67, 68,** 245, 246, 256, 257, **262, 263, 267**

312 AUTHOR INDEX

Bavelas, J.B., 231, **238**
Baylis, G.C., 8, **22**
Bechara, A., 222, **238, 242**
Becker, A.P., 9, **17**
Begg, I.M., 99, **114,** 187, **191**
Behne, T., 1, **22,** 71, **92,** 182, **196**
Behr, S.E., 51, **67**
Bem, D.J., vii, **ix,** 185, 187, **191,** 199, **214,** 254, **262**
Berger, C.R., 23, **46**
Berkowitz, L., **119, 194**
Berlin, B., 283, **285**
Berman, J., **308**
Berman, L., 139, **155**
Berndsen, M., 101, **114**
Bernieri, F.J., 231, **238**
Berre, J., **67**
Berridge, K.C., 52, 59, 60, 63, 64, **65,** 69
Berry, D., **20,** 179, **191**
Berscheid, E., 255, **262**
Besner, D., **216**
Betsch, C., **192**
Betsch, R., **115**
Betsch, T., 143, **152, 192, 193**
Bhawuk, D.P., **307**
Biernat, M., 10, **17,** 128, 139, 140, **134,** 152
Biller, B., 166, **177**
Bink, M.L., 247, **265**
Binkofski, F., **43**
Birbamer, N., **240**
Birkner, N., 297, **307, 309**
Bjork, R.A., 98, **117**
Black, A., **238**
Blair, I.V., 11, **17,** 202, 205, **214**
Blakemore, S.-J., 9, **17,** 38, **43,** 182, 191
Blaney, P.H., 234, **238**
Blank, H., 210, **215**
Blanton, H., 140, **155**
Bless, H., viii, xiii, 10, **21,** 82, 83, 85, **88, 92,** 97, **119,** 121, 122, 126, 127, 128, 129,130, **134, 136, 137,** 141, **155,** 157, 158, 160, 161, 162, 164, 166, 167, 168, 169, 170, 173, **173, 174, 175, 176, 177,** 183, 186, **195, 196,** 236, 237, **238, 242,** 251, 253, 254, **262, 266**
Blessum, K.A., 132, **134**
Block, N., 54, **65**
Blümke, M., 201, **215**
Blythe, P.W., 182, **191**
Boas, F., 269, **285**
Bodenhausen, G.V., viii, xiii, 1, 9, 10, 11, **17, 19, 20, 123,134,** 148, 149, 150, **154,** 162, **173, 175,** 181, 190, **191,** 205, 209, 212, **215,** 253, **262, 264**
Boekaerts, M., **266**
Boer, E., 57, **67**
Boettger, R., 84, **92**

Bohner, G., 123, 124, 132, 134, **136,** 141, **155,** 183, **192, 195,** 201, **217,** 253, **262**
Bolte, A., 186, **191**
Bond, R.N., **114**
Bonnefon, J.F., 79, **89**
Boring, E.G., 50, **65**
Bornstein, R.F., 167, **173**
Bos, M.W., 55, **66**
Bower, G.H., 233, 234, **238**
Bowerman, M., 283, **287**
Bowles, R.J., 7, **19**
Boyer, M., 179, **192**
Bradley, B.P., 5, **18**
Bradshaw, J.M., 83, 85, **89**
Brandimonte, M.A., 62, **65, 68**
Brandt, A., 303, **307**
Brandtstädter, J., 250, 253, **262**
Braun, F., 284, **288**
Breitmeyer, B.G., 54, **65,**
Brekke, N., 123, **137,** 143, **156,** 158, 159, **177**
Brendl, C.M., 212, **214**
Brett, M., 36, **45**
Brewer, M.B., 2, **18,** 181, 182, **191**
Brinkmann, B., 97, **115**
Brinkmann, J., 143, **152**
Briñol, P., 168, **176, 215**
Broadbent, D.E., 3, 5, **18**
Broadbent, M.H., 3, 5, **18**
Brocas, I., **68**
Brock, T.C., **19, 155**
Brooks, K., 62, **68**
Brown, D.R., 139, 141, **152**
Brown, J., 166, **174,** 187, **193,** 252, 255, **267,** 296, **306, 308**
Brown, R., 23, **45,** 162, **174,** 270, 272, 273, 274, **285, 288**
Brown, T., **21**
Brun, W., 76, **92**
Bruner, J.S., 2, 6, 9, 12, **18, 21,** 100, **114,** 180, 190, **191,** 250, **262**
Brunswik, E., 181, 183, **191**
Bryan, E.S., 247, **265**
Buccino, G., 33, **43**
Buck, G.C., **288**
Buck, R., 229, **238**
Burrows, L., 16, **17,** 37, **43**
Bush, L.K., 232, **238**
Butler, E.A., 228, **238**
Byrne, R.M., 77, 81, **88, 89**
Byrne, R.W., 2, **18**

C

Cacioppo, J.T., 131, **137,** 183, 186, **194, 196,** 231, **239**
Call, J., 1, **22,** 71, **92,** 182, **196**
Cannon, W.B., 42, **44**

AUTHOR INDEX   313

Cantor, N., 25, 29, **44**, 71, **88**
Cantril, H., 13, **19**
Caplan, A., 64, **65**
Caramazza, A., 274, **285**
Carlston, D.E., 2, **22**, 31, **44**, **45**
Carpenter, M., 1, **22**, 71, **92**, 182, **196**
Carr, T.H., 8, **18**
Carrell, S.E., 230, **237**
Carrillo, J., **68**
Carver, C.S., 57, **65**, 246, 256, 257, 262
Chabris, C.F., 54, **68**
Chafe, W.I., 273, **285**
Chaiken, S., 71, **88**, 104, **114**, 132, **134**, 183, **192**, **194**, **195**, 199, **214**, 229, **238**
Chalmers, R., 271, **285**
Chambon, M., 37, 38, **44**
Changeux, J.P., 54, **66**
Chapleau, K.M., 11, **17**
Chapman, G.B., 142, 148, **152**
Chapman, J.P., 100, 101, **114**
Chapman, L.J., 100, 101, **114**
Chartrand, T.L., 15, 16, **18**, 190, **192**, 231, 232, **238**, **240**, **243**, 246, 256, **261**, **262**, 303, **309**
Chassin, L., 202, **217**
Chater, N., 80, **91**
Chatlosh, D.L., **120**
Chee, M.W.L., 213, **214**
Chen, M., 16, **17**, 37, **43**
Chen, S., 230, **237**
Cheney, D.L., 2, **21**
Cheng, C.M., 200, **216**, 231, **238**
Cherry, E.C., 250, **262**
Chiao, J.Y., 6, **18**
Chiu, C., 301, **306**
Choi, I., 301, 302, **306**, **308**
Choi, Y.S., 3, **18**
Chua, E., 304, **307**
Chun, W., **265**
Church, R.M., 37, **45**
Churchland, P.S., 50, 64, **66**
Cialdini, R.B., 182, **192**
Clark, A., 271, 284, **285**
Clark, H.H., 141, **152**
Clark, M.S., **44**, **238**, **239**, **241**, **264**
Cleeremans, A., 50, 53, 54, **66**, 179, 192
Clement, C.A., 146, **152**
Clore, G.L., 125, 130, 131, 132, **135**, **136**, 164, 165, 168, **173**, **176**, 183, 184, **195**, 199, **216**, 219, 223, 225, 234, 235, 236, 237, **238**, **239**, **241**, **242**, 251, 254, 259, **264**, **265**, **266**
Cohen, C. E., 25, **44**
Cohen, D., **308**, **309**
Cohen, H., **43**, **134**
Cohen, J.C., **66**
Cohen, 272
Cole, M., **289**

Cole, P., **89**, **153**, **286**
Collins, A.M., 26, **44**, 131, **135**, 199, **216**, 223, **241**, 246, **262**
Collins, J.C., 187, **193**
Condon, W.S., 231, **238**
Conrey, F.R., 213, **214**
Coon, H.M., 293, **308**
Cooper, J., 185, **194**, **196**, 255, **266**, 267
Cooper, W.H., 199, **214**
Coren, S., 139, **152**
Cork, R.L., 51, **67**
Correll, J., 11, **18**
Coull, A., 162, 171, **177**
Cowan, W.B., 203, **216**
Craighero, L., 14, **21**
Craik, F.I.M., **174**
Crelia, R.A., 163, **175**, 234, **240**
Crick, F., 50, 58, **66**
Crocker, J., 100, **114**
Crombez, G., 210, **214**
Cronkie, G.W., **289**
Crowe, E., 259, **264**
Cruttenden, H., 274, **285**
Cummins, D.D., 2, **18**
Cupchik, G.C., 233, **238**, **240**
Curtis, R.C., **192**, 199, **214**
Custers, R., 257, **262**
Czyewska, M., 14, **20**

D

D'Agostino, P.R., 167, **173**
Dagenbach, D., 8, **18**
Dalgleish, T., **192**
Damasio, A.R., 34, 40, 41, 42, **44**, **238**, 242
Damasio, H., 222, **238**, **242**
Dardenne, B., **173**, **177**
Darley, J.M., 144, **153**
Darwin, C., 185, **192**, 221, 222, 226, 228, **238**
Dasgupta, N., 202, 208, **214**
Daubman, K.A., 7, **19**, 283, **286**
Davainis, D., **240**
Davidson, R.J., **65**, **67**, **134**, 229, **238**
Davies, P.G., 13, **19**
Davison, L., 227, **242**
Dawes, R.M., 99, **119**
De Bouter, C., 231, **243**, 303, **309**
De Coster, J., 31, **47**, 53, 55, **68**, 188, 195
De Fockert, J.W., 213, **216**
De Hart, T., 252, **266**
De Houwer, J., 200, 203, 207, 210, 214, 216
De Paulo, B.M., 99, **120**
De Poot, C., 277, **285**, **288**
De Tiege, X., **67**
De Vries, P., 250, **261**
De Waal, F.B.M., 231, **241**
De Wall, C.N., 55, 56, **65**, **66**

AUTHOR INDEX

De Wit, J., **136**
De Witt, M.J., 6, **20**
Deary, I.J., 221, **239**
Decety, J., 9, **17**, 34, 38, **43**, **44**, **45**, 182, **191**
Deci, E.L., 256, **262**
Dehaene, S., 54, 55, **66**
Deignan, K., **240**
Denes-Raj, V., 180, **192**
Denrell, J., 95, 98, **114**
Denzler, M., viii, xiii, 7, **19**, 245, 247, 251, 259, **262**, **263**
Dermer, M., 255, **262**
Derryberry, D., 3, 7, **18**, 251, **262**
Destrebecqz, A., 179, **192**
Deutsch, M., 182, **192**
Deutsch, R., viii, xiii, 16, **22**, 28, **47**, 53, 55, **66**, **69**, 71, 73, 87, **92**, 95, **119**, 179, 188, 189, 190, **192**, **195**, 202, **215**, 247, **266**
Devine, P.G., 23, 28, **44**, 99, **118**, 162, **173**, 182, 190, **192**
Diener, C., 296, **306**
Diener, E., **135**, **136**, 293, 296, **306**, 309
Diener, M., 296, **306**
Dienes, Z., 62, 64, **67**, 179, **191**
Dijksterhuis, A., 15, 16, **18**, 36, 37, **44**, 51, **66**, 96, **114**, 143, 149, **152**, 166, **174**, 250, 257, **261**
Dimberg, U., 229, 232, **239**
Ditto, P.H., 182, 183, **192**
Dittrich, W.H., 228, **237**
Dodd, D.H., 83, 85, **89**
Doherty, M.E., 99, **118**
Domjan, M., 97, **115**
Douglas, K.M., 281, 282, **285**
Dovidio, J.F., 23, 37, **44**, **45**, 96, **115**
Draine, S.C., 55, **66**
Drew, M.R., 38, **44**
Driver, R.E., 144, **156**
Droit-Volet, S., 37, 38, **44**
Duan, C., 27, **47**
Duckworth, K.L., 199, 207, **214**
Duffy, S., 283, **286**
Dull, V., 181, **191**
Duncan, B.L., 10, **18**
Dunn, M., 159, **177**
Dunning, D., 13, **17**, **18**, 140, **152**, 255, 262
Dunton, B.C., 23, **44**, 201, **214**
Dutton, K., 7, **19**
Dweck, C., 301, **306**
Dywan, J., 167, **174**

E

Eagly, A.H., 132, **134**
Easterbrook, J.A., 7, **18**, 251, **262**
Ebbesen, E.B., **45**

Ebbinghaus, H., 139
Eberhardt, J.L., **44**
Eccles, J.S., 97, **117**
Eddy, D., 139, **155**
Edelman, G.M., 50, **66**
Edwards, K., 131, **135**, 235, **240**
Eelen, P., 210, **214**
Effron, D.A., viii, xiii, 23
Egloff, B., 201, **214**, 226, **238**, **239**
Ehrlich, K., 274, **285**
Eisenberg, N., **238**
Eiser, J.R., 101, **119**, 139, 140, **152**
Ekman, P., 182, 185, **192**, **193**, 228, 229, **238**, **239**
Elek, S.M., **120**
Elfenbein, H.A., 182, **192**
Elliott, A., **263**
Elliott, J.M., 6, **20**
Ellis, H.C., 237, **239**
Ellsworth, P.C., 131, **134**, **135**, 235, 240
Elmehed, K., 229, **239**
Elring, P.T.A.M., **289**
Emerson, M.J., **216**
Endo, Y., 297, **307**
Enfield, N., **90**
Eng, J., 227, **239**
Engel, C.L., 222, **238**
Engle, R.W., 213, **215**
Englich, B., 71, 84, **89**, 140, 142, 150, **152**, 154
Engstler-Schooler, T.Y., 61, 62, **68**
Enns, J.T., 139, **152**
Epstein, S., 179, 180, 188, **192**
Epstude, K., 140, 141, 142, 148, 149, 150, **152**, 153, 154
Erb, H.P., 181, 183, **192**, **194**
Erdelyi, M.H., 5, **18**
Erickson, D.J., 86, **90**
Erickson, E.A., **238**
Eriksen, C.W., 7, **19**
Esteves, F., 4, **21**, 230, **241**
Etling, K.M., 143, **156**
Evans, J.St.B.T., 73, 81, **89**, 94, **115**
Evdokas, A., 224, **242**

F

Fairhurst, S., 38, **44**
Falla, S.J., 5, **18**
Farinacci, S., 99, **114**, 187, **191**
Farnham, S.D., **66**
Faymonville, M.E., **67**
Fazio, R.H., 6, 7, 11, 15, **19**, **21**, 23, **44**, 128, 133, **134**, **135**, 161, **174**, 200, 201, 202, 208, **214**, **215**, **216**, 253, **266**
Feather, N.T., **194**
Fein, S., 13, **18**, **19**, 255, **263**
Feldman Barrett, L., **46**, **69**, **135**, **242**

AUTHOR INDEX 315

Feldman, S., **285**
Fereira, V.S., 80, **91**
Ferguson, M.J., 36, **44**, 202, 205, 208, **215**, 247, **261**, **263**
Fernández-Dols, J.M., **239**
Festinger, L., vii, **ix**, 140, 144, 148, **152**, 182, **192**, 254, 258, **263**
Fiedler, K., viii, xiii, 88, **91**, 93, 94, 95, 97, 98, 100, 101, 102, 103, 106, 107, 108, 109, 110, 111, 113, **115**, **116**, **117**, **118**, **120**, 143, **152**, **192**, **195**, 201, **215**, **239**, 274, 275, 277, 279, 280, 283, **285**, **286**, **288**
Fillmore, C.J., 273, 277, **285**
Fiore, S.M., 62, **68**
Fischer, A.H., **241**, 260, **263**
Fish, D., 272, 273, 274, **285**
Fishbach, A., 166, **174**, 248, 256, **263**, 265
Fishbein, M., 133, **134**, 248, **263**
Fisher, D.L., 57, **68**
Fishman, D., 61, **66**
Fiske, S.T., viii, **ix**, 2, **19**, 35, **44**, **46**, 71, **89**, 102, **119**, 172, **174**, **264**
Fitzsimons, G.M., 57, **66**, 245, 246, 263
Fleck, S., 151, **153**
Flykt, A., 4, **21**, 230, **241**
Fodor, J.A., 25, **44**
Fong, G., 252, **266**
Fontanella, K., **240**
Forgas, J.P., **20**, **134**, 164, **173**, **177**, **194**, **195**, 234, **239**, **242**, 252, **263**, **265**, **266**
Förster, J., viii, xi, xiii, 7, 13, **19**, 57, 60, **66**, 157, 167, 170, **174**, **176**, 188, **192**, **193**, **194**, 228, **239**, 245, 246, 247, 248, 250, 251, 252, 254, 256, 258, 259, 261, **262**, **263**, **265**, 284, 292, **307**
Försterling, F., 273, **287**
Fox, E., 5, 8, **19**
Franco, F., 274, **285**
Franconeri, S., 4, **19**
Frank, M.G., 182, **193**
Frank, M.J., 50, **66**
Franklyn-Stokes, A., 304, **307**
Frederick, S., 82, 83, 85, 87, **89**, 180, 183, 188, 189, **193**
Fredrickson, B.L., 221, 236, **239**, **240**, 251, **263**
Frey, K., 221, **240**
Freytag, P., 97, 100, 101, 106, 107, 111, 113, **115**, **116**, **118**
Fridell, S.R., 222, **238**
Fridlund, J.A., 228, **239**
Friedman, N.P., **216**
Friedman, R.S., 7, **19**, 57, **66**, 247, 248, 251, 254, 259, 260, **263**, **265**, **266**
Friedrich, F.J., 3, **21**
Frier, B.M., 220, **239**
Friesen, W.V., 182, 185, **192**, 228, 229, **238**, **239**

Frijda, N.H., 229, **239**
Frith, C., **91**
Fujita, K., 227, **239**
Funder, D.C., 100, **118**
Funke, J., **115**
Fussell, S.R., **287**

G

Gabbino, P., 62, **65**
Gabriel, S., 301, **307**
Gaelick, L., 145, **155**
Gaertner, L., 298, **309**
Gaertner, S.L., 23, 28, **44**, **115**
Gaes, G., 144, **156**
Gailliot, M.T., 57, **66**
Gallese, V., 34, 39, 42, **43**, **44**, **45**
Gao, G., 304, **307**
Garcia, J., 93, **116**
Garcia, M., 199, **214**
Gärdenfors, P., 78, **89**
Gardner, W., 298, 301, **307**, **308**
Garnham, A., 274, **285**
Garst, E., 231, **238**
Garvey, C., 274, **285**
Gasper, K., 237, **239**, 251, **264**
Gastorf, J.W., 144, **156**
Gati, I., 145, **156**
Gauker, C., 271, **286**
Gaunt, R., 189, **194**
Gaver, W.W., 221, **239**
Gawronski, B., 55, **66**, 202, 205, 206, 209, 210, 211, 212, 213, **214**, **215**
Gelade, G., 2, **22**
Gemmell, A.J., 228, **237**
Genter, D., 101, **118**
Gentner, D., 145, 146, 148, **152**, **153**, 154
Gerard, H.B., 182, **192**
Gergen, K.J., 139, **154**
Gernsbacher, M.A., 274, **285**
Gibbon, J., 37, **45**
Gibson, J.J., 93, **116**
Gifford, R.K., 102, **116**
Gigerenzer, G., 56, **66**, 96, 97, 98, 99, 107, **116**, **119**, 179, 181, 182, 183, **193**, 206, **215**
Gilbert, D.T., **47**, 77, 86, **89**, 95, **116**, 158, **177**, 189, **194**, 229, 235, **239**, **243**
Gilovich, T., **89**, **90**, **91**, **92**, 96, 103, **116**, **152**, **193**, 274, **286**
Gilson, C., 272, **286**
Ginsburg, B., 229, **238**
Ginsburg, J., 88, **91**
Girard, K., 186, **196**
Girotto, V., 72, **89**
Glaser, J., 203, **215**
Glenberg, A.M., 33, 34, **45**

AUTHOR INDEX

Glöckner, A., 143, **152**
Goethals, G.R., 144, **153, 156**
Gold, A.E., 220, **239**
Goldberg, L.R., 99, **116**
Goldsmith, H.H., **65, 134**
Goldstein, D.G., , 56, **66,** 97, 99, **116,** 181, 183, **193**
Goldstone, R.L., 25, 32, **45, 68,** 101, **118,** 145, **154**
Golisano, V., **238**
Gollwitzer, P.M., **136, 176,** 189, **193, 195,** 247, 255, 256, 257, **261, 264, 265, 267**
González-Vallejo, C., **117**
Goodman, C.C., 12, **18**
Goody, E., **90**
Gordon, S.E., 201, **217**
Görts, C., 283, **288**
Goschke, T., 186, **191**
Gosling, S.D., 183, **193**
Goto, S.G., 301, **309**
Gottfried, J.A., 17, **20**
Govorun, O., 200, **216**
Grabitz, H.-J., 211, **215**
Gramm, K., 102, **115**
Graumann, C.F., **116**
Gray, H.M., 3, **18**
Graziano, W., 255, **262**
Green, B.F., **285**
Green, J.D., 253, **264, 266**
Green, M.C., **19**
Greenberg, J., **267**
Greene, R.L., 97, **116**
Greene, S.B., 274, **286, 287**
Greenslade, L., 280, **288**
Greenwald, A.G., 51, 52, 55, **65, 66, 155,** 200, 202, 205, 208, **214, 215**
Gregg, A.P., 253, **264, 266**
Greifeneder, R., 166, 167, 168, **174**
Grice, H.P., 72, 73, 74, 87, **89,** 142, **153,** 276, **286**
Griffin, D., **89, 90, 91, 92,** 96, **116, 152,** 193
Grober, E., 274, **285**
Groner, R., **289**
Groom, C., 213, **214**
Gross, J.J., 220, 226, 227, **238, 239,** 241
Gruder, C.L., 144, **153**
Grunedal, S., 229, **239**
Gschneidinger, E., 127, **137,** 161, **176,** 227, **242**
Gudykunst, W.B., 304, **307**
Gutierrez, E., 54, **67**
Gumpertz, J.J., **286**

H

Ha, Y.-W., 147, 148, **153**
Haar, T., 101, **118,** 143, **152**
Haberstroh, S., 143, **152, 193,** 305, 307
Haddock, G., 151, **153,** 166, **174,** 182, 194
Hadjichristidis, C., 78, **91**
Häfner, M., 151, **155,** 247, **266**
Hagmayer, Y., 107, **120**
Halberstadt, J.B., 5, **21,** 32, **45**
Hall, E.T., 304, **307**
Halpern, D.V., 58, **68**
Hamilton, D.L., **45,** 100, 101, 102, **116, 262**
Hamilton, L.R., 5, **18,**
Hammerl, M., 211, **215**
Hammond, K.R., 89, 180, **193**
Hampton, J., **43**
Haney, C., 103, **116**
Hannover, B., viii, xiii, 123, **137,** 163, **176, 184, 195,** 291, 297, 299, 300, 301, 303, 306, **307, 308, 309**
Hansen, C.H., 4, **19,** 230, **239,** 250, **264**
Hansen, R.D., 4, **19,** 230, **239,** 250, 264
Hardin, C., 271, **286**
Harlacher, U., 141, **155**
Harlow, T.F., 188, **194**
Harms, R.G., **285**
Harris, R.J., 81, **89**
Harris, V.A., 103, **117**
Hartmann, C., 97, **118**
Harvey, J.H., **156, 196, 267**
Hasher, L., 97, **116**
Hassin, R.R., **18,** 247, **261**
Hastie, R, 27, **45,** 251, **264**
Hastorf, A.H., 13, **19**
Hatfield, E., 231, **239**
Haun, D.B.M., 283, **287**
Haviland-Jones, J., **263**
Hawley, K.J., 6, **20**
Hayes, A.F., 140, **152**
Hayhoe, M.M., 57, **69**
Hazy, T.E., 50, **66**
Healy, A.F., **45**
Hearst, E., 102, **118**
Heck, H.E., 6, **18**
Heider, F., vii, **ix,** 10, **19,** 182, **193,** 258, **264**
Heier, H., 180, **192**
Heine, S., 296, 297, **307**
Helson, H., 139, **153**
Henderson, M., 227, **239**
Herman, P.C., **114**
Herr, P.M., 128, **134,** 139, 140, 143, 149, **153,** 161, **174**
Hertwig, R., 96, 97, **116,** 119
Hess, M., 229, **241**
Hess, U., 228, **239**
Hewstone, M., 96, **117, 136, 155, 156,** 182, **194, 287, 288**
Hicks, J.L., 247, **265**

AUTHOR INDEX 317

Higgins, E.T., 12, 13, **19**, **88**, **89**, 96, 100, **115**, **117**, **118**, 122, 124, 126, **134**, **135**, **136**, **137**, 139, 140, **153**, **154**, **156**, 157, 160, **174**, **175**, **194**, **195**, 224, **242**, **243**, 245, 246, 247, 248, 251, 252, 257, 258, 259, 260, **262**, **263**, **264**, **265**, **266**, **288**, 292, 298, 307
Hill, J.F., 144, **156**
Hill, T., 14, **20**
Hillger, L.A., 273, **288**
Hilton, D.J., viii, xiii, 71, 72, 77, 78, 79, 82, 84, 85, 87, **89**, **92**
Hilton, J.L., 6, **22**
Hintzman, D.L., 206, **215**
Hippler, H.J., **134**, **155**
Hirst, A., 213, **216**
Hodges, S.D., **69**, 133, **137**
Hodson, C., **115**
Hoffman, C., 271, 274, 283, **286**
Hoffmann, M.L., 231, **239**
Hoffrage, U., 98, 107, **116**, 183, **193**
Hofstede, G., 293, 304, **307**
Hogarth, R.M., 180, 183, 188, **193**
Hogg, M.A., **115**, **194**, **266**
Hohmann, N., 97, **118**
Holland, R.W., 232, **243**, 303, **307**
Hollander, E.P., **116**
Holtgraves, T.M., 274, 275, **286**
Holyoak, K.J., 55, **66**, **194**
Holzberg, A.D., 255, **262**
Hommel, B., **47**
Hong, J., **240**
Hong, Y., 301, **306**
Horgan, T.G., 231, **243**
Horn, L.R., 76, **89**, **92**
Horvitz, J.C., 38, **44**
Hoshino-Brown, E., 13, **19**
Houlette, M., **115**
Houston, C., 143, **156**
Houston, D.A., 139, 145, **153**, **155**
Hovland, C.I., 139, 140, **153**, **155**
Howerter, A., **216**
Hsee, C.K., 180, **194**
Hubbard, M., 10, **20**
Hugenberg, K., viii, xiii, 1, 9, 10, 13, **19**, **21**, 181, 190, 213, **214**
Hughes, J.N., **239**
Hulse, S., **285**
Hummel, J.E., 55, **66**
Humphreys, G.W., **216**
Hunt, E., 271, **286**
Hunt, J.McV., **265**
Hunt, R.G., **116**
Hurt, C.A., 51, **67**
Hutchins, E., 276, **286**
Hutchinson, J.M.C., 182, **193**
Huttenlocher, J., 140, **153**
Hymes, C., 259, **264**

I

Ickes, W.J., 38, **45**, **196**, **267**
Idson, L.C., 248, 259, **263**, **264**
Igou, E.R., viii, xiii, 129,130, 157, 161, 166, **134**, **173**, **174**
Ilmoniemi, R., 42, **46**
Inhelder, B., 100, **117**
Innes-Ker, A.H., 5, **21**, 235, **240**
Isen, A.M., 7, **19**, 252, 253, **264**, 283, 286
Israel, J., **309**
Ito, T.A., 6, **19**, **20**
Iyengar, S., 124, **135**, 303, 304, **307**
Izard, C., **47**, **239**

J

Jackson, P.L., 23, 34, 38, **44**, **45**
Jacoby, L.L., 11, **21**, 60, **66**, 166, 167, **174**, 186, 187, **193**, **196**
James, W., 3, 4, **20**, 37, 44, 42, **45**, 124, **135**, 185, **193**, 221, 222, 231, **240**, 271, **286**
Jarcho, J., 302, **308**
Jasechko, J., 166, **174**, 187, **193**
Jemmott, J.B., 182, 183, **192**
Jenkins, C., 11, **17**
Jenkins, H.M., 101, **114**, **117**
Jennings, J.M., 60, **66**
Jennings, R.J., 38, **45**
Ji, L., 305, **307**
Johansen, M.K., 99, **118**
John, O.P., 5, 7, **21**, 226, **239**, 250, 266
Johnson, B.T., 250, **267**
Johnson, C., 102, **118**
Johnson, D.N., 3, **22**
Johnson, D.R., 271, 283, **286**
Johnson, E.J., 142, 148, **152**, 184, **193**, 235, **240**
Johnson, K.M., **115**
Johnson, M.K., 170, **174**
Johnson-Laird, P.N., 77, 81, **89**
Johnston, W.A., 6, **20**
Jones, C.R., 100, 103, **117**, 122, **135**, 246, **264**
Jones, E.E., 2, **20**, **117**
Jonides, J., 4, 6, **20**, **22**
Jopling, D.A., **308**
Jose, P.E., 223, **242**
Joslyn, S., 63, **66**
Jou, J., 81, **89**
Judd, C.M., 11, **17**, **18**, 28, **45**, 124, **137**, 181, **193**, 202, **217**
Juslin, P.N., 96, 98, 99, 113, **115**, **117**, 120, 242
Jussim, L., 97, **117**

K

Kagan, J., **47**, **239**

318 AUTHOR INDEX

Kahneman, D., vii, **ix,** 50, **66,** 80, 81, 82, 83, 84, 85, 87, **89, 91, 92,** 96, 103, 114, **116, 117, 119,** 123, **136,** 139, 140, 142, 145, **152, 153, 156,** 160, 166, **174, 176,** 179, 180, 183, 188, 189, **193, 196,** 236, **239**
Kan, I.P., 36, **45**
Kane, M.J., 213, **215**
Kanouse, D.E., 272, **285, 286**
Kao, S.-F., 101, **117**
Kappas, A., 228, **239**
Karasawa, M., 284, **287,** 297, **307**
Kardes, F.R., 147, **155,** 200, **214**
Kareev, Y., 103, 113, **115, 117**
Karelaia, N., 183, **193**
Kaschak, M.P., 33, **45**
Kashima, E.S., 283, **286**
Kashima, Y., 31, **45,** 283, **286**
Kashy, D., 60, **69**
Kasimatis, M., 221, **240**
Kasoff, J., 274, **286**
Kaufman, J., **67, 68**
Kawakami, K., 37, **45,** 232, **243**
Kawamura, T., 283, **286**
Kay, P., 277, 283, **285, 286**
Keele, S.W., 28, **46**
Keil, A., 142, **153**
Kellenbach, M.L., 36, **45**
Kellenbenz, M., 141, **155**
Keller, J., viii, xiii, 130, 157, 166, **174**
Keller, M.C., 221, **240**
Kelley, C.M., 130, **135,** 166, 167, **174,** 187, **193**
Kelley, H.H., vii, **ix,** 9, **20,** 77, 78, **90,** 104, **117,** 182, **194**
Keltner, D., 131, **135,** 235, **240**
Kemmelmeier, M., 79, **89,** 293, **308**
Kerekes, A.R.Z., 31, **45**
Keren, G., 81, **92**
Kersten, A., 25, **45**
Keysar, B., 83, **89**
Kidd, R.F., **196, 267**
Kihlstrom, J.F., 50, 51, 52, 64, **67**
Kimchi, R., 283, **286**
Kinney, R.F., 256, **264**
Kipling, D., **265**
Kirk, E.R., 256, **266**
Kirker, W.S., 250, **266**
Kita, S., 283, **287**
Kitayama, S., **18, 19,** 103, **118, 262,** 283, 284, **286,** 293, 294, 295, 296, 297, 299, **307, 308**
Klaaren, K.J., **69**
Klatzky, A.L., 25, **45**
Klauer, K.C., viii, xiii, 12, **20,** 94, 102, **117,** 199, 204, 207, 213, **214, 215,** 216, 217
Klayman, J., 98, **117,** 147, 148, **153**
Klein, R., 140, **153**
Kleinbölting, H., 98, **116,** 183, **193**

Klinger, M.R., 55, **67**
Klumpp, G., **119,** 130, **136, 176, 195**
Knutson, B., 65, **69**
Ko, S.J., 183, **193**
Kobayashi, C., 296, **308**
Koch, C., 54, **67**
Koch, K., 202, **217**
Koelling, R.A., 93, **116**
Koestner, R., 144, **156**
Kommer, D., 184, **195**
Konrath, S., 127, **135**
Koole, S.L., **267**
Koomen, W., 128, **136, 152**
Koriat, A., 52, **67,** 98, **117,** 166, **174,** 227, **240**
Kornblum, S., **261**
Kosslyn, S.M., 34, **45**
Krauss, S., 94, **118**
Krauth-Gruber, S., 24, 32, **46**
Kreuz, R.J., **287**
Krosnick, J.A., 82, 83, **90**
Kross, E., 227, **240**
Krueger, J.I., 100, **118**
Kruglanski, A.W., **19, 88, 89, 115, 116, 117, 118, 134, 136, 154, 156,** 166, 172, **174, 176,** 181, 182, 190, **194, 195,** 247, 248, 249, 253, 254, 255, 256, 257, **262, 263, 264, 265, 266,** 277, 278, 282, **287, 288, 307**
Krull, D.S., 86, **89, 90,** 229, **239**
Kruschke, J.K., 28, **45**
Kübler, A., 83, **92,** 97, **119,** 122, **137,** 160, **176**
Kuhl, J., 256, **265**
Kühnen, U., viii, xiii, 291, 297, 299, 300, 301, 305, 306, **307, 308, 309**
Kuiper, N.A., 250, **266**
Kunda, Z., 26, **45,** 72, **90,** 148, **153,** 162, **174,** 250, 252, 254, **265, 266**
Kunst-Wilson, W.R., 51, **67**
Kurman, J., 296, **308**

L

LaFleur, S.J., **69**
LaFrance, M., 38, **45,** 231, **240**
Laham, S.M., **20, 194, 265**
Laird, J.D., 185, **194,** 233, **240, 243**
Lakin, J.L., 231, 232, **240**
Lalljee, M.G., 88, **91**
Lamb, R., 88, **91**
Lambert, A.J., 11, **21, 264**
Lamberts, K., **45, 46, 68**
Lambie, J.A., 62, **67**
Landwehr, R.F., 166, **175**
Lane, R., **238**
Lang, P.J., 220, 226, **240**
Lange, C., 42, 44, 222
Langendoen, D.T., **285**

AUTHOR INDEX 319

Lanzetta, J., 231, 233, **238, 243**
Larrick, R.P., 104, **118**
Larsen, J.T., 283, **286**
Larsen, R.J., 221, **240**
Larwill, L.K., 187, **193**
Latham, G.P., 256, **265**
Lau, I.J., 271, 283, **286**
Laureys, S., 51, 54, **67**
Lavie, N., 213, **216**
Lawhon, J., 144, **156**
Lazarus, R.S., 220, 223, 224, 227, 230, **240,** 242, 250, **265**
Leakey, R.E., 1, **20**
LeDoux, J., 65, **67,** 225, **240**
Lee, A., 298, 299, 301, **307, 308**
Lee, C.J., 84, **90**
Lee, J.Y., 274, **286**
Lee, K.M., 213, **214**
Lee-Chai, A., 256, **261**
Lefebvre, C., **43,** 134
Legrenzi, P., 72, **89**
Lehman, D.R., 82, **90,** 297, **307**
Lemery, C.R., **238**
Lemley, R.H., 84, **91**
Lenneberg, E.H., 270, **285, 286**
Leonesio, R.J., 166, **175**
Lépinasse, V., 37, **44**
Lepore, L., 23, **45,** 162, **174**
Lepper, M., 132, **135,** 255, **265,** 303, 304, **307**
Lerner, J., 84, **92**
Lester, V., **19**
Leuenberger, A., 255, **262**
Leung, K., 293, **309**
Levenson, R.W., 185, **192,** 220, **241**
Leventhal, H., 224, 225, 233, **238, 240**
Levin, D.T., **68**
Levine, D. **ix, 194**
Levinson, S.C., 72, 73, 74, 75, 76, 83, 85, **90,** 283, **286, 287**
Levy, J., 57, **67**
Lewicki, P., 11, 14, **20**
Lewin, K., vii, **ix,** 245, 258, **265**
Lewis, M., **263**
Li, F., 82, **90**
Li, P., 256, **266**
Li, W., 5, 17, **20**
Liberman, A., 108, **119,** 147, 148, **156**
Liberman, N., 57, **66,** 125, **135, 137,** 157, 167, **174,** 188, **192, 193, 194,** 227, 236, **239, 242,** 246, 247, 248, 259, **262, 263, 264, 265,** 292, **307**
Lieberman, M.D., 180, 188, 189, **194,** 302, **308**
Lightstone, J., 233, **241**
Likowski, K.U., 187, **196**
Lindsey, S., 201, **217**
Lindzey, G., **18, 47**
Lippman, W., 281, **286**
Lipps, T., 231, **240**

Lisle, D.J., **69**
Litwin, G.H., 183, **194**
Liu, T.J., 255, **267**
Lloyd, B.B., **156**
Locke, E.A., 256, **265**
Locke, J., 26, **45**
Locke, K.D., 235, **240**
Lockwood, P., 148, **153**
Loewenstein, G., 52, **68,** 133, **135,** 180, 190, **194,** 222, **242, 262**
Loftus, E.F., 26, **44,** 55, **67,** 83, 84, **90,** 170, 171, **174,** 246, **262**
Loftus, G.R., 5, **20**
Logan, G.D., 29, **46,** 55, **67,** 203, **216**
Lohr, B.A., 62, **65**
Lombardi, W.J., **114,** 126, **135,** 160, 175
Lonner, W.J., 292, **306**
Lopez, D.F., 220, **237**
Lord, C.G., 132, 133, **134, 135,** 255, 265
Lories, G., **173, 177**
Lui, L., 181, **191**
Lundqvist, D., 4, **21**
Luria, A.R., 86, 87, 88, **90**
Lurie, L., 139, **153**
Lynn, S., 139, **155**

M

Maass, A., 88, **90,** 272, 275, 278, 280, 281, 284, **286, 287**
Macchi, L., 81, **90**
MacDonald, J., 64, **67**
Mackie, D.M., 182, 183, **194, 262**
Mackworth, N.H., 5, **20**
MacLeod, C., 5, 7, **20**
MacLeod, K.M., 220, **239**
Macrae, C.N., 9, **20,** 151, **153,** 162, 166, **174,** 175
Maddux, W.W., 231, (Photo courtesy of James Quale, MD, Swedish Medical Center.) **243,** 303, **309**
Maher, B., **119**
Maher, B.A., **119**
Maheswaran, D., 183, **194**
Mai, H.P., 123, 126, 129, **136,** 163, 176
Maio, G.R., 182, **194**
Majid, A., 77, 78, **90,** 283, 284, **287**
Malapani, C., 38, **44**
Malle, B.F., 71, **90**
Malone, P.S., 95, **116**
Malpass, R.S., 99, **118**
Mandel, N., 149, 150, **155**
Mandelbaum, G., **287**
Mandler, G., vii, **ix,** 50, **67,** 221, **239**
Maner, J.K., **66**
Manis, M., 139, **152**
Manktelow, K.I., 78, **91**

AUTHOR INDEX

Mannarelli, T., 183, **193**
Manstead, A., **197,** 223, **241,** 260, **263**
Mantel, S.P., 147, **155**
Marcel, A.J., 50, 55, 62, **67**
Mark, M.M., 125, **136,** 165, **176,** 253, 266
Markman, A.B., **17,** 145, 146, 148, **153,** 212, 214
Markman, A.D., 145, 146, **153, 154**
Markus, H., 42, **47,** 293, 294, 295, 296, 299, **307, 308**
Marques, J.M., **115**
Marr, D., 2, **20**
Marsh, R.L., 247, **265**
Marsman, G.J., 274, 275, 280, **288**
Martin, H., **119**
Martin, L.L., 87, **92,** 123, 126, **135, 136, 137,** 141, 144, **155,** 160, 161, 163, 164, 171, **173, 175, 176,** 185, 188, **194, 196,** 234, **238, 240, 242,** 254, **265**
Martin, R., **156,** 182, **194**
Masicampo, E.J., 55, **66**
Massad, C.M., 10, **20**
Masuda, T., 301, **308**
Mathews, A., 5, **20**
Matsumoto, D., **306**
Matsumoto, H., 295, **307**
Mauss, I.B., 220, 226, **239, 241**
Mayer, J.D., 234, **238**
McArthur, L.A., 78, **90,** 272, **287**
McArthur, L.Z., 9, **20**
McCarter, L., 220, **241**
McCartney, J.J., 64, **65**
McCauley, C., 71, **90**
McClelland, J.L., 31, **46,** 55, **67**
McClure, J., 104, **118**
McDermott, K.J., 80, **90**
McGarty, C., 101, **114**
McGhee, D.E., 200, **215**
McGinnies, E., 12, **21**
McGlone, M.S., 131, **135**
McGurk, H., 64, **67**
McHugo, G.J., 232, **238**
McIntosh, D.N., 42, **47**
McKenna, M., 54, **67**
McKenzie, C.R.M., 77, 80, **90, 91,** 100, 118
McKoon, G., 208, 209, **216,** 274, **286,** 287
McLaughlin, J.P., 28, **44**
McLeod, P., 62, **67**
McMillan, D., 27, **47,** 101, **119**
McNamara, T.P., 12, **20**
McNaughton, B.L., 31, **45**
Mead, G.H., 271, **287**
Means, B., 253, **264**
Meck, W., 37, **44, 45, 46**
Medin, D.L., 28, 32, **45, 46, 68,** 101, **118,** 145, **154**
Meiser, T., 102, **117**
Melcher, J., 62, **67**

Melkman, R., 227, **240**
Melli, G., **43**
Mellott, D.S., **66**
Meltzoff, A.N., 231, **241**
Menon, D., 295, **308**
Menz, C., **289**
Merikle, P.M., 64, **67**
Mervis, C.B., 71, **91**
Messner, C., 212, **214**
Metcalfe, J., 246, **265**
Metz-Göckel, H., 299, **308**
Metzinger, T., **68**
Meyer, D.E., **261**
Meyerowitz, J.A., 255, **262**
Meyers-Levy, J., 164, **175**
Mierke, J., 207, 213, **215, 216**
Mikkelsen, L.A., 80, **91**
Milesi, A., 281, **287**
Millar, M.G., 133, **135**
Miller, C.T., 144, **154**
Miller, D.T., 139, 140, 144, 145, **153, 154,** 160, **174**
Miller, G.F., 182, **191**
Miller, J.G., 295, **308**
Miller, K., 199, **214**
Miller, N.E., 248, 255, 258, 259, **265**
Miller, R.L., **153**
Milliken, B., 8, **20**
Milne, A.B., 9, **20**
Minor, J.K., 36, **45**
Mischel, W., 25, 29, **44,** 71, **88,** 227, **240,** 246, **265**
Mitchell, J.P., 202, 208, **216**
Miyake, A., 212, **216**
Miyamoto, Y., 103, **118**
Moallem, I., 17, **20**
Mogg, K., 5, **18**
Molden, D.C., 259, **264**
Moll, H., 1, **22,** 71, **92,** 182, **196**
Monahan, J., 99, **119,** 221, **241**
Mondillon, L., viii, xiii, 23, 39, **46**
Monson, T., 255, **262**
Moonen, G., **67**
Moore, B., 231, **243**
Moore, M.K., **241**
Moors, A., 203, **216**
Mordkoff, A., 227, **242**
Morgan, J.L., 89, **153,** 286
Morris, M.E., 183, **193**
Morris, M.W., 104, **118,** 295, **308**
Morrison, R.G., **194**
Morse, S., 139, **154**
Moskowitz, G.B., **21,** 256, 257, **265, 266**
Moss, H., **43**
Mowrer, O.H., 258, **266**
Moxey, L.M., 76, **91**
Mullally, P., 294, **308**
Mullen, B., 102, **118**

AUTHOR INDEX 321

Mullett, J., **238**
Murphy, S.T., 12, **20**, 38, **47**, 221, **241**
Murphy-Berman, V., **308**
Musch, J., 12, **20**, 94, **117**, 204, 207, 213, **214, 215, 216, 217**
Mussweiler, T., viii, xiv, 33, 36, **46**, 71, **89**, 98, 113, **118, 119**, 139, 140, 141, 142, 144, 147, 148, 149, 150, **152, 153, 154, 155,** 172, **175**
Myers, D.G., 179, **194**
Mynatt, C.R,. 99, **118**

N

Naccache, L., 54, **66**
Nachev, P., 54, **69**
Nadel, L., **238**
Nakayama, K., 6, **18**
Nandram, S., 283, **288**
Narayan, S., 6, **22**
Narens, L., 166, **175**
Naumer, B., 94, **117**
Navon, D., 13, **20**, 251, 252, **266**
Neale, M.A., 142, **154**
Neely, J.H., 200, 203, 204, **216**
Neisser, U., **43, 308**
Nelson, T.O., 166, **175**
Neubauer, D.H., 226, **239**
Neuberg, S.L., 172, **174**
Neumann, O., **241, 266**
Neumann, R., viii, xiv, 172, **175,** 187, 188, **196,** 219, 221, 222, 223, 224, 226, 229, 233, **241, 242**
Newell, A., 25, **46**
Newman, J., 101, **118**
Newtson, D., 10, **20**
Nickel, S., 106, 107, 108, **115, 116**
Niedenthal, P.M., viii, xiv, 5, **18, 19, 21,** 23, 24, 32, 33, 37, 38, 39, 40, 42, **43, 44, 46, 47, 69,** 220, 234, 235, **240, 241, 242, 262**
Nisbett, R.E., vii, **ix,** 15, **21,** 51, 67, 84, **91,** 95, **118,** 121, **135,** 236, **241,** 301, 302, **306, 308**
Nomikos, M.S., 227, **240**
Noonan, K., 84, **91**
Noordman, L.G.M., 274, **289**
Norasakkunkit, V., 295, **307**
Nordgren, L.F., 51, 55, **66**
Norenzayan, A., 88, **91,** 301, 302, **306, 308**
Norman, D.A., 56, **67**
Norman, J., 15, **21**
Northcraft, G.B., 142, **154**
Nosanchuk, T.A., 233, **241**
Nosek, B.A., **66,** 200, 202, **216**
Nosofsky, R.M., 28, 29, **46,** 99, **118**

Nowicki, G., 253, **264**
Nussbaum, S., 125, **135**

O

O'Barr, D.J., 83, **90**
O'Brien, M., 106, **119**
O'Reilly, R.C., 31, **46,** 50, **66**
O'Sullivan, M., 182, **192**
Oakhill, J., 274, **285**
Oaksford, M., 80, **91**
Obayashi, J., 302, **308**
Ogmen, H., 54, **65**
Ogston, W.D., 231, **238**
Ohlsson, S., 62, **68**
Ohman, A., **240**
Öhman, A., 4, **21,** 230, **241**
Oishi, S., 293, **309**
Oleson, K.C., 162, **174**
Olson, J.M., **18, 19,** 72, **91,** 100, **114, 118,** 308
Olson, M. A., 202, 208, **216**
Olsson, A.-C., 99, **117**
Olsson, H., 96, 99, **117**
Olvermann, R., 299, **308**
Opton, E., 227, **240**
Ortony, A., 131, **135,** 199, **216,** 223, 225, 230, **238, 241**
Osgood, C.E., 10, **21,** 199, **216**
Ostrom, T.M., 141, **155**
Ostrom, T.O., **45**
Over, D.E., 73, 78, **89, 91**
Oyserman, D., 293, 301, 305, **307, 308**
Özelsel, A., 7, **19,** 251, **263**
Özgen, E., 270, 284, **287**

P

Pacini, R., 180, 188, **192**
Paller, K.A., 5, 17, **20**
Palmer, J.C., 83, 84, **90**
Palmer, S.E., 283, **286**
Pandey, J., **307**
Paquette, P., 272, **287**
Park, B., 11, **18,** 28, **45,** 124, **137,** 181, **193,** 202, **217**
Parkinson, B., 223, **241**
Parrott, W.G., 222, **241**
Pashler, H., **20,** 56, 57, 64, **67**
Patrick, R., 253, **264**
Patterson, K., 36, **45**
Paulus, M.P., 65, **69**
Payne, B.K., 11, **21,** 200, **216**
Payne, K.B., 212, 213, **216**
Pecher, D., 36, **43, 46**
Peigneux, P., **67**
Pelham, B.W., 86, **89,** 229, **239**
Peng, K., 302, **308**

322 AUTHOR INDEX

Perner, J., 71, **92**
Perrett, D., 72, **91**
Pessoa, L., 54, **67**
Petty, R.E. 37, **47**, 159, 163, 168, 171, **176, 177**, 182, 183, **194, 196, 215**, 259, **267**
Pham, M.T., 131, **135**, 184, **194**
Piaget, J., 41, **46**, 95, 100, 103, 104, 117, 118
Pichert, J.W., 252, **261**
Pichler, A., **19**
Pickering, M.J., 77, 78, **90**
Pierro, A., 181, **194**
Pinter, B., 253, **264**
Pintrich, P.R., **266**
Plant, E.A., **66**
Plessner, H., viii, xiv, 93, 94, 97, 100, 101, **115, 116, 118, 192**
Plew, S.H., 6, **20**
Plous, S., 143, **155**
Pohl, R., **154**
Pöhlmann, C., 297, 298, 299, **307**, 308, 309
Politi, F., 284, **287**
Pollatsek, A., 57, **68**
Pomerantz, J.R., 34, **45**
Posavac, S.S., 147, **155**
Posner, M.I., 3, **21**, 28, **46**, 50, **67**
Postman, L., 12, **21**, 100, **114**
Postmes, T., **152**
Powell, M.C., 6, **19**, 200, **214**
Power, M.J., **192**
Pratto, F., 5, 7, **21**, 250, **266**
Premack, A., 71, **91**
Premack, D., 71, **91**
Prentice, D.A., 140, 144, **154**, 250, **261**
Presson, C.C., 202, **217**
Preston, S.D. 231, **241**
Prinz, W., 14, **21, 47**, 231, **241**, 261, 266
Proctor, R.W., **45**
Provine, R.R. 232, **241**
Puce, A., 72, **91**
Pugh, M.A. 132, **135**
Pulvermüller, F., 42, **46**, 270, **287**
Pylyshyn, Z.W., 25, **46**
Pyszczynski, T. **267**

Q

Quinn, C.N., 62, **68**
Quinn, J., 60, **69**

R

Rabe, C. **238**
Rafal, R.D., 3, **21**
Ramachandran, V.S., 53, 64, **68**
Ramsey, S.L. 132, **135**
Rank, S. 183, **192**
Rankin, N.O. 227, **240**

Rapson, R.L. 231, **239**
Ratcliff, R. 208, 209, **216**, 274, **287**
Raven, F. **288**
Raye, C.L. 170, **174**
Raymond, S. 274, 275, **286**
Rayner, K., 57, **68**
Read, D. **262**
Real, L., **21**
Reber, R. 130, 131, **135**, 167, **175**, 187, **195**
Reed, E., **21**
Reed, N., 62, **67**
Regan, D.T. 133, **135**, 274, **286**
Regier, T. 206, **215**
Reichle, E.D., 57, 58, **68**
Reingold, E.M., 64, **67**
Reisenzein, R. 168, **176**, 219, 220, 226, 227, **241, 242**
Reitsma-van Rooijen, M. 282, **287**
Rhodes, M.G. 130, **135**
Rholes, W.S. 100, **117**, 122, **135**, 246, 264
Ric, F., 24, 32, 33, 40, **46**
Richards, J.M. 226, 227, **239, 241**
Rickard, T.C., 55, **68**
Rickheit, G. **289**
Ricoeur, P. 270, **287**
Riggio, L., **43**
Rips, L.J. 147, **155**
Ritov, I. 145, **155**
Rittenauer-Schatka, H. **119**, 130, **136**, 176, 195
Rizzo, A., 72, **89**
Rizzolatti, G., 14, **21, 43**
Roberts, J.M. 270, **286**
Robinson, M.D., 235, 236, **241**
Robinson, W.P., **92**
Robinson, W.S., 110, **118**
Rocher, S.J., 162, 171, **177**
Roeder, U., 299, 301, 303, **307, 308**
Roediger, H.L., **174**
Roese, N.J., 72, **91**, 100, **118**
Rogers, T.B., 250, **266**
Rogers, T.T., 55, **67**
Rogoff, B., **289**
Roloff, M.W., 23, **46**
Roney, C.J.R., 259, **264**
Rosch, E., 71, **91**
Rose, J., 202, **217**
Rose, T., 100, 101, **116**
Roseman, I.J., 223, 224, **242**
Rosen, E., **156**
Rosenthal, R., 99, 101, **118, 120**
Roskos-Ewoldsen, D.R., 6, 15, **19, 21**
Ross, B.H., **17, 43**
Ross, L., vii, **ix**, 10, 15, **21**, 95, **118**, 121, **135**, 255, **265**
Roßnagel, C., 204, **216**
Rothermund, K., 203, 207, 212, **217**, 250, **262, 266**
Rothman, A.J., 166, 168, 171, **175**, 186, **195**

Rubin, M., 96, **117**
Rubini, M., 277, 278, 281, 282, **287**, 288
Ruder, M., 167, **175**
Rudman, L.A., **66**
Rudolph, U., 273, **287**
Rumelhart, D.E., 29, 30, 31, **46**
Ruppert, J., 24, **43**
Russell, J.A., 185, **195**, 219, 220, **239**, 242
Russer, S., 102, **115**
Russo, R., 7, **19**
Rusting, C.L., 252, **266**
Rüter, K., 140, 144, 148, 149, **154, 155**
Ryan, R.M., 256, **262**

S

Sacco, D.F., 13, **21**
Sackur, I., 54, **66**
Sadler, M.S., 11, **17**
Sagar, H.A., 10, **21**
Sager, K., 231, **238**
Sagristano, M., 125, **135**
Salovey, P., **135**
Salvi, D., 88, **90**, 275, **287**
Sanbonmatsu, D.M., 147, **155**, 200, **214**, 253, **266**
Sanford, A.J., 76, 77, 78, **90, 91**
Sanitoso, R., 252, **266**
Sapir, E., 269, **287**
Saron, C.D., 229, **238**
Schaal, B., 257, **265**
Schachter, S., 185, **195**
Schacter, D.L., 51, **67**
Schaffer, M.M., 28, **46**
Schaller, M., 106, 107, **119**, 255, **266**
Scheflen, A.E., 231, **242**
Scheier, M.F., 246, 256, 257, **262**
Scheier, M.S., 57, **65**
Scherer, K.R., **65**, 131, **134**, 220, 221, 224, 225, 228, **240, 242**
Schimmack, U., 293, **309**
Schkade, D.A., 123, 133, **135, 136**
Schmälzle, K., 183, **192**
Schmeichel, B.J., 56, **65**, 246, **262**
Schmidt, R.A., 189, **195**
Schmukle, S.C., 201, **214**
Schneider, W., 50, **68**
Schober, M.F., 141, **152**
Schofield, J.W., 10, **21**
Schooler, J.W., viii, xiv, 52, 58, 59, 60, 61, 62, 63, **65**, **66**, **67**, **68**, **69**, 255, 257, 258, **267**
Schooler, L., 97, **119**
Schooler, T.Y., 201, **217**
Schreiber, C.A., 52, 63, **68**
Schubert, B., 299, 300, 306, **308**
Schubert, T.W., 32, 36, **47**, 151, **155**

Schulz, S., 229, **241**
Schut, H., **136**
Schwartz, G.E., **67**
Schwartz, J.L.K., 200, **215**
Schwarz, N., viii, xiv, 10, **21**, 60, **69**, 82, 83, 85, 87, 88, **88**, **89**, **91, 92**, 96, 97, **119**, 121, 122, 123, 124, 125, 126, 127, 128, 129, 130, 131, 132, 134, **134, 135, 136, 137**, 141, 142, **155**, 158, 160, 161, 162, 163, 164, 165, 166, 167, 168, 171, **173, 175, 176, 177**, 180, 183, 184, 186, 187, **195, 196**, 201, 209, **215, 216, 217**, 227, 234, 235, 236, 237, **238, 242**, 251, 253, 254, 259, **262, 266, 287, 288**, 305, **307**
Scribner, S., **289**
Sczesny, S., 284, **288**
Searle, J., 54, 64, **68**
Sedikides, C., 253, **264, 266**, 298, **309**
Sedlmeier, P., 96, 97, **119**
Segal, M., 71, **90**
Seibt, B., 219, **241**, 247, **266**
Seidel, O., 202, **215**
Seise, J., 201, **214**
Sekaquaptewa, D., 272, **288**
Semin, G.R., viii, xiv, 88, **90, 91**, 124, **136**, 269, 270, 271, 272, 274, 275, 277, 279, 280, 281, 282, 283, 284, **285, 286, 287, 288, 289**
Semin-Goossens, A., 283, **288**
Senulis, J.A., 229, **238**
Sergent, C., 54, **66**
Seta, J.J., 140, **155**, 163, **175**, 234, 240
Setterlund, M.B., 234, **241**
Seyfarth, R.M., 2, **21**
Shah, A., **308**
Shah, J.Y., 247, 248, 257, **265, 266**
Shallice, T., 56, **67**
Shanks, D.R., 30, **47**, 56, 64, **68**
Shanteau, J., 81, **89**
Shapiro, D., **67**
Shariff, A.F., 58, **68**
Sher, S., 77, **91**
Sherif, M., 139, 140, **153, 155**
Sherman, D.A., 255, **262**
Sherman, J.W., 6, **22**, 213, **214**
Sherman, S.J., 102, **116**, 128, **134**, 139, 145, **153, 155**, 161, **174**, 202, 208, **217**
Shiffrin, R., 50, **68**
Shinskey, F.G., 57, 64, **68**
Shiv, B., 222, **242**
Shoben, E.J., 147, **155**
Shtyrov, Y., 42, **46**
Shweder, R.A., 101, **119**
Sia, T.L., 133, **134**
Sieck, W.R., 62, **68**
Siemer, M., 168, **176**, 219, **242**
Simmel, M., 10, **19**, 182, **193**

AUTHOR INDEX

Simmons, W.K., 36, 41, 43, **43, 47**
Simon, H.A., 25, **45**
Simons, A., **119**, 130, **136, 176, 195**
Simons, D.J., 4, **19**, 54, **68**
Simpson, E.H., 106, 107, 109, 110, 112, 113, 115, **119**
Simpson, J.A., **239**
Sinclair, R.C., 125, **136**, 165, **176**, 253, 266
Singer, J., 185, **195**
Singer, W., 50, 54, **68**
Sinha, C., **43**
Sinha, D., **307**
Sisti, D., 64, **65**
Skrable, R.P., 80, **91**
Sleeth-Keppler, D., **265**
Sloboda, J.A., **242**
Slocic, P., **176**
Sloman, S.A., 73, **91**, 188, **195**
Slovic, P., 96, **117**
Slugoski, B.R., 72, 78, 82, 83, 84, 85, 87, 88, **89, 91, 92**
Smallwood, J., 58, 61, **66, 68**
Smeesters, D., 149, 150, **155**
Smith, E.E., 147, **155**
Smith, E.R., 26, 28, 30, 31, **46**, 52, 55, **68**, 124, **136**, 188, **195**, 206, 208, **217**, 226, **242**, 270, 271, **287, 288**
Smith, N.C., **238**
Snyder, C.R.R., 50, **67**
Snyder, D.K., **239**
Snyder, M., 148, **155**
Soldat, A.S., 125, **136**
Soll, J.B., **117**
Solomon, K.O., 36, 41, **43, 45, 47**
Solso, R., **67**
Soman, D., 183, **196**
Soon, C.S., 213, **214**
Sorrentino, R.M., **19**, **137**, **153**, **175**, **243**, **264**, **308, 309**
Spears, R., 37, **44**, 101, **114, 119, 152**, 186, **195**, 281, **289**, **308**
Speisman, J.C., 227, **242**
Spelke, E.S., 99, **119**
Spencer, S.J., 13, **18, 19**, 255, **263**
Sperber, D., 75, **91, 92**
Sperling, G., 52, **68**
Spiegel, S., 181, **194**
Springer, A., 299, **307**
Sriram, N., 213, **214**
Srull, T.K., 12, **22**, 26, 27, **47**, 122, **136, 137**, 145, **155, 217**, 251, **261, 267**
Stahlberg, D., 281, 284, **286, 287, 288**
Stangor, C., 27, **47**, 101, **119**, 139, **153**
Stanovich, K.E., 73, **92**
Stapel, D.A., **21**, 128, **136**, 140, **152, 154, 155**, 161, **175, 176**, 186, **195**, 277, 283, 284, **288**
Staudinger, U.M., **194**

Steele, C.M., 255, **267**
Steenaerts, B., 232, **243**
Steiner, V.J., **289**
Stepper, S., 166, **176**, 185, 188, **195, 196,** 221, **242**
Stewart, B., 200, **216**
Stitt, C.L., 71, **90**
Stoner, P., 254, **265**
Strack, F., viii, xi, xiv, 16, **22**, 28, **47**, 53, 55, **66, 69**, 71, 73, 82, 83, 86, **88, 89, 91**, 95, 97, 98, 113, **118, 119**, 122, 123, 126, 127, 128, 129, 130, **136, 137**, 140, 141, 142, 149, 150, **152, 154, 155**, 159, 160, 161, 163, 166, 169, 170, 173, **173, 174, 175, 176**, 179, 184, 185, 186, 187, 188, 189, 190, **192, 194, 195, 196,** 205, 210, **215,** 219, 221, 222, 227, 228, 233, 235, **239, 241, 242,** 251, 252, 253, **262, 263,** 305, **309**
Strauman, T.J., 140, **153**, 224, **242**
Strawson, P.F., 74, **92**
Strayer, J., **238**
Stroebe, M., **136**
Stroebe, W., **116, 155, 156, 194, 287**, 288
Stroehm, W., 110, **115**
Strohner, H., **289**
Stryczek, E., 107, **116**
Suci, G.J., 10, **21**, 199, **216**
Sudman, S., **134, 155**
Suga, S., 284, **287**
Sullivan, B.T., 57, **69**
Suls, J.M., **21, 136**, 144, **153, 154**, 156, 176
Sumner, P., 54, **69**
Sutton, R.M., 281, 282, **285**
Swann, W.B., 148, **155**
Swets, J., 99, 113, 114, **119**
Symons, C.S., 250, **267**

T

Tagiuri, R., 2, **18**
Tajfel, H., 305, **309**
Takata, T., 297, **309**
Tannenbaum, P.H., 10, **21**, 199, **216**
Tanur, J.M., **152**
Tasso, A., 81, **88**
Tata, P., 5, **20**
Taylor, S.E., viii, **ix**, **19**, 71, **89**, 102, **119**, 141, 143, **156**, 166, **176**, 182, **196**, 252, 255, 256, **267**
Tcherkassof, A., 229, **239**
Tchir, M.A., 274, **286**
Teige-Mocigemba, S., 204
Teigen, K.H., 76, **92**
Tesser, A., **89, 119**, 133, **135, 136**, 137, 173, 175, 176, 217, 238, 242, 265, 287

Tetlock, P.W., 84, **92**
Theeuwes, J., 4, **22**
Thiel, L., **134**, 162, **173**
Thomas, S., 210, **214**
Thomassen, A.J.W.M., **289**
Thompson-Schill, S.L., 36, **45**
Thunberg, M., 229, **239**
Tice, D.M., **66**
Ting-Toomey, S., 304, **307**
Tipper, S.P., 8, **20**, **22**
Todd, A.R., 9, **17**
Todd, P.M., 179, 182, **191**, **193**
Tofighbakhsh, J., 131, **135**
Toguchi, Y., 298, **309**
Tomasello, M., 1, **22**, 71, **92**, 182, **196**
Tononi, G., 50, 54, **69**
Topolinski, S., 186, 187, **196**
Tormala, Z.L., 168, **176**
Tota, M.E., **114**, 250, **261**
Trafimow, D., 301, **309**
Tranel, D., 222, **238**
Traxler, M., 274, **285**
Triandis, H.C., 293, 294, 296, 301, **309**
Triesch, J., 57, **69**
Triesmann, A., 2, **22**
Trope, Y., 71, **88**, 104, 107, 108, **114**, **119**, 125, **135**, **137**, 147, 148, **156**, 189, **192**, **194**, **195**, **214**, 227, 229, 236, **238**, **239**, **242**
Trötschel, R., 256, **261**
Trujillo, J.T., 65, **69**
Tsai, P.-C., 54, **69**
Tsuchiya, N., 54, **67**
Tucker, D.M., 3, 7, **18**, **22**, 251, **262**, 267
Turiel, E., **21**
Tversky, A., vii, **ix**, 80, 81, 82, 83, 84, **89**, **90**, **92**, 96, 100, 114, **117**, **119**, 140, 142, 145, **156**, 166, **176**, 179, 184, **193**, **196**, 235, **240**
Tweney, R.D., 99, **118**
Tybout, A.M., 164, **175**
Tyler, S.K., 7, **22**, 251, **267**

U

Uchida, Y., 295, **308**
Uleman, J.S., **18**, **65**
Underwood, B., 231, **243**
Ungerleider, L.G., 54, **67**
Unkelbach, C., 111, 113, **115**, 186, **196**
Upmeyer, A., **308**
Upshaw, H.S., 141, **155**
Urland, G.R., 6, **19**, **20**

V

Vallacher, R.R., 23, **47**, 125, **137**

van Baaren, R.B., 55, **66**, 231, 232, **243**, 303, **307**, **309**
van Buiten, M., 81, **92**
van den Bergh, O., 167, **177**, 210, **214**
van den Bos, K., **136**
van der Molen, M.W., 38, **45**
van der Pligt, J., 101, **114**, **119**
van der Vijver, F., 293, **309**
van Kleeck, M.H., 273, **285**, **288**
van Knippenberg, A., 16, **18**, 96, **114**, **152**, 231, 232, **243**, 303, **309**
van Leeuwen, E., 282, **287**
Vargas, P.T., 272, **288**
Vaughan, K.B., 231, **243**
Velten, E., 220, **243**
Vermeulen, N., 39, **46**
Verplanken, B., 143, **156**
Viding, E., 213, **216**
Viviani, P., 38, **47**
Vohs, K.D., 56, 58, **65**, **66**, **68**, **69**, 245, 246, 256, 257, **262**, **263**, **267**
von Hippel, W., 6, **22**, **134**, **194**, 272, **288**
von Humboldt, W., 269, 277, **288**
von Restorff, H., 102, **120**
Vonk, W., 274, **289**
Voss, A., 250, **262**
Vrana, S.R., 167, **177**
Vygotsky, L.S., 86, 88, **92**, 271, **289**

W

Wänke, M., 83, **92**, 97, 113, **115**, **119**, 122, 129, **134**, **137**, 160, 161, 166, 167, **173**, **176**, **177**, 186, **196**
Wager, T., **216**
Wagner, D., 184, **195**
Wagner, H., **197**
Wakslak, D., 125, **137**
Waldmann, M.R., 107, **120**
Walker, J.A., 3, **21**
Wallace, D.S., 132, **135**
Walther, E., 97, 98, 100, 106, 107, 108, **115**, **116**, 210, 211, **215**, **217**
Wang, X.T., 94, **118**
Ward, A., 11, **21**
Ward, G., **92**
Ward, J., 57, **69**
Ward, W.C., 101, **117**
Wasel, W., 257, **265**
Wason, P.C., 81, 83, 86, **92**
Wasserman, E.A., 101, **117**, **120**
Watson, O.M., 303, **309**
Wearden, J.H., 38, **47**
Weber, E.U., **45**, 180, **194**
Webster, D.M., 51, 253, 255, **265**
Wegener, D.T., 159, 163, 171, **177**, 182, **194**, 259, **267**

AUTHOR INDEX

Wegner, D.M., 23, **47**, 51, 61, **69**, 125, 137
Weiner, B., 78, **92**, 221, 223, 224, **243**
Weiskrantz, L., 52, 54, **69**
Welch, N., 180, **194**
Wells, G.L., 94, 99, **120**
Wentura, D., 203, 207, 212, **217**, 250, 266
Werkman, W.M., 281, **289**
Werth, L., 259, **263**
Wertsch, J.V., 271, **289**
West, R.F., 73, **91**
Weyers, P., 187, **196**
Wheatley, T., 158, **177**
Wheeler, L., 144, **156**
Wheeler, S.C., 37, **47**
Whittlesea, B.W.A., 167, **177**, 186, 187, **196**
Whorf, B.L., 269, 270, 282, **289**
Wiemer-Hastings, K., 41, **43**
Wigboldus, D., 281, **289**
Wilbarger, J.L., 59, **69**
Wild, B., 97, **115**
Wilhelm, F.H., 220, 226, **238, 239, 241**
Williams, C.J., 23, **44**
Williams, K.D., **20, 134, 194**
Williams, K.R., **194**
Willis, H., 96, **117**
Wislon, A.E., **91**
Wilson, C.D., 36, **43**
Wilson, D., 75, 83, **92**
Wilson, D.S., 51, **67**
Wilson, T.D., 51, 62, **69**, 123, 133, **137**, 143, **156**, 158, 159, **177**, 201, 205, **217**, 235, 236, **241, 243**, 255, **267**
Wimmer, H., 71, **92**
Winkielman, P., viii, xiv, 24, 32, 33, 39, **46**, 52, 59, 60, 63, 65, **69**, 128, 130, 131, **135, 137**, 167, **175**, 186, **196, 242**, 257, 258
Winman, A., 96, 98, 113, **117, 120**
Winton, W.M., 221, **243**
Wippich, W., 186, **196**
Wispé, L., 231, **243**
Witherspoon, D., 186, 187, **196**
Wittenbrink, B., 11, **18**, 124, **137**, 200, 201, 202, **215, 217, 288**
Witzki, A.H., **216**
Wolff, W.T., 101, **118**
Wolfgang, A., **242**
Wölk, M., **238**
Woloshyn, V., 187, **193**

Wolpert, D., **91**
Wood, J.V., 144, **156**
Wood, W., 60, **69**
Wright, L.W., 62, **65**
Wright, W.F., 143, **156**
Wyer, R.S., 44, 47, 122, 123, **134, 136, 137**, 201, **217**, 251, **261, 267**
Wyer, R.S. Jr., 2, 12, **22**, 26, 27, **43, 45, 47, 65**, **264**

Y

Yantis, S., 4, **20, 22**
Yates, J., 274, **285**
Ybarra, O., 221, **240**
Yeh, W., 124, **137**
Yeh, Y., 7, **19**
Yeung, C., 183, **196**
Yonelinas, A.P., 60, **66**
Young, A.W., 228, **237**
Young, H., 37, **45**
Yousem, H., 250, **265**
Yu, K., 54, **69**
Yzerbyt, G., 162, 171, **173, 177**

Z

Zabbini, S., 281, **287**
Zacks, R.T., 97, **116, 264**
Zajonc, R.B., 12, **20**, 38, 42, **47**, 51, 60, **67, 69**, 97, **120**, 167, **177**, 221, 224, **239, 241, 243**
Zanna, M.P., **18, 19**, 100, **114, 118**, 133, **134**, 144, **155, 156, 177**, 185, **194, 196**, 255, **265, 266, 267, 286, 308**
Zárate, M.A., 28, **46**, 206, 208, 209, 217
Zebrowitz, L.A., 3, **22**
Zeelenberg, R., 36, **46**
Zeeman, A., 51, **69**
Zeidner, M., **266**
Zentner, M.R., 221, **242**
Zerbes, N., 201, **214**
Zillmann, D., 185, **196, 197**
Zimbardo, P.G., 103, **116**
Zimmermann, I., 97, **118**
Zinbarg, R.E., 5, **20**
Zogmaister, C., 182, **197**
Zuckerman, M., 99, **120**
Zukier, H., 84, **91**
Zwaan, R., **43**

Subject Index

A

Aboutness principle, 122
Abstraction, 28, 125, 280, 283
Accessibility, 157, 158, 159, 190, 246
    chronic, 96, 124
    experience, 130, 183
    principle, 122
    selective, 98, 147, 148, 149, 150
    temporary, 124
Adaptation, dual, 271
Affective experiences, 184
Affective priming, 11, 12
Affective state, 5, 7, 150, 165, 195
    dysphoric, 237
    psychological, 273
    signals, 252, 259
Affective systems, 24, 25, 35
Affect
    regulation, 226
    unconscious, 59, 60
Agency
    personal, 294–295
    concepts, 303
Agent, 72, 273, 274
Amodal symbols, 25, 34, 38, 40
Anger, 230
Anxiety, 5, 7, 86, 251
Appraisal theories, 223
Arousal, autonomic, 185
Articulating experience, 62
Assimilation, 11, 121, 148–151, 161
    effect, 10, 12, 96, 126, 151, 160, 248
    size of, 129
Associations, 206
Associative network models, 23, 25, 26, 233
Attention, 35
    capture, 4–7
    driving, 282
    selective, 3, 6, 8, 29, 102
Attitudes, 6, 7, 9, 10–11, 14, 15, 199
Attribution, 301
    causal, 77, 78, 94, 108, 273
    fundamental attribution error, 107
Automatic behavior, 15–16, 49, 60, 306
Automatic control, 57, 67
Automatic evaluation, 203, 204
Automaticity
    concept, 203
    in self regulation, 256
    model of, 29
    of automatic evaluation, 204
    of accessibility, 157
Automatic processes, 157, 246, 257, 302
Automatic processing, 73, 82
Autonomy, partial, 203

B

Base-rate neglect, 97, 98
Behavior
    automatic, 15–16, 60, 306
    motivated, 303, 306
Behaviorism, 16, 50
Behaviorist, 17
Bias, 82, 96
    correspondence, 95, 255
    in-group-serving, 98
    judgmental, 73, 82, 85
    linguistic, 281
    retrieval, 252
    self-enhancement, 255, 296, 297
    self-serving, 98, 255
    semantic, 99
Bisection task, temporal, 38
Blind-sight patients, 52, 54

C

Capacity
    central-executive, 212, 213
    cognitive, 112, 182, 190, 201, 302
    restricted, 56, 97, 104
Categorization, 25, 96, 128, 161
    social, 6, 11

327

Category
    boundaries, 127
    linguistic, 279, 283
    structure, 127
Causality, implicit, 273, 274, 275
Causal schema hypothesis, 273
Cognition
    embodied, 24, 34, 40, 43
    situated, 124, 128, 132
Cognitive balance, 210
Cognitive dissonance, 13, 72
Cognitive-ecological approach, 102
Cognitive feelings, 165–167, 171, 186–187
Cognitive load, 55–56, 63, 95, 255, 302
Cognitive tuning, 251, 254
Common-coding theories, 14
Comparisons, 139–152
Communication, 228, 302
    rules, 72, 159
    spontaneous, 230
    voluntary communication uses, 230
Concepts, 24–43
    learning, 27, 28, 30
    situated, 124
Conceptual system, 16, 23
Connectionist models, 29–32, 205–209, 213 see also Distributed processing models
Conscious access, 53–54
Conscious control, 56–58, 224
Conscious feelings, 60, 65
Consciousness, 50, 59, 256
Conscious thinking, 54–56
Contagion, 230, 231, 232–233
Context model, 28
Contingencies, 100–103
    higher-order, 94, 95, 103, 104, 111, 113
    pseudo, 110–112
Contrast, 148, 149, 150, 161
Contrast effect, 10, 121, 129, 151, 159, 162, 173, 248
Control, 56–59
    automatic, 57, 67
    conscious, 56–58, 224
    self, 245, 246, 251, 256, 267
Controllability, lack of, 203
Convergence zones, 40
Conversational correction effects, 84
Conversational implicatures 73, 74, 75, 76
Conversational norms, 128, 160, 163
Conversational pragmatics, 82–83
Conversational rationality, 73
Conversational skill, 83
Cooperative planning, 78
Correction
    flexible correction model, 163, 164
    overcorrection, 123
    processes, 163, 177
Corrugator, 39, 185, 187, 221, 229, 232

Cue utilization, 181
Cue validity, 8, 181
Culture, 291–306

D

Declarative knowledge, 159–164, 166
Decision making, 179
Deontic conditionals, 78, 79, 80
Dilution effect, 84
Discounting, 104–108
Discrimination, 98–99
Dissonance theory, 210
Dispositional inferences, 86, 229, 275, 302
Dissociations, 59–63
    access, 59–60
    temporal, 60–61
    translation, 59, 61–63
Distributed processing models, 24, 29, see also Connectionist models
Dual adaptation, 271
Dual-processing model, 225, 226, 229
Dual-process theory, 55
Dual-systems perspective, in psychology, 82

E

Ease of retrieval, 166, 167, 168, 174
Ego defense, 13
Electromyographic recording, 39
Embodied simulation models, 24
EMG, see Electromyographic recording
Empathy, 34, 43, 230–231
Emotions, 131, 219, 228
    theory of, 34, 42
Encoding
    flexibility model, 6
    style, 14
Episodic memory, 28, 236
Evaluations, 199
    automatic, 203, 204
    spontaneous, 199–214
Evaluative conditioning, 210
Evaluative priming, 200, 201, 203, 209, 212, 213
Executive functions, 56, 67, 213, 189
Exemplar models, 25, 28–29, 31, 205–212, 213
Expectancies, 5, 9, 10–11, 14, 100, 248
Experiences
    accessibility, 130, 183
    affective, 184
    articulating, 62
    metacognitive, 121, 130, 131
    recollective, 168, 169, 170, 171
    subjective, 52, 129, 164, 167, 180, 187
Experiencer, 273, 274
Experiencer-stimulus schema, 273
Experiential consciousness, 59

Experiential information, 129–131
Explanations (of marked events), 77

F

Familiarity, 130
Faulty theories, 62
Fear, 184, 225, 226, 228, 230
Feature overlap, 128
Feedback
    bodily, 42
    hypothesis, 221
Feelings, 131, 164, 172, 219
    cognitive, 165–167, 171, 186–187
    conscious, 60, 65
    feeling-as-information model, 233
Flexible correction model, 163, 164
Fluency, 130, 166, 167
fMRI, *see* Functional magnet resonance imaging
Focusing
    illusions, 123
    thematic, 277
Frames, 77–82
Functional magnet resonance imaging, 36

G

GCI, *see* generalized conversational implicatures
Generalized context model, 28
Generalized conversational implicatures, 74, 76
Global workspace theory, 53
Goals, 2, 5, 245, 246
    fulfillment, 247, 278, 259
    priming, 247, 248, 249
    unconscious, 57
Grice's rules of communication, 72
Group-based stereotyping, 31

H

Happiness, 7, 39, 228
Hedonic monitoring, 60
Heuristics, 82, 96
    how do I feel about?, 165, 168
    single-cue, 99
Higher mental processes, 72

I

IAT, *see* Implicit association test
Ideomotor action, 37
Ideomotor theory, 231
Illocutionary uptake, 73, 74
Illocutionary act, 74
Illusory correlation, 100, 101, 102
Imitation, 38, 231, 232, 233, 303
Implicit association test, 200
Implicit causality, 273, 274, 275
Implicit quantifiers, 272, 275
Implicit salience, 274
Impulsive system, 55, 189
Inclusion/exclusion model, 126, 129, 160, 162, 163, 164
Independence, 299, 300, 301, 302
Indicative conditionals, 80, 81
Induction, 25, 60, 93–114, 172, 220
Inferences under uncertainty, 94
Information
    experiential, 129–131
    use, 126–129, 253
Inhibition, 87, 212, 213, 248, 249
Intelligence, interactional, 71–88
Interdependence, 299, 301, 304, 305
Internal clock models, 37
Introspection, 34, 41, 42, 50
Intuition, 61, 81, 179–191
Intuitive judgment, 179, 180, 188–190, 191

J

James, ideomotor theory, 231
James-Lange, 42, 222
Judgments, 179
    intuitive, 179, 180, 188–190, 191
    memory-based, 123
    of coherence, 186, 187
    of responsibility, 88

L

Language use, 72, 270, 276
LCM, *see* Linguistic category model
Leading questions effect, 83
Leakage, 87
Levator, 39, 40
Levels of construal, 125
Liking, 130, 223
Linguistic category model, 278, 283
Linguistic expectancy bias, 281
Linguistic intergroup bias, 281

M

Malleability, 203, 205
Matching principle, 132
Memory
    based judgments, 123
    processes, 168, 169
    semantic, 26, 28, 31
    state-dependent, 234

Mental construal, 121–134, 306
Mental processes, 55, 72
Mental representations, 121
Meta-awareness, 52, 58, 63, 64
Metacognition, 52, 157–173
Metacognitive experiences, 121, 130, 131
Metacognitive knowledge, 159, 161, 169, 171
Meta-cognitive myopia113
Metacognitive theories, 160, 161, 173
Mimicry, 231–232, 233, 303,
Mind wandering, 58
Mirror neurons, 14
Misattribution, 12, 168, 184
MODE model, 15
Monitoring, 58, 61, 256, 257
  system, 58, 61
  hedonic, 60
Mood, 131, 165, 219
Mood-congruency effect, 234
Morphological hypothesis, 274
Motivated behavior, 303, 306
Motivation, 62
Multidimensional space, 28
Multimodal simulation, 34
Muscle contractions, 185
Muscles, facial, 39, 40, 42, 185, 229

N

Naïve realism, 11
Naïve theories, 158, 159, 171
Negation, 76, 86, 87
Neglect, base-rate, 97, 98

O

Orbicularus occuli, 39

P

Parallel distributing processing, 29, *see also* Connectionist models
Patient, 273
Pattern completion, 31, 207
PDP, *see* Parallel distributing processing
Perception, 228
  temporal, 37
  self-, 9, 185, 187, 256
  selective, 15
  person, 2, 9, 151, 161, 162
Personality patterns, 293, 296
Physiological approaches, 221–222
PMM, *see* Probabilistic mental models
Postacquisition revaluation, 210, 211
Pragmatic signals, 77, 78, 79, 85
Preconditioning, sensory, 210, 211

Priming, 15, 157, 158, 160
  affective, 11, 12
  effect, 11, 14
  evaluative, 200, 201, 203, 209, 212, 213
  goal, 247, 248, 249
  negative, 8
  procedural, 150
  semantic, 11, 12, 203, 208, 247
  subliminal, 54, 247, 257
  stereotype, 209
  trait, 122
Probabilistic mental models, 98
Processing
  automatic, 73, 82, 157
  controlled, 73, 83
  fluency, 130
  strategies, 125, 172, 173, 236
Property verification, 36
Psychology of reasoning and judgment, 72

Q

Quantifiers, implicit, 272, 275

R

Rarity principle, 80
Rationality, bounded, 113
Recollective experience, 168, 169, 170, 171
Reflective-impulsive model, 16, 188, 189
Reflective system, 55, 189
Regression, 97
Regulatory focus, 13, 19
Regulatory focus theory, 14, 258, 298
Relational schemata, 230
Representational strength, 53
Representations, mental, 121
Reset, 163, 164
Restricted capacity, 56, 97, 104
RFT, *see* Regulatory focus theory
RIM, *see* Reflective-impulsive model

S

Salience, implicit, 274
Sampling, 35, 95, 96, 98, 103
Self, 140, 149, 293
  control, 245, 246, 251, 256, 267
  construals, 293, 299, 300, 304, 305
  enhancement bias, 255, 296, 297
  esteem, 252, 253, 255, 296–298
  evaluation, 144, 150, 151, 230, 255, 296
  perception, 9, 185, 187, 256
  regulation, 14, 245–261, 296
  regulatory ability, 58
Selective accessibility, 98, 147, 148, 149, 150

Selective attention, 3, 6, 8, 29, 102
Semantic memory, 26, 28, 31
Semantic priming, 11, 12, 203, 208, 247
Semantic roles, 273, 274
Sensorimotor system, 24, 34, 37, 40
Sensorimotor areas, 36
Sensorimotor states, 40, 42
Sensorimotor processes, 225
Shortcuts
    external, 181–183, 189
    internal, 183–181, 188, 190
Signals
    detection analysis, 99, 102
    pragmatic, 77, 78, 79, 85
    second signal system, 86
    theory, 79
Simpson's paradox, 106–107, 109, 110, 112, 113
Simulation, 35
Single-cue heuristics, 99
Social inference, 31, 103
Social categorization, 6, 11
Social psychology of higher mental processes, 72
Speech, directive function of, 88
Speed-accuracy setting, 212, 213
Spontaneous communication, 230
Spreading activation, 26, 189, 206
Square of opposition, 76
Stereotypes, 6, 11, 13, 16
    change, 96, 162
    expectancies, 10
    group-based, 31
    priming, 209
Stimulus, 273
Subjectivity, 64
Subjective experiences, 52, 129, 164, 167, 180, 187
Subliminal priming, 54, 247, 257
Subtraction effect, 87

T

Template matching, 2
Temporal bisection task, 38
Terms
    marked, 75
    unmarked, 74
Time perception models, 37
Truth, 130
Typicality, 161, 162

U

Unconscious affect, 59, 60
Unconscious goals, 57
Unconscious processes, 50, 54
Unconscious thinking, 55, 56
Unwanted thoughts, 61, 63

V

Value, 247
Vegetative state, 51
Verbal overshadowing, 62
Verbal reflection, 61–62
Verbal report, 53, 63
Visual imagery, 34
Volitional model, 274
Voluntary communication uses, 230

Z

Zygomaticus, 39, 40, 185, 229, 232